CONTENTS

CONTACTS

Published by
World Media Publishing Limited
Suite 11, The Linen House,
253 Kilburn Lane, London, W10 4BQ
Tel: +44 (0)20 8962 9555
Fax: +44 (0)20 8962 9550
E-mail: mail@bestlovedhotels.com

*Book sales: See insert at back of book or
go to www.bestlovedhotels.com*

United Kingdom

Best Loved Hotels of the World
FREEPOST LON16342
London W10 4BR
Tel: +44 (0)870 5862010
Fax: +44 (0)20 8962 9550

United States

c/o DDS, 20770 Westwood Drive,
Strongsville, OH 44149
Administration Tel: 440-572-7263
Book Sales (Toll Free): 800-808-7682
Fax (Toll Free): 800-572-8131

Publisher
Jeffrey M Epstein

Communications Director
Peter C H Jarvis

Marketing Executive
Joanna Whysall

Designer
Adrian Price

Editorial Assistant
Michelle Webb

Data Software Services
Chartland Associates

Reprographics by
Graphic Ideas, London

Printed by
Pindar PLC, Scarborough

Cover Image
NGS 77115 - Landscape with a Tourist at
Loch Katrine by John Knox (1778 – 1845)
National Gallery of Scotland,
Edinburgh/Bridgeman Art Library

ACKNOWLEDGMENTS
*We are grateful to the following for their
help with supplying photographs:*

The Bridgeman Art Library, Jenny
Mortimer, Steve Whiting and Jasmine
Teer of britainonview.com, Bord
Fáilte, Mark Green of Green Image
Photography, East of England Tourist
Board, Shannon Development, Scottish
Viewpoint/VisitScotland.

Final thanks go to Frida Andersson and
Katarina Oswan for all their hard work.

SCOTLAND

Highlands & Islands
The braes, burns and lochs
The Whisky Trails
Castles and Palaces

THE NORTH

The Yorkshire Moors and Dales
The Forest of Bowland
The Lake District
Hadrian's Wall

WALES

Snowdonia
The Brecon Beacons
The valleys of song
Land of castles

MIDSHIRES

The Norfolk Broads
The Derbyshire peaks and dales
The Cotswolds
Shakespeare country

WEST COUNTRY

Roman & Regency Bath
Dartmoor and Exmoor
Beaches and the coastal path
Maritime heritage

THE SOUTH

The New Forest & Dorset
Londoner's playground
Palaces and stately homes
The Thames Valley

LONDON

Heathlands and The Royal Parks
The entertainment capital
Focal point of British culture
The Royal palaces

IRELAND

The wild west of Connemara and Donegal
The romance of the lakes and mountains
Sacred myths and legends
Stones that tell tales

ACKNOWLEDGMENTS

We have used the ratings schemes from the following organisations where relevant and would like to thank each organisation's Hotel Quality Assurance Departments for their assistance:

A.A., R.A.C., E.T.C., S.T.B.,
W.T.B., N.I.T.B., I.T.B.

In addition we have acknowledged specific annual awards given by the following well-respected Guides:

The Which? Hotel Guide 2003
The Which? Good Food Guide 2003

A MESSAGE OF WELCOME FROM THE PUBLISHER

Jeffrey Epstein, Publisher/Founder

Peter Jarvis, Communications Director

Joanna Whysall, Editor

Heather Hay Ffrench, Food Editor

WWW.BESTLOVEDHOTELS.COM

I am very pleased to present the 2003 Edition of Best Loved Hotels – UK/Ireland. Like its predecessors we have endeavoured to create a broad brushstroke of the very best of all types of hotels across the breadth and width of these extraordinary islands. Last year, my introduction stressed the importance of travel and the imperative to express our freedom of movement and thought by using Best Loved Hotels to celebrate life whether business or pleasure. From speaking to numerous hotels, it appears that many of you took me at my word and the countryside hotels have done quite well. Unfortunately, those hotels dependent on international travellers have fared less well this year and I invite those readers from abroad to visit our shores during 2003.

> *I invite those readers from abroad to visit our shores during 2003*

The 2003 Edition features nearly 400 hotels and you will find some very interesting new additions alongside many others who have continued to upgrade and improve their rooms, food, and service. As always, our team have visited hundreds of hotels and we have received many reviews from readers in our quest to give you many appealing options. As Editor, Joanna Whysall, in addition to her other duties has outdone herself this year in identifying and presenting the uniqueness of each property.

The theme of this edition is Literary Britain and Ireland and our Regional Editorial Features provide ample reasons to travel based on each region's fabulously rich literary tradition. British and Irish literature provides us

> *British and Irish literature provides us with a strong appreciation and insight of our people and culture*

with a strong appreciation, insight, and understanding of these countries, the people and culture as well as its seeming timelessness. The names William Shakespeare, Jane Austin, William Wordsworth, Emily Brönte, Thomas Hardy, Sir Walter Scott, Virginia Woolf, Robbie Burns, Dylan Thomas, James Joyce, John Fowles, and Seamus Heaney are synonymous with not only great writing but each have given us as many references to the places and sights as any great map or road atlas.

Carrying on from last year I am pleased to let you know that, with the help of our acclaimed Food Editor, Heather Hay Ffrench, we have expanded our Culinary and Gastronomic editorial including more reasons to tempt you to dine out and sample the very best of modern as well as traditional British and Irish cuisine.

I hope you enjoy and use this book with great relish.

Jeffrey M Epstein
Founder/Publisher

BEST LOVED HOTELS AND GREENSTOP.NET - AN ENVIRONMENTAL PARTNERSHIP

A few years ago 'green' meant brown bread, sandals and beards. Environmental issues were for other people to worry about and we did not even think about how our purchases were packaged, how waste was disposed of or how much energy we used. Today, these issues are on the agenda of every major company, and environmental issues frequently dominate the news. Many environmental initiatives also save money: a point not to be forgotten!

The great thing about developing a more eco-friendly attitude is that it does help us re-think our lifestyle and simplify our priorities. Anyone who has stayed at a Best Loved 2 or 3 'Green Stop' hotel such as **Pool House, Strattons, Tan-y-Foel, Percy's, Isle of Eriska** or **Glenmoriston** will have been struck by the calm organisation, warm welcome and sincerity of their hosts. Business guests will equally be delighted to know that **Mere Court, Bodysgallen, Glenlo Abbey, Herbert Park** and **Longfields**, are all developing policies in keeping with Responsible Business Practice.

> *The great thing about developing an eco-friendly attitude is that it does help us re-think our lifestyle*

Strattons was acclaimed by the Sunday Times journalist Sean Newsom as his favourite of the winners in this year's Good Hotel Guide. Owner Vanessa Scott says they are used to winning environmental awards and to people writing about them but this is the first time a mainstream guide has given a green award. The Scotts are a creative and artistic couple anyway but they say that being green has made them look at things very differently.

This year, Claire Macdonald, the renowned Scottish cookery writer and owner of **Kinloch Lodge Hotel** on Skye, included **Pool House Hotel** in her list of twenty favourite friendly places to eat in the Highlands. **Pool House** does do some of the brown bread and sandals bit. They have just bought Indian runner ducks to improve even further the quality of their scones! Liz Miles reports their many

> *...Swiss guests this year have commented positively on their 'green' policies.*

Apparently their policy of leaving the Little Earth book in rooms goes down well with guests, although one honeymooner did complain that he had not expected his new wife to start nagging quite so soon and especially about dripping taps!!

Percy's, which is at the centre of a stunning, organically managed 130 acre Devon Estate, has simultaneously received a Gold Ribbon from the RAC, been made a Stylish and Chic Hotel of the Year in the 2003 Which? Hotel Guide and, for the second year in succession, has had the title of the ETC's 'Small Hotel of the Year' for the West country bestowed upon them.

Tan-y-Foel's restaurant, nominated Restaurant of the Year for Wales in 2002, holds three rosettes awarded by the AA for culinary excellence, using a predominance of fine local produce composed in a daily changing menu by Janet Pitman, chef proprietor and Master Chef of Great Britain.

So put on your 'sandals', trim that beard, book your tour of the United Kingdom and Ireland to include the Greenstop selection, and enjoy the very different 'brown bread' of these excellent hotels.

Patricia Ash
GreenStop

Glenmoriston Arms, Nr Loch Ness, Scotland

Pool House, Poolewe, Scotland

Strattons, Swaffham, Norfolk

Percy's, Nr Okehampton, Devon

WWW.GREENSTOP.NET

How to use this book

This book is about places to stay in the United Kingdom and Ireland: castles, stately homes, country house hotels, city centre hotels, town houses, leisure resorts, health spas and welcoming inns. Each has its own page with comprehensive details including a recommendation in the form of a "Best Loved" quotation from someone who has been there. When you plan a holiday, a friend's advice is usually helpful; our aim is to provide that kind of information. The structure and design of this book is aimed to make the business of making a choice as simple as possible and, given that there are over 400 places to choose from, we feel sure you will appreciate some help.

GENERAL STRUCTURE

The book is divided into eight regions starting with Scotland and moving south; the London region (starting page 354) is the last on the mainland and Ireland is the last in the book. The geographical areas are shown in the map above.

The hotels are listed in alphabetical order by name within their region.

Each region has a four-page introduction that picks out some of the highlights in the region and is designed to spark off some ideas.

At the end of the book are 16 pages of indexes to help you find the hotel of your choice.

Within the indexes are detailed regional maps to help you plan an itinerary.

THE HOTEL PAGES

Whilst every hotel page has a relaxed look (see right), it is packed with information which is broadly itemised as follows:

Good quality **pictures** to give you some idea of the look of the place.

Descriptive editorial intended to give you a feel for the character of the hotel and the people who run it.

A **"Fact column"** (with the yellow background) which brings together all the information you need about the hotel, how to make contact, its

facilities and location. The illustration opposite shows the breadth of scope and how useful this panel can be.

Directions. A green shaded panel supplies information on how to find the hotel. Some, like those in London, are easy to find by the address alone but others may be tucked away in the country where directions are essential.

THE ROUTE PLANNER MAPS

The regional route planning maps (see pages 464 to 479) are designed to give you instant help in two main ways:

- To find the nearest Best Loved Hotel to where you want, or have, to be.

- To find a Best Loved Hotel within a price band to suit your pocket or celebrate a special occasion.

All the Best Loved Hotels are denoted by colour coded rosettes as shown below:

Each colour represents a price band of the hotels room rates including applicable taxes estimating the average of the lowest to the highest tariff throughout the year. For hotels which include meals, an adjustment has been used to arrive at the average rate.

KEY TO HOTELS

The rosettes indicate the page number of the hotel. The colour of the rosette is a rough guide to the price of a twin or double room (see colour key below).

Double room: up to £95 per night

Double room: £96 - £145 per night

Double room: £146 - £195 per night

Double room: £196 + per night

Base map © MAPS IN MINUTES™ 2000
Design and modification
© 2001 Best Loved Hotels of the World

When these rosettes appear on the maps they also include the hotel's page number. At this stage, you may not know which hotel it is but you can easily find out by either going to the page number quoted OR by turning to the regional index of hotels on page 451.

REGIONAL INDEX

This index lists all the hotels in the book and gives you an 'at-a-glance' guide to hotels by price and region. The same rosette colour coding is used as well as the page, the county and the map reference so you can find all the information quickly.

CHILDREN-FRIENDLY HOTELS

Hotels that can accommodate children can be found in the A - Z index, page 448. Details also appear on the hotel page.

PET-FRIENDLY HOTELS

Hotels that can accommodate pets are listed on page 459.

MEETINGS FACILITIES

If an hotel has facilities for meetings (for 8 or more people), you will find details on the hotel page in the fact column and in the index on page 460.

GENERAL FACILITIES

Although every hotel page itemises its facilities, you may prefer to look at the index of facilities where we list hotels with swimming pools, health and beauty and tennis as well as those offering riding and tennis. The index starts on page 456.

GOLF

Hotels with their own courses or with courses nearby are listed on page 462.

Out of season reservations

If a hotel closes for the season, you can still call to make a booking or get information.

In January 2002 the Republic of Ireland converted to the Euro. Irish Punts are no longer in circulation. Therefore all prices for hotels in the Republic of Ireland are quoted in Euros, rounded to the nearest Euro.

At the time of going to press the exchange rate was €1 = £0.65, €1 = US $0.65

Address, phone number and fax so you can make your booking or get more information. Or, look for a reservation number below. Always quote Best Loved.

E-mail will also help you find out more or make a booking. NOTE: This service is closely monitored and all commercial solicitations will be discarded.

Room rates that are only a guide giving the lowest seasonal rate to the highest. Most rates are 'per room for two people sharing, per night'. There are a few exceptions where the rate is 'per person per night'.

Credit/charge cards accepted by the hotel.

Other abbreviations are as follows:
DC = Diners Club
MC = Mastercard and Access
VI = Visa
JCB = Japan Credit Card

Ratings & Awards are taken from the most recent published information from tourist boards, the Royal Automobile Club (RAC) and the Automobile Association (AA). The ratings systems are described on page 10. Awards from other industry recognised organisations are included where relevant and if permitted.

Affiliations. Some hotels belong to consortia or marketing groups and this is given as another source of information or for making a reservation. Details of affiliations are given on page 8.

Reservations are provided to make the booking process easier especially if you are trying to make contact outside Britain or Ireland. Always quote Best Loved.

The Access Codes have relevance only to travel agents.

Holbeck Lane, Windermere, Cumbria LA23 1LU
Telephone 015394 32375
Fax 015394 34743

E-mail: *holbeck@bestloved.com*

OWNERS
David and Patricia Nicholson

ROOM RATES
18 Doubles/Twins   £130 - £240
2 Four-posters/Suites   £160 - £250
Includes full breakfast and VAT.
Enquire for 5-course dinner inclusive rates

CHARGE/CREDIT CARDS

AMERICAN EXPRESS • DC • JCB • MC • VI

RATINGS & AWARDS
E.T.C. ★★★ *Gold Award*
R.A.C. *Gold Ribbon* ★★★ *Dining Award 4*
A.A. ★★★ ✿✿✿✿
Cumbria Tourist Board Hotel of the Year 2000 - 2001

FACILITIES
On site: *Garden, croquet, tennis, health spa, woodland walks, cycling, putting green*
Licensed for weddings
2 meeting rooms/max 60 people
Nearby: *Golf, riding, fishing*

RESTRICTIONS
No children under 8 years in restaurant
Limited facilities for disabled guests
No pets in public rooms

ATTRACTIONS
Wordsworth's Dove Cottage
Beatrix Potter's home, lake cruises

AFFILIATIONS
Pride of Britain
Small Luxury Hotels

NEAREST
MAJOR CITY:
Manchester - 90 miles/1½ hrs
MAJOR AIRPORT:
Manchester - 90 miles/1½ hrs
RAILWAY STATION:
Windermere - 3 miles/5 mins

RESERVATIONS
Toll free in US/Canada: 800-525-4800 or 800-544-9993 or 800-98-PRIDE
Quote Best Loved

ACCESS CODES
AMADEUS LX VEMHGC
APOLLO/GALILEO LX 21650
SABRE/ABACUS LX 31195
WORLDSPAN LX BWFHG

www.holbeck.bestloved.com

AFFILIATIONS

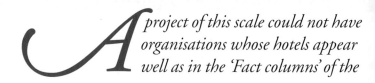

project of this scale could not have organisations whose hotels appear well as in the 'Fact columns' of the

Inverlochy Castle, page 57

The Celebrated Hotels Collection/Preston's Global Hotels

Historic deluxe country house and city town house hotels each display in their own individual way, traditional elegance and personal service reminiscent of a bygone age, and provide for the needs of the modern sophisticated traveller.

US: 3816 Briar Oak Drive, Birmingham, AL 35243
US Toll Free (CHC): 800-322-2403
US Toll Free (PGH): 800-544-9993
Tel: 205-967-7054: *Fax:* 205-967-5192

UK: Suite 11, The Linen House,
253 Kilburn Lane, London W10 4BQ
Tel: 020 8962 9555
Fax: 020 8962 9550

Hotel on the Park, page 213

Fine Individual Hotels

Havens of luxury for those who enjoy life with a certain style. The charming, personally-managed hotels offer delightful accommodation, menus ranging from classical to contemporary, a connoisseur's wine list and courteous attention.

All reservations and enquiries should be made direct with each individual hotel.

Linthwaite House, page 118

Grand Heritage Hotels

A collection of hotels that are steeped in tradition, from Manor Houses through to Palaces. Each hotel offers the best service, cuisine and comfort in order to make a journey an unforgettable experience.

1st Floor, Warwick House, 181-183 Warwick Road, London, W14 8PU
Tel: 020 7244 6699 • *Fax:* 020 7244 7799 • *Web:* www.grandheritage.com
US Toll Free: 888-93-GRAND

Hunter's Hotel, page 417

Ireland's Blue Book

High standards of accommodation, traditional hospitality and good food in the rural beauty of Ireland. Members of ICHRA offer an opportunity to enjoy quality that is fast disappearing. Guests are welcomed with 'céad mílle fáilte' at every door.

Ardbraccan Glebe, Navan, County Meath, Ireland
Tel: +353 (0)46 23416 • *Fax:* +353 (0)46 23292 • *Web:* www.irelands-blue-book.ie
US Toll Free: 800-323-5463

Butlers Town House, page 399

Manor House Hotels of Ireland

Manor House Hotels, are a superb collection of Irish Country Houses and Castles in the most picturesque of locations. They consist of three and four star properties that are as unique as you are.

1 Sandyford Office Park, Foxrock, Dublin 18, Ireland
Tel: +353(0)1 2958900 • *Fax:* +353(0)1 2958940 • *Web:* www.manorhousehotels.com

*come together without the support of many
in this book. We acknowledge them below as
pages dedicated to their hotels.*

Pride of Britain

This collection of privately owned and owner run country house properties offers a glimpse of style and tradition that is uniquely British. Each strives to produce extra special hospitality for their guests.

Cowage Farm, Foxley, Wiltshire, SN16 OJH
Tel: 01666 824666 • *Fax:* 01666 825779 • *Web:* www.prideofbritainhotels.com
US Toll Free: 800-98-PRIDE

Castle House, page 188

Relais & Chateaux

Abbeys, manor houses, mills, fine country houses and chateaux have become very comfortable hotels and elegant restaurants. They are run with an enthusiasm expressed in the famous 5 Cs: Character, Courtesy, Calm, Charm and Cuisine.

UK: Grosvenor Garden House, 35-37 Grosvenor Gardens, London SW1W 0BS
Tel: 020 7630 7667 • *Fax:* 020 7828 9476 • *Web:* www.relaischateaux.com
US: 11 East 44th Street, New York, NY 10017. *Tel:* 212-856-0115 • *Fax:* 212-856-0193

Le Manoir Aux Quat' Saison, page 216

Scotland's Hotels of Distinction

Quality hotels and inns, all individually owned and managed. World-renowned hospitality, with highest standards of ambience and quality of food and service. A warm welcome, the finest Scottish cuisine, and excellent value for money.

UK: PO Box 14610, Leven, Fife, KY8 6ZA *UK Toll Free:* 0800 975 5975
Tel: 01333 360888 • *Fax:* 01333 360809 • *Web:* www.hotels-of-distinction.com
US: McFarland Ltd, 365 Gaines School Road, Athens, GA 30605
US Toll Free: 800-437-2687 • *Fax:* 706-549-1515

Pool House, page 79

Small Luxury Hotels

The SLH stamp guarantees an unequalled level of privacy, luxury and exclusivity. These fine quality hotels embrace the sophistication of city centres, the glamour and charm of resorts, historic chateaux and country houses throughout the world.

James House, Bridge Street, Leatherhead Surrey KT22 7EP
Tel: 01372 361873 • *Fax:* 01372 361874 • *Web:* www.slh.com
US Toll Free: 800-525-4800

Bath Priory Hotel, page 252

Welsh Rarebits

They are all in interesting houses, in good locations, with superb food, imaginative decor and indefinable atmosphere. Wales's top country house hotels and traditional farmhouses, seaside hotels and historic inns are all included, and each in its own way is exceptional.

Princes Square, Montgomery Powys SY15 6PZ
Tel: 01686 668030 • *Fax:* 01686 668029 • *Web:* www.rarebits.co.uk

Bodysgallen Hall, page 152

HOTEL RATINGS & AWARDS

A Guide to Ratings

For a quick assessment of an hotel's qualities, we have used rating systems from the tourist boards, the Royal Automobile Club (RAC) and Automobile Association (AA). In addition, we have included the Consumer Association's The Good Food Guide 2003 and WHICH? Hotel Guides 2003. All ratings and awards are supplied to us by the hotels and verified by us where possible. If you need more specific information, we suggest you approach the relevant organisation direct.

Symbols are not everything!

A lack of stars, diamonds and rosettes does not necessarily convey the whole picture: some hotels are so new, they have not been rated at all as yet, while others are so non-conformist that they cannot satisfy the standard criteria but who are, nevertheless, interesting and comfortable places to stay. All the hotels in this book have been visited by at least one member of the Best Loved team and we can confirm the personal quotations at the top of every page in this book make them best-loved by someone – and for a very good reason!

 Irish Tourist Board

★★★★★

Star ratings, ranging upwards from one to five Stars are used to classify hotels throughout Ireland.

 Northern Ireland Tourist Board

---

Royal Automobile Club (R.A.C.)

★★★★★ ◆◆◆◆◆

Star ratings, from one to five, relate to hotel size and facilities; diamonds relate to guest accommodation.

Gold Ribbon & Blue Ribbon Awards

The Gold Ribbon is the highest accolade awarded by the RAC, followed by the Blue Ribbon. Due to the timings of the presentation of these awards in some cases we have published ratings from 2002.

There are other awards for Guest accommodation:

Little Gem - for all round quality
Sparkling diamonds - for hygiene
Warm Welcome - for hospitality

There are also five levels of Dining Awards for both hotels and guest houses indicating quality of *all* meals.

VisitScotland

★★★★★

The system awards stars as follows:

★ - *Fair and acceptable*
★★ - *Good*
★★★ - *Very Good*
★★★★ - *Excellent*
★★★★★ - *Exceptional*

Establishments are rated by category: small hotel, hotel, guest house, inn, restaurant with rooms and serviced apartments. They should only be compared with those within their own category.

 **BWRDD CROESO CYMRU WALES TOURIST BOARD**

★★★★★

The system awards stars as follows:

★ - *Fair*
★★ - *Good*
★★★ - *Very Good*
★★★★ - *Excellent*
★★★★★ - *Exceptional*

Establishments are rated by category: hotel, country hotel, country house, guest house, lodge, b&b, farmhouse, inn and restaurant with rooms. They should only be compared with those within their own category.

Every care has been taken in the compilation of this Directory. The hotels' factual information was supplied to us by the hotels themselves and is to the best of our knowledge accurate at the time of publication. The descriptive information is compiled by, and is the impression of, the Best Loved editorial team.

Whilst we believe that the information will prove to be reliable throughout 2003, we do not accept responsibility for errors, changes which might occur or standards which could be affected by a change of ownership or other reason since going to press. Nor can the publishers accept responsibility for consequential loss arising from such changes or other inaccuracies, or for any other loss direct or consequential arising in connection with information describing hotels in this publication.

All rights reserved.

No part of this publication may be reproduced, stored in a retrieval system, digitised or transmitted in any form, whether by means of photocopying electronically, mere copying or in any other way, without obtaining the written consent of World Media Publishing Limited.

©2003 World Media Publishing Limited
ISBN 1 898889 50 3

The Automobile Association (A.A.)

★★★★★ 76%

◆◆◆◆◆

Star ratings, from one to five Stars are related to hotel size as well as its facilities. The Diamond rating is the same but relates to guest accomodation. Percentage ratings indicate the level of quality within the category.

★★★

Red Stars are given annually to a very few hotels considered to be the best in their star category. The A.A.'s new Top 200 Awards recognise the very best hotels in Britain & Ireland.

Rosettes range from one up to five, denoting the quality of food.

 English Tourism Council

When you see the stars or diamonds you can be sure the establishment has been inspected and meets the council's standards for facilities and service under the English Tourism Council's quality assurance scheme. The more stars or diamonds, the better the facilities on a scale from one to five. Stars are awarded to hotels and diamonds for guest accommodation.

★★★★★ ◆◆◆◆◆

In addition to stars and diamonds, establishments of all kinds may receive an additional gold or silver award in recognition of the highest levels of quality in areas that guests regard as of the greatest importance.

 BITOA The British Incoming Tour Operators Association

 ASTA American Society of Travel Agents

 Hospitality BRITISH HOSPITALITY ASSOCIATION MEMBER

THE TRADITIONAL INN
Example: The Lugger Hotel, Portloe,
Cornwall

A RESTAURANT WITH ROOMS
Example: Three Choirs Vineyard,
Newent, Gloucestershire

STATELY HOMES & COUNTRY HOUSE HOTELS
Example: Gidleigh Park,
Chagford, Devon

Representing the best of their kind

This book offers a huge selection of hotels in Great Britain and Ireland from the stately palace to the welcoming inn, each the best of its kind within its locality and price range.

Here, we show a sample of that variety. There are hundreds of places where you might choose to stay. They all have character and are an integral part of the delights and attractions of their region.

And each, in its own special way, is best-loved by someone who's been there.

A RESORT HOTEL
Example: Lodge & Spa at Inchydoney Island,
Clonakilty, Ireland

A TOWN HOUSE HOTEL
Example: The Grange Hotel,
York

A LUXURY BED & BREAKFAST
Example: Sallyport House, Ireland

CASTLES
Example: Thornbury Castle, South Gloucestershire

A CITY CENTRE HOTEL
Example: The Somerset Roland, London

SCOTLAND

Sandaig, where the arc of sparkling burn that inspired Gavin Maxwell to write his classic, Ring of Bright Water, still glitters in the salt flavoured sunshine. This is where Edal the otter lies buried and the author's ashes were scattered in sight of the Sound of Sleat and views of Skye and Eig.

From purple Highlands to verdant Lowlands, Literary Scotland is a magical blend of ancient, half remembered ballads and mighty classical writers.

Edinburgh's Scott monument, and nearby Waverley Station are lasting reminders of one of Scotland's greatest patriots, Sir Walter Scott. Born, 1771, and educated in the capital, Scott was an avid collector of Scottish Ballads from the Borders. Initially coming to literary prominence as a poet, his first novels were published anonymously. They quickly captured the public imagination and the author became known as 'The Great Unknown'.

From humbler origins, Robert Burns, son of a tenant farmer, was born in Ayrshire in 1750. Despite financial constraints, his father provided a tutor, and 'Rabbie' was exceptionally well read. But an abiding love for whisky and women touched everything he did. Success with early writings spurred him to produce a vast quantity of songs; over 400 of these poetic masterpieces survive today.

Robert Louis Stevenson, 1850-94 was another son of Edinburgh. Never physically strong he travelled widely in Europe and America – marrying the American, Fanny Osbourne. Declining in health, the last years of his life were spent in the warm climes of Samoa. Treasure Island, written in 1882, may be the most famous book he wrote, but his creation of Dr Jekyll and Mr Hyde captured imaginations ever since and spawned innumerable books and films. Remarkably, the original classical horror story was written and printed in only 10 weeks.

The publication of a collection of Hugh MacDiarmid's poetry caused Ted Hughes to comment 'this is the book I have been waiting for'. Influenced by living on Whalsay for 9 years, MacDiarmid's poem 'Stony Limits' vividly captures the austerity of his life and times.

John Buchan, author and statesman, had the ability to capture the Scottish landscape in all its moods. In Witchwood, his favourite novel, he contrasts the menacing atmosphere of the ancient Caledonian Forest with sweeping, exhilarating moorland, inhabiting his world with witches, heroes and lovers.

PLACES TO VISIT

JM Barry Birthplace in Kirriemuir. A National Trust property, including the house where the writer was born in 1860 and the property next door that houses an exhibition of his works. Behind the property is Barrie's first theatre – the outhouse!

Bright Water Visitor Centre offers information, boat trips, tours and a chance to experience the superb setting that inspired Gavin Maxwell. There is a reconstruction of the room where the author wrote his enduring story, more information at www.eileanban.com

Combine laser disc technology, theatre and the immortal words of Robert Burns and you have the Tam O'Shanter Experience a t The Burns National Heritage Park in Alloway. A multitude of special events and activities throughout the year, www.burnsheritagepark.com

Extract from Song Composed in August by Robert Burns:

Now waving grain, wide o'er the plain,
Delights the weary farmer,
And the moon shines bright, when I rove at night
To muse upon my charmer.

The partridge loves the fruitful fells,
The plover loves the mountains,
The woodcock haunts the lonely dells,
the soaring hern the fountains...

BOOKS TO READ

▷ The Saga of Ring of Bright Water by Douglas Botting. The authorised biography of Gavin Maxwell: a fascinating part of the story of this eccentric romantic.

▷ Johnson and Boswell and Scotland, A Journey to the Hebrides, edited by Pat Rogers: an opportunity to compare their individual accounts of their 1773 tour.

▷ The Life of Walter Scott, A Critical Biography by John Sutherland: a fascinating insight into a many layered life.

A special place to buy books:

Mair Wilkes Books a treasure trove of Scottish and local books at Newport on Tay and also at some seasonal shows.

LITERARY ATTRACTIONS & FESTIVALS

▷ Edinburgh Book Festival takes place over 17 days in August, has over 550 authors, 650 events, book tents to browse and a writers' yurt to encourage the author in everyone. www.edbookfest.co.uk

▷ A 3 day celebration in Wigtown, Scotland's National Book Town, with readings, workshops and much more, www.booktown.co.uk

▷ The Scottish Storytelling Centre, events and exhibitions at the Netherbow, Edinburgh www.edbookfest.co.uk

Craigellachie Hotel of Speyside

A CULINARY Scotland

A vast diversity of glorious scenery gives Scotland's produce an unbeatable depth of flavour. Rocky shorelines dotted with small harbours and centuries old traditions of creel fishing are where some of the best lobsters and crabs in the world are caught. The great estates, with vast tracts of heather covered moorland and the expertise to manage them, provide game birds and venison for the table. Lush sheltered pasture produces succulent beef and lamb and fertile fields nurture soft fruit and prime vegetables. Traditional specialities from the Scottish kitchen have travelled far and wide. Crisp shortbread; rich heather honey; Dundee cakes and Scotch Broth, with its handful of barley to give it a velvety smoothness, are flavours recognised all over the world. And then there is whisky. Hundreds of single malts; a multitude of blends; whisky trails; whisky tastings and underlying it all the unique flavour and history of endeavour that captures the spirit of Scotland.

THE MENU:
Corriegour Lodge

Corriegour Lodge has an enviable reputation for food; Chef/Proprietor Ian Drew trained to be an actor and maintains that cooking is just a different art form - but just as theatrical! The following excerpt from his dinner menu offers a taste of culinary theatre:

Starter
Pressed Terrine of Wild Venison with Organic Leaves, Toasted Brioche and Crab Apple Jelly.

Timbales of Roasted Vegetables with Goats Cheese Crust and Brown Butter Vinaigrette

Main Course
Roast Breast of Partridge on Celeriac and Potato Galette with Armagnac and Orange Sauce

Whole Sea Bream with Fennel and Basil Salad and Herb New Potatoes

Dessert
Soufflé of Valhrona's Manjari Chocolate with Milk Chocolate Sauce and Grand Marnier Ice Cream

THE ROYAL CONNECTION:

There is an entry in Queen Victoria's diary that reads;' I never saw a lovelier or more romantic spot.' At the time she wrote it she was staying at Inverlochy Castle, accompanied by her ghillie. This stately, early Victorian pile is furnished in true baronial style - complete with remarkable furniture that was a gift from the King of Norway. Stylish, sophisticated food 'artfully composed without showing off' is served in three dining rooms with standards of service that would have more than satisfied the royal connections.

THE STYLE:

There is a 'certain something' about the restaurant at Kinnaird House - from 'Roasted North Sea Cod with lettuce fondue and langoustine chowder' to Warm Chocolate and Sherry 'Mouelleux' with vanilla

ice cream' there's perfection with an extra polish. It may partially be due to an American fan of current Head Chef Trevor Brooks who loved his cooking so much that he flew him to America for three weeks at a time, three years running - to cook no expense spared meals. The American connection goes further as this superb hotel is owned by American Mrs Constance Cluett Ward who, with her husband lived here and enjoyed many happy years of glorious house parties before turning it into a luxury hotel.

THE POETRY:

Robert Burns stayed several times at Kirroughtree when it was a private house Head Chef Ralf Mueller, a Masterchef of Great Britain, cooks with a larder of local specialities that reads like an inspiration for one of the bard's songs - Mull of Galloway lobster, Cree Salmon, Kirroughtree venison, Wigtown Bay wild fowl, Kilantringam laverbread and Cairnsmore cheese - and they taste as good as they sound.

THE WHISKY:

In the heart of Speyside, where the whisky flows generously, the Craigellachie Hotel is a magnate for malt whisky enthusiasts. Head Chef Addy Daggert and his team are keen to use what they call 'local malt produce' throughout their menu. 'The local Speyside malts make an excellent

compromise with the local game and poultry. The smooth malts give our base fonds a real boost, and the Island malts go with the smoked produce. A favourite is Iced Malt Whisky parfait where the honey, malt and rich double cream bring out the best in each other. Their Quaich bar displays over 430 single malts!

THE RECIPE: From Kinfauns - 'a paradise for the Bon Viveur'.

Tian of Skye Lobster and Crab with a Freshwater Prawn and Vegetable Spring Roll on a Lemon and Dill Dressing.

INGREDIENTS
For 4 to 6 servings

1 Isle of Skye Lobster
200g Isle of Skye White Crab Meat
150g Freshwater Prawn Meat
1 ripe Avocado
200g Blanched and Diced Plum Tomatoes
200g Peeled and Diced Cucumber
20g Butter
150g Julienne of Leek, Carrot, Celery
50g Chopped Shallot Seasoning
Pinch of Paprika
0.25 glass dry White Wine
2 sheets Spring roll pastry
Zest and Juice 1 Lemon
0.5 cup virgin olive oil
Fresh Dill
0.5 Tablespoon Dijon Mustard

METHOD

Cook lobster and crab in court bouillon, when cool take out of shell and chill, with crab pick take out and flake white claw meat - keep all shells for making soup.

Lightly sweat off prawns, Julienne of vegetables and half the shallots in butter. Add half white wine and cool.

Assemble spring rolls by cutting pastry into small oblongs, moisten edges and place on a spoonful of prawn and vegetable mix - roll up, tucking edges in while rolling. Deep fry.

The lemon and dill dressing is easily made in a blender or like a vinaigrette using the rest of the wine, shallots and lemon whisking in Dijon mustard and olive oil, finishing with plenty of chopped dill.

Assemble using a plain 3 inch pastry ring: build up layers of cucumber, tomato, crab, avocado and lobster on top, carefully lift off ring, drizzle dressing around plate and place a hot prawn roll on top with a lobster claw and sprig of dill to finish.

Editor's Extras

The fishing port of Eyemouth and nearby St Abbs provide one of the most popular diving areas in Britain - because of the profusion of sea life. Speaks volumes for the quality of local fish and shellfish!

A visit to Loch Lomond is a tourist 'must' and now you can even enjoy some serious shopping! A new visitor attraction, with, amongst other 'goodies' a Jenners department store and a

Food Hall, has a farmers' market planned for the car park - details at *www.lochlomondshores.com.*

Haggis is taking on a great new life transformed into all sorts of culinary delights - most of the best interpretations seem to involve a generous dash of whisky, try pouring a 'wee dram' onto the cooked haggis and then piling it on tiny croustades as an instant savoury.

" ***Warm hospitality and great food - thankyou!*** *"*

David & Tina Thompson, Edinburgh

Village hotel

ARCHIESTOWN HOTEL

SCOTLAND

Castles, fishing flies and drams, home cooking and hospitality

Sightseeing and fly fishing, a cosy hearth and good food are just a few of the favourite things guests enjoy on a visit to the Archiestown Hotel. This delightful small property sits in the middle of its namesake village (founded by Sir Archibald Grant of Monymusk in 1760), and welcomes fishers, walkers, golfers, whisky enthusiasts and others in search of traditional hospitality and atmosphere.

The hotel has recently been taken over by Philip and Rosalind Lewis, whose reputation as superb hosts is legendary. Philip is head chef and his daily changing menus specialise in the best local meat and game, fish and shellfish dishes, followed by sybaritic homemade treats such as rhubarb and strawberry crumble, crème brûlée figs and minted syrup. After dinner, relax by the fireside and enjoy a dram from one of the famous local distilleries while planning the day ahead.

Archiestown is on the Whisky Trail, and a short step from the Speyside Way. There are 15 golf courses within an hour's drive, skiing in the Cairngorms, sailing on the Moray Firth, or venture no further than a stroll around the walled garden where the hotel's fresh flowers and herbs are grown.

LOCATION

Take the A95 Spey Valley route between Grantown and Craigellachie. Archiestown is on the B9102, 4 miles from Craigellachie.

Archiestown, by Aberlour, Moray AB38 7QL

Telephone 01340 810218
Fax 01340 810239

E-mail: *archiestown@bestloved.com*

OWNERS
Philip and Rosalind Lewis

ROOM RATES
3 Singles	*£30 - £45*
8 Doubles/Twins	*£60 - £90*
Includes full breakfast and VAT

CHARGE/CREDIT CARDS

 • MC • VI

RATINGS & AWARDS
S.T.B. ★★★★ *Small Hotel*
A.A. ★★ ❀ *75%*
Taste of Scotland - 1 Medallion

FACILITIES
On site: *Garden*
1 meeting room/max 25 people
Nearby: *Golf, tennis, riding, shooting, fishing, stalking, walking*

RESTRICTIONS
No facilities for disabled guests
Pets by arrangement

ATTRACTIONS
Macallan, Glenlivet, Cardhu & Glenfordas distilleries, Loch Ness, Balmoral and Cawdor Castles, Cairngorms, The Highlands, Malt Whisky Trail, Speyside Way

AFFILIATIONS
Independent

NEAREST
MAJOR CITY:
Inverness - 50 miles/1 hr

MAJOR AIRPORT:
Aberdeen - 59 miles/1 ¼ hrs
Inverness - 50 miles/1 hr

RAILWAY STATION:
Elgin - 16 miles/20 mins

RESERVATIONS
Direct with hotel
Quote **Best Loved**

ACCESS CODES
Not applicable

" A little paradise in the middle of Scotland "

Ros & Peter Logan, Croydon, Surrey

ARDANAISEIG

19th century country house

**Kilchrenan by Taynuilt,
Argyll PA35 1HE**

**Telephone 01866 833333
Fax 01866 833222**

E-mail: *ardanaiseig@bestloved.com*

OWNER
Bennie Gray

GENERAL MANAGER
Peter Webster

ROOM RATES
Single occupancy   £69 - £155
13 Doubles/Twins   £78 - £250
3 Four-posters   £110 - £250
Includes full breakfast and VAT

CHARGE/CREDIT CARDS

 • *DC* • *MC* • *VI*

RATINGS & AWARDS
S.T.B. ★★★★ *Small Hotel*
A.A. ★★★ ✿✿ 70%
R.A.C. ★★★ *Dining Award 3*

FACILITIES
On site: *Garden, heli-pad,
croquet, tennis, boating
1 meeting room/max 30 people*
Nearby: *Fishing, snooker, walking*

RESTRICTIONS
*No facilities for disabled guests
No pets in public rooms
No smoking in restaurant or drawing room
Closed Jan*

ATTRACTIONS
*Oban and the Hebrides,
Mull and Iona, Inveraray Castle,
skiing and biking at Glencoe*

AFFILIATIONS
The Celebrated Hotels Collection

NEAREST
*MAJOR CITY:
Glasgow - 90 miles/2 hrs*

*MAJOR AIRPORT:
Glasgow - 80 miles/1 ½ hrs*

*RAILWAY STATION:
Taynuilt - 10 miles/15 mins*

RESERVATIONS
Toll free in US: 800-322-2403
Quote **Best Loved**

ACCESS CODES
Not applicable

The perfect place to discover the highlands and islands of Scotland

In a remote place of quiet tranquillity and almost surreal natural beauty, where the slopes of Ben Cruachan fall into the clear waters of Loch Awe, there is a small and wildly romantic old country house hotel. Ardanaiseig sits alone overlooking the mysterious islands and crannogs of the Loch, in deeply wooded gardens teeming with wildlife.

Built in 1834, overlooking its own island, Ardanaiseig, with its log fires, freshly picked flowers, antique furniture and fine works of art, has a special stately and timeless atmosphere. It is ideally situated for visits to Argyll's many castles and sites of historic interest.

The 100 acres of wild woodland gardens of Ardanaiseig were laid out in the 1820s. Since then thousands of exotic shrubs and trees including the famous rhododendrons have been imported from many parts of the world - including the Himalayas.

The restaurant is noted for its imaginative use of fresh produce, particularly seafood. Herbs from the walled garden enhance the subtle flavours created by the young award-winning chef.

LOCATION

On the Scottish west coast, Loch Awe side, 85 miles from Stirling and 90 miles from Glasgow. From A85 to Oban turn off at Taynuilt on B845 to Kilchrenan and on to Ardanaiseig.

" We look forward to our next opportunity to visit - Next to excellence is the appreciation of it "

Beryl Barnett

• Map p.464
ref: G9

Georgian mansion

BALBIRNIE HOUSE HOTEL

SCOTLAND

A beautiful country house between Edinburgh and St Andrews

Balbirnie House is a quite unique multi-award winning country house hotel which combines understated luxury with superb service and value. The building is a Grade 'A' listed Georgian country mansion and is set in a beautiful 400-acre estate in the heart of the Kingdom of Fife. Following a caring restoration, Balbirnie is a delightful small luxury hotel, privately owned and managed.

A natural inheritance of gracious public rooms and period reflections create an individual ambience, skillfully combined with attentive service for the needs of today's house guests.

Views from the house extend over well-manicured lawns, picturesque flowering borders and ancient yew hedges to Balbirnie Park golf course, an undulating and scenic par 71 challenge.

With its unrivalled geographical location it is possible to visit the local quaint fishing villages or explore the countryside and heritage of Fife. Visit Edinburgh and the mecca of golf, St Andrews. Balbirnie is 30 minutes equidistant between both. Varied leisure pursuits can be arranged.

LOCATION

½ hour equidistant from Edinburgh and St Andrews on the A92. Branch off on to the B9130 to Markinch Village.

Balbirnie Park, Markinch, Glenrothes, Fife KY7 6NE
Telephone 01592 610066
Fax 01592 610529
E-mail: *balbirnie@bestloved.com*

OWNERS
The Russell Family

ROOM RATES
2 Singles	£130 - £160
24 Doubles/Twins	£190 - £250
2 Four-posters	£250
2 Suites	£250

Includes full breakfast and VAT

CHARGE/CREDIT CARDS

 • DC • MC • VI

RATINGS & AWARDS
S.T.B. ★★★★ Hotel
R.A.C. *Blue Ribbon* ★★★★ Dining Award 3
A.A. ★★★★ ❀
A.A. Top 200 - 02/03
Taste of Scotland 'Hotel of the Year'
Taste of Scotland - 3 Medallions

FACILITIES
On site: *Garden, heli-pad, croquet, golf*
8 meeting rooms/max 300 people
Nearby: *Riding, fishing, shooting, golf, clay pigeon shooting, archery, off road driving*

RESTRICTIONS
Pets by arrangement

ATTRACTIONS
Falkland Castle, Scone Palace, Glamis Castle, Stirling Castle, The Royal Yacht Britannia, Edinburgh Castle, luxury guided tours

AFFILIATIONS
Pride of Britain
Small Luxury Hotels

NEAREST
MAJOR CITY:
Edinburgh - 28 miles/35 mins

MAJOR AIRPORT:
Edinburgh - 25 miles/30 mins

RAILWAY STATION:
Markinch - 1 mile/5 mins

RESERVATIONS
Toll free in US: 800-525-4800
or 800-98-PRIDE
Toll free in UK: 0800-964470
*Quote **Best Loved***

ACCESS CODES
AMADEUS LX EDIBHH
APOLLO/GALILEO LX 20905
SABRE/ABACUS LX 23430
WORLDSPAN LX EDIBH

• Map p.464
ref: F8

" Ballathie is not just a fine hotel - it is a civilized haven of rural peace "

Sir Patrick Cormack, FSA MP

BALLATHIE HOUSE HOTEL

Victorian manor house

SCOTLAND

Kinclaven by Stanley, Perth, Perthshire PH1 4QN

Telephone 01250 883268
Fax 01250 883396

E-mail: *ballathie@bestloved.com*

GENERAL MANAGER
Christopher J Longden

ROOM RATES
6 Singles   £75 - £95
33 Doubles/Twins   £150 - £230
3 Suites   £220 - £240
Includes full breakfast, newspaper and VAT

CHARGE/CREDIT CARDS

AMERICAN EXPRESS • DC • JCB • MC • VI

RATINGS & AWARDS
S.T.B. ★★★★ Hotel
A.A. ★★★ ❀❀
A.A. Top 200 - 02/03
Taste of Scotland - 3 Medallions

FACILITIES
On site: *Garden, heli-pad, fishing, croquet, shooting 5 meeting rooms/max 60 people*
Nearby: *Golf, riding*

RESTRICTIONS
Limited facilities for disabled guests
No pets in public rooms

ATTRACTIONS
Scone Palace, Stirling Castle, Perth, Speyside and Aviemore, Edinburgh, Glamis Castle

AFFILIATIONS
Scotland's Heritage Hotels

NEAREST
MAJOR CITY:
Perth - 10 miles/15 mins

MAJOR AIRPORT:
Edinburgh - 60 miles/1 hr

RAILWAY STATION:
Perth - 10 miles/15 mins

RESERVATIONS
Toll free in US: 800-934-6374
*Quote **Best Loved***

ACCESS CODES
Not applicable

In the heart of Perthshire, Ballathie is an enviable touring base on the River Tay

A winding driveway through the woodlands leads to Ballathie's handsome facade crowned by trio of pointy witches' hat roofs. In spring the woods are ablaze with rhododendrons, while in autumn the 1,500-acre estate is bathed in the red-gold of turning leaves. This is a tranquil haven for all seasons, ideally placed for sightseeing, and for sportsmen, who can fish for salmon on the Tay, shoot game in season, and play a round or two of golf at the championship Rosemount course nearby (St Andrews and Carnoustie are also within easy reach). On the sightseeing front, Perth, the cathedral town of Dunkeld, and Scone Palace are within a 20-minute drive, while Edinburgh, Dundee, and the Queen Mother's childhood home of Glamis Castle are under an hour away. Inverness and the West Coast can be reached on day trips.

After a busy day, Ballathie's welcoming country house atmosphere beckons. The attractive bedrooms have been thoughtfully equipped and have lovely views, and the dining room has a reputation for fine Scottish cuisine accompanied by a wide-ranging wine list. After dinner guests can settle in front of a log fire with a glass of malt to plan the next day's diversions.

LOCATION

From Perth, continue north on A9 for 2 miles. Then take the B9099 through Stanley and then turn right at sign for Kinclaven and Ballathie.

21

❝ *An exceptional meal, beautifully presented, all the staff so accomodating - it couldn't have have been improved on* ❞

Willie and Marilyn Hunter, Exeter

• *Map p.464*
ref: H7

SCOTLAND

19th century estate

BANCHORY LODGE

First class fishing fit for a king!

Banchory Lodge is just 40 miles away from Balmoral Castle and set amongst breathtaking woodland and countryside. Thus, visitors will undoubtedly come to understand why this remote corner of Scotland is so popular with the Queen and her family. Situated on the banks of the Dee, which is renowned as one of the best salmon rivers in the world, this traditional, family-run hotel has its own beat, and as such is nothing short of an anglers' paradise.

August sees the opening of the 'glorious 12th' season for grouse, and arrangements can be made for this, and rough and pheasant shooting, on nearby estates. Also within walking distance are two 18-hole golf courses, and anyone wishing to tour locally can do so on bicycles which the hotel loans for free.

The 22-bedroom lodge is conveniently located in the middle of three specialist trails: the Victorian Heritage is self-explanatory, the Castle Trail includes some 40 National Trust properties, while The Whisky Trail incorporates a mind-boggling 50 local distilleries.

Whether guests spend the day standing waist high in water or visiting historic sites, breakfast is

a hearty Scottish affair; local game, Scottish salmon and Aberdeen Angus are also on the menu.

LOCATION

From Aberdeen take A93 to Banchory.
In town centre take left turning into
Bridge Street, hotel is well signed.

Dee Street, Banchory,
Kincardineshire AB31 5HS

Telephone 01330 822625
Fax 01330 825019

E-mail: *banchory@bestloved.com*

OWNER
Margaret Jaffray

GENERAL MANAGER
Donald Law

ROOM RATES
2 Singles   £70 - £85
12 Doubles/Twins   £110
2 Four-posters   £110
6 Family rooms   £110 - £130
Includes full breakfast and VAT

CHARGE/CREDIT CARDS

 • DC • JCB • MC • VI

RATINGS & AWARDS
R.A.C. Blue Ribbon ★★★ *Dining Award 3*
A.A. ★★★ ❀ *75%*

FACILITIES
On site: *Garden, river*
2 meeting rooms/max 130 people
Nearby: *Golf, fishing, riding,*
swimming, shooting

RESTRICTIONS
Limited facilities for disabled guests

ATTRACTIONS
Balmoral and Crathes Castles,
Victorian Heritage Trail,
Whisky and Castles Trail,
Fettercairn and Royal Lochnagar Distilleries

AFFILIATIONS
The Tartan Collection

NEAREST
MAJOR CITY:
Aberdeen - 18 miles/ ½ hr

MAJOR AIRPORT:
Aberdeen - 22 miles/35 mins

RAILWAY STATION:
Aberdeen - 18 miles/ ½ hr

RESERVATIONS
Direct with hotel
Quote **Best Loved**

ACCESS CODES
Not applicable

22 • Map p.464 ref: F7

SCOTLAND

THE BOAT HOTEL

Victorian station hotel

**Boat of Garten,
Highland PH24 3BH**

**Telephone 01479 831258
Fax 01479 831414**

E-mail: *boat@bestloved.com*

OWNERS
Ian and Shona Tatchell

ROOM RATES
4 Singles £50
26 Doubles/Twins £100
2 Suites £120
Includes full breakfast and VAT

CHARGE/CREDIT CARDS
MC • JCB • VI

RATINGS & AWARDS
S.T.B. ★★★★
A.A. ★★★ ❀❀ 70%
*Taste of Scotland - 3 Medallions
Scotch Beef Club
Investors in People*

FACILITIES
On site: *Garden, snooker, golf (adjacent)
2 meeting rooms/max 80 people*
Nearby: *Skiing, fishing, riding, shooting,
off-roading, rafting, watersports*

RESTRICTIONS
*No facilities for disabled guests
Closed 7 - 31 Jan*

ATTRACTIONS
*Cawdor Castle, Loch Ness,
Malt Whisky Trail, Fort George,
Rothiemurchus Sporting Estate,
Cairngorm Mountains & Mountain Railway,
Culloden Battlefield*

AFFILIATIONS
Independent

NEAREST
*MAJOR CITY:
Inverness - 30 miles/40 mins*

*MAJOR AIRPORT:
Inverness - 35 miles/45 mins*

*RAILWAY STATION:
Aviemore - 6 miles/10 mins*

RESERVATIONS
Direct with hotel
Quote **Best Loved**

ACCESS CODES
Not applicable

All aboard for a Highland special firmly anchored in the Spey Valley

Just north of the Cairngorm Mountains, Boat of Garten is a peaceful Highland village set amongst heather-clad hills. This was once a stop on the Great North of Scotland railway route, and The Boat occupies the fine old Victorian station hotel where anglers and other sporting types would install themselves for Highland holidays.

A recent refurbishment has seen the public areas restored to their Victorian splendour complete with polished wooden floors, Oriental rugs and marble fireplaces. The bedrooms are comfortably traditional, while The Capercaillie restaurant has a bolder contemporary feel to match the chef's stylish cuisine. Signature dishes include a tian of home-cured salmon and Shetland crabmeat and Cairngorm beef fillet. Whilst the food is largely Scottish produce, their French Canadian restaurant manager Joel brings a touch of diversity to the restaurant, and being a countertenor - perhaps a little operetta too! Informal meals can be taken in the relaxing lounge bar and there is a lively and popular public bar with occasional live music.

The Boat's sporting pedigree lives on - adjacent to the hotel is the 18-hole, Championship Boat of Garten golf course. Nearby Rothiemurchus Estate offers numerous outdoor activities, including shooting and fishing. It is also home to a charming old shooting lodge, Drumintoul - a wonderful venue for weddings and great for conferences.

LOCATION

From the A9, take the A95 just north of Aviemore. Follow signs to Boat of Garten.

" The most charming and stylish stay ever "

Nicola Conyers, Scotland

Victorian town house

THE BONHAM

**35 Drumsheugh Gardens,
Edinburgh EH3 7RN**
**Telephone 0131 623 6060
Fax 0131 226 6080**
E-mail: *bonham@bestloved.com*

OWNER
Peter Taylor

GENERAL MANAGER
Shaune Ayers

ROOM RATES
10 Singles   £145 - £165
36 Doubles/Twins   £170 - £240
2 Suites   £325
Includes continental breakfast and VAT

CHARGE/CREDIT CARDS

 • *DC* • *MC* • *VI*

RATINGS & AWARDS
S.T.B. ★★★★
A.A. ★★★★ ❀❀ *Town House*
A.A. Top 200 - 02/03
WHICH? Hotel of the Year 2000
Taste of Scotland - 2 Medallions

Voted one of the world's coolest hotels

Without doubt The Bonham belongs to the new generation of 'hip and happening' town house hotels. In fact it was one of the first of this new breed to hit the scene back in 1998. More recently the hotel was voted one of the world's coolest hotels by Condé Naste Traveller Magazine.

The interiors have been created by a leading designer and cleverly incorporate high contemporary style around the existing Victorian features. There is not a shred of chintz in sight. Spacious rooms, large windows and tall ceilings of the period accentuate the uncluttered and bright atmosphere. Colour schemes are fantastic, and the fabrics and furnishings are simply the epitome of modern luxury. Huge, vibrant canvasses adorn the walls.

Whilst stylishly 'cool', there is certainly nothing pretentious about The Bonham. It is an exceptional place in every sense, run with expert professionalism with a wonderful team of staff.

The restaurant is striking and lively and serves European inspired dishes. It is located just five minutes walk from Edinburgh's West End which makes it a very central place to stay when in town.

FACILITIES
On site: *1 meeting room/max 70 people*
Nearby: *Golf, fitness centre*

RESTRICTIONS
No pets, guide dogs only

ATTRACTIONS
*Edinburgh Castle, Royal Yacht Britannia,
Botanical Gardens, Edinburgh Castle,
Holyrood House, Royal Mile,
National Art Gallery of Scotland*

AFFILIATIONS
Preston's Global Hotels

NEAREST
MAJOR CITY:
Edinburgh

MAJOR AIRPORT:
Edinburgh - 6 miles/25 mins

RAILWAY STATION:
Waverley - 1 ½ miles/10 mins
Haymarket - ½ mile/5 mins

RESERVATIONS
Toll free in US: 800-544-9993
Quote **Best Loved**

ACCESS CODES
AMADEUS HK EDIDRU
APOLLO/GALILEO HT 88207
SABRE/ABACUS HK 1451
WORLDSPAN HK DRUMS

LOCATION

*5 minutes walk from Edinburgh's
West End/City Centre.*

www.bonham.bestloved.com

SCOTLAND

BRIDGE OF ORCHY

Highland hotel

**Bridge of Orchy,
Argyll PA36 4AD**

**Telephone 01838 400208
Fax 01838 400313**

E-mail: *orchy@bestloved.com*

MANAGERS
Andrew and Sharon McKnight

ROOM RATES
Single occupancy	£50
8 Doubles/Twins	£85
2 Family rooms	£127

Includes full breakfast and VAT

CHARGE/CREDIT CARDS

• MC • VI

RATINGS & AWARDS
S.T.B. ★★★★
A.A. ★★ ❀❀ 75%
Welcome Host Award - Walkers Welcome

FACILITIES
On site: *2 meeting rooms/max 60 people*
Nearby: *Fishing, climbing, watersports,
white water rafting*

RESTRICTIONS
*No facilities for disabled guests
No smoking in bedrooms
No pets, guide dogs only*

ATTRACTIONS
*West Highland Way, Loch Lomond,
Kilchurn & Inverary Castles,
The Trossachs, Glencoe,
Oban Distillery,
Fort William*

AFFILIATIONS
Scotland's Hotels of Distinction

NEAREST
*MAJOR CITY:
Glasgow - 60 miles/1 ¼ hrs*

*MAJOR AIRPORT:
Glasgow - 60 miles/1 ¼ hrs*

*RAILWAY STATION:
Bridge of Orchy - ½ mile/5 mins*

RESERVATIONS
Toll free in US: 800-437-2687
*Quote **Best Loved***

ACCESS CODES
Not applicable

Highland hospitality and spectacular scenery on the road to Glencoe and Skye

Set beside the Orchy River, the Bridge of Orchy hotel lies amidst some of the most breathtaking scenery the Highlands have to offer. This is the gateway to rugged Rannoch Moor with fabulous views away to the 1,000-metre heights of Beinn Dorain and Beinn An Dòthaidh. The Bridge of Orchy is a staging post on the famous West Highland Way footpath and an ideal base for outdoor pursuits from salmon and trout fishing to skiing, canoeing and white water rafting. A favourite outing from the hotel is a train ride on the West Highland Line - the stretch between Orchy and Fort William is arguably the best journey of all.

Once inside the hotel, the grandeur of the landscape is tempered by warmth and comfort. There are 10 bright and attractive bedrooms, each with its own character. The restaurant offers traditional Scottish cuisine at breakfast and dinner and there is a spacious window-lined lounge with comfy chairs. The Caley Bar is another fine place to relax after a busy day. Bar meals are served here as well as cask ales and a good selection of malt whisky. There is also a new decked terrace area which is great on fine days and has a spectacular panorama of the river and mountains.

LOCATION
60 miles north of Glasgow on the A82.

Baronial mansion — BUNCHREW HOUSE HOTEL

Timelessness and tranquillity by the banks of the Beauly Firth

Steeped in history and tradition, this beautiful 17th century Scottish mansion stands in 20 acres of landscaped gardens whose wall is lapped by the sea in the Beauly Firth. It was built by Simon Fraser, the eighth Lord Lovat, whose marriage to Jean Stewart in 1621 is commemorated by a stone marriage lintel above the fireplace in the drawing room.

Magnificent views from the hotel include the Black Isle and Ben Wyvis. While the dining room - filled with contemporary paintings of the Frasers - overlooks the sea. Traditional cuisine includes prime Scottish beef, fresh lobster and langoustines, local game and venison, and fresh vegetables cooked with herbs from the hotel's own herb garden. These superb dishes are complemented by a comprehensive wine list.

Fourteen comfortable guest rooms include two with luxurious four-posters and one with a sumptuous half-tester; all are furnished to an extremely high standard and all benefit from 24-hour room service.

This is an area offering a number of outdoor sporting activities and a diversity of castles, glens, gardens, and, of course, the intriguing legend of the Loch Ness Monster.

LOCATION

A short distance from both Inverness Airport and railway station, off the A862 between Inverness and Beauly.

SCOTLAND

**Bunchrew,
Inverness IV3 8TA**

**Telephone 01463 234917
Fax 01463 710620**

E-mail: *bunchrew@bestloved.com*

OWNERS
Graham and Janet Cross

ROOM RATES
Single occupancy	£85 - £138
12 Doubles/Twins	£120 - £200
2 Four-posters	£150 - £200

Includes full breakfast and VAT

CHARGE/CREDIT CARDS

 • *JCB* • *MC* • *VI*

RATINGS & AWARDS
S.T.B. ★★★★ *Small Hotel*
A.A. ★★★ ❀❀ 76%
Taste of Scotland - 3 Medallions
Scotch Beef Club

FACILITIES
On site: *Garden, heli-pad, fishing
3 meeting rooms/max 100 people*
Nearby: *Golf, riding, fishing, shooting, skiing, walking*

RESTRICTIONS
*No facilities for disabled guests
No pets in public rooms*

ATTRACTIONS
*Loch Ness, Culloden Battlefield,
Glens of Affric, Cannich,
Strathfarrar & Strathglass,
Cawdor Castle, Isle of Skye*

AFFILIATIONS
*Preston's Global Hotels
Grand Heritage Hotels*

NEAREST
MAJOR CITY:
Inverness - 3 miles/10 mins

MAJOR AIRPORT:
Inverness - 9 miles/20 mins
Edinburgh - 150 miles/ 2 ½ hrs

RAILWAY STATION:
Inverness - 3 miles/10 mins

RESERVATIONS
*Toll free US: 800-544-9993
or 888-93-GRAND*
Quote **Best Loved**

ACCESS CODES
*AMADEUS UI INVBUN
APOLLO/GALILEO UI 41478
SABRE/ABACUS UI 62868
WORLDSPAN UI 42581*

● *Map p.464*
ref: D9

« *So relaxed, our kind of place* »

Jean & Ken Hooper, USA

SCOTLAND

CAIRNBAAN HOTEL

Traditional coaching inn

**By the Crinan Canal,
Near Lochgilphead,
Argyll PA31 8SJ**

**Telephone 01546 603668
Fax 01546 606045**

E-mail: *cairnbaan@bestloved.com*

OWNERS
Darren and Christine Dobson

DEPUTY MANAGER
James McEachern

ROOM RATES
Single occupancy £66
10 Doubles/Twins £105 - £125
Includes full breakfast and VAT

CHARGE/CREDIT CARDS
MC • VI

RATINGS & AWARDS
S.T.B. ★★★★ *Small Hotel*
A.A. ★★★ ✿ 71%
Taste of Scotland - 2 Medallions

FACILITIES
On site: *Garden*
2 meeting rooms/max 150 people
Nearby: *Golf, fishing, water skiing,
yachting, tennis, fitness, shooting, riding,
forest walks, mountain biking*

RESTRICTIONS
*No facilities for disabled guests
No smoking in bedrooms
No pets in public rooms*

ATTRACTIONS
*Inveraray Castle, Islands of Islay and Jura,
Ancient Cairns & Standing, Dunadd Fort,
The Crinan Canal, Sea Life Centre,
Kilmartin House*

AFFILIATIONS
Scotland's Heritage Hotels

NEAREST
MAJOR CITY:
Glasgow - 80 miles/2 hrs

MAJOR AIRPORT:
Glasgow - 80 miles/2 hrs

RAILWAY STATION:
Glasgow - 80 miles/2 hrs
Oban - 35 miles/52 mins

RESERVATIONS
Direct with hotel
Quote **Best Loved**

ACCESS CODES
Not applicable

The perfect place to watch the world slip by

Cairnbaan Hotel was built in the late 18th century as a coaching inn to serve fishermen and puffers trading on the Crinan Canal. Now refurbished, it offers you the warm welcome typical of the West Coast. Traditional and special dishes are served at dinner in the restaurant. Lunches, snacks and a variety of home-baking can be enjoyed in the 'Bar Lock 5' or The Conservatory.

It is an ideal base from which to tour Argyll and the Islands of Islay and Jura. Local places of interest include Inveraray Castle, where some of Scotland's finest treasures are on show, Dunadd Fort where the ancient Kings of Scotland were crowned, and ancient cairns and standing stones.

Inveraray Jail is an unusual holiday attraction: guides dressed in the uniforms of prisoners and warders re-enact its 19th century past. At newly opened Kilmartin House Argyll's ancient past comes alive. The Highland Wildlife Park at Kincraig features herds of red deer, Highland cattle and many species now extinct to the wild: bison, ancient breeds of sheep and Przewalski's horses, one of the world's rarest mammals.

LOCATION
*2 hours from Glasgow Airport via A82 and A83
to Lochgilphead. Take A816 to Cairnbaan.*

" There's good food, fine wine, a beautiful setting and a warm and friendly atmosphere. When it's done this well, what more could you want? "

Alan Wilkinson, Glasgow Herald

18th century country house — CAVENS HOUSE HOTEL

SCOTLAND

A spacious and gracious country retreat in the heart of Burns Country

Cavens was built by tobacco baron Sir Richard Oswald in 1752 as the centrepiece of his extensive Dumfriesshire estates. The influential Oswalds were friends of Benjamin Franklin through their American connections and also contemporaries of Scottish poet Robert Burns, who wrote an 'Ode sacred to the memory of Mrs Oswald' on her death. Tranquil, relaxing and surrounded by mature parkland gardens, Cavens is now home to Angus and Jane Fordyce.

Throughout the house there is a marvellous sense of space so guests never feel crowded. The comfortable bedrooms are particularly generously proportioned – one has a six-foot bed, while the Oswald Room has its own veranda overlooking the garden. Angus, who spent 20 years working in various top London hotels, is responsible for most of the cooking. The four-course dinner menu features the best of local produce from smoked salmon, venison and Highland beef to delicious Scottish cheeses.

Cavens is a great base for touring Burns Country, and for golfers who will find 12 golf courses nearby including the renowned Southerness just a mile away. Travellers heading north will find this an excellent stopover and the house can be made exclusively available for house parties (16-18 guests).

LOCATION

Follow the A710 'Solway Coast road' South from Dumfries for 12 miles, passing through New Abbey and on to Kirkbean. From Kirkbean Village, the driveway to Cavens is clearly signposted on the left.

Cavens, Kirkbean, Dumfries & Galloway DG2 8AA

Telephone 01387 880234 Fax 01387 880467

E-mail: cavens@bestloved.com

OWNERS
Angus and Jane Fordyce

ROOM RATES

Single occupancy	£55 - £70
7 Doubles/Twins	£90 - £110

Includes full breakfast and VAT

CHARGE/CREDIT CARDS

MC • JCB • VI

RATINGS & AWARDS
S.T.B. ★★★★ Small Hotel
A.A. ★★ ❀ 75%
Taste of Scotland - 3 Medallions

FACILITIES
On site: Garden, fishing, croquet
1 meeting room/max 50 people
Nearby: Golf, shooting, fishing, riding

RESTRICTIONS
Limited facilities for disabled guests
Smoking in main lounge only
Pets by arrangement

ATTRACTIONS
Threave Garden and Estate,
Shambellie House,
Burns Cottage and Museum,
The Tam O'Shanter Experience,
Drumlanrig Castle,
John Paul Jones Cottage

AFFILIATIONS
Independent

NEAREST
MAJOR CITY:
Dumfries - 13 miles/15 mins

MAJOR AIRPORT:
Glasgow - 100 miles/2 hrs

RAILWAY STATION:
Dumfries - 13 miles/15 mins

RESERVATIONS
Direct with hotel
Quote **Best Loved**

ACCESS CODES
Not applicable

" You have achieved a simple perfection. Thank you. P.S. Great staff "

Kenneth H Millstein

CHANNINGS

Edwardian town house

SCOTLAND

15 South Learmonth Gardens, Edinburgh EH4 1EZ
Telephone 0131 332 3232
Fax 0131 332 9631
E-mail: *channings@bestloved.com*

OWNER
Peter Taylor

GENERAL MANAGER
Hans Rissmann

ROOM RATES
5 Singles	£130 - £160
37 Doubles/Twins	£170 - £205
1 Four-poster	£195 - £210
3 Suites	£245 - £250

Includes full breakfast and VAT

CHARGE/CREDIT CARDS

• DC • MC • VI

RATINGS & AWARDS
S.T.B. ★★★★
A.A. ★★★★ ❀❀ *Town House*
Taste of Scotland - 3 Medallions

FACILITIES
On site: *Garden, patio,*
Channings Restaurant,
Ochre Vita Mediterranean Food and Wine Bar
2 meeting rooms/max 35 people
Nearby: *Golf, fitness centre*

RESTRICTIONS
No facilities for disabled guests
No pets, guide dogs only

ATTRACTIONS
Dynamic Earth, Royal Yacht Britannia,
Botanical Gardens, Edinburgh Castle,
Holyrood House, Royal Mile,
National Art Gallery of Scotland

AFFILIATIONS
Scotland's Hotels of Distinction
Preston's Global Hotels
Classic British Hotels

NEAREST
MAJOR CITY:
Edinburgh

MAJOR AIRPORT:
Edinburgh - 6 miles/20 mins

RAILWAY STATION:
Waverley - 1 ½ miles/5 mins
Haymarket - 1 ½ miles/5 mins

RESERVATIONS
Toll free in US: 800-544-9993
or 800-437-2687
*Quote **Best Loved***

ACCESS CODES
AMADEUS UI EDICHA
APOLLO/GALILEO UI 22312
SABRE/ABACUS UI 22560
WORLDSPAN UI 14126

You'll be charmed by the staff at this country-style town house

Situated in the cobbled streets of 'old' Edinburgh, this 4 star hotel provides a country-style ambience and pace within the centre of this vibrant, thriving city. The overriding distinctive edge, however, is supplied by a team of outstanding staff who are collectively responsible for the Channings moniker of 'Edinburgh's friendliest hotel'.

The 46 bedrooms are up-to-the-minute and have been designed with great expertise, using a collection of striking fabrics in bold colour ways. Ideal for those romantic getaways, some rooms have roll-top, or double-sized Jacuzzi baths as well as great views across the historic skyline. Impressively, all rooms are equipped with international modem points, voice mail, 55 cable channels, e-TV with internet access, DVD, video, games and hi-fi system. Channings Restaurant has long since been regarded as one of the city's premier eateries, and now hot on the scene is Ochre Vita which offers a taste of the Mediterranean in colourful surroundings.

Unlike many hotels, Channings really does cater appropriately for both the leisure and business customer and the Library and Kingsleigh Suite (located in part of the building that was once home to explorer Ernest Shackleton) are ideal for conferences, meetings and other corporate events.

LOCATION

Channings is only ½ mile from the city centre (10 minutes walk) and only 20 minutes from the airport by taxi.

*" **Better food than some of the top London restaurants and a view to die for** "*

The Mirror

Highland lodge

CORRIEGOUR LODGE

**Loch Lochy, By Spean Bridge,
Inverness-shire PH34 4EB**

**Telephone 01397 712685
Fax 01397 712696**

E-mail: *corriegour@bestloved.com*

OWNERS
Christian and Ian Drew

RATES PER PERSON
2 Singles   £80
7 Doubles/Twins   £80
Includes full breakfast, dinner and VAT

CHARGE/CREDIT CARDS

 • *DC* • *JCB* • *MC* • *VI*

RATINGS & AWARDS
S.T.B. ★★★★ *Small Hotel*
Taste of Scotland - 3 Medallions

FACILITIES
On site: *Garden, fishing*
Nearby: *Riding, shooting, walking,
climbing, pony trekking, sailing,
cycling, fishing, absailing,
white water rafting*

RESTRICTIONS
*No facilities for disabled guests
No children under 8 years*

ATTRACTIONS
*Eilean Donan Castle,
Glencoe, Urquhart Castle,
Culloden Battlefield,
Isle of Skye, Blair Castle,
Glenfinnan, Loch Ness*

AFFILIATIONS
Independent

NEAREST
MAJOR CITY:
Inverness - 58 miles/1 ½ hrs

MAJOR AIRPORT:
Inverness - 66 miles/1 ¾ hrs
Glasgow - 110 miles/3 hrs

RAILWAY STATION:
Fort William - 12 miles/20 mins

RESERVATIONS
Direct with hotel
Quote **Best Loved**

ACCESS CODES
Not applicable

An experience to savour amidst the dramatic scenery of the Great Glen

One of the first things to say about Corriegour Lodge is that it is situated in one of the finest and most dramatic settings in the Great Glen - an area famed for its outstanding natural beauty.

The location is something the owners, Ian and Christian enthuse about with a great passion, a passion, incidentally, that is apparent in every aspect of their business. Refreshingly, their aim is to provide guests with the modern comforts of today with the standards and service of yesteryear - without charging a premium for it. They describe the hotel as a 'total experience', a retreat where guests can come and relax and enjoy the sheer beauty and tranquillity of the area.

An integral part of this 'experience' is the dining, which, by all accounts, is show stopping. Head Chef Ian is one of Scotland's youngest, most talented chefs and he is of course spoilt by the abundance and quality of the area's natural larder.

For the finale guests may be treated to a rare sighting of Lizzie, distant cousin of Nessie, who is believed to lurk in the loch below (or is it perhaps a case of just one whisky too many).

An excellent new addition to Best Loved.

LOCATION
*From Edinburgh follow the A9 from the south
and turn off at Dalwinnie. Then follow signs for
Spean Bridge. From Glasgow follow the A82 to
Crianlarich and Fort William. Then follow signs
to Spean Bridge. From Spean Bridge the hotel is
on the Inverness road, on the right.*

30

• Map p.464
ref: E6

" Very much the country house with a relaxed and welcoming atmosphere, and refreshingly unpretentious "

D J Robertson, A.A. Inspector

COUL HOUSE HOTEL

Highland country house

**Contin, by Strathpeffer,
Near Inverness,
Ross-shire IV14 9ES**
Telephone 01997 421487
Fax 01997 421945

E-mail: *coulhouse@bestloved.com*

OWNERS
Martyn and Ann Hill

ROOM RATES
3 Singles	£54 - £72
12 Doubles/Twins	£78 - £128
1 Four-poster	£106 - £142
1 Suite	£120 - £170
3 Triple/Family rooms	£78 - £171

Includes full breakfast and VAT

CHARGE/CREDIT CARDS

• DC • JCB • MC • VI

RATINGS & AWARDS
S.T.B. ★★★★ Hotel
A.A. ★★★ ❀ 74%
Taste of Scotland - 2 Medallions

FACILITIES
On site: *Garden, pitch and putt
2 meeting rooms/max 80 people*
Nearby: *Golf, fishing*

RESTRICTIONS
None

ATTRACTIONS
*Strathpeffer Spa Victorian Village,
Loch Ness, Strathconon,
Cromarty Firth, Beauly Priory,
Loch Achonachie salmon lift, Castle Leod,
Rogie Falls and Torrachilty Forest Trail*

AFFILIATIONS
Scotland's Hotels of Distinction

NEAREST
*MAJOR CITY:
Inverness - 20 miles/30 mins*

*MAJOR AIRPORT:
Inverness - 25 miles/35 mins
Glasgow - 180 miles/4 hrs*

*RAILWAY STATION:
Inverness - 20 miles/30 mins*

RESERVATIONS
Toll free in US: 800-437-2687
Quote **Best Loved**

ACCESS CODES
*AMADEUS BW INV511
APOLLO/GALILEO BW 32880
SABRE/ABACUS BW 30594
WORLDSPAN BW 83511*

So much to see and enjoy in such a perfect Highland setting

The ancient Mackenzies of Coul picked the supreme situation for this secluded country mansion, with magnificent, uninterrupted views over forest and mountain. For 25 years, it has been the home of Martyn and Ann Hill, who offer high standards, friendly service and a warm Highland welcome.

The candlelit Mackenzie's Restaurant and Tartan Bistro are appointed for 'Taste of Scotland' cooking, which is personally supervised by head chef, Karl Taylor, who has been at Coul for many years. Smoked seafoods, fresh salmon and succulent roasts are on the menu. The wine list is equally superb, and the Mackenzie's Bar has a fine selection of single malts. The three elegant lounges all have log fires. The bedrooms are individually designed and decorated, and thoroughly well equipped.

The hotel is a favourite with anglers and golfers. It has salmon and trout fishing nearby, and offers a 5-course golf package that includes Royal Dornoch. Using the hotel as a base you can easily cruise Loch Ness, visit Macbeth's Cawdor Castle, or sail to the Summer Isles. You can also pony-trek and go on guided 'Insight' rambling, or follow the Highland Heritage Trail.

LOCATION

From south, by-passing Inverness, continue on A9 over Moray Firth Bridge. After 5 miles, follow A835 to Contin. Hotel is ½ mile up private drive to the right.

❝ *Deep-cushioned comfort amongst the historic castles of Scotland* ❞

Mr & Mrs Miller, Vancouver, Canada

Victorian hotel CRAIGELLACHIE HOTEL OF SPEYSIDE

SCOTLAND

Boundless Highland hospitality on the banks of the River Spey

The Craigellachie Hotel occupies a pre-eminent position crowning a low rise above lawns that lead down to the banks of the River Spey. The fast-flowing Spey is one of Scotland's top salmon fishing rivers and a magnet for keen anglers, while the surrounding countryside proves equally appealing to guests who just want to enjoy some of the Highlands' finest scenery. At the very heart of the Malt Whisky Trail, the award winning Quaich Bar serves over 500 single malts and is a celebration to the hotel's many world famous neighbours.

Generously proportioned rooms give a welcome sense of space and provide many quiet corners where guests can steal themselves away either to read a good book by the fire, have a game of snooker or sit and chat over tomorrow's touring plans. Recent refurbishments have garnered considerable praise for the elegant yet unfussy décor which blends cleverly with the period of the building and extends to the charming bedrooms decorated with subtle combinations of colours and fabrics.

Modern Scottish cuisine with an international twist is the order of the day in the ambient Ben

Aigan restaurant and after dinner, what better way to spend the rest of the evening than sampling a dram, or two!

LOCATION

12 miles from Elgin on the A941 Aviemore/Elgin road.

Craigellachie, Speyside, Banffshire AB38 9SR

**Telephone 01340 881204
Fax 01340 881253**

E-mail: *craigellachie@bestloved.com*

GENERAL MANAGER
Duncan Elphick

ROOM RATES
12 Doubles/Twins   £100 - £120
8 Superior Doubles/Twins   £115 - £135
5 Deluxe Doubles/Twins   £130 - £150
Includes full breakfast and VAT

CHARGE/CREDIT CARDS

 • DC • JCB • MC • VI

RATINGS & AWARDS
S.T.B. ★★★★ *Hotel*
A.A. ★★★ ❀❀ 76%
Taste of Scotland - 3 Medallions

FACILITIES
On site: *Garden, tennis, bicycles*
3 meeting rooms/max 50 people
Nearby: *Golf, fishing, riding,*
cycling, off road driving

RESTRICTIONS
No facilities for disabled guests
Small pets very welcome, but not in
public rooms

ATTRACTIONS
Loch Ness, the Highlands,
Balmoral Castle, Malt Whisky Trail,
Culloden Battlefield, Cairngorms

AFFILIATIONS
The Celebrated Hotels Collection
Grand Heritage Hotels

NEAREST
MAJOR CITY:
Inverness - 50 miles/1 hr

MAJOR AIRPORT:
Aberdeen - 55 miles/1 hr

RAILWAY STATION:
Elgin - 12 miles/20 mins

RESERVATIONS
Toll free in US: 800-322-2403
or 888-93-GRAND
*Quote **Best Loved***

ACCESS CODES
AMADEUS UI ABZCRG
APOLLO/GALILEO UI 33029
SABRE/ABACUS UI 56409
WORLDSPAN UI 42062

❝ *A magical experience! By far our best ever in many years of quality travel. A must on any quality itinerary. Authentic excellence* ❞

Sally Miller, California

CROMLIX HOUSE

Baronial mansion and estate

SCOTLAND

Kinbuck By Dunblane, Near Stirling, Perthshire FK15 9JT

Telephone 01786 822125
Fax 01786 825450

E-mail: *cromlix@bestloved.com*

OWNERS
David and Ailsa Assenti

ROOM RATES
Single occupancy	£125 - £190
6 Doubles/Twins	£200 - £260
8 Suites	£245 - £360

Includes full breakfast and VAT

CHARGE/CREDIT CARDS

 ● *DC* ● *MC* ● *VI*

RATINGS & AWARDS
S.T.B. ★★★★★ *Small Hotel*
A.A. ★★★ ❀❀
A.A. Top 200 - 02/03
Taste of Scotland - 4 Medallions
Andrew Harper Hideaway of 2000

FACILITIES
On site: *Garden, heli-pad, fishing, croquet, riding, tennis*
3 meeting rooms/max 70 people
Nearby: *Golf, riding, salmon & trout fishing*

RESTRICTIONS
No facilities for disabled guests
No pets in public rooms

ATTRACTIONS
Stirling Castle, Scone Palace, Glenturret Distillery, The Trossachs

AFFILIATIONS
Pride of Britain
The Celebrated Hotels Collection

NEAREST
MAJOR CITY:
Glasgow - 30 miles/35 mins
Edinburgh - 38 miles/45 mins

MAJOR AIRPORT:
Edinburgh - 35 miles/40 mins
Glasgow - 40 miles/55 mins

RAILWAY STATION:
Dunblane - 4 miles/10 mins

RESERVATIONS
Toll free in US: 800-322-2403
or 800-98-PRIDE
Quote **Best Loved**

ACCESS CODES
Not applicable

An absolute treasure close to Edinburgh and Glasgow

Built in 1874 as a family residence in a 2000 acre estate, Cromlix retains its original character and features, including a charming chapel perfect for weddings. The imposing exterior belies a 'comfortable' and 'homely' interior. The feeling is that of a much loved home which invites relaxation. In the true traditions of country house hospitality, nothing is 'too precious' or pretentious everything about Cromlix is genuine, including the sense of history.

As you would expect, Cromlix is furnished throughout with antiques, fine furniture and paintings. The six bedrooms and eight very spacious suites with private sitting rooms, offer comfort and luxury. Two of the five public rooms are typical of a Victorian shooting lodge.

Dining at Cromlix is an experience to be savoured. The award winning staff prepare a fresh menu daily. Vegetarian, special and lighter diets are readily catered for.

Country pursuits include fishing, shooting or simply enjoying the wildlife. By advance arrangement: trout and salmon fishing; sporting, clay shooting. Nearby : 10 golf courses.

LOCATION
5 minutes off the A9 north of Dunblane through Kinbuck Village on the B8033.

*" **The small hotel with the big personality** "*

Ray Schoenke, Baltimore

● *Map p.464*
ref: F6

SCOTLAND

Country house

CULDEARN HOUSE

True Scottish warmth, hospitality and a kilted laird

Voted 'Scotland's Best Small Hotel' by the RAC, this beautifully furnished hotel makes an ideal place to sample Scottish country life.

Culdearn House is situated in the lush surroundings of picturesque Grantown-on-Spey. Each of the nine immaculate guest rooms is individually styled and named after the famous and romantic castles of Scotland. All inclusive in the price of your room are breakfast and dinner so the generosity of the hospitality is quickly apparent.

The elegant lounge provides a relaxing place to mingle with the other guests before dinner. Whilst enjoying a locally produced whisky, perhaps (for which the area is renowned), one can anticipate the pleasures suggested by the menu.

Alasdair Little, 'the kilted laird' himself, a perfect host, with his wife, Isobel, the award-winning chef, will ensure your complete satisfaction. With her staff, she will prepare your meal using fresh produce from nearby estates and the Moray coast. To complement the food, the laird will suggest a wine or two from his personal selection while kilted girls will attend you with smiling, efficient service.

LOCATION

Approaching Grantown from the south west on A95 turn left at the 30 mph sign. Culdearn faces you.

Woodlands Terrace, Grantown-on-Spey, Moray PH26 3JU

Telephone 01479 872106
Fax 01479 873641

E-mail: *culdearn@bestloved.com*

OWNERS
Isobel and Alasdair Little

RATES PER PERSON
1 Single	*£75*
8 Doubles/Twins/Kings	*£75*

Includes full breakfast, dinner and VAT

CHARGE/CREDIT CARDS

 ● DC ● JCB ● MC ● VI

RATINGS & AWARDS
S.T.B. ★★★★ *Small Hotel*
R.A.C. ★★ *Dining Award 3*
A.A. ★★ ❀ *77%*
Taste of Scotland - 3 Medallions
Green Tourism Business - Gold Award
Scotch Beef Club

FACILITIES
***On site:** Garden*
***Nearby:** Golf, fishing, riding, birdwatching*

RESTRICTIONS
Limited facilities for disabled guests
No children under 10 years
No pets
Closed 1 Nov - 18 Mar

ATTRACTIONS
Ballindalloch,
Cawdor and Brodie Castles,
Culloden Battlefield,
Malt Whisky distilleries

AFFILIATIONS
The Circle Group

NEAREST
MAJOR CITY:
Inverness - 30 miles/35 mins

MAJOR AIRPORT:
Edinburgh - 140 miles/2 ½ hrs
Inverness - 35 miles/40 mins

RAILWAY STATION:
Aviemore - 15 miles/20 mins

RESERVATIONS
Direct with hotel
*Quote **Best Loved***

ACCESS CODES
Not applicable

❝ Princes past and present have enjoyed the ambience and hospitality of this elegant Palladian mansion ❞

Captain Edmund Burt, Letters from a Gentleman in the North of Scotland, c 1730

CULLODEN HOUSE

18th century country house

SCOTLAND

Culloden, Inverness, Inverness-shire IV2 7BZ

Telephone 01463 790461
Fax 01463 792181

E-mail: *cullodenhse@bestloved.com*

GENERAL MANAGER
Stephen Davies

ROOM RATES
3 Singles	£135 - £160
17 Doubles/Twins	£199
8 Suites	£295

Includes full breakfast, newspaper and VAT

CHARGE/CREDIT CARDS

 • DC • JCB • MC • VI

RATINGS & AWARDS
S.T.B. ★★★★ *Hotel*
A.A. ★★★★ ❀

FACILITIES
On site: *Garden, heli-pad, croquet, tennis boules, sauna, golf driving net 3 meeting rooms/max 100 people*
Nearby: *35 golf courses, fishing, riding, fitness centre, tennis, yachting*

RESTRICTIONS
No facilities for disabled guests
No children under 10 years
Smoking in bar only
Pets by arrangement

ATTRACTIONS
Cawdor Castle, Clava Cairns, Loch Ness, Caladonian Canal, Fort George, Aviemore, 21 Distilleries, Culloden Battlefield

AFFILIATIONS
The Celebrated Hotels Collection
Scotland's Heritage Hotels

NEAREST
MAJOR CITY:
Inverness - 3 miles/10 mins

MAJOR AIRPORT:
Inverness - 3 miles/10 mins

RAILWAY STATION:
Inverness - 3 miles/10 mins

RESERVATIONS
Toll free in US: 800-322-2403
Toll free tel/fax in US: 800-373-7987
Toll free in UK: 0800-980-4561
Quote **Best Loved**

ACCESS CODES
AMADEUS UZ INVCHH
APOLLO/GALILEO UZ 24800
SABRE/ABACUS UZ 49776
WORLDSPAN UZ 41006

Princely Palladian hospitality in a very special Highland setting

Culloden House is a gracious Georgian mansion, refurbished in 1788 incorporating a fortified mid-16th century castle, set in 40 acres of stately parkland. As early as 1730, the Forbes family established a tradition of fine hospitality. On arrival guests could refresh themselves with a pint of fine claret, and stay the night if they chose to. They always chose to.

The house's history features spies, sieges, proud Highland chieftains and romance. Bonnie Prince Charlie buckled his sword as he dashed from the house to fight his last battle. The recent guest list includes politicians, film stars and royalty. The house is decorated and furnished in Palladian style. The main rooms feature ornate Adam plasterwork and fireplaces. Here you can listen to Scottish folk music played on pedal harp, bagpipes and clarsach. Bedrooms are appointed to a very high standard, many having four-poster beds or tester. Dinners are a delight, featuring fresh and smoked Scottish game, meat, fowl and produce cooked and presented imaginatively.

Close by are Culloden Battlefield, the Highland glens, Cawdor Castle, Clava Cairns, the Caledonian Canal and 35 golf courses. Dolphins wait near Inverness harbour, and so may something else in Loch Ness.

LOCATION

1 mile down the A96 from Inverness, turn right at sign for Culloden. 1 mile further, turn left at Culloden House sign.

" *This is a place I can relax* "

Dwight D Eisenhower, Former President of the USA

SCOTLAND

18th century castle CULZEAN CASTLE - EISENHOWER APARTMENT

Rooms with a view atop one of Scotland's premier tourist attractions

Possibly one of the grandest bachelor pads ever constructed, Culzean Castle perches on the Ayrshire sea cliffs commanding views across the water to the mountains of Arran and the Mull of Kintyre. Until the latter part of the 18th century, Culzean was a relatively modest castle keep belonging to the Kennedy family. Enter David Kennedy, the newly succeeded 10th Earl of Cassillis, who commissioned the great Scottish architect Robert Adam to provide him with a fabulous bachelor abode where he could entertain his friends in high old style. Adams obliged, creating his final masterpiece, which was completed in 1792.

In 1945, the Kennedys relinquished their home to the National Trust for Scotland, but not before gifting a six-bedroom apartment on the top floor of the castle to General Eisenhower as a thank you to the wartime hero from the Scottish nation. During his retirement, Eisenhower spent some time painting and walking in the castle grounds. The self-contained Eisenhower Apartment is now available to discerning guests, elegantly furnished in country house style with a cosy dining room where guests enjoy fine Scottish food, and a round drawing room offering spectacular sea views.

LOCATION

From Maybole take the B7023 and then the A719, signed Turnberry. Culzean is signed off this road on the right hand side, just 4 miles from Maybole.

**Maybole,
Ayrshire KA19 8LE**

**Telephone 01655 884455
Fax 01655 884503**

E-mail: *culzean@bestloved.com*

GENERAL MANAGER
Jonathan Cardale

ROOM RATES
Single occupancy   £140 - £250
4 Doubles/Twins   £225 - £275
1 Four-poster   £325
1 Suite   £375
*Includes full breakfast, afternoon tea,
complimentary drinks and VAT*

CHARGE/CREDIT CARDS

 • *MC* • *VI*

RATINGS & AWARDS
Taste of Scotland - 1 Medallion

FACILITIES
On site: *Garden, shoreline and
woodland walks*
Nearby: *Golf, shooting, fishing*

RESTRICTIONS
*Limited facilities for disabled guests
Children by arrangement
No smoking throughout
No pets*

ATTRACTIONS
*Turnberry & Royal Troon Golf Courses,
Culzean Castle, Isle of Arran Distillery,
Ayr Racecourse, Isle of Arran,
Tam O'Shanter Experience*

AFFILIATIONS
Independent

NEAREST
MAJOR CITY:
Glasgow - 45 miles/1 hr

MAJOR AIRPORT:
*Prestwick - 15 miles/30 mins
Glasgow - 47 miles/1 hr*

RAILWAY STATION:
Ayr - 12 miles/20 mins

RESERVATIONS
Direct with hotel
Quote **Best Loved**

ACCESS CODES
Not applicable

● *Map p.464*
ref: G10

66 To all, to each, a fair good-night, and pleasing dreams, and slumbers light! 99

Sir Walter Scott whilst staying at Dalhousie in 1808

DALHOUSIE CASTLE & SPA

Historic castle

SCOTLAND

**Bonnyrigg,
Edinburgh EH19 3JB**

**Telephone 01875 820153
Fax 01875 821936**

E-mail: *dalhousie@bestloved.com*

MANAGING DIRECTOR
Neville S Petts

ROOM RATES

Single occupancy	*£90 - £285*
27 Doubles/Twins	*£110 - £285*
3 Triples/Quads	*£175 - £240*
2 Themed suites	*£245 - £285*

Includes full breakfast and VAT

CHARGE/CREDIT CARDS

 • *DC* • *JCB* • *MC* • *VI*

RATINGS & AWARDS
S.T.B. ★★★★ *Hotel*
A.A. ★★★ ❀❀ *77%*
Taste of Scotland - 1 Medallion

FACILITIES
On site: *Heli-pad, health & beauty,
spa, falconry, archery, Private Chapel
5 meeting rooms/max 150 people*
Nearby: *Fishing, clay shooting, golf, riding,
fitness, tennis, off-road driving*

RESTRICTIONS
*Limited facilities for disabled guests
No smoking in bedrooms
No pets in public rooms
Closed 5 - 19 Jan (midweek only)*

ATTRACTIONS
*Edinburgh City and Castle,
Edinburgh Crystal, Holyrood House,
Royal Yacht Britannia, Glasgow City,
Glenkinchie Distillery*

AFFILIATIONS
*Preston's Global Hotels
Grand Heritage Hotels*

NEAREST
MAJOR CITY:
Edinburgh - 7 miles/20 mins

MAJOR AIRPORT:
Edinburgh - 14 miles/30 mins

RAILWAY STATION:
Waverley - 7 miles/20 mins

RESERVATIONS
*Toll free in US: 800-544-9993
or 888-93-GRAND*
Quote **Best Loved**

ACCESS CODES
*AMADEUS UI EDIDCH
APOLLO/GALILEO UI 78139
SABRE/ABACUS UI 30846
WORLDSPAN UI 40637*

A 13th-century castle with a state-of-the-art spa

The Ramsays of Dalhousie laid the foundations of their family seat over 700 years ago and its ancient stones have witnessed a fascinating procession of historical events and famous guests from Edward I and Oliver Cromwell to Queen Victoria and Sir Walter Scott. However, the new millennium has probably heralded the most revolutionary development in the castle's long and distinguished history with the arrival of the Aqueous Spa.

A short drive south of Edinburgh, the castle is set in its own estate of forest and parkland. Thirteen of its 27 sumptuously furnished and thoughtfully-equipped bedrooms are historically themed, for example the Sir William Wallace Room, and there are a further five rooms in the century-old Lodge a two-minute walk away overlooking the South Esk River. The "Aqueous" hydrotherapy spa is the first of its kind in Scotland offering invigorating and rejuvenating hydro facilities combined with relaxing treatments to reduce stress and promote a healthy body and mind. Spa packages or individual treatments are available. Adjacent to the spa, the Orangery offers a Scottish-Mediterranean menu with light and healthy options as a counter-balance to the traditional Scottish-French cuisine served in the more formal vaulted Dungeon Restaurant.

LOCATION

From Edinburgh take A7 south through Newtongrange. Right at junction onto B704. The hotel entrance is ½ mile along on right.

" *Let us hope that the Sturman's achieve in Scotland what they achieved south of the border* **"**

A.A. Inspector

● *Map p.464*
ref: F11

18th century vicarage | DRYFESDALE COUNTRY HOUSE HOTEL

SCOTLAND

A convenient and comfortable break just across the Border

In rolling countryside, just minutes off the main A74(M) Carlisle to Glasgow road, The Dryfesdale makes an ideal overnight break on the road north, or extend your stay for a few days to explore the Solway Coast and Dumfries, a notable stop on the Robert Burns Trail.

The Dryfesdale's elevated parkland setting affords panoramic views across the Borders landscape a short distance outside the market town of Lockerbie. It is an unassuming spot in a former manse, or vicarage, dating from 1762. There is a cosy bar and sun lounge offering informal meals and a rich choice of some 160 single malt whiskies, or guests can dine in the more formal restaurant, which specialises in local Scottish cuisine.

With time to spare, there is plenty to see and do in the area. The 'Queen of the South', bustling Dumfries is the gateway to southwest Scotland and home to the Robert Burns Centre. Scotland's most famous poet spent his twilight years here and was buried in St. Michael's Church. South of Dumfries, triangular Caerlaverock Castle is an unusual and fascinating construction founded in the 13th century. Nearby, the Wildfowl and Wetlands Centre on the marshy Solway shore is a real birdwatcher's haven.

LOCATION
½ *mile from Junction 17 of the M74.*
The hotel is well signposted from the motorway roundabout.

Lockerbie,
Dumfries & Galloway DG11 2SF

Telephone 01576 202427
Fax 01576 204187

E-mail: *dryfesdale@bestloved.com*

OWNERS
Clive and Heather Sturman

ROOM RATES
3 Singles £65 - £85
12 Doubles/Twins £95 - £140
Includes full breakfast and VAT

CHARGE/CREDIT CARDS

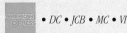 ● *DC* ● *JCB* ● *MC* ● *VI*

RATINGS & AWARDS
S.T.B. ★★★★ *Hotel*
A.A. ★★★ 🏵🏵 *77%*
Taste of Scotland - 3 Medallions

FACILITIES
On site: *Garden, heli-pad, fishing, croquet, putting green*
3 meeting rooms/max 150 people
Nearby: *Fishing, shooting, riding*

RESTRICTIONS
Pets by arrangement

ATTRACTIONS
Edinburgh, Solway Coast, Gretna Green, Caerlaverock Castle, Lockerbie Garden of Remembrance, Burn's House & Museum

AFFILIATIONS
Independent

NEAREST
MAJOR CITY:
Dumfries - 10 miles/15 mins

MAJOR AIRPORT:
Glasgow - 73 miles/1 hr

RAILWAY STATION:
Lockerbie- 3 miles/10 mins

FERRY PORT:
Stranraer - 70 miles/1 ½ hrs

RESERVATIONS
Direct with hotel
Quote **Best Loved**

ACCESS CODES
Not applicable

38

● *Map p.464*
ref: E6

" We travel around a great deal. No other hotel in the British Isles has so invariably combined caring service and beautiful cooking all in a completely relaxed atmosphere "

Sonia & Patrick Stevenson

DUNAIN PARK HOTEL

Georgian shooting lodge

**Inverness,
Inverness-shire IV3 8JN**

**Telephone 01463 230512
Fax 01463 224532**

E-mail: *dunain@bestloved.com*

OWNERS
Ann and Edward Nicoll

ROOM RATES
3 Doubles/Twins	£158
2 Superior doubles	£198
6 Suites	£198
2 Cottages	£158

Includes full breakfast and VAT

CHARGE/CREDIT CARDS

 ● *DC* ● *JCB* ● *MC* ● *VI*

RATINGS & AWARDS
S.T.B. ★★★★ *Hotel*
Taste of Scotland - 3 Medallions

FACILITIES
On site: *Garden, croquet,
indoor pool, sauna*
Nearby: *Golf, fishing, riding, walking*

RESTRICTIONS
Limited facilities for disabled guests

ATTRACTIONS
*Loch Ness, Cawdor Castle,
Culloden Battlefield, Whisky Trail,
Eden Court Theatre*

AFFILIATIONS
Independent

NEAREST
MAJOR CITY:
Inverness - 2 miles/5 mins

MAJOR AIRPORT:
Inverness - 8 miles/30 mins
Glasgow - 188 miles/3 ¾ hrs

RAILWAY STATION:
Inverness - 2 miles/5 mins

RESERVATIONS
Direct with hotel
Quote **Best Loved**

ACCESS CODES
Not applicable

www.dunain.bestloved.com

*A seasoned traveller's delight.
Something to write home about*

Located just three miles from Loch Ness, Dunain Park Hotel was originally a shooting lodge, built in Georgian times by the Duke of Gordon, and extended in Victorian times. Edward and Ann Nicoll have owned and run Dunain Park as an hotel for sixteen years, which they have upgraded and refurbished to the highest standard. The five original bedrooms, all with private facilities, were complemented by the addition of six deluxe king-bedded suites. Open fires in the main lounges help to create a welcoming atmosphere for guests to relax in. The two garden cottages, overlooking the walled garden, are fully serviced and furnished to the same high standard of the main building. Dunain Park's six acres of gardens and woodlands have recently been replanted with thousands of new bulbs, trees and shrubs, guaranteeing a glorious display of colour and variety.

Mrs Nicoll is in charge of the kitchen and produces an à la carte menu which changes daily and uses the best local produce such as salmon, venison and highland beef. Accompanied by soft fruits, lettuce, vegetables and herbs from the kitchen garden, as well as home-made jams, jellies and chutneys, the meals prove to be innovative and irresistible.

LOCATION
Heading west from Inverness on the A82, 1 mile from the town boundary on the left hand side.

Highland hotel

THE DUNALASTAIR HOTEL

SCOTLAND

A fairytale location in idyllic Highland 'adventureland'

So, you fancy getting away from it all! Dunalastair Hotel should be your destination, especially if you also fancy adventure in the great outdoors. Start the adventure on your journey there. In spite of its remoteness, an overnight Perth-London sleeper train can drop you at Pitlochry just a taxi ride from the hotel or, from Glasgow, a branch line - is this the last one left? - will take you through breathtaking scenery right to Loch Rannoch on one of Europe's greatest train journeys.

The little village snuggled beneath mountains at the end of the loch, with its burn flowing under the bridge, was surely the inspiration for Brigadoon. Dominating the village square, with its small shops and cottages, is the hotel, where you can be absolutely sure of a tremendous Highland welcome. The Edwards family are wildly enthusiastic about all the Highlands have to offer and will be happy to spirit you away from beside the roaring log fires and a heart-warming selection of whiskies.

If you can resist the call to fishing, hill-walking, orienteering, mountain-biking, sailing, white-water rafting and various extreme sports, you will find a kaleidescope of delights within this well-run, Victorian sporting lodge.

LOCATION

Take the A9 to Pitlochry, then take the B8019 via 'Queens View' to Kinloch Rannoch. Dunalastair is situated in the village square.

The Square, Kinloch Rannoch, Perthshire PH16 5PW

**Telephone 01882 632323
Fax 01882 632371**

E-mail: dunalastair@bestloved.com

MANAGING DIRECTOR
Paul Edwards

ROOM RATES
2 Singles	£35 - £45
17 Doubles/Twins	£70 - £99
4 Four-posters	£89 - £110
1 Rob Roy room	£100 - £130
1 Family room	£70 - £90

Includes full breakfast and VAT

CHARGE/CREDIT CARDS

 • MC • VI

RATINGS & AWARDS
S.T.B. ★★★ Hotel
Walkers Welcome
Cyclists Welcome
Taste of Scotland - 1 Medallion

FACILITIES
On site: 3 meeting rooms/max 70 people
Nearby: Golf, fishing, riding, shooting, biking, white water rafting, off-roading, watersports, walking

RESTRICTIONS
Limited facilities for disabled guests
Closed Jan

ATTRACTIONS
Blair Castle, Scone Palace, West Highland Railway tour, House of Bruar, Distillery Tours, Outdoor Activity Centre

AFFILIATIONS
Independent

NEAREST
MAJOR CITY:
Perth - 46 miles/1 ¼ hrs

MAJOR AIRPORT:
Edinburgh - 87 miles/2 hrs
Glasgow - 90 miles/2 hrs

RAILWAY STATION:
Pitlochry - 18 miles/30 mins
Rannoch - 18 miles/30 mins

RESERVATIONS
Direct with hotel
Quote **Best Loved**

ACCESS CODES
AMADEUS HK DNDDUN
APOLLO/GALILEO HT 43977
SABRE/ABACUS HK 22476
WORLDSPAN HK DUNAL

SCOTLAND

HOTEL EILEAN IARMAIN

Victorian house

**Isle Ornsay, Sleat,
Isle of Skye IV43 8QR**

**Telephone 01471 833332
Fax 01471 833275**

E-mail: *eilean@bestloved.com*

OWNERS
Sir Iain and Lady Noble

ROOM RATES
Single occupancy	£90
9 Doubles/Twins	£120
1 Four-poster	£150
2 Triples	£160
4 Suites	£180 - £250

Includes full breakfast and VAT

CHARGE/CREDIT CARDS

 ● *DC* ● *MC* ● *VI*

RATINGS & AWARDS
S.T.B. ★★★ *Hotel*
R.A.C. ★★ *Dining Award 3*
A.A. ★★ ✿✿ *74%*
Les Routiers Best Hotel of the Year 2001
Taste of Scotland - 2 Medallions

FACILITIES
On site: *Garden, heli-pad, fishing,
shooting, stalking
2 meeting rooms/max 50 people*
Nearby: *Golf, riding, pool*

RESTRICTIONS
*No facilities for disabled guests
No pets in public rooms*

ATTRACTIONS
*Armadale Castle & Gardens,
Talisker Distillery, Aros Heritage Centre,
Dunvegan Castle, Serpentarian Reptile Centre,
'Bella Jane' Boat trips, Hotel Art Gallery*

AFFILIATIONS
Independent

NEAREST
MAJOR CITY:
Glasgow - 148 miles/4 hrs

MAJOR AIRPORT:
Inverness - 93 miles/2 hrs

RAILWAY STATION:
Kyle of Lochalsh - 14 miles/30 mins

FERRY PORT:
Mallaig/Armadale - 8 miles/15 mins

RESERVATIONS
*Direct with hotel
Quote* **Best Loved**

ACCESS CODES
Not applicable

An enchanted atmosphere reflecting the legends and romance of Skye

Built in 1888, this small, privately owned hotel has retained its Victorian charm and old-world character. Hotel Eilean Iarmain is situated on the small rocky bay of Isle Ornsay in the south of Skye, with expansive views over the Sound of Sleat to the Knoydart hills.

The 16 bedrooms are decorated and furnished in traditional style and include four new suites, housed in the restored stables, one of which is specially suitable for disabled guests. Each bedroom has its own charm: 'The Tower Room', panelled in old pine, and 'The Leabaidh Mhor', with a canopied bed from nearby Armadale Castle, to name two of them. There are log fires in the reception rooms, and a panelled dining room where candlelit dinners can be enjoyed overlooking the bay.

The dinner menu, of five courses, combines imaginative cooking with the variety of fresh local produce, including fish and shellfish landed at the old stone pier, oysters and game from the estate, home baked bread and oatcakes. The extensive wine list has been selected by the proprietors with the aim of offering some unusual wines with fascinating historical provenances, as well as a very good range of more famous wines. Hotel Eilean Iarmain is open year round.

LOCATION

*Approximately 20 minutes from Skye Bridge;
20 minutes from Kyle of Lochalsh Rail Station;
30 minutes from Kylerea ferry.*

❝ *At the Enmore Hotel everything doth gel* ❞

Anne & John Mancino, Plymouth

Gentleman's retreat

ENMORE HOTEL

SCOTLAND

**Marine Parade, Dunoon,
Argyll PA23 8HH**

**Telephone 01369 702230
Fax 01369 702148**

E-mail: *enmore@bestloved.com*

OWNERS
Angela and David Wilson

ROOM RATES
Single occupancy	£59 - £89
5 Doubles/Twins	£90 - £120
4 Four-posters	£150 - £170

Includes full breakfast and VAT

CHARGE/CREDIT CARDS

 • MC • VI

RATINGS & AWARDS
S.T.B. ★★★★ *Small Hotel*
A.A. ★★ ✿ *78%*
A.A. Courtesy & Care Award
Taste of Scotland - 2 Medallions

FACILITIES
On site: *Garden, squash,
private shingle beach*
2 meeting rooms/max 30 people
Nearby: *Golf, riding, fishing*

RESTRICTIONS
No facilities for disabled guests
No smoking in bedrooms
Closed mid Dec - mid Feb

ATTRACTIONS
*Dunoon Golf Course, Inverary,
Loch Lomond, Stirling,
Dumbarton Castle, Rothesay Castle,
Mount Stuart, Benmore Gardens*

AFFILIATIONS
Scotland's Hotels of Distinction

NEAREST
MAJOR CITY:
Glasgow - 50 miles/1 ½ hrs (via ferry)

MAJOR AIRPORT:
Glasgow - 50 miles/1 hr (via ferry)

RAILWAY STATION:
Glasgow - 40 miles/1 hr (via ferry)

FERRY PORT:
Gourock - 20 mins

RESERVATIONS
Toll free in US: 800-437-2687
*Quote **Best Loved***

ACCESS CODES
Not applicable

Freshly cut flowers and binoculars on the windowsill

It is often the small things that count. A thoughtful gesture, an unexpected treat, someone remembering how to fix your favourite drink or how you take your coffee. David and Angela Wilson are experts at adding the personal touch and take great delight in surprising their guests with little extras such as carefully chosen books in the bedrooms and a pair of binoculars balanced on the windowsill to bring the maritime bustle on the Firth of Clyde into focus.

Enmore dates back to 1785, when it was built as a gentleman's retreat for a wealthy Glasgow businessman. The location is stunning affording clear views out across the Firth and there are private romantic gazebos in the well-tended gardens. The pretty and imaginatively furnished bedrooms have sea, garden or mountain views, there are three lounges and a small bar so guests can always find somewhere quiet, and David, who is also chief chef, prepares excellent value Taste of Scotland evening meals.

Dunoon is a picturesque seaside resort with an 18-hole championship golf course, sailing, fishing and pony trekking opportunities. Loch Lomond, Glasgow, the Younger Botanic Garden at Benmore, and the Kyles of Bute are all within striking distance.

LOCATION

*Travel from Glasgow either on the M8/A8
through Greenock and Gourock and over on
one of the two ferries or via Loch Lomond
and the A815 to Dunoon.*

" To die for, we will return "

Mr & Mrs D Smyth, South Carolina, USA

ENTERKINE HOUSE

Country hotel

SCOTLAND

***Annbank, By Ayr,
Ayrshire KA6 5AL***

**Telephone 01292 520580
Fax 01292 521582**

E-mail: *enterkine@bestloved.com*

OWNER
Oswald Browne

ROOM RATES
Single occupancy	£125
6 Suites	£230

Includes full breakfast and VAT

CHARGE/CREDIT CARDS

 ● *MC* ● *VI*

RATINGS & AWARDS
S.T.B. ★★★★★ *Small Hotel*
Taste of Scotland - 4 Medallions

FACILITIES
On site: *Garden, croquet, putting green,
clay shooting, sauna, gym equipment
1 meeting room/max 24 people*
Nearby: *Golf, shooting, fishing, riding*

RESTRICTIONS
*Limited facilities for disabled guests
No children under 11 years
Pets by arrangement*

ATTRACTIONS
*Culzean Castle,
Tam O'Shanter Experience,
Burns Cottage,
Isle of Arran, Glentrool,
Royal Troon & Turnberry Golf Courses*

AFFILIATIONS
*Preston's Global Hotels
Grand Heritage Hotels*

NEAREST
*MAJOR CITY:
Glasgow - 38 miles/50 mins*

*MAJOR AIRPORT:
Prestwick - 8 miles/12 mins
Glasgow - 42 miles/55 mins*

*RAILWAY STATION:
Ayr - 5 miles/10 mins*

RESERVATIONS
*Toll free in US: 800-544-9993
or 888-93-GRAND
Quote **Best Loved***

ACCESS CODES
*AMADEUS UI PIKKIN
APOLLO/GALILEO UI 37468
SABRE/ABACUS UI 59801
WORLDSPAN UI42460*

www.enterkine.bestloved.com

Small and exclusive Ayrshire retreat for business and pleasure

A winding avenue of mature trees leads visitors up to Enterkine, providing a gentle transition between the hustle and bustle of the real world and the serenity of this secluded country house retreat. The house dates from the 1930s, when it was built as a private residence, and with just six bedroom suites it still maintains an intimate ambience while providing a luxurious degree of comfort and service for individuals and small groups.

Enterkine is beautifully positioned in its own 310-acre estate with views over woodland, meadows and the Ayr valley. The attractive guest rooms are very comfortable and particularly spacious. Guests have a choice of three elegant reception rooms, there is the oval book-lined library for a quiet read, and two dining rooms where the menu is prepared by Douglas Smith, who is widely recognised as one of Scotland's top young chefs.

This corner of Ayrshire offers plenty of sporting and sightseeing diversions. Both Glasgow and Edinburgh are within easy driving distance, while golfers will find seven championship courses (including Turnberry and Royal Troon) no more than 30 minutes away. The hotel can also arrange game shooting and fishing on request.

LOCATION
***From A77 take B742, signed Annbank.
The entrance to the estate is on the B742
just 50 metres past Annbank.***

43

> *We had a wonderful time at the hotel. The staff are super and we will recommend Fernie Castle to everyone* **"**

Dianne & Janis Howe, Ontario, Canada

● Map p.464
ref: G9

16th century castle

FERNIE CASTLE

SCOTLAND

The romance of the past with the comforts of the present

The first glimpse of Fernie Castle is a moment to remember as the drive emerges from the woods to reveal the castle's white linewash and distinctive corner tower. There has been a castle here since 1353, though the present building dates back a mere four-and-a-half centuries, and stands in 17 acres of private woodland close to a small loch.

Hosts Neil and Mary Blackburn extend a warm welcome symbolized by the crackling open fire in the grate. The traditional décor is warm and cosy with the odd suit of armour to remind you where you are! There are quiet corners for relaxing such as the Wallace Lounge's turret snuggery and atmospheric Keep Bar. Informal meals are served here, or guests can dine in the elegant Auld Alliance Room beneath a grand Georgian chandelier. Romance is alive in the hotel's deluxe rooms, known as Kings and Queens, some of which feature four-poster beds; the Squires and Ladies standard rooms are also very comfortable and thoughtfully equipped.

Golfers are spoilt for choice with 59 golf courses nearby including St Andrews.

Picturesque fishing villages such as East Neuk are within easy reach, as are Falkland Palace and Kellie Castle.

LOCATION

The hotel is located at the intersection of the A9 and the A92, between Edinburgh and Dundee.

Letham,
Ladybank,
Fife KY15 7RU

Telephone 01337 810381
Fax 01337 810422

E-mail: *fernie@bestloved.com*

OWNERS
Neil and Mary Blackburn

RATES PER PERSON
3 Singles	£85 - £109
17 Doubles/Twins	£85 - £109
Includes full breakfast, dinner and VAT

CHARGE/CREDIT CARDS

 ● *MC* ● *VI*

RATINGS & AWARDS
A.A. ★★★ 65%

FACILITIES
On site: *Garden, croquet*
3 meeting rooms/max 180 people
Nearby: *Golf, fishing, watersports*

RESTRICTIONS
No facilities for disabled guests
No smoking in bedrooms

ATTRACTIONS
St Andrews, Falkland Palace,
Edinburgh Castle, Stirling Castle,
Inchcolm Abbey, Deep-Sea World

AFFILIATIONS
Independent

NEAREST
MAJOR CITY:
Dundee - 15 miles/25 mins

MAJOR AIRPORT:
Dundee - 15 miles/25 mins

RAILWAY STATION:
Cupar - 7 miles/10 mins

RESERVATIONS
Direct with hotel
Quote **Best Loved**

ACCESS CODES
Not applicable

SCOTLAND

> ❝ *It is worth beating a path to Flodigarry which enjoys one of the finest situations of any country house in Scotland* ❞
>
> *Neil MacLean, Sunday Times*

FLODIGARRY COUNTRY HOUSE HOTEL   *19th century country house*

Staffin,
Isle of Skye IV51 9HZ
Telephone 01470 552203
Fax 01470 552301

E-mail: *flodigarry@bestloved.com*

OWNERS
Andrew and Pam Butler

ROOM RATES
Single occupancy	£58 - £99
13 Doubles/Twins	£116 - £120
4 Family rooms	£116 - £140
2 Four-posters	£116 - £170

Includes full breakfast and VAT

CHARGE/CREDIT CARDS

 • MC • VI

RATINGS & AWARDS
S.T.B. ★★★★ *Small Hotel*
Macallan Country House Hotel of the Year
Talisker Awards for Best Service &
Best Accommodation

FACILITIES
On site: *Garden, heli-pad, fishing, croquet*
1 meeting room/max 40 people
Nearby: *Yachting, fishing,*
watersports, riding

RESTRICTIONS
No smoking in bedrooms or lounge
No pets in public rooms

ATTRACTIONS
Dunvegan Castle, Quiraing,
Trotternish ridge walk, Talisker Distillery,
Skye Museum of Island Life,
Boat Trips to Outer Hebrides,
Old Man of Storr

AFFILIATIONS
Independent

NEAREST
MAJOR CITY:
Inverness - 120 miles/3 hrs

MAJOR AIRPORT:
Glasgow - 250 miles/5 hrs
Inverness - 120 miles/3 hrs

RAILWAY STATION:
Kyle of Lochalsh - 50 miles/1 hr

FERRY PORT:
Uig - 8 miles/20 mins

RESERVATIONS
Direct with hotel
*Quote **Best Loved***

ACCESS CODES
Not applicable

A romantic castle with dreamy views, good food, fine wine and Gaelic charm

The quintessential escapists dream, Flodigarry Country House Hotel is set amidst one of the most stunningly beautiful and dramatic landscapes in the British Isles. Nestling beneath the towering pinnacles of the Quiraing Mountain in the remote north east of Skye, the hotel overlooks the magnificent broad sweep of Staffin Bay, one of the most beautiful on Skye.

Unspoilt by progress, the area is steeped in history from the Vikings to the more recent Jacobite rising of 1745. The family home of Highland heroine, Flora MacDonald stands in the hotel grounds (see right).

The comfortable public rooms and cosy bedrooms all enjoy superb views over the mountains and sea. In addition, there are seven luxury bedrooms in Flora's cottage now lovingly restored and refurbished.

Winning awards for both its fine cuisine and accommodation, Flodigarry prides itself on the warmth of its old-fashioned Highland hospitality where there's a sense of Victorian ease without stuffiness. Named the Macallan Country House Hotel of the Year and recommended by The Sunday Times, Flodigarry is a breath of fresh air.

Bide a while, soak up the wonderfully timeless atmosphere, the superb panoramic views and Gaelic charm of this island gem.

LOCATION
From Portree, A855 north 20 miles to Staffin.
Hotel is a further 4 miles north on right.

> ❝ *I always thought that Scotland held way too many beautiful places to discover to ever need to re-visit the same place - until the Four Seasons* ❞
>
> *Ailean Graham, Aberdeen*

Map p.464
ref: E9

Lochside hotel

THE FOUR SEASONS HOTEL

SCOTLAND

An inspiring loch side setting with the most spectacular of views and food to match

Set against a steep, forested backdrop on the shores of Loch Earn, the Four Seasons occupies one of the most enviably picturesque locations in the whole of Scotland. The main house was built in the early 1800s for the manager of the local limekilns. Later it served a term as a schoolmaster's house before being gradually extended into a small and comfortable hotel.

Here you will find spacious bedrooms, many with views over the loch, and for the privacy minded, six secluded chalets on the wooded hillside behind the hotel, which are perfect for families.

The view from the Four Seasons stretches southwest down the loch and can honestly be described as magnificent. Spectacular sunsets, mist-wreathed mornings and the snow-covered Bens exercise a mesmeric fascination.

Perhaps one of the best places to watch the ever-changing scenery is from one of the hotel's two restaurants. Both restaurants offer the things you dream of; Orkney scallops, Loch Fyne mussels, Tweed Valley partridge, East Coast halibut and Border lamb. Nearby, there are all sorts of day trips to choose from such as the steam train to Mallaig on the West Coast, a visit to Scotland's smallest whisky distillery, fishing and sailing, or hill walkers can conquer a Munro or two.

LOCATION

On the north east edge of Loch Earn on the A85, Comrie to Lochearnhead road.

***St Fillans,
Perthshire PH6 2NF***

***Telephone 01764 685333
Fax 01764 685444***

E-mail: *fourseasons@bestloved.com*

OWNER
Andrew Low

ASSISTANT MANAGER
Mary McDiarmid

RATES PER PERSON
Single occupancy	*£61 - £100*
12 Doubles/Twins	*£61 - £75*
6 Chalets	*£35*

Includes full breakfast, dinner and VAT

CHARGE/CREDIT CARDS

 • *MC* • *VI*

RATINGS & AWARDS
S.T.B. ★★★ *Small Hotel*
R.A.C. ★★★ *Dining Award 3*
A.A. ★★★ ✿✿ *69%*
Taste of Scotland - 1 Medallion

FACILITIES
On site: *Garden, fishing*
3 meeting rooms/max 140 people
Nearby: *Golf, fishing, riding, shooting, mountain biking, watersports*

RESTRICTIONS
No facilities for disabled guests
Closed 1 Jan - 1 Mar

ATTRACTIONS
Edinburgh, Scone Palace, Devil's Cauldron, Rob Roy's Grave, Mull & Iona, Loch Tay Crannog

AFFILIATIONS
Independent

NEAREST
MAJOR CITY:
Perth/Stirling - 30 miles/45 mins

MAJOR AIRPORT:
Edinburgh - 60 miles/1 ¼ hrs

RAILWAY STATION:
Perth/Stirling - 30 miles/45 mins

RESERVATIONS
Direct with hotel
*Quote **Best Loved***

ACCESS CODES
Not applicable

" Glenapp Castle is now the standard by which we shall judge all other hotels "

Mr & Mrs Kenneth Ley, Renfrewshire

GLENAPP CASTLE

Scottish baronial castle

SCOTLAND

**Ballantrae,
Ayrshire KA26 0NZ**
Telephone 01465 831212
Fax 01465 831000
E-mail: *glenapp@bestloved.com*

OWNER
Graham and Fay Cowan

ROOM RATES
13 Luxury Doubles/Twins	*£440*
2 Luxury suites	*£490*
2 Master rooms	*£550*

*Includes all meals, house
wines & spirits and VAT*

CHARGE/CREDIT CARDS

 • *MC* • *VI*

RATINGS & AWARDS
A.A. ★★★ ✿✿
A.A. Top 200 - 02/03
Andrew Harper's Recommended Hotels

FACILITIES
On site: *Garden, heli-pad, croquet, tennis
3 meeting rooms/max 34 people*
Nearby: *Shooting, fishing, curling,
walking, boat trips, golf*

RESTRICTIONS
*Smoking in Library only
No pets in public rooms
Closed Nov - Mar (except for exclusive use)*

ATTRACTIONS
*Culzean Castle & Country Park,
Logan Botanical Gardens,
Galloway Forest Park,
Ayrshire - Robert Burns country,
Castle Kennedy Gardens,
Mull of Galloway*

AFFILIATIONS
*Relais & Chateaux
The Celebrated Hotels Collection*

NEAREST
MAJOR CITY:
Glasgow - 70 miles/1 ½ hrs

MAJOR AIRPORT:
Glasgow Prestwick - 35 miles/50 mins

RAILWAY STATION:
Stranraer - 17 miles/20 mins

RESERVATIONS
*Toll free in US: 800-322-2403
or 800-735-2478*
*Quote **Best Loved***

ACCESS CODES
*AMADEUS WB GLAB26
APOLLO/GALILEO WB 41722
SABRE/ABACUS WB 05587
WORLDSPAN WB GB26*

A unique experience in a fairytale Scottish Castle

High above the village of Ballantrae, looking out over the Irish Sea towards Ailsa Craig and the Mull of Kintyre, Glenapp Castle is indeed a magical sight. The ancestral seat of the Earls of Inchcape is now the home of the Cowan family and opened as a luxury hotel in April 2000.

In order to preserve the peaceful ambience of a traditional country house, Glenapp Castle is only open to guests who have made an advance reservation. On arrival, you will find that everything you could possibly wish for, including the splendid meals prepared by head chef Laurent Gueguen and his team, and specially selected house wines and spirits from the comprehensive cellar lists are included in your daily rate.

The interior of this spectacular Scottish Baronial castle has been totally preserved including the magnificent Austrian Oak-panelled entrance hall and staircase. The bedrooms and suites are spacious, elegant and furnished with antiques and original oil paintings to provide an ambience of traditional luxury.

The thirty acres of delightful gardens and woodland that surround the castle abound with specimen rhododendrons and many rare and unusual shrubs and trees. The showpiece walled-garden boasts a 150-foot Victorian glasshouse.

The Cowans' intention was to create something unique at Glenapp: they have truly succeeded!

LOCATION
*Approximately 15 miles north of Stranraer
and 35 miles south of Ayr and Prestwick
Airport on the A77 near village of Ballantrae.*

> **" In a world full of hotels advertising wonderful accommodation, it is a game of roulette picking out real gems. Glenmoriston is one of these. "**
>
> *C Halford, South Yorkshire*

• *Map p.464*
ref: E7

Highland hotel and restaurant GLENMORISTON ARMS HOTEL

SCOTLAND

Character, comfort and creative cuisine just a short stroll from Loch Ness

Glenmoriston Arms Hotel lies at the foot of one of the most beautiful Highland glens, close to Loch Ness. Every turn of the road brings fresh views of mystical mountains and lochs, and ancient Caledonian forests - scenery that is literally breathtaking.

Owners Neil and Carol Scott make sure that guests enjoy a unique blend of warmth, elegance and informality, and with just eight bedrooms each guest is welcomed as an individual. The atmosphere carries over to the hotel's restaurant which was deemed recently by one guest as 'one of the most superb culinary experiences in Scotland'.

Located in the very heart of Highland history, day trips include touring the enchanting Isle of Skye where you can visit Dunvegan Castle and the Clan Donald Centre. You can also follow the route of Bonnie Prince Charlie by visiting the Battlefield at Culloden, where, after his defeat, he escaped to Skye passing through Glenmoriston en route. The hotel was recently described by an A.A. Inspector: 'small is beautiful is certainly an appropriate way to describe this delightful hotel'.

This is one of the last unspoilt regions of Europe, where fresh air is just one of many great simple pleasures.

LOCATION

From south follow A82 from Fort William; continue 6 miles north of Fort Augustus. From north follow A82 from Inverness; continue 12 miles south of Drumnadrochit.

Invermoriston,
Near Loch Ness,
Inverness-shire IV63 7YA

Telephone 01320 351206
Fax 01320 351308

E-mail: *glenmoriston@bestloved.com*

OWNERS
Neil and Carol Scott

ROOM RATES
Single occupancy	*£55 - £65*
7 Doubles/Twins	*£70 - £100*
1 Four-poster	*£90 - £120*
Includes full breakfast and VAT	

CHARGE/CREDIT CARDS
 • *JCB* • *MC* • *VI*

RATINGS & AWARDS
S.T.B. ★★★★ *Small Hotel*
A.A. ★★ ✿✿ 77%

FACILITIES
On site: *Garden, fishing, jacuzzi, Bistro*
1 meeting room/max 24 people
Nearby: *Fishing, stalking, riding, golf, boat trips, walking*

RESTRICTIONS
No facilities for disabled guests
No pets
Closed Jan - 1 Mar

ATTRACTIONS
Loch Ness, Isle of Skye, Ben Nevis, Inner and Outer Hebrides, Aonach Mor Ski Centre, Culloden Moor Battlefield, Urquhart and Eilean Donan Castles, Great Glen Way

AFFILIATIONS
Preston's Global Hotels

NEAREST
MAJOR CITY:
Inverness - 26 miles/35 mins

MAJOR AIRPORT:
Inverness - 26 miles/35 mins

RAILWAY STATION:
Inverness - 26 miles/35 mins

RESERVATIONS
Toll free in US: 800-544-9993
*Quote **Best Loved***

ACCESS CODES
Not applicable

www.glenmoriston.bestloved.com

• *Map p.464*
ref: G9

GREEN CRAIGS

Seaside country house

SCOTLAND

***Aberlady,
East Lothian EH32 0PY***

**Telephone 01875 870301
Fax 01875 870440**

E-mail: *greencraigs@bestloved.com*

OWNERS
Ray and Olly Craig

MANAGER
Lucy Wood

ROOM RATES
Single occupancy	£65 - £85
2 Doubles/Twins	£110
1 Suite	£140
3 Family rooms	£115

Includes full breakfast and VAT

CHARGE/CREDIT CARDS

• *DC* • *JCB* • *MC* • *VI*

RATINGS & AWARDS
Independent

FACILITIES
On site: *Garden, heli-pad, croquet
1 meeting room/max 300 people*
Nearby: *Golf, tennis, fitness centre, riding,
water skiing, shooting*

RESTRICTIONS
*Limited facilities for disabled guests
Pets by arrangement*

ATTRACTIONS
*Edinburgh, Edinburgh Castle,
Glenkinchie Distillery, Deep Sea World,
Museum of Flight,
Tantallon & Hailes Castles,
numerous golf courses*

AFFILIATIONS
Independent

NEAREST
*MAJOR CITY:
Edinburgh - 18 miles/25 mins*

*MAJOR AIRPORT:
Edinburgh - 25 miles/30 mins*

*RAILWAY STATION:
Longniddry - 3 miles/5 mins*

RESERVATIONS
Direct with hotel
Quote **Best Loved**

ACCESS CODES
Not applicable

At the 'white house on The Point' your complete satisfaction is a pleasure

Dramatically situated by the sea, Green Craigs enjoys spectacular views across Gosford Bay to Edinburgh and over the shoreline of Fife. It is an exceptional country house, a small hotel of quality, and the family home of Ray and Olly Craig. Built in 1924, the high ceilings, cornices, nooks and crannies are decorated in sympathy with the original style. 'As a family,' says Olly Craig, 'we have loved each minute of bringing out the individuality of each room, and making it sparkle with warmth and delight.'

The dining room glows with the colours of the setting sun across the bay. The food is fantastic. Exceedingly pleasant menus are devised by chef MacInnes. The modestly priced bar meals are also something special.

Green Craigs is next to the eighth green of Kilspindie golf course. Muirfield and 17 other courses are nearby. So are Edinburgh Castle, and the Glenkinchie Distillery. Green Craigs itself is part of the holiday environment. The Craigs look on it as 'their little piece of heaven'. They are happy when guests share their enjoyment of the house and garden.

LOCATION
One mile west of Aberlady on the A198.

" *Long live Greywalls, so dear in our hearts* "

Edouard Van Vyve, Antwerp

• Map p.464
ref: G9

49

Country retreat

GREYWALLS

SCOTLAND

Follow in the footsteps of Nicklaus, Faldo, Edward VII and King Hussein

Sir Edwin Lutyens, architect of the British Embassy in Washington and the Cenotaph in Whitehall, designed Greywalls in 1901. King Edward VII stayed here: you can write your postcards in the panelled library he loved. King Hussein of Jordan was a more recent visitor.

Greywalls is next to Muirfield golf course. Past guests including Arnold Palmer, Jack Nicklaus, Lee Trevino, Greg Norman and Nick Faldo are all part of the Greywalls story.

Greywalls still feels like a family home. The warmth of hospitality from Giles and Ros Weaver today makes guests feel like honoured family friends. There are 23 comfortable, cosy bedrooms each with its own bathroom; many are furnished with antiques. There is a Steinway grand piano, a sunny Edwardian tea room and a small bar with a fine stock of whiskies. The very best of local produce is used to create outstanding meals from hearty breakfasts to fulsome dinners!

Outside are the gardens that Lutyens himself helped to plan. Within eight miles are 10 golf courses, long sandy beaches, nature reserves renowned for bird life, and ancient ruined castles.

LOCATION

Link from M8, M9 or M90 Motorways to A198 via Edinburgh City Bypass A720.

Muirfield, Gullane,
East Lothian EH31 2EG

Telephone 01620 842144
Fax 01620 842241

E-mail: *greywalls@bestloved.com*

OWNERS
Giles and Ros Weaver

MANAGER
Sue Prime

ROOM RATES
4 Singles   £120 - £220
19 Doubles/Twins   £200 - £240
Includes full breakfast and VAT

CHARGE/CREDIT CARDS

 • DC • MC • VI

RATINGS & AWARDS
S.T.B. ★★★★ Hotel
AA. ★★★ ❀❀
A.A. Top 200 - 02/03
Taste of Scotland 4 Medallions

FACILITIES
On site: *Garden, croquet, tennis,*
putting green
1 meeting room/max 30 people
Nearby: *Golf, shooting, fishing,*
walking, beaches

RESTRICTIONS
No facilities for disabled guests
No pets in public rooms
Closed 17 Oct - 15 April

ATTRACTIONS
Tantallon Castle, Dirleton Castle,
Edinburgh and Edinburgh Castle,
Holyrood House, Muirfield Golf Course

AFFILIATIONS
Independent

NEAREST
MAJOR CITY:
Edinburgh - 18 miles/35 mins

MAJOR AIRPORT:
Edinburgh - 25 miles/40 mins

RAILWAY STATION:
Drem - 2 miles/5 mins

RESERVATIONS
Direct with hotel
*Quote **Best Loved***

ACCESS CODES
Not applicable

« Absolutely fantastic in every way - many, many thanks »

Lady Clare Macdonald, Isle of Skye

THE HOWARD

Georgian town house

SCOTLAND

**34 Great King Street,
Edinburgh EH3 6QH**
Telephone 0131 315 2220
Fax 0131 557 6515
E-mail: *howard@bestloved.com*

OWNER
Peter Taylor

MANAGER
Johanne Falconer

ROOM RATES
2 Singles	£175 - £275
11 Doubles/Twins	£235 - £295
5 Suites	£325 - £475

Includes full breakfast and VAT

CHARGE/CREDIT CARDS

 • *DC* • *MC* • *VI*

RATINGS & AWARDS
S.T.B. ★★★★★
A.A. ★★★★ *Town House*
A.A. Top 200 - 02/03

FACILITIES
On site: *Guests' dining room, car park,
2 meeting rooms/max 18 people*
Nearby: *Golf, swimming pool,
cycling & jogging route*

RESTRICTIONS
*No facilities for disabled guests
No pets, guide dogs only
Closed Christmas*

ATTRACTIONS
*Edinburgh Castle, Holyrood House,
National Gallery, Old Town and New Town,
Edinburgh Festival & Military Tattoo,
Dynamic Earth, Royal Yacht Britannia*

AFFILIATIONS
*The Celebrated Hotels Collection
The Small Hotel Company
Small Luxury Hotels*

NEAREST
MAJOR CITY:
Edinburgh

MAJOR AIRPORT:
Edinburgh - 8 miles/25 mins

RAILWAY STATION:
Waverley - 1 mile/25 mins

RESERVATIONS
*Toll free in US: 800-322-2403
or 800-525-4800*
Quote **Best Loved**

ACCESS CODES
*AMADEUS LX EDIHWO
APOLLO/GALILEO LX 96963
SABRE/ABACUS LX 8591
WORLDSPAN LX HOWAE*

A place where elegance and discretion are the watchwords

It has to be said that there is something distinctively different about The Howard. The first impression is that it's reminiscent of the town house residences of the late 1800's - ultimately elegant and unobtrusive. This is evident from the most discreet of check-ins, to the dedicated butler service; upon arrival bags are unpacked and tea is served in the Drawing Room, through to the Floris toiletries in the bathroom.

However, it is important to note that there is nothing 'old fashioned' about The Howard and it is the result of considerable skill that the hotel retains this genuine traditional air whilst providing guests with the most up-to-the-minute facilities. All rooms are fully equipped with every modern convenience and more, including International modem points, Nicam TV and e-TV providing a hi-fi system, DVD, games and Internet access. Some rooms feature freestanding roll-top bathtubs, Jacuzzis or power showers.

The Howard's dining room, The Atholl provides an unsurpassed 5-star dining experience in lovely Georgian surroundings, but dinner can also be served in your room if you wish.

The hotel has two private rooms ideal for holding small, high-level, corporate events.

A truly spectacular pied á terre.

LOCATION
Travelling west along Queen Street, turn right into Queen Street Gardens East. Great King Street is the 3rd on the right.

« Very friendly staff. Everything runs very efficiently. Delicious food »

J Trumper

● *Map p.464*
ref: F8

Edwardian hotel

HUNTINGTOWER HOTEL

SCOTLAND

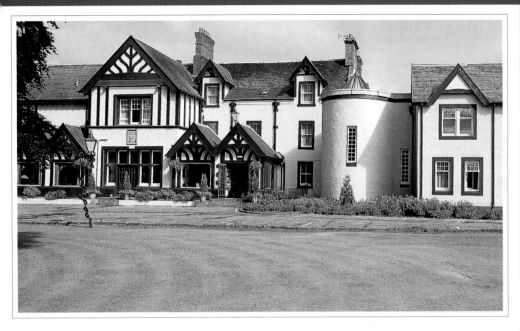

**Crieff Road, Perth,
Perthshire PH1 3JT**

**Telephone 01738 583771
Fax 01738 583777**

E-mail: *huntingtower@bestloved.com*

**GENERAL MANAGER
AND DIRECTOR**
Michael Lee

ROOM RATES

3 Singles	£70 - £90
12 Doubles/Twins	£90 - £120
3 Suites	£110 - £140
16 Executive suites	£110 - £140

Includes full breakfast and VAT

CHARGE/CREDIT CARDS

 ● *DC* ● *MC* ● *VI*

RATINGS & AWARDS
S.T.B. ★★★★ *Hotel*
A.A. ★★★ ❀ *75%*
Taste of Scotland - 2 Medallions
Sunday Times Golden Pillow Award

FACILITIES
On site: *Garden, heli-pad, pitch & putt*
6 meeting rooms/max 200 people
Nearby: *Golf, tennis, fitness, fishing, water
skiing, shooting, riding*

RESTRICTIONS
Pets by arrangement

ATTRACTIONS
*Scone Palace, Ochil Hills
Pitlochry Salmon Ladder
Crieff, Glenshee Ski Centre
Blair Castle*

AFFILIATIONS
Independent

NEAREST
*MAJOR CITY:
Perth - 3 miles/10 mins*

*MAJOR AIRPORT:
Edinburgh - 30 miles/40 mins
Glasgow - 60 miles/1 hr*

*RAILWAY STATION:
Perth - 3 miles/10 mins*

RESERVATIONS
*Direct with hotel
Quote* **Best Loved**

ACCESS CODES
Not applicable

King James VI was very sorry to leave the Huntingtower!

The Huntingtower is an elegant Edwardian house set in its own four acres of glorious landscaped gardens, ten minutes from the centre of Perth. In recent years, the hotel has been completely and lovingly restored to its original splendour, and has seen the edition of 16 Junior Suites, with family rooms available. For dining there are two superb options: the award-winning oak-panelled Restaurant or the more informal Conservatory for lighter meals.

The area provides many leisure opportunities including salmon and trout fishing on the river Tay, hillwalking and horse riding in the Highlands, shooting, cycling, or simply relaxing in the peaceful and tranquil surroundings. Golf courses abound - with St Andrews, Carnoustie and Gleneagles all less than one hour away. There are also interesting historic connections. In 1582, at Huntingtower Castle, James VI of Scotland was kidnapped by discontented Protestant nobles. Other examples worth visiting are Blair Castle and the Black Watch Museum at Balhousie Castle.

Glasgow, Edinburgh, Stirling, Loch Lomond and the Trossachs are within an hour's drive.

LOCATION

10 minutes west of Perth on the A85.

● *Map p.464*
ref: D8

" What a wonderful place. Dinner was excellent and the room enchanting. Will come back when we return to Scotland "

Mr Cary, Dallas

THE INN AT ARDGOUR

Highland inn

Ardgour, Fort William, Inverness-shire PH33 7AA

Telephone 01855 841225
Fax 01855 841214

E-mail: *ardgour@bestloved.com*

OWNERS
David and Mary Allen

ROOM RATES
8 Doubles/Twins	£80 - £120
3 Family rooms	£70 - £150
1 Family suite	£80 - £165

Includes full breakfast and VAT

CHARGE/CREDIT CARDS

 • *JCB* • *MC* • *VI*

RATINGS & AWARDS
S.T.B. ★★★★ *Inn*

FACILITIES
On site: *Drying room, cycle storage*
Nearby: *Golf, fishing, water skiing, climbing, sailing*

RESTRICTIONS
Limited facilities for disabled guests
No smoking in bedrooms or restaurant
Closed two weeks over Christmas

ATTRACTIONS
Ben Nevis, Glencoe, Sea Life Centre, Glennfinnan, Isle of Skye, Castle Tioram, cycle tours

AFFILIATIONS
Preston's Global Hotels

NEAREST
MAJOR CITY:
Glasgow - 95 miles/2 ½ hrs

MAJOR AIRPORT:
Glasgow - 80 miles/2 hrs

RAILWAY STATION:
Fort William - 8 miles/15 mins

RESERVATIONS
Toll free in US: 800-544-9993
Quote **Best Loved**

ACCESS CODES
Not applicable

A traditional Highland inn with a captivating location

This welcoming old Highland hostelry lies at the mouth of the Great Glen on the shores of Loch Linnhe. The inn has the most spectacular mountain-framed view of the loch and in the foreground the ferry plies back and forth as it has done for many hundred's of years, because this is the original 'Road to the Isles'.

The Inn at Ardgour is now owned and run by Mary and David Allen, a charming, genuinely hospitable couple who have brought a great of deal of warmth to the Inn. They have been busy in their first year redecorating bedrooms, introducing new furnishings, upgrading bathrooms and generally adding that personal touch such as naming all the rooms after local birds and wildlife. The Inn has both a traditional, rather cosy dining room serving excellent Scottish fare as well as the slightly less formal But n' Ben restaurant.

The Western Highlands offer outdoor diversions from hiking and wildlife watching to day trips to the Hebridean islands, and the bar is an excellent place to unwind after an interesting day's activities. It is also a great place to join the locals in a 'wee dram and a bit of craich'.

LOCATION
From A82 Onich to Fort William take the ferry (4 mins) across to Ardgour from Corran.

" Personal service, a family atmosphere with food comparable to Gleneagles and Turnberry "

John Huncharek, Houston, Texas

16th century coaching inn

INN AT LATHONES

By Largoward, St Andrews, Fife KY9 1JE
Telephone 01334 840494
Fax 01334 840694

E-mail: lathones@bestloved.com

OWNERS
Nick and Jocelyn White

ROOM RATES
2 Singles   £75 - £100
10 Doubles/Twins   £120 - £140
2 Master rooms   £160
Includes full breakfast and VAT

CHARGE/CREDIT CARDS

 • DC • MC • VI

RATINGS & AWARDS
S.T.B. ★★★★ Inn
A.A. ★★ ✿✿ 78%
Investors in People
Scotch Beef Club

FACILITIES
On site: *Patio, outdoor play area*
1 meeting room/max 60 people
Nearby: *Golf, fishing, water skiing, yachting, tennis, fitness centre, riding, clay pigeon shooting*

RESTRICTIONS
Limited facilities for disabled guests
No pets in public rooms
Closed 6 - 22 Jan

ATTRACTIONS
Kellie Castle, Isle of May, St Andrews Cathedral, 18 hole golf courses, Sea-Life Centre, Secret Bunker, Royal and Ancient Golf Museum

AFFILIATIONS
Preston's Global Hotels
Grand Heritage Hotels

NEAREST
MAJOR CITY:
St Andrews - 5 miles/10 mins

MAJOR AIRPORT:
Edinburgh - 50 miles/1 ½ hrs
Dundee - 10 miles/20 mins

RAILWAY STATION:
Leuchars - 7 miles/15 mins

RESERVATIONS
Toll free in US: 800-544-9993
or 888-93-GRAND
*Quote **Best Loved***

ACCESS CODES
AMADEUS UI ADXINN
APOLLO/GALILEO UI 27836
SABRE/ABACUS UI 52266
WORLDSPAN UI 41354

A first choice for the gourmet and the golfer

Fine food, great golf - and maybe even the odd ghost - all await visitors to the historic coaching Inn at Lathones. Situated just five miles from St Andrews, and in the heart of Fife, which is home to more than 40 top quality golf courses, this 400 year-old hotel is the ideal location for anyone who enjoys a round. Staff will be happy to arrange tee times, tuition and practice sessions, whatever your handicap, at the course that most suits you.

Easy access to first-class sporting facilities is matched by the Inn's highly regarded restaurant: proprietors Nick and Jocelyn White and head chef Marc Guibert have always made it their business to hand-source all their local suppliers, from fishermen to organic farmers. The result is a regionally focused yet diverse menu that has earned the unique accolade of being the only four-star inn listed by the Scottish Tourist Board.

Patrons have long enjoyed atmospheric hospitality at Lathones - and some, like The Grey Lady, have even been said to return from beyond the grave! The deluxe room named after her, as is

typical of the hotel's high standards, boasts its own log fire, power shower and Jacuzzi bath.

LOCATION
Situated 5 miles south from St Andrews on the A915, which is the main road between St Andrews and Leven.

● Map p.464
ref: E10

> **" Keen attention to detail and decor. Every member of staff provided a personalised touch, it was the highlight of our stay "**
>
> *Mr & Mrs Butler, London*

THE INN ON THE GREEN

Hotel & restaurant

**25 Greenhead Street,
Glasgow G40 1ES**

**Telephone 0141 5540165
Fax 0141 5564678**

E-mail: *onthegreen@bestloved.com*

GENERAL MANAGER
Mark Calpin

ROOM RATES
1 Single   £55
17 Doubles/Twins   £75 - £90
Includes full breakfast and VAT

CHARGE/CREDIT CARDS

AMERICAN EXPRESS ● *MC* ● *VI*

RATINGS & AWARDS
S.T.B. ★★★ *Small Hotel*
Taste of Scotland - 3 Medallions

FACILITIES
On site: *Bar & Restaurant*
Nearby: *Golf, tennis, fitness centre*

RESTRICTIONS
No facilities for disabled guests
No pets

ATTRACTIONS
*Glasgow Cathedral, The Burrell Collection,
Kelvingrove Art Gallery,
Rennie Mackintosh's Hill House,
Loch Lomond, The Trossachs*

AFFILIATIONS
Preston's Global Hotels

NEAREST
MAJOR CITY:
Glasgow

MAJOR AIRPORT:
Glasgow - 10 miles/12 mins

RAILWAY STATION:
Glasgow - 3 miles/5 mins

RESERVATIONS
Toll free in US: 800-544-9993
Quote **Best Loved**

ACCESS CODES
AMADEUS LM GIA864
APOLLO/GALILEO LM 26168
SABRE/ABACUS LM 51722
WORLDSPAN LM 05864

Innovative design marks out a winner in the 'dear green place'

The Inn on the Green restaurant has been a local institution since the 1980's. Across the street from Glasgow Green and the People's Palace, this cosy basement bistro combines its role as a favourite watering hole renowned for great live piano jazz with that of a gallery showcasing contemporary art.

The hotel itself displays considerable creative flair in its innovative styling. Each room at the Inn is custom-designed from the textured hessian, silk, grass and bamboo wallcoverings to the chunky wooden beds and Burberry bed linen. Individually-forged wrought iron curtain rails and picnic hampers chockfull of tea, coffee, hot chocolate and biscuits add another distinctive note. Even the mirrors are special - steam one over if you can, they are designed to remain reflective however hot your shower!

Glasgow was nominated the UK's City of Architecture & Design in 1999, and offers a wealth of museums, galleries and architectural highlights such as Charles Rennie Mackintosh's Art Nouveau Glasgow School of Art. Reinvented as both fashionable and dynamic in the 1990's,

it is the third most popular British destination for foreign visitors after London and Edinburgh.

LOCATION

From M74 follow London Road to Bridgton. Pass Bridgton Station and at major lights take slip road left into Arcadia Street. Follow road round bend and take 1st left and left again into Greenhead Street. Hotel is on right.

55

> ❝ *The courtesy and care of all your staff is of such an exceptionally high standard* ❞
>
> *Mrs & Mrs K J Grey, Bristol*

• Map p.464
ref: D4

Country hotel

INVER LODGE HOTEL

Unwind amidst one of Europe's last great unspoilt wildernesses

High on a hill above the fishing village of Lochinver, Inver Lodge looks out to the hazy outline of the Western Isles. Inland lie the rugged hills and moorlands of Sutherland generously sprinkled with woodlands, lochs and dozens of clear running rivers and streams. This untamed wilderness is a natural refuge for wildlife and offers visitors the space and tranquillity to relax and recharge far from the bustle of everday life.

Inver Lodge is a purpose-built contemporary hotel, which emphasises high standards of comfort and service. Large windows ensure there are wonderful views wherever you look from the traditionally furnished lounge with its roaring log fire to the exceptionally spacious guest rooms equipped with every modern convenience. The dining room is a showcase for imaginative menus featuring fine local ingredients, while the wine list offers a selection that encircles the globe.

A wide range of leisure activities runs the gamut from the hotel's own snooker room, sauna and solarium to hiking. Salmon and trout fishing are available on local rivers and lochs, while birdwatchers may spot golden eagles or visit a rare

puffin colony. Sightseeing opportunities include the famous Inverewe Gardens and Britain's highest waterfall.

LOCATION

Take the A837 towards Lochinver. Once in the town, head towards the harbour. The hotel is first on the left after the Tourist Information Centre.

Lochinver,
Sutherland IV27 4LU
Telephone 01571 844496
Fax 01571 844395

E-mail: *inverlodge@bestloved.com*

GENERAL MANAGER
Nicholas Gorton

ROOM RATES
Single occupancy £80 - £150
14 Doubles/Twins £140
6 Superior Doubles/Twins £160 - £200
Includes full breakfast and VAT

CHARGE/CREDIT CARDS
 • DC • JCB • MC • VI

RATINGS & AWARDS
S.T.B. ★★★★ Hotel
R.A.C. ★★★ Dining Award 3
A.A. ★★★ ❀
A.A. Top 200 - 02/03
Scotch Beef Club

FACILITIES
On site: *Garden, heli-pad, salmon & trout fishing, sauna, solarium, snooker*
1 meeting room/max 40 people
Nearby: *Golf, deer stalking, fishing, riding*

RESTRICTIONS
No facilities for disabled guests
No children under 7 years
No pets in public rooms
Closed Nov - Easter

ATTRACTIONS
Inverewe Gardens, Western Isles, Inverpolly Nature Reserve, Handa Island Puffin Colony, Smoo Caves, Fas a Chual Aluinn Falls

AFFILIATIONS
Scotland's Hotels of Distinction

NEAREST
MAJOR CITY:
Inverness - 95 miles/2 ¼ hrs

MAJOR AIRPORT:
Inverness - 100 miles/2 ½ hrs

RAILWAY STATION:
Lairg - 45 miles/1 ¼ hrs

RESERVATIONS
Toll free in US: 800-437-2687
Quote Best Loved

ACCESS CODES
Not applicable

INVERBEG INN

Highland hotel

SCOTLAND

Luss, Loch Lomond, Dunbartonshire G83 8PD

Telephone 01436 860678
Fax 01436 860686

E-mail: *inverbeg@bestloved.com*

GENERAL MANAGER
Andrew Scott

ROOM RATES
Single occupancy	£65
15 Doubles/Twins	£70 - £130
3 Suites	£120
2 Family rooms	£110 - £150

Includes full breakfast and VAT

CHARGE/CREDIT CARDS

 • MC • VI

RATINGS & AWARDS
S.T.B. ★★★★ *Inn*
Welcome Host and Walkers Welcome Quality Awards

FACILITIES
On site: *Garden*
2 meeting rooms/max 60 people
Nearby: *Sailing, windsurfing, jet skiing, biking, riding*

RESTRICTIONS
Pets by arrangement

ATTRACTIONS
Inverary Castle, Carrick Castle, The Trossachs, West Highland Way, Loch Lomond National Park, Glencoe

AFFILIATIONS
Scotland's Hotels of Distinction

NEAREST
MAJOR CITY:
Glasgow - 33 miles/45 mins

MAJOR AIRPORT:
Glasgow - 33 miles/45 mins

RAILWAY STATION:
Balloch - 9 miles/15 mins

RESERVATIONS
Toll free in US: 800-437-2687
Quote **Best Loved**

ACCESS CODES
Not applicable

A 'roadside blessing' on the bonnie, bonnie banks of Loch Lomond

Among the numerous plaudits that have come its way, the Inverbeg Inn has been described as a 'roadside blessing'. It is a particularly apt description, because this is just the kind of intimate, friendly and superbly positioned small hotel every traveller dreams of finding.

Thirty minutes from Glasgow, bordering Rob Roy country and the Trossachs, the Inn and its lochside Lodge offer a touring and sightseeing location that is second to none. It is also an ideal overnight stop on the road to the West Coast, and tailored packages are available for special events such as weddings or small conferences. The Inn lies just beyond the village of Luss, which enjoyed a starring role as Glendarroch in the TV series Take the High Road.

The majority of the comfortable guest rooms are found in the main building, which also houses the traditional Caledonian Bar and a restaurant specialising in local produce from scallops and salmon to beef and venison. There are three special suites in the Lodge, which boasts wonderful views east across the loch to the island of Inchlonaig and off to the distant peaks of Ben Lomond and Ben Vrakie.

LOCATION

On the A82 towards Tarbert,
2 miles north of Luss.

❝ *I never saw a lovelier or more romantic spot* ❞

Queen Victoria, 1873

Highland castle   INVERLOCHY CASTLE

A passionate commitment to your needs in the grandeur of the Highlands

Inverlochy was built by the first Lord Abinger in 1863, near the site of the original 13th century fortress. It is set against some of the most magnificent scenery in the Western Highlands, and stands amongst the foothills of Ben Nevis in its own 500-acre estate. The castle is surrounded by landscaped gardens and rhododendrons.

The baronial Great Hall has beautiful frescoed ceilings, with crystal chandeliers and a handsome staircase. Fine decorations throughout befit the Victorian proportions of the rooms which have been recently refurbished to provide an even higher standard of comfort and luxury. There are 17 individual suites and bedrooms with private bathroom and all modern facilities.

Centrepiece of the dining room is an elaborate carved breakfont sideboard, presented as a gift to Inverlochy by the King of Norway. The menu features international cuisine with emphasis on fresh Scottish produce which changes on a daily and seasonal basis.

Tennis, loch fishing and many beautiful walking paths are within the grounds. Highland scenic attractions, and sports and leisure activities are situated within a short drive. Such is the reputation of Inverlochy that it is advisable to book well in advance!

LOCATION

From Fort William, take A82 north. After 4 miles pass Fort William Golf Club and take next left to Inverlochy - the hotel is clearly signposted.

**Torlundy,
Fort William,
Inverness-shire PH33 6SN**
**Telephone 01397 702177
Fax 01397 702953**

E-mail: inverlochy@bestloved.com

GENERAL MANAGER
Niall Edmondson

ROOM RATES
14 Doubles/Twins	*£290 - £345*
3 Suites	*£440 - £550*
Includes VAT	

CHARGE/CREDIT CARDS

 ● MC ● VI

RATINGS & AWARDS
S.T.B. ★★★★★ *Hotel*
R.A.C. Gold Ribbon ★★★★ *Dining Award 4*
A.A. ★★★★ ❁❁❁
A.A. Top 200 - 02/03

FACILITIES
On site: *Garden, snooker, heli-pad, fishing, croquet, tennis*
1 meeting room/max 50 people
Nearby: *Golf, fishing, skiing, riding, stalking, guided hill walking, yachting, shooting*

RESTRICTIONS
No facilities for disabled guests
Pets by arrangement

ATTRACTIONS
Glencoe, Glenfinnan, Culloden, Isle of Skye, Blair Castle

AFFILIATIONS
Relais & Châteaux
Connoisseurs Scotland
Celebrated Hotels Collection

NEAREST
MAJOR CITY:
Glasgow - 100 miles/2 ½ hrs

MAJOR AIRPORT:
Glasgow - 100 miles/2 ½ hrs
Inverness - 70 miles/1 ¾ hrs

RAILWAY STATION:
Fort William - 4 miles/15 mins

RESERVATIONS
Toll free in US: 888-424-0106
or 800-322-2403
*Quote **Best Loved***

ACCESS CODES
AMADEUS WB FWMINV
APOLLO/GALILEO WB 14748
SABRE/ABACUS WB 40329
WORLDSPAN WB GB22

" It's quirky and eccentric, but they really know about country living "

Lord Lichfield

SCOTLAND

ISLE OF ERISKA

Victorian baronial mansion

Ledaig, Oban,
Argyll PA37 1SD

Telephone 01631 720371
Fax 01631 720531

E-mail: *eriska@bestloved.com*

OWNERS
The Buchanan-Smith Family

ROOM RATES
Single occupancy	£190
17 Doubles/Twins	£245 - £290
1 2-Bedroom suite	£450

Includes full breakfast, complimentary
newspaper, afternoon tea and VAT

CHARGE/CREDIT CARDS

 • MC • VI

RATINGS & AWARDS
S.T.B. ★★★★★ *Hotel*
A.A. ★★★★ ❀❀❀
A.A. Top 200 - 02/03
WHICH? Secluded Charm Award 2001

FACILITIES
On site: *Garden, gym, heli-pad, fishing,*
croquet, golf, tennis, indoor pool,
health & beauty, sauna, sea fishing,
6-hole golf course
3 meeting rooms/max 40 people
Nearby: *Golf, riding, river and lake fishing*

RESTRICTIONS
No pets in public rooms
Closed Jan

ATTRACTIONS
Sea-Life Centre, Glencoe
Distilleries, Isle of Mull
Dunstaffnage Castle, Loch Linnhe

AFFILIATIONS
Pride of Britain
The Celebrated Hotels Collection

NEAREST
MAJOR CITY:
Glasgow - 90 miles/2 ½ hrs

MAJOR AIRPORT:
Glasgow - 90 miles/2 ½ hrs

RAILWAY STATION:
Oban - 12 miles/20 mins

RESERVATIONS
Toll free in US: 800-322-2403 or
800 -98-PRIDE
Quote Best Loved

ACCESS CODES
Not applicable

Accessed by private bridge, Eriska is all about fulfilling dreams

Eriska is a small, secluded island less than 100 miles from Glasgow and Edinburgh. It is the only island in Britain solely devoted to the care and wellbeing of guests. The Big House was built in 1884 at the height of Scottish baronial style. Blazing log fires in the burr oak panelled Hall make for a very Scottish holiday. So does a glass of malt whisky in the library. Since 1973 Eriska has been owned by the Buchanan-Smith family. They set high priority on peace and tranquillity, and these qualities attract people back to the island again and again.

Eriska lives up to the Scottish country house requirement for 'A good table' throughout the day from the delicious breakfasts to the acclaimed formal candlelit dinners.

Sporting facilities include 6-hole golf course, 17-metre swimming pool, steamroom, sauna, gymnasium, all weather tennis court, croquet, golf putting and clay pigeon shooting. The island is virtually a nature reserve with designated nature trails. Seals, otters, badgers and roe deer are all around. Eriska has its own road bridge to link with the mainland. It is only 30 minutes to the seaport of Oban, whence steamers ply to Iona and Staffa. Mainland attractions include Glencoe and Inverary Castle, seat of the Clan Campbell.

LOCATION

From Edinburgh and Glasgow, drive to Tyndrum, then follow the A85 towards Oban. At Connel proceed by bridge on the A828 for 4 miles to north of Benderloch. Then follow the signs to the hotel.

Highland hotel

KINFAUNS CASTLE

Family history and wonderful food in the fair land of Gowrie

Kinfauns Castle stands in 26 acres of parkland whose history dates back to the 12th century. Built in the Gothic style, there are many features that express an impressive provenance: the handsome carriage way whose steps lead to the Hall of Entrance in which the tartans of previous families are displayed, the ribbed and panelled gold leaf ceiling of The Gallery, the stained glass bay windows and the richly carved chimney piece bearing armorial insignia. The wallpaper is by William Morris and seven magnificent marble fireplaces grace the public rooms.

The oak staircase ornamented by two foot high heraldic wood carvings, one of the most outstanding features, grandly leads to the suites and bedrooms, some with four-poster beds. It is a continuing theme; the bathrooms feature Verona Rosa marble and every convenience is on hand to make your stay both comfortable and memorable.

Kinfauns Castle has quickly achieved a culinary reputation. Continental overtones have a definite Scottish touch which is no surprise - this part of Scotland has an astonishing larder

from both land and sea. The wine list is well-chosen and includes a wide range of wines from Europe and the New World - all properly priced.

LOCATION

2 miles east of Perth on the main A90 Dundee Road. Follow signs for Kinfauns Castle.

Kinfauns, Perth, Perthshire PH2 7JZ

Telephone 01738 620777
Fax 01738 620778

E-mail: *kinfauns@bestloved.com*

OWNERS
James and Julia Smith

GENERAL MANAGER
Nigel W Liston

ROOM RATES
Single occupancy   £125 - £190
16 Doubles/Twins   £190 - £320
Includes full breakfast, newspaper and VAT

CHARGE/CREDIT CARDS

 • DC • JCB • MC • VI

RATINGS & AWARDS
S.T.B. ★★★★ *Hotel*
A.A. ★★★ 🏵🏵
A.A. Top 200 - 02/03

FACILITIES
On site: *Garden, heli-pad, croquet, parkland, health & beauty treatments available by arrangement*
3 meeting rooms/max 70 people
Nearby: *Golf, fishing, tennis, fitness, riding*

RESTRICTIONS
No facilities for disabled guests
Children by arrangement
No pets in public areas
Closed Jan

ATTRACTIONS
Pitlochry, Edinburgh
St Andrews, Carnoustie
Glamis Castle, Scone Palace
Loch Tay

AFFILIATIONS
The Celebrated Hotels Collection

NEAREST
MAJOR CITY:
Perth - 2 miles/5 mins

MAJOR AIRPORT:
Edinburgh - 50 miles/1 hr

RAILWAY STATION:
Perth - 2 miles/5 mins

FERRY PORT:
Rosythe - 30 miles/40 mins

RESERVATIONS
Toll free in US: 800-322-2403
*Quote **Best Loved***

ACCESS CODES
Not applicable

• Map p.464
ref: F8

SCOTLAND

> **" This excellence really precludes us from wanting to go elsewhere. Your Head Chef's imaginative cuisine continues to give us great pleasure "**
>
> *Brian McKibbin, Ludlow, Shropshire*

KINLOCH HOUSE HOTEL

Victorian manor house

**By Blairgowrie,
Perthshire PH10 6SG**
Telephone 01250 884237
Fax 01250 884333
E-mail: *kinlochhse@bestloved.com*

OWNERS
The Allen Family

RATES PER PERSON
4 Singles	£110 - £155
9 Doubles/Twins	£75 - £120
5 Four-posters	£75 - £120
2 Suites	£120 - £160

Includes full breakfast, dinner and VAT

CHARGE/CREDIT CARDS

 • *DC* • *JCB* • *MC* • *VI*

RATINGS & AWARDS
S.T.B. ★★★★★ Hotel
A.A. ★★★ ❀❀
A.A. Top 200 - 02/03
Macallan Taste of Scotland Award 2001
Taste of Scotland - 4 Medallions

FACILITIES
***On site:** Garden, gym, heli-pad, fishing, croquet, indoor pool, health & beauty, jacuzzi, steam room*
1 meeting room/max 30 people
***Nearby:** Golf, fishing, tennis, shooting*

RESTRICTIONS
No children under 7 years in dining room
Pets by arrangement, Closed 19 - 29 Dec

ATTRACTIONS
Scone Palace, Black Watch Museum, Glenshee Ski Centre, Blair Castle, Glamis Castle and Cluny Gardens

AFFILIATIONS
The Celebrated Hotels Collection
Small Luxury Hotels

NEAREST
MAJOR CITY:
Perth - 18 miles/30 mins
MAJOR AIRPORT:
Edinburgh - 70 miles/1 ¼ hrs
Dundee - 20 miles/35 mins
RAILWAY STATION:
Dunkeld - 8 miles/15 mins

RESERVATIONS
Toll free in US: 800-525-4800
or 800-322-2403
Toll free in UK: 0800 964 470
*Quote **Best Loved***

ACCESS CODES
AMADEUS LX PSLKLH
APOLLO/GALILEO LX 57720
SABRE/ABACUS LX 31056
WORLDSPAN LX EDIKH

The art of good living in the very heart of Scotland

Some hotels seem to spring up, others, like a good wine, mature and mellow with age. Kinloch House is an example of the latter. It starts off propitiously with its location; put your finger on the centre of Scotland and you're spot on.

It was built in 1840, extended in 1911 becoming an hotel in 1981. But the transition is seamless; it still has the look and feel of a private house. It stands in 25 acres of parkland grazed by highland cattle, with views over the Marlee Loch to the Sidlaw Hills beyond. The walled garden is a recent resurrection which serves two purposes: as a place to relax and as a kitchen garden much of whose goodness ends up on your plate. The gifted Bill McNicoll, head chef for 17 years, is to be envied, supplied as he is from coast to coast; Aberdeen Angus Beef, lobsters from Kyle of Lochalsh, game from the highlands. His efforts are blessed by a wide-ranging wine list. 'Dinner is regarded as the signature to an enjoyable day', says the brochure. True, but a single malt from a choice of 160 adds a certain flourish before bedtime!

Working up an appetite is easy. There are 30 golf courses within an hour's drive and fishing can be arranged. The state-of-the-art health, beauty, fitness and therapy facilities are beautifully tucked away so that the character of this great house is not compromised.

LOCATION
Located 3 miles west of Blairgowrie on the A923 to Dunkeld.

" The welcome is wonderfully warm, service is immaculate and discreet, comfort is considerable, and the food is famously good. Balm for body and soul "

Philippa Davenport, Financial Times Weekend

• Map p.464
ref: D7

Lochside island hotel

KINLOCH LODGE

SCOTLAND

**Sleat, Isle of Skye,
Highland IV43 8QY**

**Telephone 01471 833214
Fax 01471 833277**

E-mail: *kinlochlodge@bestloved.com*

OWNERS
Lord and Lady Macdonald

RATES PER PERSON

14 Doubles/Twins   £85 - £125
Includes full breakfast, dinner and VAT

CHARGE/CREDIT CARDS

 • MC • VI

RATINGS & AWARDS
S.T.B. ★★★★ Small Hotel
Courvoisier's Book of the Best
Taste of Scotland - 3 Medallions

FACILITIES
On site: *Garden, heli-pad,
fishing, stalking*
1 meeting room/max 20 people
Nearby: *Golf, riding*

RESTRICTIONS
*No facilities for disabled guests
Children by arrangement
Pets by arrangement
No smoking in bedrooms or dining room
Closed Christmas*

ATTRACTIONS
*Isle of Skye, Clan Donald Centre,
Inverewe Gardens, Dunvegan Castle*

AFFILIATIONS
*The Celebrated Hotels Collection
Great Little Hotels of Scotland*

NEAREST
MAJOR CITY:
Inverness - 100 miles/3 ½ hrs

MAJOR AIRPORT:
Inverness - 100 miles/3 ½ hrs

RAILWAY STATION:
Kyle of Lochalsh - 12 miles/45 mins

FERRY PORT:
Armadale - 10 miles/20 mins

RESERVATIONS
Toll free in US: 800-322-2403
Quote **Best Loved**

ACCESS CODES
Not applicable

At home with
Lord and Lady Macdonald

Kinloch Lodge is an elegant country house dating from the early 1600s, whose gardens slope down to meet the sea loch, Na Dal, on the Isle of Skye in the Highlands of Scotland. It is the ancestral home of Lord Macdonald of Macdonald, High Chief of Clan Donald, who runs it as a small, very personal hotel with his wife, the world-renowned cookery writer Claire Macdonald. In 1998 the Macdonalds built a new house adjacent to the Lodge and in similar style, known as Kinloch, providing 14 bedrooms in all.

The setting is romantic, beautiful and incomparably peaceful. Secluded between a wooded hillside and the sea loch on two sides, the surrounding area is fascinating for those who love and appreciate nature, with notable flowers and plants, five golden eagles on the hill behind the house, seals galore and a colony of otters. The bird life is varied and plentiful.

Here, in view of Skye and the spectacular Cuillin Hills, the Macdonalds dispense the warmest hospitality from their family home. The atmosphere is very relaxed, with comfortable rooms decorated in traditional country house style, log fires and a five-course dinner that features the freshest of ingredients that are naturally available in season.

LOCATION

*1 mile off A851. 6 miles south of Broadford
and 10 miles north of Armadale.*

SCOTLAND

" *Spectacular - we promise to return! Wonderful, a true home from home* "

Bob & Sandra Baker

KINNAIRD

Country mansion

Kinnaird Estate, Dunkeld, Perthshire PH8 0LB

Telephone 01796 482440
Fax 01796 482289

E-mail: *kinnaird@bestloved.com*

OWNER
Constance Ward

GENERAL MANAGER
Douglas Jack

RATES PER PERSON
Single occupancy   £122 - £148
8 Doubles/Twins   £122 - £148
1 Suite   £238
Includes dinner, breakfast and VAT

CHARGE/CREDIT CARDS

 • MC • VI

RATINGS & AWARDS
S.T.B. ★★★★★ *Small Hotel*
R.A.C. Gold Ribbon ★★★ *Dining Award 4*
A.A. ★★★ ❀❀❀
A.A. Top 200 - 02/03

FACILITIES
On site: *Garden, snooker, heli-pad, fishing, croquet, tennis, health & beauty, shooting 3 meeting rooms/max 25 people*
Nearby: *Golf, riding*

RESTRICTIONS
Limited facilities for disabled guests
No pets, heated kennels available

ATTRACTIONS
Pitlochry, Loch Ness, Glamis Castle, Scone Palalce, Glenshee Ski Centre, Blair Castle

AFFILIATIONS
The Celebrated Hotels Collection
Relais & Châteaux

NEAREST
MAJOR CITY:
Perth - 14 miles/20 mins

MAJOR AIRPORT:
Edinburgh - 55 miles/1hr

RAILWAY STATION:
Dunkeld - 7 miles/10 mins

RESERVATIONS
Toll free in US: 800-322-2403
Toll free in US: 800-735-2478
Quote **Best Loved**

ACCESS CODES
Not applicable

An exquisite Edwardian mansion 'sunk among trees' in the Tay Valley

Set back from the River Tay on a thickly wooded hillside crowned by rocky crags, Kinnaird is indeed 'sunk among trees' as the Scottish writer Thomas Carlyle noted of the original mansion in the 1820s.

The house occupies an emerald green clearing fringed by lawns and its mellow stone façade conceals an elegant and utterly charming Edwardian interior furnished in traditional style with antiques, fine pictures and family mementoes belonging to owner, Constance Ward. The bedrooms are large, light and stylish with luxuriously appointed bathrooms and gas log fires. For guests who prefer greater privacy, there is a brace of courtyard cottages close to the main house, or six beautifully converted self-catering cottages located around the 9,000-acre estate.

The estate offers a wide range of activities from a game of tennis on the all-weather court to clay pigeon, pheasant and grouse shooting, deer stalking and trout or salmon fishing on the Tay or one of the three lochs. A good walk is another way to build up an appetite for the excellent restaurant which features the best of local and estate produce accompanied by an impressive wine list and extensive selection of traditional malt whiskies.

LOCATION
From Perth take A9 north, signed for Inverness.
Exit A9 on to B898, signed Dalguise & Kinnaird.
Follow road for 4 ½ miles & the hotel is on the right hand side.

18/19th century farmstead

KIRKTON HOUSE

SCOTLAND

A great little country place in easy reach of Glasgow Airport

Commanding panoramic views of the River Clyde and the Argyll Hills, Kirkton House is handy for Glasgow Airport, Loch Lomond, the West Highlands and Glasgow City. There are excellent local walks and golf courses.

Kirkton House is a conversion of a traditional 18/19th century Scottish farmhouse and barns around a courtyard. The lounge and dining areas have exposed stone walls and rustic fireplaces (including the original 'swee' for hanging the pots). Guests can enjoy a drink in the guest lounge (beside a roaring open fire on chilly evenings), and savour the 'homey', informal and unpretentious ambience. Your well-travelled proprietors have a natural gift for hospitality.

All the well-appointed bedrooms (two on the ground floor) are en-suite, some only with shower. All rooms have television, writing table, iron and ironing board, and hospitality tray. Wholesome home cooked dinners are served at individual tables per party: orders are taken at about 7 pm. Tables should be pre-booked for this house party experience.

'A luxurious and delightful experience' JF, Mass, USA. 'How does one improve on perfection?' HH, Pinner, UK. - just two of many compliments from the guest book.

LOCATION

Turn north off A814 at west end of Cardross village, up Darleith Road. Proceed ½ mile out of housing line and Kirkton House drive is on right after 3 cottages.

Darleith Road, Cardross, Argyll and Bute G82 5EZ

Telephone 01389 841951
Fax 01389 841868

E-mail: *kirkton@bestloved.com*

OWNERS
Stewart and Gillian Macdonald

ROOM RATES
Single occupancy	£40 - £50
2 Doubles/Twins	£60 - £80
4 Family rooms	£73 - £96

Includes full breakfast and VAT

CHARGE/CREDIT CARDS

 • *DC* • *JCB* • *MC* • *VI*

RATINGS & AWARDS
S.T.B. ★★★★ *Guest House*
R.A.C. ◆◆◆◆◆ *Dining Award 1*
*Warm Welcome, Sparkling Diamond 2001
and Little Gem Awards*
A.A. ◆◆◆◆◆ *Premier Collection*
Taste of Scotland - 4 Medallions

FACILITIES
On site: *Garden, paddock, stabling*
Nearby: *Golf, riding, fishing*

RESTRICTIONS
*Limited facilities for disabled guests
No smoking in bedrooms
Closed 1 Dec - 1 Feb*

ATTRACTIONS
*Loch Lomond, The Trossachs
Hill House, Glasgow
Burrell Collection
Loch Lomond International Golf Club
Scottish Exhibition Centre*

AFFILIATIONS
The Circle Group

NEAREST
MAJOR CITY:
Glasgow - 18 miles/35 mins

MAJOR AIRPORT:
Glasgow - 15 miles/25 mins

RAILWAY STATION:
Cardross - 1 mile/2 mins

RESERVATIONS
Direct with hotel
*Quote **Best Loved***

ACCESS CODES
Not applicable

SCOTLAND

" A delightful experience "

Professor & Mrs Ian Richardson, Auchterarder

KIRROUGHTREE HOUSE

18th century mansion

**Newton Stewart,
Wigtownshire DG8 6AN**

**Telephone 01671 402141
Fax 01671 402425**

E-mail: *kirroughtree@bestloved.com*

OWNER
Douglas McMillan

GENERAL MANAGER
Jim Stirling

ROOM RATES
2 Singles	£75 - £135
11 Doubles/Twins	£130 - £150
1 Four-poster	£150
3 Suites	£150 - £170

Includes full breakfast and VAT

CHARGE/CREDIT CARDS

AMERICAN EXPRESS • *MC • VI*

RATINGS & AWARDS
S.T.B. ★★★★ *Hotel*
A.A. ★★★ ❀❀
A.A. Top 200 - 02/03
Taste of Scotland - 4 Medallions

FACILITIES
On site: *Garden, croquet, tennis
1 meeting room/max 30 people*
Nearby: *Golf, riding, fitness, shooting,
fishing, curling*

RESTRICTIONS
*No facilities for disabled guests
Closed Jan - mid Feb*

ATTRACTIONS
*Gem Rock Museum, Culzean Castle,
Whithorn Dig, Drumlanrig Castle,
Logan Botanical Gardens,
Mill on the Fleet*

AFFILIATIONS
Independent

NEAREST
*MAJOR CITY:
Glasgow - 90 miles/2 hrs*

*MAJOR AIRPORT:
Glasgow - 90 miles/2 hrs*

*RAILWAY STATION:
Barhill - 18 miles/30 mins*

RESERVATIONS
Direct with hotel
*Quote **Best Loved***

ACCESS CODES
WORLDSPAN RX KIRNE

An award winning hotel that inspired Robert Burns

Kirroughtree House is an inspiringly beautiful mansion built by the Heron family in 1719. The Rococo furnishings of its oak-panelled lounge reflect the style and grace of the period. From the lounge rises the original staircase where Robert Burns recited his poems to the Heron family and their guests. He composed four of his ballads, and a song to Elizabeth Heron's music, in this house.

Kirroughtree House is owned and managed by the McMillan family. Individual attention is given to guests by the friendly management and staff. The elegant restaurant has a fine reputation for excellent food. The very best of local produce is used in creating meals of great originality and finesse. Kirroughtree's past awards include Scotland's Hotel of the Year, a standard that it has maintained with its two rosettes for cuisine.

The hotel stands in eight acres of landscaped gardens on the edge of Galloway Forest Park in the foothills of the Cairnsmore of Fleet. You can relax on the terrace and enjoy the spectacular views or play tennis, pitch and putt or croquet. Special golf packages on the exclusive Cally course, salmon and trout fishing, rough shooting and deer stalking can all be arranged.

LOCATION
Travelling west on the A75, take the A712 towards New Galloway. The hotel driveway is 300 yards on the left.

" *Why would anyone stay in a stuffy, impersonal hotel when places like this exist - brilliant concept and spot-on realization "*

Elaine Bishop, Isle of Wight

Serviced Apartments

THE KNIGHT RESIDENCE

Stylish private apartments in the shadow of Edinburgh Castle

Serviced apartments offer an increased sense of privacy and the opportunity to relax as if you were at home, without having to worry about keeping things in order when you're on holiday or travelling for business. The Knight Residence takes this ethic and adds to it by offering well thought-out and attentive concierge service with a personal touch. Colin Stone, the General Manager is proud of his team who provide daily housekeeping and aim to be efficient, friendly and yet unobtrusive.

Each of the 19 apartments has its own kitchen and lounge, and is equipped with video, cable TV and hi-fi with extension speakers into the bathroom; business facilities include fax, email, internet access and secretarial support.

Whether you are visiting in August for the festival or otherwise, Scotland's capital city is renowned worldwide for its cultural heritage, and many tourist attractions are within easy reach. The Residence has a commitment to showcasing the work of local artists and throughout the property original paintings, sculpture and designs are permanently on show. The best thing is if you

fall in love with any particular piece, you can arrange to buy it, and either take it home immediately, or have it sent on.

LOCATION

From Princes Street turn right into Lothian Road. Take first left into King Stables Road and then a right onto the West Port. Turn left into Lauriston Street and the hotel is on your right.

12 Lauriston Street, Edinburgh EH3 9DJ

Telephone 0131 622 8120 Fax 0131 622 7363

E-mail: *knightres@bestloved.com*

GENERAL MANAGER
Colin Stone

ROOM RATES
Single occupancy   £85 - £140
9   1-Bedroom apts   £95 - £150
10   2-Bedroom apts   £130 - £205
Includes VAT

CHARGE/CREDIT CARDS

 • *DC* • *JCB* • *MC* • *VI*

RATINGS & AWARDS
S.T.B. ★★★★★ *Serviced Apartments*
R.A.C. ◆◆◆◆◆ *Sparkling Diamond and Warm Welcome Awards*

FACILITIES
On site: *Private parking*
Nearby: *Golf, leisure centre*

RESTRICTIONS
No facilities for disabled guests
No smoking throughout
Pets by arrangement

ATTRACTIONS
*Edinburgh Castle,
Holyrood House,
Dynamic Earth,
Royal Yacht Britannia,
National Gallery,
Edinburgh Festival and Military Tattoo*

AFFILIATIONS
Independent

NEAREST
MAJOR CITY:
Edinburgh

MAJOR AIRPORT:
Edinburgh - 7 miles/20 mins

RAILWAY STATION:
Waverley - 1 ½ miles/5 mins

RESERVATIONS
Direct with hotel
Quote Best Loved

ACCESS CODES
AMADEUS IP EDI 012
APOLLO/GALILEO IP 46358
SABRE/ABACUS IP 29353
WORLDSPAN IP 2900

• *Map p.464*
ref: D12

" The epitome of what a fine country house hotel should be - warm, inviting and totally enjoyable "

Helen Worth & Michael Angelis, TV personalities

KNOCKINAAM LODGE

19th century hunting lodge

**Portpatrick, Near Stranraer,
Dumfries & Galloway DG9 9AD**

**Telephone 01776 810471
Fax 01776 810435**

E-mail: *knockinaam@bestloved.com*

OWNERS
Michael Bricker and Pauline Ashworth

RATES PER PERSON
1 Single	*£125 - £145*
5 Doubles/Twins	*£105 - £135*
4 Master rooms	*£130 - £170*

Includes full breakfast, dinner and VAT

CHARGE/CREDIT CARDS

• DC • MC • VI

RATINGS & AWARDS
S.T.B. ★★★★ Small Hotel
Taste of Scotland - 4 Medallions

FACILITIES
On site: *Garden, heli-pad, croquet*
1 meeting room/max 45 people
Nearby: *Fishing, shooting, golf, walking*

RESTRICTIONS
No facilities for disabled guests
*No children under 12 years in
the restaurant for dinner*
No pets in public rooms

ATTRACTIONS
*Logan, Ardwell and Glenwhan Gardens,
Castle Kennedy, Culzean Castle,
Galloway Castle*

AFFILIATIONS
*The Celebrated Hotels Collection
Pride of Britain*

NEAREST
MAJOR CITY:
Stranraer - 8 miles/15 mins

MAJOR AIRPORT:
Glasgow - 98 miles/2 hrs

RAILWAY STATION:
Stranraer - 8 miles/15 mins

FERRY PORT:
Stranraer - 8 miles/15 mins

RESERVATIONS
*Toll free in US: 800-322-2403
or 800-98-PRIDE*
*Quote **Best Loved***

ACCESS CODES
Not applicable

One of Churchill's and Eisenhower's best kept secrets

In its beautiful 30-acre setting beside the Irish Sea, Knockinaam enjoys one of Scotland's most romantic settings. Built in 1869 as a hunting lodge by Lady Hunter-Blair and extended to its present size in 1901, it has marvellous sea views and sunsets, gardens, public rooms with open log fires and 10 comfortable en suite bedrooms. It is the ideal place for a relaxing getaway. Sir Winston Churchill chose Knockinaam as his secret meeting place with General Dwight D. Eisenhower during the Second World War.

The restaurant serves the most delicious and innovative cuisine, using only the freshest ingredients. The menu features Scottish beef and lamb, as well as local seafood. To complement the food, the wine list has over 500 varieties. The hotel is noted for its display of over 124 malt whiskies, a pleasure for the connoisseur and an education for the novice!

Knockinaam has an international reputation for service, hospitality and attention to details, provided by proprietors Pauline Ashworth, Michael Bricker and their wonderful staff.

There is superb fishing and shooting close by, and the nearby golf clubs include Turnberry,

Royal Troon, Prestwick, Brunston Castle, Southerness, Stranraer and Portpatrick

LOCATION

*From A75 or A77, follow signs to Portpatrick.
2 miles west of Lochans, turn left at sign to
Knockinaam Lodge, pass Colfin Smokehouse and
follow signs for 3 miles to the Lodge.*

" We had the opportunity to experience some very fine hotels in Scotland, but the most comfortable and cosy one was definitely Knockomie "

Annette & Roy Scwalbe, Weisswasser, Germany

Arts and crafts house

KNOCKOMIE HOTEL

Pampered comfort surrounded by a wealth of sights and sports

Overlooking the Royal Burgh of Forres, Knockomie is ideally situated to visit castles, distilleries and golf courses, while salmon and deer await the keen sportsman. The front hall is panelled in Scots Pine, while all 15 bedrooms are individually decorated with soft furnishings and period furniture. Some have four-poster or half-tester beds; others, with patios, are on the ground floor, including one for the disabled.

Knockomie House was built in 1821, added to in the Arts and Crafts style in 1914 and extended in 1993. Their grill and bistro serve the best of Scottish produce to specialise in the Taste of Scotland. This is complemented by an extensive wine list and a large collection of malt whiskies.

An ideal location to visit the many castles, including Cawdor, Brodie and Ballindalloch or the unique Whisky Trail in the Spey Valley. Loch Ness is less than an hour away waiting to reveal its secret. Other opportunities include stalking and shooting in the glens, or fishing in the lochs and rivers. Local golf courses include Lossiemouth, Hopeman, Forres, Nairn (championship) and Dornoch (championship).

LOCATION

1 mile south of Forres on A940.

Grantown Road, Forres, Moray IV36 2SG

**Telephone 01309 673146
Fax 01309 673290**

E-mail: *knockomie@bestloved.com*

DIRECTOR
Gavin Ellis

ROOM RATES
Single occupancy £82 - £95
11 Doubles/Twins £93 - £148
1 Family room £140
2 Four-posters £165
1 Suite £196
Includes full breakfast and VAT

CHARGE/CREDIT CARDS

 • DC • JCB • MC • VI

RATINGS & AWARDS
S.T.B. ★★★★ *Small Hotel*
Taste of Scotland - 3 Medallions

FACILITIES
On site: *Garden, heli-pad, croquet*
2 meeting rooms/max 70 people
Nearby: *Golf, fishing, shooting, stalking, walking*

RESTRICTIONS
Limited facilities for disabled guests

ATTRACTIONS
Brodie Castle, Cawdor Castle, Ballindalloch Castle, Johnston's of Elgin, Benromach and Glen Grant Distilleries, Findhorn Foundation, Malt Whisky Trail

AFFILIATIONS
*Preston's Global Hotels
Great Little Hotels of Scotland
Grand Heritage Hotels*

NEAREST
MAJOR CITY:
Inverness - 27 miles/30 mins

MAJOR AIRPORT:
Inverness - 25 miles/30 mins
Aberdeen - 79 miles/2 hrs

RAILWAY STATION:
Forres - 1 mile/5 mins

RESERVATIONS
*Toll free in US: 800-544-9993
or 888-93-GRAND*
Quote **Best Loved**

ACCESS CODES
*AMADEUS UI FSSKNO
APOLLO/GALILEO UI 73447
SABRE/ABACUS UI 32407
WORLDSPAN UI 40671*

> *" Ladyburn exemplifies life as it used to be lived and ought to be lived "*
>
> *Jack Macmillan MBE, Edinburgh*

LADYBURN

SCOTLAND

**by Maybole,
Ayrshire KA19 7SG**

**Telephone 01655 740585
Fax 01655 740580**

E-mail: *ladyburn@bestloved.com*

OWNERS
David and Jane Hepburn

ROOM RATES
Single occupancy   £60 - £80
3 Doubles/Twins   £100 - £170
2 Four-posters   £154 - £170
1 2-Bedroom apartment   £90 - £180
Includes full breakfast and VAT

CHARGE/CREDIT CARDS

 • *MC* • *VI*

RATINGS & AWARDS
R.A.C. Blue Ribbon ★★ *Dining Award 3*
A.A. ★★ ❀
A.A. Top 200 - 02/03

FACILITIES
On site: *Garden, heli-pad, croquet
1 meeting room/max 20 people*
Nearby: *Golf, fishing, stalking,
clay pigeon shooting*

RESTRICTIONS
*Limited facilities for disabled guests
Smoking in Library only
No children
No pets
Closed 1 - 14 Nov*

ATTRACTIONS
*Burns' Centre, Crossraguel Abbey,
Culzean Castle, Glentrool,
Tam O'Shanter Experience*

AFFILIATIONS
Independent

NEAREST
*MAJOR CITY:
Glasgow - 45 miles/1 hr*

*MAJOR AIRPORT:
Glasgow - 50 miles/1 ¼ hrs
Prestwick - 12 miles/30 mins*

*RAILWAY STATION:
Ayr - 12 miles/20 mins*

RESERVATIONS
*Direct with hotel
Quote* **Best Loved**

ACCESS CODES
Not applicable

Character, comfort and good food tied with a Blue Ribbon of excellence

Ladyburn and Jane Hepburn are, as they say, an item! Indivisible. Praise one and you praise the other. It's not obvious from the picture above but there is a clue in the yellow column on the right: you will not find another Blue Ribbon (the second highest accolade the RAC can give) sitting next to only two stars (representing size and facilities).

Ladyburn is about as original as you can get! With service and comfort it could shame the best five stars in the world. Ladyburn is a combination of irrepressible enthusiasm, total understanding of what people want when away from home and an instinctive genius for cooking. There are only five rooms in the house but what rooms! What comfort! Real coffee on the side and, at bedtime, not just chocolates but a hot water bottle, too!

You will not find a menu in sight; Jane will ask you what you would like and make a suggestion or two if you need a prompt, then go out and buy whatever is necessary.

The gardens, too, are more than worthy of a mention - recently accepted into Scotland's

Garden Scheme, tours can be arranged between Ladyburn and other gardens throughout Ayrshire.

Ladyburn - there is nothing to match it!

LOCATION
*Take the A77 to Maybole. Turn onto B7023
to Crosshill and right at War Memorial.
2 miles further along, turn left. Ladyburn
is ¾ mile on right.*

" This is a magical place "

Dr & Mrs A Mitchell, Bray -on-Thames

• Map p.464
ref: E9

Lakeside hotel — THE LAKE OF MENTEITH HOTEL

Good food and magnificent lakefront views to the Trossachs

On a sunny day the only hotel on Scotland's only lake (the rest are 'lochs') casts its reflection over the glassy calm water a few feet away and it is as pretty and tranquil a picture as you can imagine. From the hotel, the views stretch down the lake to the Isle of Inchmahome, site of a 12th-century priory, and beyond to the ever-changing scenery of the Trossachs. The story behind the 'lake' is a little murky, but the most likely explanation is the visit of a mid-19th century Dutch cartographer who probably misheard the local word 'laigh' meaning 'lowland' and translated it as 'lake'.

This charming family-run hotel makes a terrific base for an active holiday with hillwalking and fishing on the doorstep, golf and riding nearby. There is plenty to see, too, from doughty Stirling Castle to Glasgow and Edinburgh. Another option, of course, is to relax and savour the view from the conservatory restaurant renowned for its fine French cuisine prepared from the finest Scottish produce. In winter, the hotel offers wine evenings with guest experts. It may also be possible to build up an appetite skating on the lake which occasionally freezes over!

LOCATION

M9 Exit 10. Take the A84/A873/A81 to Port of Menteith. The hotel is on the left next to the church.

Port of Menteith, Perthshire FK8 3RA

**Telephone 01877 385258
Fax 01877 385671**

E-mail: *lakementeith@bestloved.com*

OWNERS
Graeme and Ros McConnachie

ROOM RATES
Single occupancy   £45 - £85
16 Doubles/Twins   £90 - £170
Includes full breakfast and VAT

CHARGE/CREDIT CARDS

 • MC • VI

RATINGS & AWARDS
S.T.B. ★★★ *Small Hotel*
A.A. ★★ ❀❀ *76%*
Taste of Scotland - 3 Medallions

FACILITIES
On site: *Garden, fishing
2 meeting rooms/max 40 people*
Nearby: *Golf, riding, leisure centre*

RESTRICTIONS
*Limited facilities for disabled guests
No children under 8 years
No smoking in bedrooms
Closed 2 -20 Jan*

ATTRACTIONS
*Inchmahome Priory, The Trossachs,
Stirling Castle, Rob Roy Centre,
Loch Katrine*

AFFILIATIONS
Independent

NEAREST
MAJOR CITY:
Glasgow - 29 miles/50 mins

MAJOR AIRPORT:
Glasgow - 32 miles/50 mins

RAILWAY STATION:
Stirling - 17 miles/25 mins

RESERVATIONS
Direct with hotel
Quote **Best Loved**

ACCESS CODES
Not applicable

> *" It is the kind of view you could watch all day and it accompanies everything you do in the hotel like silent music - the food matches the setting "*
>
> *Iain Crawford, freelance journalist*

LOCH MELFORT

Hotel and restaurant

SCOTLAND

Arduaine, by Oban, Argyll PA34 4XG

Telephone 01852 200233
Fax 01852 200214

E-mail: *lochmelfort@bestloved.com*

OWNERS
Nigel and Kyle Schofield

ROOM RATES
Single occupancy	£49 - £79
24 Doubles/Twins	£78 - £118
2 Superior doubles	£110 - £158

Includes full breakfast and VAT

CHARGE/CREDIT CARDS

 ● *MC* ● *VI*

RATINGS & AWARDS
S.T.B. ★★★★ *Hotel*
A.A. ★★★ ❀❀ *76%*
Taste of Scotland - 3 Medallions

FACILITIES
On site: *Garden*
1 meeting room/max 40 people
Nearby: *Fishing, riding, sailing, windsurfing, walking, mountain biking*

RESTRICTIONS
Limited facilities for disabled guests
Pets by arrangement

ATTRACTIONS
Arduaine Gardens, Mull & Iona, Gigha and Arran Islands, Kerrera, Kilmartin Glen, Inveraray, Glencoe, Dunstaffnage Castle and Chapel

AFFILIATIONS
Scotland's Hotels of Distinction
Les Routiers

NEAREST
MAJOR CITY:
Glasgow - 110 miles/2 hrs

MAJOR AIRPORT:
Glasgow - 100 miles/2 hrs

RAILWAY STATION:
Oban - 19 miles/30 mins

RESERVATIONS
Toll free in US: 800-223-6510
or 800-437-2687

Quote **Best Loved**

ACCESS CODES
AMADEUS UI GLALOC
APOLLO/GALILEO UI 83670
SABRE/ABACUS UI 21454
WORLDSPAN UI LOCHA

Spectacular location on the west coast with uninterrupted views

The finest location on the west coast of Scotland awaits visitors to this award-winning hotel and restaurant, the perfect place for a relaxing holiday or short break at any time of the year. Personally run by Nigel and Kyle Schofield, they and their friendly and attentive staff are always on hand to make sure your stay is an enjoyable one.

The comfortable bedrooms all have private bathrooms, TV, radio and direct dial telephones. Most have stunning views across Asknish Bay to the islands of Jura, Shuna and Scarba.

The restaurant, with its two AA rosettes for cuisine, offers superb dining comprising only the best of fresh local produce particularly locally-caught fish and shellfish, meats and cheeses. Mouth-watering home-made puddings and ice-creams provide the perfect finale to the menu which changes daily. A carefully chosen and comprehensive wine list offers an excellent choice. Lunches, suppers and afternoon teas are served in the hotel's Skerry Bistro.

The hotel lies next to the National Trust of Scotland's famous Arduaine Gardens, one of 20 National Trust properties within easy reach, all revelling in the mountain grandeur of Argyll.

LOCATION

Midway between Oban and Lochgilphead on A816.

" Your staff were courteous and greatly contributed to my new found love of Scotland "

Kyle Gibson, USA

• Map p.464
ref: G10

Edinburgh town house

MELVIN HOUSE HOTEL

Stop Press! Excellent value in Edinburgh's fashionable West End

In 1766, 22-year-old James Craig won a public competition to design a New Town for Edinburgh which would expand the city beyond the confines of the rocky outcrop dominated by Edinburgh Castle. Craig's neo-Classical plan extended north of Princes Street, and by the late-19th century the final piece of the New Town development, the West End, neared completion.

It was here, in 1883, that John Ritchie Findlay, legendary owner, of Scotland's national newspaper, 'The Scotsman', built himself a handsome terraced house, which has now been transformed into this first class hotel. Renowned Architect, Sidney Mitchell was instructed to 'cut no corners' in the construction of his elegant and spacious home. Extensively restored, Melvin House remains full of grand Victorian character, intricate mouldings, dark wood panelling and imposing marble fireplaces in the public rooms. The generously sized bedrooms, which can provide exceptional value-for-money family accommodation, boast views over the city to the castle or the ancient kingdom of Fife. A short walk from the Princes Street shops and major attractions such as the National Gallery of

Scotland, Melvin House's location is hard to beat and business travellers are well-placed for the city's financial and business communities as well as the hotel's own stately conference rooms.

LOCATION
5 mins from the west end of Princes Street.

**3 Rothesay Terrace,
Edinburgh EH3 7RY**

**Telephone 0131 225 5084
Fax 0131 226 5085**

E-mail: *melvinhouse@bestloved.com*

OWNERS
The McKenzie Family

ROOM RATES
Single occupancy   £75 - £115
10 Doubles/Twins   £120
6 Executive Doubles/Twins   £160
6 Family rooms   £160 - £180
Includes full breakfast and VAT

CHARGE/CREDIT CARDS

 • *DC* • *MC* • *VI*

RATINGS & AWARDS
S.T.B. ★★★ *Hotel*

FACILITIES
On site: *4 meeting rooms/max 75 people*
Nearby: *Golf, swimming*

RESTRICTIONS
*No facilities for disabled guests
Suitable for children over 12 years
No smoking in bedrooms
Pets by arrangement*

ATTRACTIONS
*Edinburgh Castle, Holyrood House,
Royal Mile, Dynamic Earth,
National Art Gallery of Scotland,
Royal Yacht Britannia*

AFFILIATIONS
Preston's Global Hotels

NEAREST
*MAJOR CITY:
Edinburgh*

*MAJOR AIRPORT:
Edinburgh - 6 miles/25 mins*

*RAILWAY STATION:
Haymarket - ¼ mile/10 mins*

RESERVATIONS
Toll free in US: 800-544-9993
Quote **Best Loved**

ACCESS CODES
Not applicable

Map p.464
ref: E9

" *What a super place, really enjoyed the comfort, tranquility and especially the food* "

Hazel & Gerry Oates, Somerset

MONACHYLE MHOR

Highland hotel

SCOTLAND

Balquhidder, Lochearnhead, Stirlingshire FK19 8PQ

**Telephone 01877 384622
Fax 01877 384305**

E-mail: *monachyle@bestloved.com*

OWNERS
Angela and Tom Lewis

ROOM RATES
Single occupancy   £55 - £95
10 Doubles/Twins   £90 - £150
Includes full breakfast and VAT

CHARGE/CREDIT CARDS
MC • VI

RATINGS & AWARDS
S.T.B. ★★★ *Small Hotel*
A.A. ★★ 🌸🌸 74%
*S.T.B. Scottish Thistle Award
Macallan Taste of Scotland Award for best
'Out of Town Restaurant'
Taste of Scotland - 4 Medallions*

FACILITIES
On site: *Garden, fishing,
deer stalking, shooting
1 meeting room/max 16 people*
Nearby: *Golf, water skiing,
sailing, jet skiing*

RESTRICTIONS
*No facilities for disabled guests
No children under 12 years
No smoking in bedrooms
Pets by arrangement*

ATTRACTIONS
*The Trossachs, Loch Lomond,
Stirling Castle, Wallace Memorial,
Rob Roy Centre*

AFFILIATIONS
Independent

NEAREST
*MAJOR CITY:
Perth - 42 miles/1 hr
Stirling - 30 miles/45 mins*

*MAJOR AIRPORT:
Glasgow - 55 miles/ 1 ½ hrs*

*RAILWAY STATION:
Perth - 42 miles/1 hr
Stirling - 30 miles/45 mins*

RESERVATIONS
*Direct with hotel
Quote* **Best Loved**

ACCESS CODES
Not applicable

Farmhouse hospitality and memorable food in the heart of Rob Roy country

Monachyle Mhor farmhouse presides over a 2,000-acre estate that encompasses two lochs to the west of Balquhidder. It takes its name from the Gaelic word describing the narrow strait where the lochs meet and this wild and beautiful Trossachs landscape is a fitting backdrop to the legend of Rob Roy, the Scottish folk hero, whose exhilarating Jacobite era adventures were later immortalised by Sir Walter Scott.

The Lewis family (Rob, Jean and Tom) have spent some 20 years perfecting their warm and welcoming small hotel. The original farmhouse has been equipped with every modern comfort while retaining its character and charm. There are 10 attractive country style bedrooms and two self-catering cottages cleverly converted from the old byre and coach house across the cobbled courtyard. Tom Lewis is the chef and masterminds the imaginative seasonal menu. Most of the ingredients come from within a 30-mile radius, including herbs and vegetables from the hotel's organic garden, and Tom's own homemade jams, pickles, cured beef and bacon.

Working up an appetite is no problem with such fantastic walking country on the doorstep.

Salmon and trout fishing, deer stalking and grouse shooting can also be arranged in season.

LOCATION

*From Stirling, take the A84 north.
11 miles north of Callander, follow signs
for Kinghouse/Balquhidder. The road
doubles back on itself, to head left.
The hotel is 6 miles along this road.*

" *The Old Manor is our very special retreat for year round breaks - good food, friendly staff - and lots to see and do* "

Tony and Elizabeth Welton, Edinburgh

Country house hotel   OLD MANOR HOTEL

A country house where the dining is excellent and golfers are spoilt for choice

This pleasant hotel is only 20 minutes from St Andrews itself, looking out on to the Lundin Links and Leven Open qualifying golf courses. The Old Manor is a fine old country house, situated in its own grounds with impressive views over Largo Bay. All of the public rooms are comfortably furnished to provide an easy place to relax. Many of the comfortable bedrooms have delightful sea views, several with balconies; all are en suite.

In the fine dining Aithernie Restaurant (two AA rosettes) Chef James McKay and his team make imaginative use of local produce, game and seafood. At the popular Coachman's Grill, Head Chef Roberta Drummond, runner up in the Female Chef of the Year competition, offers fine chargrilled steaks and seafood in a less formal atmosphere with choice real ales and over 100 malt whiskies.

Golf enthusiasts will enjoy the hotel's complimentary booking service, where you can choose convenient tee times at over 30 courses within an hour's drive. There is also a great deal for non-golfers. St Andrews has beautiful beaches and Scotland's oldest university. The surrounding area has plenty of leisure parks, museums, castles, stately homes and gardens. A wonderful venue for a wedding reception or a honeymoon.

LOCATION

Exit 2a from M90 on to A92 to St Andrews. At roundabout take third exit - A915 to St Andrews. Lundin Links is 1 mile past Leven. The Old Manor is on right as you enter village.

Lundin Links, Near St Andrews, Fife KY8 6AJ
Telephone 01333 320368
Fax 01333 320911
E-mail: *oldmanor@bestloved.com*

OWNERS
The Clark Family

ROOM RATES
1 Single	£35 - £80
14 Doubles/Twins	£70 - £140
5 Superior Doubles/Twins	£150 - £190
3 Four-posters	£160 - £200

Includes full breakfast and VAT

CHARGE/CREDIT CARDS
 ● DC ● JCB ● MC ● VI

RATINGS & AWARDS
S.T.B. ★★★★
A.A. ★★★ ✿✿ 77%
Taste of Scotland - 3 Medallions
Scotch Beef Club

FACILITIES
On site: *Garden*
3 meeting rooms/max 180 people
Nearby: *Golf, fishing, riding, tennis, squash, bowls, beaches*

RESTRICTIONS
Limited facilities for disabled guests
No children in restaurant after 7 pm
No smoking in bedrooms
No pets in public areas

ATTRACTIONS
Deep Sea World, Crail, Anstruther, St Andrews Cathedral, Falkland Palace St Andrews Golf Course,

AFFILIATIONS
Scotland's Hotels of Distinction
Preston's Global Hotels
Great Little Hotels of Scotland

NEAREST
MAJOR CITY:
St Andrews - 12 miles/20 mins
Edinburgh - 35 miles/40 mins

MAJOR AIRPORT:
Edinburgh - 30 miles/45 mins

RAILWAY STATION:
Markinch - 6 miles/10 mins

RESERVATIONS
Toll free in US: 800-437-2687
or 800-544-9993
Toll free in UK: 0800 980 2420
Quote **Best Loved**

ACCESS CODES
AMADEUS HK EDIOLD
APOLLO/GALILEO HT 28503
SABRE/ABACUS HK 53935
WORLDSPAN HK OLDMS

Map p.464
ref: E10

" *Loved it!* "

Neil Sedaka

ONE DEVONSHIRE GARDENS

Victorian town house

**1 Devonshire Gardens,
Glasgow G12 0UX**

**Telephone 0141 339 2001
Fax 0141 339 1663**

E-mail: *devonsglas@bestloved.com*

GENERAL MANAGER
Stephen G. McCorkell

ROOM RATES
Single occupancy   £125 - £195
24 Doubles   £145 - £495
8 Four-posters   £225 - £495
4 Suites   £250 - £550
Includes VAT

CHARGE/CREDIT CARDS

 • *DC* • *MC* • *VI*

RATINGS & AWARDS
S.T.B. ★★★★★ *Hotel*
A.A. ★★★★ *82%*
A.A. Romantic Hotel

FACILITIES
On site: *Private dining room,
House '5' Restaurant
Gordon Ramsey's Amaryllis Restaurant
3 meeting rooms/max 50 people*
Nearby: *Golf, riding*

RESTRICTIONS
*No facilities for disabled guests
Pets at manager's discretion*

ATTRACTIONS
*The Burrell Collection,
Rennie Mackintosh's Hill House,
Dumbarton and Bothwell Castles,
Glasgow University, Loch Lomond,
The Trossachs*

AFFILIATIONS
The Celebrated Hotels Collection

NEAREST
*MAJOR CITY:
Glasgow - 1 ½ miles/10 mins*

*MAJOR AIRPORT:
Glasgow - 12 miles/20 mins*

*RAILWAY STATION:
Glasgow - 130 miles/10 mins*

RESERVATIONS
Toll free in US: 800-322-2403
Quote **Best Loved**

ACCESS CODES
*AMADEUS HK GLADEV
APOLLO/GALILEO HT 25902
SABRE/ABACUS HK 31789
WORLDSPAN HK DEVOS*

An establishment of distinction and stylish splendour

One Devonshire Gardens, renowned for its comfort and hospitality, is set in the city's fashionable West End, minutes from many famous attractions; The Burrell Collection, Glasgow University, Kelvingrove Art Gallery & Museum to name a few.

One of the hotel's charms is a fine Victorian Terrace, painstakingly restored to the glory of a bygone era. Subdued lighting and countless original paintings put this amongst the best hotels in the city. The bedrooms, including some four-posters, are spacious and airy with designer décor and considerate touches such as DVD and CD players.

In addition to the hotel's existing restaurant, the great news is that One Devonshire is now home to Gordon Ramsey's Amaryllis Restaurant which has been causing a buzz within Glasgow's 'serious' dining circles and, of course, provides an excellent new reason for a visit.

Loch Lomond is just 30-minute's away. Edinburgh is 45 minutes by train, which runs twice - hourly. The hotel is the ideal place to enjoy some of a vast collection of malt whiskies. Famous past guests include Michael Jackson, Whitney Houston and Bryan Adams, to name a few.

An elegant hotel with unrivalled Scottish cuisine, where guests are assured of individual and traditional grand hospitality.

LOCATION

Exit 17 off M8. Turn right onto A82. After Grosvenor Hotel turn left at 2nd traffic lights into Hyndland Road. Take first right and right at roundabout. Hotel is at end of road on right.

" *My most favourite hotel in Scotland* "

Barbara Cartland

● *Map p.464*
ref: F9

Georgian residence

PARK LODGE HOTEL

SCOTLAND

A taste of France in the heart of Scotland

The Park Lodge Hotel near Stirling is what might be described as small yet perfectly formed. An ivy-clad Georgian country house that was built in 1825, it has a rear walled garden and is situated right opposite Stirling Golf course, with commanding views of the castle.

The Sir William Wallace monument - around whom the film Braveheart was based - is also close by. However, what gives this establishment its particularly personal touch is its proprietors, Georges and Anne Marquetty, who have been there for 30 years - Anne, having furnished each of the hotels' 10 bedrooms in keeping with the character of the building. And Georges, who was born in the south of France, having brought a flavour of the Mediterranean with him.

As chef at the hotel's Heritage Restaurant Georges has created a menu that combines first-rate Scottish produce with a distinctly French flair. He is also a Chevalier du Taste de Vin, so is thus fully equipped to advise you on the wine to accompany your food, whether it is

at a dinner for two, a wedding reception or an important business conference, all of which can be hosted at the hotel.

LOCATION

From Kings Park Road take a left into Drummond Place and first right into Park Terrace.

**32 Park Terrace,
Stirling FK8 2JS**

**Telephone 01786 474862
Fax 01786 449748**

E-mail: *parklodge@bestloved.com*

OWNERS
Georges and Anne Marquetty

ROOM RATES
2 Singles	£60
7 Doubles/Twins	£95
1 Four-poster	£95 - £110

Includes full breakfast and VAT

CHARGE/CREDIT CARDS

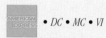 ● *DC* ● *MC* ● *VI*

RATINGS & AWARDS
S.T.B. ★★★ *Small Hotel*

FACILITIES
On site: *Garden,
3 meeting rooms/max 180 people*
Nearby: *Golf, tennis, riding, fishing*

RESTRICTIONS
*Limited facilities for disabled guests
Pets by arrangement*

ATTRACTIONS
*Stirling Castle, Wallace Monument,
Stirling Smith Art Gallery and Museum,
Edinburgh, St Andrews, Glasgow,
Loch Lomond Millenium Wheel*

AFFILIATIONS
Independent

NEAREST
*MAJOR CITY:
Edinburgh - 38 miles/50 mins
Glasgow - 30 miles/45 mins*

*MAJOR AIRPORT:
Edinburgh - 32 miles/40 mins
Glasgow - 37 miles/45 mins*

*RAILWAY STATION:
Stirling - 4 miles/15 mins*

RESERVATIONS
Direct with hotel
Quote **Best Loved**

ACCESS CODES
Not applicable

• Map p.464
ref: G9

" One of the most honest and enterprising restaurants in Britain "

R W Apple Jnr, The New York Times

THE PEAT INN

Restaurant with rooms

SCOTLAND

**Peat Inn, by Cupar,
Fife KY15 5LH**

Telephone 01334 840206
Fax 01334 840530

E-mail: *peat@bestloved.com*

OWNERS
David and Patricia Wilson

ROOM RATES
8 Suites £145 - £155
Includes continental breakfast and VAT

CHARGE/CREDIT CARDS

• MC • VI

RATINGS & AWARDS
S.T.B. ★★★★★ *Restaurant with Rooms*
A.A. ★★ ❀❀❀
A.A. Top 200 - 02/03
A.A. Romantic Hotel
A.A. Wine List of the Year
Andrew Harper Award - Hideaway Report
Taste of Scotland - 4 Medallions

FACILITIES
On site: *Garden*
1 meeting room/max 12 people
Nearby: *Riding, golf, fishing, shooting*

RESTRICTIONS
Closed every Sunday and Monday

ATTRACTIONS
*St Andrews, East Neuk fishing villages,
Falkland Palace, Inchcolm Abbey,
Kellie Castle*

AFFILIATIONS
Independent

NEAREST
*MAJOR CITY:
Edinburgh - 40 miles/1 hr
Dundee - 19 miles/30 mins*

*MAJOR AIRPORT:
Edinburgh - 40 miles/1 hr*

*RAILWAY STATION:
Cupar - 6 miles/10 mins*

RESERVATIONS
Direct with hotel
*Quote **Best Loved***

ACCESS CODES
Not applicable

A celebrated restaurant just a short drive from St Andrews

Food lovers the world over are attracted to The Peat Inn in the tiny rural village named after the inn itself. David Wilson, Chef Laureate, Master Chef and Proprietor, is well known as one of the nation's first TV Chef celebrities and is still active in encouraging high standards of cuisine as a director of The Taste of Scotland.

As if the food and wine at The Peat Inn were not enough, the accommodation is the envy of many large country house hotels. Sympathetically designed by Patricia Wilson, seven of the suites are split level, while one is single level, and each and every suite features a marble bathroom, a pretty sitting room and welcome extras such as a selection of homemade cakes and fresh fruit.

St Andrews is of course synonymous with golf, but the area also offers plenty more to keep guests interested. The Kingdom of Fife is a land of contrasts, from the fishing villages of the East Neuk of Fife to Falkland Palace, country residence of the Stewart monarchs. Other attractions include Scone Palace, Deep Sea World and the birthplace of J M Barrie.

LOCATION
Situated in the village of Peat Inn at the junction of the B940/B941, 6 miles south west of St Andrews.

This is by far the friendliest and best hotel, with delicious food that is beautifully presented. I love all the little extras

Angela Taylor, Ashton-under-Lyne, Lancashire

Whisky family home — PIERSLAND HOUSE HOTEL

SCOTLAND

Enjoy Royal Troon - in the world's finest setting for a single malt

Piersland was built in 1899 for Alexander Walker, grandson of Johnnie Walker, founder of the Scotch whisky firm. A Grade A listed building, Piersland has two extra reasons to be chosen for a Scottish holiday. Royal Troon Golf Club, venue of the 1997 British Open and the 2004 British Open, is directly opposite. Sir Alexander's own Walker Lounge, luxuriously panelled in oak and with its original wood carvings and fireplaces today offers the choice of 200 fine single malts. There is no better place in the world to enjoy Scotland's most famous product.

Piersland is set in landscaped grounds. You enter through the elegant Minstrel Hall. Sumptuous meals are served in two restaurants and the verandah is the perfect place to enjoy a traditional afternoon tea. Within ten miles is the county town of Ayr, birthplace of Robert Burns, and Culzean Castle, seat of the Clan Kennedy. Turnberry, Old Prestwick and eight other top golf courses are within 30 minute's drive. Glasgow, Edinburgh, Stirling, Loch Lomond and the Trossachs are within easy reach.

LOCATION

5 miles north of Ayr, directly opposite Royal Troon Golf Club.

Craigend Road, Troon, Ayrshire KA10 6HD

**Telephone 01292 314747
Fax 01292 315613**

E-mail: *piersland@bestloved.com*

GENERAL MANAGER
Karel Kuhler

ROOM RATES
1 Single	£63 - £90
13 Doubles/Twins	£80 - £119
15 Suites	£115 - £135
1 Four-poster	£115 - £165

Includes full breakfast and VAT

CHARGE/CREDIT CARDS
 • DC • MC • VI

RATINGS & AWARDS
S.T.B. ★★★★ Hotel
A.A. ★★★ ❀❀ 72%
Taste of Scotland - 4 Medallions

FACILITIES
On site: *Garden*
3 meeting rooms/max 150 people
Nearby: *Golf, riding, fitness, yachting, tennis, shooting*

RESTRICTIONS
Pets by arrangement

ATTRACTIONS
*Turnberry,
Culzean Castle,
Burns Cottage,
Isle of Arran,
Brodick Castle*

AFFILIATIONS
Independent

NEAREST
*MAJOR CITY:
Glasgow - 25 miles/30 mins*

*MAJOR AIRPORT:
Prestwick/Glasgow - 3 miles/10 mins*

*RAILWAY STATION:
Troon - ½ mile/5 mins*

RESERVATIONS
Direct with hotel
Quote **Best Loved**

ACCESS CODES
Not applicable

● *Map p.464*
ref: D6

" *Apstootly brilyant and the staf is nice* "

Helen Conner, aged 5

THE PLOCKTON HOTEL

Highland hotel

Harbour Street, Plockton,
Wester Ross IV52 8TN

Telephone 01599 544274
Fax 01599 544475

E-mail: *plockton@bestloved.com*

OWNERS
Dorothy, Tom and Alan Pearson

ROOM RATES
1 Single	£40
13 Doubles/Twins	£80 - £90
1 Family	£90 - £100

Includes full breakfast and VAT

CHARGE/CREDIT CARDS

 ● *MC* ● *VI*

RATINGS & AWARDS
S.T.B. ★★★
A.A. ★★ 69%
Best Seafood Pub in Scotland 2002

FACILITIES
Nearby: *Golf, fishing, sailing*

RESTRICTIONS
Limited facilities for disabled guests
No smoking in bedrooms
No pets, guide dogs only

ATTRACTIONS
Eilean Donan Castle,
Isle of Skye,
Inverewe Gardens,
Highland Games,
Walking & climbing

AFFILIATIONS
Independent

NEAREST
MAJOR CITY:
Inverness - 82 miles/2 hrs

MAJOR AIRPORT:
Inverness - 82 miles/2 hrs

RAILWAY STATION:
Kyle of Lochalsh - 8 miles/15 mins

RESERVATIONS
Direct with hotel
Quote **Best Loved**

ACCESS CODES
Not applicable

An unsurpassed location and an outstanding reputation for seafood

When I arrived at Plockton my breath was taken away. To be truthful my breath was taken away several times on my train journey trundling up through the West Highland Way past mirrored lochs, soaring mountains and palm trees! But still Plockton, with its houses curving along the lochside, caught me by surprise. I thought I'd found a hidden gem, only to discover it was a National Trust village - one of the most beautiful in Scotland and so close to Skye.

There is a hidden gem too in the form of the Plockton Hotel. Modest in scale, it was created from several fishermen's crofts, with the 13 charming, bedrooms decorated in a delightful cottagey style but the restaurant is the jewel in the crown. With such access to seafood it is not surprising that it specialised in delicious locally caught, prawns, salmon and haddock, but for it to have been voted Best Seafood Pub in Scotland is an added bonus.

I totally endorse the sentiments from the visitor book - 'If the big place in the sky is anything like this then take me now - but just one more pickled herring before I go!' Almost too good to be true.

LOCATION
Located in the centre of the village facing the sea. Not to be confused with the Plockton Inn.

" A visit to Pool House is a warm and happy memory for life "

Lord Macaulay of Bragar, QC

Highland hotel

POOL HOUSE HOTEL

SCOTLAND

A MacKenzie laird chose this spot for his home right on the shores of Loch Ewe

Pool House is a very special place, and not just for its magnificent views which draw the eye across the bay to the famous Inverewe Gardens.

It is owned and run by two generations of the Harrison family, who have created a gem of a small hotel. The house has just four suites, each one impeccably furnished and decorated to a different theme, from high Victoriana to the Renaissance. Mrs Harrison is a descendant of the RMS Titanic's Captain Smith and the Diadem Suite is in the style of one of the liner's first class cabins. The nautical theme is in evidence once again with each of the suites being named after Royal Navy Ships, acting as a reminder that the house was once the headquarters of the North Atlantic and Murmansk convoys during World War II.

The kitchen is the domain of son-in-law John Moir whose classical French cuisine has a Scottish twist, drawing on superb local ingredients such as lobster, scallops, and Loch Ewe langoustine. Guests are welcome to join him collecting mussels or fishing on the loch in the hotel's own boat - keep an eye out for the porpoise and seals!

A rare and magical place that everyone should experience at least once.

LOCATION

From Inverness take A835 towards Ullapool. At Garve take A832 for Gairloch. The hotel is located 6 miles north of Gairloch and is well signed.

by Inverewe Gardens, Poolewe, Wester Ross IV22 2LD
Telephone 01445 781272
Fax 01445 781403
E-mail: *poolhouse@bestloved.com*

OWNERS
Peter and Margaret Harrison

GENERAL MANAGER
Elizabeth Miles

ROOM RATES
1 Single	£65 - £95
4 Suites	£190 - £330

Includes full breakfast and VAT

CHARGE/CREDIT CARDS

 ● *JCB* ● *MC* ● *VI*

RATINGS & AWARDS
S.T.B. ★★★★ *Small Hotel*
R.A.C. *Blue Ribbon* ★★★ *Dining Award 3*
A.A. ★★★ ✿✿ *80%*
A.A. Scottish Hotel of the Year 2001/2002
Business Commitment to the
Environment Award 2002
Taste of Scotland - 3 Medallions

FACILITIES
On site: *Garden, billiard room*
1 meeting room/max 12
Nearby: *Golf, fishing, tennis, riding,*
cycling, sailing, swimming, leisure centre

RESTRICTIONS
No facilities for disabled guests
No children under 10 years
Smoking in bar only
No pets, guide dogs only
Closed Jan

ATTRACTIONS
Inverewe Gardens, Applecross Peninsula,
Gairloch Heritage Museum,
Inverpolly National Nature Reserve,
Beinneighe Nature Reserve,
Summer Isles, Loch Broom

AFFILIATIONS
Scotland's Hotels of Distinction
The Great Inns of Britain
Celebrated Hotels Collection

NEAREST
MAJOR CITY:
Inverness - 75 miles/1 ¾ hrs
MAJOR AIRPORT:
Inverness - 75 miles/1 ¾ hrs
RAILWAY STATION:
Inverness - 75 miles/1 ¾ hrs

RESERVATIONS
Toll Free in the US: 800-437-2687
Toll Free in the US: 800-322-2403
Quote **Best Loved**

ACCESS CODES
Not applicable

" *Cosy, very Scottish and a lovely atmosphere* "

Sonia & William Macleod, Auckland, New Zealand

PRESTONFIELD HOUSE
17th century Scottish mansion

SCOTLAND

**Priestfield Road,
Edinburgh EH16 5UT**

**Telephone 0131 6683346
Fax 0131 6683976**

E-mail: *prestonfield@bestloved.com*

OWNERS
The Stevenson Family

GENERAL MANAGER
Richard Scott

ROOM RATES
Single occupancy   £90 - £225
29 Doubles/Twins   £120 - £225
2 Suites   £250 - £450
Includes full breakfast, newspaper and VAT

CHARGE/CREDIT CARDS

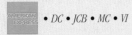 • DC • JCB • MC • VI

RATINGS & AWARDS
S.T.B. ★★★★ *Hotel*

FACILITIES
On site: *Garden, heli-pad, golf
Licensed for weddings
6 meeting rooms/max 1000 people*
Nearby: *Riding, golf*

RESTRICTIONS
None

ATTRACTIONS
*Edinburgh Castle, National Art Gallery
Royal Mile, Botanical Gardens
Holyrood House, Princes Street*

AFFILIATIONS
Independent

NEAREST
*MAJOR CITY:
Edinburgh*

*MAJOR AIRPORT:
Edinburgh - 10 miles/25 mins*

*RAILWAY STATION:
Waverley - 2 miles/7 mins*

RESERVATIONS
Direct with hotel
Quote **Best Loved**

ACCESS CODES
*AMADEUS HK EDIPRE
APOLLO/GALILEO HK 92198
SABRE/ABACUS HK 25739
WORLDSPAN HK PREST*

The elegant country mansion in the heart of Edinburgh

Prestonfield House is one of Scotland's finest historic mansions. Its location, five minutes from Princes Street, makes it ideal for visiting Edinburgh. The house and the unique early 19th century Round Stables are surrounded by a golf course and set in 13 acres of parkland and gardens which are designated as a landscape of outstanding historical and scenic beauty.

Prestonfield was built in 1687 for Sir James Dick, Lord Provost of Edinburgh. The Tapestry, Leather and Italian Rooms contain their distinctive late 17th and early 18th century decorative schemes and much of the family collection of paintings and furniture remain in their original settings. Great care has been taken to ensure that the introduction of modern facilities does not conflict with the historic fabric nor the character of this important building.

Continuing the tradition of 'kindness on kindness, cheerful meals and balmy rest' that Benjamin Franklin found in 1759, Prestonfield has a high quality à la carte restaurant in the Old Dining Room. Few hotels in any capital city anywhere in the world match Prestonfield for its comfort as a country house hotel, combined with its nearness to the city centre. There is ample parking, and shops and historic sites of Edinburgh are nearby.

LOCATION

Turn off the A7 Dalkeith Road into Priestfield Road, a little to the north of Cameron Toll roundabout. Prestonfield House is signposted.

" **If there's anywhere better than here then it must have pearly gates** *"*

Lyn Foggo & Walter Butler, Edinburgh

17th century hunting lodge ROMAN CAMP COUNTRY HOUSE

SCOTLAND

Historic house centrally situated for Callander and the Trossachs

The house takes its name from earthworks to the east of its walled gardens, believed to be the site of a Roman fort. It was built originally as a hunting lodge in 1625 for the Dukes of Perth. It passed into the ownership of Viscount Esher in 1897. The turrets that give the building its unique character were added at that time. The house became an hotel in 1939.

Each of the 14 bedrooms has its own distinctive style and character. Some have coombed walls and furniture dating back 200 years. All are equipped with the little thoughtful extras that make your stay comfortable and enjoyable.

The library, panelled in 16th century oak, has a log fire, lit even in summer. The oval-shaped restaurant features tapestries of English cathedrals woven by Elizabeth Esher in the 1930s. Menus are prepared from local ingredients in season. There are tasty à la carte and vegetarian menus.

Beyond the 20 acres of tranquil parkland and gardens with views of the River Teith are the Trossachs and the Highlands. This is a land of mountain and glen, rolling pasture and heather

moor. It is a marvellous base for your Scottish holiday.

LOCATION

From M9 Exit 10, head north on the A84 through the village of Callander, then turn left down a 300-yard drive at the east end of Callander main street.

**Off Main Street,
Callander,
Perthshire FK17 8BG**

**Telephone 01877 330003
Fax 01877 331533**

E-mail: *roman@bestloved.com*

OWNERS
Eric and Marion Brown

ROOM RATES
Single occupancy	£90 - £120
4 Doubles/Twins	£110
7 Superior doubles	£160
3 Suites	£180
Includes full breakfast and VAT	

CHARGE/CREDIT CARDS

 • *DC* • *MC* • *VI*

RATINGS & AWARDS
S.T.B. ★★★★ *Small Hotel*
A.A. ★★★ ❀❀❀
Taste of Scotland - 4 Medallions
A.A. Top 200 - 02/03

FACILITIES
On site: *Garden, heli-pad, fishing
2 meeting rooms/max 100 people*
Nearby: *Golf, fishing, shooting*

RESTRICTIONS
Pets by arrangement

ATTRACTIONS
*Rob Roy country, Trossachs National Park,
Inchmahome Priory, Stirling Castle,
Loch Lomond, Castle Campbell*

AFFILIATIONS
Independent

NEAREST
*MAJOR CITY:
Edinburgh - 52 miles/1 hr*

*MAJOR AIRPORT:
Edinburgh - 46 miles/50 mins*

*RAILWAY STATION:
Stirling - 17 miles/30 mins*

RESERVATIONS
Direct with hotel
Quote **Best Loved**

ACCESS CODES
Not applicable

" We lost all concept of time! "

A & M Anderson, Dunedin, New Zealand

ROXBURGHE HOTEL & GOLF COURSE *18th century retreat*

**Heiton, by Kelso,
Roxburghshire TD5 8JZ**
Telephone 01573 450331
Fax 01573 450611

E-mail: *roxburgh@bestloved.com*

OWNERS
The Duke and Duchess of Roxburghe

GENERAL MANAGER
William Kirby

ROOM RATES
2 Singles   £120
13 Doubles/Twins   £125 - £175
5 Four-posters   £215
2 Suites   £265
Includes full breakfast and VAT

CHARGE/CREDIT CARDS

 • *DC* • *MC* • *VI*

RATINGS & AWARDS
S.T.B. ★★★★ *Hotel*
A.A. ★★★ ✿✿ *76%*
Taste of Scotland - 3 Medallions

FACILITIES
On site: *Garden, heli-pad, fishing,
croquet, golf, tennis, health & beauty
trout loch, clay pigeon shooting,
18-hole championship golf course
3 meeting rooms/max 70 people*
Nearby: *Fishing*

RESTRICTIONS
*Pets by arrangement
Closed Christmas*

ATTRACTIONS
*Floors Castle, Kelso Abbey,
Jedburgh Abbey, Edinburgh,
Lindisfarne, St Abb's Head*

AFFILIATIONS
*The Celebrated Hotels Collection
The European Connection*

NEAREST
*MAJOR CITY:
Edinburgh - 58 miles/1 hr
Newcastle - 60 miles/1 hr*

*MAJOR AIRPORT:
Edinburgh - 58 miles/1 hr*

*RAILWAY STATION:
Berwick-upon-Tweed - 20 miles/35 mins*

RESERVATIONS
Toll free in US: 800-322-2403
*Quote **Best Loved***

ACCESS CODES
Not applicable

'Old style' country house with ample outdoor pursuits

This big 'old style' country house hotel is situated within a 500 acre estate in the mellow landscape of the Scottish Borders. Owned by the Duke and Duchess of Roxburghe, it is the Duchess with her expertise in interior design who has managed to preserve the sense of history whilst creating a truly comfortable and relaxed environment complete with deep comfy sofas and open log fires. The bedrooms, some with four-posters, are pretty and traditionally furnished. Dining, as can be easily imagined, is a great affair with the menu featuring produce from the estate.

The vast acreage provides not only complete peace and privacy but also an extensive range of outdoor pursuits including woodland walks, fishing, clay pigeon shooting and off-road driving and of course the 18-hole championship golf course. It is an ideal venue for corporate events and incentives and the hotel caters for the beginner through to the experienced sportsmen.

There is much to see and do in the local area including visits to the picturesque Border towns of Kelso and Melrose with their quaint old shops and fantastic cashmere bargains. With regular flights into Edinburgh or Newcastle the Roxburghe is now a very accessible short break destination.

LOCATION

From the A68 Edinburgh-Newcastle route, take A698 Jedburgh-Kelso road. The hotel is 3 miles south of Kelso on the outskirts of Heiton village.

" It is rare that you can find a hotel with such high standards of accommodation, food and service in such warm and friendly surroundings "

Angela Cairns, Edinburgh

Victorian hotel

ROYAL HOTEL

Getting here is a pleasure, being here is a delight!

It's true: Winston Churchill (no relation) supplies Roger and Bea McKie's venison, while every morning Peter, Arthur and Mary catch the fish and the shellfish served in the restaurant that night. For head chef Roger McKie, it is essential to know and trust your suppliers. He's a firm believer that the best and freshest ingredients should be treated with respect allowing their true flavours to shine through and you only need taste his 'simple, modern Scottish cooking' to concur wholeheartedly.

If Roger's cooking is one of the prime reasons to visit the Royal, another is the journey through Argyll itself. There is an absolutely beautiful drive, striking up over the mountains from Dunoon before descending to the West Coast, where the hotel sits across from the rocky shore. The Royal's entrance hall features an intricate mosaic marble floor laid by Italian prisoners of war. They have given the spacious bedrooms a bright and stylish look with bold but unfussy Victorian colour schemes and painted woodwork and all but three have spectacular views across a busy maritime thoroughfare to the Isle of Bute.

LOCATION

From Glasgow take the A82 to Tarbert, then the A83, A815, A886, and A8003. Or take the ferry from Gourock to Dunoon and then the B836.

Shore Road, Tighnabruaich, Argyll PA21 2BE

**Telephone 01700 811239
Fax 01700 811300**

E-mail: *royalargyll@bestloved.com*

OWNERS
Roger and Bea McKie

ROOM RATES
Single occupancy   £67 - £107
11 Doubles/Twins   £74 - £124
Includes full breakfast and VAT

CHARGE/CREDIT CARDS

MC • VI

RATINGS & AWARDS
S.T.B. ★★★★ *Small Hotel*
A.A. ★★ ❀ *78%*
Taste of Scotland - 2 Medallions

FACILITIES
On site: *Loch shore*
1 meeting room/max 40 people
Nearby: *Golf, windsurfing, sailing, fishing*

RESTRICTIONS
*No facilities for disabled guests
No smoking in bedrooms
Pets by arrangement
Closed 25 - 27 Dec*

ATTRACTIONS
*Inverary Castle, Mount Stuart,
Ostel Bay, Kilmartin Glen,
Argyll Wildlife Park, Oban*

AFFILIATIONS
Independent

NEAREST
MAJOR CITY:
Glasgow - 50 miles/1 ½ hrs

MAJOR AIRPORT:
Glasgow - 50 miles/ 1 ½ hrs

RAILWAY STATION:
Gourock - 25 miles/1 ¼ hrs

RESERVATIONS
Direct with hotel
Quote **Best Loved**

ACCESS CODES
Not applicable

• Map p.464
ref: F5

SCOTLAND

ROYAL MARINE HOTEL

Edwardian country house

*Golf Road, Brora,
Sutherland KW9 6QS*

Telephone 01408 621252
Fax 01408 621181

E-mail: *royalmarine@bestloved.com*

GENERAL MANAGER
Robert Powell

ROOM RATES
Single occupancy £68 - £88
18 Doubles/Twins £110 - £130
2 Master rooms £120 - £150
1 Family room £120 - £150
Includes full breakfast and VAT

CHARGE/CREDIT CARDS

 • *DC* • *MC* • *VI*

RATINGS & AWARDS
S.T.B. ★★★★ *Hotel*
A.A. ★★★ ✿ 72%
Taste of Scotland - 2 Medallions

FACILITIES
On site: *Garden, gym, indoor pool,
curling, snooker, sauna, steam rooms,
spa bath, solarium, disabled bedroom
2 meeting rooms/max 100 people*
Nearby: *Golf, fishing, tennis*

RESTRICTIONS
Pets by arrangement

ATTRACTIONS
*Dunrobin Castle, Orkney Islands,
Clynelish Malt Whisky Distillery,
Hunters of Brora Woollen Mills,
Glenmorangie Whisky Distillery,
Falls of Shin*

AFFILIATIONS
Scotland's Hotels of Distinction

NEAREST
MAJOR CITY:
Inverness - 60 miles/1 hr

MAJOR AIRPORT:
Inverness - 70 miles/1 ¼ hrs
Glasgow - 283 miles/5 ¼ hrs

RAILWAY STATION:
Brora - ¼ mile/2 mins

RESERVATIONS
Toll free fax in US: 888-307-0705
*Quote **Best Loved***

ACCESS CODES
Not applicable

A place of comfort and calm in a wild and beautiful environment

The renowned Scottish architect, Sir Robert Lorimer, originally designed this as a private country house in the 1900s. A recent extensive restoration has taken place providing the modern amenities expected of a quality hotel. Features include a number of carved wooden fireplaces and an elegant stairway and reception foyer, all complemented by the chef's cuisine in the traditionally styled dining room.

The hotel is especially attractive to sportsmen. Nearby are local championship links golf courses including Brora, Golspie, Royal Dornoch and Tain. It has its own boat on Loch Brora for fly fishing; its newly built leisure centre has a host of activities and facilities available to all residents.

Situated midway between Inverness and John O'Groats, Brora is ideal as a centre for touring the Northern Highlands and the Orkney Islands. The sparsely populated region abounds with birds and wild life. The rock formations are of particular interest to geologists and provide excellent hill walking.

LOCATION

*One hour north of Inverness, just
off A9 adjacent to James Braid's
18 hole links golf course.*

❝ *Thank you for a most relaxing stay... Good food, good wine, good staff* ❞

Mr G McIntyre, Glasgow

• *Map p.464*
ref: D10

Victorian castle

STONEFIELD CASTLE HOTEL

SCOTLAND

Baronial elegance with an exotic touch of the Himalayas

High on the Kintyre peninsula commanding magnificent views over Loch Fyne, Stonefield Castle represents the epitome of baronial elegance rising gracefully from conifer woodlands. The castle was built in 1837 for the Campbell family, but its famous gardens were the work of Himalayan plant collector Sir Joseph Hooker.

Stonefield simply oozes character and a timeless ambience complemented by many original period furnishings. Guests will discover a beguiling serenity in the traditional wood panelled lounges and comfortable country house style bedrooms. The restaurant is almost as renowned for its views as it is for the award-winning Scottish cuisine of head chef Angus Macfarlane, whose skills are brought to bear on the freshest local seafood, Loch Fyne oysters and Buccleuch beef accompanied by homegrown vegetables.

One of the most breathtaking sights here is the morning mist rising from the loch. Another is the woodland garden where a century ago Sir Joseph planted the first seeds in what is now the finest collection of rhododendrons outside Kew Gardens. Here, winding paths thread through the woods in a scene more reminiscent of the Himalayan kingdom of Bhutan than Argyll!

LOCATION

On the A83 between Ardrishaig and Tarbert.
The hotel is 2 miles before Tarbert on the left.

Tarbert,
Argyll PA29 6YJ

Telephone 01880 820836
Fax 01880 820929

E-mail: *stonefield@bestloved.com*

GENERAL MANAGER
Alistair Wilkie

RATES PER PERSON
4 Singles	*£90 - £110*
25 Doubles/Twins	*£90 - £110*
4 Suites	*£125*

Includes dinner, breakfast and VAT

CHARGE/CREDIT CARDS

 • *DC* • *MC* • *VI*

RATINGS & AWARDS
S.T.B. ★★★★ *Hotel*
R.A.C. ★★★ *Dining Award 2*
Taste of Scotland - 2 Medallions

FACILITIES
On site: *Garden, snooker, heli-pad*
4 meeting rooms/max 200 people
Nearby: *Golf, fishing, boating, riding, swimming, tennis, walking, sailing, shooting*

RESTRICTIONS
Limited facilities for disabled guests
Pets by arrangement

ATTRACTIONS
Inverary Castle, Achamore Gardens, Kilmartin House Museum, Machrihanish Golf Course, Mount Stuart

AFFILIATIONS
Independent

NEAREST
MAJOR CITY:
Glasgow - 95 miles/1 ¼ hrs

MAJOR AIRPORT:
Glasgow - 92 miles/1 ¼ hrs

RAILWAY STATION:
Oban - 40 miles/1 hr

RESERVATIONS
Direct with hotel
*Quote **Best Loved***

ACCESS CODES
Not applicable

SCOTLAND

SUMMER ISLES

19th century fishing inn

**Achiltibuie,
Ross-shire IV26 2YG**

**Telephone 01854 622282
Fax 01854 622251**

E-mail: *summer@bestloved.com*

OWNERS
Mark and Geraldine Irvine

ROOM RATES
Single occupancy	£70 - £110
9 Doubles/Twins	£110 - £170
4 Suites	£170 - £235

Includes full breakfast and VAT

CHARGE/CREDIT CARDS
MC • VI

RATINGS & AWARDS
S.T.B. ★★★★ *Small Hotel*
*The Good Food Guide -
Restaurant of the Year 2000*
Taste of Scotland - 4 Medallions

FACILITIES
Nearby: *Birdwatching, walking, fishing,
scuba diving, sailing, beach*

RESTRICTIONS
*No facilities for disabled guests
No children under 6 years
No pets in public rooms
Closed 13 Oct - Easter*

ATTRACTIONS
*Inverewe Gardens, Sutherland coast,
Inverpolly Nature Reserve, Western Isles,
Highlands*

AFFILIATIONS
Independent

NEAREST
*MAJOR CITY:
Inverness - 85 miles/2 hrs*

*MAJOR AIRPORT:
Edinburgh - 220 miles/5 hrs*

*RAILWAY STATION:
Inverness - 85 miles/2 hrs*

RESERVATIONS
Direct with hotel
Quote **Best Loved**

ACCESS CODES
Not applicable

An oasis of civilisation in wild, untouched landscape

Mark and Geraldine Irvine run this individual but sophisticated hotel which has belonged to the family since the late 1960s. It has established itself as an oasis of civilisation hidden away in a stunningly beautiful, but still wild and untouched landscape.

Nearly everything you eat there is home produced or locally caught. Scallops, lobsters, langoustines, crabs, halibut, turbot, salmon, venison, big brown eggs, wholesome brown bread fresh from the oven - the list of real food is endless. With such fresh ingredients, Michelin-starred chef Chris Firth-Bernard provides delicious, healthy fare.

Two new additions to the family of very finely appointed bedrooms, are The Boathouse and William's Cottage, the latter sleeping four. Both are exquisite with stunning views. After breakfast, Mark and Geraldine are happy to talk to you about fishing, walking or bird-watching. A local boat, the Hectoria, sails round the islands to show off seals and rare birds. You can also explore the scenery sub-aqua with the local diving school.

Inverewe Gardens, Inverpolly Nature Reserve and the Sutherland coast are all within easy reach. This place has a huge amount to offer.

LOCATION

*10 miles north of Ullapool, turn left
on to a single track road. After 15 miles
you reach the village of Achiltibuie.
The hotel is just past the post office.*

" An amazing hotel - every detail had been thought of - the food was fantastic and the staff made us feel special "

J Money, London

Drover's inn

TAYCHREGGAN

SCOTLAND

Mountain grandeur, fascinating wildlife and lochside beauty

Surrounded by the grandeur of mountains, Taychreggan Hotel has nestled on the shores of magnificent Loch Awe for the past 300 years. Originally a cattle drover's inn, the old stone house and its courtyard form the centrepiece of the hotel where the aim is to woo visitors into feeling like house guests. Most of the beautiful bedrooms overlook the loch; all offer high standards of quality, style and comfort.

The friendly and experienced staff have received great trade and consumer recognition and have scooped many prestigious awards. The magnificent view from the dining room is matched by superb Scottish cuisine, a comprehensive list of French wines and fine single malt whiskies.

You can visit historic places such as Inveraray or Kilchurn Castle, or choose from many outdoor activities. For hill walkers there are 13 peaks over 3,000 feet within an hour's drive. The hotel has its own fishing rights and boats. Birds of prey and rare species can be seen in these breathtaking surroundings. Horse riding, deer stalking, water sports, loch cruises, golf and rough shooting can all be arranged.

Kilchrenan, by Taynuilt, Argyll PA35 1HQ

Telephone 01866 833211
Fax 01866 833244

E-mail: taychreggan@bestloved.com

GENERAL MANAGER
Alistair Stevenson

ROOM RATES
13 Doubles/Twins £127
6 Superior Doubles/Twins £198 - £237
Includes full breakfast and VAT

CHARGE/CREDIT CARDS

 • JCB • MC • VI

RATINGS & AWARDS
S.T.B. ★★★★ Hotel
R.A.C. ★★★ Dining Award 3
A.A. ★★★ ❁❁ 75%
Taste of Scotland - 2 Medallions
Scotland The Brand
Investors in People

FACILITIES
On site: Garden, fishing
2 meeting rooms/max 30 people
Nearby: Walking, gliding

RESTRICTIONS
No facilities for disabled guests
No children under 14 years
Pets by arrangement

ATTRACTIONS
Kilchurn Castle, Inveraray,
loch cruises, forest walks,
the gardens of Argyll

AFFILIATIONS
Preston's Global Hotels

NEAREST
MAJOR CITY:
Glasgow - 90 miles/2 hrs

MAJOR AIRPORT:
Glasgow - 90 miles/2 hrs

RAILWAY STATION:
Taynuilt - 7 miles/15 mins

RESERVATIONS
Toll free in US: 800-544-9993
Quote **Best Loved**

ACCESS CODES
Not applicable

LOCATION

From Edinburgh: exit 10/M9 to Stirling, A84 to Callander, A85 to Crianlarich/ Oban & left on to B845 to Kilchrenan/ Taychreggan. Hotel is 7 miles on, at end of this single track road.

• *Map p.464*
ref: D6

> ❝ *A warm welcome, the freshest local food; and a great night's rest ... a charming hotel set in the most spectacular scenery* ❞
>
> *Sir Chris Bonington*

TIGH AN EILEAN

Seaside hotel

SCOTLAND

Shieldaig, by Strathcarron, Ross-shire IV54 8XN

Telephone 01520 755251
Fax 01520 755321

E-mail: *tighan@bestloved.com*

OWNERS
Christopher and Cathryn Field

ROOM RATES
3 Singles   £52
8 Doubles/Twins   £120
Includes full breakfast and VAT

CHARGE/CREDIT CARDS
 • MC • VI

RATINGS & AWARDS
S.T.B. ★★★★
R.A.C. ★ Dining Award 3
A.A. ★ ❀ 77%

FACILITIES
On site: *Fishing, boat hire, kayaks*
Nearby: *Hill walking, mountain climbing*

RESTRICTIONS
No facilities for disabled guests
No dogs in public rooms
Closed Nov - April

ATTRACTIONS
Applecross Peninsula,
Inverewe Gardens,
Torridon loch and mountains,
Beinn Eighe Nature Reserve,
Isle of Skye

AFFILIATIONS
Independent

NEAREST
MAJOR CITY:
Inverness - 68 miles/1 ¾ hrs

MAJOR AIRPORT:
Glasgow - 223 miles/4 ¼ hrs
Inverness - 75 miles/2 hrs

RAILWAY STATION:
Strathcarron - 12 miles/30 mins

RESERVATIONS
Direct with hotel
Quote Best Loved

ACCESS CODES
Not applicable

A highland inn surrounded by dramatic sea and landscapes

Tigh-an-Eilean (House of the island) stands in a 200-year old fishing village on the seafront within a short stroll from the old jetty where the fishing boats unload their catch. This quiet unspoilt village, set in the Torridon Mountains, faces the Scottish National Trust's Isle of Pines, and has glorious views over Loch Shieldaig to Loch Torridon and the open sea beyond.

Cathryn and Christopher Field greet you with a warm welcome. There are two lounges and a cosy residents' honesty bar. The dining room, looking across the sea towards the sunset, offers menus that place emphasis on the finest local and regional produce from sea, river and hill. Specialities include seafood delivered direct from boat to the kitchen door that day. The reasonably priced wine list is short but thoughtfully chosen.

All bedrooms are en suite, most with a sea view. The furnishings, prints and paintings give each of them a character and charm all of their own.

This is the great outdoors where the aromatherapy of heather, Caledonian Pines and the sea is free; where the hill walker, the angler and the golfer will find their own paradise and sightseers by car can take in the spectacular scenery - try the the Beinn Eighe Nature Reserve

or the 2000 ft Benlach na Bo pass to Applecross with its views across the sea to Skye. Astronomers will find a soul-mate in Christopher whose telescope is set up in the garden. The lure of Tigh an Eilean is ever present; one visit is never enough.

LOCATION
Take the A832 from Inverness to Kinlochewe.
Turn left on to the A896 to Shieldaig.

" We spent 12 nights in Scotland this summer and this was definitely the best "

Katharine Kirkland, Suffolk

Victorian hunting lodge

TONGUE HOTEL

SCOTLAND

Tongue, Sutherland IV27 4XD

**Telephone 01847 611206
Fax 01847 611345**

E-mail: *tongue@bestloved.com*

GENERAL MANAGER
Karen Stoltman

ROOM RATES
Single occupancy   £40 - £50
17 Doubles/Twins   £70 - £110
2 Family rooms   £105 - £120
Includes full breakfast and VAT

CHARGE/CREDIT CARDS

MC • JCB • VI

RATINGS & AWARDS
S.T.B. ★★★★ *Small Hotel*
*Taste of Scotland - 2 Medallions
Warm Welcome and Walkers
Welcome Awards
Green Tourism Award*

FACILITIES
On site: *Garden*
1 meeting room/max 50 people
Nearby: *Golf, fishing, pony trekking*

RESTRICTIONS
*No facilities for disabled guests
No smoking in bedrooms
No pets, guide dogs only
Closed mid Nov - mid March*

ATTRACTIONS
*Cape Wrath, Orkney Islands,
John O'Groats, Lochinver,
Castle Varrich, Sandwood Bay*

AFFILIATIONS
Scotland's Hotels of Distinction

NEAREST
MAJOR CITY:
Inverness - 100 miles/2 hrs

MAJOR AIRPORT:
Inverness - 100 miles/2 hrs

RAILWAY STATION:
Lairg - 50 miles/1 hr

RESERVATIONS
Toll free in the US: 800-437-2687
Quote **Best Loved**

ACCESS CODES
Not applicable

A traditionally warm and stylish welcome in the wilds of Sutherland

The most northerly hotel in this book, the Tongue Hotel really does deserve a special trip. Intrepid travellers, reach for your road maps and seek out the Kyle of Tongue, a deep slash of a sea loch carved into the coast between Cape Wrath and John O'Groats in the mountainous shadows of Ben Loyal and Ben Hope.

The hotel was built as a shooting lodge by the Duke of Sutherland in the late 1800s, and nestles against a sloping bank which conceals its true proportions. The bright, spacious and impeccably restored interior is redolent with the charm and character of an altogether more gracious age. Blessed with fabulous views, many original furnishings, and lovely bedrooms, it provides the perfect environment from which to enjoy the peace and beauty of this rare setting. There is good food too with menus built around local delicacies such as Loch Erribol King prawns and Kyle of Tongue oysters.

Beyond the cosy confines of the hotel, Sutherland's dramatic landscape is a paradise for walkers. Trout fishing and birdwatching may appeal and at the end of the day there's a warm welcome in the bar and a handy drying room – in case of rain!

LOCATION

From the A836 the hotel is on the right as you enter the village.

• *Map p.464*
ref: G9

" A truly remarkable find "

Gordon Walker, Inverness, Scotland

THE WOODSIDE HOTEL

Victorian hotel

SCOTLAND

**Aberdour,
Fife KY3 0SW**

**Telephone 01383 860328
Fax 01383 860920**

E-mail: *woodside@bestloved.com*

OWNER
Stuart Dykes

GENERAL MANAGER
Carole-Anne Patterson

ROOM RATES
2 Singles	£45 - £80
14 Doubles/Twins	£50 - £80
1 Four-poster	£60 - £80
2 Family rooms	£55 - £75
1 Suite	£100 - £120

Includes full breakfast, newspaper and VAT

CHARGE/CREDIT CARDS

AMERICAN EXPRESS • *JCB • MC • VI*

RATINGS & AWARDS
S.T.B. ★★★ *Hotel*
A.A. ★★ ✿ *70%*

FACILITIES
On site: *2 meeting rooms/max 120 people*
Nearby: *Golf, tennis, fitness, yachting,
fishing, riding, shooting*

RESTRICTIONS
No facilities for disabled guests

ATTRACTIONS
*St Andrews town & golf course,
Edinburgh City & Castle,
Blair Castle, Glasgow,
Bells Whisky Distillery,
Stirling Castle*

AFFILIATIONS
Independent

NEAREST
MAJOR CITY:
Edinburgh - 15 miles/25 mins

MAJOR AIRPORT:
Edinburgh - 13 miles/20 mins

RAILWAY STATION:
Aberdour - ¼ mile/10 mins

RESERVATIONS
Direct with hotel
Quote **Best Loved**

ACCESS CODES
Not applicable

Modern comforts, good food and a warm welcome in an historic mansion

The influence of the sea can be felt throughout this warm and friendly hotel. The original owner's great grandfather founded the Russian Navy, but it is the elaborate mahogany and glass ceiling in the smoking lounge which grabs the most attention. It was brought to the hotel in 1926 from the steamship 'Orontes' which sailed between Australia and the UK.

The hotel was completely refurbished in 1995 and is located in the centre of the picturesque town of Aberdour. Each of the hotel's bedrooms is decorated and furnished in a very individual style and is named after a Scottish clan. The Rennie Room, for example, is an apartment with four-poster bed and private sitting room, while the Thomson Room is a luxury family room with views across the Firth of Forth to Edinburgh.

Fresh fish are taken directly to the hotel's excellent restaurant from the local harbour quayside. In fact, the hotel's consistently good food and imaginative menus have earned the owner, Stuart Dykes, a deserved reputation. A bar bistro offers lighter variations of the fare you can enjoy in the fine dining room.

Aberdour has the distinction of being the only Scottish Beach to have been awarded a blue flag; just one of many attractions besides Edinburgh that makes Woodside an ideal touring base.

LOCATION

From Forth Road Bridge take exit 1/M90. Turn right under M90, to Kirkcaldy. Pass over five roundabouts and enter Aberdour; hotel is on left after a garage.

BESTLOVEDHOTELS.com

Family Travel

Lots of great ideas for places to take the family for short breaks, weekends or the school holidays. From Country Houses to B&B's, from the seaside to the city.

For all your family travel needs visit BESTLOVEDHOTELS.COM and register your details on-line now to receive special offers, discounts and benefits.

- Special 'Children Welcome' search capability
- Comprehensive Hotel Leisure Facilities search, including; Swimming, Riding, Tennis, Fishing, Golf, Health & Beauty
- Over 3000 Things to Do and Places to See, all close to a Best Loved Hotel
- Up to date information on Zoo's, Wildlife Parks, Museums, Historic Sites, Theme Parks and Tourist Attractions

For all your family travel needs - register today at bestlovedhotels.com

NORTH

The compelling beauty and mirrored reflections of this splendid countryside was the home, spiritual and actual of many of The Great Romantics.

Wordsworth was born here, in 1770 at Wordsworth House in Cockermouth. He took his first steps on the soft, green lawns, grew with the sight of kites wheeling above. Later, as a young man in his creative prime, he lived at Dove Cottage, the perfect Lakeland home at Town End in Grasmere, and finally to Rydal Mount, where he wrote as Poet Laureate.

John Ruskin, another literary giant, chose to live amongst craggy splendour and walked in his 'ziggy zaggy garden that ducks and weaves through the trees' leading to the shores of Lake Conniston. Brantwood was his home from 1872 until 1900. Poet, artist and critic he was also a social revolutionary, his quicksilver mind given free rein in the solitude and splendour of the Lakes. Byron found 'things in Derbyshire as noble as in Greece or Switzerland,' whilst John Keats, archetypal Romantic writer, toured the Lakes in 1818, and was so moved by the area's rugged beauty that it became part of the setting for his Hyperion.

The wild and windswept Yorkshire Moors are close to the Old Parsonage at Haworth, home of the Reverend Bronte and his children. Charlotte's novel, Jane Eyre, made her the best known of the sisters in their day, but Emily's Wuthering Heights, that portrays so chillingly, the moor's brooding power and influence continues to inspire numerous film and television interpretations.

Agatha Christie's link with Harrogate is as mysterious as one of her plots. In 1926, after a furious row with her husband, the best selling novelist disappeared without trace. Her fans – and the police - were convinced she'd been murdered, and the hunt for her was headline news. After eleven hectic days she was found, staying under a pseudonym, at the Harrogate Hydro Hotel.

The watery adventures of the Walker and Blackett families, written by Arthur Ransome in the 1930's have captured the imagination of children and adults ever since. There are 12 books in this evocative series that paints so memorable a portrait of childhood.

The solid, handsome Wordsworth House in Main Street, Cockermouth where Wordsworth was born. Built only some 20 years before the Wordsworth family moved in, today it is a house of mature beauty, with a comfortable, impressive interior. Tel: 01900 824805.

The magnificent position of Brantwood House, Ruskin's Lakeland home overlooking Lake Conniston, provides a good reason to visit, but there is so much more. 250 acres of gardens and grounds offer a fascinating glimpse of just some of Ruskin's interests and abilities. Tel: 015394 41396.

BOOKS TO READ

▶ Agatha Christie and the Eleven Missing Days by Jared Cade: an intriguing solution to the apparently unsolvable puzzle.

▶ Lives of the Great Romantics I, II and III published by Pickering and Chatto. A scholarly collection of memoirs by the writers' contempories.

▶ The Infernal World of Branwell Bronte by Daphne du Maurier: the life and times of the reprobate brother of Charlotte, Emily and Anne – A very Gothic life, and death.

A special place to buy books:

Bookends, The Carlisle Bookshop have a comprehensive range of Cumbrian titles amongst their wide stock and are more than happy to order modern titles from Britain and America for you. Tel: 01228 529067.

LITERARY ATTRACTIONS & FESTIVALS

▶ The Beatrix Potter Society holds Biennial International study conferences in the Lake District and Scotland. For further details go to www.beatrixpottersociety.org.uk.

▶ Derbyshire Literature Festival: a focus on the county's writers, such as Allison Uttley and DH Lawrence. Tel: 01773 831359.

▶ The Armitt Museum and Library at Ambleside: an extensive collection of early guide books including editions of the renowned Rev W Gilpin's 'Observations on Several Parts of England, Particularly The Mountains and Lakes of Cumberland and Westmoreland, Relative Chiefly to Picturesque Beauty, Made in the Year 1776.'

Beatrix Potter's love of Cumbria began as a child when her family first holidayed there in 1882. It was an enduring affection that lead to her eventual purchase of Hill Top Farm from the proceeds of her writing and illustration. She willed the property and its 4000 acres to the National Trust.

Elizabeth Gaskell, contemporary and writer of an acclaimed biography of Charlotte Bronte, wrote of the Bronte's home, the Old Parsonage, 'I don't know that I ever saw a spot more exquisitely clean. Everything fits into, and is in harmony with, the idea of a country parsonage…' Tel: 01535 642323.

Middlethorpe Hall - Restaurant

The Samling - Starter Dish   John Connell - Seaham Hall

THE CULINARY North

This is a land of contrasts, of rocky crags and gentle Dales, of lively seaside towns and quiet harbours. Another northern contrast is the tradition of serving a square of Parkin, rich, aromatic, sticky and darkly sweet relative of the gingerbread family, with a chunk of crumbly, tangy Wensleydale cheese. Flavours are rich here, enjoy Cumberland sausage – a tasty blend of pork and herbs in a coil up to a metre long, with dry cured bacon, crisp and sizzling with the succulence of slowly reared pork and generations of careful husbandry. Rum butter spread on crisp biscuits is still a treat at local Christenings, Kendal Mint Cake, a thin, mint flavoured 'cake' of sugar, has accompanied heroic climbers up Everest and innumerable walkers on panoramic fells. Noisettes of moorland lamb are set off by jelly made with tart fruits from windblown hedges - tastes to savour.

THE MENU:
The Devonshire Arms
Bolton Abbey, Yorkshire

The Duchess of Devonshire is famous world wide for her dedication to superb, locally produced fare. A visit to her amazing Chatsworth Farm Shop – currently celebrating its quarter century - is a must for anyone with a passion for great food.

The Devonshire Arms, in the family of the Duke and Duchess since 1733, is – not surprisingly - the perfect Country House Hotel. The following 'snippet' is from their dinner menu.

Starter
Assiette of Magret Duck and Foie Gras
Loin of Rabbit, Jus Vanilla, Truffle Scented Greens
Red Mullet with Langoustines and Confit Tomatoes

Main Course
Wild Salmon with a Roast Scallop and Foam of Haricot Blanc
Ravioli of Shellfish with a Fricassee of Frogs Legs
Loin of Venison with Ravioli of Black Pudding

Dessert
Bramley Apple Mousse with a Granny Smith Sorbet
Rhubarb and Vanilla Cassonade, Confit Pineapple
Warm Bitter Chocolate Fondant with Agen Prune Ice Cream

A Selection of British and French Cheese with Fresh Fruit

THE SURPRISE:

The opportunity to combine dishes from some of the Orient's most exciting cuisines makes Studley Hotel's Orchid Restaurant - under Thai Head Chef, Miss Vilialak Boonyoo - a gastronomic 'find'. Thai, Malaysian, Japanese. Korean, Indonesian or Chinese specialities, such as Fragrant Chicken and Lemongrass Noodle Soup from Vietnam, could be followed by Gai Gratien Prik Thai – a spicy chicken dish from Thailand. Add the perfect finishing touch by unwrapping a banana leaf to find Steamed Banana and Sticky Rice, or be tempted by

Studley Hotel

delicious twist on Crème Brulee as French and Indochine influences combine to add a rich touch of coconut to the well-loved classic.

THE STYLE:

Swinton Park, ancestral home of the Cunliffe-Listers, is a magnificent hotel with 200 acres of gardens and grounds, surrounded by the 20,000-acre family estate. This splendid castle, beautifully restored and furnished with family antiques and portraits, offers dining in the grand manner. Menus feature estate produce such as venison – served with crushed celeriac, braised red cabbage and a date reduction; and saddle of wild rabbit with red onion marmalade and aged balsamic. The restaurant, called Samuel's after the current owner's great-great-great grandfather, has everything from gold-leaf ceiling, to estate logs burning in an open fire.

THE SPORT:

Racing is the Sport of Kings – and Queen's - the atmosphere is heady, the excitement intense, and it's a great sharpener of appetite. Racing at York is a magical mix of top class sporting occasion - including Europe's richest handicap race - and prestigious social event. Uniquely positioned Middlethorpe Hall overlooks the racecourse. The sumptuous panelled dining room offers superb food and drink in luxurious surroundings, service is impeccable - there's a beautiful Spa and a testing gym, it's the perfect place to spend some winnings!.

THE CHEF:

John Connel is head chef at Seaham Hall - the 'hottest' new hotel to open in the North-East last year. Originally from New Zealand, John has previously worked at L'Odeon, the Savoy and the Putney Bridge Restaurant, under chefs such as Bruno Loubet and Anton Edelman.

Using an eclectic mix of French rustic through to Pacific-rim fusion his menus are innovative and talented.

His ambition - to offer the very best of International dining and take Seaham Hall forward from the Three AA rosettes the restaurant currently holds.

Seaham Hall

THE SIGNATURE:

Roasted woodpigeon with Swede puree, foie gras, galette potato and Madeira raisin jus'.

Linthwaite House

Chef Andy Nicholson, at Linthwaite House Hotel, chose his seasonal signature dish because 'pigeon's a nice game bird without being too strong, woodpigeon is locally abundant…the dish has a good balance:

a contrast of the sweetness of the puree, richness of the foie gras and the mellow woodpigeon.'

Having started his career at the Dorchester, Andy worked at a number of prestigious kitchens including the Devonshire Arms, where he opened the highly successful Brasserie.

> *'If you come to the Lakes you want to eat the food that is of the time and place'*

says Chris Meredith, recently appointed head chef at the Samling. Chris's menus draw upon the influences of the Lake District, maximising the use of quality local produce and recipes.

He says, 'It will be very much the theme for what we'll provide for our guests here. We'll also be introducing an afternoon tea menu - something of a Lake District tradition.'

Editor's Extras

Teashops are a great English tradition (even before Agatha Christie's Miss Marple!) and a visit to Elizabeth Botham and Sons' wonderful shop and tearoom at Skiner Street in Whitby shows why. Your waitress will wear a white lace 'pinny', the tea will be strong and hot and the choice between delicious home baked specialities is hard.

A Victorian way of enjoying *Char – a fish caught in Lake Windermere* – was to pot it. Cook the fish gently in court bouillon, skin, fillet and cover with clarified butter, bake again until just bubbling, cool and cover with a little more butter, chill and serve with toast.

Dark and mysterious, *Secret Kingdom Ale* is brewed by the Northumberland Brewery at Bedlington – ask for at pubs within the region or find where it's made at the Cat and Sawdust.

Craster Kippers are absolutely delicious grilled for breakfast or high tea, they also make an excellent starter, poached, chilled and served with thin onion rings - in fact they are so good that they are inspirational - visit Craster on the Northumberland coast to see them being smoked, or watch on *www.kipper.co.uk.*

Heather Hay Ffrench
Best Loved Food Editor

" A house of perfect and irresistible atmosphere "

Hugh Walpole

ARMATHWAITE HALL HOTEL

17th century hall

**Bassenthwaite Lake,
Cumbria CA12 4RE**

**Telephone 017687 76551
Fax 017687 76220**

E-mail: *armathwaite@bestloved.com*

OWNERS
The Graves Family

ROOM RATES
3 Singles	£67 - £110
36 Doubles/Twins	£124 - £220
1 Four-poster	£260 - £280
3 Studio suites	£260 - £280

Includes full breakfast and VAT

CHARGE/CREDIT CARDS

 • DC • MC • VI

RATINGS & AWARDS
A.A. ★★★★ ❀ 71%

FACILITIES
On site: *Gardens, heli-pad, fishing, croquet, tennis, indoor pool, sauna, spa, steam room, gym, holistic beauty salon, wildlife park, archery, clay shooting, quad bike safaris by prior arrangement
Licensed for weddings
4 meeting rooms/max 100 people*
Nearby: *Golf*

RESTRICTIONS
*Limited facilities for disabled guests
No pets in public rooms*

ATTRACTIONS
*Beatrix Potter Museum & House,
William Wordsworth's homes,
Rheged Discovery Centre,
Hadrian's Wall, Roman wall and forts*

AFFILIATIONS
Independent

NEAREST
*MAJOR CITY:
Carlisle - 20 miles/40 mins
Newcastle - 70 miles/1 ½ hrs*

*MAJOR AIRPORT:
Manchester - 120 miles/2 ½ hrs*

*RAILWAY STATION:
Carlisle - 20 miles/40 mins*

RESERVATIONS
Direct with hotel
Quote **Best Loved**

ACCESS CODES
Not applicable

A stately home that will appeal to sportsman and connoisseur alike

Armathwaite Hall is set in a magnificent private estate encompassing park and woodlands and lake frontage. The present hall, part of which dates from 1650, stands on the site of an ancient manor owned by Sir Adam de Bassenthwaite in the reign of Edward II.

The Hall is run personally by the owners who pursue the continuing development of their hotel, its leisure and conference facilities with painstaking regard for the warm, elegant nature of this genuine English stately home.

Connoisseurs of fine cuisine will find much to appreciate at Armathwaite Hall. Master Chef Kevin Dowling takes full advantage of a wealth of local seasonal produce and Cumbrian specialities to create a variety of gastronomic delights.

Management training, personnel motivation courses and corporate hospitality days are popular with delegates and guests making full use of the extensive sports and leisure facilities available on the estate.

An interesting feature is a safari on Quad bikes in an area famed for its spectacular views. This is

the perfect centre for either business or pleasure to explore the Lake District.

LOCATION

Turn off the M6 at Exit 40 and follow the A66 to the Keswick roundabout. Then take the A591 to Carlisle for 8 miles and turn left at Castle Inn. The hotel is 300 yards ahead.

NORTH

" *A very special stay, excellent food, service and comfort* "

Nicola and Robert Dunn

● *Map p.466*
ref: D6

18th century coaching inn

THE BLUE LION

The perfect base for English country sport and leisure

Fishing, walking, shooting, racing. Experience the simple pleasures of the Yorkshire Dales, from one of only three Best-Loved Hotels in the region. Wensleydale may be famous the world over for its deliciously crumbly cheese, but a stay at the The Blue Lion in East Witton will reveal a host of additional local treasures, whether culinary, equine or pedestrian!

The historic ruins of Jervaulx Abbey are certainly worth a visit. Catterick, Wetherby, Ripon and York race tracks are all within an hour's drive, and the nearby town of Middleham is making its name as the 'Newmarket of the North'.

On your return from an evening stroll along the river bank, or if you prefer a taxing ten-mile challenge hike, you may decide to put up your aching feet and order dinner at the hotel. If so, you can choose to eat in the flag-stoned bar with its open fire and ample selection of hand-pulled beers, or at the warm and inviting restaurant. Either way, local game and fish - all procured from one of three provincial estates - should be available.

Originally an 18th-century coaching inn, the hotel has undergone an 'extensive yet sympathetic' renovation. Other activities available include golf, tennis and pony-trekking.

LOCATION

From A1, take B6267 towards Masham. Then follow the A6108 to East Witton. The hotel is situated on the right on entering the village.

NORTH

East Witton, Near Leyburn,
North Yorkshire DL8 4SN

Telephone 01969 624273
Fax 01969 624189

E-mail: bluelion@bestloved.com

OWNERS
Paul and Helen Klein

ROOM RATES
Single occupancy	£54
11 Doubles/Twins	£69 - £89
1 Family room	£89 - £105

Includes full breakfast and VAT

CHARGE/CREDIT CARDS

MC ● VI

RATINGS & AWARDS
Independent

FACILITIES
On site: *Garden*
2 meeting rooms/max 50 people
Nearby: *Tennis*

RESTRICTIONS
Limited facilities for disabled guests

ATTRACTIONS
Bolton Castle,
Jervaulx Abbey,
Raby Castle, York,
Fountains Abbey & Studley Royal,
Yorkshire Moors

AFFILIATIONS
Independent

NEAREST
MAJOR CITY:
Harrogate - 29 miles/45 mins

MAJOR AIRPORT:
Leeds/Bradford - 40 miles/1 hr

RAILWAY STATION:
Northallerton - 25 miles/30 mins

RESERVATIONS
Direct with hotel
Quote **Best Loved**

ACCESS CODES
Not applicable

❝ *Our most favourite place - the perfect balance between peacefulness, efficient service, friendly staff and outstanding food* **❞**

T A Knowlton, Chairman, The Kellogg Company of Great Britain

BORROWDALE GATES COUNTRY HOUSE HOTEL *Victorian house*

NORTH

Grange-in-Borrowdale, Keswick, Cumbria CA12 5UQ

Telephone 017687 77204
Fax 017687 77254

E-mail: *borrowdale@bestloved.com*

OWNERS
Terry and Christine Parkinson

RATES PER PERSON
3 Singles   £65 - £90
26 Doubles/Twins   £65 - £90
Includes full breakfast, dinner and VAT

CHARGE/CREDIT CARDS

 • MC • VI

RATINGS & AWARDS
E.T.C. ★★★ *Silver Award*
R.A.C. ★★★ *Dining Award 2*
A.A. ★★★ ❀ *77%*
WHICH? Hotel of the Year 2003

FACILITIES
On site: *Garden*
Nearby: *Fishing, riding, golf, boating, cycling, biking, climbing*

RESTRICTIONS
Limited facilities for disabled guests
No children in restaurant after 7 pm
No pets
Closed Jan

ATTRACTIONS
Borrowdale Valley, Cockermouth, Grasmere, Wordsworth's birthplace and Dove Cottage, Carlisle Castle, Muncaster Castle, Hadrian's Wall

AFFILIATIONS
Independent

NEAREST
MAJOR CITY:
Carlisle - 30 miles/45 mins

MAJOR AIRPORT:
Manchester - 120 miles/2 hrs
Glasgow Airport - 145 miles/2 ½ hrs

RAILWAY STATION:
Penrith - 22 miles/30 mins

RESERVATIONS
Direct with hotel
*Quote **Best Loved***

ACCESS CODES
Not applicable

A rich stroke of fortune amongst the majestic Lakeland mountains

Baddeley's Guide to the English Lakes says: '... there can be no doubt that Borrowdale holds the first position amongst its (the Lake District's) valleys'. In the north of the valley is Derwentwater, 'The Queen of the Lakes' and all around are the majestic Lakeland mountains, changing colour with the weather and the seasons. Within this idyllic picture is Borrowdale Gates secluded in its own two acres of wooded gardens.

The house was built in 1860 as a private residence and its air of comfortable informality continues; this is a wonderful place to shed one's cares and release the tensions. The furniture and fabrics contribute to the feeling of mellow good living. Antiques and fresh flowers add a personal touch that can only come from the owners Christine and Terry Parkinson. The bedrooms (ten on the ground floor) make the most of the breathtaking views, as do the lounges and restaurant with their picture windows.

The restaurant, which has won critical acclaim from numerous food guides, serves award-winning food from a daily-changing menu which is inspired by the use of the finest local produce.

LOCATION

Exit 40 off M6, A66 to Keswick. From there take B5289 and after 4 miles, turn right at the double humpback bridge into Grange. The hotel is about a quarter of a mile past the village on the right.

Country house hotel | BROADOAKS COUNTRY HOUSE

A certain 'special something'

Broadoaks is situated in a beautiful area high above Lake Windermere in an utterly peaceful corner of the Lakes. It seems far from the hustle and bustle of the lakeside towns yet is only really a stone's throw from all the main attractions.

This lovely Victorian mansion house has been decorated to the highest standard and is furnished throughout with lovely antiques and extravagant, soft furnishings. All twelve bedrooms are delightful and feature anything from four-poster beds to Victorian claw-footed baths. There is also an eight-foot, fully sunken rose petal bath, which creates its own whirlpool. Attention to detail is evident in every aspect of this delightful house.

Broadoaks holds the coveted Blue Ribbon Award from the RAC and its restaurant too is the recipient of many accolades. Both the a la carte and table d'hote are excellent and are constantly changing. There is also a fine selection of wines to choose from. The original open fire adds to the ambience of the overall dining experience. Perhaps the best way to sum up a visit to Broadoaks is in the words of a past guest who described it as a 'place where treasured memories are made.'

LOCATION

From Windermere take A591 signed Ambleside. Just after Royal Mail building veer round to the right, following signs for Troutbeck. The hotel is signed from here

NORTH

Bridge Lane, Troutbeck,
Windermere, Cumbria LA23 1LA
Telephone 015394 45566
Fax 015394 88766

E-mail: *broadoaks@bestloved.com*

OWNERS
Joan and Trevor Pavelyn

ROOM RATES
Single occupancy	£65 - £160
3 Standard Doubles	£99 - £110
3 Half-testers	£140 - £150
7 Four-posters	£140 - £220

Includes full breakfast and VAT

CHARGE/CREDIT CARDS
MC • VI

RATINGS & AWARDS
R.A.C. Blue Ribbon ★★ *Dining Award 3*
Les Routiers Newcomer Award

FACILITIES
On site: *Garden, fishing, croquet, pitch & putt, mountain bike hire*
Licensed for weddings
1 meeting room/max 25 people
Nearby: *Private lesiure club, golf, shooting, riding, cycling*

RESTRICTIONS
Limited facilities for disabled guests
No children under 5 years
Smoking in lounge only
Dogs by arrangement

ATTRACTIONS
Wordsworth's House,
Carlisle Castle,
The Lake District,
Beatrix Potter's Home and Museum,
Rydal Mount,
Castlerigg Stone Circle

AFFILIATIONS
Independent

NEAREST
MAJOR CITY:
Carlisle - 45 miles/1 hr

MAJOR AIRPORT:
Manchester - 100 miles/1 ½ hrs

RAILWAY STATION:
Windermere - 1 ½ miles/5 mins

RESERVATIONS
Direct with hotel
Quote **Best Loved**

ACCESS CODES
Not applicable

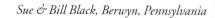

" One year on and still idyllic "

Sue & Bill Black, Berwyn, Pennsylvania

BROXTON HALL   *17th century Tudor house*

NORTH

**Whitchurch Road,
Broxton, Chester,
Cheshire CH3 9JS**

**Telephone 01829 782321
Fax 01829 782330**

E-mail: *broxton@bestloved.com*

OWNERS
Angela and John Ireland

ROOM RATES
Single occupancy	£75
8 Doubles/Twins	£90
1 Four-poster	£110
1 Junior suite	£130
Includes full breakfast and VAT

CHARGE/CREDIT CARDS
 • DC • MC • VI

RATINGS & AWARDS
R.A.C. ★★★ Dining Award 1
A.A. ★★★ 68%

FACILITIES
On site: *Garden
Licensed for weddings
1 meeting room/max 45 people*
Nearby: *Golf, riding, fishing*

RESTRICTIONS
*No facilities for disabled guests
No children under 12 years*

ATTRACTIONS
*Peckforton and Beeston Castles,
Snowdonia National Park, Chester,
Erdigg Hall, Staveley Water Gardens,
Chester & Bangor-on-Dee Racecourses*

AFFILIATIONS
Independent

NEAREST
*MAJOR CITY:
Chester - 10 miles/15 mins*

*MAJOR AIRPORT:
Manchester - 30 miles/40 mins
Liverpool - 25 miles/35 mins*

*RAILWAY STATION:
Chester - 10 miles/15 mins
Crewe - 12 miles/15 mins*

RESERVATIONS
*Direct with hotel
Quote **Best Loved***

ACCESS CODES
Not applicable

An historic house of character a league or so from Roman Chester

Built in 1671, Broxton Hall is a black-and-white half-timbered Tudor house set in five acres of grounds and extensive gardens. The historical walled city of Chester, famed for its Roman and medieval remains and buildings, is eight miles away.

The hotel provides modern comfort yet retains the ambience of a bygone age. The reception area reflects its character in the furnishings, mahogany panelled walls, carved mahogany staircase and a massive Jacobean fireplace, where a welcoming log fire burns most evenings.

All ten bedrooms are beautifully furnished with antiques and offer every facility for your comfort. All have full central heating.

The Cestria restaurant overlooks the fountain terrace and gardens, and is much praised by regular diners. International cuisine is served throughout the year, with local game in season and freshly caught fish.

Broxton Hall is ideally placed for visiting the delightful North Wales seaside and the dramatic scenery of Snowdonia. There are excellent golf courses locally and for the racing enthusiast, Chester and Bangor-on-Dee races are nearby.

LOCATION
From Chester, take the A41, signposted to Whitchurch. After 9 miles, you cross the A534. Broxton Hall is shortly after the A534 junction, on the left.

> **The surroundings are beautiful, the hotel clean and well cared for and your staff extremely helpful and polite**
>
> *Mr Nicholl, Glasgow*

● *Map p.466*
ref: D7

Woodland lodge — CHEVIN COUNTRY PARK HOTEL

NORTH

A country park with pine lodges - a stone's throw from the Yorkshire Dales

Set within 50 acres of private woodland, lakes and gardens this luxurious country park hotel provides a variety of styles of accommodation including top quality Finnish log lodges that are unique to the region. In fact, the award-winning Lakeside Restaurant is the centrepiece of the largest log building in Britain. Open wood fires add a cosy feel to this seemingly remote forested location, which is in reality only two miles from Leeds/Bradford Airport.

This peaceful setting is ideal for weekends away, although the excellent conference facilities instantly recommend it as a blue-chip corporate venue. The on-site Business Centre provides an office 'away from home' and the air-conditioned Woodlands Conference and Banqueting Suite has a total capacity of 120 in a variety of combinations.

The well-equipped Lodgix Leisure Club adds to the sense of splendid isolation: it contains a gym, heated swimming pool, hot tub, sauna, all-weather tennis court, tanning facilities and aromatherapy, massage and reflexology are available by appointment. Guests receive free membership for the duration of their stay, and numbers are strictly controlled to avoid overcrowding. Fishing in the lakes for roach and carp is also possible, although rods are not provided. Local attractions include the Dales, Harrogate and the walled city of York.

LOCATION

*Exit A1 at Wetherby on to A58 towards Leeds.
At Collingham take A659 signed Harewood/Otley.
At Pool take A658 signed Leeds/Bradford Airport.
Go up the hill and turn right towards Carlton,
then 2nd left to Yorkgate. Hotel is ½ mile on left.*

**Yorkgate, Otley,
Yorkshire LS21 3NU**

**Telephone 01943 467818
Fax 01943 850335**

E-mail: *chevin@bestloved.com*

OWNER
Amanda and Anthony Saint Claire

ROOM RATES
2 Singles £65 - £95
48 Doubles/Twins £89 - £175
Includes full breakfast and VAT

CHARGE/CREDIT CARDS

 ● DC ● MC ● VI

RATINGS & AWARDS
E.T.C. ★★★
R.A.C. ★★★
A.A. ★★★ ❀ 67%

FACILITIES
On site: *Garden, fishing, tennis,
indoor pool, health & beauty
Licensed for weddings
5 meeting rooms/max 200 people*
Nearby: *Golf, riding*

RESTRICTIONS
*Limited facilities for disabled guests
Pets by arrangement*

ATTRACTIONS
*York, Harrogate,
The Dales, Fountains Abbey,
Bronte Country, Newby Hall*

AFFILIATIONS
Best Western

NEAREST
MAJOR CITY:
Leeds - 9 miles/20 mins

MAJOR AIRPORT:
Leeds/Bradford - 2 miles/5 mins

RAILWAY STATION:
Guiseley - 3 miles/6 mins

RESERVATIONS
Toll free in US: 800-528-1234
*Quote **Best Loved***

ACCESS CODES
Not applicable

"To say I was stunned by the place would be an understatement ... everything was perfect, we couldn't fault the arrangements in any way ..."

Jayne Fergurson, Leicester

CREWE HALL

Jacobean mansion

NORTH

Weston Road, Crewe, Cheshire CW1 6UZ

Telephone 01270 253333
Fax 01270 253322

E-mail: *crewehall@bestloved.com*

DIRECTORS
Philip Humphreys and Glyn Newman

ROOM RATES
Single occupancy	£130 - £310
39 Doubles/Twins	£155
13 Superior Doubles/Twins	£180
8 Four-posters	£200
5 Suites	£295 - £370

Includes full breakfast and VAT

CHARGE/CREDIT CARDS

 • *DC* • *MC* • *VI*

RATINGS & AWARDS
A.A. ★★★★ ❀❀ 70%
Cheshire Life 'Hotel of the Year'

FACILITIES
On site: *Garden, croquet, tennis, football pitch*
17 meeting rooms/max 350 people
Nearby: *Golf*

RESTRICTIONS
None

ATTRACTIONS
Arley Hall & Gardens, Beeston Castle, Biddulph Grange, Chester, The Potteries, Tatton Park, Bridgemere Garden World

AFFILIATIONS
Grand Heritage Hotels

NEAREST
MAJOR CITY:
Chester - 20 miles/40 mins
Manchester - 35 miles/40 mins

MAJOR AIRPORT:
Manchester - 35 miles/30 mins

RAILWAY STATION:
Crewe - 2 miles/5 mins

RESERVATIONS
Toll free in US: 888-93-GRAND
Toll free in UK: 0800 0560457
Quote **Best Loved**

ACCESS CODES
AMADEUS UI XVCCWE
APOLLO/GALILEO UI 24840
SABRE/ABACUS UI 49965
WORLDSPAN UI 41056

A stately home setting a standard by which all other country houses will be judged

Looks are deceiving at Crewe Hall, an imposing Jacobean pile that was built in 1615 and refurbished in 1866 by architect Edward Barry, who worked on the Houses of Parliament. The exterior is everything you would expect from a significant stately home, but the addition of a contemporary building known as the West Wing concludes a long tradition of blending the old and new.

There are 26 superior rooms in the original Hall, including 10 four-posters; and 39 new accommodations with air conditioning and modern furnishing throughout. Connected to the old hall via a glass link and rotunda, with pleasing views of the gardens, they benefit from ample proportions, even by four-star standards. The reception is light and airy with limestone flooring and a feature glass and brushed steel staircase.

Similar contrast is achieved in the dining options: the oak-panelled Ranulph Restaurant offers traditional English cuisine amidst roaring log fires, whereas an inventive international menu is the order of the day at the sleek and sophisticated Café Bar Brasserie.

Conference facilities are first-class, and corporate guests will impress their clients if they take them to the aptly-named πr^2 - a revolving bar that offers a gradual indoor panorama.

LOCATION

Leave the M6 at J16. Follow A500 towards Crewe. First roundabout take last exit. At next roundabout take the 1st exit. Crewe Hall is a few hundred yards on the right.

Best Loved Hotels of the World

" *What a treasure* "

Colin McKenzie, The Great British Experience

● *Map p.466*
ref: B4

103

Georgian house

CROSBY LODGE

The splendours of good living in the neighbourhood of the Scottish border

This romantic and splendid Georgian house, is the home of the Sedgwick family. The lodge stands high above the village of Low Crosby, with a marvellous view of the River Eden and surrounded by wooded areas and parkland. The house, built in 1802 and altered some years later to the castellated appearance of today, is beautifully furnished with family antiques, complemented by stunning flower arrangements.

Perfectionist and Chef Patron James Sedgwick and his young team serve up deliciously exciting menus featuring authentic continental cuisine and the very best of traditional British fare. The Crosby Lodge sweet trolley, along with their home-made bread and preserves, are renowned far and wide.

Patricia looks after front of house and will greet you personally. The wine list, written and supplied by daughter Philippa, is exceptional.

The house has eleven bedrooms tastefully designed by Patricia. The friendly, efficient staff make this the ideal venue for a peaceful holiday, short break, shooting party or golfing holiday.

LOCATION

Situated just off the A689, 5 miles east of Carlisle. 3 ½ miles from Exit 44 on M6, on the right, just through Low Crosby.

NORTH

**High Crosby,
Crosby-on-Eden, Carlisle,
Cumbria CA6 4QZ**

**Telephone 01228 573618
Fax 01228 573428**

E-mail: *crosby@bestloved.com*

OWNERS
Patricia and Michael Sedgwick

ROOM RATES
Single occupancy	£85
6 Doubles/Twins	£120
2 Four-posters	£120 - £160
3 Family rooms	£150 - £176

Includes full breakfast and VAT

CHARGE/CREDIT CARDS

 ● *JCB* ● *MC* ● *VI*

RATINGS & AWARDS
E.T.C. ★★★ *Silver Award*
A.A. ★★★ 78%

FACILITIES
On site: *Garden*
2 meeting rooms/max 20 people
Nearby: *Golf, fishing, shooting*

RESTRICTIONS
Limited facilities for disabled guests
Pets by arrangement
Closed 24 Dec - 15 Jan

ATTRACTIONS
*Hadrian's Wall, Lake District,
Carlisle Castle and Cathedral,
Wetheral Woods, Penrith Castle,
Lanercost Priory, Brougham Castle*

AFFILIATIONS
Independent

NEAREST
MAJOR CITY:
Carlisle - 5 miles/8 mins

MAJOR AIRPORT:
Newcastle - 58 miles/1 hr
Glasgow - 100 miles/1 ½ hrs

RAILWAY STATION:
Carlisle - 5 miles/15 mins

RESERVATIONS
Direct with hotel
*Quote **Best Loved***

ACCESS CODES
Not applicable

❝ Thank you so much for many wonderful vacations ❞

Laura Clark, New York

DALE HEAD HALL

Elizabethan manor house

Lake Thirlmere, Keswick, Cumbria CA12 4TN

Telephone 017687 72478
Fax 017687 71070

E-mail: *dalehead@bestloved.com*

OWNERS
Alan and Shirley Lowe

GENERAL MANAGER
Hans Bonkenburg

RATES PER PERSON
Single occupancy	£108
6 Doubles/Twins	£83 - £93
4 Superior Doubles/Twins	£98
3 Four-posters	£98
2 Suites	£125

Includes dinner, full breakfast and VAT

CHARGE/CREDIT CARDS

AMERICAN EXPRESS • *JCB* • *MC* • *VI*

RATINGS & AWARDS
E.T.C. ★★★ *Gold Award*
A.A. ★★★ ❀❀ *74%*
WHICH? Hotel of the Year 2003

FACILITIES
On site: *Garden, fishing, croquet*
Nearby: *Golf, sailing, canoeing, riding*

RESTRICTIONS
Limited facilities for disabled guests
No children in restaurant under 10 years
Smoking in bar only
No pets

ATTRACTIONS
Wordsworth's Dove Cottage,
Beatrix Potter's museum and house,
Cumbrian fells, Ruskin's Brantwood

AFFILIATIONS
Independent

NEAREST
MAJOR CITY:
Carlisle - 40 miles/45 mins

MAJOR AIRPORT:
Manchester - 100 miles/2 hrs

RAILWAY STATION:
Penrith - 10 miles/20 mins

RESERVATIONS
Direct with hotel
*Quote **Best Loved***

ACCESS CODES
Not applicable

Blissful solitude on the shores of Lake Thirlmere

Beside Lake Thirlmere, surrounded by lush woodland, stands this glorious 16th century house. Rich green lawns sweep towards the water. The tranquillity of the location cannot be surpassed, since the house stands alone on the shores of the 3 ¼ mile lake.

The Leathes family came to Dale Head Hall in 1577; in 1877 lake and hall were purchased by Manchester to provide the city with clean drinking water and successive Lord Mayors with an idyllic summer retreat.

Today Alan and Shirley Lowe and their family offer exceptional accommodation and service. In restoring the hall, they set high priority on recreating its 16th century authenticity. The bar and lounge are delightful.

The 5-course table d'hôte dinner is served in the oak-beamed Elizabethan dining room, which has an inglenook fireplace. The food is fresh and imaginatively prepared. It is complemented with a good choice of fine wines.

All the splendours of the Lake District are adjacent. Helvellyn is on the doorstep and Borrowdale is close by. Fishing, sailing and canoeing can all be enjoyed; please be sure to take your own equipment as this cannot be supplied by the hotel.

LOCATION

On A591, halfway between Keswick and Grasmere. Hotel is situated along ¼ mile of private driveway overlooking Lake Thirlmere.

Best Loved Hotels of the World

" It is a home from home for me "

The Duchess of Devonshire

● Map p.466
ref: D7

105

18th century country house

THE DEVONSHIRE

**Bolton Abbey, Near Skipton,
North Yorkshire BD23 6AJ**
Telephone 01756 710441
Fax 01756 710564
E-mail: *devonskip@bestloved.com*

OWNERS
Duke and Duchess of Devonshire
MANAGING DIRECTOR
Jeremy Rata
ROOM RATES
Single occupancy   £145 - £300
31 Doubles/Twins   £200
7 Four-posters   £250 - £300
3 Suites   £350
*Includes full breakfast, daily
newspaper and VAT*

CHARGE/CREDIT CARDS

 ● DC ● MC ● VI

RATINGS & AWARDS
A.A. ★★★ ❀❀ *Top 200 - 02/03*
FACILITIES
On site: *Garden, gym, heli-pad,
fishing, croquet, tennis, indoor pool,
health & beauty, sauna, solarium, spa,
beauty therapy, steam room
Licensed for weddings
4 meeting rooms/max 150 people*
Nearby: *Golf*
RESTRICTIONS
None
ATTRACTIONS
*Bronte Parsonage, Bolton Priory,
Skipton Castle, Castle Howard,
Fountains Abbey, Harewood House*
AFFILIATIONS
*The Celebrated Hotels Collection
Small Luxury Hotels
Pride of Britain*
NEAREST
*MAJOR CITY:
Leeds - 17 miles/30 mins*

*MAJOR AIRPORT:
Manchester - 60 miles/1¼ hrs
Leeds/Bradford - 12 miles/20 mins*

*RAILWAY STATION:
Ilkley - 5 miles/10 mins*
RESERVATIONS
*Toll free in US: 800-322-2403
or 800-525-4800 or 800-98-PRIDE*
Quote **Best Loved**
ACCESS CODES
*AMADEUS LX MANDCH
APOLLO/GALILEO LX 44518
SABRE/ABACUS LX 11172
WORLDSPAN LX MANDC*

NORTH

Fabulous facilities in the breathtaking Yorkshire Dales

Everyone who comes to Wharfedale for the first time is struck by the beauty of the countryside. The 30,000 acre Bolton Abbey Estate is owned by the Duke of Devonshire and there are 80 miles of footpaths along the riverbank to the spectacular ruins of the 12th century Bolton Priory, through woodland and over the moors. All this is on the doorstep of the hotel, originally a 17th century coaching inn.

The hotel reveals a wonderfully warm and welcoming interior furnished and decorated under the supervision of the Duchess of Devonshire using antiques and fine paintings from the family home at nearby Chatsworth in Derbyshire. Understated elegance best describes the comfortable lounges and exquisitely appointed bedrooms which include eight romantic four-poster rooms.

Michael Wignall is Head Chef of The Burlington Restaurant where guests are treated to outstanding cooking and service. The wine list is stunning with over 1200 bins including 60 'house wines'. The Devonshire Brasserie and Bar provides a lively and less formal alternative. A converted 17th century barn is home to the

exceptional leisure facilities of the Devonshire Club. Here guests can use the gym, pool, steam room, sauna and tennis court or enjoy a relaxing therapy treatment.

LOCATION

*On the B6160 to Bolton Abbey, 250 yards north
from its roundabout junction with the A59
Skipton to Harrogate Road.*

" You'll talk about it. Most important you'll enjoy it "

Yorkshire Life

THE DEVONSHIRE FELL

Country house

NORTH

**Burnsall, Skipton,
North Yorkshire BD23 6BT**

**Telephone 01756 729000
or 718111
Fax 01756 729009**

E-mail: *devonfell@bestloved.com*

OWNERS
Duke and Duchess of Devonshire

MANAGING DIRECTOR
Jeremy Rata

ROOM RATES
Single occupancy	*£70 - £110*
10 Doubles/Twins	*£110 - £140*
2 Suites	*£160*
Includes full breakfast and VAT

CHARGE/CREDIT CARDS

 • *DC* • *MC* • *VI*

RATINGS & AWARDS
E.T.C. ★★
*Country Life Taittinger Independent
Hotel of the Year in 2001
Les Routiers Newcomer for the North East*

FACILITIES
On site: *Garden, fishing*
Licensed for weddings
1 meeting room/max 100 people
Nearby: *Golf, tennis, fitness, fishing*

RESTRICTIONS
Limited facilities for disabled guests

ATTRACTIONS
*Bolton Abbey, Skipton Castle,
Fountains Abbey, Harewood House,
Castle Howard, Bronte Parsonage*

AFFILIATIONS
Preston's Global Hotels

NEAREST
MAJOR CITY:
Leeds - 26 miles/1 hr

MAJOR AIRPORT:
Skipton - 8 miles/10 mins

RAILWAY STATION:
Leeds/Bradford - 20 miles/30 mins

RESERVATIONS
Toll free in US: 800-544-9993
*Quote **Best Loved***

ACCESS CODES
Not applicable

The best views in Wharfedale

The Devonshire Fell is blessed with a truly glorious position poised on a hillside overlooking the River Wharfe to the rolling uplands of the Yorkshire Dales beyond. A few years ago it underwent a complete transformation under the direction of Lady Hartington, daughter-in-law of the owner, the Duke of Devonshire.

Chic, vibrant colour schemes; huge comfy sofas and chairs with a wood burning stove in the bar area; smart conservatory restaurant and original contemporary art complements the dynamic decor. Rooms are well equipped, each with lively furnishings and spectacular views.

Chef Patron Neil Waterfield has earned good reviews for his cooking which incorporates many local specialities including game and fish. Their wine list, as one would expect, is well chosen and extensive. Jointly awarded the Country Life Taittinger Independent Hotel of the Year in 2001 (with its sister hotel The Devonshire), Newcomer for the North East in Les Routiers 2001 and a Michelin Bib Gourmand. Another big plus is the Fell's young and enthusiastic staff who add a real buzz to the friendly and informal atmosphere. All guests staying at The Devonshire Fell

have free use of the leisure facilities at The Devonshire Club in nearby Bolton Abbey.

LOCATION
**Take B6160 past Bolton Abbey from junction
with A59 (Skipton to Harrogate road).
Follow for 6 miles, hotel is on left.**

● *Map p.466*
   ref: C8

Victorian residence — ELEVEN DIDSBURY PARK

A stylish urban retreat reflecting Manchester's new-found dynamism

Prosperous mill owners and industrialists founded the exclusive south Manchester suburb of Didsbury in the 1850's. Just 15 minutes from the city centre, this leafy neighbourhood of imposing Victorian homes has metamorphosed into a cosmopolitan enclave brimming with hip restaurants and bars.

Eamonn and Sally O'Loughlin have transformed a series of outbuildings arranged around a Victorian walled garden into a classic town house hotel. There is not a shred of chintz or an over-stuffed armchair in sight, but instead a vision of artful contemporary chic and the odd quirky feature such as the Chinese sideboard which serves as a bar. Sally's work as a TV make-up artist may account for her creative flair with colours. Eamonn's innate sense of Irish hospitality is echoed by the boy Fergal the tabby cat - just so long as you don't sit on His chair.

The O'Loughlins offer a scrumptious breakfast and there are plenty of restaurants nearby for dining out (and a courtesy four wheel drive to take you when available). There is a small conference room for up to 15 people, and a beauty spa and gym at their sister hotel, Didsbury House, just down the road.

LOCATION

From M60 take A34, signposted Manchester City Centre. Turn left on to A5145 and continue down Wilmslow Road. Turn right into Didsbury Park. The hotel is half way down on the left hand side.

**11 Didsbury Park,
Didsbury Village,
Manchester M20 5LH**

**Telephone 0161 448 7711
Fax 0161 448 8282**

E-mail: *11didsbury@bestloved.com*

OWNER
Eamonn O'Loughlin

ROOM RATES
Single occupancy   £70 - £115
13 Doubles/Twins   £70 - £125
1 Junior suite   £125 - £155
Includes service and VAT

CHARGE/CREDIT CARDS

 • *DC* • *JCB* • *MC* • *VI*

RATINGS & AWARDS
Sunday Times Top Five Hotel Town Houses

FACILITIES
On site: *Garden, gym, croquet*
1 meeting room/max 30 people
Nearby: *Tennis, entertainment centre*

RESTRICTIONS
*No facilities for disabled guests
No smoking throughout
No pets*

ATTRACTIONS
*Lowry Centre, Bridgewater Hall,
Old Trafford, Manchester United Museum,
The Opera House, Lyme Park*

AFFILIATIONS
Design Hotels

NEAREST
MAJOR CITY:
Manchester - 3 ½ miles/10 mins

MAJOR AIRPORT:
Manchester - 4 miles/10 mins

RAILWAY STATION:
Stockport - 3 miles/10 mins

RESERVATIONS
Direct with hotel
Quote **Best Loved**

ACCESS CODES
Not applicable

NORTH

THE FEVERSHAM ARMS

Coaching inn

NORTH

**1/8 High Street,
Helmsley, York,
North Yorkshire YO62 5AG**

**Telephone 01439 770766
Fax 01439 770346**

E-mail: *feversham@bestloved.com*

GENERAL MANAGER
Phillip Bolson

ROOM RATES
Single occupancy	£80 - £100
12 Doubles/Twins	£100 - £120
5 Suites	£120 - £150

Includes full breakfast and VAT

CHARGE/CREDIT CARDS

 • MC • VI

RATINGS & AWARDS
E.T.C. ★★★ *Silver Award*
R.A.C. *Blue Ribbon* ★★★ *Dining Award 2*
A.A. ★★★ ❀ 77%

FACILITIES
On site: *Garden, tennis,
outdoor pool, fitness suite
1 meeting room/max 30 people*
Nearby: *Riding, shooting*

RESTRICTIONS
*No smoking in bedrooms
Pets by arrangement*

ATTRACTIONS
*Helmsley Castle, Duncombe Park,
Rievaulx Abbey, Castle Howard,
Jorvik Viking Centre, York,
Yorkshire Moors*

AFFILIATIONS
Independent

NEAREST
MAJOR CITY:
York - 22 miles/30 mins

MAJOR AIRPORT:
Leeds/Bradford - 50 miles/1 ¼ hrs

RAILWAY STATION:
York - 22 miles/30 mins

RESERVATIONS
Direct with hotel
*Quote **Best Loved***

ACCESS CODES
Not applicable

An exciting new look for a long-standing favourite Yorkshire retreat

If you haven't paid a visit to the Feversham Arms in a while, you are urged to renew your acquaintance with this historic North Yorkshire inn. The Feversham has welcomed travellers to Helmsley since 1855, but over the last year it has undergone a transformation which needs to be seen to be believed.

From the minute you cross the threshold, Feversham promises stylish relaxation. Deep sofas in the subtly-lit lounges invite guests to sink in mellow comfort before open log fires. There are two dining venues: the intimate Dining Room; and the great value, chic and contemporary Brasserie at the Fev with its banquette seating, modern art and decorative display of wine bottles arranged as a frieze above the names of famous wines scrolled across the walls. In summer, the poolside terrace and corner garden provide an al fresco setting for a special seafood menu. Stone-walled corridors lead to boldly decorated bedrooms with satellite television and CD systems, and there is a well-equipped Health and Fitness Club.

The gateway to the North York Moors, Helmsley is well placed for expeditions to Castle Howard and Rievaulx Abbey, as well as hiking and sporting opportunities.

LOCATION

From York take the A19 to Thirsk. At Thirsk take the A170 towards Scarborough. Helmsley is 14 miles along the A170 and the hotel is situated in the town centre, just off the Square.

" A far more personal, tailored and exacting standard of hospitality than frequently offered by other establishments "

Tim & Heather Erridge, Lancashire

Coaching inn   THE GENERAL TARLETON INN

Mmm! - delicious food, a lovely coaching inn and proprietors with a magic touch

When you have been incredibly successful in one venture, you may not do so well in another, as any sensible Yorkshireman will tell you! Well, the Watkins/Topham partnership need not worry, for their latest venture - The General Tarleton - is giving their other famous inn, The Angel at Hetton, a run for its money. They have laid their magic touch on this 250-year-old coaching inn, turning it into a charming hotel with pretty, top-quality bedrooms and an outstanding, and growing, reputation for good food.

Chef-patron John Topham leads a kitchen brigade who take food seriously, and have been showered with awards to prove it. For traditional dishes such as sausage and mash, with Lishman's of Ilkley prize-winning sausages, to carpaccio of beef or seared sea bass on a tomato tart, everything is sourced with the utmost care and loyalty to local suppliers. Choose from the intimate restaurant, covered courtyard for 'al fresco' eating or the oak-beamed bar with its nooks and crannies and log fires for a less formal atmosphere.

Surrounded by unspoilt countryside The General Tarleton is ideal for visiting historic York,

elegant Harrogate and bustling Leeds or touring the Yorkshire moors and dales.

LOCATION

Exit A1(M) at Junction 47 onto the A59 to Knaresborough. Then take the A6055 to Ferrensby.

Boroughbridge Road, Ferrensby, Knaresborough, North Yorkshire HG5 0QB

**Telephone 01423 340284
Fax 01423 340288**

E-mail: *tarleton@bestloved.com*

OWNERS
John Topham and Denis Watkins

GENERAL MANAGER
Ken Hardy

ROOM RATES
Single occupancy   £75
13 Doubles/Twins   £96
1 Four-poster   £106
Includes full breakfast and VAT

CHARGE/CREDIT CARDS

 • *MC* • *VI*

RATINGS & AWARDS
E.T.C. ★★★
A.A. ★★★ ❀❀ 71%

FACILITIES
On site: *Garden*
Licensed for weddings
1 meeting room/max 40 people
Nearby: *Golf, riding, fishing*

RESTRICTIONS
No facilities for disabled guests
Pets by arrangement

ATTRACTIONS
City of York,
Spa town of Harrogate,
Fountains Abbey,
Harewood House,
Ripon Cathedral,
Beningborough Hall

AFFILIATIONS
Independent

NEAREST
MAJOR CITY:
York - 50 miles/1 ½ hrs

MAJOR AIRPORT:
Leeds/Bradford - 16 miles/25 mins

RAILWAY STATION:
Harrogate - 6 miles/20 mins

RESERVATIONS
Direct with hotel
Quote **Best Loved**

ACCESS CODES
Not applicable

Map p.466
ref: B6

NORTH

> **❝** *Sets standards that other hotels only dream of achieving* **❞**
>
> A & S Sturrock, Bedfordshire

GILPIN LODGE HOTEL

Edwardian country house

Crook Road, Windermere, Cumbria LA23 3NE

Telephone 015394 88818
Fax 015394 88058

E-mail: *gilpin@bestloved.com*

OWNERS
John and Christine Cunliffe

DIRECTORS
Richard Marriott and Barney Cunliffe

RATES PER PERSON
9 Doubles/Twins   £75 - £125
5 Four-posters   £95 - £125
Includes full breakfast, dinner and VAT

CHARGE/CREDIT CARDS

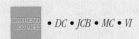 • DC • JCB • MC • VI

RATINGS & AWARDS
E.T.C. ★★★ Gold Award
R.A.C. Gold Ribbon ★★★ Dining Award 3
A.A. ★★★ ❀❀❀

FACILITIES
On site: *Garden, croquet*
Nearby: *Golf, riding, tennis, fishing*

RESTRICTIONS
Limited facilities for disabled guests
No children under 7 years
No pets

ATTRACTIONS
Wordsworth's Dove Cottage,
World of Beatrix Potter, Lake Windermere,
Holker Hall, Levens Hall,
Blackwell Arts & Crafts House

AFFILIATIONS
Pride of Britain

NEAREST
MAJOR CITY:
Manchester - 80 miles/1 ¼ hrs

MAJOR AIRPORT:
Manchester - 90 miles/1 ¾ hrs

RAILWAY STATION:
Windermere - 2 miles/10 mins

RESERVATIONS
Toll free in US: 800-98-PRIDE
Quote **Best Loved**

ACCESS CODES
Not applicable

A true gourmet retreat amidst idyllic Cumbrian scenery

A charming Edwardian lodge set in 20 secluded acres of woodlands, moors and glorious country gardens just two miles from Lake Windermere might be reason enough to book into Gilpin Lodge. Add a warm welcome from hosts John and Christine Cunliffe and their splendidly professional staff, all of whom have perfected the art of attentive but unobtrusive service, and it would seem an opportunity that shouldn't be missed. However, the real heart of this luxurious and appealing small hotel is the kitchen where head chef Mark Jordan works his culinary magic. Jordans' modern interpretation of classical cuisine has garnered numerous awards and is complemented by an impressive wine list with over 190 labels from 14 countries. The choice extends from well-priced wines by the glass to the dizzy heights of vintages selected to interest the wine connoisseur.

Guests are put completely at their ease by the Cunliffes' special brand of relaxed and informal hospitality. Fresh garden flowers, picture-lined walls and roaring log fires in cooler weather set the tone, while several of the pretty and thoughtfully

furnished bedrooms have four posters and whirlpool baths, and six rooms boast French windows leading out onto private garden patios.

LOCATION
Gilpin Lodge is 12 miles from the M6.
Leave motorway at Exit 36 and take the
A590/591 to roundabout north of Kendal.
Then take the B5284 for 5 miles.

" A charming place, I hope you didn't mind me bringing my own wine, your food complements it perfectly "

Baron Eric de Rothschild, Château Lafite

111

● Map p.466
ref: E7

Regency town house   THE GRANGE HOTEL

NORTH

**1 Clifton, York,
North Yorkshire YO30 6AA**
Telephone 01904 644744
Fax 01904 612453

E-mail: *grange@bestloved.com*

OWNER
Jeremy Cassel

GENERAL MANAGER
Peter Bate

ROOM RATES
3 Singles   £105
24 Doubles/Twins   £125 - £195
2 Four-posters   £195
1 Suite   £230
Includes full breakfast and VAT

CHARGE/CREDIT CARDS

 ● *DC* ● *JCB* ● *MC* ● *VI*

RATINGS & AWARDS
E.T.C. ★★★ *Silver Award*
R.A.C. Blue Ribbon ★★★ *Dining Award 3*
A.A. ★★★ ✿✿
A.A. Top 200 - 02/03
*Yorkshire Tourist Board White Rose
Award for Tourism 2001
& Small Hotel of the Year 2001*

FACILITIES
On site: *Licensed for weddings
2 meeting rooms/max100 people*
Nearby: *Golf, fitness*

RESTRICTIONS
*Limited facilities for disabled guests
Pets by arrangement*

ATTRACTIONS
*York Minster, The Shambles,
National Railway Museum,
Castle Howard, York Racecourse,
Yorkshire Moors & Dales*

AFFILIATIONS
The Celebrated Hotels Collection

NEAREST
MAJOR CITY:
York

MAJOR AIRPORT:
Leeds/Bradford - 30 miles/50 mins

RAILWAY STATION:
York - 1 mile/10 mins

RESERVATIONS
Toll free in US: 800-322-2403
Quote **Best Loved**

ACCESS CODES
Not applicable

Luxury, fine cuisine and all the splendours of York and The Dales

Given its history of conquerors, (Roman, Saxon, Viking and Norman), it is not surprising that York boasts of being one of Britain's most interesting cities - and you would be hard pressed to find anywhere more convenient or comfortable for its exploration than The Grange. Within walking distance are the Minster (dating from 1100) and its remarkable stained glass, the City Walls, the Jorvik Viking Centre, the National Railway Museum and the medieval Shambles. Within easy driving distance are stately homes, The Yorkshire Dales and the renowned York Racecourse.

The Grange itself is a listed Regency townhouse, built in 1834 and carefully restored to create a luxurious 30 bedroom hotel. Light streams down the vine leaf cast iron staircase which leads from finely decorated bedrooms. English chintz and fine antiques pervade and all rooms offer satellite television.

Not only is the hotel ideally situated for the explorer, the gourmet has a choice of three restaurants. From the elegance of the award-winning Ivy Restaurant - mixing classic French and modern British cuisine, or the Seafood Bar with the freshest of fish and seafood (recommended with a glass or two of chilled champagne), to the relaxed Brasserie converted from the old brick-vaulted cellars. Eat, drink, relax, explore - The Grange Hotel conquers all.

LOCATION

**About 500 yards from York city centre
on the A19 York - Thirsk road.**

Map p.466
ref: D7

" *The best of Yorkshire and a great deal besides* "

Gina Lazenby

GRANTS HOTEL

Victorian town house

**Swan Road, Harrogate,
North Yorkshire HG1 2SS**

**Telephone 01423 560666
Fax 01423 502550**

E-mail: *grants@bestloved.com*

GENERAL MANAGER
Pam Grant

ROOM RATES
13 Singles	£75 - £114
26 Doubles/Twins	£95 - £148
1 Four-poster	£115 - £160
2 Suites	£120 - £170

Includes full breakfast and VAT

CHARGE/CREDIT CARDS

 • *DC • JCB • MC • VI*

RATINGS & AWARDS
E.T.C. ★★★
R.A.C. ★★★ Dining Award 1
A.A. ★★★ 72%

FACILITIES
On site: *Patio gardens
5 meeting rooms/max 100 people*
Nearby: *Golf, health & leisure club,
riding, fishing*

RESTRICTIONS
No pets in public rooms

ATTRACTIONS
*Fountains Abbey, Harrogate,
Middleham and Bolton Castles,
Herriot Country, Yorkshire Dales, York*

AFFILIATIONS
Independent

NEAREST
*MAJOR CITY:
Leeds - 15 miles/25 mins*

*MAJOR AIRPORT:
Leeds/Bradford - 12 miles/20 mins*

*RAILWAY STATION:
Harrogate - ½ mile/5 mins walk*

*FERRY PORT:
Hull - 70 miles/1 ½ hrs*

RESERVATIONS
Toll free in UK: 0800 371343
Quote **Best Loved**

ACCESS CODES
*APOLLO/GALILEO RM 48485
SABRE/ABACUS RM 04297*

www.grants.bestloved.com

Elegant and individual hospitality in the heart of historic England

Harrogate is a beautiful spa and floral town in the heart of an area rich in English history. James Herriot, the world's most celebrated vet, was a regular weekly visitor for many years, finding a convivial refuge from the nearby Yorkshire Dales, scene of his adventures.

Within a short distance is the Roman city of York with its Jorvik Viking Centre. Alternatively, Fountains Abbey, England's largest Cistercian Monastery, disestablished by Henry VIII - now preserved as a World Heritage Site.

You can explore Middleham Castle, home of Richard III, immortalised by William Shakespeare, visit Bolton Castle where Mary Queen of Scots was imprisoned or Haworth, home of the Brontë Family.

Grants is a family-run hotel with a reputation for quality service, combining modern efficiency with old fashioned hospitality. Each of the tastefully decorated bedrooms offers a full range of facilities and a lift serves all floors. Chimney Pots Bistro provides an imaginative menu in an elegant air-conditioned atmosphere and is a firm favourite with local gourmets.

LOCATION

From M1 or M62 at Leeds, take A61 to Harrogate, then 2nd left after The Royal Hall traffic lights into Swan Road.

" As always everything was first class. It doesn't seem possible but you seem to improve things every year! "

R H Wilcox, Altrincham

• Map p.466
ref: B6

Victorian country house — GRAYTHWAITE MANOR HOTEL

**Fernhill Road,
Grange-over-Sands,
Cumbria LA11 7JE**

**Telephone 015395 32001
Fax 015395 35549**

E-mail: *graythwaite@bestloved.com*

GENERAL MANAGER
Chris Hartley

RATES PER PERSON

5 Singles	*£60 - £85*
15 Doubles/Twins	*£53 - £85*
1 Family suite	*£53 - £85*

Includes full breakfast, dinner and VAT

CHARGE/CREDIT CARDS

 • *JCB* • *MC* • *VI*

RATINGS & AWARDS
E.T.C. ★★★
R.A.C. ★★★ *Dining Award 1*
A.A. ★★★ *65%*
Britain in Bloom Gardening Award

FACILITIES
On site: *Garden, tennis, putting green
2 meeting rooms/max 50 people*
Nearby: *Golf, riding, fishing, leisure centre*

RESTRICTIONS
*Limited facilities for disabled guests
Children by arrangement
No pets*

ATTRACTIONS
*Holker Hall,
Cartmel Priory and Village,
Hill Top - Beatrix Potter's House,
Wordsworth's Dove Cottage*

AFFILIATIONS
Independent

NEAREST
MAJOR CITY:
*Manchester - 80 miles/1½ hrs
Lancaster - 30 miles*

MAJOR AIRPORT:
*Manchester - 90 miles/1½ hrs
Liverpool - 90 miles*

RAILWAY STATION:
*Grange-over-Sands - 1 mile/5 mins
Oxenholme - 14 miles*

RESERVATIONS
Direct with hotel
Quote **Best Loved**

ACCESS CODES
Not applicable

High levels of comfort in a beautiful country manor

Graythwaite Manor is one of many excellent reasons for choosing Grange-over-Sands as your weekend or holiday venue. The hotel is owned and operated by the Auchlochan Trust - whose constant aim is to provide guests with a warm welcome and personal care and attention.

This beautifully furnished country house provides an exclusive, comfortable and tranquil setting in which to relax. It is set in eight acres of landscaped gardens and woodland, on the hillside looking out over Morecambe Bay.

Elegant, spacious lounges with fresh flowers and antiques are part of the atmosphere. Each bedroom is tastefully furnished, and has a private bathroom, colour television, telephone and tea/coffee-making facilities. Many provide superb views across the gardens and bay to the Pennines beyond.

The hotel is noted for its superb cuisine, the head chef working closely with the manager to ensure the highest standards. You can look forward to a five-course dinner, a choice of carefully prepared dishes and good wine from

their extensive cellar. They use fresh local produce as much as possible. A traditional English roast is a regular feature on the menu.

LOCATION

*Exit junction 36 on M6 and take the
A590 for 14 miles to Grange. Fernhill
road is opposite the firestation.*

NORTH

Map p.466
ref: C6

" It's not a hotel, it's an experience! "

Ben & Claire, London

HIPPING HALL — *17th century country house*

Cowan Bridge, Kirkby Lonsdale, Cumbria LA6 2JJ

**Telephone 015242 71187
Fax 015242 72452**

E-mail: *hipping@bestloved.com*

OWNERS
Richard and Jean Skelton

MANAGER
Philip Montgomery

ROOM RATES
Single occupancy £75 - £85
5 Doubles/Twins £96
2 Suites £116
Includes full breakfast and VAT

CHARGE/CREDIT CARDS
AMERICAN EXPRESS • MC • VI

RATINGS & AWARDS
A.A. ★ ❀
A.A. Top 200 - 02/03

FACILITIES
On site: *Garden*
1 meeting room/max 40 people
Nearby: *Golf, riding, fishing*

RESTRICTIONS
*No facilities for disabled guests
No children under 12 years
Smoking limited
Pets by arrangement*

ATTRACTIONS
*Yorkshire Dales National Park,
Lake District National Park,
Settle-Carlisle Railway,
Wordsworth's Dove Cottage,
Beatrix Potter's House and Museum*

AFFILIATIONS
Independent

NEAREST
MAJOR CITY:
Lancaster - 18 miles/25 mins

MAJOR AIRPORT:
Manchester - 70 miles/1 ½ hrs

RAILWAY STATION:
Oxenholme - 12 miles/20 mins

RESERVATIONS
Direct with hotel
Quote **Best Loved**

ACCESS CODES
Not applicable

Enjoy this friendly country house party style

Dating from the 15th century, Hipping Hall is set in four acres of walled gardens and home to the Skelton family, whose generous hospitality makes guests feel wonderfully welcome and cosseted. The five comfortable bedrooms in the main house are furnished with antiques (Jean keeps a teddy and curio shop in the cellar!) and enjoy lovely orchard or garden views. Two pretty courtyard cottages offer sitting room, kitchen and a bedroom and bathroom reached by spiral staircases. An à la carte menu is served in the cosy dining room or in the impressive great hall for larger parties (Hipping is perfect for a family get-together, sporting weekend or private business meeting).

Cowan Bridge, where the Brontë sisters attended school, is conveniently situated for both the Lake District and Yorkshire Dales. It lies two miles from the pretty market town of Kirkby Lonsdale in the Lune Valley, the view Ruskin described as 'one of the loveliest scenes in England - therefore in the world!'.

Whether you make the Hall your base for a tour of the Lakes and Dales, an overnight stay on the road to Scotland, or a house party, you will remember your visit with great affection.

LOCATION
On A65 2 ½ miles east of Kirkby Lonsdale, 8 ½ miles from M6, Junction 36.

" *Not only was the view unbelievable, it was quite easily the best and friendliest service we have ever experienced* *"*

Will Carling, former England Rugby Captain

19th century hunting lodge HOLBECK GHYLL HOTEL & SPA

A connoisseur's hotel with sensational views of Lake Windermere

Back in 1888, Lord Lonsdale (of boxing's Lonsdale Belt fame) was so taken by the views across Lake Windermere and the Langdale Fells that he bought Holbeck Ghyll for use as his Hunting Lodge. His idea of the perfect country residence has made a lasting impression on its style and appearance. Over 100 years on, the view has hardly altered at all but the house is now an hotel of outstanding character, chosen by the Cumbria Tourist Board as Hotel of the Year 2000 - 2001. Our congratulations go to David and Patricia Nicholson whose quest for excellence has made this charming hotel such a pleasure to visit.

The interiors are styled in the manner of Charles Rennie Mackintosh with a wealth of oak panelling and stained glass. Into this magnificence are interwoven the luxuries of a first class hotel and a connoisseur's clutter of a home; antiques, original paintings, flowers, really comfortable furniture ... Success is evident in the recent addition of six luxury, lake view rooms in The Lodge, only 45 metres from the old house itself.

Part of the Holbeck experience is the five-course dinner which features dishes classically prepared and artistically presented, much in the

English style with a hint of France. Exciting and unusual vegetarian items are included in every course. Gourmets should go for the inclusive rate that includes dinner; they won't be disappointed.

LOCATION

M6 Exit 36. To Windermere, pass Brockhole Visitors' Centre, then after ½ mile turn righ into Holbeck Lane (signed Troutbeck). Hotel is ½ mile on left.

Holbeck Lane, Windermere, Cumbria LA23 1LU
Telephone 015394 32375
Fax 015394 34743
E-mail: *holbeck@bestloved.com*

OWNERS
David and Patricia Nicholson

ROOM RATES
18 Doubles/Twins   £150 - £260
2 Four-posters/Suites   £170 - £270
Includes full breakfast and VAT.
Enquire for 5-course dinner inclusive rates

CHARGE/CREDIT CARDS

 ● *DC* ● *JCB* ● *MC* ● *VI*

RATINGS & AWARDS
E.T.C. ★★★ *Gold Award*
R.A.C. Gold Ribbon ★★★ *Dining Award 4*
A.A. ★★★ ❀❀❀
A.A. Top 200 - 02/03
Cumbria Tourist Board Hotel of the Year 2000 - 2001

FACILITIES
On site: *Garden, croquet, tennis, health & beauty, health spa, woodland walks, cycling, putting green*
Licensed for weddings
2 meeting rooms/max 60 people
Nearby: *Golf, riding, fishing*

RESTRICTIONS
Limited facilities for disabled guests
No children under 8 years in restaurant
No pets in public rooms

ATTRACTIONS
Wordsworth's Dove Cottage, Lake cruises, Beatrix Potter's home, Holker Hall, Levens Hall

AFFILIATIONS
The Celebrated Hotels Collection
Pride of Britain
Small Luxury Hotels

NEAREST
MAJOR CITY:
Manchester - 90 miles/1 ½ hrs

MAJOR AIRPORT:
Manchester - 90 miles/1 ½ hrs

RAILWAY STATION:
Windermere - 3 miles/5 mins

RESERVATIONS
Toll free in US/Canada: 800-525-4800
or 800-322-2403 or 800-98-PRIDE
*Quote **Best Loved***

ACCESS CODES
AMADEUS LX VEMHGC
APOLLO/GALILEO LX 21650
SABRE/ABACUS LX 31195
WORLDSPAN LX BWFHG

NORTH

● *Map p.466*
ref: D5

" An overall outstanding stay. We will be back "

Steve & Sue Becker

JUDGES COUNTRY HOUSE HOTEL   *Victorian hall*

**Kirklevington, Yarm,
North Yorkshire TS15 9LW**
Telephone 01642 789000
Fax 01642 782878

E-mail: *judges@bestloved.com*

OWNERS
Michael and Shirley Downs

GENERAL MANAGER
Scott Wilshaw

ROOM RATES
Single occupancy	£123 - £225
20 Doubles/Twins	£159 - £225
8 King-sized rooms	£159 - £225
4 Four-posters	£159 - £225
1 Suite	£159 - £225

Includes full breakfast and VAT

CHARGE/CREDIT CARDS

 • *DC* • *MC* • *VI*

RATINGS & AWARDS
R.A.C. Blue Ribbon ★★★ *Dining Award 3*
A.A. ★★★ 🏵🏵
A.A. Top 200 - 02/03

FACILITIES
On site: *Garden, gym, heli-pad, croquet,
sauna, jacuzzi, solarium, bowls, pitch &
putt, scittles lawn, mountain biking,
basketball, badminton, archery
Licensed for weddings
7 meeting rooms/max 300 people*
Nearby: *Golf, tennis, riding, fishing,
swimming, health & beauty*

RESTRICTIONS
None

ATTRACTIONS
*Whitby Abbey, Yorkshire Moors,
Rievaulx Abbey, High Force Falls,
Pickering Castle, H.M. Bark Endeavour*

AFFILIATIONS
Grand Heritage Hotels

NEAREST
MAJOR CITY:
Middlesborough - 8 miles/20mins

MAJOR AIRPORT:
Teeside - 5 miles/30 mins

RAILWAY STATION:
Yarm - 1 mile/5 mins

RESERVATIONS
Toll free in the US: 888-93-GRAND
Quote **Best Loved**

ACCESS CODES
*AMADEUS UI MMEJCH
APOLLO/GALILEO UI 51228
SABRE/ABACUS UI 64360
WORLDSPAN UI 42867*

The verdict is unanimous approval for this former judges' lodging

Judges Country House was built on the edge of the North Yorkshire Moors in 1881, as a family residence for the Richardsons of Hartlepool, prosperous engineering entrepreneurs. In the 1970s the building was transformed into a country lodging for circuit court judges - hence the name.

The carefully restored house, replete with glossy Victorian woodwork, has a comfortably clubby atmosphere that is known to play havoc with guests' short stay plans! Part of the charm is the lovely garden with its sunny terraces, the Victorian walled garden where fruit and vegetables are grown for the kitchens, and the extensive woodlands walkways.

Judges is a delightful getaway for families, couples and business travellers alike. There are no fewer than 21 special breaks available, such as the 'Anniversary Celebration', or 'Mother and Daughter Retreat', which include health treatments, tickets to local attractions and other great treats. Other breaks include the, 'Wine Appreciation Weekend' or the 'Helicopter Flying Experience'.

A terrific base for exploring the moors, visiting the ancient abbeys of Rosedale and Rievaulx or Mount Grace Priory, and heading to the coast for Whitby, where Bram Stoker wrote Dracula, fossil-hunting is a must, and Captain Cook is celebrated with his own museum and monument.

LOCATION

*From A19, take A67 towards Yarm.
The hotel is on left hand side just
after Kirklevington village.*

NORTH

❝ *Let me die here!* ❞

Barry Wilton, Berkshire

Lakeside house

LAKESHORE HOUSE

Simply the best view in England

That's according to the Robinsons, who have turned their much-loved family home into a stunning bed and breakfast hotel and relaxing base for exploring the Lake District.

Cast aside any prejudices about B&B because this is the deluxe end of the market offering three architect-designed suites in a modern guest wing projecting from the main house. On the first floor, the Wordsworth and Ruskin suites have private balconies overlooking the lake, while below the Beatrix Potter suite boasts its own sitting room and patio. The rooms have been furnished in a cosy and comfortable mix of antique and modern pieces and there is a strong sense of unwinding in the atmosphere of a private home.

Guests can wander in the gardens and enjoy the huge, airy conservatory with its indoor swimming pool. Keith and Penelope's hearty English or continental breakfasts are served here, and it is a great place to plan the day ahead. The Lake District National Park Visitor Centre is right next door, where ferries depart for destinations around the lake. Climbing, boating and waterski-ing can be arranged locally,

and there are numerous good pubs and restaurants for dining out.

LOCATION

Exit M6 at Junction 36. Turn left onto A591. Drive through Windermere following signs for Brockhole Visitor Centre. The hotel entrance is on the left, just after Brockhole.

Ecclerigg, Windermere, Cumbria LA23 1LJ

**Telephone 015394 33202
Fax 015394 33213**

E-mail: *lakeshore@bestloved.com*

OWNERS
Keith and Penelope Robinson

ROOM RATES
Single occupancy	£85
3 Suites	£130 - £170

Includes breakfast, service and VAT

CHARGE/CREDIT CARDS
MC • JCB • VI

RATINGS & AWARDS
E.T.C. ◆◆◆◆◆
A.A. ◆◆◆◆◆ *Premier Collection
Guest Accomodation of the Year -
Best in England 2002/2003
Cumbria Tourist Board
'Best B & B Award 2001'*

FACILITIES
On site: *Garden, croquet, indoor pool,
health & beauty, sauna
3 meeting rooms/max 10 people*
Nearby: *Golf, fishing, riding*

RESTRICTIONS
*No facilities for disabled guests
No children under 12 years
No smoking throughout
No pets*

ATTRACTIONS
*Lake Windermere, Levens Hall,
Wordsworth's Dove Cottage,
Beatrix Potter's Home and Museum,
Steamboat Museum, lake cruises*

AFFILIATIONS
Independent

NEAREST
*MAJOR CITY:
Manchester - 90 miles/1 ½ hrs*

*MAJOR AIRPORT:
Manchester - 90 miles/1 ½ hrs*

*RAILWAY STATION:
Windermere - 3 miles/5 mins*

RESERVATIONS
*Direct with hotel
Quote **Best Loved***

ACCESS CODES
Not applicable

NORTH

● *Map p.466*
ref: B6

> ❝ *The welcoming atmosphere, good food and magnificent views will mean you'll readily return to Linthwaite . . .* ❞
>
> *Los Angeles Times*

LINTHWAITE HOUSE

Victorian country house

NORTH

**Crook Road, Windermere,
The Lake District LA23 3JA**
Telephone 015394 88600
Fax 015394 88601

E-mail: *linthwaite@bestloved.com*

OWNER
Mike Bevans

ROOM RATES
1 Single	£94 - £127
9 Doubles/Twins	£99 - £165
3 Superior Doubles/Twins	£176 - £198
12 Lake/Garden views	£198 - £231
1 Suite	£242 - £286

Includes full breakfast and VAT

CHARGE/CREDIT CARDS

 • DC • JCB • MC • VI

RATINGS & AWARDS
E.T.C. ★★★ *Gold Award*
R.A.C. Blue Ribbon ★★★ *Dining Award 3*
A.A. ★★★ ❀❀ *Top 200 - 02/03*
England for Excellence Award
A.A. Courtesy & Care Award

FACILITIES
On site: *Garden, fishing, croquet, bicycles
Licensed for weddings
3 meeting rooms/max 60 people*
Nearby: *Golf, riding, tennis,
watersports, leisure spa*

RESTRICTIONS
*Limited facilities for disabled guests
No children under 7 years in restaurant
Smoking in bar only, No pets*

ATTRACTIONS
*Beatrix Potter's Home & Museum,
Wordsworth's Dove Cottage,
Lake Windermere, Sizergh Castle,
Levens Hall & Topiary Gardens*

AFFILIATIONS
*The Celebrated Hotels Collection
Grand Heritage Hotels*

NEAREST
MAJOR CITY:
Manchester - 95 miles/1 ¾ hrs
MAJOR AIRPORT:
Manchester - 95 miles/1 ¾ hrs
RAILWAY STATION:
Windermere - 3 miles/10 mins

RESERVATIONS
*Toll free in US: 800-322-2403
or 888-93-GRAND*
Quote **Best Loved**

ACCESS CODES
*AMADEUS UI CAXLHH
APOLLO/GALILEO UI 48735
SABRE/ABACUS UI 35752
WORLDSPAN UI 40645*

A relaxing break among the hills and valleys of the Lake District

Situated in 14 acres of glorious hilltop gardens overlooking Lake Windermere and 'Coniston Old Man', Linthwaite House is a haven for those with distinctive tastes, who appreciate the finer things in life. Breathtaking sunsets, superb scenery and a multitude of places of special interest within easy reach, including the home of William Wordsworth, Beatrix Potter's home, museum and gallery, historic houses, theatre and cinema. Sweeping fells and Lakeland villages have been the source of inspiration for poets and writers alike since time began.

Good food and fine wine served in a relaxed, unstuffy atmosphere and unpretentious surroundings combine to give you a rewarding break in the heart of the Lake District.

There are 26 rooms, some with lakeview, and a garden suite with separate lounge. Each has en suite bath/shower, bathrobes, direct-dial telephone, radio, trouser press, hairdryer and tea/coffee making facilities and stereo/CD player.

Whatever the occasion, whatever the season, Linthwaite House will be there to pamper you.

LOCATION

***On eastern side of Lake Windermere. Exit 36/M6
and A591 for 8 miles; first left at roundabout
onto B5284 to Crook. Hotel is 7 miles on left
(1 mile past Windermere Golf Club).***

" I have stayed in many small, highly rated hotels in Europe and at home. I have never found any to better this one "

Harold Goodman, Shropshire

● Map p.466
ref: C5

Georgian country house

LOVELADY SHIELD

Nenthead Road, Alston, Cumbria CA9 3LF

**Telephone 01434 381203
Fax 01434 381515**

E-mail: *lovelady@bestloved.com*

OWNERS
Peter and Marie Haynes

RATES PER PERSON
9 Doubles/Twins	£90 - £110
1 Four-poster	£110

Includes full breakfast, dinner and VAT

CHARGE/CREDIT CARDS

 ● JCB ● MC ● VI

RATINGS & AWARDS
E.T.C. ★★ *Silver Award*
A.A. ★★ ❀ 74%
Les Routier Hotel of the Year Award 2001

FACILITIES
On site: *Garden, heli-pad, croquet
Licensed for weddings
2 meeting rooms/max 45 people*
Nearby: *Golf, fishing, shooting,
riding, walking*

RESTRICTIONS
*No facilities for disabled guests
No children under 7 years in the restaurant
No pets in public rooms*

ATTRACTIONS
*Lake District, Hadrian's Wall,
Holy Island, High Force Waterfall,
Barnard Castle, Durham Cathedral*

AFFILIATIONS
Fine Individual Hotels

NEAREST
*MAJOR CITY:
Penrith - 19 miles/30 mins*

*MAJOR AIRPORT:
Newcastle - 42 miles/1 hr*

*RAILWAY STATION:
Penrith - 19 miles/30 mins*

RESERVATIONS
Toll free in US: 800-544-9993
Quote **Best Loved**

ACCESS CODES
Not applicable

NORTH

Hidden atop the Pennine moors is a guest book swelling with compliments

At Alston, you are at a watershed. As England's highest market town, it stands amongst the moors and fells of the North Pennines; located in a heatherclad wilderness with a choice of The Lake District, The Yorkshire Dales or the Border Forest to explore. Indecision has its own rewards: simply by staying put, you will discover a prolific wildlife and heritage galore: for example, the South Tyneside narrow-gauge railway starts here.

At Lovelady Shield, the pleasures start even before you arrive - winding up through scenery reminiscent of the south of France, the drive up to the house is truly one of the most beautiful in Europe. Once there, first impressions are to be trusted. Lovelady, nestled in three acres of garden upon a wooded hillside on the banks of the Nent, looks an absolute gem of a place - and it is. The guest book positively swells with compliments particularly about the friendliness of the owners, Peter and Marie Haynes and their staff. So, too, does the food which owes everything to Master Chef Barrie Gordon. Alas, Lovelady Shield is a secret that's hard to keep; but who could deny a friend such pleasure?

LOCATION

*2 ¼ miles east of Alston. The entrance
to the drive is at the junction of the
A689 and the B6294.*

THE MANOR HOUSE

19th century retreat

NORTH

**Northlands,
Walkington, Beverley,
East Yorkshire HU17 8RU**

**Telephone 01482 881645
Fax 01482 866501**

E-mail: *manoryorks@bestloved.com*

OWNERS
Derek and Lee Baugh

ROOM RATES
Single occupancy   £70 - £80
7 Doubles/Twins   £80 - £100
Includes VAT

CHARGE/CREDIT CARDS

• DC • MC • VI

RATINGS & AWARDS
E.T.C. ★★
R.A.C. ★★ *Dining Award 3*
A.A. ★★ ❀❀ 73%

FACILITIES
On site: *Garden, heli-pad
Licensed for weddings
1 meeting room/max 40 people*
Nearby: *Golf, riding, clay pigeon shooting*

RESTRICTIONS
*No facilities for disabled guests
No children under 10 years*

ATTRACTIONS
*York, Lincoln Cathedral,
Museum of Army Transport,
Beverley Minster, Thornton Abbey,
The Deep Hole*

AFFILIATIONS
Independent

NEAREST
*MAJOR CITY:
Hull - 9 miles/12 mins*

*MAJOR AIRPORT:
Humberside - 20 miles/30 mins*

*RAILWAY STATION:
Hull - 9 miles/12 mins*

RESERVATIONS
*Direct with hotel
Quote* **Best Loved**

ACCESS CODES
Not applicable

A civilised retreat surrounded by rolling wooded countryside

Overlooking horse paddocks and parkland, and set in three acres of tree-lined grounds, The Manor House occupies a tranquil position on the rolling Yorkshire Wolds. This 19th-century retreat is perfect for those seeking relaxation and luxury. Lee and Derek Baugh maintain a high standard in all aspects of entertaining.

The bedrooms have open, attractive views; guests will find themselves pampered with unexpected personal comforts. Relax in the drawing room with an aperitif as you anticipate the delights being prepared for you by Chef-patron Derek Baugh, formerly of The Dorchester.

Through his inspired culinary approach, there has evolved a distinctive, creative style of cuisine. Lee Baugh's confections are irresistible. The wine list reflects an informed interest in the best European wines. As an alternative to the restaurant, the conservatory is an ideal place to wine and dine on a summer evening.

A wealth of activities lies on the doorstep - the vastness of the North Yorkshire Moors, the rugged grandeur of the coastline from Bridlington to the old whaling port of Whitby and the many stately homes and villages.

LOCATION

Exit 38/M62 to North Cave and then B1230 to Beverley. After passing through Walkington turn left at traffic lights, following brown hotel signs. At first minor cross-roads, turn left again. Hotel is 400 yards on left.

" My guests were very impressed with the hotel, the food, the high standards of the rooms but more especially the friendliness and helpfulness of the staff "

C Hara, Lincoln Financial Group

Regency mansion

MATFEN HALL

A magnificent Northumberland landmark

As soon as you enter the impressive two mile driveway, you just know that you are going to find something special at the end. Sir Hugh and Lady Blackett have carefully restored the Hall into a magnificent country house hotel, set in some of Northumberland's most stunning countryside.

Nestled alongside the extremely pretty village of Matfen with an equally pretty pub where guests can become temporary 'regulars', Matfen Hall is finished to exacting standards. Each of the 31 bedrooms are wonderfully opulent, but traditionally so. At the same time, all the modern amenities are there. Great care has been taken to preserve many original features such as the ornate ceilings, the Drawing Room fireplace, and the Library, now a cosy, book-lined dining room. The quite magnificent Great Hall with its massive pillars is breathtaking and unique as a venue for private dining, wedding receptions and corporate use.

You don't have to be a golfer to enjoy Matfen, but if you are then the highly-rated course boasts a variety of teasing water features and several holes where dry stone 'ha ha' walls add a distinctly local note to the proceedings. Around

Matfen, take time out to visit Hadrian's Wall and Durham Cathedral to the south, and the glorious Northumberland National Park to the north.

LOCATION

From A1 take the A69 signposted Hexham and Carlisle. At Heddon on the Wall take the B6318 towards Chollerford. The hotel is on the right hand side after 7 miles.

**Matfen,
Near Newcastle-upon-Tyne,
Northumberland NE20 ORH**

**Telephone 01661 886500
Fax 01661 886055**

E-mail: *matfenhall@bestloved.com*

OWNERS
Sir Hugh and Lady Blackett

ROOM RATES
Single occupancy	£98 - £138
29 Doubles/Twins	£130 - £210
2 Four-posters	£226
Includes full breakfast and VAT	

CHARGE/CREDIT CARDS

 • MC • VI

RATINGS & AWARDS
E.T.C. ★★★ *Silver Award*
A.A. ★★★ ✿✿ 74%
*Excellence in England Award for
Tourism 2002 Gold Winner
Pride of Northumbria Small
Hotel of the Year 2001
Investors in People*

FACILITIES
On site: *Garden, heli-pad, croquet, golf
Licensed for weddings
7 meeting rooms/max 200 people*
Nearby: *Riding, fishing*

RESTRICTIONS
Pets by arrangement

ATTRACTIONS
*Alnwick Castle & Gardens, Millennium Bridge,
Angel of the North, Hadrian's Wall,
Bamburgh Castle,
Baltic Centre for Contemporary Art*

AFFILIATIONS
Independent

NEAREST
*MAJOR CITY:
Newcastle - 15 miles/20 mins*

*MAJOR AIRPORT:
Newcastle - 8 miles/15 mins*

*RAILWAY STATION:
Newcastle - 15 miles/20 mins*

RESERVATIONS
Direct with hotel
Quote ***Best Loved***

ACCESS CODES
*AMADEUS HK NCLMAT
APOLLO/GALILEO HT 22362
SABRE/ABACUS HK 49495*

NORTH

" Hotel of dreams, it's that extra special care that has given Mere Court such a first class reputation "

Living Edge Magazine

MERE COURT HOTEL

Edwardian country house

NORTH

**Warrington Road,
Mere, Knutsford,
Cheshire WA16 0RW**

**Telephone 01565 831000
Fax 01565 831001**

E-mail: *merecourt@bestloved.com*

OWNERS
Les and Lesley Hampson

ROOM RATES
Single occupancy	£80 - £140
31 Doubles/Twins	£86 - £140
2 Four-poster suites	£140 - £180
1 Suite	£140 - £180

Includes full breakfast and VAT

CHARGE/CREDIT CARDS

 • *DC* • *JCB* • *MC* • *VI*

RATINGS & AWARDS
E.T.C. ★★★★
R.A.C. ★★★★ *Dining Award 2*
A.A. ★★★★ ❀ 70%

FACILITIES
On site: *Garden, croquet
10 meeting rooms/120 people*
Nearby: *Golf, tennis, fitness, fishing, riding*

RESTRICTIONS
*Limited facilities for disabled guests
No pets, guide dogs only*

ATTRACTIONS
*The Trafford Centre, Granada Studios,
Historic Chester and Chester Zoo,
Liverpool Albert Dock,
Blue Planet Aquarium,
Everton & Goodison Park Football Clubs*

AFFILIATIONS
Fine Individual Hotels

NEAREST
MAJOR CITY:
Manchester - 8 miles/15 mins

MAJOR AIRPORT:
Manchester - 5 miles/10 mins

RAILWAY STATION:
Knutsford - 2 miles/5 mins
Warrington Bank Key - 9 miles/20 mins

FERRY PORT:
Liverpool - 30 miles/30 mins

RESERVATIONS
Direct with hotel
Quote **Best Loved**

ACCESS CODES
Not applicable

A heritage home making a dramatic entrance into the realms of hospitality

Right in the middle of the vale that sweeps between Roman Chester and the picturesque peaks and stately homes of Derbyshire is Mere Court. It was built as an Edwardian Country House in an area famous for its 'Magpie Houses', those half-timbered cottages you will have seen caricatured in story books. Set in seven acres of delightful gardens that include an ornamental lake, it is hard to believe that Manchester, its airport and its affluent neighbourhoods like Altrincham and Knutsford all lie so close.

Mere Court has recently been given a new lease of life by Lesley Hampson who has put her heart and soul, not to mention many of her own family treasures, into recreating the grandeur of this fine, listed building. She has a natural eye for design: subtle colours harmonise with luxuriant fabrics; the ample bedrooms are attended by stately bathrooms graced with double Jacuzzis. Two restaurants, fine food, light lunches in the lounge bar and afternoon tea continue a theme that is as elegant as the period setting in which it all comes so delightfully together.

This is a meeting place par excellence: within a year, it has become the place to celebrate a wedding and, with its state-of-the-art facilities, an ideal conference venue. A fine achievement well patronised by the locals and deserving of wider recognition.

LOCATION

**On the A50, Knutsford to Warrington Road,
1 mile west of junction with A556 on the
right-hand side.**

« The finest accommodation I have ever stayed in - not only in luxury, but more importantly, service and attention to detail at all levels »

Ms W Butler, Arlington, Virginia, USA

● Map p.466
ref: E7

123

Queen Anne country house

MIDDLETHORPE HALL

An impeccable William III country residence overlooking York racecourse

'Tis a very pretty place' wrote the diarist Lady Mary Wortley Montagu, who made her home here in the early 18th century, and she would probably feel quite at home revisiting Middlethorpe today. The beautifully restored hall dates from 1699. Antique furnishings and paintings have been carefully selected to blend with their period surroundings and the public rooms are decorated in mellow tones with fresh garden flowers lending a charmingly informal note. In particular, the pale green drawing room has a marvellously relaxing and timeless feel, as do the comfortable guest rooms which are divided between the main house and an adjoining courtyard.

Middlethorpe is set in 20 acres of parkland and gardens, where guests can stroll in the glorious rose garden and admire the magnificent Cedar of Lebanon standing sentinel behind the house. They can also enjoy a gentle game of croquet or a session in the well-equipped health and fitness spa with its large indoor pool, sauna and steam rooms, gym and beauty salons. In addition to its prime location for racing enthusiasts,

Middlethorpe is ideally placed for visiting the historic city of York. Further afield are ancient abbeys, Castle Howard and the Yorkshire Dales.

LOCATION

From the A64 follow signs to York West (A1036) then follow signs to York Racecourse and Bishopthorpe. Middlethorpe Hall is on the right just before the racecourse.

Bishopthorpe Road, York, North Yorkshire YO23 2GB

**Telephone 01904 641241
Fax 01904 620176**

E-mail: *middlethorpe@bestloved.com*

GENERAL MANAGER
Milton Hussey

ROOM RATES
4 Singles	£109 - £140
17 Doubles/Twins	£160 - £205
2 Four-posters	£265
7 Suites	£230 - £340

Includes service and VAT

CHARGE/CREDIT CARDS
MC ● JCB ● VI

RATINGS & AWARDS
R.A.C. Gold Ribbon ★★★ Dining Award 4
A.A. ★★★ ❀❀❀
A.A. Top 200 - 02/03

FACILITIES
On site: *Garden, heli-pad, croquet, indoor pool, health & beauty 2 meeting rooms/max 55 people*
Nearby: *Golf, riding*

RESTRICTIONS
*No facilities for disabled guests
No children under 8 years
No pets*

ATTRACTIONS
Castle Howard, Fairfax House, Newby Hall, Fountains Abbey, National Railway Museum, Castle Museum, York Racecourse

AFFILIATIONS
*The Celebrated Hotels Collection
Historic House Hotels
Relais & Châteaux*

NEAREST
*MAJOR CITY:
York - 2 miles/5 mins*

*MAJOR AIRPORT:
Manchester - 84 miles/1 ½ hrs*

*RAILWAY STATION:
York - 2 miles/5 mins*

RESERVATIONS
*Toll free in US: 800-735-2478
or 800-322-2403*
Quote **Best Loved**

ACCESS CODES
*AMADEUS WB QQYTHO
APOLLO/GALILEO WB 14942
SABRE/ABACUS WB 4540
WORLDSPAN WB GB17*

NORTH

Map p.466
ref: B6

" *Diners are treated more like friends at Miller Howe* "

OK Magazine

MILLER HOWE HOTEL

Country house hotel & restaurant

**Rayrigg Road, Windermere,
Cumbria LA23 1EY**

**Telephone 015394 42536
Fax 015394 45664**

E-mail: *millerhowe@bestloved.com*

OWNER
Charles Garside

RATES PER PERSON
Single occupancy	£95 - £165
5 Standard Doubles/Twins	£80 - £135
6 Master Doubles/Twins	£99 - £135
1 Mini suite	£95 - £125
3 Cottage suites	£135 - £175

Includes full breakfast, dinner and VAT

CHARGE/CREDIT CARDS

 • DC • MC • VI

RATINGS & AWARDS
*R.A.C. Gold Ribbon ★★ Dining Award 3
A.A. ★★ ❀❀
A.A. Top 200 - 2002/2003
Courvoisier's Book of the Best*

FACILITIES
On site: *Garden, heli-pad, croquet
Licensed for weddings
2 meeting rooms/max 40 people*
Nearby: *Golf, riding,
fishing (permits provided),
complimentary use of leisure club*

RESTRICTIONS
*No facilities for disabled guests
No children under 8 years
No pets in public rooms*

ATTRACTIONS
*Lake District National Park,
Beatrix Potter's home and museum,
Steamboat Museum,
Wordsworth's Dove Cottage,
Holebird Gardens*

AFFILIATIONS
Independent

NEAREST
*MAJOR CITY:
Manchester - 90 miles/1 ½ hrs*

*MAJOR AIRPORT:
Manchester - 100 miles/1 ½ hrs*

*RAILWAY STATION:
Windermere - 1 mile/5 mins*

RESERVATIONS
*Direct with hotel
Quote* **Best Loved**

ACCESS CODES
Not applicable

NORTH

Priceless views and a peerless restaurant overlooking Lake Windermere

Charles Garside is so taken with the magical view from Miller Howe that he has a web-cam linked to his website so browsers can enjoy a remarkable real time lakeland vista 24 hours a day. This is typical of Garside's enthusiastic approach to running one of the Lake District's most renowned hotel-restaurants. A former international newspaper editor, he has returned to his Cumbrian roots and relishes every aspect of his newfound role from cherishing his superb long-time staff to entertaining his guests.

Miller Howe began as a restaurant with rooms founded by celebrated chef John Tovey, who remains a consultant. However, the handsome Edwardian hotel is a destination in its own right, stylishly furnished with oodles of antiques, paintings and objets d'art. The country house bedrooms have fabulous new bathrooms and are thoughtfully equipped with music centres, books, games and even umbrellas! The delectable Cottage at Miller Howe is close to the herb garden and has three suites, a kitchen and patio - ideal for private get-togethers.

New Head Chef, Paul Webster, has recently joined amidst much excitement. Undoubtedly,

there is a great deal to live up to but Garside is in no doubt that Paul will continue to delight guests and impress the critics.

LOCATION
A592 between Windermere and Bowness.

" The comfort and charm of the Hall, the welcome when arriving and the whole atmosphere, has to be experienced to be appreciated "

T Long, Newark, Nottinghamshire

• *Map p.466*
ref: D7

17th century manor house

MONK FRYSTON HALL

NORTH

Monk Fryston, Near York, North Yorkshire LS25 5DU

Telephone 01977 682369 Fax 01977 683544

E-mail: *fryston@bestloved.com*

OWNER
Lord Edward Manners

GENERAL MANAGER
Pam Smith

ROOM RATES
Single occupancy	£88 - £98
28 Doubles/Twins	£109 - £119
2 Four-posters	£140 - £155

Includes full breakfast and VAT

CHARGE/CREDIT CARDS
 • DC • MC • VI

RATINGS & AWARDS
E.T.C. ★★★
R.A.C. ★★★
A.A. ★★★ 70%

FACILITIES
On site: *Garden, croquet*
Licensed for weddings
3 meeting rooms/max 80 people
Nearby: *Golf, riding, flying*

RESTRICTIONS
Limited facilities for disabled guests

ATTRACTIONS
City of York, Castle Howard, York, Doncaster & Pontefract Racecourses, Harewood House, Yorkshire Dales, National Trust properties, Royal Armouries

AFFILIATIONS
Rutland Hotels Ltd

NEAREST
MAJOR CITY:
York - 15 miles/30 mins
Leeds - 14 miles/30 mins

MAJOR AIRPORT:
Leeds/Bradford - 18 miles/40 mins
Manchester - 75 miles/1 ½ hrs

RAILWAY STATION:
Selby - 7 miles/15 mins
Leeds - 14 miles/30 mins

RESERVATIONS
Direct with hotel
Quote **Best Loved**

ACCESS CODES
Not applicable

Heritage and hospitality close to historic York

The 17th century Hall of Monk Fryston is built on a site that dates back to the time of William the Conqueror. The Hall was purchased in 1954 by the late 10th Duke of Rutland. Its grey stone walls, mullioned windows and the coat of arms of the previous owners above the doorway certainly gives it the appearance of a gracious manor house.

The lovely gardens, with wisteria and rambling rose, are elaborate with ornamental lake and fountain. For all the grandeur though it is by no means stuffy and in fact the overall atmosphere is a very relaxed one. The staff are efficient but friendly and really go out of their way to make each and everyone feel comfortable. The bedrooms are elegantly styled and have the best of modern facilities including modems in most rooms. There are homely touches too such as fresh flowers.

The restaurant has an excellent, extensive menu with many international influences. The cheese menu is a treat and includes some local favourites. All manner of snacks are available too - something that is welcomed by corporate visitors.

All these things, plus its accessible location, makes Monk Fryston a great base for both business and leisure guests.

LOCATION
Situated on the A63, 3 miles east of the A1.

● Map p.466
ref: C7

"The food was so fantastic that the Palace would have approved and the atmosphere so relaxed I kicked off my shoes "

Carol Chester, travel writer

NORTHCOTE MANOR

Victorian manor house

Northcote Road, Langho, Near Blackburn, Lancashire BB6 8BE

**Telephone 01254 240555
Fax 01254 246568**

E-mail: *northcote@bestloved.com*

OWNERS
Craig Bancroft and Nigel Haworth

ROOM RATES
Single occupancy	£100 - £120
13 Doubles/Twins	£130 - £150
1 Four-poster	£150

Includes full breakfast and VAT

CHARGE/CREDIT CARDS

 ● *MC* ● *VI*

RATINGS & AWARDS
E.T.C. ★★★ *Gold Award*
A.A. ★★★ ❀❀❀ 70%

FACILITIES
On site: *Garden, heli-pad
Licensed for weddings
1 meeting room/max 100 people*
Nearby: *Golf, fishing*

RESTRICTIONS
*Limited facilities for disabled guests
No pets*

ATTRACTIONS
*Ribble Valley, Clitheroe,
Stonyhurst College, Whalley Abbey,
Pendle Witches, Ribchester*

AFFILIATIONS
Independent

NEAREST
*MAJOR CITY:
Manchester - 28 miles/40 mins*

*MAJOR AIRPORT:
Manchester - 40 miles/45 mins
Blackpool - 29 miles/35 mins*

*RAILWAY STATION:
Preston - 11 miles/20 mins*

RESERVATIONS
*Direct with hotel
Quote **Best Loved***

ACCESS CODES
Not applicable

Where lovers of fine food and wine may want to stay forever

Northcote Manor in the Ribble Valley, one of the great beauty spots of England, is owned and run, with great talent, by partners Craig Bancroft and Nigel Haworth. Together they have built up this small hotel in eighteen years to become one of the most successful in the country.

Northcote Manor is best known for its outstanding food and award-winning restaurant and was awarded its first Michelin star in 1996. Nigel Haworth, holder of the 1999 'Wedgwood Chef & Potter Trophy' for Britain's Top Chef, has a special love of traditional Lancashire cooking and he has recreated many of those dishes in a very different style, including a sticky toffee pudding that has been voted one of the best in the country.

While Nigel cooks and presides over the kitchen, Craig looks after the guests' needs in the restaurant and rooms. His special love is wine and he delights in personally matching food and wine for the guests.

There are fourteen bedrooms and one four-poster. Games, books, interesting ornaments and tea and coffee making facilities add to the home-from-home atmosphere. The very comfortable beds have prompted many visitors to ask where they can buy them. In 1999

Northcote Manor was proud to have been voted 'Independent Hotel of the Year' by the Caterer & Hotelkeeper - an 'Oscar' of the hospitality industry. On a final note, their policy regarding children reads, 'all welcome to experience fine dining' - admirable and refreshing we think!

LOCATION
**M6 Exit 31. Take A59 towards Clitheroe.
Langho is close to junction with A666.**

NORTH

Best Loved Hotels of the World

" Many hotels try what you have achieved - well done! "

Mr & Mrs R Lewis, London

127

• Map p.466
ref: C8

Country house hotel

NUNSMERE HALL

The style of a great transatlantic liner in the idyllic Cheshire countryside

The Brocklebanks' shipping company dates back to the early 1700s. In the 20th century, Sir Aubrey designed the Queen Mary. His son Sir John designed the QEII and became chairman of Cunard. It was Sir Aubrey who built Nunsmere Hall as his family home in 1898. Today, Nunsmere Hall echoes the style and eminence of the great transatlantic liners.

The setting is idyllic. This exquisite manor house is surrounded on three sides by a lake in its own wooded grounds. It has 36 comfortable bedrooms, an elegant lounge, a fine wood-panelled cocktail bar and a library.

The Garden Restaurant overlooks the sunken garden and in every way matches the quality of the house. Owners Malcolm and Julie McHardy are determined to achieve excellence. They have won a high reputation for exceptional country house food with a modern Mediterranean influence. Service by their young team is impeccable and the wine list is a classic.

Nunsmere Hall is close to North Wales, the historic Roman city of Chester and Manchester Airport. Liverpool, the Lake District, Stoke and the other Potteries towns are all easily reached by motorway.

LOCATION

On the A49 at Oakmere, near Northwich. From the north, leave M6 at Exit 19. From the south, leave M6 at Exit 18.

Tarporley Road, Oakmere, Near Chester, Cheshire CW8 2ES

Telephone 01606 889100
Fax 01606 889055

E-mail: *nunsmere@bestloved.com*

OWNERS
Malcolm and Julie McHardy

ROOM RATES
3 Single occupancy	£125 - £145
29 Doubles/Twins	£175 - £195
3 Four-posters	£250 - £350
4 Junior suites	£325 - £350
	Includes VAT

CHARGE/CREDIT CARDS

 • DC • MC • VI

RATINGS & AWARDS
A.A. ★★★ ❀❀
A.A. Top 200 - 02/03
A.A. Romantic Hotel

FACILITIES
On site: *Garden, croquet, snooker*
Licensed for weddings
4 meeting rooms/max 80 people
Nearby: *Golf, riding, fitness, tennis, racing*

RESTRICTIONS
Limited facilities for disabled guests
No children under 12 years
in restaurant after 7 pm
No pets

ATTRACTIONS
Chester, The Potteries,
Stapeley Water Gardens, Delamere Forest,
Lake District, North Wales,
Aintree and Haydock Race courses,
Oulton Park racing circuit

AFFILIATIONS
Independent

NEAREST
MAJOR CITY:
Chester - 12 miles/20 mins

MAJOR AIRPORT:
Manchester - 20 miles/30 mins

RAILWAY STATION:
Hartford - 5 miles/10 mins

RESERVATIONS
Direct with hotel
Quote Best Loved

ACCESS CODES
AMADEUS HK CEGNUN
APOLLO/GALILEO HT 26042
SABRE/ABACUS HK 51639
WORLDSPAN HK NUNSM

NORTH

• Map p.466
ref: E6

> **The skies were grey, the wind blew cold, but the warmth and comfort of the Pheasant's welcome shined on us throughout our short stay**
>
> *J & M Wix, Hessle*

PHEASANT HOTEL

17th century blacksmith's forge

*Harome, Helmsley,
North Yorkshire YO62 5JG*

**Telephone 01439 771241
Fax 01439 771744**

E-mail: *pheasant@bestloved.com*

OWNERS
The Binks Family

RATES PER PERSON
2 Singles	£63 - £68
8 Doubles/Twins	£63 - £68
1 Thatched Cottage	£65 - £72

Includes full breakfast, dinner and VAT

CHARGE/CREDIT CARDS

 • *DC* • *JCB* • *MC* • *VI*

RATINGS & AWARDS
E.T.C. ★★★
R.A.C. ★★★
A.A. ★★★ *71%*

FACILITIES
On site: *Garden, indoor pool*
Nearby: *Golf, riding, swimming, fishing*

RESTRICTIONS
*Limited facilities for disabled guests
Pets by arrangement
No children under 10 years
Closed 1 Dec - 1 Mar*

ATTRACTIONS
*Castle Howard, Rievaulx Abbey,
North York Moors National Park,
Byland Abbey, Nunnington Hall*

AFFILIATIONS
Independent

NEAREST
MAJOR CITY:
York - 22 miles/40 mins

MAJOR AIRPORT:
*Manchester - 90 miles/2 ½ hrs
Leeds/Bradford - 55 miles/1 ½ hrs*

RAILWAY STATION:
York - 22 miles/40 mins

RESERVATIONS
*Direct with hotel
Quote **Best Loved***

ACCESS CODES
Not applicable

NORTH

A picturesque hotel by the mill stream and village pond

The hotel, established from what was at one time the village blacksmith's two cottages and the shop, has been renovated and extended to make a very comfortable country hotel with 12 bedrooms, all with private bathroom. All bedrooms face either south or south-west, some overlooking the village pond and mill stream, the remainder, the courtyard and walled garden.

There is a small oak-beamed bar with log fire, a large drawing room which, together with the dining room, opens onto the stone-flagged terrace looking over the mill stream.

A large garden and paddock provide fresh eggs, vegetables and fruit to the hotel kitchen where the best of English food is produced under the supervision of Mrs Tricia Binks. Ample car parking is provided.

Harome is a small village less than three miles from the attractive market town of Helmsley and the North York Moors National Park; it is unspoilt, still retaining six thatched cottages (probably more than any village in North Yorkshire). There are seven farms, an inn and both a church and chapel.

LOCATION
Leave Helmsley A170 direction Scarborough, after ¼ mile turn right for Harome. The hotel is near the church in centre of village.

" *Quebecs will be my home from home in the North of England!* "

Peter Carraud, Donald Russell

● *Map p.466*
ref: D7

Victorian town house

QUEBECS TOWN HOUSE

Leeds City centre's newest boutique hotel is a Liberal success

Nothing confirms the rejuvenation of a city centre better than the opening of a first class boutique hotel. The Eton Group, who own a handful of chic townhouse hotels in London including The Academy and The Colonnade, have branched out beyond the capital and made Leeds their first stop.

Quebecs opened in February 2002 and is located in the former Leeds and County Liberal Club, a handsome high Victorian building right in the heart of town. The City Square, central station, business and fashionable shopping districts are a few minutes walk away. The historic redbrick building has been completely renovated from top to bottom and the original Victorian features immaculately restored. The magnificent main staircase constructed of dark polished oak is lit by stained glass panels depicting the Three Ridings of Yorkshire, and the first floor Oak Room is a work of art, decorated with delicately carved oak panels. Each of the supremely comfortable bedrooms feature controllable air-conditioning, CD players and music library, satellite television, and full communications hook-ups for the business traveller, including personal voice mail. Beds are made with crisp Egyptian cotton bed linen, fresh fruit, tea and coffee are provided and there is 24-hour room service.

LOCATION

Entering the city centre follow signs for the railway station. Join the 'Loop Road' which is clearly signed, and which leads into Quebec Street.

9 Quebec Street, Leeds,
Yorkshire LS1 2HA

Telephone 0113 244 8989
Fax 0113 244 9090

E-mail: *quebecs@bestloved.com*

GENERAL MANAGER
Grant Lowe

ROOM RATES
5 Singles	*£125*
5 Doubles/Twins	*£135*
13 Deluxe Doubles/Twins	*£155*
9 Executive Doubles/Twins	*£170*
4 Studio Suites	*£185*
9 Suites	*£195*
Includes service and VAT	

CHARGE/CREDIT CARDS

 ● *DC* ● *JCB* ● *MC* ● *VI*

RATINGS & AWARDS
WHICH? Hotel of the Year 2003

FACILITIES
On site: *3 meeting rooms/max 6 people*
Nearby: *Golf, leisure club*

RESTRICTIONS
No pets, guide dogs only

ATTRACTIONS
The Royal Armouries, Bolton Abbey, Leeds City Centre Art Gallery, Yorkshire Sculpture Park, Harewood House, York, The Dales, Harvey Nichols

AFFILIATIONS
The Eton Group
Summit Hotels and Resorts

NEAREST
MAJOR CITY:
Leeds

MAJOR AIRPORT:
Leeds/Bradford - 10 miles/20 mins

RAILWAY STATION:
Leeds - ½ mile/2 mins

RESERVATIONS
Toll free in US: 800-457-4000
Quote **Best Loved**

ACCESS CODES
AMADEUS XL LBALEE
APOLLO/GALILEO XL 29470
SABRE/ABACUS XL 54498
WORLDSPAN XL 41590

NORTH

In theory, you should be just like other hotels with high standards, but you're not. You must be doing something different, I just like it here

J J Hammond, Winchester

ROTHAY MANOR

Regency manor house

Rothay Bridge, Ambleside, Cumbria LA22 0EH

Telephone 015394 33605
Fax 015394 33607

E-mail: *rothay@bestloved.com*

OWNERS
Nigel and Stephen Nixon

ROOM RATES
1 Singles	£72 - £80
13 Doubles/Twins	£120 - £145
3 Suites	£160 - £175

Includes full breakfast and VAT

CHARGE/CREDIT CARDS

AMERICAN EXPRESS • DC • MC • VI

RATINGS & AWARDS
E.T.C. ★★★ *Silver Award*
R.A.C. ★★★ *Dining Award 2*
A.A. ★★★ ❀ *76%*

FACILITIES
On site: *Garden, croquet*
1 meeting room/max 35 people
Nearby: *Golf, fishing, free use of local leisure club*

RESTRICTIONS
No children under 8 years in dining room for dinner
No pets
Closed 3 Jan - 7 Feb

ATTRACTIONS
Wordsworth's Homes -
Rydal Mount & Dove Cottage,
Beatrix Potter's House & Exhibition,
Lake Windermere, Holker Hall,
Levens Hall, Lake Cruises

AFFILIATIONS
Fine Individual Hotels
Preston's Global Hotels

NEAREST
MAJOR CITY:
Carlisle - 50 miles/1 hr

MAJOR AIRPORT:
Manchester - 95 miles/1 ½ hrs

RAILWAY STATION:
Windermere - 4 miles/10 mins

RESERVATIONS
Toll free in US: 800-544-9993
Quote **Best Loved**

ACCESS CODES
Not applicable

www.rothay.bestloved.com

Relax and enjoy a Regency gem in the heart of Wordsworth country

William Wordsworth described the Lake District as 'the loveliest spot that man has ever known'. He shared his passion for its inspirational landscape of rugged mountains and reflective lakes, doughty stone villages and valleys with fellow poets and artists, as well as generations of visitors who come here to hike, sail, fish or just admire their surroundings from a lake cruise.

A quarter of a mile from the head of Lake Windermere, and within a short walk of Ambleside, Rothay Manor is a wonderful base for exploring the region. The elegant Regency house is set in its own peaceful grounds and has been personally managed by the Nixon family for over 30 years (brothers Nigel and Stephen are currently at the helm). There is a real sense of family pride in the hotel's warm and welcoming style, the thoughtfully decorated bedrooms and imaginative and beautifully presented food in the restaurant. Guests can pick up a free fishing permit or use the pool, sauna and steam room at a nearby leisure club without charge. The Nixons also offer a programme of special interest breaks between October and May ranging from painting and photography to walking, gardening and bridge. In particular, for one week in March

you can enjoy a Lake District Heritage Holiday, during which fascinating walks and visits will give an insight into the area's history and beauty.

LOCATION
¼ mile from Ambleside on the B5286 Coniston Road or B5285 from Windemere. The A593 passes by the hotel.

❝ Everything was up to and even surpassed your usual high standards that we have come to expect... One of my challenges is to find an excuse to return as soon as possible! ❞

Brett Warburton, London

131

• Map p.466
ref: B6

Country hotel

THE SAMLING

NORTH

Ambleside Road, Windermere, Cumbria LA23 1LR

Telephone 015394 31922
Fax 015394 430400

E-mail: *samling@bestloved.com*

GENERAL MANAGER
Nigel Parkin

ROOM RATES
Single occupancy   £135 - £295
10 Suites   £135 - £295
Includes early morning tea,
full breakfast, newspaper and VAT

CHARGE/CREDIT CARDS

 • DC • MC • VI

RATINGS & AWARDS
R.A.C. Blue Ribbon ★★★ *Dining Award 3*
A.A. ★★★ ❀❀ 79%

FACILITIES
On site: *Garden*
1 meeting room/max 18 people
Nearby: *Leisure centre, golf*

RESTRICTIONS
Limited facilities for disabled guests
No pets, guide dogs only

ATTRACTIONS
Wordsworth's Dove Cottage, Holker Hall,
World of Beatrix Potter, Lake Windermere,
Levens Hall & Topiary Gardens

AFFILIATIONS
Pride of Britain
Grand Heritage Hotels

NEAREST
MAJOR CITY:
Manchester - 90 miles/1 ½ hrs

MAJOR AIRPORT:
Manchester - 90 miles/ 1 ½ hrs

RAILWAY STATION:
Windermere - 3 miles/5 mins

RESERVATIONS
Toll free in US: 800-98-PRIDE
or 888-93-GRAND
Quote **Best Loved**

ACCESS CODES
AMADEUS UI CAXSAM
APOLLO/GALILEO UI 40415
SABRE/ABACUS UI 61298
WORLDSPAN UI 42537

An idyllic Lakeland hideaway with inspirational views

A few hundred feet above the shores of Lake Windermere, The Samling nestles amongst woodlands and landscaped gardens overlooking one of the finest vistas in Cumbria. The house was built for its views some 200 years ago and the timeless majesty of the scenery remains as magical as ever. Some things, however, are a little different and although this is the heart of Beatrix Potter and Wordsworth country, do not expect to find anything twee or olde-worlde about The Samling.

An hotel in the country that is emphatically not a country house hotel, The Samling combines the informality of a private house with profound comfort and thoughtful yet unobtrusive service that hints at telepathy. There are ten suites divided between the house and adjacent buildings set into the hillside. Deep baths, power showers, TV, CD, video, phone and fax come as standard; all rooms have seating areas, some have sitting rooms and open fires. Guests can relax in the drawing room with a drink, enjoy light and delicious cuisine and sample the excellent wine cellar. The Samling was designed with house parties in mind and can be taken in its entirety for 24 hours or longer.

LOCATION

Between Windermere and Ambleside.
From Windermere pass the Low Wood
Hotel and take the next right.

● *Map p.466*
ref: D5

SEAHAM HALL HOTEL & ORIENTAL SPA   *Luxury hotel*

**Lord Byron's Walk, Seaham,
Co Durham SR7 7AG**

**Telephone 0191 516 1400
Fax 0191 516 1410**

E-mail: *seaham@bestloved.com*

MANAGING DIRECTOR
Simon Rhatigan

GENERAL MANAGER
Jason Adams

ROOM RATES
Single occupancy	£185 - £600
18 Suites	£195 - £395
1 Penthouse	£600

*Includes early morning tea, continental
breakfast, newspaper and VAT*

CHARGE/CREDIT CARDS

 ● *DC* ● *MC* ● *VI*

RATINGS & AWARDS
E.T.C. ★★★★ *Gold Award*
R.A.C. Blue Ribbon ★★★★ *Dining Award 3*
A.A. ★★★★ ❀❀❀
A.A. Top 200 - 02/03
WHICH? Newcomer of the Year 2003

FACILITIES
On site: *Garden,
Oriental Spa, health & beauty,
Licensed for weddings
4 meeting rooms/max 120 people*
Nearby: *Golf, riding, tennis, leisure centre*

RESTRICTIONS
No pets

ATTRACTIONS
*Durham Castle, Durham Cathedral,
Crook Hall and Gardens,
Hadrian's Wall,
Newcastle and Quayside*

AFFILIATIONS
Pride of Britain

NEAREST
*MAJOR CITY:
Newcastle-upon-Tyne - 18 miles/25 mins*

*MAJOR AIRPORT:
Newcastle-upon-Tyne - 18 miles/25 mins*

*RAILWAY STATION:
Durham - 14 miles/25 mins*

RESERVATIONS
Toll free in US: 800-98-PRIDE
Quote **Best Loved**

ACCESS CODES
Not applicable

*Byron, Bang & Olufsen
and breakfast in bed*

Romantic, state-of-the-art, and unashamedly luxurious, Seaham Hall stands poised above the rugged North Sea coast and offers a sensational new take on the hotel scene. The house where 'mad, bad and dangerous to know' poet Lord Byron married is a truly contemporary chintz-free zone where the queue for reception has been replaced by a personal greeting at the door and guests can enjoy levels of comfort that verge on the decadent.

Each stylish suite is equipped with mood lighting, open fires, high speed Internet connection ports, and entertainment systems complete with the aforementioned Bang & Olufsen TVs, extensive film and music libraries. Most have fantastic sea views as well. In the generous bathrooms, baths are big enough for two and hands-free phones actually filter out water noises. You won't only want breakfast here, it can be quite difficult to emerge for dinner.

However, it is essential to sample the rest of the hotel from the restaurant, where the food eschews the over elaborate in favour of fine ingredients intelligently prepared, to the walk-through wine cellars. There are specially commissioned artworks, an Oriental Spa, and four superb meeting rooms featuring all the latest technology.

LOCATION

*From junction 62 of the A1M take the A690
towards Sunderland. At the A19 junction
turn right for Seaham.*

" *Whether for business or pleasure a stay at the Studley is like visiting old friends* *"*

L Ackerman, London

Contemporary hotel

STUDLEY HOTEL

NORTH

**Swan Road, Harrogate,
North Yorkshire HG1 2SE**

**Telephone 01423 560425
Fax 01423 530967**

E-mail: *studleyhtl@bestloved.com*

OWNER
Chan Bokmun

ROOM RATES
11 Singles £69 - £90
23 Doubles/Twins £85 - £120
2 Suites £100 - £140
Includes full breakfast and VAT

CHARGE/CREDIT CARDS

 • *DC* • *MC* • *VI*

RATINGS & AWARDS
A.A. ★★★ 66%

FACILITIES
On site: *Orchid Restaurant*
1 meeting room/max 50 people
Nearby: *Golf, swimming, leisure centre*

RESTRICTIONS
No facilities for disabled guests
Pets by arrangement

ATTRACTIONS
*Fountains Abbey,
Harewood House,
Yorkshire Dales,
Herriot Country,
York, Ripley Castle,
Horse racing*

AFFILIATIONS
Independent

NEAREST
MAJOR CITY:
Leeds - 16 miles/30 mins

MAJOR AIRPORT:
Manchester - 78 miles/1 ½ hrs
Leeds/Bradford - 15 miles/30 mins

RAILWAY STATION:
Harrogate - 3 miles/5 mins

RESERVATIONS
Direct with hotel
Quote **Best Loved**

ACCESS CODES
Not applicable

Lift the lid off an Oriental taste sensation in deepest Yorkshire

Adjacent to the beautiful 120-acre Valley Gardens and a convenient stone's throw from Harrogate's International Conference Centre, popular sightseeing and shopping opportunities, the Studley rejoices in one of the best locations in town. The hotel occupies a traditional Yorkshire town house and is well-known to discerning travellers.

The Orchid is their first class Oriental restaurant, where you can see the chefs cooking and which has a menu that reads like a gourmet journey through the Far East. In a clean-cut modern setting, authentic Thai, Malaysian, Indonesian, Japanese and Philippino dishes are skilfully prepared and presented. If the choice seems a little overwhelming the staff are more than willing to discuss your personal food preferences before making their recommendations. Meanwhile the comfortable guest rooms are being spruced up too. Traditional bedrooms are being renovated to be light and airy with a continental look and feel. Owner, Bokmun Chan, has used his international experience and flair to make this hotel an extraordinary asset to the area.

Harrogate offers a busy year-round calendar of events and there are many places of interest in the vicinity and curists can still enjoy a Turkish bath!

LOCATION

***30 minutes from York, Leeds, the M1
and M62, and 20 minutes from the A1
(main north/south route).***

● *Map p.466*
ref: B6

❝ My wife lectures in Tourism & Marketing, and she feels that your hotel displays levels of customer service that the rest of the industry should aspire to ❞

Mr David Abbott, Manchester

THE SWAN HOTEL

17th century coaching inn

NORTH

Newby Bridge, Near Ulverston, Cumbria LA12 8NB

Telephone 015395 31681
Fax 015395 31917

E-mail: *swancumbria@bestloved.com*

GENERAL MANAGER
Paul Roebuck

ROOM RATES
Single occupancy	£98 - £133
2 Singles	£78
47 Doubles/Twins	£150
6 Suites	£185

Includes full breakfast and VAT

CHARGE/CREDIT CARDS

● *JCB* ● *MC* ● *VI*

RATINGS & AWARDS
E.T.C. ★★★★
A.A. ★★★★ ❀ 71%

FACILITIES
On site: *Garden, fishing, indoor pool, spa, sauna, steam room, fitness studio, fishing, marina 3 meeting rooms/max 140 people*
Nearby: *Golf, pony-trekking, hot air ballooning, clay pigeon shooting*

RESTRICTIONS
No pets, guide dogs only

ATTRACTIONS
Lake Windermere, Beatrix Potter's House, Wordsworth's Dove Cottage, Levens Hall, National Park Visitor Centre, Holker Hall Lakeside Aquarium

AFFILIATIONS
Independent

NEAREST
MAJOR CITY:
Manchester - 80 miles/1 ½ hrs

MAJOR AIRPORT:
Manchester - 90 miles/1 ½ hrs

RAILWAY STATION:
Grange-over-Sands - 6 miles/10 mins
Oxenholme - 12 miles/20 mins

RESERVATIONS
Direct with hotel
Quote **Best Loved**

ACCESS CODES
Not applicable

A Lakeland hotel for all seasons

The River Leven begins its short journey to the sea from the southern tip of Lake Windermere. A few miles from its source, the river flows past the landmark Swan Hotel, a former 17th-century coaching inn by Newby Bridge. Today, after an impressive multi-million pound refurbishment, it has emerged as one of the most comfortable and well-equipped hotels in the region.

Very much an antidote to the classic country house hotel, the Swan offers all the facilities and service of a city centre hotel yet in a beautiful setting. Guests can still enjoy cosy traditional lounges with roaring log fires, the traditional décor and beamed ceilings of Revells Restaurant, and charming, thoughtfully appointed guest rooms. However the superb spa facilities are strictly 21st century and include a pool, sauna, steam room, state-of-the-art gym and a range of health and beauty treatments for the ultimate in pampering.

At the gateway to the Lake District National Park, the Swan is set in 14 acres. At the adjacent Swan Marina there are peaceful waterfront pathways inviting a gentle stroll. More active guests can participate in watersports and outdoor activities from golf and pony trekking to hot air ballooning.

LOCATION
At Newby Bridge on the A590 Kendal to Barrow-in-Furness road, 20 mins from Junction 36 of M6.

" The whole of the Swinside experience has been magic "

Paddy Burt, Daily Telegraph

• *Map p.466*
ref: B5

Victorian house

SWINSIDE LODGE HOTEL

A real discovery just a stroll away from the 'Queen of the Lakes'

Swinside Lodge is a delightful Victorian house within one of the most beautiful and tranquil corners of the English Lakes. It stands in its own grounds at the foot of 'Cat Bells', one of many favourite mountain walks and is a mere five minutes stroll from the shores of Derwentwater - 'Queen of the Lakes'. A regular launch service operates on the lake, providing a leisurely mode of travel to the nearby bustling market town of Keswick and other local beauty spots.

Wild life abounds and the area is a paradise for birdwatchers and for walkers of all ages. Others will find it an ideal base from which to explore the natural beauty of the countryside.

Swinside Lodge is fast gaining a reputation for its very comfortable and well-appointed accommodation and, in particular, for its award-winning cuisine served in the intimate ambience of the candlelit dining room by friendly and attentive staff. For your added comfort the hotel has a no smoking policy.

You are invited to share in the relaxing and hospitable atmosphere of Swinside Lodge where caring staff will help to make your stay an enjoyable and memorable experience.

LOCATION

M6 Exit 40. Take A66 bypassing Keswick.
Over main roundabout take 2nd left.
Go through Portinscale, towards Grange.
Hotel is 2 miles further on the right.

NORTH

Grange Road,
Newlands, Keswick,
Cumbria CA12 5UE

Telephone 017687 72948
Fax 017687 72948

E-mail: *swinside@bestloved.com*

OWNERS
Kevin and Susan Kniveton

RATES PER PERSON
Single occupancy	£77 - £98
7 Doubles/Twins	£75 - £95

Includes full breakfast, dinner and VAT

CHARGE/CREDIT CARDS

MC • JCB • VI

RATINGS & AWARDS
E.T.C. ★ *Gold Award*
R.A.C. *Blue Ribbon* ★ *Dining Award 3*
A.A. ★ ❀
A.A. Top 200 - 02/03

FACILITIES
On site: *Garden*
1 meeting room/max 20 people
Nearby: *Golf, riding, fishing, sailing*

RESTRICTIONS
No facilities for disabled guests
No children under 5 years
No smoking throughout
No pets, guide dogs only

ATTRACTIONS
Lake District, Brough Castle,
Beatrix Potter's House, Dove Cottage,
Rydal Mount, Arthur's Round Table,
Castlerigg Stone Circle

AFFILIATIONS
Independent

NEAREST
MAJOR CITY:
Carlisle - 38 miles/45 mins

MAJOR AIRPORT:
Newcastle - 100 miles/2 hrs
Carlisle - 38 miles/45 mins

RAILWAY STATION:
Penrith - 17 miles/20 mins

RESERVATIONS
Direct with hotel
*Quote **Best Loved***

ACCESS CODES
Not applicable

SWINTON PARK

Stately home

NORTH

**Masham, Near Ripon,
North Yorkshire HG4 4JH**

**Telephone 01765 680900
Fax 01765 680901**

E-mail: *swintonpark@bestloved.com*

OWNERS
The Cunliffe-Lister Family

ROOM RATES
Single occupancy	£100
26 Doubles/Twins	£100 - £250
4 Suites	£250 - £350

Includes full breakfast and VAT

CHARGE/CREDIT CARDS

AMERICAN EXPRESS • *JCB • MC • VI*

RATINGS & AWARDS
E.T.C. ★★★★ *Silver Award*
A.A. ★★★★ ❀❀ *79%*

FACILITIES
On site: *Garden, heli-pad, fishing, golf, croquet, riding, cricket, health & beauty, shooting, walking trails, cricket, model boat racing, boules, bowls, mountain biking, falconry, off-road driving
Licensed for weddings
7 meeting rooms/max 120 people*
Nearby: *Golf*

RESTRICTIONS
*No smoking in bedrooms
Pets by arrangement*

ATTRACTIONS
*Brewery Tours, Wensleydale,
Ripon Cathedral, Herriot Centre,
Fountains Abbey, Jervaulx Abbey,
Newby Hall, Harewood House*

AFFILIATIONS
*The Celebrated Hotels Collection
European Connection*

NEAREST
*MAJOR CITY:
York - 37 miles/50 mins*

*MAJOR AIRPORT:
Leeds/Bradford - 33 miles/50 mins*

*RAILWAY STATION:
Northallerton - 14 miles/25 mins*

RESERVATIONS
Toll free in US: 800-322-2403
Quote **Best Loved**

ACCESS CODES
Not applicable

A grand country-house experience near the beautiful Yorkshire Dales

Not many people lose the 'family seat' and then get it back again. The Cunliffe-Listers recently bought back Swinton Park and have turned this modest little pad - only 30 bedrooms - into a super hotel. In a 200 acre park with lakes and gardens, it developed over the years with the addition of battlements and turrets and enormous reception rooms as a Victorian 'castle'. For that real 'castley' feel you could chose the Turret room with its steep stairs between rooms, or one of the vast suites on both floors with fabulously draped half-tester beds.

Rooms are classified as dukes, earls, barons, down to mere knights and there is plenty of opportunity to do 'knightly' things - with falconry, riding, game and clay shooting, stalking and fishing. Alternatively try cricket or croquet, bowls or kite flying or, for more modern pastimes, there are mountain bikes, quad bikes, a fitness centre and spa treatments. Inside the gracious reception rooms include a private cinema, a snooker and Victorian games room and in the superb dining-room, the excellent Samuels restaurant where venison and other delicacies

from the 20,000 acre estate feature on the contemporary menu served.

LOCATION
From A1 take B6267 to Masham. Drive through town and follow signs for Swinton.

❝ We were staying in a real English home in another more peaceful and serene century ❞

Janet & George Railey, New York

Country house

UNDERSCAR MANOR

The jewel of the Lakes

'Today my companion and I took tea with the Oxleys at their exquisite house, Underscar. The house has been constructed on one of the most breathtaking locations that I have ever seen; set against the slopes of Skiddaw, and overlooking the tranquil Derwentwater. A lush garden surrounds the house filled with flowers and shrubs; with places to sit and admire the view. As I sipped my tea in the drawing room, a gem with its ornate plaster-work ceiling, I gazed down towards the lake and watched the sun setting on the water; it was a moment of rare, joyous beauty and I wish I could have stayed at Underscar forever.'

'The Diary of a Victorian Country Gentlewoman' - 11th May 1860

Today, 140 years on, Underscar Manor is a family owned and operated country house in the experienced and caring hands of Pauline and Derek Harrison. This breathtaking location is now in the Lake District National Park, designated an Area of Outstanding Natural Beauty.

The house is surrounded by forty acres of gardens and woodland walks, by a cascading stream. Its beautiful Victorian restaurant provides award-winning fine cuisine.

LOCATION

M6 Exit 40 towards Workington on A66 for 17 miles. At large roundabout, take 3rd exit and turn immediately right up lane signposted 'Underscar'. Entrance to drive ¼ mile on right.

Applethwaite, Near Keswick, Cumbria CA12 4PH

**Telephone 017687 75000
Fax 017687 74904**

E-mail: *underscar@bestloved.com*

OWNERS
*Pauline and Derek Harrison
Gordon Evans*

ROOM RATES
Single occupancy £120
11 Doubles/Twins £90 - £125
Includes full breakfast, dinner and VAT

CHARGE/CREDIT CARDS

 • MC • VI

RATINGS & AWARDS
Independent

FACILITIES
On site: *Garden, indoor pool, health & beauty*
Nearby: *Golf, riding, fishing, walking*

RESTRICTIONS
*No facilities for disabled guests
No children under 12 years
No pets*

ATTRACTIONS
*Lake District National Park,
Castlerigg Stone Circle,
Beatrix Potter's House,
Wordsworth's Dove Cottage,
Brougham Castle,
Penrith Castle*

AFFILIATIONS
Independent

NEAREST
*MAJOR CITY:
Manchester - 120 miles/2 hrs*

*MAJOR AIRPORT:
Manchester - 120 miles/2 hrs*

*RAILWAY STATION:
Penrith - 17 miles/20 mins*

RESERVATIONS
Direct with hotel
Quote **Best Loved**

ACCESS CODES
Not applicable

NORTH

Best Loved Hotels of the World

" The staff did more than necessary to make us feel welcome! "

Mr & Mrs J Capes, York

WAREN HOUSE HOTEL

Country house

NORTH

**Waren Mill, Belford,
Northumberland NE70 7EE**

**Telephone 01668 214581
Fax 01668 214484**

E-mail: *warenhse@bestloved.com*

OWNERS
Anita and Peter Laverack

ROOM RATES
8 Doubles/Twins   £120 - £140
1 Four-poster   £140 - £165
3 Suites   £165 - £195
Includes full breakfast and VAT

CHARGE/CREDIT CARDS

 • DC • JCB • MC • VI

RATINGS & AWARDS
E.T.C. ★★★
R.A.C. ★★★ Dining Award 1
A.A. ★★★ 68%
A.A. Romantic Hotel

FACILITIES
On site: *Garden*
1 meeting room/max 25 people
Nearby: *Golf, riding*

RESTRICTIONS
*No facilities for disabled guests
No children under 14 years
Smoking in Library only
Pets by arrangement*

ATTRACTIONS
*Alnwick Castle and Gardens,
Bamburgh Castle, Holy Island,
Farne Islands*

AFFILIATIONS
Independent

NEAREST
MAJOR CITY:
Edinburgh - 70 miles/1 ½ hrs
Newcastle-upon-Tyne - 45 miles/1 hr

MAJOR AIRPORT:
Newcastle - 45 miles/45 mins

RAILWAY STATION:
Berwick-upon-Tweed - 15 miles/20 mins

FERRY PORT:
Newcastle - 40 miles/45 mins

RESERVATIONS
Direct with hotel
*Quote **Best Loved***

ACCESS CODES
Not applicable

A gem of a country house amongst the treasures of the North East

One of England's most northerly Best Loved Hotels might well be summed up, 'we kept the best till last'. Waren House is the home of Anita and Peter Laverack who, during the last twelve years, have renovated and restored this lovely old house into an elegant 'Country Inn'. Set in six acres of mature grounds and walled garden, the hotel looks out over Budle Bay towards the Holy Island of Lindisfarne, only reached by causeway at low water.

This is the least populated part of the United Kingdom and even at the height of summer you can walk on miles of deserted golden beaches; visit ancient castles including Bamburgh, Alnwick, Lindisfarne and the ruins at Dunstanburgh; clamber over battlements including Hadrian's Wall; or have a round of golf on one of the numerous nearby courses before returning to Waren House, where a warm welcome, elegant accommodation, excellent food and a choice of over 250 wines awaits. For an extended stay there are two suites and one, the Edwardian, looks out over the walled garden and Cheviot Hills.

Waren House is within five miles of Northumberland's three main attractions: Farne Islands, Bamburgh Castle and Holy Island.

LOCATION

2 miles east of A1 on coast just south of Holy Island. There are advance signs from both north and south. Take B1342 to Waren Mill. The hotel (floodlit at night) is 2 miles from Bamburgh.

" A pleasant surprise for a weary traveller "

David Roberts, New York

• Map p.466
ref: C5

Country hotel

WESTMORLAND HOTEL

**Orton, Penrith,
Cumbria CA10 3SB**

**Telephone 01539 624351
Fax 01539 624354**

E-mail: *westmorland@bestloved.com*

MANAGER
Clive Watts

ROOM RATES
Single occupancy	£57 - £77
40 Doubles/Twins	£57 - £73
4 Suites	£84 - £100
6 Family rooms	£73 - £91

Includes breakfast and VAT

CHARGE/CREDIT CARDS

 • DC • MC • VI

RATINGS & AWARDS
E.T.C. ★★★
R.A.C. ★★★ *Dining Award 1*
A.A. ★★★ ❀ 71%

FACILITIES
On site: *Licensed for weddings
6 meeting rooms/max 120 people*
Nearby: *Riding*

RESTRICTIONS
*Limited facilities for disabled guests
No pets in public rooms*

ATTRACTIONS
*Rheged Discovery Centre, Dalemain House,
The World of Beatrix Potter, Lake Cruises,
Wetheriggs Pottery, Yorkshire Dales,
Lake District*

AFFILIATIONS
Independent

NEAREST
*MAJOR CITY:
Carlisle - 40 miles/45 mins*

*MAJOR AIRPORT:
Manchester - 95 miles/2 ¼ hrs*

*RAILWAY STATION:
Penrith - 17 miles/20 mins*

RESERVATIONS
Direct with hotel
Quote **Best Loved**

ACCESS CODES
Not applicable

An inspirational spot for business and leisure travellers

Nestled into the hillside where the Pennines meet the Lake District, the Westmorland commands spectacular views across moorland, hill and dale. It is hard to believe this country hotel lies a matter of minutes from the M6 making it both a convenient break on a long journey, a longer stay base for touring Lakeland and the Yorkshire Dales, and an inspired choice for special events from a wedding to a conference.

The hotel's bright and airy interior is an attractive blend of warm colours, Cumberland stone and handsome timber beams. There are picture windows in the award-winning Bretherdale Restaurant where the scenery does battle with the menu for your attention and each of the 50 thoughtfully appointed rooms comes with its own glorious view. As well as very comfortable standard rooms, there are Executive Rooms with extras like heated bathroom floors and little treats including cafetières and Kendal mint cake, and more spacious Junior Suites.

The Westmorland's high service standards make it a favourite with corporate clients. The six meeting rooms and conference suites are fully air-conditioned with plentiful natural light.

Audio-visual equipment, business services, tailor-made delegate packages and team-building activities are all available on request.

LOCATION
Easily approached from exits 38 and 39 of the M6 motorway. At the Westmorland Service Station, follow the 'Hotel' signs.

NORTH

NORTH

> *An intimate jewel. Warm and sophisticated with the gracious personal touch of Judith and Ryland* "

Olysia Tresznewsky, Wilmington, Delaware, USA

THE WHITE HOUSE MANOR

Georgian town house

New Road, Prestbury, Macclesfield, Cheshire SK10 4HP

Telephone 01625 829376 Fax 01625 828627

E-mail: *whitehsemanor@bestloved.com*

OWNERS
Ryland and Judith Wakeham

ROOM RATES
3 Singles	£40 - £95
6 Doubles/Twins	£70 - £120
2 Four-posters	£110 - £120
Includes VAT	

CHARGE/CREDIT CARDS

 • *DC* • *MC* • *VI*

RATINGS & AWARDS
E.T.C. ★★★★ *Silver Award*
A.A. ★★★★ *73% Town House*

FACILITIES
On site: *Garden*
4 meeting rooms/max 40 people
Nearby: *Golf, riding*

RESTRICTIONS
No facilities for disabled guests
No children under 10 years
No pets

ATTRACTIONS
Tatton Hall, Styal Mill and Park, Trafford Centre, Staffordshire Potteries, Chatsworth House, Lowry Centre Manchester United Museum

AFFILIATIONS
Independent

NEAREST
MAJOR CITY:
Manchester - 13 miles/30 mins

MAJOR AIRPORT:
Manchester - 7 miles/20 mins

RAILWAY STATION:
Macclesfield - 3 miles/10 mins

RESERVATIONS
Direct with hotel
*Quote **Best Loved***

ACCESS CODES
Not applicable

An entertaining hotel themed for the Millennium

Three reasons spring to mind for travelling to this part of Cheshire: Great antiques, superb stately homes and The White House Manor.

On entering The White House Manor, a beautifully restored Georgian house, you immediately realise that something different is afoot. For this Georgian shell has been transformed into a luxurious private sanctuary. The Wakeham's vision has given this small prosperous village a hotel of 21st century sophistication that defies its quaint rural setting.

To call the 11 bedrooms 'individually furnished' is an understatement. Each of the themed bedrooms exhibit an imagination, humour and laser sense of detail. Rich fabrics and fine antiques mingle comfortably with space-age bathrooms with Turkish steam room, whirlpool baths, and power showers with body jets. The year 2000 saw the addition of the Millennium suite, the Wakeham's idea of the future. Natural fabrics and colours form the backdrop for an ultra-modern glass bed.

The hotel provides breakfast and room service, other meals are taken at the award-winning White House Restaurant a short walk (and well worth the trip) to the village centre. The location also makes it a great first or last night stop before flying out of nearby Manchester Airport.

LOCATION

From M6, exit 17 take A534 to Congleton then left on to A536 to Prestbury. Passing Prestbury Golf Course, take right at first roundabout. Go over bridge and the hotel is on the right.

We really enjoyed our stay in Pickering and above all at The White Swan, the staff were attentive and the food the best we have ever tasted in England

M Irflinger, Germany

• *Map p.466*
ref: E6

Coaching inn

THE WHITE SWAN

Really good in every respect - with feasts to compete with a Hogwart's banquet!

Over the last few years almost every newspaper or a guidebook has waxed lyrical about the White Swan; about the charming bedrooms, the excellent food, the extraordinarily rich wine cellar, the top-class service or the even just the laid-back charm of this old coaching inn.

The talented Buchanans have exceptional skills. Deidre - one of the first Dames de la Jurade de Saint Emilion - has stocked the wine cellar unusually well with clarets back to 1934, and an outstanding range of Saint Emilion. They haven't overlooked a warming selection of malt whiskies and well-kept Yorkshire ales either. These accompany a well-executed menu of top quality but unpretentious food, made with plenty of Yorkshire produce.

After Marion refurbished the 12 bedrooms so effectively, she was invited to redesign a large five star hotel! Cashmere throws, antique French and brass beds, a Tuscan-style patio, giant baths, subtle colours and pretty views all add up to really delightful accommodation. The Buchanans are enthusiastic about the level of service they offer - including how to ask for a ghostly 'please haunt

my room' door hangar- a legacy of Harry Potter filming on the nearby North York Moor railway?

LOCATION

Pickering is on the junction of the A169 and A170 Helmsley to Scarborough road. The hotel is in the Market Place.

The Market Place, Pickering,
Yorkshire YO18 7AA

Telephone 01751 472288
Fax 01751 475554

E-mail: *whiteswan@bestloved.com*

OWNERS
The Buchanan Family

ROOM RATES
Single occupancy	£70 - £105
11 Doubles/Twins	£100 - £130
1 Suite	£130 -£150

Includes full breakfast and VAT

CHARGE/CREDIT CARDS

 • *MC* • *VI*

RATINGS & AWARDS
E.T.C. ★★ *Silver Award*
A.A. ★★ ✿ 75%

FACILITIES
On site: *Garden*
1 meeting room/max 45 people
Nearby: *Golf, riding, fishing, shooting, mountain biking, outdoor activities, para-gliding, gliding*

RESTRICTIONS
No facilities for disabled guests
No smoking in bedrooms

ATTRACTIONS
North York Moors Railway, Pickering Castle, York Minster, Castle Howard, Rievaulx Abbey, The Races, Outdoor pursuits

AFFILIATIONS
Independent

NEAREST
MAJOR CITY:
York - 26 miles/40 mins

MAJOR AIRPORT:
Leeds/Bradford - 60 miles/1 ¼ hrs

RAILWAY STATION:
Malton - 8 miles/15 mins

RESERVATIONS
Direct with hotel
Quote **Best Loved**

ACCESS CODES
Not applicable

NORTH

● Map p.466
ref: C8

"The food, the service and the rooms were all excellent, thank you for making our wedding day a memorable one "

S Hudson, Chester

WILLINGTON HALL

Elizabethan-style manor house

NORTH

Willington, Tarporley, Cheshire CW6 0NB

Telephone 01829 752321 Fax 01829 752596

E-mail: *willington@bestloved.com*

OWNERS
Stuart and Diana Begbie

ROOM RATES
1 Single	£70
9 Doubles/Twins	£100 - £120
Includes full breakfast and VAT

CHARGE/CREDIT CARDS

• DC • MC • VI

RATINGS & AWARDS
E.T.C. ★★★
R.A.C. ★★★ *Dining Award 1*
A.A. ★★★ 65%

FACILITIES
On site: *Garden, riding*
Licensed for weddings
4 meeting rooms/max 150 people
Nearby: *Golf*

RESTRICTIONS
No facilities for disabled guests
Closed 24 - 27 Dec

ATTRACTIONS
Chester, Beeston Castle, Tatton Park, Erdigg Hall, Staveley Water Gardens, Tabley - Tirley Garth, Delamere Forest, Oulton Park Race Circuit

AFFILIATIONS
Independent

NEAREST
MAJOR CITY:
Chester - 7 miles/15 mins

MAJOR AIRPORT:
Manchester - 28 miles/40 mins

RAILWAY STATION:
Chester - 7 miles/15 mins

RESERVATIONS
Direct with hotel
*Quote **Best Loved***

ACCESS CODES
Not applicable

The personal touch creates a memorable stay

Willington Hall enjoys a truly wonderful position at the foot of the Willington Hills with views that stretch across miles of unspoilt Cheshire countryside to the Welsh mountains in the distance. The Elizabethan-style brick house was actually founded in 1829, and remained in the same family for over 170 years before it was bought recently by Diana and Stuart Begbie.

The Begbie's have done a splendid job of rejuvenating the interior while preserving the integrity of the house. The traditionally decorated and comfy bedrooms offer oodles of space and large windows allow the light to pour in (together with those lovely views). The restaurant is open for lunch and dinner and there are bars in the Study and Drawing Room, or drinks can be taken out on the terrace. One of Willington Hall's chief charms is the relaxed and friendly atmosphere created by the Begbie's and their staff, which makes it a particular favourite with guests who value the personal touch.

Peace and quiet is ensured by the rural setting and 17 acres of gardens and parkland, but Willington is also conveniently located for road, rail and air connections. The historic city of

Chester is nearby, and North Wales and the Peak District are easily accessible for a day trips, as are Beeston Castle, Liverpool, Manchester, Staffordshire and The Potteries.

LOCATION

Take the A51 from Tarporley to Chester and turn right at the Bull's Head at Clotton. Willington Hall is 1 mile ahead on the left.

Different from even the best run hotel in the south

Sir Peregrine Worsthorne, *Sunday Telegraph*

● *Map p.466*
ref: B8

Victorian mansion   WOOLTON REDBOURNE HOTEL

Entertaining the entertainers in The Beatles home ground

Woolton is recorded in the Domesday Book and surviving reminders of its past are to be seen in 15th century houses and a sandstone cross in the centre of the village. It has also survived the urban grip of Liverpool's expansion by being declared a Conservation Area. Of its many listed buildings is The Woolton Redbourne Hotel, built by Sir Henry Tate in 1884.

The conversion from home to hotel is never easy and the wishful cliché, home away from home, not always completes what the imagination couldn't grasp. But here, we have an exception, not just because the transition has been very cleverly achieved, but because the rooms include the random clutter you find in your own home - albeit the clutter has class and comes from various antiquaria specialising in Victoriana. There are 20 luxury bedrooms including the Redbourne Suite which features a four-poster bed and a four-poster jacuzzi no less.

The service is exceptional: one guest reported that, on arriving late one evening, dinner was served in his room by the chef himself and a retinue of staff. You cannot get better than that!

And the food? Like the eclectic contents of the house, an entertainment to be savoured and appreciated by the connoisseur. No wonder visiting celebrities to Liverpool choose the Woolton Redbourne above any ordinary hotel.

LOCATION

From the M62 take Exit 4 and turn left onto the A5058. After roundabout turn left at traffic lights, the hotel is 2 miles further on.

**Acrefield Road,
Woolton, Liverpool,
Merseyside L25 5JN**

**Telephone 0151 421 1500
Fax 0151 421 1501**

E-mail: *woolton@bestloved.com*

OWNER
Paul Collins

GENERAL MANAGER
Debbie Owen

ROOM RATES
5 Singles	£68 - £112
12 Doubles/Twins	£99
3 Four-posters	£99 - £160
2 Suites	£135 - £160

Includes full breakfast and VAT

CHARGE/CREDIT CARDS

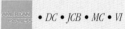 ● *DC* ● *JCB* ● *MC* ● *VI*

RATINGS & AWARDS
E.T.C. ◆◆◆◆ *Silver Award*

FACILITIES
On site: *Garden*
1 meeting room/max 20 people
Nearby: *Golf*

RESTRICTIONS
Limited facilities for disabled guests

ATTRACTIONS
*Beatles Museum and Tour,
Merseyside Waterfront and Albert Dock,
Catholic and Anglican Cathedrals,
Speke Hall National Trust Property,
St George's Hall,*

AFFILIATIONS
Independent

NEAREST
MAJOR CITY:
Liverpool - 7 miles/20 mins

MAJOR AIRPORT:
Manchester - 24 miles/30 mins

RAILWAY STATION:
Liverpool - 7 miles/20 mins

FERRY PORT:
Liverpool - 7 miles/20 mins

RESERVATIONS
Direct with hotel
Quote **Best Loved**

ACCESS CODES
Not applicable

● *Map p.466*
ref: B5

"*Gracious service, courtesy, consideration and attention to detail*"

P Heal

THE WORDSWORTH HOTEL

Village hotel

**Grasmere,
Cumbria LA22 9SW**

**Telephone 015394 35592
Fax 015394 35765**

E-mail: *wordsworth@bestloved.com*

GENERAL MANAGER
J G van Stipriaan

ROOM RATES
4 Singles		£70
28 Doubles/Twins	£130 - £180	
3 Four-posters		£180
2 Suites		£220

Includes full breakfast and VAT

CHARGE/CREDIT CARDS

 ● DC ● MC ● VI

RATINGS & AWARDS
A.A. ★★★★ ❀❀ 68%

FACILITIES
On site: *Garden, gym, heli-pad,
fishing, croquet, indoor pool,
solarium, sauna, jacuzzi
Licensed for weddings
3 meeting rooms/max 120 people*
Nearby: *Golf, riding, sailing,
walking, fishing*

RESTRICTIONS
*Limited facilities for disabled guests
No pets*

ATTRACTIONS
*Wordsworth's Dove Cottage and museum,
John Ruskin's home, Levens Hall,
Hilltop - Beatrix Potter's home,
Castlerigg Stone Circle, Keswick,
Brougham, Penrith and Sizergh Castles*

AFFILIATIONS
Preston's Global Hotels

NEAREST
*MAJOR CITY:
Manchester - 95 miles/1 ½ hrs*

*MAJOR AIRPORT:
Manchester - 100 miles/2 hrs*

*RAILWAY STATION:
Windermere - 9 miles/20 mins*

RESERVATIONS
*Toll free in US: 800-544-9993
Quote **Best Loved***

ACCESS CODES
Not applicable

NORTH

You'll wax poetic after staying at this lovely Lakeland beauty

In the very heart of English Lakeland, and the centre of one of its loveliest villages, The Wordsworth combines the sophistication of the first-class hotel with the magnificence of the surrounding countryside. Situated in two acres of landscaped grounds, next to the churchyard where William Wordsworth is buried, its name honours the memory of the area's most famous son. The scenery that so inspired the Lake Poets can be enjoyed from the peaceful lounges, furnished with fine antiques, or in the conservatory and cocktail bar, with the aid of a favourite aperitif or specially mixed drink.

The two suites and 37 bedrooms combine great character with comfort. There is an attractive indoor pool with jacuzzi and mini-gym.

The Prelude Restaurant named after Wordsworth's well-known poem, is the place to enjoy lighter or more substantial meals, skillfully prepared from a variety of fresh produce. 24-hour room service is available and the hotel has its own charming pub, The Dove and Olive Branch, a friendly meeting place for a traditional beer or tasty snacks.

The Wordsworth, known for its welcome, is very convenient for Lakeland's principal beauty spots and places of interest.

LOCATION
***Exit 36/M6 northbound, (A591). Follow A591
past Kendal, Windermere and Ambleside.
4 miles north of Ambleside, turn left into
Grasmere and hotel is on right next to church.***

Magnifico - great place, superb food and hospitality - top drawer

David B Macintosh Snr, Quincy, Mass, USA

• Map p.466
ref: D6

18th century shooting lodge

THE YORKE ARMS

Culinary marvel at work deep in the glorious Yorkshire Dales

Snuggled cosily into the Nidderdale Valley, Ramsgill enjoys one of the loveliest settings in the Yorkshire Dales and also harbours one of Britain's leading restaurants with rooms. Since 1997, when chef Frances Atkins and her husband Bill took over The Yorke Arms, this creeper-covered old shooting lodge has featured regularly in any list of Britain's Top 50 restaurants.

The Yorke Arms is everything a good country inn should be from the warm glow of log fires in the warren of downstairs rooms that contain the bar, the informal brasserie and the restaurant to the comfy en suite bedrooms upstairs. The nerve centre of the operation is Frances' kitchen, recently doubled in size and totally refurbished to cater for a new Cookery School offering regular two-day cookery courses for a maximum of six people. Frances stylish but uncomplicated culinary style encompasses the light and inventive and well as more traditional dishes accompanied by Bill's excellent wine list.

Naturally, Ramsgill is perfectly positioned for superb walks and exploring the beauties of the Dales. Further afield, favourite attractions include Fountains Abbey, the gardens at Newby Hall, or maybe a spot of shopping and sightseeing in the spa town of Harrogate.

LOCATION

In Ramsgill on the north western tip of Gouthwaite Reservoir on the Low Wath Road 4 miles north of Pateley Bridge.

Ramsgill-in-Nidderdale, Pateley Bridge, Near Harrogate, North Yorkshire HG3 5RL

Telephone 01423 755243
Fax 01423 755330

E-mail: *yorke@bestloved.com*

OWNERS
Bill and Frances Atkins

RATES PER PERSON
3 Singles	*£85 - £110*
6 Doubles/Twins	*£85 - £115*
3 Superior suites	*£105 - £150*
1 Four-poster	*£105 - £150*
1 Family room	*£85 - £115*

Includes full breakfast, dinner and VAT

CHARGE/CREDIT CARDS

 • DC • MC • VI

RATINGS & AWARDS
A.A. ★★ ❀❀❀❀ 75%
Yorkshire Life Magazine
'Chef of the Year Award 2002'

FACILITIES
On site: *Garden, heli-pad*
2 meetings rooms/max 40 people
Nearby: *Riding, fitness, shooting*

RESTRICTIONS
No facilities for disabled guests
No children under 12 years
Pets by arrangement

ATTRACTIONS
Ripon Cathedral, Harrogate,
Ripley Castle, Fountains Abbey,
The Nidderdale Reservoirs,
Yorkshire Dales

AFFILIATIONS
Independent

NEAREST
MAJOR CITY:
Harrogate - 20 miles/35 mins

MAJOR AIRPORT:
Leeds/Bradford - 25 miles/45 mins

RAILWAY STATION:
Harrogate - 20 miles/35 mins

RESERVATIONS
Direct with hotel
*Quote **Best Loved***

ACCESS CODES
Not applicable

NORTH

WALES

This is the land of song, of poetry set to music, of unique talents such as the irreplaceable Dylan Thomas and of a literary tradition that stretches back before the written word.

Welsh bards of ancient time used Triads, a literal device linking people, places or events in threes, to help them remember and pass on the oral traditions and histories of their land   During the thirteenth century many of these Triads were written down; a further major compilation during the fifteenth century created an abundant store of writings that mingled history with legend. These Welsh Triads have been dipped into time and time again for literary inspiration.

Lady Charlotte Guest, 1812-1895, daughter of an English earl, was one of a number of translators of the original Welsh to English who enabled a wider world to appreciate their beauty – and remarkable store of fact. Both Tennyson and Coleridge turned to these pages for inspiration.

Not only the literature of ancient Wales inspired the Great, the majestic beauty of Snowdonia has challenged experienced climbers for generations and William Wordsworth celebrated his climb to the summit in the closing of his epic poem, The Prelude. Wordsworth found more than mountains to inspire him in the scenery of Wales, in 1798, on a walking holiday with his sister Dorothy, he visited Tintern Abbey, the romantic ruins and the nearby majestic River Wye, the poetry his visit inspired is some of his best loved work.

The mystical beauty of ancient Wales lives on in this sheltered valley where, as in the old way, New Year is still celebrated on Jan 13th. Lady Charlotte Guest's translation of early welsh folk tales was published under the title The Mabinogion. Tennyson based his Idylls of the King – the most popular poem of Victorian times - on her work.

Like slate in a quarry the poems of RS Thomas are sharp and hard. There is an underlying reality that comes from Thomas' own life and observations and many of his works are social histories in themselves. When his collected poems 1945 - 90 were published Ted Hughes wrote,' this is the book I've been waiting for'.

Legend says Arthur's magician, Merlin sleeps on Bardsey Island, attended by 9 bards, in a castle made of glass. Present day, internationally recognised, poet and playwright Gillian Clarke takes schoolchildren to the island, using its mixture of myth and beauty to inspire their creative writing. The concept of a glass castle is a very Celtic one, here, in the sparkling spray it is easy to imagine its reality.

Dylan Thomas came here in 1949, it was to be his last home, The Boat House at Laugharne overlooks the glorious Taf Estuary and you can still see fishermen working in coracles. Thomas wrote Under Milk Wood here, the fictitious Llareggub is based on the town.

Hay on Wye is in border country. The town itself is at the junction of 3 borders – England, Brecknockshire and Radnockshire. Fertile soil, and an important local trade route mean that this is a place that has been fought over on many, historic occasions by the battling English and Welsh. The now peaceful town hosts the annual book fair that attracts visitors from all over the world. (www.hay-on-wye.co.uk).

Music and poetry are often intricately linked in Wales and many visitors to the National Eisteddfod find that even if they speak no Welsh they hear music in the spoken word. A fascinating mixture of song, dance, poetry and prose this event has its origins in the far past, druids walk amongst garlanded school children and competition for artistic recognition is fierce. (www.international-eisteddfod.co.uk).

Once again
Do I behold these steep and lofty cliffs,
That on a wild secluded scene impress
Thoughts of more deep seclusion; and connect
The landscape with the quiet of the sky.
The day is come when I again repose
Here, under this dark sycamore, and view
Those plots of cottage-ground, these orchard tufts,
Which at this season, with their unripe fruits
Are clad in one green hue, and lose themselves
'Mid groves and copses.

William Wordsworth: Lines Written a few Miles Above Tintern Abbey, on revisiting the Banks of the Wye during a tour. 13 July 1798

BOOKS TO READ

▶ Collected Poems by Gillian Clarke: one of the best-known poets living and working in Wales today. The poetry evokes clear, strong images; and this is one of the most popular works of welsh poetry.

▶ Lady Charlotte- a Biography of the Nineteenth Century by Revel Guest and Angela V. John. A Classic biography written from the subjects diaries – and she wrote them for 70 years.

▶ Dylan Thomas – Under Milk Wood: available to read or on tape or CD. Still inspiring inventive and dynamic direction and performances.

A special place to buy books:

Nooks and crannies to browse in at The Great Oak Bookshop, Llanidloes, Powys in the heart of mid Wales, new and 2nd hand books. Tel: 01686 412959.

LITERARY ATTRACTIONS & FESTIVALS

▶ Dylan Thomas – The Celebration at the Dylan Thomas Centre, Swansea. This year is the 50th anniversary of the writer's death. Tel: 01792 463980.

▶ Hay on Wye Literary Festival - www.hayfestival.co.uk.

▶ Museum of Welsh Life at St Fagins – a fascinating library of welsh cultural and social history -www.nmgw.ac.uk.

Felin Fach Griffin

Wendy Vaughan

Bodysgallen Hall

Fairyhill

A CULINARY Wales

Contemporary cuisine and an ancient culinary heritage, a remarkable combination to find hidden in tree lined valleys, on vantage spots with views of snow topped mountains or perched close to the sea. The places to find fine food in Wales are in some of the loveliest spots in Britain. And at times the ingredients used are as foreign as the language - laverbread, the tasty seaweed that once appeared only at occasional breakfasts is now offered in intriguing starters, flavourful canapés and other gastronomic delights devised by inventive chefs with a passion for local specialities. Cockles have always been a part of the Welsh culinary scene; family recipes for cockle pies and flans are part of the coastal tradition - now they're as often served with a Mediterranean flavour. The plump, succulent fish, cooked to perfection, that diners enjoy in elegant restaurants may have been caught from a coracle - stone-age design, tar lined, without rudder or sail. These tiny vessels, that once crossed oceans, can still be seen on rivers such as the majestic Teifi, not only at festivals but also at work, silently drifting over rippling silver water.

THE RECIPE: *Fairyhill Seabass - from Paul Davies, Chef Proprietor, Fairyhill*

INGREDIENTS

1 to 1.5 generous fillets of sea bass per person
2 shallots
half pint dry white wine
1 tablespoon cream
250g unsalted butter
Mixed greens - spinach, rocket, chard, leek, shredded mange tout

METHOD

Ask the fishmonger to fillet, scale and pin bone sea bass. Allow 1 generous fillet per person. If bass is not large enough allow 1 _ fillets. Cut to make 3 equal pieces per person.

To make butter sauce, chop 2 shallots, place in a small stainless steel pan with half pint dry white wine, reduce to syrup. Add tablespoon of cream and bring back to the boil.

Remove from the heat and beat in gently 250g butter (unsalted) in walnut sized pieces. When all butter is whisked in strain and keep warm.

In a very hot pan sear sea bass fillets turning once. Do not overcook. Heat a wok until hot add a little oil and stir fry the greens until just cooked, arrange on plate and place sea bass on top. Surround with seasoned butter sauce.

Tan-y-Foel

THE SIGNATURE: Tucked in the heart of the Conwy Valley, but with culinary influences as diverse as Europe and the Far East, menus at the prize winning Tan-y-Foel restaurant offer daily changing delights. Head Chef Janet Pitman's signature dishes combine the superb quality of local produce with imagination and colour - Mediterranean Melin-y-Coed goats cheese, Turbot with pasta nero and coral sauce, Rack of Welsh Lamb with minted redcurrant jus.

THE TRADITION: Culinary adventures at Egerton Grey grow from traditional Welsh specialities - Fillet of Welsh Lamb is seared and served with a roasted garlic and red wine sauce. Rack of Welsh lamb is with spinach and parsnip puree and a thyme jus. Tradition is a feature in this luxurious retreat where superb antiques, fine porcelain and paintings abound - the views are splendid and there's not another dwelling in sight.

THE SURPRISE: It's a pub - no it's not, it's Felin Fach Griffin, a real 'find' on the wild, unspoilt Welsh borders. A haven of comfort and wonderful food - with serious style. Recently opened by Huw Evans Bevan and

Felin Fach Griffin

Charles Inkin (trained at the world famous Ballymaloe Cookery School) this is a place to really enjoy the food - you can feel the care that has gone into sourcing the ingredients, and the talent that has gone into the cooking and presentation. This is laid-back sophistication that works.

THE VIEW: The superb food served at Bodysgallen has to compete for the attention of even the most dedicated diner - the views from the dining room are riveting. First, the gardens, overflowing with roses, with follies, with a rare, 17th century parterre where tightly clipped box hedges border scented herbs. Each season highlights new features to admire, in autumn a riot of rosehips, in winter the structure of the garden, a designer's delight. Spring's passage follows sweeps of flowering bulbs and then summer, luxuriant and scented. And for a backdrop? Conwy Castle and the mighty Snowdon.

THE CHEF: Wendy Vaughan, Chef/Proprietor at The Old Rectory Country House, is a Masterchef of Great Britain, a Member of the World Master Chef Society and has won a Michelin Star for several years running. Her restaurant absolutely drips with accolades. A recent reviewer for the Independent was typical of the enthusiastic multitude - 'The first night we had staggeringly tasty roast spiced monkfish with vanilla risotto in a red wine sauce and basil oil - and that was just for starters.'

THE WALLED GARDENS: Not one, but two kitchen gardens are being restored at Maes-y-Neuadd where precious slate walls create a micro climate in this mild corner of Wales. The possibilities for producing an abundance of succulent, fresh fruit and vegetables for the hotel and a unique setting for guests to enjoy are being fully appreciated and exploited. Strawberries and peaches, globe artichokes and a multitude of herbs will flank garden paths that would have delighted Peter Rabbit. Under the guidance of Chef Peter Jackson - and using his recipes - the hotel produces preserves called The Welsh Mountain Garden - as delicious as you would expect from such a setting.

Maes-y-Neuadd

Editor's Extras

St David's Day is celebrated all over Wales - and far beyond. The 'Get Welsh in Swansea' event held on March 1st includes a Welsh Food Fair, details at www.swansea.gov.uk.

Visiting a farmers' market always gives a great feeling of the food of the area. Aberystwyth Farmers Market is held once a month and there's produce from all around Cardigan Bay, dates from 01970 633066.

Welsh honey makes a perfect gift to take home - and goes well with Welsh Lamb; an easy way to add its flavour is to roast a small leg of lamb adding a few spoonfuls of wine and honey to the pan and baste often, finish with some finely chopped herbs.

Heather Hay Ffrench
Best Loved Food Editor

> ❝ *A haven of tranquillity within a haven of tranquillity. We left with a great deal more than we came* ❞
>
> Phil Jupituse, Comedian

Contemporary country house

BAE ABERMAW

Contemporary style overlooking Cardigan Bay and Snowdonia

Architects Simon Atkinson and Robin Abrams (he is British, she American) have brought their considerable skill and vision to bear on transforming this old Victorian hotel into a superbly stylish contemporary property with a spectacular position above Cardigan Bay. Enormous care has gone into restoring the handsomely proportioned rooms, polished wood floors, and marble and slate open fireplaces. The colour scheme is white on white, but far from being intimidating it is chic and fresh, and guests are positively encouraged to go and explore Snowdonia National Park or the beach, returning muddy (or sandy) and relaxed to enjoy deep baths and great food.

Food is a compelling reason to discover Bae Abermaw. Executive Head Chef Martin James and Head Chef, Kevin Williams are passionate about this corner of the world - something that is evident by the wonderful local produce used in many dishes. Refreshingly, they make everything themselves, even the ice cream and sorbet.

The national park literally begins at the back door and there are many great local walks, including a hike up Cader Idris. Golfers can sample notable courses at Aberdovey and Royal St David's, while a multitude of other sporting activities are close by.

LOCATION

From Dolgellau take the A496 to Barmouth. At Barmouth turn right, signposted Bae Abermaw. The hotel is 100 yards up the hill on the right.

Panorama Hill, Barmouth, Gwynedd LL42 1DQ
Telephone 01341 280550
Fax 01341 280346
E-mail: *baeabermaw@bestloved.com*

OWNER
Simon Atkinson

GENERAL MANAGERS
Martin James and Jan Williams

ROOM RATES
Single occupancy	£75
10 Doubles/Twins	£80 - £110
2 Suites	£100
3 Family rooms	£100
Includes full breakfast and VAT	

CHARGE/CREDIT CARDS

 ● MC ● VI

RATINGS & AWARDS
W.T.B. ★★★★

FACILITIES
On site: *Garden, croquet, Licensed for weddings*
1 meeting room/max 120 people
Nearby: *Golf, fishing, cycling trails, walking, climbing*

RESTRICTIONS
No facilities for disabled guests
Smoking permitted in bar only
No pets

ATTRACTIONS
Snowdonia & Cader Idris, Harlech & Caernarfon Castles, Portmeirion Italianate village, Ffestiniog Railway and Slate Mine, Mawwdach Estuary and Bird Sanctuary

AFFILIATIONS
Welsh Rarebits

NEAREST
MAJOR CITY:
Chester - 69 miles/1 ¾ hrs

MAJOR AIRPORT:
Manchester - 100 miles/2 ¼ hrs

RAILWAY STATION:
Barmouth - ¼ mile/5 mins

FERRY PORT:
Holyhead - 65 miles/1 ¾ hrs

RESERVATIONS
Direct with hotel
Quote **Best Loved**

ACCESS CODES
Not applicable

WALES

BODYSGALLEN HALL

17th century country house

WALES

*Llandudno,
Conwy LL30 1RS*

**Telephone 01492 584466
Fax 01492 582519**

E-mail: *bodysgallen@bestloved.com*

GENERAL MANAGER
Matthew Johnson

ROOM RATES
3 Singles	£109 - £160
15 Doubles/Twins	£145 - £260
16 Cottage suites	£170 - £260
2 Four-poster	£220 - £250

Includes service and VAT

CHARGE/CREDIT CARDS
MC • VI

RATINGS & AWARDS
W.T.B. ★★★★★ *Country Hotel*
R.A.C. Gold Ribbon ★★★ *Dining Award 4*
A.A. ★★★★ ❀❀
A.A. Top 200 - 02/03

FACILITIES
On site: *Garden, heli-pad, croquet,
tennis, indoor pool, health & beauty
2 meeting rooms/max 60 people*
Nearby: *Golf, sailing, watersports,
riding, fishing*

RESTRICTIONS
*No children under 8 years
No pets*

ATTRACTIONS
*Caernarfon Castle, Bodnant Gardens,
Swallow Falls, Penrhyn Castle,
Snowdonia, Ffestiniog Railway*

AFFILIATIONS
*Historic House Hotels
The Celebrated Hotels Collection
Relais & Châteaux*

NEAREST
MAJOR CITY:
Chester - 50 miles/55 mins

MAJOR AIRPORT:
Manchester - 85 miles/1 ½ hrs

RAILWAY STATION:
Llandudno Junction - 1 mile/3 mins

RESERVATIONS
*Toll free in US: 800-322-2403
or 800-735-2478*
Quote **Best Loved**

ACCESS CODES
*AMADEUS WB CEGBOD
APOLLO/GALILEO WB 14944
SABRE/ABACUS WB 11426
WORLDSPAN WB GB16*

Jewel-like formal gardens vie for attention with spectacular views of Snowdonia

One of the prime joys of handsome 17th-century Bodysgallen Hall is the 200-acre private parkland setting nestled on a ridge with views stretching off to the rugged heights of Snowdonia. Arranged around the main house and enclosed by mellow stone walls, the lovely gardens include a rare and intricate parterre planted with sweet-smelling herbs, a rose garden and several follies as well as a croquet lawn and tennis courts. The kitchen garden is also an important feature, contributing fresh ingredients for the dining room, which skilfully presents the best of local produce.

The interior of the hall has been beautifully restored and furnished with an eye to both comfort and style. Of special note is the oak-panelled drawing room with its tiled fireplaces and stone mullioned windows providing a relaxing and peaceful retreat for guests. There are 19 attractive and very comfortable bedrooms in the main house and 16 cottages in the grounds for guests who prefer a greater degree of privacy. Several cottages are adjacent to the first class spa, where guests enjoy unlimited use of the large indoor pool, spa bath, sauna, steam room and gym, while three beauty salons offer a range of treatments.

LOCATION

*Take the A55 expressway from Chester to its intersection with the A470 then follow A470 towards Llandudno for 2 miles.
The hotel is on the right.*

*" **We look forward to future visits with eager anticipation** "*

Tony & Judy Asbury, Buckinghamshire

Victorian mansion — BONTDDU HALL HOTEL

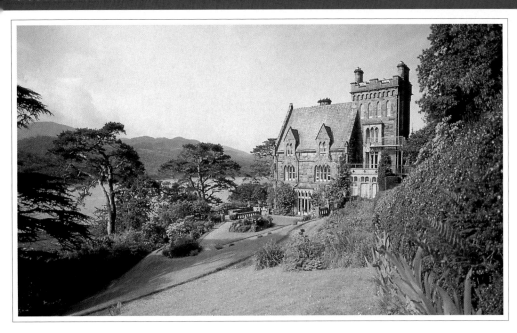

WALES

Bontddu, Near Dolgellau, Gwynedd LL40 2UF

Telephone 01341 430661
Fax 01341 430284

E-mail: *bontddu@bestloved.com*

GENERAL MANAGER
Noel Williams

ROOM RATES
2 Singles	£61 - £71
13 Doubles/Twins	£110 - £130
1 Four-poster	£160
3 Suites	£160

Includes full breakfast and VAT

CHARGE/CREDIT CARDS
DC • JCB • MC • VI

RATINGS & AWARDS
R.A.C. ★★★ *Dining Award 2*
A.A. ★★★ ❀❀ *70%*
A.A. Courtesy & Care Award

FACILITIES
On site: *Garden*
Licensed for weddings
2 meeting rooms/max 140 people
Nearby: *Golf, riding, mountain walking*
& biking, fishing, dry ski slope

RESTRICTIONS
No facilities for disabled guests
No children under 3 years
Pets by arrangement, £10 surcharge

ATTRACTIONS
Snowdon Mountain Railway,
Harlech Castle, Caernarfon Castle,
Dinas Oleu, Bala Lake,
Portmeirion Italianate village

AFFILIATIONS
Independent

NEAREST
MAJOR CITY:
Chester - 70 miles/1 ½ hrs

MAJOR AIRPORT:
Manchester - 120 miles/2 hrs

RAILWAY STATION:
Barmouth - 5 miles/10 mins

FERRY PORT:
Holyhead - 75 miles/1 ½ hrs

RESERVATIONS
Direct with hotel
*Quote **Best Loved***

ACCESS CODES
Not applicable

An historic home that has played host to three great Prime Ministers

This Victorian mansion is set in 14 acres of grounds with a profusion of azaleas, camellias, and rhododendrons against a backdrop of mountains and a river estuary. The magical views are amongst the finest in Wales. The house was built by Charles Beale in 1873, father-in-law of Joseph Chamberlain, a Victorian politician, whose son, Neville Chamberlain, became Prime Minister in the 1930s.

Bontddu Hall has a well-earned reputation for high standards and attention to detail. There are 19 well-appointed bedrooms and three suites - Churchill, Chamberlain, and Lloyd George - named after previous guests. There is also some self-catering accommodation for two to six people.

The cuisine is classic in style, using the best of fresh local produce - Welsh mountain lamb, Mawddach salmon, Cardigan Bay lobster. A fine wine cellar complements the food.

Bontddu Hall is in Snowdonia National Park. There are championship links golf courses at Harlech and Aberdyfi and historic castles in all directions. The locality provides for hillwalking,

pony trekking, exploring slate and gold mines, bird watching, sea and river fishing and even narrow gauge steam railways.

LOCATION
Turn off A470 north of Dolgellau, on to A496 (direction Barmouth). 2 miles to village of Bontddu, hotel is on the right as you come into the village.

❝ Never fails to live up to all expectations. A haven! ❞

George & Vicki Walker, Cheshire

- Map p.468
  ref: C5

THE CROWN AT WHITEBROOK

17th century inn

Whitebrook, Monmouth, Monmouthshire NP25 4TX

Telephone 01600 860254
Fax 01600 860607

E-mail: *crownwales@bestloved.com*

OWNERS
Angela and Elizabeth Barbara

ROOM RATES
Single occupancy	£55
10 Doubles/Twins	£90
1 Four-poster	£95
Includes full breakfast and VAT	

CHARGE/CREDIT CARDS
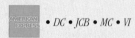 • *DC • JCB • MC • VI*

RATINGS & AWARDS
W.T.B. ★★★ *Restaurant with Rooms*
A.A. ❀❀

FACILITIES
On site: *Garden, croquet*
2 meeting rooms/max 22 people
Nearby: *Golf, riding, fishing*

RESTRICTIONS
No facilities for disabled guests
No children under 12 years
Smoking in lounge only
Closed Christmas & New Year

ATTRACTIONS
Tintern Abbey, Chepstow Castle,
Forest of Dean, Raglan Castle,
Brecon Beacons, Wye Valley,
The Sugar Loaf Mountain,
Ross on Wye

AFFILIATIONS
Welsh Rarebits

NEAREST
MAJOR CITY:
Cardiff - 20 miles/40 mins

MAJOR AIRPORT:
London Heathrow - 100 miles/1 ½ hrs

RAILWAY STATION:
Chepstow - 12 miles/15 mins

RESERVATIONS
Direct with hotel
Quote **Best Loved**

ACCESS CODES
Not applicable

WALES

A delectable auberge in the depths of the Wye Valley

A mile from the River Wye, a tiny lane burrows between steep green banks into the remote heart of the Whitebrook Valley. Here, all but enveloped in the leafy embrace of Tintern Forest and a silence so profound it is almost unnerving (no mobile phone signal either - joy!), the Crown is essentially a restaurant with rooms, an unpretentious, intimate haven of tranquillity in an unspoilt Area of Outstanding Natural Beauty.

The Crown's front door opens into a comfortable lounge where guests can relax, or gather for chat over after-dinner drinks and coffee. The informal atmosphere encouraged by proprietors-sisters Angela and Elizabeth Barbara-is one of the hotel's great strengths. However, the food is the main draw and the French-inspired menu employs the very best Welsh ingredients from new season lamb to delicious cheeses such as Harlech flavoured with parsley and horseradish, yet still surprisingly mild.

The bedrooms are comfortable, fastidiously clean and utterly peaceful with thoughtful little touches like home baked Welsh cakes.

Working up an appetite is no problem. Walkers can join the Lower Wye Valley Walk or the Offa's Dyke Path to Tintern Abbey direct from the hotel

grounds. Interesting local towns include Monmouth and the antique book capital of Hay-on-Wye and South Wales offers a veritable embarrassment of historic castles and keeps.

LOCATION

From Heathrow: M4 & M48 west, take first exit after crossing Severn Bridge & A466 (to Monmouth). At Bigsweir Bridge bear left for Whitebrook, hotel is 2 miles up on left.

66 *This is surely a piece of Welsh Heaven* 99

Janet Appleby, Cheshire

● *Map p.468*
ref: D6

Country house

EGERTON GREY HOTEL

Porthkerry, Rhoose, Nr Cardiff
Vale of Glamorgan CF62 3BZ

Telephone 01446 711666
Fax 01446 711690

E-mail: *egerton@bestloved.com*

OWNERS
Richard Morgan-Price and Huw Thomas

ROOM RATES
1 Single	£75
2 Doubles	£95
4 Superior Doubles/Twins	£105
1 Four-poster	£130
1 Suite	£130
Include full breakfast and VAT	

CHARGE/CREDIT CARDS

 ● *MC* ● *VI*

RATINGS & AWARDS
W.T.B. ★★★★ *Country Hotel*
A.A. ★★★ ❀❀ *73%*

FACILITIES
On site: *Garden, croquet*
Licensed for weddings
1 meeting room/max 40 people
Nearby: *Golf, leisure centre*

RESTRICTIONS
No facilities for disabled guests
Pets by arrangement
No smoking in bedrooms

ATTRACTIONS
Welsh Folk Museum, Cardiff Castle,
Cardiff Bay, Llancaich Fawr,
National Botanical Gardens,
Coch Castell, Brecon Beacons

AFFILIATIONS
Welsh Rarebits

NEAREST
MAJOR CITY:
Cardiff - 11 miles/25 mins

MAJOR AIRPORT:
Cardiff - ½ mile/5 mins

RAILWAY STATION:
Barry - 3 miles/10 mins

RESERVATIONS
Direct with hotel
Quote **Best Loved**

ACCESS CODES
Not applicable

WALES

The best of Edwardian splendour with service to satisfy even Jeeves

If you visit the excellent Welsh Life Museum at St Fagans, you will see many interesting buildings recreating Welsh life in the past. One missing exhibit though is that of the grand country house, but you only need to drive a few miles to find the perfect example. Just minutes from beautiful coast, mountains, Cardiff Airport and the M4, but totally secluded in seven acres of manicured gardens, Egerton Grey is a country house with the style of its Victorian heyday - try croquet on the lawn - and the facilities of the 21st century.

Furnished with a wealth of antiques and paintings, the elegantly comfortable public rooms include a grand Edwardian drawing room - ideal for weddings or conferences. The bedrooms are unusually large and have original Edwardian bathrooms with deep, free-standing tubs. However, the eccentricities of Edwardian plumbing are not part of the deal! Everything has been up-dated for the discerning traveller.

Dine in the mahogany-panelled billiard room where graceful table settings and fine china complement well-executed traditional country house recipes, the pride of the kitchen brigade.

Sparkling with loving care and smoothly professional service, Egerton Grey constantly delights its guests.

LOCATION
Exit M4 at junction 33. Follow signs to Cardiff Airport, bypassing Barry and turn left at small roundabout, signposted Porthkerry. After 500 yards turn left at hotel signpost.

• *Map p.468*
ref: C2

❝ We enjoyed your lovely hotel and found Wales to be filled with delightful attractions and great people like yourselves ❞

Louis & Molly Webber, New York

THE EMPIRE

Victorian resort hotel

WALES

Church Walks, Llandudno, Conwy LL30 2HE

Telephone 01873 860330
Fax 01492 860791

E-mail: *empire@bestloved.com*

OWNERS
Len and Elizabeth Maddocks

MANAGERS
Elyse and Michael Waddy

ROOM RATES
Single occupancy	£55 - £75
51 Doubles/Twins	£90 - £110
7 Suites	£100 - £250
Includes full breakfast and VAT

CHARGE/CREDIT CARDS

 • *DC • JCB • MC • VI*

RATINGS & AWARDS
W.T.B. ★★★★
A.A. ★★★ ❀ 74%

FACILITIES
On site: *Indoor pool, heated outdoor pool, health & beauty treatments, sauna, whirlpool & spa bath, steamroom, roof garden & patio*
1 meeting room/max 40 people
Nearby: *Golf, riding, fishing, sailing*

RESTRICTIONS
No facilities for disabled guests
No pets, guide dogs only
Closed Christmas

ATTRACTIONS
Snowdonia National Park, Conwy and Caenarfon Castles, Portmeirion Italianate Village, Bodnant Gardens

AFFILIATIONS
Independent

NEAREST
MAJOR CITY:
Chester - 50 miles/50 mins

MAJOR AIRPORT:
Manchester - 84 miles/1 ½ hrs

RAILWAY STATION:
Llandudno Junction - 3 miles/10 mins

FERRY PORT:
Holyhead - 45 miles/45 mins

RESERVATIONS
Direct with hotel
*Quote **Best Loved***

ACCESS CODES
Not applicable

Affordable luxury for all occasions

The Empire is privately owned and has been run by the Maddocks family for over 50 years. Helping Len and Elizabeth, are daughter Elyse and her husband Michael Waddy who, between them, offer some of the kindest hospitality in the region. Amongst the family treasures are wonderful antiques and one of the largest private collections of artists' prints by Sir William Russell Flint. You will feel at home here: the generously appointed bedrooms are complete with marbled bathrooms, TV and VCR (the videos are free) and modem connections for the traveller who wants to keep up to the minute.

There is an indoor heated pool with sauna, steam room and spa bath. Outside, there is another heated pool around which you can recline on sun loungers amongst the flowers. If you feel the need for greater relaxation, the therapist has a range of beauty treatments, aromatherapy, reflexology and Indian head massage.

Michael, with a gifted team of young chefs at his elbow, serves innovative fresh food daily in the award-winning Watkins & Co restaurant. Do not overlook the home-made bread and wicked desserts.

The Empire, set on the picturesque Victorian promenade and near the pier, offers special two-night breaks.

LOCATION

Exit the A55 at the A470 intersection for Llandudno. Follow signs for town centre, drive down the main street (Mostyn Street). The hotel is at the end and faces the town.

" **Peace, beauty and wonderful food and a great welcome** *"*

P D James

Map p.468
ref: C6

157

Georgian manor house

FAIRYHILL

Relaxed luxury at the heart of the Gower peninsula

The rolling green hills and moorland of the Gower Peninsula tumble down to the sea fringed by broad curving bays and wide sandy beaches. This was the very first landscape in Britain to be declared an Area of Outstanding Natural Beauty and where better to establish a gourmet sanctuary of character and distinction?

Fairyhill is a charming 18th-century house set in 24 acres of gardens and woodland with a trout stream and tranquil lake reached by meandering paths. Here, the atmosphere is intimate and informal, there is a warm welcome in the cosy, well-stocked bar and a supremely relaxing lounge which opens onto the garden terrace. Eight delightful and thoughtfully appointed bedrooms offer every comfort from CD players to soft lighting.

For many visitors the highlight of Fairyhill is the restaurant , which is widely regarded as one of the finest in Wales. Seasonal menus reflect the very best of fresh local produce from scrambled eggs with Penclawdd cockles to fillet of Welsh Black beef and seared local sea bass, and there is an award-winning wine list.

Local diversions include lovely beaches, the spectacular National Trust site at Worm's Head, and the National Botanical Garden of Wales.

LOCATION

Take Exit 47 off M4 and follow signs to Gower/Gowerton. From Gowerton go through Penclawdd, signposted Llanridian and Crofty. Fairyhill is 1 mile past Greyhound Inn.

Reynoldston, Gower, Swansea SA3 1BS

Telephone 01792 390139
Fax 01792 391358

E-mail: *fairyhill@bestloved.com*

OWNERS
Andrew Hetherington and Paul Davies

ROOM RATES
Single occupancy   £120 - £225
8 Doubles   £140 - £245
*Includes early morning tea,
full breakfast and VAT*

CHARGE/CREDIT CARDS

 • *JCB* • *MC* • *VI*

RATINGS & AWARDS
W.T.B. ★★★★★ *Country Hotel*
R.A.C. Gold Ribbon ★★ *Dining Award 3*
A.A. ★★ ✿✿✿
A.A. Top 200 - 02/03
A.A. Wine List of the Year

FACILITIES
On site: *Garden, heli-pad, croquet
1 meeting room/max 40 people*
Nearby: *Riding, fishing, surfing, sailing*

RESTRICTIONS
*No facilities for disabled guests
No children under 8 years
No pets
Closed 1 - 17 Jan*

ATTRACTIONS
*The Gower Peninsula, Swansea,
Weobley Castle, Aberglasney Gardens,
National Botanical Garden of Wales*

AFFILIATIONS
Welsh Rarebits

NEAREST
*MAJOR CITY:
Swansea - 12 miles/25 mins*

*MAJOR AIRPORT:
London Heathrow - 170 miles/2 ½ hrs
Cardiff - 50 miles/1 hr*

*RAILWAY STATION:
Swansea - 12 miles/25 mins*

*FERRY PORT:
Swansea - 12 miles/25 mins*

RESERVATIONS
Direct with hotel
Quote **Best Loved**

ACCESS CODES
Not applicable

WALES

❝ Too many pillows, too cosy, too difficult to leave... ❞

Louise Sanders

THE FELIN FACH GRIFFIN

Restaurant with rooms

Felin Fach, Brecon,
Powys LD3 0UB

Telephone 01874 620111
Fax 01874 620120

E-mail: *felinfach@bestloved.com*

OWNERS
Huw Evans-Bevan and Charles Inkin

ROOM RATES
4 Doubles/Twins   £73 - £82
3 Four-posters   £83
Includes breakfast and VAT

CHARGE/CREDIT CARDS
MC • VI

RATINGS & AWARDS
W.T.B. ★★★★
A.A. ❀❀
WHICH? Hotel of the Year 2002

FACILITIES
On site: *Garden, croquet*
Nearby: *Golf, sailing, fishing,*
windsurfing, game shooting,
clay pigeon shooting, pony trekking

RESTRICTIONS
Limited facilities for disabled guests
Smoking in bar only
Pets by arrangement
Closed 25 Jan - 7 Feb

ATTRACTIONS
Hay-on-Wye, Powis Castle,
Brecon Beacons, Elan Valley,
Caerphilly Castle, Brecon Cathedral,
Black Mountains

AFFILIATIONS
Welsh Rarebits

NEAREST
MAJOR CITY:
Cardiff - 48 miles/1 hr

MAJOR AIRPORT:
Cardiff - 58 miles/1 ¼ hrs

RAILWAY STATION:
Abergavenny - 25 miles/30 mins

RESERVATIONS
Direct with hotel
Quote **Best Loved**

ACCESS CODES
Not applicable

WALES

Tradition, simplicity and comfort, brimming with press reports

The first sign that things are not altogether orthodox at the Felin Fach Griffin is the pink paintwork transforming this former farmhouse from rustic afterthought to eyecatching landmark. Welcome to a Welsh country inn entirely devoid of horsebrasses, Welsh love spoons and lashings of chintz. It is the brainchild of Huw Evans-Bevan and chef Charles Inkin who have carried their uncompromising belief in 'the simple things in life – done well' to a quiet Welsh valley in the shadow of the Black Mountains and the Brecon Beacons.

Tradition, simplicity and comfort are watchwords at the Griffin, rigorously applied to three of the most basic but vital human needs: to eat; to drink; to sleep. This, however, is tradition without unnecessary frills – the simplicity of cottage pine and fresh garden flowers tempered by the luxury of crisp bed linen and the dark gloss on a handsomely carved antique four poster. Charles Inkin's food is utterly delicious and beautifully presented but essentially uncomplicated and accompanied (naturally) by good wines and traditional ales. The atmosphere is informal, the setting impeccable. In fact, the

Griffin's seductive contemporary take on traditional innkeeping should be sampled at the earliest opportunity.

LOCATION
Located on the A470 Brecon to Builth Wells road. The hotel is set back on the left.

"*Of all the hotels that I stay at in the world, The George is where I choose to spend my leisure, pleasure and peace*"

Graham Smith, Toyota GB Ltd

● Map p.468
ref: C3

17th century inn

GEORGE III HOTEL

A house of great character in a wonderful location

The George III Hotel is situated on the magnificent Mawddach Estuary. The main hotel was built around 1650 as two separate buildings, pub and ship chandlers. The adjacent Lodge is a Victorian building built as a Waiting Room, Ticket Office and Station Master's house for the railway station, now closed.

Guests may choose between accommodation in the hotel or in the lodge. Every room is full of character, comfortably furnished and has a wonderful view of the estuary.

Great emphasis is placed on the food with Welsh lamb and seafood being the specialities. On fine days, bar lunches are served on the balcony and the non-smoking cellar bar is ideal for families.

The area is packed with romantic ruins and fairytale castles and a great way to sightsee is either on foot or on mountain bikes which can be hired locally. Or you can fish for salmon and trout, go clay pigeon shooting or power trekking or take a ride on one of the little railways in the area.

LOCATION

Turn left off A470 signposted Tywyn, approximately 2 miles, turn right for toll bridge, then first left for hotel.

Penmaenpool, Dolgellau, Gwynedd LL40 1YD

Telephone 01341 422525
Fax 01341 423565

E-mail: *george3@bestloved.com*

MANAGER
Jason Cartwright

ROOM RATES
Single occupancy £45 - £58
11 Doubles/Twins £80 - £98
Includes full breakfast and VAT

CHARGE/CREDIT CARDS

 ● *JCB* ● *MC* ● *VI*

RATINGS & AWARDS
W.T.B. ★★★
R.A.C. ★★
A.A. ★★ 72%

FACILITIES
On site: *Garden, fishing*
1 meeting room/max 30 people
Nearby: *Golf, pony trekking, walking, clay pigeon shooting, mountain bike hire*

RESTRICTIONS
Limited facilities for disabled guests
Pets by arrangement

ATTRACTIONS
Snowdonia National Park, Cymer Abbey, Harlech Castle, Ffestiniog Railway, Difi Furnace, Dinas Oleu, Cader Idris

AFFILIATIONS
Mortal Man Inns

NEAREST
MAJOR CITY:
Chester - 70 miles/1 ½ hrs

MAJOR AIRPORT:
Manchester - 90 miles/2 hrs

RAILWAY STATION:
Barmouth - 8 miles/15 mins

RESERVATIONS
Direct with hotel
Quote Best Loved

ACCESS CODES
Not applicable

WALES

160

*« **Absolutely wonderful - accommodation lovely and food delicious.
Staff incredibly nice** »*

Mr & Mrs Kay, Clitheroe, Lancashire

THE GROES INN

16th century inn

**Tyn-y-Groes, Near Conwy,
Conwy LL32 8TN**

**Telephone 01492 650545
Fax 01492 650855**

E-mail: *groesinn@bestloved.com*

OWNERS
Dawn and Justin Humphreys

ROOM RATES
Single occupancy	£68 - £100
11 Doubles/Twins	£85 - £102
2 Junior suites	£121
1 Family room	£85 - £105

Includes full breakfast and VAT

CHARGE/CREDIT CARDS

 • *DC* • *MC* • *VI*

RATINGS & AWARDS
W.T.B. ★★★★ *Hotel*
R.A.C. ★★★ *Dining Award 1*
A.A. ★★★ *73%*

FACILITIES
On site: *Garden*
1 meeting room/max 25 people
Nearby: *Golf, fishing, yachting, tennis,
fitness centre, riding*

RESTRICTIONS
Limited facilities for disabled guests

ATTRACTIONS
*Snowdonia National Park,
Conwy and Caenarfon Castles,
Portmeirion Italianate Village,
Bodnant Gardens,
Ffestiniog and Llanberis railways,
hill and mountain walks*

AFFILIATIONS
Welsh Rarebits

NEAREST
MAJOR CITY:
Chester - 50 miles/1 hr

MAJOR AIRPORT:
Manchester - 75 miles/1 ½ hrs

RAILWAY STATION:
Llandudno Junction - 5 miles/7 mins

FERRY PORT:
Holyhead - 30 miles/40 mins

RESERVATIONS
Direct with hotel
*Quote **Best Loved***

ACCESS CODES
Not applicable

WALES

*The fine art of inn keeping at its best
in the foothills of Snowdonia*

The Groes Inn is a revelation for those who mourn the passing of the great British inn - a traditional refuge of travellers blending the warm welcome of a local pub with the homely comforts of a good bed and wholesome food. These words, taken from The Groes' brochure, are something of an understatement. There is a much deeper satisfaction in prospect here and it starts with the proprietors who have the fine art of innkeeping bred into them for three generations.

The inn is just two miles south of the walled town of Conwy, set in the Conwy River valley amongst the foothills of Snowdonia. It first had its license in 1573 and, ever since, has kept the spirit of hospitality alive. Today's visitors will be reassured to find there have been subtle changes to hoist the facilities to present-day standards. Its character, however, remains unchanged. A recent addition to these facilities is the Gallery Suite, comprising of two elegantly furnished rooms which are not only ideal for weddings and private dinner parties but also make an incredible setting for a small meeting or conference.

The area is well-known for the excellence of its produce: beef, home cured ham and of course Welsh lamb. From Anglesey comes crab, wild salmon, plaice, oysters and mussels. The Groes Inn gets its pick and works wonders with it! And if you can manage it, do try the puddings.

LOCATION

*From Conwy Castle, take the B5106
towards Trefriw passing under the double
arches of the town walls. The inn is about
2 miles further on the right.*

" *You've bought a hotel and turned it into a home* "

John J Howells, Cardiff

• *Map p.468*
ref: D5

Victorian country house

LAKE COUNTRY HOUSE

WALES

Llangammarch Wells,
Powys LD4 4BS

Telephone 01591 620202
Fax 01591 620457

E-mail: *lakecountry@bestloved.com*

OWNERS
Jean-Pierre and Janet Mifsud

ROOM RATES
Single occupancy	*£95 - £150*
8 Luxury doubles	*£155*
11 Suites	*£185 - £250*
Includes full breakfast and VAT	

CHARGE/CREDIT CARDS
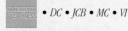 • *DC* • *JCB* • *MC* • *VI*

RATINGS & AWARDS
W.T.B. ★★★★★ *Country Hotel*
R.A.C. Gold Ribbon ★★★ *Dining Award 3*
A.A. ★★★ ❀❀
A.A. Inspectors Selected Hotel
A.A. Top 200 - 02/03

FACILITIES
On site: *Garden, heli-pad, fishing, croquet,*
golf, tennis, snooker, clay pigeon shooting,
salmon/trout fishing, 9-hole par 3 golf
course & putting area, billiards room
Licensed for weddings
1 meeting room/max 150 people

RESTRICTIONS
Limited facilites for disabled guests
Pets by arrangement

ATTRACTIONS
Powis Castle, The Elan Valley,
Brecon Beacons, Hay-on-Wye's bookshops,
Aberglasney, National Botanical Gardens

AFFILIATIONS
Welsh Rarebits
Pride of Britain

NEAREST
MAJOR CITY:
Hereford - 40 miles/45 mins

MAJOR AIRPORT:
Cardiff - 60 miles/1 ¼ hrs

RAILWAY STATION:
Llangammarch Wells - 1 mile/5 mins

RESERVATIONS
Toll free in US: 800-98-PRIDE
Quote **Best Loved**

ACCESS CODES
Not applicable

If you can't relax here,
you can't relax anywhere!

An air of elegance and calm informality pervades this exquisitely furnished Welsh country house. Warmly welcoming, this award-winning retreat stands serenely in 50 acres of parkland including a large trout lake, a haven for fascinating wildlife. In such a setting, guests experience the true feeling of Wales.

One may enjoy a mouth-watering, traditional Welsh afternoon tea in front of log fires in the lounge or in the garden in summer. Dining by candlelight in the restaurant is a memorable experience; the cuisine has been winning prestigious awards for its excellence.

Suites and bedrooms are delightfully appointed, each having a private bathroom, television, direct-dial telephone, period furniture and fine pictures and books.

Excellent salmon and trout fishing is available on the rivers Wye and Irfon and the hotel's own picturesque lake which regularly yields trout of five pounds and over and has no closed season. There is tennis, croquet, clay pigeon shooting and a nine-hole golf course within the grounds. The hotel's billiards room is a popular evening venue. There are four 18-hole courses in the vicinity and pony trekking can be arranged.

LOCATION
A40 to Abergavenny-Brecon; after Brecon veer left onto B4519, then left for Llangammarch Wells. Cross Mount Eppynt (6 miles) & turn left at foot of hill. Hotel is one mile along on right.

" It was indeed splendid. Everything was absolute perfection - the staff were wonderful and the food excellent "

Kate Dunkley, Cheshire

LAKE VYRNWY HOTEL

Victorian country house

Lake Vyrnwy, Llanwddyn, Montgomeryshire SY10 0LY

Telephone 01691 870692
Fax 01691 870259

E-mail: *vyrnwy@bestloved.com*

OWNERS
The Bisiker Family

ROOM RATES
34 Doubles/Twins   £120 - £190
1 Suite   £190
Includes full breakfast and VAT

CHARGE/CREDIT CARDS

AMERICAN EXPRESS • *DC* • *MC* • *VI*

RATINGS & AWARDS
W.T.B. ★★★★ *Country Hotel*
A.A. ★★★ ❀❀ *73%*

FACILITIES
On site: *Garden, heli-pad, fishing, tennis, fly-fishing, shooting, cycling, walking trails, rowing, sailing, clay shooting, quad-trekking*
Licensed for weddings
3 meeting rooms/max 125 people
Nearby: *White water rafting, canoeing, walking trails*

RESTRICTIONS
Limited facilities for disabled guests
No pets in public rooms

ATTRACTIONS
Powis Castle, Great Little Trains of Wales, Vyrnwy Visitor Centre, Lake Vyrnwy, Ffestiniog and Llanberis railways, RSPB Hides, hill and mountain walks

AFFILIATIONS
Welsh Rarebits

NEAREST
MAJOR CITY:
Shrewsbury - 32 miles/45 mins
Chester - 43 miles/1 hr

MAJOR AIRPORT:
Birmingham/Manchester - 90 miles/1 ¾ hrs

RAILWAY STATION:
Welshpool - 22 miles/30 mins
Shrewsbury - 32 miles/45 mins

RESERVATIONS
Direct with hotel
*Quote **Best Loved***

ACCESS CODES
Not applicable

Magical views from the Roof of Wales and a great sporting pedigree

Set high on the slopes of the Berwyn Mountains with views stretching off across lake and moorland to Snowdonia, the Vyrnwy really does sit atop the Roof of Wales. It is the centrepiece of the vast Vyrnwy Estate, which has its origins back in the late 19th century when the city fathers of Liverpool dammed the Vyrnwy Valley to create a fresh water supply for the city. They ensured its purity by purchasing the surrounding 24,000-acre catchment area and transformed it into a sporting estate with a splendid lodge - the present day hotel.

The former lodge has delighted country lovers with its magnificent position, comfort and style for more than a century. The guest rooms are spacious and individually decorated, many furnished with antiques, and some have four-posters, jacuzzis and private balconies. The head chef takes pride in sourcing most of his ingredients from local suppliers, while the estate provides game in season.

Vyrnwy offers unrivalled opportunities for outdoor pursuits such as tennis, sailing, clay shooting, quadtrekking, archery, trout-fishing on the lake and walking, cycling and birdwatching around the estate. Further afield, Powis Castle, the Offa's Dyke Path and several great little mountain train rides are within easy reach.

LOCATION

Follow brown tourist signs for Lake Vyrnwy from Shrewsbury A458 or from Oswestry A5.

❝ Service, food and facilities are all superb. We've had a great weekend ❞

Clive Benham, Ilminster, Somerset

• Map p.468
ref: B6

Country house hotel

LAMPHEY COURT HOTEL

Georgian charm and modern comfort in Pembrokeshires National Park

A country house hotel in its own spacious grounds, bordered by Pembrokeshire National Park and the coast - only three miles from one of the county's best beaches. A popular location for business travellers and tourists, not to mention a favourite with artists, Pembrokeshire has a beautiful coastline with abundance of cliffs, sand dunes and wildlife.

Lamphey Court, a Georgian mansion carefully restored by the Lain family, caters for both leisure and business with 37 comfortable bedrooms and purpose-built Coach House studios across the courtyard, perfect for families or corporate travellers. Delegates can choose from three conference rooms with modern facilities, including the Georgian and Windsor rooms and the newly refurbished Ruby room caters for high-level meetings and banquets. To help guests unwind, the hotel's leisure centre has a range of facilities including heated swimming pool, Jacuzzi and aerobics hall. Guests can dine in the Georgian a la carte restaurant serving Teifi salmon and Freshwater Bay Lobster, or the less formal Conservatory - great for lunches.

Lamphey Court has easy access to the M4 and is ideally located for touring the Pembrokeshire

Coast, Oakwood Leisure Park, Pembroke Castle and the seaside town of Tenby. There are also plenty of activities nearby such as island expeditions and whale and dolphin watching.

LOCATION

M4 to Carmarthen, A477 towards Pembroke. Turn left at Milton village for Lamphey. The hotel is well sign-posted both from M4 and the Irish ferry.

Lamphey, Pembroke, Pembrokeshire SA71 5NT

Telephone 01646 672273
Fax 01646 672480

E-mail: *lamphey@bestloved.com*

OWNER
The Lain Family

ROOM RATES
2 Singles	£72 - £85
20 Doubles/Twins	£100 - £140
15 Suites	£100 - £120
Includes full breakfast and VAT	

CHARGE/CREDIT CARDS

 • DC • MC • VI

RATINGS & AWARDS
W.T.B. ★★★★
R.A.C. ★★★ Dining Award 1
A.A. ★★★ 74%

FACILITIES
On site: *Garden, gym, heli-pad, tennis, sauna, jacuzzi*
3 meeting rooms/max 100 people
Nearby: *Golf, riding, fishing, water skiing*

RESTRICTIONS
Pets by arrangement

ATTRACTIONS
Pembrokeshire coast, St David's Cathedral, Oakwood Leisure Park, Pembroke Castle, Tenby, Dylan Thomas Boathouse

AFFILIATIONS
Best Western
Welsh Rarebits

NEAREST
MAJOR CITY:
Cardiff - 95 miles/1 ½ hrs

MAJOR AIRPORT:
Cardiff - 95 miles/ 1 ½ hrs

RAILWAY STATION:
Lamphey - ½ mile/5 mins

RESERVATIONS
Toll free in US: 800-528-1234
Quote Best Loved

ACCESS CODES
AMADEUS BW HAW424
APOLLO/GALILEO BW 13378
SABRE/ABACUS BW 12484
WORLDSPAN BW 83424

WALES

164

• *Map p.468*
ref: D5

LLANGOED HALL

Country house

WALES

Llyswen, Brecon, Powys LD3 0YP

Telephone 01874 754525
Fax 01874 754545

E-mail: *llangoed@bestloved.com*

OWNER
Sir Bernard Ashley

ROOM RATES
Single occupancy	£120 - £300
11 Doubles/Twins	£160 - £295
7 Four-posters	£160 - £340
3 Suites	£320 - £340
Includes full breakfast and VAT	

CHARGE/CREDIT CARDS
AMERICAN EXPRESS • DC • JCB • MC • VI

RATINGS & AWARDS
W.T.B. ★★★★★ *Country Hotel*
A.A. ★★★★ 🌸🌸
A.A. Top 200 - 02/03

FACILITIES
On site: *Garden, heli-pad, fishing, croquet, tennis, snooker, mountain bikes, clay pigeon shooting*
Licensed for weddings
3 meeting rooms/max 70 people
Nearby: *Golf, shooting, riding, 4x4, canoeing, gliding*

RESTRICTIONS
No facilities for disabled guests
No children under 8 years
No pets, kennels available

ATTRACTIONS
Brecon Beacons, Cardiff, Hay-on-Wye, Tintern Abbey, Powis & Raglan Castles

AFFILIATIONS
The Celebration Hotels Collection
Welsh Rarebits

NEAREST
MAJOR CITY:
Cardiff - 55 miles/55 mins

MAJOR AIRPORT:
Cardiff - 65 miles/1 ½ hrs

RAILWAY STATION:
Abergavenny - 23 miles/40 mins

RESERVATIONS
Toll free in US: 800-322-2403
Toll free in UK: 0321 ASHLEY
Quote **Best Loved**

ACCESS CODES
Not applicable

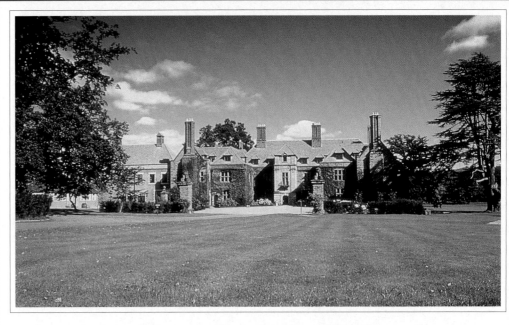

Designed by a distinguished architect, recreated by a great designer

Llangoed Hall may have been the legendary White Palace, home of the first Parliament at the dawn of Welsh history. In AD 560, Prince Iddon donated it to the church in expiation of his sins. A mansion was built here in 1632. The great architect Sir Clough Williams-Ellis designed it as a gracious country house in 1912, retaining the surviving Jacobean porch as part of the south wing.

Sir Bernard Ashley saw it as the place where he could fulfil his ambition to recreate the atmosphere of an Edwardian house party. There is no reception desk, just friendly staff to carry the bags. In summer the Great Hall's French windows are open so that guests can enjoy the garden. In winter, the huge stone fireplace has a merry log blazing. In the Picture Gallery are fine portraits and works by Whistler and the Edwardians. The handsome dining room offers modern classical cooking. It makes the most of fresh local produce, such as Welsh lamb, Wye salmon and laverbread.

The secluded Wye Valley and the Black Mountains are all around; the Brecon Beacons, Cardiff, the bookshops of Hay-on-Wye,

Caerphilly, Raglan and Powis Castles and Wordsworth's Tintern Abbey are nearby.

LOCATION
On A470. 11 miles south east of Builth Wells; 11 miles north east of Brecon.

" Single-handedly, Maes-y-Neuadd seems to embody the virtues of all this year's Good Hotel Guide, Cesar Award Winners "

Sean Newsom, The Times

600-year old manor house   HOTEL MAES-Y-NEUADD

Elegance and serenity in the midst of magnificent Snowdonia

Deep in Snowdonia, amongst some of the most beautiful scenery in Britain, the manor house of Maes-y-Neuadd has watched over this timeless, magnificent scene for more than 600 years. For centuries the home of one family, the house is now owned by two couples, Lynn and Peter Jackson and Doreen and Peter Payne. They have lovingly restored and refurbished the house, creating a warm and welcoming haven for travellers from all over the world. The rooms are furnished using the best of modern craftsmanship, filled with fine antiques and many paintings by local artists. The eight acres of grounds reflect the beauty of the seasons, nurtured by the mild Gulf Stream climate.

Chef proprietor Peter Jackson revels in the quality of the 'natural larder' on his doorstep. To complement the fine lamb, cheese, fish and game for which Wales is renowned, many vegetables, fruit and herbs are grown in the kitchen garden.

The ancient language, culture and music set this area of Wales apart from the rest of Britain. Above all the welcome, 'Croeso', for which Wales is so famous, is nowhere warmer than at Maes-y-Neuadd.

LOCATION

Located 1 ½ miles off B4573, 3 ½ miles north of Harlech. Hotel sign on corner of lane.

Talsarnau, Near Harlech, Gwynedd LL47 6YA
Telephone 01766 780200
Fax 01766 780211
E-mail: *maes@bestloved.com*

OWNERS
Doreen and Peter Payne
Lynn and Peter Jackson

ROOM RATES
1 Single	£75
12 Doubles/Twins	£165 - £220
1 Four-poster	£185
2 Suites	£195 - £210

Includes full breakfast and VAT

CHARGE/CREDIT CARDS

 • DC • MC • VI

RATINGS & AWARDS
W.T.B. ★★★★
A.A. ★★ ✿✿
A.A. Top 200 - 02/03
The Good Food Guide -
Restaurant of the Year 2000

FACILITIES
On site: *Garden, heli-pad, putting green*
Licensed for weddings
1 meeting room/max 16 people
Nearby: *Golf, riding, fishing, shooting*

RESTRICTIONS
Limited facilities for disabled guests
Pets by arrangement

ATTRACTIONS
Mount Snowdon, Slate Caverns
Portmeirion Italianate Village,
Caernarfon and Harlech Castles,
Royal St David's Golf Course,
Narrow Gauge Railway

AFFILIATIONS
The Celebrated Hotels Collection
Welsh Rarebits
Pride of Britain
Grand Heritage Hotels

NEAREST
MAJOR CITY:
Bangor - 35 miles/1 hr

MAJOR AIRPORT:
Manchester - 100 miles/2 hrs

RAILWAY STATION:
Harlech - 3 miles/10 mins

RESERVATIONS
Toll free in US: 800-322-2403,
800-98-PRIDE or 888-93-GRAND
*Quote **Best Loved***

ACCESS CODES
AMADEUS UI CEGMAE
APOLLO/GALILEO UI 34651
SABRE/ABACUS UI 31036
WORLDSPAN UI 42175

WALES

“ The torch for cooking on the North Wales coast is carried by Wendy Vaughan. Faultless throughout! ”

Vogue Magazine

OLD RECTORY COUNTRY HOUSE *Georgian country house*

Llansanffraid Glan Conwy, Near Conwy, Conwy LL28 5LF

Telephone 01492 580611 Fax 01492 584555

E-mail: *orectconwy@bestloved.com*

OWNERS
Michael and Wendy Vaughan

ROOM RATES
Single occupancy	£99 - £129
5 Doubles/Twins	£129 - £169
1 Four-poster	£149 - £169

Includes full breakfast and VAT

CHARGE/CREDIT CARDS
MC • JCB • VI

RATINGS & AWARDS
W.T.B. ★★★★★
R.A.C. Gold Ribbon ★★ *Dining Award 4*
A.A. ★★ ✸✸✸
A.A. Top 200 - 02/03

FACILITIES
On site: *Garden*
Nearby: *Golf, riding, fishing*

RESTRICTIONS
No facilities for disabled guests
No children under 5 years
Pets by arrangement
No smoking throughout
Closed 30 Nov - 1 Feb

ATTRACTIONS
*Conwy Castle, Llandudno,
Bodnant Gardens,
Snowdonia National Park*

AFFILIATIONS
Welsh Rarebits

NEAREST
MAJOR CITY:
Chester - 40 miles/45 mins

MAJOR AIRPORT:
Manchester - 70 miles/1 ½ hrs

RAILWAY STATION:
Llandudno Junction - 1 ½ miles/5 mins

FERRY PORT:
Holyhead - 35 miles/1 hr

RESERVATIONS
Direct with hotel
*Quote **Best Loved***

ACCESS CODES
AMADEUS HK CEGOLD
APOLLO/GALILEO HK 25905
SABRE/ABACUS HK 31998
WORLDSPAN HK OLDRE

'Outstanding comfort, welcome, service and food' - lovely place, too!

The charming Old Rectory Country House, idyllically set in beautiful gardens, panoramically overlooks the grand sweep of Conwy estuary, historic Conwy Castle and the Snowdonia Mountains. There are many things to delight the eye in this elegant Georgian country house. Its highly polished rooms are decorated with old paintings, antiques and porcelain.

The Vaughans have created a calm, relaxing, unfussy atmosphere and have received an award for 'Welsh Hospitality at its Best'. They have also been granted Red Star status by the A.A. and a coveted Gold Ribbon by the R.A.C. for 'outstanding comfort, welcome, service and food'. Indeed, this six-bedroom country house is deserving of its many accolades. Wendy Vaughan's acclaimed cuisine - she is a 'Master Chef of Great Britain' - is complemented by an award-winning wine cellar.

Situated midway between Chester and Caernarfon and near Betwys-Y-Coed, it is an ideal centre for touring North Wales. Within three miles there are three championship golf courses. Michael's help with touring routes and his knowledge of all things Welsh, guarantee a memorable stay. You are assured of personal attention at this 'beautiful haven of peace'.

LOCATION

On the A470, ½ mile south of its junction with the A55.

> *" It's a real treat to have such spacious rooms in a hotel, with so many unusual features and a feeling of real luxury "*
>
> *Jennifer & Andrew Parker, Solihul*

Victorian resort hotel

OSBORNE HOUSE

A romantic High Victorian gem on the seafront

For many visitors to Llandudno, the only address worth considering is The Empire, a stately and much loved grande dame of a Victorian resort hotel owned and managed by the Maddocks family (see page 156). Now, The Empire's faithful are about to be thrown into utter confusion by the arrival of The Osborne, a recent and splendiferous Maddocks venture that has seen a crumbling 1851 seafront property restored and refurbished in spectacular style and transformed into stunning all-suites hotel.

To say Len and Elizabeth Maddocks are excited about their new hotel is something of an understatement. It has taken time to complete as every huge, high-ceilinged room has been immaculately finished and furnished with antiques. The spacious bedrooms have fabulous views of Conwy Bay and Great Ormes Head, king size brass beds and marble bathrooms. Guests are greeted with a complimentary bottle of champagne and a cosy gas log fire twinkling in the grate in winter. Downstairs, the restaurant (opening May 2003) boasts impressively ornate ceilings, a large fireplace and a high quality brasserie menu served from 11am-11pm.

Within easy reach of Llandudno are the wilds of Snowdonia, the lovely Bodnant Garden in the Vale of Conwy, and Caernafon.

LOCATION

Exit the A55 Junction 19 for Llandudno. Follow signs for town centre, drive down the main street (Mostyn Street). Check-in at The Empire Hotel, which is at the end and faces the town.

Promenade, Llandudno, Conwy LL17 2LP

**Telephone 01873 860330
Fax 01492 860791**

E-mail: *osbornewales@bestloved.com*

OWNERS
Len and Elizabeth Maddocks

DIRECTOR
Elyse Waddy

ROOM RATES
6 Suites £150 - £250
Includes continental breakfast and VAT

CHARGE/CREDIT CARDS

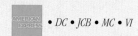 • *DC* • *JCB* • *MC* • *VI*

RATINGS & AWARDS
W.T.B. ★★★★★ *Town House*
A.A. ★★★★ *Town House*
A.A. Top 200 - 02/03

FACILITIES
Nearby: *Golfing, riding, fishing, sailing*

RESTRICTIONS
*No facilities for disabled guests
No pets, guide dogs only
No children*

ATTRACTIONS
*Snowdonia National Park,
Portmeirion Italianate Village,
Bodnant Gardens,
Conwy and Caernarfon Castles,
Ffestiniog and Llanberis railways,
Lechwedd Slate Caverns*

AFFILIATIONS
Independent

NEAREST
MAJOR CITY:
Chester - 50 miles/50 mins

MAJOR AIRPORT:
Manchester - 85 miles/1 ½ hrs

RAILWAY STATION:
Llandudno Junction - 3 miles/10 mins

RESERVATIONS
Direct with hotel
Quote Best Loved

ACCESS CODES
Not applicable

WALES

PÁLE HALL COUNTRY HOUSE

Manor house

WALES

**Pale Estate,
Llandderfel,
Bala, Gwynedd LL23 7PS**

**Telephone 01678 530285
Fax 01678 530220**

E-mail: *pale@bestloved.com*

OWNERS
Saul and Judith Nahed

ROOM RATES
1 Single	£69 - £125
16 Doubles/Twins	£100 - £185

Includes full breakfast and VAT

CHARGE/CREDIT CARDS

● *JCB* ● *MC* ● *VI*

RATINGS & AWARDS
W.T.B. ★★★★ *Country Hotel*
A.A. ★★★ 🌸🌸 *76%*

FACILITIES
On site: *Garden, heli-pad, fishing, croquet, clay pigeon shooting, salmon and trout fishing, game and pheasant shooting, 4x4 off road driving
Licensed for weddings
2 meeting rooms/max 40 people*

RESTRICTIONS
*No facilities for disabled guests
Children by arrangement
No pets*

ATTRACTIONS
Snowdonia, Powis Castle & Gardens, Bodnant Gardens, Lechwedd Slate Caverns, Conwy and Penrhyn Castles, Portmeirion, Erddig House, Chirk Castle, Pistyll Rhaeadr Waterfall

AFFILIATIONS
Independent

NEAREST
MAJOR CITY:
Chester - 38 miles/50 mins

MAJOR AIRPORT:
Manchester - 77 miles/1 ¾ hrs
Liverpool - 55 miles/1 ½ hrs

RAILWAY STATION:
Welshpool - 30 miles/40 mins
Wrexham - 32 miles/45 mins

RESERVATIONS
Direct with hotel
Quote **Best Loved**

ACCESS CODES
Not applicable

A magnificent house once graced by the presence of Queen Victoria

Palé Hall, a luxurious Victorian mansion set in acres of parkland, was built in 1870 for a wealthy Scottish gentleman and railway engineer. His brief to the architects was that 'no expense should be spared' in building this family home.

This splendid house has stunning interiors including exquisite features like the magnificent entrance hall with its lofty vaulted ceiling and galleried oak staircase, the boudoir with its handpainted ceiling, the marble bar and fireplaces. The public rooms express a quiet confidence reflecting the more leisured times in which they were built.

All bedrooms are individually decorated and en suite with television, direct dial telephone, luxury toiletries and hospitality tray. They all enjoy a commanding view of the gardens and surrounding panoramic scenery, including the entrance to the Queen's Walk named after a stay by Queen Victoria in 1889. The original bath and half tester bed used by Her Majesty during her stay are still available for the comfort of guests.

The restaurant is acclaimed for its food, including vegetarian and other diets, the emphasis on the fresh and natural with a regular change of menu. The restaurant possesses a restful intimate atmosphere for dinner by candlelight. Palé Hall is easily accessible by road and is an excellent base for touring.

LOCATION
The house is situated just off the B4401 Corwen to Bala road 4 to 5 miles from Llandrillo. Hotel is signposted from main road.

" *A little paradise in the UK* "

17th century abbey

PENALLY ABBEY

All the beauty and drama of Britain's only coastal National Park

Penally Abbey sits high above Carmarthen Bay, calmly surveying the easternmost portion of the spectacular Pembrokeshire Coast National Park from its lovely Gothic windows. This is a ringside seat for seascapes that change from hour to hour and season to season. In summer warm, glittering seas beckon holidaymakers down to glorious sandy beaches, while spring and autumn are ideal for invigorating walks, a round at the Tenby golf course, horse-riding and sailing. In the depths of winter the best place to watch the elements battle it out over gale-swept seas is one of Penally's comfy armchairs with a log fire crackling in the grate.

Little remains of the abbey's monastic origins save a ruined chapel in the five-acre grounds. However, the listed house is full of character and elegant old-world charm. The bedrooms, both in the main house and adjoining coach house, have been furnished in period style (some have four posters) and equipped with every modern comfort. In the evening, there is a terrace for drinks in fine weather and dinner is a romantic, candlelit affair in the dining room where the emphasis is on delicious food created from local ingredients.

LOCATION

Penally Abbey is situated adjacent to the 12th century church on the village green in the village of Penally, 1 ½ miles from Tenby. Off the A4139 Tenby-Pembroke coast road.

Penally, Near Tenby,
Pembrokeshire SA70 7PY

Telephone 01834 843033
Fax 01834 844714

E-mail: *penally@bestloved.com*

OWNERS
Stephen and Elleen Warren

ROOM RATES
Single occupancy	£104
5 Doubles/Twins	£128
7 Four-posters	£146

Includes full breakfast, newspaper and VAT

CHARGE/CREDIT CARDS

 • *MC* • *VI*

RATINGS & AWARDS
W.T.B. ★★★★ *Country Hotel*
A.A. ★★★ ❀ 75%

FACILITIES
On site: *Garden, croquet,*
indoor pool, snooker
Licensed for weddings
1 meeting room/max 20 people
Nearby: *Golf, riding, fishing,*
clay pigeon shooting

RESTRICTIONS
No facilities for disabled guests
No children under 7 years allowed
in restaurant for dinner
No pets

ATTRACTIONS
Tenby, Dylan Thomas's Boathouse,
Pembroke Castle, Manorbear Castle,
Pembokeshire National Park

AFFILIATIONS
Welsh Rarebits

NEAREST
MAJOR CITY:
Cardiff - 90 miles/1 ¾ hrs

MAJOR AIRPORT:
London Heathrow - 250 miles/4 hrs
Cardiff - 90 miles/1 ¾ hrs

RAILWAY STATION:
Tenby - 1 ½ miles/5 mins

RESERVATIONS
Direct with hotel
Quote **Best Loved**

ACCESS CODES
Not applicable

WALES

www.penally.bestloved.com

170

● *Map p.468*
ref: C3

Every now and then life does you a good turn, you find a 'gem'; something you want to keep to yourself. I cannot be that selfish about my stay at Penmaenuchaf Hall

Mr Alan T Mumby, Welsh Design Advisory Service, Cardiff

PENMAENUCHAF HALL

Victorian mansion

Penmaenpool, Dolgellau, Gwynedd LL40 1YB

Telephone 01341 422129
Fax 01341 422787

E-mail: *penhall@bestloved.com*

OWNERS
Mark Watson and Lorraine Fielding

ROOM RATES
Single occupancy   £75 - £115
14 Doubles/Twins   £116 - £176
Includes full breakfast and VAT

CHARGE/CREDIT CARDS

 • *DC* • *JCB* • *MC* • *VI*

RATINGS & AWARDS
W.T.B. ★★★★ *Country Hotel*
A.A. ★★★ ❀❀ 76%
WHICH? Hotel of the Year 2003

FACILITIES
On site: *Garden, snooker, fishing, croquet*
Licensed for weddings
2 meeting rooms/max 50 people
Nearby: *Riding, golf, clay pigeon shooting, quad biking, abseiling, mountain biking*

RESTRICTIONS
Limited facilities for disabled guests
No children under 6 years
(does not apply to babes-in-arms)
Pets by arrangement

ATTRACTIONS
Portmeirion, Harlech Castle, Ffestiniog Railway, Llechwedd Slate Caverns, Celtica: a celtic experience, Centre of Alternative Technology

AFFILIATIONS
Welsh Rarebits

NEAREST
MAJOR CITY:
Chester - 69 miles/1 ¼ hrs

MAJOR AIRPORT:
Manchester - 100 miles/2 hrs

RAILWAY STATION:
Fairbourne - 6 miles/10 mins

RESERVATIONS
Direct with hotel
Quote Best Loved

ACCESS CODES
Not applicable

WALES

Imposing and stylish in the romantic foothills of Snowdonia

Cader Idris, the Chair of Arthur, stands 2927ft high amongst the peaks of Snowdonia where folklore and legend intertwine with history told in romantic ruins that grace this spectacular part of Britain. Iron Age forts, Roman roads and fortresses and splendid Norman castles gather in haphazard profusion. A fascinating place to come for pony-trekking, walking and fishing.

And especially for the food! This stunning countryside sets the scene for some of the most memorable cuisine to be had in Wales. Bass, lobster and crab; Welsh lamb, black beef and game; fresh fruit, vegetables and Welsh dairy products - all prepared with the authority and flair of an award-winning chef.

Penmaenuchaf Hall was built in 1860 and is set amidst 21 extensive acres of landscaped gardens and woodland with views of the Mawddach Estuary and the mountains beyond. Its dedicated owners have kept a family home atmosphere whilst indulging their guests in every way they can. Your room will be luxurious and well-appointed and the hospitality as warm as the glowing oak and mahogany interiors and the crackling log fires of winter.

It's said that he who sleeps the night on Cader Idris will wake blind, mad or a poet. Not here; you will awake refreshed, wiser too for having stayed at Penmaenuchaf Hall.

LOCATION
From Dolgellau by-pass (A470) take A493 towards Tywyn and Fairbourne. The entrance is 1 mile on left.

" Excellent service, manager and staff superb. Wonderful venue "

Sandra Neale, Abergavenny

Georgian country house

PETERSTONE COURT

Overlooking the River Usk and the Brecon Beacons all within the National Park

Whether you stay in an elegantly furnished period bedroom or in one of the hotel's four converted split-level studio accommodations, you can expect to find quality and comfort at every turn. Ten years ago Peterstone Court was voted as the best new hotel in Wales. Set on the banks of the River Usk, amid the rugged splendour of Brecon Beacons National Park, which comprises a breathtaking 520 square miles, it is easy to see why. Remote mountain ranges, hidden waterfalls and wooded river valleys complete a stunning rural environment. The land the hotel is built on has a history of occupation since the 14th century and magical stories of a ghost who once haunted the drive persist.

The restaurant makes the most of local produce, including succulent Welsh lamb from nearby Green Mountains Farm. Corporate events can be accommodated in the bespoke function rooms, which can take up to 130, and are kitted out with a television, flip charts, overhead projectors and screens. The hotel is also suited to wedding celebrations, private parties and is often booked for exclusive use. The gym and health spa

include a sauna, jacuzzi and solarium in addition to an outdoor heated pool in the summer months.

LOCATION

On the A40 in the village of Llanhamlach 3 miles east of Brecon and 16 miles west of Abergavenny.

Llanhamlach, Brecon, Powys LD3 7YB

**Telephone 01874 665387
Fax 01874 665376**

E-mail: *peterstone@bestloved.com*

OWNER
George Keppe

MANAGING DIRECTOR
Anthony Evans

ROOM RATES
Single occupancy £98
10 Doubles/Twins £109
2 Four-posters £135
Includes full breakfast and VAT

CHARGE/CREDIT CARDS
MC • VI

RATINGS & AWARDS
W.T.B. ★★★ *Country Hotel*
R.A.C. ★★★
A.A. ★★★ 73%

FACILITIES
On site: *Garden, gym, heated pool, health & beauty, outdoor pool, sauna, snooker Licensed for weddings 3 meeting rooms/130 people*
Nearby: *Golf, riding, canoeing, walking*

RESTRICTIONS
*No facilities for disabled guests
Pets by arrangement
No smoking in bedrooms*

ATTRACTIONS
Brecon Beacons National Park, Hay-on-Wye, Caerphilly Castle, Llanthony Abbey, Danyr Ogaf Caves, Cardiff

AFFILIATIONS
Independent

NEAREST
*MAJOR CITY:
Swansea - 40 miles/45 mins*

*MAJOR AIRPORT:
Cardiff - 60 miles/1 ½ hrs*

*RAILWAY STATION:
Abergavenny - 16 miles/30 mins*

RESERVATIONS
Direct with hotel
Quote **Best Loved**

ACCESS CODES
Not applicable

WALES

« It was difficult to find, it was even more difficult to leave »

Gabriel Pety, Belgium

• Map p.468
ref: C2

TAN-Y-FOEL COUNTRY HOUSE

17th century house

Capel Garmon, Betws-y-Coed, Conwy LL26 0RE

**Telephone 01690 710507
Fax 01690 710681**

E-mail: *tanyfoel@bestloved.com*

OWNERS
Peter and Janet Pitman

ROOM RATES
Single occupancy	£99 - £120
4 Doubles/Twins	£120 - £150
2 Four-posters	£136 - £150

Includes full breakfast and VAT

CHARGE/CREDIT CARDS

 • DC • JCB • MC • VI

RATINGS & AWARDS
W.T.B. ★★★★★ *Country House*
A.A. ★★ ✿✿✿✿
A.A. Top 200 - 02/03

FACILITIES
On site: *Garden*
Nearby: *Golf, fishing, riding, walking*

RESTRICTIONS
*No facilities for disabled guests
No children under 7 years
No smoking throughout
No pets
Closed 1 - 31 Dec*

ATTRACTIONS
*Snowdonia National Park,
Caernarfon Castle, Conwy Castle,
Plas Newydd, Chester,
Bodnant Gardens*

AFFILIATIONS
Welsh Rarebits

NEAREST
*MAJOR CITY:
Chester - 50 miles/1 ¼ hrs*

*MAJOR AIRPORT:
Manchester - 80 miles/1 ¾ hrs*

*RAILWAY STATION:
Llandudno Junction - 11 miles/25 mins*

RESERVATIONS
*Direct with hotel
Quote **Best Loved***

ACCESS CODES
Not applicable

WALES

An oasis of tranquility and culinary excellence in the Snowdonia National Park

Tan-y-Foel means 'the house under the hillside' and perfectly describes this delectable hideaway set in eight acres of woodland and pasture with views stretching away to Snowdonia and the Conwy Valley. Garlanded with praise from all quarters, Tan-y-Foel is the only five star country house in Snowdonia National Park, its six guest rooms have secured an Imaginative Bedroom Award from The Which? Hotel Guide, whilst Janet Pitman, a Master Chef of Great Britain, has earned a Restaurant of the Year Award from The Good Food Guide for her outstanding cuisine.

The bedroom award offers a gentle hint as to what to expect. A traditional Welsh stone-built country house from the outside, Tan-y-Foel's contemporary interior design comes as a complete surprise. Earthy tones through beige and jute to terracotta predominate and dark teak ornaments suggest an Oriental influence, which is echoed in Janet's cooking. Her signature dish is a superbly presented Welsh loin of pork with pakoras and an oriental marinade served with organic carrot and ginger sauce.

In the surrounding area, Conwy and Caernarfon castles are bastions of Welsh history,

Bodnant Gardens are a must for garden lovers, as well as the wilds of Snowdonia.

LOCATION

From the A55 take the A470 to Llanrwst. Keep on the A470 through Llanrwst and after 2 miles take the turning signposted Capel Garmon/Nebo. The hotel is on the left handside after 1 ½ miles.

" *Found on a stormy night we have returned again and again . . . it's a special treat at all times of the year* **"**

Jill Tweedie & Alan Brien, Authors

Georgian country house TYDDYN LLAN COUNTRY HOUSE

A stylish oasis in the midst of this magical Welsh valley

Tyddyn Llan is a lovely Georgian country house surrounded by some of the most magnificent countryside in Wales. A one-time shooting lodge for the Dukes of Westminster, it was converted in 1983 by Peter and Bridget Kindred into an hotel that they, after much travelling, would like to stay in. Peter's career as a set designer in television and films has been used to advantage to create the elegant decor and Bridget's knowledge and love of food has established a much acclaimed restaurant.

Friendly and informal with antiques, interesting paintings, some by Peter himself, comfortable furniture and encircled by its own beautiful gardens, it is an oasis amidst the mountains, rivers and the great outdoors. This unspoilt valley of the River Dee provides excellent walking over the Berwyn Mountains, fishing (with a ghillie if required), horseriding and shooting in season.

The hotel is also well placed to explore the splendour of Snowdonia with its many castles and monuments and it is not far from the Roman City of Chester and the majestic Mawddach and Dyfi Estuaries. The Kindreds look forward to wishing you 'Croeso I Cymru' - 'Welcome to Wales'.

LOCATION

From A5 in Corwen, take 1st left turning to Llandrillo B4401 for 4 ½ miles. Tyddyn Llan is on the right side on the way out of the village to Bala.

Llandrillo, Near Corwen,
Denbighshire LL21 0ST

Telephone 01490 440264
Fax 01490 440414

E-mail: *tyddyn@bestloved.com*

OWNERS
Peter and Bridget Kindred

ROOM RATES
10 Doubles/Twins   £105 - £140
Includes full breakfast and VAT

CHARGE/CREDIT CARDS

 ● DC ● JCB ● MC ● VI

RATINGS & AWARDS
W.T.B. ★★★★ *Country Hotel*
A.A. ★★ ❀❀
A.A. Top 200 - 02/03

FACILITIES
On site: *Garden, fishing, croquet, health & beauty*
Licensed for weddings
2 meeting rooms/max 50 people
Nearby: *Golf, shooting, windsurfing, sailing, canoeing*

RESTRICTIONS
Limited facilities for disabled guests
No pets in public rooms

ATTRACTIONS
Snowdonia National Park, Bodnant Gardens, Portmeirion Village, Harlech, Chirk and Caernarfon Castles, Golf at Bala and Llangollen courses, Erddig Hall, Chester

AFFILIATIONS
Welsh Rarebits

NEAREST
MAJOR CITY:
Chester - 35 miles/50 mins

MAJOR AIRPORT:
Manchester - 65 miles/1 ¼ hrs

RAILWAY STATION:
Chester - 35 miles/50 mins
Wrexham - 28 miles/45 mins

RESERVATIONS
Direct with hotel
Quote Best Loved

ACCESS CODES
Not applicable

WALES

> " *We found an historic but friendly country house which combines peace,*
> *unsurpassed views and excellence in every way* "
>
> *T H Davies, LVO*

WARPOOL COURT HOTEL | *Country house*

**St Davids,
Pembrokeshire SA62 6BN**

**Telephone 01437 720300
Fax 01437 720676**

E-mail: *warpool@bestloved.com*

GENERAL MANAGER
Rupert Duffin

ROOM RATES
2 Singles	£77 - £97
23 Doubles/Twins	£134 - £230

Includes full breakfast and VAT

CHARGE/CREDIT CARDS

AMERICAN EXPRESS • *DC* • *MC* • *VI*

RATINGS & AWARDS
W.T.B. ★★★★ *Country Hotel*
A.A. ★★★ ❀❀ 77%

FACILITIES
On site: *Garden, gym, croquet, tennis,
indoor pool, sauna
Licensed for weddings
2 meeting rooms/max 180 people*
Nearby: *Riding, sea fishing, surfing,
windsurfing*

RESTRICTIONS
*No facilities for disabled guests
Pets by arrangement
Closed Jan*

ATTRACTIONS
*St Davids' Cathedral, Pembroke Castle,
St Davids' Bishops Palace,
Pembrokeshire Coast National Park,
Colby Woodland Garden*

AFFILIATIONS
Welsh Rarebits

NEAREST
*MAJOR CITY:
Swansea - 75 miles/1 ½ hrs*

*MAJOR AIRPORT:
Cardiff - 115 miles/2 hrs*

*RAILWAY STATION:
Fishguard - 15 miles/30 mins
Haverfordwest - 15 miles/30 mins*

*FERRY PORT:
Fishguard/Pembroke - 15 miles/30 mins*

RESERVATIONS
*Direct with hotel
Quote* **Best Loved**

ACCESS CODES
Not applicable

*Some of the most spectacular
sea views you'll find in this book*

Originally built as St Davids' Cathedral choir school in the 1860s this privately owned hotel enjoys spectacular scenery at the heart of the Pembrokeshire National Park, with views over the coast and St Brides Bay to the islands beyond.

First converted to an hotel 30 years ago, the Court offers a unique antique tile collection and 28 comfortable and individually decorated bedrooms, many of which have glorious sea-views.

The dining room enjoys a splendid reputation offering imaginative menus, and vegetarian dishes, using local produce - crab, lobster, sewin and seabass are caught just off the coast and the hotel smokes its own salmon and mackerel.

Set in seven acres, the tranquil gardens offer pre-dinner drinks on the lawns or peaceful strolls. For those wishing for a more active pursuit, the covered heated pool (open April to October), exercise rooms, sauna or tennis court beckon - croquet, pool and table tennis are also available.

A five minute walk will take you either to the coastal path with its spectacular scenery or the Cathedral and Bishops Palace in St Davids.

The area boasts many sandy beaches, and offers a wealth of history and natural beauty.

LOCATION

*From Cross Square in St Davids, bear
left between Cartref Restaurant and Midland
Bank. Go down Goat Street. At bottom,
fork left and follow hotel signs.*

Tastes of Lincolnshire

Lincolnshire people feel strongly about their food and are justifiably proud of the county's tradition of producing the finest produce.

The new quality branding mark - Tastes of Lincolnshire - represents all that is best in their local food and drink, and identifies restaurants pubs and shops throughout the county who believe in the exceptional quality of local produce and are using it in their menus.

This rural county, with its rich fertile soils, is one of the chief food producing areas of England. Lincolnshire produce - vegetables, cereals and meat as well as bulbs and flowers are sent all over Britain. Long a farming county, with a strong small-holders tradition and horticultural skills particularly in the Fens, many of today's farmers are re-finding their craft - farmers' markets are thriving and their Quality Beef and Lamb scheme helps reduce the distances that animals travel. The local breed of cattle, the Lincoln Red, has always been popular in the area and has begun to find fans outside the county for its succulence and flavour. One producer of this memorable beef is Woodlands Organic Farm near Boston - they also raise bronze turkeys and run a local organic box scheme. The Tomlinsons at Redhill Farm sell dry cured bacon, hams and

sausages at their farm shop near Gainsborough and at local farmers' markets. The lush pastures of the rolling Wolds are home to the Holstein cows that supply the milk Simon Jones uses to make award winning Lincolnshire Poacher Cheese - matured for twelve to eighteen months. Fourteen windmills - wind willing - are still working. Many produce organic flours and because grinding by stone generates less heat than modern techniques the flavour and nutritional value is greater.

The Fens in the south of the county have their own special character, a great, flat land, with big skies, magnificent churches and some of the most fertile fields to be found anywhere. This is where much of England's finest potatoes come from as well as a huge range of vegetables ranging from crunchy cabbages to delicate asparagus. And amongst the vegetables are sunny fields of daffodils - Lincolnshire is the largest producer in the world.

Grimsby, in the northeast of the county, handles more fish than any other port in Britain - for a taste not to be missed try fish that has been slowly smoked in one of their traditional smoke houses such as Alfred Enderby's, one of the few independent family run smoking firms left in England. Here haddock

and salmon are slowly smoked overnight in traditional smoke houses using just wood chippings and 60 years of experience. There is much else to discover - ice cream makers, jam makers, ostrich farmers, fudge makers and chocolatiers.

Lincolnshire farmers and butchers supply some of Britain's finest meat. Free range poultry, pork, home cured hams and bacon, local lamb, venison, game and Lincoln Red Beef are featured on Tastes of Lincolnshire menus - alongside traditional local specialities from chine to haslet and famous Lincolnshire sausages.

This is a county with a long heritage of great food. There are splendid historic kitchens, such as the medieval one at Gainsborough Hall, Victorian ones at Burghley House and Belvoir Castle and a beautifully restored kitchen garden at Normanby Hall - all offering tantalising glimpses of Lincolnshire's flavourful past.

For further information contact:

Tastes of Lincolnshire
Lincolnshire Development
Beech House
Waterside South,
Lincoln
LN5 7JH

Tel 01522 823438

MIDSHIRES

This is a landscape painted with a broad brush: sweeping hills and rolling dales, fertile fens and industrial heartland. The influence on literature of this Middle England has been immense.

AE Houseman's poem, A Shropshire Lad, made him one of England's most popular poets in the late 1800s. As a child, living at Bromsgrove in Worcester, he had a far view of the Shropshire Hills that he later immortalised in the as, '…blue, remembered hills…'.

The medieval character of Newstead Abbey the former Augustinian priory in Nottinghamshire that was the poet Byron's ancestral home forms the perfect background for an icon of the Romantic age. He was dashingly handsome, and the self destructive model for many of his literary creations.

DH Lawrence's childhood home, Eastwood in Nottinghamshire, gave him a very different view of the world from the aristocratic Byron's. With an illiterate father and middle class mother who had been a school teacher, he was set apart from his contempories in the coal mining town where he was born. Many of his novels involve the contrast between unspoilt countryside and a town despoiled by mining.

George Crabbe was born in Suffolk in 1754, he became curate at Aldeburgh and was known as the poet of the poor for his descriptions of life in poor fishing settlements. He was greatly admired by Byron, amongst others, and his story of Peter Grimes was the inspiration for Benjamin Britten – another son of Suffolk – to write his opera of the same name.

The watery calm, rustling rushes and remarkable beauty of the Norfolk Broads have inspired generations of writers. George Christopher Davies, writer, naturalist and yachtsman was credited with having discovered the Broads – in reality his works brought them to a wider audience than just those people who lived on them, fishing from punts and following an age-old way of life.

Perhaps the finest World War II thriller of all – The Eagle has Landed by Jack Higgins, was inspired by the remoteness of the wind swept dunes of the Norfolk Coast. John Sturges' film adaptation, starring Michael Caine, Donald Sutherland and many other cinema greats, captures the 'page turning' plot and the sense of infinite space in this quiet corner of England.

The writing of Colin Dexter and the activities of his created detective, Inspector Morse, played by the late John Thaw, are a present day representation of life beneath the 'dreaming spires' of Oxford. Morse's driving of his classic red Jaguar car, real ale drinking and choral singing in vaulted, gothic halls are all to a background of swelling, splendid music. There are guided tours of Morse's Oxford, visiting places where he solved fictitious crimes, and the pubs he enjoyed.

PLACES TO VISIT

The thatched roof and idyllic country garden would make Anne Hathaway's Cottage a very desirable residence today. When she was born there, in 1556, it was the comfortable home of a farmer and his family. Anne married William Shakespeare when she was 26 and he was 18, she brought a dowry of £6 13s and 4d to the marriage, he brought literary genius and everlasting fame.

Newstead Abbey is the magnificent house that the poet, Lord Byron, was forced to sell in 1818 after fleeing England to escape his creditors and increasing scandals about his personal life. Set in 300 acres of glorious gardens and grounds; there are many events and exhibitions with literary themes through the year. A monument to Boatswain, Byron's beloved dog that died of rabies, is just one of many tangible reminders of the short-lived poet.

A small terraced house in Eastwood, Nottinghamshire, with a haberdashery shop in the front room, was the birthplace of DH Lawrence. The house is furnished in the style it would have been when he was born in the room above the shop. The mines are no longer active, but the countryside where he walked is still quiet, providing the same contrast with industrial life as it does in many of his famous novels. Tel: 01773 763312.

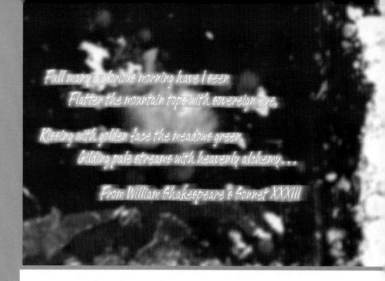

Full many a glorious morning have I seen
Flatter the mountain tops with sovereign eye,

Kissing with golden face the meadows green
Gilding pale streams with heavenly alchemy...

From William Shakespeare's Sonnet XXXIII

BOOKS TO READ

▶ Shakespeare's Dark Lady by Ian Wilson, an intriguing novel investigating the identity of the mysterious woman in the great bard's life.

▶ The Complete Critical Guide to DH Lawrence by Fiona Becket: the number of books written about Lawrence is greater than those he wrote himself. This work contains some of his contempories comments as well as current ones.

▶ Byron, Prince of Passion, Benita Eisler worked from the full range of Byron's papers and writings to produce this in depth biography.

A special place to buy books:

Readers' Rest, Steep Hill, Lincoln. Fantastic position halfway up (or down!) the steep hill between the Cathedral and the riverside town. New and second-hand books, lots of shelves to browse and a good reason to explore the area.

LITERARY ATTRACTIONS & FESTIVALS

▶ The Swan Theatre at Stratford upon Avon stages Royal Shakespearean Company Productions and has many pre and after theatre literary events. Tel: 01789 295623.

▶ The University of East Anglia's Literary Festival attracts present day 'greats' such as Harold Pinter and Seamus Heaney to talk, present and inspire. Tel: 01603 508050.

▶ The Oxford Literary Festival is based at the Oxford Union: focus on writers past and present, talks, readings and walking tours. Tel: 01865 514149.

The Raven Hotel

THE CULINARY Midshires

The very heartland of England, a broad sweep encompassing fertile acres, forest and much of the agricultural life of the Nation. It's an area where endeavour and enterprise sit side by side with good living. Initiatives such as the recently launched Tastes of Lincolnshire are helping to bring the rich diversity and supreme quality of produce of these regions to broader notice. Specialities such as Lincolnshire Chine - fine, local pork 'stuffed' with an abundance of parsley, cured like a ham and then sliced to serve as an hors d'oeuvre or with locally grown salads - are beginning to cross borders. Lincolnshire Poacher cheese has reached Paxton and Whitfields' superb Jermyn Street shop in London. Growers such as Ros and Nick Loweth at Abbey Farms sell their produce direct from their farm shop - and distribute to a wider market appreciative of the quality and flavour of asparagus and herbs grown on the silt fens. Lincoln Red beef is magnificent, FC Phipps, Q Guild butchers at Mareham le Fen sells this superb beef alongside Rare Breed meats, home cured hams and bacon - not surprising that FC Phipps was judged the winner in Country Life magazine's Best British Butcher Competition.

THE MENU:
Restaurant Des Clos

The following is one of a choice of degustation menus served at the Hotel Des Clos to introduce the style and saveur of cuisine at their outstanding Restaurant Des Clos.

Starter
Roast Scallop: Indian spices, parsley coulis, confit garlic, sweet garlic puree

Foie Gras Parfait: rhubarb confit, pain d'epice

Main Course
Cured Organic Salmon: Billingtons sugar syrup, citrus salad

'Plate of Pork': belly, trotter, tete, black pudding, creamed cabbage, honey and clove jus

Dessert
Cropwell Bishop Stilton

Raspberry Yoghurt

'Taste of Strawberries': salad, sauté, jelly, sorbet

'Banoffi pie'

THE VILLAGE: Burnham Market is one of the prettiest villages in Norfolk, it has over 40 delightful, privately owned shops to enjoy and one of the very best hostelries - The Hoste Arms. Proprietor Paul Whittome is a man in love with his hotel - he makes that clear in the title of his book, 'the hoste, my passionate affair'. The menus and food are full of promise - that they live up to. Lots of choice from Burnham Creek oysters to Hoi Sin Marinated Pork Belly. The restaurant and on warm days the tables outside are busy with appreciative regulars and visitors attracted by The Hoste's enviable reputation.

THE HEART: Nuthurst Grange is at the very centre of England. Within a twelve-mile radius you can find the National Exhibition Centre, the International Convention Centre, the Royal Show Ground, Warwick and Kenilworth Castles, Shakespeare's birthplace and a multitude of other attractions. The hotel itself nestles in rural tranquillity, over 7 acres of landscaped garden and woodland provide leafy avenues for a stroll before dinner, and it's worth building an appetite for. Contemporary French and British cuisine; everything from the canapés served with predinner drinks to the petit fours served with coffee are made in the kitchen by Head Chef Ben Davies and his enthusiastic team.

THE SIGNATURE: Steve Biggs, Head Chef at The Raven Hotel, has lived and worked in Shropshire for the last fourteen years - creating a valuable network of local suppliers. His signature dishes include Shank of Stottesdon Lamb - braised lamb, slow cooked in port and redcurrant, scented with rosemary and Confit of Duck with homemade beetroot and ginger chutney and a balsamic dressing. Spectacular views of the Derwent Valley and rural Northumbria from the Conservatory add additional spice to the delicious regional flavours.

THE CHEF: Raymond Blanc, Chef/Proprietor of Le Manoir aux Quat'Saisons is that very rare thing, a legend in his own lifetime. Never formally trained,' his expertise and experience grew from intuition, enhanced by experimenting and accumulating technical experience and surrounding himself with people who share the same vision'. He's also a very entertaining speaker - sharing his thoughts on the ultimate importance of the very best ingredients, reminiscing on his mother's delicious cooking - the flavours he still remembers so vividly, the scents that take him back in time. Food at his restaurant has that same precious quality, to evoke wonderful memories and a feeling of well being. Amongst his numerous awards is a recent Special Award from the Craft Guild of Chefs, based upon 'the individuals commitment and contribution to the industry as a whole.'

THE VINEYARD: 70 acres of vines, grape varieties from the world renowned Pinot Noir to modern, carefully selected varieties and cultivation methods from around the world, new techniques and traditional skills side by side. A tour of Three Choirs Vineyard's is a fascinating insight into how, after an absence of nearly 900 years, vines are flourishing and delicious wines are being made in England. The vineyard's viticulturist, Mike Garfield's highly sought after guided tours are a great reason to visit this leading vineyard - as is their restaurant. Excellent, award winning food, and of course wonderful wines to enjoy in the beautiful tranquillity of this special place.

THE HISTORY: An entry in the Domesday Book has the assets of the Mill at Shipston-on Stour as 16 acres and taxes of 10 shillings. Today called the Old Mill, this historic venue's present assets are an enviable combination of relaxed atmosphere, delightful ambiance and good food. There's also a private 2 acre island, formed by the River Stour and the Mill Race - the perfect place for a marquee in summer, for parties, Pimms and warm, riverside evenings.

Editor's Extras

One of the few remaining independent family run brewers left in the UK, *Batemans* brews a wide range of beers - including the memorably named 'Yellow Belly'. A fascinating visitor centre at Wainfleet, (and their beer's delicious anywhere...). Details at *www.bateman.co.uk*

Fish and chip fanciers from far and wide visit the 'chippy' in Upton in Lincolnshire where they still use the original coal-fired fryer! The Art Deco interior is well worth a look, too.

Taste of the area? Thornton Novice cheese hand crafted from unpasteurised ewes' milk has a delicate nutty flavour, made by Jo and Ray North who are full of useful information about their cheese, you can often find them at regional food fairs, more info at 01507 524398

Heather Hay Ffrench
Best Loved Food Editor

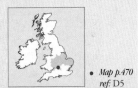
❝ Warwickshire's best kept secret, anything but run of the mill ... ❞

Sue & Wes Anson, La Jolla, CA, USA

ARROW MILL HOTEL

Ancient mill

**Arrow, Alcester,
Warwickshire B49 5NL**

**Telephone 01789 762419
Fax 01789 765170**

E-mail: *arrowmill@bestloved.com*

OWNERS
The Woodhams Family

ROOM RATES
3 Singles	£75
9 Doubles/Twins	£85 - £120
5 Family rooms	£90
1 Four-poster	£140
Includes full breakfast and VAT	

CHARGE/CREDIT CARDS

 • DC • MC • VI

RATINGS & AWARDS
Independent

FACILITIES
On site: *Garden, fishing*
2 meeting rooms/max 60 people
Nearby: *Golf, shooting*

RESTRICTIONS
No facilities for disabled guests
Pets by arrangement
Closed Christmas week

ATTRACTIONS
*Stratford-upon-Avon, Warwick Castle,
The Cotswolds, Coughton Court,
National Exhibition Centre*

AFFILIATIONS
Independent

NEAREST
MAJOR CITY:
Stratford-upon-Avon - 8 miles/20 mins

MAJOR AIRPORT:
Birmingham - 25 miles/40 mins

RAILWAY STATION:
Stratford-upon-Avon - 8 miles/20 mins

RESERVATIONS
Direct with hotel
*Quote **Best Loved***

ACCESS CODES
Not applicable

An ancient mill at the heart of England's culture and history

Arrow Mill was valued in the Domesday Book in 1086 at three shillings and sixpence (17pence), a severe underestimate. It continued as a working flour mill for centuries. Arrow Mill's supremely beautiful, secluded riverside setting in its own 60 acre grounds has hardly changed. There is still the same panoramic vista across the mill pond. The mill building retains its historic character. Ancient oak beams and roaring log fires recall England's countryside of long ago. The bedrooms are tastefully furnished, and the modern facilities are discreetly unobtrusive.

The Millstream Restaurant incorporates the original floor of the mill. The River Arrow continues to turn the wheel. The à la carte menu depends on high quality local ingredients from this garden area of England, as well as the excellent team of chefs. Lunches from the Miller's Table are similarly delectable.

Alcester is close to the centre of England, and to its historic and cultural heart. The North Warwickshire mines and Birmingham's smiths produced over 15,000 swords to arm Cromwell's army. Warwick, Leamington, Kenilworth and

Shakespeare's Stratford-upon-Avon are all nearby and make Arrow Mill an enviable spot from which to base a holiday.

LOCATION
Set back from the A435 1 mile south of Alcester.

MIDSHIRES

" We wanted you to know how much we enjoyed our stay. You have made it into a fantastic place. We will be back "

Anthony & Vicky Smee, London

181

● Map p.470
ref: E6

18th century country house — BIGNELL PARK HOTEL

A cosy and characterful retreat close to Blenheim and Oxford

Originally an 18th-century Cotswold stone farmhouse, Bignell Park Hotel combines traditional, old-world charm with the easy grace of a beautifully-run country house. The hotel is set in 2 ½ acres of secluded informal gardens and orchard close to the renowned Kirtlington Polo Club. It is also ideally situated for side trips to Blenheim Palace, ancestral home of the Dukes of Marlborough, the dreaming spires of Oxford, Warwick Castle, Stratford-upon-Avon, and a clutch of enchanting honey-coloured Cotswold villages.

Recently refurbished, each of the hotel's 23 bedrooms (including three with four-poster beds) has been attractively decorated and furnished with care. The comfortably elegant drawing room overlooks the garden and guests relax beside log fires in the colder months. The food at Bignell Park has never been better and the atmospheric candlelit restaurant with its wood beamed ceiling, open fire and minstrels' gallery is a wonderful setting to enjoy it. An extensive and carefully compiled wine list includes both fine New and Old World wines which complement

the English/French menu perfectly. A private dining room offers the perfect answer for small, intimate gatherings.

LOCATION

From M40 Junction 9, take the A41 towards Bicester. After about 1 ½ miles, turn left to Chesterton. Leaving Chesterton towards Bicester, Bignell Park is on the A4095.

**Chesterton, Bicester,
Oxfordshire OX26 1UE**

**Telephone 01869 326550
Fax 01869 322729**

E-mail: *bignell@bestloved.com*

MANAGING DIRECTOR
Ian Davies

GENERAL MANAGER
Mark Stevens

ROOM RATES
Single occupancy   £65 - £95
20 Doubles/Twins   £90 - £110
3 Four-posters   £125 - £155
Includes full breakfast and VAT

CHARGE/CREDIT CARDS

 ● *MC* ● *VI*

RATINGS & AWARDS
E.T.C. ★★ *Silver Award*
A.A. ★★★ ❀ 76%

FACILITIES
On site: *Garden*
2 meeting rooms/max 60 people
Nearby: *Golf, fishing*

RESTRICTIONS
No pets, guide dogs only

ATTRACTIONS
*Oxford Colleges, Blenheim Palace,
The Cotswolds, Warwick Castle,
Kirtlington Polo Club,
Silverstone Race Circuit,
Bicester Shopping Village*

AFFILIATIONS
Independent

NEAREST
MAJOR CITY:
Oxford - 10 miles/25 mins

MAJOR AIRPORT:
London Heathrow - 40 miles/1 hr

RAILWAY STATION:
Bicester North - 2 miles/10 mins
Bicester Town - 1 ½ miles/6 mins

RESERVATIONS
Direct with hotel
*Quote **Best Loved***

ACCESS CODES
Not applicable

MIDSHIRES

" This hotel has to be the nicest we know. The treatment we receive each time from the staff could not be bettered - please don't change anything "

Mrs S Barker, Question of Service

THE BROADWAY HOTEL

15th century abbot's retreat

The Green, Broadway, Worcestershire WR12 7AA

Telephone 01386 852401
Fax 01386 853879

E-mail: *broadway@bestloved.com*

GENERAL MANAGER
Simon Foster

ROOM RATES
3 Singles	*£80*
12 Doubles/Twins	*£118 - £125*
4 Superior doubles	*£138 - £145*
1 Four-poster	*£138 - £145*
Includes full breakfast and VAT

CHARGE/CREDIT CARDS

• DC • JCB • MC • VI

RATINGS & AWARDS
E.T.C. ★★★ *Silver Award*
A.A. ★★★ *68%*

FACILITIES
On site: *Garden*
Licensed for weddings
2 meeting rooms/max 20 people
Nearby: *Golf, tennis, fitness, riding*

RESTRICTIONS
No facilities for disabled guests
Pets by arrangement

ATTRACTIONS
The Cotswolds, Stratford-upon-Avon, Sudeley and Warwick Castles, Gardens of Hidcote and Kiftsgate, Bourton-on-the-Water, walking and cycling

AFFILIATIONS
Grand Heritage Hotels

NEAREST
MAJOR CITY:
Birmingham - 35 miles/45 mins

MAJOR AIRPORT:
London Heathrow - 90 miles/1 ¼ hrs
Birmingham - 40 miles/45 mins

RAILWAY STATION:
Evesham - 5 miles/10 mins

RESERVATIONS
Toll free in US: 888-93-GRAND
Quote **Best Loved**

ACCESS CODES
AMADEUS UI BHXBDH
APOLLO/GALILEO UI 10139
SABRE/ABACUS UI 40453
WORLDSPAN UI 40734

The Broadway descent to the temptations of good living

Broadway lays claim to be the prettiest village in England and, to heighten the excitement of its discovery, you have to sneak up on it - from Oxford. The road has been straight for miles riding across the undulating Cotswold hills when, suddenly, it arrives at a steep escarpment to reveal a vast panorama, The Vale of Evesham, aka The Garden of England. On a clear day you can see Wales, Worcester Cathedral, the Malvern Hills and 13 counties. At the base of the hairpin descent, is Broadway and you begin to understand why it's called broad way and how it earned its picturesque title.

The Broadway Hotel is set back on the green at the bottom of the village. It used to be a retreat for the Abbots of Pershore 600 years ago and it still has an aura of tranquillity though the monastic privations have given way to the sinful luxuries and comforts expected by today's travellers. It has all the low-beamed, mellow Cotswold charm of a traditional inn with attractive, modern fabrics and furnishings.

On race days, the Jockey Bar can get a bit lively but there is a secluded garden if you prefer. The Courtyard Restaurant will also entertain you with its à la carte dishes that earn the right to be accompanied by a decent bottle of wine.

Altogether, something surprisingly special.

LOCATION

Off the A44 on the village green at the bottom of Broadway.

"Tranquillity and beauty only surpassed by the excellence of the food and service"

Henry Blofeld, cricket commentator

• *Map p.470*
ref: D5

Victorian country mansion | BROCKENCOTE HALL

Authentic French enclave in the heart of the Worcestershire countryside

The builders of the original Victorian mansion that is now the beautiful Brockencote Hall Hotel, certainly knew a thing or two about finding a perfect place for relaxation.

Nestling in the heart of the Worcestershire countryside, Brockencote Hall is set in 70 acres of private parkland yet is close to the motorway network, just half an hour from Birmingham - the perfect location for touring the sites of an area rich in history and culture. From here, you are equally well-placed to visit Shakespeare's Stratford-upon-Avon, Warwick Castle, the idyllic Cotswolds and the wonders of Wales.

Guests at Brockencote Hall will experience something else that is unique in the area: the hotel is renowned for its authentic French ambience. Proprietors Joseph and Alison Petitjean have created a charming Gallic oasis in the heart of England, combining traditional French comfort and friendliness with superb French cuisine.

The hotel offers a choice of 17 superb bedrooms, all with en suite facilities, including one that has been especially designed to make stays comfortable for disabled guests.

LOCATION
Exit 1 (M42 west bound only) or Exit 4 (M5). Go into Bromsgrove and take the A448 towards Kidderminster. The hotel is 5 miles along on the left.

**Chaddesley Corbett,
Near Kidderminster,
Worcestershire DY10 4PY**
**Telephone 01562 777876
Fax 01562 777872**

E-mail: *brockencote@bestloved.com*

OWNERS
Alison and Joseph Petitjean

ROOM RATES
Single occupancy	£120 - £140
15 Doubles/Twins	£145 - £180
2 Four-posters	£180

Includes full breakfast and VAT

CHARGE/CREDIT CARDS

 • DC • MC • VI

RATINGS & AWARDS
E.T.C. ★★★ *Gold Award*
R.A.C. Blue Ribbon ★★★ *Dining Award 4*
A.A. ★★★ ❀❀
A.A. Top 200 - 02/03
Heart of England Excellence in Tourism
Silver Award - Small Hotel of the Year

FACILITIES
On site: *Garden, fishing, croquet, tennis 2 meeting rooms/max 50 people*
Nearby: *Golf, riding, fishing, water sports, clay pigeon shooting, archery*

RESTRICTIONS
No pets
Closed 1 Jan - 9 Jan

ATTRACTIONS
Warwick Castle, Worcester, Hereford Cathedral, Stratford-upon-Avon, Black Country Museum, Cotswolds, Ironbridge, Cadbury World, West Midlands Safari Park

AFFILIATIONS
Grand Heritage Hotels

NEAREST
MAJOR CITY:
Birmingham - 18 miles/30 mins

MAJOR AIRPORT:
Birmingham - 20 miles/30 mins

RAILWAY STATION:
Kidderminster - 4 miles/10 mins

RESERVATIONS
Toll free in US: 888-93-GRAND
Toll free in UK: 0800 056 0457
Quote **Best Loved**

ACCESS CODES
AMADEUS UI BHXBHC
APOLLO/GALILEO UI 27837
SABRE/ABACUS UI 52406
WORLDSPAN UI 41367

MIDSHIRES

Map p.470
ref: E4

> **" *I am sure that when you decide to stay at the Brookhouse you will find comfort and relaxation* "**
>
> *D Fotheringham-Kidd*

THE BROOKHOUSE

17th century farmhouse

Brookside, Rolleston-on-Dove, Burton-upon-Trent, Staffordshire DE13 9AA

Telephone 01283 814188
Fax 01283 813644

E-mail: *brookhouse@bestloved.com*

OWNER
John Westwood

ROOM RATES
7 Singles   £74 - £79
13 Doubles/Twins   £95 - £105
Includes full breakfast, complimentary newspaper and VAT

CHARGE/CREDIT CARDS

 • *DC* • *JCB* • *MC* • *VI*

RATINGS & AWARDS
Independent

FACILITIES
On site: *Garden*
1 meeting room/max 20 people
Nearby: *Golf, riding*

RESTRICTIONS
Limited facilities for disabled guests
No children under 12 years

ATTRACTIONS
Tutbury Castle, Tutbury Crystal, Haddon Hall, Keddleston Hall, Calke Abbey, Derbyshire Dales

AFFILIATIONS
Independent

NEAREST
MAJOR CITY:
Derby - 8 miles/15 mins

MAJOR AIRPORT:
Birmingham - 25 miles/40 mins
Manchester - 70 miles/1 ½ hrs

RAILWAY STATION:
Burton-upon-Trent - 3 miles/10 mins
Derby - 9 miles/20 mins

RESERVATIONS
Direct with hotel
Quote **Best Loved**

ACCESS CODES
Not applicable

MIDSHIRES

House of character, where dining is a pleasure and the beds amazing

After the River Dove abandons the cascades of the Derbyshire Dales, it winds languorously through the fertile flatlands between Burton-on-Trent and Derby. The area has a pastoral beauty scarcely known and barely touched by modern times. Rolleston-on-Dove is the quintessential Old English village complete with thatched cottages and a babbling brook, The Dove no less, running through it. This is the setting for The Brookhouse, not just posing postcard-pretty by the river but a charming village character.

The Brookhouse has woven a kind of magic over the people who work there. They are all local and as loyal as can be, two of the staff have been there more than 20 years and the only new boy is the owner, John Westwood, who has been there only 15 years! The service is nimble and comes wreathed in smiles and a winning country accent.

The restaurant has an excellent reputation for good food. Soft lights and candlelight reflect in silver and crystal; fresh flowers are everywhere. Freshness is the order of the day and the wine list offers imaginative, rare and unusual wines.

The bedrooms are splendidly appointed but do ask to see the other bedrooms; you will find a truly remarkable collection of antique beds, all gorgeously caparisoned. Comfortable, too! One of the great 'finds' in this book.

LOCATION

Rolleston is just outside Burton-upon-Trent between the A50 to Stoke-on-Trent and the A38 to Derby.

● *Map p.470*
ref: H4

185

BROOM HALL COUNTRY HOTEL

A charming family-run country home close to the Norfolk Broads

Broom Hall is a real family concern run by Nigel, Angela and Simon Rowling - and, of course, Hector the dog, who doubles as chief greeter and PR officer. The comfortable Victorian house lies at the end of a winding driveway flanked by lime trees in traditional English gardens planted with flourishing herbaceous borders. The gardens in turn are surrounded by 13 acres of paddocks and parkland ensuring utter peace and quiet.

This is a great place to wind down and relax, enjoy Angela and Simon's generous home cooking, and contemplate the views from the terrace or snuggle up to an open fire in the winter months. Telephones are banned from the bedrooms to further allow the setting to work its magic, but there is gentle exercise to be had in the heated indoor pool, or perhaps a game of snooker.

While staying at Saham Toney, you are in easy reach of the Norfolk Broads, the beaches and nature reserves of the North Norfolk Coast, and the royal Sandringham, where the Queen traditionally spends Christmas. The Jacobean glories of Blickling Hall are also nearby, and walkers can stretch their legs along the trans-Norfolk Peddars Way.

LOCATION

From the A11 take the A1075. At Watton turn left and then at the next roundabout turn right to Saham Toney on the B1077. Continue into Richmond Road and hotel entrance is on the left hand side.

Richmond Road,
Saham Toney, Near Thetford,
Norfolk IP25 7EX

Telephone 01953 882125
Fax 01953 882125

E-mail: *broomhall@bestloved.com*

OWNERS
Nigel, Angela and Simon Rowling

ROOM RATES
1 Single   £45 - £55
8 Doubles/Twins   £70 - £100
1 Four-poster   £120
Includes full breakfast and VAT

CHARGE/CREDIT CARDS
MC • VI

RATINGS & AWARDS
A.A. ★★ 68%

FACILITIES
On site: *Garden, heli-pad, indoor pool, snooker*
Licensed for weddings
1 meeting room/max 60 people
Nearby: *Golf, fishing, cycling, clay pigeon shooting, go-karting*

RESTRICTIONS
No facilities for disabled guests
Smoking in bar only
Pets by arrangement

ATTRACTIONS
Sandringham Royal Residence, Holkham Hall, Blickling Hall, Norwich, Heacham Lavender Farm, Cambridge and Ely, Newmarket

AFFILIATIONS
Independent

NEAREST
MAJOR CITY:
Norwich - 22 miles/40 mins

MAJOR AIRPORT:
Stansted - 60 miles/1 hr

RAILWAY STATION:
Thetford - 13 miles/20 mins

FERRY PORT:
Harwich - 65 miles/ 1 ¼ hrs

RESERVATIONS
Direct with hotel
Quote **Best Loved**

ACCESS CODES
Not applicable

MIDSHIRES

BURFORD HOUSE

Tudor town house

99 High Street, Burford, Oxfordshire OX18 4QA

**Telephone 01993 823151
Fax 01993 823240**

E-mail: *burford@bestloved.com*

OWNERS
Simon and Jane Henty

ROOM RATES
Single occupancy	£80 - £105
5 Doubles/Twins	£95 - £125
3 Four-posters	£115 - £140

Includes full breakfast and VAT

CHARGE/CREDIT CARDS

 • *JCB* • *MC* • *VI*

RATINGS & AWARDS
E.T.C. ◆◆◆◆◆ *Gold Award*
A.A. ◆◆◆◆◆ *Premier Collection*

FACILITIES
On site: *Garden*
Nearby: *Golf, fishing, riding*

RESTRICTIONS
*No facilities for disabled guests
No smoking in bedrooms
No pets*

ATTRACTIONS
*Oxford, Bath,
Stratford-upon-Avon,
Blenheim Palace,
Warwick Castle*

AFFILIATIONS
*Cotswolds Finest Hotels
Preston's Global Hotels*

NEAREST
*MAJOR CITY:
Oxford - 18 miles/20 mins*

*MAJOR AIRPORT:
London Heathrow - 60 miles/1 ½ hrs*

*RAILWAY STATION:
Kingham - 5 miles/10 mins
Charlbury - 5 miles/10 mins*

RESERVATIONS
Toll free in US: 800-544-9993
Quote **Best Loved**

ACCESS CODES
Not applicable

MIDSHIRES

Unashamed luxury at the gateway to the Cotswolds

Said to be the 'Gateway to The Cotswolds' in the 'most beautiful countryside in England' Burford just goes on getting prettier and prettier as time matures the same golden Cotswold stone that built Blenheim Palace and St Paul's Cathedral. In the centre of town, built on a steeply sloping High Street, amongst the quaint antique shops, tea rooms and traditional butchers and grocers is Burford House. It is a focal point in a scene of rural peace and plenty.

Though the house dates back to Tudor times, Simon and Jane Henty bring a freshness to their special kind of hospitality and already, this gift has made many friends. It appears effortless but that is the hallmark of professionals. Burford House is fast becoming a Cotswold landmark.

Described as a luxury Bed and Breakfast Town House Hotel, it is, indeed, very attractively furnished and decorated. Simon and Jane have made this their home - and it shows. The welcome is warm and friendly; the whole atmosphere is that of a private house. Four-poster beds and gleaming luxury bathrooms are there to indulge you. A flower-filled courtyard and cosy sitting rooms refresh the flagging spirit.

LOCATION

Burford is situated just north of the junction of the A424 and the A40 Oxford to Cheltenham road. The hotel is on the High Street in the middle of the town.

14th century manor house

CALCOT MANOR

Ancient and modern ...
an enduring family favourite

Calcot was originally converted in 1984 and is now run by Richard Ball. The hotel is located in an unspoilt part of the Cotswold Hills, well-placed for visiting Bath and within reach of the country's finest antique centres. There is a heated swimming pool, two tennis courts and a croquet lawn in the grounds and bicycles can be provided for touring the famous Cotswold villages.

This charming Cotswold manor house was originally a farmhouse dating back to the 15th century. Its beautiful stone barns and stables, now converted into further superb bedrooms, include a 14th century tithe barn that was built by Cistercian Monks in 1300 and is amongst the oldest in Britain.

The hotel is beautifully furnished and the service is friendly and unobtrusive. In the award-winning restaurant, guests can linger over delicious meals whilst enjoying wonderful views of the countryside.

Calcot welcomes families and has a number of suites with sofa beds, toys, child-listening facilities, a playroom and an outdoor play area. Additionally, guests can soon enjoy the use of a fitness studio, health and beauty treatments, sauna, steam room and hot tub in what is set to be a superb new health and leisure spa, due to open in Spring 2003.

LOCATION

Ideally situated on the edge of the Cotswolds, only 35 minutes north of Bath. Exit 18 off M4, Calcot is 4 miles west of Tetbury at junction of A46 and A4135.

**Near Tetbury,
Gloucestershire GL8 8YJ**
Telephone 01666 890391
Fax 01666 890394

E-mail: *calcot@bestloved.com*

MANAGING DIRECTOR
Richard J G Ball

ROOM RATES
Single occupancy £130 - £145
24 Doubles/Twins/Family £145 - £185
4 Family suites £185 - £200
Includes full breakfast and VAT

CHARGE/CREDIT CARDS

 ● DC ● MC ● VI

RATINGS & AWARDS
E.T.C. ★★★ *Gold Award*
R.A.C. Gold Ribbon ★★★ *Dining Award 3*
A.A. ★★★ ❀❀
A.A. Top 200 - 02/03

FACILITIES
On site: *Garden, heli-pad,
heated pool, croquet, tennis,
Health & Leisure Spa opening Spring 2003
Licensed for weddings
2 meeting rooms/max 100 people*
Nearby: *Golf, clay pigeon shooting, riding*

RESTRICTIONS
No pets

ATTRACTIONS
*Westonbirt Arboretum, Bath,
Badminton Horse Trails, The Cotswolds,
Berkeley Castle, Slimbridge Wildfowl Trust,
Cheltenham Racecourse*

AFFILIATIONS
*Preston's Global Hotels
Pride of Britain*

NEAREST
MAJOR CITY:
Bath - 22 miles/35 mins

MAJOR AIRPORT:
London Heathrow - 100 miles/1 ½ hrs
Bristol - 30 miles/45 mins

RAILWAY STATION:
Kemble - 15 miles/10 mins

RESERVATIONS
*Toll free in US: 800-544-9993
or 800-98-PRIDE*
Quote **Best Loved**

ACCESS CODES
*AMADEUS HK LHRCAL
APOLLO/GALILEO HT 41198
SABRE/ABACUS HK 34714
WORLDSPAN HK CALCO*

MIDSHIRES

CASTLE HOUSE

Luxury hotel

**Castle Street, Hereford,
Herefordshire HR1 2NW**

Telephone 01432 356321
Fax 01432 365909

E-mail: *castlehse@bestloved.com*

OWNERS
Dr and Mrs Albert Heijn

GENERAL MANAGER
Lisa Eland

ROOM RATES
4 Singles	£90
1 Double	£155
10 Suites	£165 - £210

Includes continental breakfast and VAT

CHARGE/CREDIT CARDS

 • *JCB* • *MC* • *VI*

RATINGS & AWARDS
E.T.C. ★★★ *Gold Award*
R.A.C. Gold Ribbon ★★★ *Dining Award 5*
A.A. ★★★ ✿✿✿✿✿
A.A. Top 200 - 02/03
A.A. Hotel of the Year 2001

FACILITIES
On site: *Garden*
Nearby: *Golf, swimming, tennis,
riding, fishing*

RESTRICTIONS
None

ATTRACTIONS
*Hereford Cathedral, Mappa Mundi,
Offas Dyke, Cider Museum, Eastnor Castle,
Black and White Village Trail*

AFFILIATIONS
*The Celebrated Hotels Collection
Small Luxury Hotels
Pride of Britain*

NEAREST
MAJOR CITY:
Hereford

MAJOR AIRPORT:
Birmingham - 65 miles/1 ½ hrs

RAILWAY STATION:
Hereford - 1 mile/5 mins

FERRY PORT:
Swansea - 74 miles/1 ¾ hrs

RESERVATIONS
*Toll free in US: 800-322-2403
or 800-525-4800 or 800-98-PRIDE*
Quote **Best Loved**

ACCESS CODES
*AMADEUS LX BHXCAS
APOLLO/GALILEO LX 30262
SABRE/ABACUS LX 55135
WORLDSPAN LX BHXCH*

MIDSHIRES

One of the most talked about hotels in the country

Close to the cathedral and its famed exhibition, this gracious small hotel occupies a handsome Grade II-listed mansion fashioned out of a pair of 18th-century Georgian villas over 100 years ago. A sensitive restoration programme has preserved many of the original features and the elegant décor and discrete, well-polished service recreate the feel of a timeless and hospitable private home.

Attention to detail is a watchword at Castle House. The lovely bedrooms are thoughtfully equipped with mini hi-fis and fridges stocked to guests requirements. Late arrival suppers can be pre-ordered so that upon arrival you could find a light supper - maybe smoked salmon and chilled white wine - waiting in the room. There is also a decanter of Hereford apple brandy for a night cap. Guests have use of a fully-equipped office suite and dining in is essential. Noted chef Stuart McLeod (ex-Savoy and Gleneagles Hotel) has created a series of delicious menus with a regional flavour including the seven-course Taste of the Marches gourmet experience. The hotel is very fortunate to have its own farm, Ford Abbey, which keeps the Kitchen supplied with Hereford beef and Gloucester Old Spot pork and bacon.

On first impressions, Hereford may appear slow and sleepy, but think again. You would need to extend your stay indefinitely to sample a fraction of the local attractions on offer, including the Mappa Mundi and chained library.

LOCATION

In the centre of Hereford. Follow signs for City Centre and then City Centre East. From St Owen's Street turn right into St Ethelbert Street, then veer right into Castle Street.

" *Charingworth Manor stands for unadulterated pleasure and I am not ashamed to enjoy it* *"*

Patrick Maclagan, Berkshire

• Map p.470
ref: D5

14th century manor

CHARINGWORTH MANOR

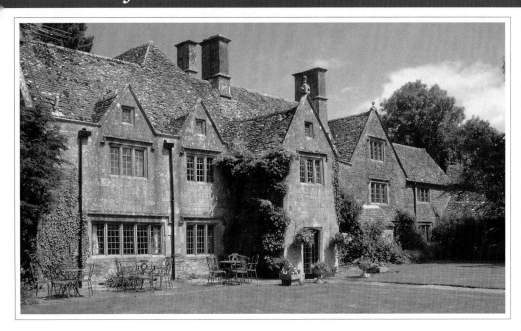

Near Chipping Campden, Gloucestershire GL55 6NS
Telephone 01386 593555
Fax 01386 593353
E-mail: *charingworth@bestloved.com*

GENERAL MANAGER
Walter Fallon

ROOM RATES
Single occupancy	£115 - £180
21 Doubles/Twins	£150 - £235
2 Four-posters	£250
3 Suites	£275

Includes full breakfast, early morning tea or coffee, newspaper and VAT

CHARGE/CREDIT CARDS

 • DC • MC • VI

RATINGS & AWARDS
R.A.C. Blue Ribbon ★★★ *Dining Award 3*
A.A. ★★★ ❀❀ *79%*

The perfect retreat from the twenty-first century

The ancient manor of Charingworth lies amidst the gently rolling Cotswold countryside, three miles from Chipping Campden, described as having 'the most beautiful High Street in the whole of England'. The 14th century manor house is set in its own peaceful grounds of fifty acres and offers breathtaking views.

Inside Charingworth is an historic patchwork of intimate public rooms with log fires burning during the colder months. The atmosphere is warm and relaxed, the service friendly and attentive with a real focus on customer care. There are 26 bedrooms, all furnished with antiques and fine fabrics.   The hotel has undergone great improvements over the past two years to ensure optimum comfort for guests.

The Chefs create imaginative dishes where great emphasis is placed on the finest produce available. Recognition has come in the form of dining awards from the AA and RAC.

To enhance your stay there is an elegant romanesque leisure spa, entirely in keeping with the relaxed comfort found throughout Charingworth. It offers an indoor heated pool, sauna, steam room, solarium and gym.

The hotel is in great proximity to local tourist attractions - Cotswold villages, Warwick Castle and famous gardens of Hidcote and Kiftsgate are very close by. Also easily reached are the historic Stratford-upon-Avon and Oxford.

FACILITIES
On site: *Garden, gym, heli-pad, croquet, tennis, indoor pool, sauna, steam room, solarium*
Licensed for weddings
3 meeting rooms/max 60 people
Nearby: *Clay shooting, archery*

RESTRICTIONS
No facilities for disabled guests
No children under 10 years in restaurant after 6.30 pm
No pets

ATTRACTIONS
The Cotswolds, Broadway, Warwick Castle, Stratford-upon-Avon, Cheltenham Races, Oxford, Chipping Campden

AFFILIATIONS
Grand Heritage Hotels
English Rose Hotels

NEAREST
MAJOR CITY:
Stratford-upon-Avon - 12 miles/30 mins

MAJOR AIRPORT:
Birmingham - 36 miles/1 hr

RAILWAY STATION:
Moreton-in-Marsh - 8 miles/10 mins

RESERVATIONS
Toll free in US: 888-93-GRAND
or 800-322-2403
Toll free in UK: 0800 282811
Quote **Best Loved**

ACCESS CODES
AMADEUS UI BHXCMH
APOLLO/GALILEO UI 84371
SABRE/ABACUS UI 57686
WORLDSPAN UI 40634

MIDSHIRES

LOCATION
Charingworth is situated on the B4035 between Chipping Campden and Shipston-on-Stour. 2 ½ miles from the A429.

" The service was efficient yet unobtrusive and the attention to the little details was commented on by all present "

Daphne Pearson, Monmouth

THE CLOSE HOTEL

16th century country house

**8 Long Street, Tetbury,
Gloucestershire GL8 8AQ**

**Telephone 01666 502272
Fax 01666 504401**

E-mail: *close@bestloved.com*

MANAGERS
Daren and Louise Bale

ROOM RATES
Single occupancy   £60 - £120
12 Doubles/Twins   £80 - £140
3 Four-posters   £125 - £150
*Includes full breakfast,
early morning tea and VAT*

CHARGE/CREDIT CARDS

 • *MC* • *VI*

RATINGS & AWARDS
A.A. ★★★ ❀❀❀
A.A. Top 200 - 02/03

FACILITIES
On site: *Garden
Licensed for weddings
4 meeting rooms/max 80 people*
Nearby: *Golf, tennis, riding*

RESTRICTIONS
*Limited facilities for disabled guests
No children under 12 years in
the restaurant for dinner
Pets by arrangement*

ATTRACTIONS
*The Cotswolds, Cheltenham Races,
Sudeley & Berkeley Castles,
Westonbirt Arboretum,
Badminton Horse Trials,
Highgrove & Gatcombe Royal Estates*

AFFILIATIONS
Independent

NEAREST
*MAJOR CITY:
Cheltenham - 25 miles/40 mins*

*MAJOR AIRPORT:
Birmingham - 83 miles/1 ½ hrs*

*RAILWAY STATION:
Kemble - 7 miles/15 mins*

RESERVATIONS
*Direct with hotel
Quote **Best Loved***

ACCESS CODES
Not applicable

MIDSHIRES

Traditional elegance in one of the Cotswold's finest 16th-century town houses

Just off the Market Square in the lovely old wool town of Tetbury, The Close dates from 1585. According to the town records, the house was so grand that its owner had to pay out one pound a year in rates while most of the other properties on Long Street were rated at a penny! Much altered over the years, and painstakingly restored, this gracious small hotel combines warmth and elegance with exacting standards of service.

The business of relaxation has been elevated to an art form at The Close. Guests can unwind in their spacious and richly decorated bedrooms, take tea in the antique splendour of the Withdrawing Room, or retreat to the cosy Sitting Room with its garden views, log fires and deep sofas. The delightful dining room boasts an 18th-century Adam ceiling and each chairback has been individually designed to match a special feature in the room. Daren Bale's highly acclaimed traditional yet imaginative cuisine has been awarded 3 AA rosettes, making the Close a great find for conoisseurs of good food.

Tetbury's antiques shops are a favourite haunt for enthusiasts. Other local attractions include the Westonbirt Arboretum, the Cotswolds, Cheltenham and Bath.

LOCATION

From Junction 18 of the M4, take A46 heading north, then onto A433. In Tetbury, turn left at Market Square. The hotel is on the left.

“ *The most amazing place! Everything was just perfect. Thank you* ”

Jon & Hilary Rowel, Sidney, Australia

17th century manor COCKLIFFE COUNTRY HOUSE HOTEL

A secret hideout in Sherwood Forest but with a modern slant

Romance is in the air at Cockliffe House, brought by the spirits of those romantic heroes Robin Hood and Lord Byron. A near neighbour at Newstead Abbey, his family home, it is quite possible that Byron was a frequent visitor, or that Robin Hood hid in this part of the mighty Sherwood Forest. Just six miles from Nottingham, it is ideally placed for visiting the city's castle and widely acclaimed, interactive Galleries of Justice, the Peak District or the Lincolnshire Wolds, but is secreted away down a tranquil country lane.

Of an intriguing design with half turrets at each corner, this 17th century manor was rescued from neglect by owners Dane and Jane Clark. Their affection for the house shows in their eclectic restoration, utilising items and styles from the past and contemporary design ideas in paint finishes and fabrics. The overall effect is stunning and the comfortably appointed rooms delight even the most discerning guest. The location is so perfect for weddings that receptions are a speciality, as are conferences, which enjoy the benefit of the relaxing setting and high-tech

facilities. With an award winning chef-patron to boot, Cockliffe House makes the ideal hideout!'

LOCATION
From city centre pick up signs for A60 Mansfield. Follow road through Arnold and at major roundabout continue on A60. At the Seven Mile pub turn right signed Police HQ. Follow road to top of hill and turn right (hidden turning). Hotel is ½ mile along on right.

**Burnt Stump Country Park,
Burnt Stump Hill,
Nottingham,
Nottinghamshire NG5 8PQ**

**Telephone 0115 9680179
Fax 0115 9680623**

E-mail: *cockliffe@bestloved.com*

OWNERS
Dane and Jane Clarke

ROOM RATES
Single occupancy   £95
10 Doubles/Twins   £105 - £150
Includes full breakfast and VAT

CHARGE/CREDIT CARDS

 • *DC* • *MC* • *VI*

RATINGS & AWARDS
Independent

FACILITIES
On site: *Garden*
1 meeting room/max 50 people
Nearby: *Golf, riding, fishing, fitness centre*

RESTRICTIONS
No facilities for disabled guests
Pets by arrangement

ATTRACTIONS
*Belvoir Castle, Chatsworth House,
Southwell Minster and Lincoln Cathedral,
Sherwood Forest, Hardwick Hall,
Belton House, Haddon Hall*

AFFILIATIONS
Independent

NEAREST
MAJOR CITY:
Nottingham - 4 miles/10 mins

MAJOR AIRPORT:
East Midlands Airport - 20 miles/25 mins

RAILWAY STATION:
Nottingham - 4 miles/10 mins

RESERVATIONS
Direct with hotel
Quote **Best Loved**

ACCESS CODES
Not applicable

MIDSHIRES

> **" It was lovely to get personal attention and you and your colleagues made the evening a great success "**
>
> *Jeremy Budden, Willis National, London*

COLWALL PARK HOTEL — *Country house*

Colwall, Malvern, Worcestershire WR13 6QG

Telephone 01684 540000
Fax 01684 540847

E-mail: *colwallpark@bestloved.com*

OWNERS
Iain and Sarah Nesbitt

ROOM RATES
3 Singles £65 - £80
17 Doubles/Twins £110 - £130
2 Suites £150
Includes full breakfast and VAT

CHARGE/CREDIT CARDS

 • *MC* • *VI*

RATINGS & AWARDS
E.T.C. ★★★ *Silver Award*
A.A. ★★★ ❀❀ 73%
A.A. Courtesy & Care Award 2000

FACILITIES
On site: *Garden, croquet, boules*
4 meeting rooms/max 150 people
Nearby: *Golf, riding, health club*

RESTRICTIONS
Limited facilities for disabled guests

ATTRACTIONS
Elgar Route, Eastnor Castle, Royal Worcester Porcelain, Shopping in historic Ledbury, Cheltenham, The Cotswold villages, Hereford & Gloucester

AFFILIATIONS
Independent

NEAREST
MAJOR CITY:
Worcester - 12 miles/20 mins

MAJOR AIRPORT:
Birmingham International - 40 miles/1 hr

RAILWAY STATION:
Colwall - 20 yds/ ½ min

RESERVATIONS
Direct with hotel
Quote **Best Loved**

ACCESS CODES
Not applicable

Inspirational surroundings on the sunny side of the Malvern Hills

Long celebrated as one of Britain's most alluring landscapes, the Malvern Hills have inspired generations of artists and writers, most notably the composer Sir Edward Elgar. From the undulating ridge of the hills, the views stretch over 10 counties, east across the Cotswolds, and west over the Severn Valley to the Welsh Mountains. This is wonderful countryside to explore, virtually untainted by tourism and full of interest.

Nestled on the western flanks of the hills, Colwall Park combines high standards of traditional comfort and noticeably professional, and efficient service, in equal measure. The hotel was awarded the English Courtesy and Care Award 2000 by the A.A.

The 22 bedrooms and suites are comfortable and prettily furnished, whilst downstairs guests can curl up in deep armchairs in the Lounge. The oak panelled Seasons Restaurant, so called because its menus change accordingly, offers guests a range of classic modern British cooking and has earned two AA rosettes, not to mention a significant local following. As an alternative to this excellent and well-priced menu, simpler dishes, particularly good for the business traveller, are available from the popular Lantern bar.

Colwall Park offers instant access to the hills that inspired Elgar's Pomp and Circumstance and is close to his birthplace and grave. Other side trips include Malvern and the Royal Worcester Porcelain Factory.

LOCATION
Situated in the centre of Colwall Village on the B4218 between Malvern and Ledbury.

" **The epitome of the English country hotel** *"*

Hilary Rubinstein, The Good Hotel Guide

Georgian country house

CONGHAM HALL

MIDSHIRES

Norfolk's finest country house experience

Not enough has been written extolling the virtues of Norfolk. In summer, acres of golden fields give way to the wilds of the Broads, a paradise to wildlife enthusiasts. In winter, its rugged coastline provides the perfect backdrop for reflective walks.

Another Norfolk virtue must be Congham Hall, the very essence of the country house experience. Its many acres of parkland include one of England's finest herb gardens. For Congham throws up romantic images of a seemingly vanishing rural England but here it is, thankfully, as fresh as ever.

The atmosphere can be described as relaxed luxury. A member of staff is never far away to attend your every need. Whether enjoying a book in the pot pourri-scented lounges or enjoying the pool, all has been designed to achieve an air of 'no hassle, no pressure, no noise!', as a guest put it. The spotless bedrooms are prettily furnished and exude a warmth and homeliness throughout.

If you come to Congham Hall in need of a good rest, your expectations will be met and exceeded. As a touring base for Norfolk and East Anglia you will find no better choice of hotel. Pilots should note the following heli-pad grid reference: OS 132 TF 712 229 N52 46.8 E000 31.9

LOCATION

From the A148/A149 interchange north east of Kings Lynn, follow the A148 towards Cromer for 100 yards. Turn right towards Grimston and the hotel is 2 ½ miles on left hand side.

Grimston, Kings Lynn, Norfolk PE32 1AH

Telephone 01485 600250
Fax 01485 601191

E-mail: *congham@bestloved.com*

OWNER
Countess von Essen

GENERAL MANAGER
Julie Woodhouse

ROOM RATES
1 Single   £99
15 Doubles/Twins   £155 - £185
4 Suites   £240

Includes full breakfast and VAT

CHARGE/CREDIT CARDS

 ● DC ● MC ● VI

RATINGS & AWARDS
R.A.C. Gold Ribbon ★★★ Dining Award 3
A.A. ★★★ ❀❀
A.A. Top 200 - 02/03

FACILITIES
On site: *Garden, heli-pad,
croquet, tennis, outdoor pool
Licensed for weddings
4 meeting rooms/max 100 people*
Nearby: *Golf, fishing, riding,
shooting, sailing*

RESTRICTIONS
*Limited facilities for disabled guests
Smoking permitted in lounge & bar only
No pets, kennels available*

ATTRACTIONS
*Holkham Hall, Sandringham Estate,
Houghton Hall, RSPB Bird Reserves,
Newmarket Racecourse, Ballooning*

AFFILIATIONS
*von Essen hotels - A Private Collection
Pride of Britain*

NEAREST
*MAJOR CITY:
Cambridge - 43 miles/1 hr*

*MAJOR AIRPORT:
London Stansted - 76 miles/1 ½ hrs*

*RAILWAY STATION:
Kings Lynn - 6 miles/15 mins*

RESERVATIONS
Toll free in US: 800-98-PRIDE
*Quote **Best Loved***

ACCESS CODES
*AMADEUS HK STNCON
APOLLO/GALILEO HK CONGH
SABRE/ABACUS HK 34243
WORLDSPAN HT 41199*

" A stay here is worthwhile for Baba Hine's food, Denis Hine's wine list and the air of bonhomie they create "

Vogue magazine

CORSE LAWN HOUSE HOTEL

18th century house

**Corse Lawn,
Gloucestershire GL19 4LZ**

**Telephone 01452 780771
Fax 01452 780840**

E-mail: *corselawn@bestloved.com*

OWNERS
Baba and Denis Hine

GENERAL MANAGER
Giles Hine

ROOM RATES
1 Single	*£80*
16 Doubles/Twins	*£100 - £145*
2 Suites	*£160*
Includes full breakfast and VAT

CHARGE/CREDIT CARDS

 • *DC* • *MC* • *VI*

RATINGS & AWARDS
E.T.C. ★★★ *Silver Award*
A.A. ★★★ ❀❀ *77%*
A.A. Half Bottle Wine List of the Year

FACILITIES
On site: *Garden, heli-pad, croquet,
tennis, indoor pool,
Licensed for weddings
2 meeting rooms/max 70 people*
Nearby: *Golf, riding, fishing*

RESTRICTIONS
None

ATTRACTIONS
*Berkeley Castle, Tewkesbury Abbey,
Slimbridge Wildfowl Trust, Wye Valley,
The Royal Forest of Dean, Malvern Hills*

AFFILIATIONS
Preston's Global Hotels

NEAREST
MAJOR CITY:
Gloucester - 9 miles/10 mins

MAJOR AIRPORT:
Birmingham - 30 miles/45 mins

RAILWAY STATION:
Gloucester - 9 miles/15 mins

RESERVATIONS
Toll free in US: 800-544-9993
*Quote **Best Loved***

ACCESS CODES
Not applicable

www.corselawn.bestloved.com

MIDSHIRES

Grace and flavour between the Malverns and Cotswolds

A Rip van Winkle style hamlet dozing peacefully amidst rolling Gloucestershire farmland, Corse Lawn appears blissfully unaware that the 21st century has arrived. It is hard to believe that the M5 and M50 motorways are just six miles away, and you can be in Cheltenham, Gloucester or Worcester within 20 minutes.

At the heart of the tiny settlement, a graceful Queen Anne house set in mature gardens overlooks the village green and the large duck pond which once served as a drive-in coach wash for a stage-and-four. Corse Lawn House has been the home of the Hine family, of cognac fame, and an intimate country house hotel for over 20 years.

Denis, Baba and Giles Hine are superlative hosts and have a natural ability to make you feel like one of their guests, rather than a hotel guest. Baba's renowned culinary skills have inspired several of today's leading modern British chefs. The varied menu, including seasonal grouse and partridge and a wine selection to drool over are all part and parcel of a great stay. As you would expect, the house cognac has been specially selected for Mr Hine and the cellar stocks many rare Hine vintages.

Winter or summer, this is a place to really unwind and enjoy, and a great location for exploring the Cotswolds, the Malvern Hills and the Forest of Dean.

LOCATION

**On B4211, 1 mile off A438. 5 miles from
Tewkesbury and 9 miles from Ledbury.**

❝ *Thank you for making our first visit to England so very memorable* ❞

James Lamberti, Vermont, USA

● *Map p.470*
ref: E5

Regency house — COTSWOLD HOUSE HOTEL

A top of the range hotel full of great surprises

This renowned Regency hotel, with its trademark spiral staircase, now incorporates five new luxury cottage rooms in the grounds. One has its own private garden and outdoor hot tub, another boasts a sitting room, log fire and private dining facilities. Here, as is the case throughout, sumptuous surroundings and décor are complemented by state-of-the-art technology. This means ISDN lines, Bang & Olufsen entertainment systems in the bedrooms and televisions in the bathrooms, where you can watch DVDs or listen to CDs at your leisure. Aromatherapy bath oils, along with pillows and bedding are on a bespoke menu where you can select from a range that includes cashmere blankets and Frette linen sheets.

Staff at this intimate country hotel, run by Ian and Christa Taylor, are dedicated to providing a truly individualised service that is sure to please even the most demanding guest. Dining is of course equally sophisticated. Simon Hulstone the Head Chef and the Garden Room Restaurant enjoys considerable acclaim. Here elegance is not just confined to the dining room itself, which has

French windows leading out onto the garden and terrace, it also extends to the food which he describes as 'modern, wholesome and seasonal'.

LOCATION
On B4081, 2 miles north of A44 between Moreton-in-Marsh and Broadway.

**Chipping Campden,
Gloucestershire GL55 6AN**
Telephone 01386 840330
Fax 01386 840310

E-mail: *cotswoldhouse@bestloved.com*

OWNERS
Ian and Christa Taylor

ROOM RATES
1 Single	£120
14 Deluxe Doubles/Twins	£175 - £245
5 Cottage Rooms	from £275

Includes full breakfast and VAT

CHARGE/CREDIT CARDS

 ● *MC* ● *VI*

RATINGS & AWARDS
R.A.C. Gold Ribbon ★★★ *Dining Award 4*
A.A. ★★★ ❀❀
A.A. Top 200 - 02/03

FACILITIES
On site: *Garden, croquet*
1 meeting room/max 80 people
Nearby: *Golf, riding, fishing, clay shooting,
walking, hot air ballooning*

RESTRICTIONS
No facilities for disabled guests
Pets by arrangement

ATTRACTIONS
*The Cotswolds, Stratford-upon-Avon,
Hidcote & Kiftsgate Gardens,
Warwick, Snowshill Manor,
Batsford Arboretum,
Berkeley & Sudeley Castles*

AFFILIATIONS
*Preston's Global Hotels
Pride of Britain*

NEAREST
MAJOR CITY:
Oxford - 33 miles/45 mins
Stratford - 10 miles/15 mins

MAJOR AIRPORT:
London Heathrow - 78 miles/1 ¾ hrs
Birmingham - 30 miles/30 mins

RAILWAY STATION:
Moreton-in-Marsh - 7 miles/10 mins

RESERVATIONS
Toll free in US: 800-544-9993
or 800-98-PRIDE
*Quote **Best Loved***

ACCESS CODES
AMADEUS HK BHXCOT
APOLLO/GALILEO HT 14869
SABRE/ABACUS HK 30593
WORLDSPAN HK COTSW

MIDSHIRES

" The welcome, comfort, service and food were second to none and I now have a new yardstick by which to judge other hotels "

A Pollard, Salisbury

COTTAGE COUNTRY HOUSE HOTEL *17th century cottages*

MIDSHIRES

Easthorpe Street, Ruddington, Nottinghamshire NG11 6LA

Telephone 0115 984 6882
Fax 0115 921 4721

E-mail: *cottage@bestloved.com*

OWNERS
Tim and Christina Ruffell

ROOM RATES
1 Single	£80
12 Doubles/Twins	£95 - £145
2 Suites	£150

Includes full breakfast and VAT

CHARGE/CREDIT CARDS

 • *JCB* • *MC* • *VI*

RATINGS & AWARDS
Independent

FACILITIES
On site: *Garden*
4 meeting rooms/max 60 people
Nearby: *Golf, tennis, water skiing, yachting, hunting/shooting, go-karting, fishing, riding,*

RESTRICTIONS
Limited facilities for disabled guests
Children by arrangement
No smoking in bedrooms or restaurant
No pets

ATTRACTIONS
Nottingham City and Castle,
Belvoir Castle, Newstead Abbey,
Holmepierrepoint National Watersports
Centre, Wollaton Hall,
Robin Hood Experience

AFFILIATIONS
Independent

NEAREST
MAJOR CITY:
Nottingham - 5 miles/10 mins

MAJOR AIRPORT:
London Heathrow - 130 miles/2½ hrs
East Midlands -13 miles/20 mins

RAILWAY STATION:
Nottingham - 5 miles/10 mins

RESERVATIONS
Direct with hotel
*Quote **Best Loved***

ACCESS CODES
Not applicable

www.cottage.bestloved.com

Impeccable hospitality with a touch of the Med

Such is the welcome at The Country Cottage House Hotel that you are greeted as soon as you pull up and escorted straight to your room without the usual form-filling formalities. And, while drinks or light snacks are offered, your luggage is portered and your car parked.

Having settled into your room, all en-suite with direct dial telephones, colour TV's and tea and coffee making facilities, you begin to appreciate the hotel's unique personality created by its owners Tim and Christina Ruffell. Mediterranean influences are everywhere (both lived and worked in the region for some years) from the yacht cabin-style single room to the eclectic menu and the many ornaments and pictures collected over the years. The hotel, renovated by local craftsmen to the Ruffell's design (winning three conservation awards), is formed by 17th century cottages around a private, gated courtyard and walled garden. Inside, a superb Inglenook fireplace and a well-stocked barrel-vaulted wine cellar heighten its authentic character.

Should you wish to get to know the area, Christina loves Nottingham and its environs and happily shares her vast local knowledge with you.

'The Cottage' is aptly named: small, cosy, full of character, old-fashioned values and boundless hospitality, with excellent facilities for conferences and weddings. Don't miss it.

LOCATION
3 miles south of Nottingham in Ruddington.
Turn right off main A60. Turn right into High Street and right again into Easthorpe St.
The hotel is 150 metres on right.

" *Restores one's confidence in English hotels. Wonderful setting, superb food, super atmosphere. Most enjoyable* "

Terry & Irene Cockle, Surrey

● *Map p.470*
ref: D5

Country hotel | THE COTTAGE IN THE WOOD

Wine, dine and savour one of the finest views in England

High in the Malvern Hills, there is a secluded hideaway embraced by woodlands on three sides. The fourth is open to the view and a truly breathtaking vista that unfurls across the Severn Vale for 30 miles or more. There is no doubt that the Cottage in the Wood occupies a magical position, but it is also a delightful family-run hotel and restaurant, spread over a trio of attractive historic buildings.

The hands-on Pattin family, headed up by John and Sue, are involved in every aspect of the hotel creating a genuinely relaxed and welcoming atmosphere. The fine Georgian Dower House contains the restaurant and a handful of bedrooms, while Beech Cottage offers pretty, cottagey-style accommodation, and the guest rooms in the newly rebuilt Folly House (opening May 2003) command the finest views of all. Good food is assured in the dining room and John has collected a superb wine list featuring over 600 bottles and halves at astonishingly affordable prices.

Guests can enjoy bargain breaks year round and discounted rates at the nearby Worcestershire Golf Course. Walks in the Malverns begin at the front door and sightseeing opportunities include three cathedral cities, Warwick Castle and Stratford-upon-Avon.

LOCATION

10 miles from the M5 - from the south take junction 8, from the north take junction 7. The hotel is signposted 3 miles south of Great Malvern off the A449.

**Holywell Road,
Malvern Wells,
Worcestershire WR14 4LG**

**Telephone 01684 575859
Fax 01684 560662**

E-mail: *cottagewood@bestloved.com*

OWNERS
John and Sue Pattin

ROOM RATES
Single occupancy	£79 - £92
20 Doubles/Twins	£98 - £160

Includes full breakfast and VAT

CHARGE/CREDIT CARDS

 ● *MC* ● *VI*

RATINGS & AWARDS
E.T.C. ★★★ *Silver Award*
A.A. ★★★ ❀❀ *75%*

FACILITIES
On site: *Garden
1 meeting room/max 20 people*
Nearby: *Golf, walking, shooting, fishing, riding*

RESTRICTIONS
*No facilities for disabled guests
Pets by arrangement*

ATTRACTIONS
Malvern Hills, Worcester Cathedral, Warwick Castle, Stratford-upon-Avon, Gloucester Cathedral, The Cotswolds, Royal Worcester Porcelain, Elgar Trail

AFFILIATIONS
Independent

NEAREST
*MAJOR CITY:
Birmingham - 43 miles/1 hr*

*MAJOR AIRPORT:
Birmingham - 48 miles/1 hr*

*RAILWAY STATION:
Great Malvern - 3 miles/5 mins*

RESERVATIONS
Direct with hotel
Quote **Best Loved**

ACCESS CODES
Not applicable

MIDSHIRES

❝ Superb food, good wine, even forgot the weather ❞

Patrick Dewitt

THE CROWN AT BLOCKLEY

16th century coaching inn

**High Street, Blockley,
Moreton-in-Marsh,
Gloucestershire GL56 9EX**

**Telephone 01386 700245
Fax 01386 700247**

E-mail:
crownmoreton@bestloved.com

OWNERS
Andrew Kertai and Mandy Eden

ROOM RATES
Single occupancy	£60
18 Doubles/Twins	£90 - £110
4 Four-posters	£120
3 Suites	£120

Includes full breakfast and VAT

CHARGE/CREDIT CARDS

 • DC • MC • VI

RATINGS & AWARDS
R.A.C. ★★★ *Dining Award 2*

FACILITIES
On site: *1 meeting room/max 50 people*
Nearby: *Golf, leisure centre, clay pigeon
shooting, archery, riding*

RESTRICTIONS
No facilities for disabled guests

ATTRACTIONS
*Broadway, Stratford-upon-Avon,
Warwick Castle, Oxford,
Cotswold villages, Wildlife Park*

AFFILIATIONS
Independent

NEAREST
MAJOR CITY:
Oxford - 25 miles/30 mins

MAJOR AIRPORT:
Birmingham - 40 miles/1 hr

RAILWAY STATION:
Moreton-in-Marsh - 5 miles/10 mins

RESERVATIONS
Direct with hotel
Quote **Best Loved**

ACCESS CODES
Not applicable

A comfortable and traditional inn with an award-winning restaurant

This charming, award-winning, mellow-stoned 16th century coaching inn, with its trademark archways, is set in a picturesque village in the heart of the Cotswolds. The friendly staff are always on hand to make your stay memorable. The 24 well-equipped and tastefully furnished bedrooms are all en suite and include colour television and tea making facilities.

In summer, the Crown provides the perfect setting to enjoy a drink and fine food under a cooling parasol on the patio or in the garden. On colder days you can relax and enjoy the home comforts of the friendly atmosphere of this family-run hotel in front of a log fire.

The Rafters Restaurant has a fine menu of traditional English and European cuisine. The Bar offers a lighter meal and chance to meet one of the many local characters. For smaller business meetings, there is a conference room making a pleasant change from the office environment.

The Crown Hotel reflects the tranquil nature of the Cotswolds with walks along tree-lined footpaths and horse riding from local stables. There is a golf club nearby.

LOCATION
**2 miles off the A44 Evesham
to Moreton-in-Marsh road.**

" *Superb! The sex was nearly as good as the food!* *"*

Paul and Sally Whitmore, Ipswich, Suffolk

Guest house

DANNAH FARM

A real working farm on The Chatsworth Estate

Wake up to a traditional country breakfast with home-made bread and free-range eggs on a real working farm that is part of The Chatsworth Estate. Originally a royal deer park, Dannah is home to tenant farmers Joan and Martin Slack, who have a mixed working farm, high above the Ecclesbourne valley.

Despite its rural isolation, the hotel is only 20 minutes from the M1 and very close to both Nottingham and Derby. It is also within easy reach of Derbyshire's many tourist attractions, including Bakewell, Haddon Hall - where the classic novel Jane Eyre was set - and Alton Towers. Despite its beauty, the area has less tourists than one might expect, with golf, fishing and riding facilities nearby. It is ideal for those who love walking and touring, as well as families with children and the single business traveller who wants a few home comforts at the end of a long day.

Dinner is good, home-made food; made from local produce, cooked and prepared by Joan Slack herself and served at 7pm. As winners of a Best of Tourism Award, Dannah combines classic country (think cats, chickens, pigs and an English

Setter called Cracker) with a few little luxuries, like four-poster beds and whirlpool baths, thrown in.

LOCATION

From Belper take the A517 signed Ashbourne. Shortly after Blackbrook, turn right towards Shottle. The hotel is on the junction of Chequer Lane and Palace Lane.

Bowman's Lane,
Shottle, Near Belper,
Derbyshire DE56 2DR

Telephone 01773 550273
Fax 01773 550590

E-mail: *dannah@bestloved.com*

OWNERS
Joan and Martin Slack

ROOM RATES
Single occupancy	£54 - £65
5 Doubles/Twins	£79 - £120
3 Suites	£120
Includes full breakfast and VAT

CHARGE/CREDIT CARDS

MC • VI

RATINGS & AWARDS
A.A. ◆◆◆◆◆ *Premier Collection*

FACILITIES
On site: *Garden*
1 meeting room/max 15 people
Nearby: *Golf, fishing, riding,
clay pigeon shooting*

RESTRICTIONS
*Limited facilities for disabled guests
Smoking in sitting room only
No pets
Closed Christmas*

ATTRACTIONS
*Chatsworth House, Haddon Hall,
Bakewell, Blue John Mines,
Alton Towers, Dovedale,
Denby Pottery*

AFFILIATIONS
Independent

NEAREST
MAJOR CITY:
Derby - 9 miles/20 mins

MAJOR AIRPORT:
East Midlands - 23 miles/30 mins

RAILWAY STATION:
Derby - 9 miles/20 mins

RESERVATIONS
Direct with hotel
Quote **Best Loved**

ACCESS CODES
Not applicable

MIDSHIRES

> *It is said to be a mistake to return - not here. Wonderful again*
>
> Jenny & Colin, Surrey

THE DIAL HOUSE HOTEL

Manor house

**The Chestnuts, High Street,
Bourton-on-the-Water,
Gloucestershire GL54 2AN**

**Telephone 01451 822244
Fax 01451 810126**

E-mail: *dial@bestloved.com*

OWNERS
Adrian and Jane Campbell-Howard

ROOM RATES
1 Single	£57
9 Doubles/Twins	£114
3 Four-posters	£138
Includes full breakfast and VAT

CHARGE/CREDIT CARDS

 • *JCB • MC • VI*

RATINGS & AWARDS
E.T.C. ★★ *Silver Award*
A.A. ★★ ❀❀ 74%
*West Country Cooking 'Best Hotel in
Gloucestershire 2002'*

FACILITIES
On site: *Garden, croquet, putting lawn
1 meeting room/max 20 people*
Nearby: *Golf, riding, fishing*

RESTRICTIONS
*No facilities for disabled guests
No children under 5 years
Smoking in bar area only
No pets*

ATTRACTIONS
*The Cotswolds, Blenheim Palace, Oxford,
Sudeley Castle, Hidcote Gardens,
Stratford -upon-Avon*

AFFILIATIONS
Independent

NEAREST
*MAJOR CITY:
Cheltenham - 17 miles/25 mins*

*MAJOR AIRPORT:
London Heathrow - 74 miles/1 ½ hrs*

*RAILWAY STATION:
Moreton-in-Marsh - 9 miles/12 mins*

RESERVATIONS
*Direct with hotel
Quote **Best Loved***

ACCESS CODES
Not applicable

A secret and luxurious hideaway in the Cotswolds

Imagine: it's a rare blue English summer's day, and you are lazing in the leaf-green walled garden of a classic, Cotswold stone house. All is calm around you and picture-postcard pretty; somewhere in the distance you can hear the gentle thwack of croquet on the lawn. You are staying in the Dial House Hotel, and from your four-poster bedroom window you can see the River Windrush, which meanders right through the centre of a quintessentially English country village.

Known locally as the Venice of the Cotswolds, Bourton-on-the-Water is an idyllic, romantic location. In centuries past, Shakespeare himself might even have been inspired by its tranquil waters, as Stratford upon Avon is only half-an hour's drive away. But here, just as it is in Italy, food is the music of love: the oak-beamed restaurant boasts two AA rosettes, and its head chef, Jonathan Lane-Robinson has mastered his craft at some of the most prestigious establishments in the UK. The menu is British with a modern European influence and includes local game and fish. It's hard to believe that London is just 40 miles away.

LOCATION
*In the centre of Bourton village on the corner
of the High Street and Sherborne Street.*

MIDSHIRES

" A place where time for living has not been overtaken by the pace of life "

Mr J Harris, New York

● *Map p.470*
ref: C5

18th century town house

DINHAM HALL

An extraordinary hotel in an extraordinary town

There is something very special about Ludlow. Only a small market town, it has everything anyone could wish for - delightful shops, outstandingly pretty streets, a romantic castle, a river, all set in beautiful countryside and - to cap it all - more top-quality restaurants than any town in Britain outside London! Obviously a place not to be missed, and the same can be said of Dinham Hall.

Hard by the castle, centre of the Ludlow Festival, the hotel's elegant furnishings complement its 1792 origins. Two bedrooms are in a cottage in the grounds, but all have modern facilities and decor in an appealing country style. With food standards so high in Ludlow, Dinham Hall proudly offers tempting French cuisine in several settings: the elegant main restaurant with wonderful views; the Green room for intimate private parties or the Merchant suite with its attractive beamed roof.

With a wealth of things to do here -shopping for antiques, fishing, golfing, walking on the hills, visiting the award -winning Ironbridge Gorge Industrial Museum or some fine castles. In fact, the hotel is delighted to arrange a day out, often at preferential rates.

LOCATION

On the A49, 20 miles north of Hereford and 25 miles south of Shrewsbury.

Dinham, Ludlow, Shropshire SY8 1EJ

Telephone 01584 876464
Fax 01584 876019

E-mail: *dinham@bestloved.com*

OWNER
Jean-Pierre Mifsud

GENERAL MANAGER
Alex Grainger

ROOM RATES
2 Singles £75
9 Doubles/Twins £130 - £180
3 Four-posters £160
Includes full breakfast and VAT

CHARGE/CREDIT CARDS

 ● *DC* ● *MC* ● *VI*

RATINGS & AWARDS
E.T.C. ★★★
R.A.C. ★★★ *Dining Award 2*
A.A. ★★★ ❀❀ 72%

FACILITIES
On site: *Garden*
1 meeting room/max 60 people
Nearby: *Golf, riding, fishing, tennis, clay pigeon shooting*

RESTRICTIONS
Limited facilities for disabled guests
No children under 8 years in restaurant
Pets by arrangement

ATTRACTIONS
Ludlow Castle, Stokesay Castle, Hereford Cathedral & the Mappa Mundi, Ironbridge Museum, Shrewsbury, Burford House

AFFILIATIONS
Independent

NEAREST
MAJOR CITY:
Shrewsbury - 25 miles/30 mins

MAJOR AIRPORT:
Birmingham - 59 miles/1 ¼ hrs

RAILWAY STATION:
Ludlow - ¼ mile/5 mins

RESERVATIONS
Direct with hotel
Quote ***Best Loved***

ACCESS CODES
Not applicable

MIDSHIRES

❝ I have travelled extensively and this is one of the best hotels I can honestly say I have ever stayed in ❞

Paul Dane, Leicestershire

THE DOG AND PARTRIDGE

15th century inn

**High Street, Tutbury,
Burton-on-Trent,
Staffordshire DE13 9LS**

**Telephone 01283 813030
Fax 01283 813178**

E-mail: *dogpartridge@bestloved.com*

GENERAL MANAGER
Frederick Muddiman

ROOM RATES
3 Singles £75
23 Doubles/Twins £85 - £100
3 Four-posters £110
Includes full breakfast and VAT

CHARGE/CREDIT CARDS

● MC ● VI

RATINGS & AWARDS
Independent

FACILITIES
On site: *Garden*
Nearby: *Leisure club, complimentary use of Golf & Country Club*

RESTRICTIONS
*Limited facilities for disabled guests
Pets by arrangement*

ATTRACTIONS
*Tutbury Castle, Tutbury Crystal,
Bass Brewery Museum, Alton Towers,
Sudbury Hall & Museum,
Peak District National Park*

AFFILIATIONS
Independent

NEAREST
MAJOR CITY:
Derby - 12 miles/20 mins

MAJOR AIRPORT:
East Midlands - 19 miles/35 mins

RAILWAY STATION:
Hatton - ¼ mile/5 mins

RESERVATIONS
Direct with hotel
*Quote **Best Loved***

ACCESS CODES
Not applicable

An amazing array of food choices and very comfortable too

Behind a superb half-timbered façade gently bowed with age and adorned with colourful window boxes, the Dog & Partridge is a storybook village inn at the heart of historic Tutbury. This venerable hostelry dates back to 1440, and sits neatly positioned on the border between Staffordshire and its famous potteries and the rugged upland landscape of Derbyshire.

The Dog & Partridge is a friendly place, family-owned and run by charming and enthusiastic staff. Great importance is placed on good food with two dining rooms to choose from. The renowned Carvery is a local institution, while the cosy Brasserie with its ox-blood walls, leather armchairs and subtle lighting offers a modern British menu with a few Mediterranean inspired dishes. And so to bed - perhaps in one of the beautifully restored Heritage rooms. These have been stylishly furnished without losing their traditional appeal and feature such treats as CD players, luxurious bathrooms, and modem facilities for business travellers. Romantic weekends are catered for with four poster and half tester beds.

Around and about there is plenty to see and do from visits to stately homes to a round of golf at the impressive Branston Golf & Country Club.

LOCATION
Take junction 22 from the M1, onto the A50. Turn left onto the A511. At the roundabout just past Tutbury & Hatton station, turn onto Bridge Street towards Tutbury. Take the 2nd left, and follow the road round to the right, onto High Street.

MIDSHIRES

" Everything and everyone was wonderful. We feel fortunate to have happened upon you "

Freling & Linda Smith, New York

17th century farmhouse

DORMY HOUSE

A haven for Stratford-upon-Avon, The Cotswolds and Broadway itself

Dormy House is set high in the beautiful Cotswold countryside amid picturesque, medieval villages. Originally a 17th century farmhouse, the hotel blends its historic past with 21st century facilities and personalised service. Each of the 48 bedrooms is beautifully decorated and provides every comfort for a good night's rest.

The charming lounges, enhanced with bowls of fresh flowers, have deep armchairs in which to relax. In winter, roaring log fires provide a welcoming atmosphere. The candlelit Tapestries Restaurant offers diners the choice of cosy alcoves in the old farmhouse or the elegant conservatory style dining room. The food is of a truly international standard; the freshest ingredients of the highest quality ensure an unforgettable experience. Lunch and evening meals are also served in the oak-beamed Barn Owl bar.

Surrounding the hotel on three sides is the Broadway Golf Club where guests can play by arrangement. Alternatively, guests can explore the numerous National Trust properties and gardens nearby, such as Hidcote, Kiftsgate and the Brockhampton Estate. The friendly staff are a mine of information on the surrounding attractions, including Cotswold villages, Stratford's theatres and sporting facilities.

LOCATION

On the A44, at the top of Fish Hill 1 ½ miles from Broadway Village, take the turn signposted Saintbury and Picnic Area. After ½ mile fork left and Dormy House is on the left.

Willersey Hill, Broadway,
Worcestershire WR12 7LF
Telephone 01386 852711
Fax 01386 858636
E-mail: *dormy@bestloved.com*

DIRECTOR
Ingrid Philip-Sorensen

GENERAL MANAGER
David Field

ROOM RATES
Single occupancy   £80 - £110
40 Doubles/Twins   £150 - £160
4 Four-posters   £185
4 Suites   £195
    Includes full breakfast and VAT

CHARGE/CREDIT CARDS

 ● *DC* ● *MC* ● *VI*

RATINGS & AWARDS
E.T.C. ★★★ *Silver Award*
R.A.C. ★★★ *Dining Award 3*
A.A. ★★★ ✿✿ *78%*

FACILITIES
On site: *Garden, gym, croquet, putting green, sauna, billiards*
Licensed for weddings
5 meeting rooms/max 170 people
Nearby: *Golf, riding, fishing, tennis, clay pigeon shooting, archery*

RESTRICTIONS
Limited facilities for disabled guests
No pets in public rooms
Closed 25 - 27 Dec

ATTRACTIONS
Warwick Castle, Blenheim Palace, Stratford-upon-Avon, The Cotswolds, Broadway, Chipping Campden, Gardens of Hidcote and Kiftsgate

AFFILIATIONS
Independent

NEAREST
MAJOR CITY:
Oxford - 40 miles/1 hr

MAJOR AIRPORT:
Birmingham - 40 miles/1 hr
London Heathrow - 90 miles/2 hrs

RAILWAY STATION:
Moreton-in-Marsh - 6 miles/10 mins

RESERVATIONS
Direct with hotel
Quote **Best Loved**

ACCESS CODES
Not applicable

MIDSHIRES

❝ Not since Château de Bagnols in France has there been such attention to detail in an historic house hotel. It should be an inspiration to English hoteliers ❞

Lyn Middlehurst, Gallivanter's Guide

FAWSLEY HALL

15th century manor

Fawsley, Near Daventry, Northamptonshire NN11 3BA

Telephone 01327 892000
Fax 01327 892001

E-mail: *fawsley@bestloved.com*

GENERAL MANAGER
Jeffrey Crockett

ROOM RATES
4 Singles	£125 - £135
19 Doubles/Twins	£150 - £180
12 Superior rooms	£185 - £215
6 Four-posters	£195 - £260
3 Suites	£200 - £295

Includes continental breakfast and VAT

CHARGE/CREDIT CARDS

 • *DC* • *MC* • *VI*

RATINGS & AWARDS
A.A. ★★★★ ✿✿

FACILITIES
On site: *heli-pad, tennis, health & beauty, fitness studio*
Licensed for weddings
7 meeting rooms/max 120 people
Nearby: *Golf, fishing, shooting, riding*

RESTRICTIONS
Limited facilities for disabled guests

ATTRACTIONS
Althorp, Sulgrave Manor, Warwick Castle, Silverstone, Stratford-upon-Avon, Towcester Racecourse

AFFILIATIONS
The Celebrated Hotels Collection

NEAREST
MAJOR CITY:
Birmingham - 40 miles/ 1 hr

MAJOR AIRPORT:
Birmingham - 35 miles/50 mins
Heathrow - 80 miles/1 ½ hrs

RAILWAY STATION:
Rugby - 18 miles/30 mins

RESERVATIONS
Toll free in US: 800-322-2403
Quote Best Loved

ACCESS CODES
Not applicable

www.fawsley.bestloved.com

MIDSHIRES

Spend a little time living in the lap of history

Shakespeare's Cottage at Stratford-upon-Avon, the ancestral homes Sulgrave Manor (George Washington), and Althorp, (Diana, Princess of Wales) form a triangle (all within 30 minutes drive) whose heart is Fawsley Hall. Each place marks an important aspect of England's colourful heritage.

Fawsley Hall in many respects is as historically and architecturally important - better yet you can stay here! This 500 year old stately house consists of three expertly and sensitively restored Tudor, Georgian, and Victorian wings allowing the guest ample choice of historic accommodation. Topping off the house are the glorious Capability Brown designed views. A more idyllic setting has rarely been realised. Luxury pervades every aspect of the Hall. From the decorative features to the staff's enthusiastic attentiveness you can easily begin to believe that you too are the Lord of the Manor.

While the decor is left to history, the restaurant provides a refreshing contemporary contrast. Here you will find serious cutting edge European cuisine excellently prepared and lovingly served. Additionally, Fawsley has a new fitness studio and beauty treatment rooms, with a relaxation room, sauna and hot tub planned for 2003. This is a great place for an intimate romantic getaway or a grand memorable gathering. In any event, Fawsley Hall should not be missed.

LOCATION
Take exit 11 off the M40 and follow the A361 signposted for Daventry. The hotel is situated between Charwelton and Badby.

Best Loved Hotels of the World

> *" Comfortable, charming and unpretentious . . . it is one of the places to which I keep coming back "*

Elizabeth Ortiz, Gourmet Magazine

17th century town house hotel

THE FEATHERS

Warmth and charm next to Sir Winston Churchill's birthplace

This privately owned 17th century town hotel is located in the heart of picturesque Woodstock which nestles by the gates of Blenheim Palace, the home of the 11th Duke of Marlborough and birth place of Sir Winston Churchill. The Feathers offers the ideal base from which to explore the dreaming spires of the university city of Oxford and the beautiful Cotswolds, yet it is only 1 ½ hours from London.

The hotel has 17 individually designed rooms and five suites all with antiques, books and interesting pictures. All rooms have private bathrooms, colour televisions with satellite channels and direct dial telephones.

In winter, log fires blaze in all the sitting rooms and the bar. In warmer months, the courtyard garden provides the ideal location to take a light meal or refreshment.

The well renowned restaurant has received much critical acclaim. The interesting dishes on the menu are carefully but simply created using only the finest ingredients. Guests may select from the constantly changing à la carte menu.

LOCATION

From the south, take the A44 to Woodstock. After Blenheim Palace gates take first left after traffic lights - the hotel is on left.

Market Street, Woodstock, Oxfordshire OX20 1SX

Telephone 01993 812291 Fax 01993 813158

E-mail: *feathers@bestloved.com*

RESIDENT MANAGER
Gavin Thomson

ROOM RATES
Single occupancy £115 - £135
16 Doubles/Twins £135 - £185
4 Suites £240 - £290
Includes full breakfast and VAT

CHARGE/CREDIT CARDS
 • DC • JCB • MC • VI

RATINGS & AWARDS
R.A.C. *Blue Ribbon* ★★★ *Dining Award 3*
A.A. ★★★ 🏵🏵 77%

FACILITIES
On site: *Garden, Courtyard garden, mountain bikes*
2 meeting rooms/max 50 people
Nearby: *Golf, riding, fishing*

RESTRICTIONS
No facilities for disabled guests
Pets by arrangement

ATTRACTIONS
Blenheim Palace, Broughton Castle, Oxford, Stratford-upon-Avon, The Cotswolds, Silverstone

AFFILIATIONS
The Celebrated Hotels Collection
Grand Heritage Hotels

NEAREST
MAJOR CITY:
Oxford - 8 miles/15 mins

MAJOR AIRPORT:
London Heathrow - 40 miles/1 hr

RAILWAY STATION:
Oxford - 8 miles/15 mins

RESERVATIONS
Toll free in US: 800-322-2403
or 888-93-GRAND
Quote Best Loved

ACCESS CODES
AMADEUS UI OXFFEA
APOLLO/GALILEO UI 25900
SABRE/ABACUS UI 30576
WORLDSPAN UI 42150

MIDSHIRES

" I'm hard pressed to name any family enterprise, in France or Britain, that can match the remarkable efforts of the Morris team "

Richard Binns, travel writer

GRAFTON MANOR

Manor house

MIDSHIRES

Grafton Lane, Bromsgrove, Worcestershire B61 7HA

Telephone 01527 579007
Fax 01527 575221

E-mail: *grafton@bestloved.com*

OWNER
The Lord of Grafton

MANAGER
Stephen Morris

ROOM RATES
1 Single	£85 - £95
5 Doubles/Twins	£105 - £125
1 Four-poster	£125 - £150
2 Suites	£150

Includes full breakfast and VAT

CHARGE/CREDIT CARDS

AMERICAN EXPRESS • DC • MC • VI

RATINGS & AWARDS
Member of Master Chefs Institute

FACILITIES
On site: *Garden, heli-pad, fishing, croquet, special wedding marquee*
Licensed for weddings
2 meeting rooms/max 180 people
Nearby: *Golf, riding*

RESTRICTIONS
No facilities for disabled guests
No pets

ATTRACTIONS
Stratford-upon-Avon, Worcester, The Cotswolds, Warwick Castle, Stourbridge Glass, Welsh Marches

AFFILIATIONS
Independent

NEAREST
MAJOR CITY:
Birmingham - 17 miles/30 mins

MAJOR AIRPORT:
Birmingham - 22 miles/30 mins

RAILWAY STATION:
Bromsgrove - 2 miles/5 mins

RESERVATIONS
Direct with hotel
*Quote **Best Loved***

ACCESS CODES
AMADEUS HK BHXGRA
SABRE/ABACUS HK 36237
WORLDSPAN HK GRAFT

A great house with an illustrious past now the epitome of modern elegance

The Manor of Grafton has an illustrious history; from its foundation before the Norman Conquest, Grafton has been recognised as one of Worcestershire's great historic houses. This splendid house, for centuries the home of king makers, was opened as an hotel in 1980 by the present owners John (now The Lord of Grafton) and June Morris who, together with their family, ensure guests receive attentive, friendly service.

The elegant 17th century dining room is the focal point of a visit to Grafton, with imaginative menus created by Simon Morris and Will Henderson, who aim to produce only the best for guests, complemented by a fine wine list. Damask-rose petal and mulberry sorbets are indicative of the inspired style of cuisine. The guest bedrooms have been painstakingly restored, introducing the comforts demanded today while retaining the grace and elegance of another age.

There is much to enjoy at Grafton: a superb formal Herb Garden in 26 acres of beautiful grounds, a two-acre lake, a 16th century fish stew (brick building in the stream), and a 15th century private chapel. Grafton Manor is an ideal base from which to explore the Worcestershire countryside.

LOCATION
From M5 Exit 5 proceed via A38 towards Bromsgrove. Bear left at second roundabout. Grafton Lane is first left after half a mile.

" It was a delight to be able to return to such a pleasant hotel "

The Rt Hon John Major, former Prime Minister

Elizabethan country manor

THE GREENWAY

A long-standing reputation for excellence in the Cotswolds

One of Britain's first country house hotels, The Greenway retains an enviable reputation for its peerless style and welcoming atmosphere. Guests can enjoy a genuine country house experience with all the personalised attention to detail you would expect from the hostess of an elegant private home. The setting is glorious, too, with the Cotswold Hills for a backdrop and extensive gardens where the huge old yew hedges look like a scene straight out of Alice in Wonderland.

Recently, The Greenway's public rooms have been classically refurbished in fresh and pretty yellow and green tones. Gleaming antique furniture adds a mellow note and there are cosy log fires in winter. In summer there is a lovely indoor-outdoor feel as the bar opens onto the lawn, while the restaurant overlooks a sunken garden and lily pond. Bedrooms are generously proportioned and traditionally furnished. They are divided between the main house and a Georgian coach house where original elements such as the wooden beams and stalls have been cleverly incorporated in the design.

The Greenway is ideally placed for visiting the Cotswolds' numerous beauty spots, quaint villages and the spa town of Cheltenham, as well as Shakespeare's hometown, Stratford-upon-Avon.

LOCATION

Leave M5 at Exit 11A and join A417 towards Cirencester. At A46 turn left direction Cheltenham. Hotel is 1 mile on the right.

Shurdington, Cheltenham,
Gloucestershire GL51 4UG

Telephone 01242 862352
Fax 01242 862780

E-mail: greenway@bestloved.com

GENERAL MANAGER
Andrew Mackay

ROOM RATES
1 Single   £89
20 Doubles/Twins   £140 - £200
Includes full breakfast and VAT

CHARGE/CREDIT CARDS

 ● *DC* ● *MC* ● *VI*

RATINGS & AWARDS
R.A.C. Blue Ribbon ★★★ *Dining Award 3*
A.A. ★★★ ❀❀❀
A.A. Top 200 - 02/03

FACILITIES
On site: *Garden, heli-pad, croquet*
Licensed for weddings
2 meeting rooms/max 40 people
Nearby: *Golf, fishing, clay pigeon shooting,*
tennis, swimming, riding

RESTRICTIONS
None

ATTRACTIONS
The Cotswolds, Stratford-upon-Avon,
Bath, Cheltenham Spa,
Painswick, Wye Valley,
Sudeley Castle, Forest of Dean,
Cirencester Polo Park

AFFILIATIONS
The Celebrated Hotels Collection
Grand Heritage Hotels

NEAREST
MAJOR CITY:
Cheltenham - 2 ½ miles/5 mins
Gloucester - 5 miles/15 mins

MAJOR AIRPORT:
Birmingham - 60 miles/1 ¼ hrs
Bristol - 45 miles/50 mins

RAILWAY STATION:
Cheltenham - 2 ½ miles/5 mins

RESERVATIONS
Toll free in US: 800-322-2403
Toll free in US: 888-96-GRAND
Quote Best Loved

ACCESS CODES
AMADEUS UI GLOGRE
APOLLO/GALILEO UI 8838
SABRE/ABACUS UI 30477
WORLDSPAN UI 42525

MIDSHIRES

● *Map p.470*
   ref: E6

> " *What an amazing evening, congratulations for such a well organized evening. We have had nothing but praise and requests for more and more...* "
>
> *Hilary, London*

HEYTHROP PARK

Victorian stately home

**Enstone,
Chipping Norton,
Oxfordshire OX7 5UE**

**Telephone 01608 673 333
Fax 01608 673 799**

E-mail: *heythrop@bestloved.com*

OWNER
Firoz Kassam

ROOM RATES
7 Standard doubles	£150 - £185
6 Deluxe doubles	£250 - £285
1 Suite	£400 - £450

Includes full breakfast and VAT

CHARGE/CREDIT CARDS

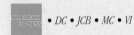

● DC ● JCB ● MC ● VI

RATINGS & AWARDS
Awards Pending

FACILITIES
On site: *Garden, snooker, heli-pad, croquet, golf, tennis, indoor pool, football, squash, cricket, bowls, quad biking
Licensed for weddings
60 meeting rooms/max 300 people*

RESTRICTIONS
*Limited facilities for disabled guests
Smoking in bar only
No pets*

ATTRACTIONS
Oxford, the Cotswolds, Blenheim Palace, Stratford-upon-Avon, Warwick Castle, Silverstone Race Circuit

AFFILIATIONS
Grand Heritage Hotels

NEAREST
MAJOR CITY:
Oxford - 20 miles/30 mins

MAJOR AIRPORT:
London Heathrow - 65 miles/1 ¼ hrs

RAILWAY STATION:
Charlbury - 6 miles/10 mins

RESERVATIONS
*Toll free in US: 888-93-GRAND
Toll free in UK: 0800 856 0457*
*Quote **Best Loved***

ACCESS CODES
*AMADEUS UI OXFHEY
APOLLO/GALILEO UI 43637
SABRE/ABACUS UI 3498
WORLDSPAN UI 42674*

Classical grandeur in the Oxfordshire countryside

In 1701, Charles Talbot, Duke of Shrewsbury, began a four-year sojourn in Rome that left him with an abiding love of classical architecture. On his return to England, Talbot commissioned Thomas Adam, a pupil of the Sir John Vanbrugh architect of Blenheim Palace a few miles away, to design him a house in the Roman style. Heythrop's honey coloured stone was quarried locally and the duke's stately Oxfordshire residence was completed in 1716.

Adam's handsome classical edifice has led a chequered career over the centuries. From a hunting lodge for the Duke of Beaufort, the house lay derelict after a terrible fire in 1831, and was later converted into a Victorian family home. Two additional wings were constructed in the 1920s and state-of-the-art conference facilities added in the 1980s. Recently the house has been completely refurbished in Victorian style and transformed into an exceptional hotel with grand public rooms and 14 enormous bedrooms with views over the extensive grounds. The side wings will add another 160 rooms over the next year. Within the park there are beautiful formal gardens, immaculate lawns and mature woodlands. Recreational facilities include a nine-hole golf course, putting green, croquet and bowls lawns.

LOCATION

From the A44 Chipping Norton to Oxford Road, take the road signed for Bicester. The hotel is a short way along on the left and is well signed.

MIDSHIRES

" *Our 27th favourite hotel in the world* "

The Times, London

17th century manor house

THE HOSTE ARMS

Good food, drink, music and art in one of England's most beautiful villages

Since the railways abandoned North Norfolk, its treasures and its character happily co-exist in unhurried peace. For example, of all Britain's villages, Burnham Market is arguably the most beautiful. It is in an area now designated as of Outstanding Natural Beauty and has a fascinating coastline populated with all sorts of interesting gems.

In the centre of Burnham Market is the Hoste Arms, once frequented by Lord Nelson, and now thriving under the ownership of Paul Whittome. Its renaissance is in part due to a well-established reputation for good food; the menu revels in temptation.

The original bedrooms are pretty and well appointed but it is the new South African wing that needs a special mention here. It houses eight bedrooms including a Penthouse and a Zulu Suite. Designed by Paul's South African wife, Jeanne, there are beds with leather headboards and Zebra print throws, ostrich feathered lampshades, walk-in wardrobes and TV's that appear at a flick of a switch - described by one critic as James Bondesque.

'My aim has been to develop the Hoste to the most popular inn in England combining my love of people, food, drink, music and art', says Paul. What a success he has made of it!

LOCATION
Located approximately 2 miles from the A149 between Brancaster and Wells-next-the-Sea.

The Green,
Burnham Market,
Norfolk PE31 8HD
Telephone 01328 738777
Fax 01328 730103

E-mail: *hostearms@bestloved.com*

OWNER
Paul Whittome

GENERAL MANAGER
Emma Tagg

RATES PER PERSON

3 Singles	£71 - £95
19 Doubles/Twins	£44 - £58
4 Four-posters	£60 - £70
1 Penthouse	£75 - £100

Includes full breakfast and VAT
Special midweek dinner, bed & breakfast
rates available

CHARGE/CREDIT CARDS
MC • VI

RATINGS & AWARDS
E.T.C. ★★ *Silver Award*
A.A. ★★ ❀❀ 74%

FACILITIES
On site: *Garden*
3 meeting rooms/max 50 people
Nearby: *Golf, yachting, tennis, fitness*
centre, shooting, riding

RESTRICTIONS
Limited facilities for disabled guests
Children by arrangement

ATTRACTIONS
Caithness Crystal, Holkham Hall,
Sealife Centre, Pensthorpe Waterfowl Park,
Sandringham, Norfolk Broads

AFFILIATIONS
The Great Inns of Britain

NEAREST
MAJOR CITY:
Norwich - 35 miles/45 mins

MAJOR AIRPORT:
Norwich - 35 miles/45 mins
Stansted - 75 miles/1½ hrs

RAILWAY STATION:
Kings Lynn - 22 miles/35 mins

RESERVATIONS
Direct with hotel
*Quote **Best Loved***

ACCESS CODES
Not applicable

MIDSHIRES

" *It is the restaurant that really does stand out in this hotel. It will certainly leave you wanting to return for more* "

Lisa Piddington, Travel Editor, Birmingham Post

HOTEL DES CLOS

Restaurant with rooms

MIDSHIRES

Old Lenton Lane, Nottingham, Nottinghamshire NG7 2SA

Telephone 0115 986 6566
Fax 0115 986 0343

E-mail: *desclos@bestloved.com*

OWNERS
The Ralley Family

ROOM RATES
Single occupancy	£80 - £120
4 Doubles/Twins	£90 - £130
5 Suites	£90 - £130
Includes full breakfast and VAT	

CHARGE/CREDIT CARDS

 • DC • MC • VI

RATINGS & AWARDS
A.A. ❀❀❀ *Restaurant with rooms*
A.A. Top 200 - 02/03
R.A.C. Dining Award 4
Les Routiers Hotel of the Year 2003

FACILITIES
On site: *Garden, croquet*
1 meeting room/max 20 people
Nearby: *Golf, fishing, swimming*

RESTRICTIONS
Limited facilities for disabled guests
No pets, guide dogs only
No children under 2 years

ATTRACTIONS
Nottingham City and Castle,
Belvoir Castle, Newstead Abbey,
Caves of Nottingham,
Wollaton Hall,
Angel Row Gallery

AFFILIATIONS
Les Routiers

NEAREST
MAJOR CITY:
Nottingham

MAJOR AIRPORT:
East Midlands - 13 miles/15 mins

RAILWAY STATION:
Nottingham - 3 miles/10 mins

RESERVATIONS
Direct with hotel
Quote **Best Loved**

ACCESS CODES
Not applicable

The complete hotel and dining experience

The Hotel des Clos and Restaurant Sat Baines are conveniently situated on the banks of Nottingham's River Trent, just five minutes from the city centre. The hotel lives up to its claim of being 'not quite town' yet 'not quite country'. One thing for sure, however, is that it is home to one of the foremost restaurants in the region. The kitchen bakes fresh bread twice daily, and head chef Sat Baines who won the Roux Scholarship, is passionate about cooking and quality of produce. Above all he endeavours to 'excite people with food', and with a dinner menu that includes such creations as carpaccio of tuna with candied violets and roast Cornish turbot with artichoke and wild asparagus, he is well on his way to achieving that aim. For an all-round flavour of the place, the 9-course 'degustation' menu offers a great value introduction.

A converted Victorian farm with 9 bedrooms, all antique furnished, this family-run establishment boasts a stream of awards, including four dining awards from the R.A.C. and three A.A. rosettes. It is also one of the A.A.'s Top 200 hotels in the country. For the business traveller, proximity to town makes this the ideal

stop-off, while the hotel's pretty courtyard gardens are the finishing touch to an intimate wedding celebration.

LOCATION
10 minutes from the City Centre.
Advisable to call first for driving directions.

> **" Birmingham has been waiting a long time for this! "**
>
> *John F Davies III, New York City, USA*

Victorian city centre hotel — HOTEL DU VIN & BISTRO

The talk of the town

Where, we all wondered, would the contemporary and steadfastly stylish 'micro-chain' strike next. Well, it was Birmingham, and it opened last April. The hotel has been welcomed by the city's many business visitors who want something other than the bland international alternatives.

In keeping with the Hotel du Vin's established trademark, this new hotel has been converted out of an elaborate Victorian red brick building. A grand double staircase leads to the bedrooms, which are furnished with specially commissioned furniture and natural fabrics sourced from some of the finest interior design houses. There are sensibly sized desks, complete with all necessary data ports. The bathrooms are particularly noteworthy, with many featuring enormous walk-in showers and twin cast iron baths.

The central focus is the courtyard, which lends itself to alfresco dining, more reminiscent of medieval Brussels perhaps than Birmingham! The food is simple, modern cuisine at its very best and the theme of wine is as evident as you would expect from an Hotel du Vin with a wine list featuring 400 bins and over 60 champagnes.

For those guests wishing to eat, drink and stay trim an exciting concept has been introduced in the form of Health du Vin - a state of the art gym and spa. Sante!

LOCATION

Take A32(M) to city centre & proceed over flyover, keeping left. At end of flyover, before underpass, take exit signed Jewellery Quarter. At roundabout take 2nd exit. Take 1st left and 3rd right. Turn right at junction with Church Street. Hotel is on right.

Church Street, Birmingham B3 2NR

Telephone 0121 200 0600
Fax 0121 236 0889

E-mail: *duvinbirm@bestloved.com*

GENERAL MANAGER
Michael Warren

ROOM RATES
Single occupancy £110 - £395
56 Doubles/Twins £110 - £145
10 Suites £185 - £395
Includes VAT

CHARGE/CREDIT CARDS
 ● DC ● MC ● VI

RATINGS & AWARDS
A.A. ★★★★ ❀ Town House
A.A. Top 200 - 02/03

FACILITIES
On site: *gym, health & beauty*
3 meeting rooms/max 80 people

RESTRICTIONS
No pets, guide dogs only

ATTRACTIONS
Cadbury World, Warwick Castle, Stratford-upon-Avon, Jewellery Quarter, Sealife Centre

AFFILIATIONS
*Hotel du Vin Ltd
The European Connection
Preston's Global Hotels*

NEAREST
MAJOR CITY: Birmingham

MAJOR AIRPORT: Birmingham - 20 miles/20 mins

RAILWAY STATION: Birmingham New Street - ½ mile/5 mins

RESERVATIONS
Toll free in US: 800-544-9993
Quote **Best Loved**

ACCESS CODES
Not applicable

MIDSHIRES

www.duvinbirm.bestloved.com

● *Map p.470*
ref: G5

" At last a first-class, luxury hotel in Cambridge "

Preston Epstein, The Celebrated Hotels Collection

HOTEL FELIX

Luxury hotel

**Whitehouse Lane,
Huntingdon Road,
Cambridge,
Cambridgeshire, CB3 0LX**

**Telephone 01223 277977
Fax 01223 277973**

E-mail: *felix@bestloved.com*

OWNER
Jeremy Cassel

GENERAL MANAGER
Shara Ross

ROOM RATES
Single occupancy	*from £125*
48 Doubles/Twins	*£155 - £195*
4 Junior suites	*£240 - £260*

Includes continental breakfast and VAT

CHARGE/CREDIT CARDS

 • *DC* • *JCB* • *MC* • *VI*

RATINGS & AWARDS
Awards Pending

FACILITIES
On site: *Garden*
4 meeting rooms/max 100 people
Nearby: *Golf, riding*

RESTRICTIONS
No pets in public rooms

ATTRACTIONS
*King's College Chapel, Punting,
Fitzwilliam Museum,
Botanic Gardens,
Great St Mary's Church,
Houghton Mill,
Newmarket Racecourse*

AFFILIATIONS
Grand Heritage Hotels

NEAREST
*MAJOR CITY:
Cambridge*

*MAJOR AIRPORT:
Stansted - 30 miles/40 mins*

*RAILWAY STATION:
Cambridge - 1 mile/5 mins*

RESERVATIONS
Toll free in US: 888-93-GRAND
*Quote **Best Loved***

ACCESS CODES
Not applicable

MIDSHIRES

Long awaited contemporary luxury in Cambridge

Historic Cambridge has long lacked a luxurious and privately owned hotel, but all that has just changed with the opening in November 2002 of Hotel Felix. Originally built as a Victorian mansion in 1852, the Hotel Felix is now a chic and contemporary property, providing 52 wonderfully stylish bedrooms. For those in the know, this is the sister hotel of the luxury, red-starred Grange Hotel in York.

Graffiti, the hotels restaurant, serves excellent modern Mediterranean food in lovely surroundings where the walls are hung with large specially commissioned canvasses. It overlooks the terrace and gardens where al fresco dining is available during summer months. The adjoining bar is a relaxed and welcoming area for less formal dining and drinks. There are also three connecting rooms ideal for private functions and meetings. All bedrooms are generously sized and elegantly styled. For special occasions there is a sumptuous and very private suite up in the eaves.

Set in landscaped gardens and surrounded by fields, Hotel Felix is the perfect location from which to explore Cambridge and the surrounding countryside. It's less than a mile from the city centre and just 20 minutes drive from the famous Newmarket racecourse. There are ample car parking facilities.

LOCATION
Exit M11 at junction 13 onto A1303 for Cambridge. Then follow signs for Huntingdon A14 to reach the A1307. White House Lane is halfway down road on right.

Regency town house   HOTEL ON THE PARK

Regency elegance in the centre for the Cotswolds

This beautifully restored Regency building is the finest town house hotel in the Cheltenham area and is perfectly located for touring the Cotswolds and surrounding towns of interest such as Stratford-upon-Avon and Bath. It is in a superb position overlooking Pittville Park yet only a short walk from the town centre and the National Hunt Racecourse.

This exclusive privately-owned hotel has the air of a private club yet offers welcoming and unstuffy hospitality. The bedrooms are individually designed and dressed with traditional fabrics, crisp Egyptian cotton sheets, fine antiques and porcelain with original paintings adorning the walls.

All rooms feature en suite bathrooms, some with ball and claw baths. Facilities include complimentary hot and cold drinks. There is an elegant, candlelit drawing room and bar or an intimate library with crackling log fire to read and relax in. The hotel is privileged to have as its restaurant, The Bacchanalian, with food prepared by Stewart Allen, whose modern British food reveals its European influences.

LOCATION

In the Regency spa town of Cheltenham. Take A435 signposted Evesham from town centre. Hotel on left opposite Pittville Park.

Evesham Road, Cheltenham, Gloucestershire GL52 2AH

**Telephone 01242 518898
Fax 01242 511526**

E-mail: *onthepark@bestloved.com*

OWNER
Darryl Gregory

ROOM RATES
Single occupancy	£85
10 Doubles/Twins	£108 - £128
1 Junior suite	£138
1 Four-poster	£158
Includes VAT	

CHARGE/CREDIT CARDS

 • DC • MC • VI

RATINGS & AWARDS
E.T.C. ★★★ *Gold Award*
R.A.C. Gold Ribbon ★★★ *Dining Award 4*
A.A. ★★★ ❀❀
A.A. Top 200 - 02/03

FACILITIES
On site: *Garden,
'The Bacchanalian' Restaurant
1 meeting room/max 18 people*
Nearby: *Golf, riding, fishing*

RESTRICTIONS
*No facilities for disabled guests
No children under 8 years
No smoking in bedrooms
No pets*

ATTRACTIONS
*The Cotswolds, Pittville Pump Room,
Gustav Holst birthplace, Sudeley Castle,
Cheltenham Races*

AFFILIATIONS
*Preston's Global Hotels
Fine Individual Hotels
Cotswolds Finest Hotels*

NEAREST
*MAJOR CITY:
Birmingham - 49 miles/1 hr*

*MAJOR AIRPORT:
Birmingham - 49 miles/1hr*

*RAILWAY STATION:
Cheltenham - 2 miles/10 mins*

RESERVATIONS
*Toll free in US: 800-544-9993
Toll free fax UK: 0800 7311053*
Quote **Best Loved**

ACCESS CODES
Not applicable

MIDSHIRES

It's so rare to receive such fantastic service, I hope you are very proud of your staff!

Sarah Hardaker

LACE MARKET HOTEL

Contemporary hotel

**29 - 31 High Pavement,
Nottingham,
Nottinghamshire NG1 1HE**

**Telephone 0115 8523232
Fax 0115 8523223**

E-mail: *lacemarket@bestloved.com*

GENERAL MANAGER
Mark Cox

ROOM RATES
6 Singles	£89
17 Doubles/Twins	£105
11 King-bedded rooms	£125
5 Superior doubles	£155
3 Studios	£179
Includes VAT	

CHARGE/CREDIT CARDS

 • *MC* • *VI*

RATINGS & AWARDS
A.A. ★★★★ ⊛ *Town House*

FACILITIES
On site: *Restaurant, bar
3 meeting rooms/max 60 people*
Nearby: *Complimentary use of local
health club*

RESTRICTIONS
*No children in restaurant after 8 pm
Pets by arrangement*

ATTRACTIONS
*Nottingham Castle, Wollaton Hall,
National Watersports Centre,
Shopping, Belvoir Castle,
Southwell Minster*

AFFILIATIONS
*Design Hotels
The European Connection*

NEAREST
*MAJOR CITY:
Nottingham*

*MAJOR AIRPORT:
East Midlands Airport - 10 miles/20 mins*

*RAILWAY STATION:
Nottingham - ½ mile/5 mins*

RESERVATIONS
*Direct with hotel
Quote* **Best Loved**

ACCESS CODES
*AMADEUS DS NOTLAC
APOLLO/GALILEO DS 17730
SABRE/ABACUS DS 47815
WORLDSPAN DS 05887*

MIDSHIRES

New and old combined for a really successful combination of radical chic

In spite of the name there isn't a lace doily or antimacassar in sight at the Lace Market hotel. The exterior may be mature Georgian elegance but the interior is very much of today - radical chic and cool minimalist.

Past the Georgian façade with its stately sash windows and classical portico, the interior is a totally refreshing juxtaposition of original architraves and coving with the sleek modern lines of brushed steel, smooth polished wood and custom-designed furniture. The wonderful sense of space is counterbalanced by warming earth colours for a comfortable ambiance. Of course all the bedrooms have every modern convenience including trendy bathrooms with glass basins and large, self-indulgent baths in some rooms.

The hotel reflects the ambience of the newly restored Lace Market area of Nottingham, which buzzes with lively restaurants, wine bars, clubs, boutiques - happily mixing young and old in every dimension. This small townhouse hotel is right in the heart of this contemporary revival and its bar and restaurant, 'Merchants', is one of the hippest venues in town. The restaurant is equally at the forefront of all that is new today, combining European influences with modern British cuisine for a thoroughly modern flavour.

LOCATION
*Follow signs for City Centre and then follow
brown signs for the Lace Market, Galleries of
Justice and St Mary's Church.*

« Once in a blue moon it is still possible to come across a country house that makes one want to jump for joy »

Craig Brown, Sunday Times

● Map p.470
ref: F3

George IV mansion

LANGAR HALL

A house of special charm in the beautiful Vale of Belvoir

Langar Hall was built in 1837 on the site of a great historic house, the home of Admiral Lord Howe. It stands in quiet seclusion overlooking lovely gardens beyond which sheep graze among the ancient trees in the park. Below the croquet lawn, lies a romantic network of medieval fishponds stocked with carp.

This charming hotel is the family home of Imogen Skirving, who combines the standards of good hotel keeping with the hospitality of an informal country house where children are welcome. Most of the bedrooms enjoy lovely views and every one is quiet, comfortable and well-equipped particularly for guests who have business in Nottingham.

Downstairs, you will find the study, a quiet room for reading and meetings, the white sitting room, for afternoon tea and drinks before dinner, the Indian room, ideal for private parties and conferences and the dining room. This elegant pillared hall is open every day for lunch and dinner, a popular neighbourhood restaurant serving fresh seasonal food with an emphasis on game in winter and fish in summer.

We can recommend Langar Hall as being particularly suited to exclusive house parties.

LOCATION

Langar is on A52 between Nottingham and Grantham - turn at Bingham. Between Newark and Leicester on A46 - drive through Cropwell Bishop. Both roads are sign-posted.

Langar, Nottinghamshire NG13 9HG

Telephone 01949 860559
Fax 01949 861045

E-mail: *langar@bestloved.com*

OWNER
Imogen Skirving

ROOM RATES
Single occupancy	£65 - £100
8 Doubles/Twins	£100 - £140
1 Four-poster	£185
1 Suite	£185

Includes full breakfast and VAT

CHARGE/CREDIT CARDS
 ● DC ● MC ● VI

RATINGS & AWARDS
E.T.C. ★★★ Silver Award
A.A. ★★★ ❀❀ 72%

FACILITIES
On site: *Garden, heli-pad, fishing, croquet, children's adventure play area*
Licensed for weddings
2 meeting rooms/max 40 people
Nearby: *Golf, riding, fitness, fishing, shooting, parachuting/parasending/hang-gliding, motorsport*

RESTRICTIONS
No facilities for disabled guests
No smoking in bedrooms
Pets by arrangement

ATTRACTIONS
Newark antique fairs, Trent Bridge cricket, Nottingham Forest football, Belvoir Castle, Chatsworth House, Sherwood Forest, Southwell and Lincoln Cathedrals, Hardwick Hall, Belton House

AFFILIATIONS
Independent

NEAREST
MAJOR CITY:
Nottingham - 12 miles/20 mins

MAJOR AIRPORT:
East Midlands - 20 miles/30 mins

RAILWAY STATION:
Grantham/Bingham - 4 miles/15 mins

RESERVATIONS
Direct with hotel
*Quote **Best Loved***

ACCESS CODES
Not applicable

MIDSHIRES

> ❝ *Le Manoir is one of the most sumptuous country house hotels in Great Britain and its restaurant the best in the nation* ❞
>
> *Michael Balter, Bon Appetit*

LE MANOIR AUX QUAT' SAISONS — *15th century manor*

Church Road, Great Milton, Oxford, Oxfordshire OX44 7PD

Telephone 01844 278881
Fax 01844 278847

E-mail: *manoir@bestloved.com*

OWNER
Raymond Blanc

GENERAL MANAGER
Philip Newman-Hall

ROOM RATES
2 Standard doubles	£245 - £275
4 Deluxe doubles	£295 - £325
13 Superior doubles	£375 - £450
5 Junior suites	£450 - £495
7 Suites	£600 - £825
1 2-Bedroom suite	£1,150
Includes VAT	

CHARGE/CREDIT CARDS

 • *DC* • *JCB* • *MC* • *VI*

RATINGS & AWARDS
R.A.C. Gold Ribbon ★★★★ *Dining Award 5*
A.A. ★★★★ ✿✿✿✿✿

FACILITIES
On site: *Heli-pad, croquet, cookery school*
Licensed for weddings
1 meeting room/max 50 people
Nearby: *Fishing, golf, clay pigeon shooting, riding*

RESTRICTIONS
Pets by arrangement

ATTRACTIONS
The Cotswolds, Blenheim Palace, Windsor Castle, Waddesdon Manor, Oxford

AFFILIATIONS
Orient Express Hotels
Relais & Châteaux
Relais Gourmands

NEAREST
MAJOR CITY:
Oxford - 7 miles/15 mins

MAJOR AIRPORT:
London Heathrow - 40 miles/45 mins

RAILWAY STATION:
Oxford - 7 miles/15 mins

RESERVATIONS
Toll free in US: 800-845-4274
or 800-735-2478
Quote **Best Loved**

ACCESS CODES
APOLLO/GALILEO WB 14966
SABRE/ABACUS WB 11557
WORLDSPAN WB GB04

Discover the magic of Le Manoir

In secluded and beautiful grounds a few miles south of the historic university town of Oxford, Le Manoir aux Quat' Saisons is one of Europe's finest restaurants and a lovely country house hotel. Le Manoir is the inspired creation of chef, Raymond Blanc, whose extraordinary cooking has received the highest tributes from all international guides to culinary excellence. Uniquely, the London Times gives Blanc's cooking 10 out of 10 and rates it 'the best in Britain'.

The restaurant is the natural focus of this lovely 15th century manor house which stands in landscaped gardens, its sweeping lawns set against a backdrop of fine trees. A feature of the estate is a carefully tended vegetable garden which supplies the kitchen with the finest and freshest organic produce.

The atmosphere throughout is one of understated elegance, whilst all 32 bedrooms and suites offer guests the highest standards of comfort and luxury. Every need is anticipated, for service is a way of life here, never intrusive but always present. 'It is as if the entire staff has been touched by spirits beyond the reach of sordid commerce', writes the Daily Telegraph.

LOCATION

From London, take the M40 and exit at Junction 7. Turn left onto A329 to Wallingford. The hotel is signed after 1 mile.

" *A veritable haven of peace and tranquillity* "

Anthony Donaldson, London

17th century manor — LORDS OF THE MANOR

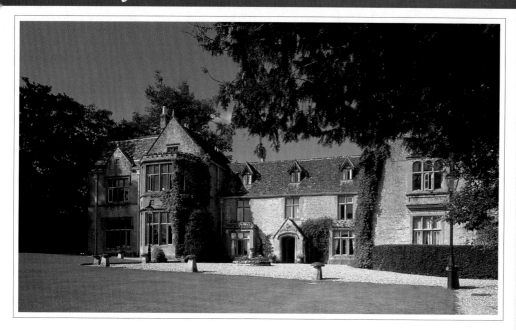

Paradise found in the heart of The Cotswolds

The Lords of the Manor is a 17th Century country house hotel in the heart of the Cotswolds. Built in 1650, this former rectory stands in eight acres of secluded gardens and parkland in Upper Slaughter, one of the Cotswolds' prettiest and most unspoilt villages.

Comfortable surroundings and big roaring fires, beautifully tended, well-loved gardens and croquet on the lawn create an idyllic setting.

The award-winning restaurant at the Lords of the Manor has a fine reputation for modern English cooking and uses only the best local produce. The rambling cellar produces a wine list to complement even the most diverse palate. All the bedrooms are furnished with period pieces giving each room its individual character.

For leisure activities, guests can enjoy a game of croquet or coarse fishing on the lake. Riding, golf, game and clay pigeon shooting can be arranged locally.

The Lords of the Manor is ideally situated to explore many of the honey-stoned villages which have made the Cotswolds an ideal area for a truly memorable stay.

LOCATION

2 miles off the A429 between Stow-on-the-Wold and Bourton-on-the-Water. Signed to 'The Slaughters'.

Upper Slaughter,
Near Bourton-on-the-Water,
Gloucestershire GL54 2JD
Telephone 01451 820243
Fax 01451 820696
E-mail: *lords@bestloved.com*

GENERAL MANAGER
Philip Mason-Gordon

ROOM RATES
2 Singles	£99
16 Doubles/Twins	£155 - £195
6 Old Rectory rooms	£235 - £309
3 Suites	£265 - £309

Includes full breakfast and VAT

CHARGE/CREDIT CARDS
 ● *DC* ● *JCB* ● *MC* ● *VI*

RATINGS & AWARDS
E.T.C. ★★★ *Gold Award*
R.A.C. Gold Ribbon ★★★ *Dining Award 4*
A.A. ★★★ ❀❀❀ *Top 200 - 02/03*

FACILITIES
On site: *Garden, croquet*
Licensed for weddings
1 meeting room/max 20 people
Nearby: *Clay pigeon shooting, archery, golf, riding, fishing, quad-biking*

RESTRICTIONS
No facilities for disabled guests
No children under 9 years
No smoking in bedrooms
No pets

ATTRACTIONS
The Cotswolds, Blenheim Palace, Oxford, Stratford-upon-Avon, Sudeley Castle, Hidcote Gardens

AFFILIATIONS
The Celebrated Hotels Collection
Small Luxury Hotels
Cotswolds Finest Hotels

NEAREST
MAJOR CITY:
Oxford - 35 miles/40 mins
MAJOR AIRPORT:
London Heathrow - 80 miles/1 ¾ hrs
Birmingham - 45 miles/1 ¼ hrs
RAILWAY STATION:
Moreton-in-Marsh - 8 miles/20 mins

RESERVATIONS
Toll free in US: 800-322-2403
or 800-872-4564
Quote **Best Loved**

ACCESS CODES
AMADEUS LX BRSLOM
APOLLO/GALILEO LX 32333
SABRE/ABACUS LX 31994
WORLDSPAN LX GLOLM

MIDSHIRES

❝ *Full of ambience, full of charm, full of lovely food - full of regrets at leaving* **❞**

Mr & Mrs B, Ashby de la Zouch

THE MALT HOUSE

16th century malting house

**Broad Campden,
Gloucestershire GL55 6UU**

**Telephone 01386 840295
Fax 01386 841334**

E-mail: *malt@bestloved.com*

OWNER
Judi Wilkes

ROOM RATES
6 Doubles/Twins   £95 - £125
1 Suite   £105 - £150
Includes full breakfast and VAT

CHARGE/CREDIT CARDS

AMERICAN EXPRESS • MC • VI

RATINGS & AWARDS
A.A. ◆◆◆◆

FACILITIES
On site: *Garden, croquet*
1 meeting room/max 25 people
Nearby: *Golf, riding, fishing*

RESTRICTIONS
No facilities for disabled guests
No smoking throughout
Children by arrangement
No pets
Closed 22 - 29 Dec

ATTRACTIONS
*Stratford-upon-Avon,
Cotswold villages,
Warwick Castle,
Chipping Campden,
Cheltenham Races,
Oxford, Bath*

AFFILIATIONS
Independent

NEAREST
MAJOR CITY:
Oxford - 35 miles/1 ¼ hrs

MAJOR AIRPORT:
Birmingham - 32 miles/1 hr

RAILWAY STATION:
Moreton-in-Marsh - 2 miles/15 mins

RESERVATIONS
Direct with hotel
Quote **Best Loved**

ACCESS CODES
Not applicable

Feel at home at this Cotswold hideaway

This 16th century building originally provided the malt to make the ale for the village of Broad Campden. About a hundred years ago the malting house and its neighbouring cottages were combined together, creating this charming property that we see today.

The general atmosphere is utterly relaxed. Downstairs are a number of beautifully appointed rooms providing many a cosy corner where guests can curl up with one of the hotel's good books - the window seat and fireside are particularly perfect places for this inactivity.

The bedrooms, some with king-sized beds, are pretty and traditional in décor and it is evident that a great deal of thought has gone into making each one of them completely distinctive. There are many considerate details too such as flowers from the garden and nice bath oils. Each one has a view of the garden, which is almost indescribably beautiful with its orchard, stream and summerhouse. When the weather permits there are many quite corners here too!

Owner, Judi Wilkes is a mind of formation when it comes to the surrounding attractions of the Cotswolds and she will even create itineraries for special interest groups.

This is the kind of place you could happily recommend to anyone.

LOCATION

*In the village of Broad Campden off the B4081
just 1 mile west of Chipping Campden.*

Best Loved Hotels of the World

" *An oasis of peace and perfection* "

H Wood, London

• Map p.470
ref: H3

219

500-year old manor house

THE MANOR HOUSE

An historic home cradled in the timeless serenity of rural Norfolk

The Manor House at Great Snoring - even the name has a Rip van Winkle charm redolent of cottage gardens and church bells, cricket on the village green and afternoon tea served in delicate porcelain with scones and lashings of homemade jam. A nostalgic vision perhaps, but if this England still exists there is no better place to find it than right here in the unspoilt countryside of North Norfolk just inland from the Heritage Coast.

Tucked behind the local church, the Grade II listed Manor House is an architectural gem dating from 1500. It is home to the Scoles family and has just six homely bedrooms ensuring a truly relaxed and personal atmosphere making you feel like a private quest rather than a paying one. This is a real English country house full of character and furnished with family antiques in that apparently effortless style which interior designers struggle to recreate. The good news now is that the Manor is also available for exclusive use and really is the perfect place for a house party, ideal for a family get-together or a group of friends. The house can

sleep 12 and from £850 per night, provides outstanding value for money. Truly a Best Loved Hotel in every sense!

LOCATION

Great Snoring is situated 3 miles north east of Fakenham from the A148. The hotel is behind the church on the road signposted to Barsham from the village street.

**Barsham Road,
Great Snoring, Fakenham,
Norfolk NR21 0HP**

**Telephone 01328 820597
Fax 01328 820048**

E-mail: *manornorfolk@bestloved.com*

OWNER
Rosamund M Scoles

ROOM RATES
Single occupancy	£85
6 Doubles/Twins	£110 - £130
2 Sheltons Cottages	£135

*Includes early morning tea,
full breakfast and VAT*

CHARGE/CREDIT CARDS

 • *JCB* • *MC* • *VI*

RATINGS & AWARDS
Independent

FACILITIES
On site: *Garden, heli-pad
Licensed for weddings
2 meeting rooms/max 40 people*
Nearby: *Riding, fishing, watersports*

RESTRICTIONS
*No facilities for disabled guests
Children by arrangement
No pets
Closed 24 Dec - 27 Dec*

ATTRACTIONS
*Norfolk Heritage Coast,
Sandringham House,
Holkham Hall,
Norwich, Cambridge,
National Trust properties*

AFFILIATIONS
Independent

NEAREST
*MAJOR CITY:
Norwich - 22 miles/30 mins*

*MAJOR AIRPORT:
London Heathrow - 115 miles/3 hrs
Stansted - 90 miles/2 ½ hrs*

*RAILWAY STATION:
King's Lynn - 22 miles/40 mins*

RESERVATIONS
Direct with hotel
Quote **Best Loved**

ACCESS CODES
Not applicable

MIDSHIRES

THE NEW INN AT COLN

16th century inn

MIDSHIRES

**Coln-St-Aldwyns,
Near Cirencester,
Gloucestershire GL7 5AN**

**Telephone 01285 750651
Fax 01285 750657**

E-mail: *newinn@bestloved.com*

OWNERS
Brian and Sandra-Anne Evans

ROOM RATES
Single occupancy	£80 - £125
12 Doubles/Twins	£110 - £140
1 Four-poster	£110 - £140

Includes full breakfast, newspaper and VAT

CHARGE/CREDIT CARDS

 • *MC* • *VI*

RATINGS & AWARDS
R.A.C. Blue Ribbon ★★ *Dining Award 3*
A.A. ★★ ❀❀
A.A. Top 200 - 02/03

FACILITIES
On site: *1 meeting room/max 12 people*
Nearby: *Golf, riding, fishing, water skiing*

RESTRICTIONS
*No facilities for disabled guests
No children under 10 years
No smoking in bedrooms
Pets by arrangement*

ATTRACTIONS
*Westonbirt Arboretum, Oxford,
Cotswold villages, Bath,
Barnsley House, Hidcote Gardens,
Sudeley & Berkeley Castles*

AFFILIATIONS
*The Great Inns of Britain
Cotswolds Finest Hotels*

NEAREST
MAJOR CITY:
Oxford - 30 miles/40 mins

MAJOR AIRPORT:
London Heathrow - 70 miles/1 ¼ hrs
Birmingham - 70 miles/1 ¼ hrs

RAILWAY STATION:
Swindon - 18 miles/30 mins

RESERVATIONS
Direct with hotel
*Quote **Best Loved***

ACCESS CODES
Not applicable

Founded in the reign of Elizabeth I - honoured in the reign of Elizabeth II

The New Inn At Coln was built 400 years ago when Queen Elizabeth I decreed there should be a coaching inn within a day's travel of every major centre of population, for the comfort and security of her subjects. It is still a great place to stay today. Owners Brian and Sandra-Anne Evans and staff welcome guests as friends, willingly providing any help needed to enjoy the Cotswolds.

Each bedroom is a private castle of comfort, richly adorned with floral prints and English chintz curtains. The renowned restaurant serves food with flair: the emphasis is on local produce and fresh ingredients. Old English recipes, long forgotten are now triumphantly revived. Real ales and fine malt whiskies are there to be savoured beneath the ancient beams in the bar.

Away from the ivy-covered stone walls and the Dovecote, lie some of England's finest attractions. Dreamy cottages and lazy streams are on every Cotswold trail. Oxford's quadrangles, Bath's regal squares and crescents and Cheltenham's racecourse are all within a short drive.

LOCATION
A40 to Burford, take the B4425 towards Bibury, turn left shortly after Aldsworth.

Best Loved Hotels of the World

" *The perfect antidote to real life* "

Anonymous

• Map p.470
ref: 14

221

Georgian manor — THE NORFOLK MEAD HOTEL

As fine a place for rest and relaxation as you will find on the Norfolk Broads

The villages surrounding Norwich are the essence of East Anglian life: Thatched roofs, white-washed characterful pubs, friendly easy-going folk and, as a bonus, the untamed beautiful Norfolk Broads. This is definitely 'R & R country'. An area of great tranquillity and peace where you can cruise along a latticework of rivers or lounge by a pool enjoying a Pimms.

One such place is situated only 15 minutes north of Norwich; The Norfolk Mead Hotel is a real find. The day we arrived, the scene looked like something straight out of a travel programme: boats cruising up the River Bure and a Labrador playing on the sunlit lawn. All very idyllic. On entering this fine Georgian House, lunch was over, clearly an enjoyable affair as contented diners were singing its praises as they took their coffee. Meanwhile, tanning themselves by the pool, were other guests working up an appetite for dinner, occasionally sauntering over to the convivial bar overlooking the walled garden.

Jill and Don Fleming have put a lot of work into the hotel and it shows. The bedrooms are comfortable and tastefully decorated with views of the pool, the garden, and, of course the river.

The Norfolk Mead makes an excellent place to explore the Broads, or to escape from doing business in town. Thoroughly recommended

LOCATION

From Norwich: take ring road to B1150, head for North Walsham. At Coltishall turn right at petrol station and right again in front of church.

Coltishall, Norwich,
Norfolk NR12 7DN

Telephone 01603 737531
Fax 01603 737521

E-mail: *norfolkmead@bestloved.com*

OWNERS
Jill and Don Fleming

ROOM RATES
Single occupancy £65 - £90
8 Doubles/Twins £80 - £100
3 Junior Suites £140
Includes full breakfast and VAT

CHARGE/CREDIT CARDS
 • DC • MC • VI

RATINGS & AWARDS
E.T.C. ★★ Silver Award

FACILITIES
On site: *Garden, heli-pad, fishing, croquet, tennis, health & beauty, outdoor pool, marina, rowing boat 2 meeting rooms/max 80 people*
Nearby: *Golf, sea fishing, water skiing, yachting, tennis, fitness centre, shooting, riding*

RESTRICTIONS
No facilities for disabled guests
No smoking in bedrooms
No pets in public rooms

ATTRACTIONS
Sandringham, Blickling Hall, Norwich, Norfolk Broads, North Norfolk coast & beaches, nature reserves, antiques hunting

AFFILIATIONS
Independent

NEAREST
MAJOR CITY:
Norwich - 7 miles/15 mins

MAJOR AIRPORT:
Stansted - 80 miles/2 hrs
Norwich - 5 miles/15 mins

RAILWAY STATION:
Norwich - 7 miles/15 mins

FERRY PORT:
Harwich - 84 miles/2 hrs

RESERVATIONS
Direct with hotel
Quote **Best Loved**

ACCESS CODES
Not applicable

MIDSHIRES

"Sheer perfection . . . faultless"

Olwyn & Bill Payne, California

• *Map p.470*
ref: D5

NUTHURST GRANGE

Country house

Nuthurst Grange Lane,
Hockley Heath,
Warwickshire B94 5NL

Telephone 01564 783972
Fax 01564 783919

E-mail: *nuthurst@bestloved.com*

OWNERS
David and Karen Randolph

ROOM RATES
Single occupancy	£139
13 Doubles/Twins	£159 - £179
1 Four-poster	£189
1 Suite	£189

Includes full breakfast and VAT

CHARGE/CREDIT CARDS

 • *DC* • *MC* • *VI*

RATINGS & AWARDS
E.T.C. ★★★ *Gold Award*
A.A. ★★★ ❀❀❀
A.A. Top 200 - 02/03

FACILITIES
On site: *Garden, heli-pad, croquet*
Licensed for weddings
3 meeting rooms/max 180 people
Nearby: *Golf, riding, fishing,*
tennis, gym, pool

RESTRICTIONS
Pets by arrangement

ATTRACTIONS
Stratford-upon-Avon, Warwick Castle,
Kenilworth Castle, The Cotswolds,
National Exhibition Centre

AFFILIATIONS
Independent

NEAREST
MAJOR CITY:
Birmingham - 12 miles/25 mins

MAJOR AIRPORT:
Birmingham - 7 miles/15 mins

RAILWAY STATION:
Birmingham Intl - 7 miles/15 mins

RESERVATIONS
Direct with hotel
Quote **Best Loved**

ACCESS CODES
Not applicable

MIDSHIRES

Unashamed luxury in the very heart of England

A long tree-lined drive takes you to Nuthurst Grange nestling in 7 ½ acres of gardens and woodlands.

The restaurant is the centrepiece of the hotel, providing an intimate and relaxing setting for luncheon or dinner. Head Chef Ben Davies and his team have won many ratings & awards for their imaginative menus which feature the freshest seasonal produce. Complemented by a fine wine list, the cuisine embraces the best of modern and classical French/British cooking. The pre-meal canapes, the selection of bread, biscuits and petits fours are all home-made.

All 15 spacious bedrooms are furnished and decorated in soft country house style. Each has superb rural views through traditional leaded windows and private bathrooms with air-spa baths.

The seclusion of the hotel belies its easy accessibility. Just off the Stratford-upon-Avon to Birmingham road, the hotel is within 15 minutes of Birmingham International Airport and the heart of England's motorway network.

LOCATION

M42, Exit 4 and M40 Exit 16. ½ mile
south of Hockley Heath on A3400,
turning by hotel signboard into
Nuthurst Grange Lane.

" For those in need of a little luxurious indulgence, this is exactly what the doctor of hedonism would order "

Alison Davidson, Birmingham Evening Post

Restaurant with rooms

THE OLD MILL

A Gallic island of excellence

Twenty years after he invaded England in 1066, William the Conqueror ordered that every piece of land and building should be registered in what is now famously known as The Domesday Book. The Old Mill at Shipston-on-Stour was one such entry, and its association with France, albeit a very different one, continues today. The hotel is a converted flour mill, and all its rooms have been extensively refurbished and named after a specific French region; so the Burgundy Room's exposed brick chimney breast and stripped wood floor work perfectly with the rich, colour palette and original old beams.

Much of the produce for the Chavignol Restaurant onsite is sourced from the company's own estate or throughout Europe. This commitment to great food, fine wine and a relaxed luxury may sound quintessentially Gallic, but proprietor Mark Maguire and chef Marcus Ashenford have created their own island of excellence - quite literally in this case, as the hotel's 1½ acre garden is completely surrounded by water - in the heart of the Warwickshire countryside. And for those who want to take a small piece of the experience home with them, Chavignol import wine and cheeses which can be ordered online.

LOCATION

10 miles south of Stratford-upon-Avon. From the village centre turn down Church Street, which then becomes Mill Street.

Mill Street, Shipston-on-Stour, Warwickshire CV36 4AW

**Telephone 01608 663888
Fax 01608 663188**

E-mail: oldmillship@bestloved.com

OWNER
Mark Maguire

ROOM RATES
Single occupancy   £95
4 Doubles   £190
1 Family room   £85 - £95
Includes full breakfast and VAT

CHARGE/CREDIT CARDS

 • MC • VI

RATINGS & AWARDS
A.A. ❀❀❀ *Restaurant with rooms*
A.A. Top 200 - 02/03

FACILITIES
On site: *Garden*
Nearby: *Riding, fishing, boating, tennis, swimming, golf*

RESTRICTIONS
*Limited facilities for disabled guests
Pets by arrangement*

ATTRACTIONS
*The Cotswolds,
Stratford-upon-Avon,
Broughton Castle,
Hidcote Gardens,
Charlecote Park,
Snowshill Manor,
Warwick Castle*

AFFILIATIONS
Independent

NEAREST
*MAJOR CITY:
Oxford - 28 miles/45 mins*

*MAJOR AIRPORT:
Birmingham - 36 miles/45 mins
London Heathrow - 74 miles/1 ½ hrs*

*RAILWAY STATION:
Moreton-in-Marsh - 7 miles/10 mins*

RESERVATIONS
Direct with hotel
Quote **Best Loved**

ACCESS CODES
Not applicable

MIDSHIRES

> *My wife and I have spent some of our happiest times, outside our own home, at The Old Parsonage. We feel the Parsonage has been one of our real finds*
>
> *James Nelson, Cumbria*

OLD PARSONAGE

17th century town house

1 Banbury Road, Oxford, Oxfordshire OX2 6NN

Telephone 01865 310210
Fax 01865 311262

E-mail: *oldparsoxon@bestloved.com*

OWNER
Jeremy Mogford

MANAGER
Steven Vanozzi

ROOM RATES
1 Single £130
25 Doubles/Twins £155 - £190
4 Suites £200
Includes full breakfast and VAT

CHARGE/CREDIT CARDS
 • DC • JCB • MC • VI

RATINGS & AWARDS
E.T.C. ★★★★ *Silver Award Town House*
A.A. ★★★★ 66%
A.A. Town House

FACILITIES
On site: *Garden, private parking*
Nearby: *Golf, flying, punting*

RESTRICTIONS
Limited facilities for disabled guests
No pets
Closed 25 - 26 Dec

ATTRACTIONS
Oxford University, Ashmolean Museum, Botanical Gardens, Sheldonian Theatre, Oxford University Colleges,

AFFILIATIONS
Preston's Global Hotels
The European Connection

NEAREST
MAJOR CITY:
Oxford

MAJOR AIRPORT:
London Heathrow - 47 miles/1 hr

RAILWAY STATION:
Oxford - 2 miles/5 mins

RESERVATIONS
Toll free in US: 800-544-9993
*Quote **Best Loved***

ACCESS CODES
AMADEUS HK OXFOLD
APOLLO/GALILEO HT 14857
SABRE/ABACUS HK 30442
WORLDSPAN HK OLDPA

The spirit of Oxford in the heart of this famous university city

The Old Parsonage site dates back to 1308. The building is a much-loved Oxford landmark. It played its part in the city's history; as a sanctuary for persecuted clergy in the Middle Ages, as a stronghold for Royalists in the Civil War of the 1640s, and as a home for 19th century literati including Oscar Wilde. The historic character of the building has been preserved. The hotel is small, individually run, with a distinct personality.

Each of the 30 bedrooms is furnished in a style of its own. Many enjoy views over the secluded walled garden or the unique roof garden. Each has a luxurious marble bathroom.

The much praised Parsonage Bar and Restaurant opens for breakfast and continues serving all day until late. The menu is most imaginative and is complemented by a well - researched wine list. It has become famous amongst residents and the local Oxford community for a quiet cappuccino, a glass of champagne or sumptuous cream teas. Meals are served on the terrace in fine weather. Gee's Restaurant, housed in a spectacular Victorian conservatory and owned by the hotel, is less than five minutes walk along the Banbury Road.

Located between Keble and Somerville Colleges, the hotel is a short walk from Oxford's shops, theatres, museums and art galleries.

LOCATION

Leave northern ring road at roundabout at top of Banbury Road. Follow Banbury Road through Summertown towards city centre. Hotel is on right, next to St Giles Church.

> *The entire family were delighted with their rooms, the delicious food, the helpfulness of all the staff and the beautiful setting*
>
> Joyce & Hugh Croydon, Herts

Edwardian country house

OLD VICARAGE

A breathtakingly beautiful county just waiting to be discovered

Shropshire lies on the Welsh border, seemingly hidden from the rest of Britain by Birmingham's urban sprawl. Yet just 15 minutes from the motorway, the tiny conservation village of Worfield is as far from the fast lane as it is possible to get. Originally an Edwardian vicarage, the hotel retains all the charm and elegance that characterises quintessential village life.

Each of the bedrooms is named after a local hamlet, such as Claverly, Shipton, Chesterton or even Badger Dingle, where many of P G Wodehouse's famous Jeeves and Wooster stories were set. Furnishings are often antique, and all rooms have an individual character, particularly the luxury Allscot room, which has French windows onto its own private garden with views down to the River Worfe.

Proprietors, Sarah and David Blakstad have also added their personal touch to the restaurant, and they follow a philosophy that ensures a fine balance between formality and fun, where traditional dishes are prepared with locally sourced produce to high culinary standards. The hotel has won many awards and particularly it has been acclaimed for its provision for disabled guests. Worfield is an ideal touring base, and the many historic local attractions include Stratford-on-Avon and Ironbridge Gorge.

LOCATION

From Kidderminster, follow signs to Wolverhampton on A454. Look for left hand turn to Worfield about 3 miles from Bridgnorth. Hotel is 1 mile along on right.

Worfield, Bridgnorth, Shropshire WV15 5JZ

Telephone 01746 716497
Fax 01746 716552

E-mail: *oldvicshrop@bestloved.com*

OWNERS
David and Sarah Blakstad

ROOM RATES
Singles	£78 - £113
8 Doubles/Twins	£118 - £178
1 Family room	£153
1 Four-poster	£168
4 Suites	£168 - £178

Includes full breakfast, newspaper and VAT

CHARGE/CREDIT CARDS

 • DC • MC • VI

RATINGS & AWARDS
E.T.C. ★★★ *Gold Award*
R.A.C. Blue Ribbon ★★★ *Dining Award 3*
A.A. ★★★ ❀❀❀
A.A. Top 200 - 02/03

FACILITIES
On site: *Garden, croquet*
3 meeting rooms/max 40 people
Nearby: *Golf, fishing, riding*

RESTRICTIONS
No smoking in bedrooms or dining rooms

ATTRACTIONS
Stratford-upon-Avon, The Cotswolds, Weston Park Stately Home, Ludlow Castle, Ironbridge Gorge, Severn Valley Railway, Royal Worcester & Royal Doulton Potteries,

AFFILIATIONS
Pride of Britain

NEAREST
MAJOR CITY:
Wolverhampton - 10 miles/30 mins

MAJOR AIRPORT:
Birmingham - 45 miles/1 hr

RAILWAY STATION:
Wolverhampton - 10 miles/30 mins

RESERVATIONS
Toll free in US: 800-98-PRIDE
*Quote **Best Loved***

ACCESS CODES
AMADEUS HK BHXOLD
APOLLO/GALILEO HT 20216
SABRE/ABACUS HK 33865
WORLDSPAN HK OLDVI

MIDSHIRES

" *Owlpen is a Gloucestershire Shangri-la where those in the know come year after year for absolute peace and seclusion* **"**

The Sunday Times

OWLPEN MANOR

15th century manor

Owlpen, Near Uley, Gloucestershire GL11 5BZ

Telephone 01453 860261
Fax 01453 860819

E-mail: *owlpen@bestloved.com*

OWNERS
Nicholas and Karin Mander

ROOM RATES
9 Self-catering cottages £60 - £140
Includes VAT

CHARGE/CREDIT CARDS
• *MC* • *VI*

RATINGS & AWARDS
E.T.C. ★★★★

FACILITIES
On site: *Garden, heli-pad, fishing, shooting*
2 meeting rooms/max 40 people
Nearby: *Golf, riding, gliding*

RESTRICTIONS
No facilities for disabled guests
Pets by arrangement

ATTRACTIONS
Owlpen Manor House,
The Cotswolds,
Berkeley Castle,
Roman City of Bath,
Slimbridge Wildfowl Trust,
Westonbirt Arboretum

AFFILIATIONS
Independent

NEAREST
MAJOR CITY:
Bath - 25 miles/40 mins

MAJOR AIRPORT:
London Heathrow - 105 miles/2 hrs

RAILWAY STATION:
Stroud - 7 miles/20 mins

RESERVATIONS
Direct with hotel
Quote **Best Loved**

ACCESS CODES
Not applicable

Your own historic cottage in one of the most romantic estates in the country

HRH The Prince of Wales described Owlpen as the epitome of the English village. Set in its own peaceful wooded valley, Owlpen is one of the most romantic, historic estates in the country. Its Tudor manor house remains a family home; Queen Margaret, Henry VI's queen, slept in its Great Chamber, during the Wars of the Roses in 1471 and it is famed for its 16th and 17th century formal gardens and the great yew trees. The medieval Cyder House with its huge oak cider press serves as a restaurant and reception area for visitors who stay in the distinctive, historic cottages. The cottages include a medieval barn, a watermill restored in 1464, the 1620 Court House and weavers' and keepers' cottages. Several are listed buildings in their own right.

The cottages are furnished and decorated in the style of an English country house where family possessions have accumulated over the generations. Modern comforts are discreetly and fully provided. The cottages have their own gardens providing a sheltered spot in which to relax and breathe the scents of flowers.

Owlpen is in the Royal Triangle in the heart of the Cotswolds. Limestone villages, prehistoric barrows, quiet lanes and antique shops are all here to be explored. Bath, Cheltenham, Cirencester and Gloucester are all about 20 miles away.

LOCATION

Situated ½ mile east of Uley, off the B4066. From the M4 take exit 18 and follow the signs from the A4135.

> *What a fabulous place! Warm and relaxing, friendly and unpretentious. Food to die for and what a wine list! Please never, ever change a thing and we will be back*
>
> J & J Blake, Shipton Bellinger

18th century country house

THE PAINSWICK HOTEL

"Sheer poetry", said His Majesty. A sentiment as true today as ever it was

"The valleys around Painswick are sheer poetry, in this Paradise" - King Charles I's words. The village comprises medieval cottages lying cheek-by-jowl with the 17th and 18th century merchants' houses and has been accorded the title: The Queen of the Cotswolds. The former rectory, built in 1790 in the Palladian style is today The Painswick Hotel.

The hotel has 19 luxury bedrooms, all with luxury toiletries, baskets of fresh fruit, mineral water, books, magazines and other amenities. The stunning fabrics, soft furnishings, antique furniture, period engravings and objets d'art all contribute to the sense of well-being. In the pine panelled dining room, simply delicious and tempting food is served with an emphasis on seafood, local game and Gloucestershire cheeses.

The public rooms, all with distinct elegance and character, have antique furniture and fine pictures, together with open fires. They express a quiet confidence reflecting the more leisured times in which they were built.

Painswick is a superb touring, sporting and cultural centre. All the pleasures of The Cotswolds, Regency Cheltenham and Bath, Gloucester and Stratford-upon-Avon are within an easy drive.

LOCATION

In the centre of Painswick behind Parish church. 8 miles off M5 Exit 13 take A419 to A46 north. 28 miles off M4 Exit 15 take A419 to A46 north.

Kemps Lane, Painswick, Gloucestershire GL6 6YB

Telephone 01452 812160
Fax 01452 814059

E-mail: *painswick@bestloved.com*

OWNERS
Gareth and Helen Pugh

ROOM RATES
2 Singles	£75 - £90
15 Doubles/Twins	£125 - £175
2 Four-posters	£200

Includes full breakfast, newspaper and VAT

CHARGE/CREDIT CARDS

 • *JCB* • *MC* • *VI*

RATINGS & AWARDS
E.T.C. ★★★ *Silver Award*
R.A.C. Blue Ribbon ★★★ *Dining Award 3*
A.A. ★★★ ❀❀ *75%*

FACILITIES
On site: *Garden, croquet*
Licensed for weddings
3 meeting rooms/max 80 people
Nearby: *Golf, riding, gliding, hot air ballooning, clay pigeon shooting*

RESTRICTIONS
No facilities for disabled guests
Pets by arrangement

ATTRACTIONS
Sudeley Castle, Berkeley Castle, Bath, Stratford-upon-Avon, Rococco gardens, The Cotswolds

AFFILIATIONS
Preston's Global Hotels
Cotswold's Finest Hotels

NEAREST
MAJOR CITY:
Gloucester - 5 miles/10 mins

MAJOR AIRPORT:
London Heathrow - 90 miles/1 ¾ hrs

RAILWAY STATION:
Stroud - 3 miles/5 mins

RESERVATIONS
Toll free in US: 800-544-9993
*Quote **Best Loved***

ACCESS CODES
AMADEUS HK GLOPAI
SABRE/ABACUS HK 50497

MIDSHIRES

● *Map p.470*
ref: E6

" Neither of us have experienced such discreet and polite hospitality. So, for 'running such a beautiful ship' and for your friendliness, thank you very much "

Richard White, High Wycombe

THE PLOUGH AT CLANFIELD   *16th century manor house*

**Bourton Road, Clanfield,
Oxfordshire OX18 2RB**

**Telephone 01367 810222
Fax 01367 810596**

E-mail: *plough@bestloved.com*

OWNERS
John and Rosemary Hodges

ROOM RATES
Single occupancy	£90
8 Doubles/Twins	£120
3 Four-posters	£130
1 Suite	£165

*Includes continental or
full breakfast and VAT*

CHARGE/CREDIT CARDS

 • *DC • JCB • MC • VI*

RATINGS & AWARDS
A.A. ★★★ 69%

FACILITIES
On site: *Garden
2 meeting rooms/max 40 people*
Nearby: *Golf, fishing, tennis,
fitness centre, shooting, riding*

RESTRICTIONS
*No children under 12 years
Smoking in lounge bar only
No pets, guide dogs only
Closed Christmas*

ATTRACTIONS
*Blenheim Palace, Rousham House,
Kelmscott Manor, Stonor Park,
Oxford, Waterperry Gardens*

AFFILIATIONS
Independent

NEAREST
*MAJOR CITY:
Oxford - 18 miles/25 mins*

*MAJOR AIRPORT:
London Heathrow - 65 miles/1 ½ hrs*

*RAILWAY STATION:
Oxford - 18 miles/25 mins*

RESERVATIONS
*Direct with hotel
Quote **Best Loved***

ACCESS CODES
Not applicable

MIDSHIRES

Deep-piled comfort and wonderful country food in a classic manor

In Cirencester, a short drive from Clanfield there is a marvellously intact Roman amphitheatre which is said to date from 1BC. The structure is a symbol of ancient Roman ingenuity. And if, in a 1,000 years, you stumbled upon the honey-coloured Cotswolds manor house that is The Plough, you might be similarly struck with respect for Elizabethan architecture. This is a classic in every respect!

John and Rosemary Hodges have lovingly turned this graceful old house into a welcoming hostelry renowned throughout the region for fine food. The Plough is very much the ideal of the country house experience. Voluminous sofas and oversized armchairs invite you to sink into comfort and pass an afternoon with a good book. In the evening, candle-lit tables with proper napery beckon the guest to enjoy a wonderful repast.

The bedrooms, in keeping with the rest of the house, have been tastefully and traditionally decorated and and include lovely little extras like a decanter of sherry and plush bathrobes.

The Plough is the perfect base from which to explore Oxford, Bath, Stratford-upon-Avon and the pretty Cotswold villages.

LOCATION
*Located on the edge of the village of Clanfield,
at the junction of the A4095 and the B4020
between Witney and Faringdon.*

" We came to discover Shropshire but our best find was this most excellent hotel. We will remember our stay with affection and will be spreading the word "

Michael and Joan Tice, Bognor Regis

• Map p.470
ref: C4

15th century coaching inn | THE RAVEN HOTEL & RESTAURANT

Much praised in Much Wenlock on the gourmet circuit of Shropshire

The modern Olympic Games owe much to a certain Dr Penny Brookes who lived in Much Wenlock. He founded the Wenlock Olympian Society in 1850 and, years later, worked with Baron Coubertin to found the modern Olympic movement. In 1890, the Baron wrote: "And of the Olympic Games ... it is not a Greek to whom one is indebted but rather to Dr W P Brookes".

Since the games began the Raven has been the haunt of spectators and competitors alike. Then, as now, the traditional welcome is as warm as a 500-year old coaching inn can muster. The place has immense character. The flower-filled courtyard gives access to a number of bedrooms which have been delightfully furnished and provided with every modern comfort. There are four-poster rooms and an imaginatively designed galleried suite, a good example of a blend of old and new.

Before you dine, have a look at the Olympian memorabilia on display in the public rooms, then prepare yourself for a treat. The two rosette AA rating is a clue but a look at the menu, and you will agree with Paddy Burt of the Daily Telegraph, "This is what I call serious food". It's imaginative and delicious with a good choice of something traditional or much higher up the culinary scale.

The Raven is without doubt an absolute winner!

LOCATION

10 miles from Telford between Shrewsbury and Bridgnorth where the A4169 meets the A458. Proceed down Much Wenlock High St, turn right, hotel is 100 yards on right.

**Barrow Street,
Much Wenlock,
Shropshire TF13 6EN**

**Telephone 01952 727251
Fax 01952 728416**

E-mail: *ravenhotel@bestloved.com*

OWNER
Kirk Heywood

ROOM RATES
Single occupancy	£75
12 Doubles/Twins	£95
1 Four-poster	£105
1 Family room	£120
1 Suite	£125
Includes full breakfast and VAT	

CHARGE/CREDIT CARDS

 • DC • JCB • MC • VI

RATINGS & AWARDS
A.A. ★★★ ❀❀ 73%

FACILITIES
On site: *Garden, health & beauty
1 meeting room/max 16 people*
Nearby: *Golf, tennis, fishing,
riding, swimming*

RESTRICTIONS
*No facilities for disabled guests
No pets
Closed Christmas*

ATTRACTIONS
*Ironbridge, Dudmaston Hall,
Coalport Pottery, Stokesay Castle,
Wenlock Priory, Wroxeter Roman City,
Wenlock Edge, Attingham Park*

AFFILIATIONS
Independent

NEAREST
*MAJOR CITY:
Telford - 10 miles/15 mins
Shrewsbury - 13 miles/20 mins*

*MAJOR AIRPORT:
Birmingham - 53 miles/1 hr*

*RAILWAY STATION:
Shrewsbury - 13 miles/20 mins*

RESERVATIONS
*Direct with hotel
Quote **Best Loved***

ACCESS CODES
Not applicable

MIDSHIRES

❝ *We loved our stay in your beautiful hotel. The grounds, the service, the atmosphere were all exquisite. This is one of the best kept secrets of Derbyshire.* ❞

Mr and Mrs Holman, Salt Lake City

RISLEY HALL

Victorian manor

MIDSHIRES

Derby Road, Risley, Derbyshire DE72 3SS

Telephone 0115 939 9000
Fax 0115 939 7766

E-mail: *risley@bestloved.com*

OWNER
Mike Crosbie

GENERAL MANAGER
Julie Dunkley

ROOM RATES
Single occupancy	£100 - £194
14 Doubles/Twins	£112 - £235
4 Four-posters	£112 - £235
17 Suites	£165 - £235

Includes VAT

CHARGE/CREDIT CARDS

 • *MC* • *VI*

RATINGS & AWARDS
E.T.C. ★★★ *Silver Award*
A.A. ★★★ ❀❀ 73%

FACILITIES
On site: *Garden, croquet*
Licensed for weddings
4 meeting rooms/max 120 people
Nearby: *Golf, tennis, fitness, riding*

RESTRICTIONS
Limited facilities for disabled guests
No pets

ATTRACTIONS
Nottingham Castle, Sherwood Forest,
Peak District National Park,
Chatsworth House, Belvoir Castle

AFFILIATIONS
Independent

NEAREST
MAJOR CITY:
Nottingham - 7 miles/15 mins
Derby - 7 miles/15 mins

MAJOR AIRPORT:
East Midlands - 10 miles/15 mins

RAILWAY STATION:
Long Eaton - 3 miles/5 mins

RESERVATIONS
Direct with hotel
*Quote **Best Loved***

ACCESS CODES
Not applicable

A Victorian home purpose-built for the pleasures of good living

This is Saxon country whose prosperity grew with the lace industry in the last century. Risley Hall itself has a history that goes back to the 11th century. It prospered into the grand house it is in Victorian times under the ownership of a flamboyant entrepreneur called Ernest Terah Hooley.

Today, the splendours of this baronial hall have been restored; the house and its gardens once again receive guests intent on the pleasures of good food and amusing company in luxury surroundings. A country retreat offering fine cuisine, luxurious bedchambers and outstanding service in a majestic setting.

There are 35 bedrooms and suites. Tasteful colour schemes, elegant furnishings, beautiful brocades and original oak beams create a relaxing environment with a character of its own. From soft sophistication to a cosy cottage feel or a dramatic four-poster style, there's a room to suit every mood and occasion.

he chef de cuisine indulges his diners in his own distinctive style. They can opt for the à la carte or menu du jour menus. Whatever the choice, Abbey's restaurant could not be a more beautiful place in which to enjoy it.

LOCATION

Exit 25 off M1, take Sandiacre exit from
Bostock Lane. At cross roads, turn left towards
Risley. Follow A5010 Derby road for ½ a mile.
Risley Hall is on left hand side.

Georgian manor   RIVERSIDE HOUSE HOTEL

Fennel Street,
Ashford-in-the-Water,
Bakewell,
Derbyshire DE45 1QF

Telephone 01629 814275
Fax 01629 812873

E-mail: riverside@bestloved.com

GENERAL MANAGER
James Lamb

ROOM RATES
Single occupancy	*£85 - £120*
14 Doubles/Twins	*£120 - £135*
1 Four-poster	*£135 - £155*
Includes full breakfast and VAT	

CHARGE/CREDIT CARDS

 • *DC* • *MC* • *VI*

RATINGS & AWARDS
A.A. ★★★ ❀❀ 77%
A.A. Customer Care Hotel of the Year
Karen Brown Recommended

FACILITIES
On site: *Garden, croquet*
Licensed for weddings
1 meeting room/max 30 people
Nearby: *Golf, river fishing,*
shooting, riding

RESTRICTIONS
No children
No smoking in bedrooms
No pets

ATTRACTIONS
Derbyshire Dales, Hardwick Hall,
Chatsworth House, Plague Village,
Haddon Hall, Blue John Mines

AFFILIATIONS
Independent

NEAREST
MAJOR CITY:
Sheffield - 16 miles/30 mins

MAJOR AIRPORT:
Manchester - 40 miles/1 hr

RAILWAY STATION:
Chesterfield - 12 miles/30 mins

RESERVATIONS
Direct with hotel
*Quote **Best Loved***

ACCESS CODES
Not applicable

The height of hospitality in the splendour of The Peaks

It is no wonder the striking and magnificent Peak District's moor-like landscape was established as Britain's first National Park. The interesting bit is that the 'Peak District' doesn't have a single 'Peak', the highest elevation being Kinder Scout, a mere 680 metres. But what this area lacks in height it makes up in mountains of hospitality. It is an area enormously popular with British travellers and only recently discovered by foreign visitors seeking a glimpse of 'real England'. In a picturesque village by the River Wye, is the aptly named Riverside House Hotel. This secluded and cosy, ivy-clad Georgian house, is the ideal spot from which to explore the Peaks and Dales of Derbyshire, Chatsworth and Dovedale.

Recently the hotel underwent a major upgrading to the public rooms and bedrooms which has significantly improved on its much admired reputation. Informality and friendliness are the order of the day at the Riverside. Customer care, tastefully designed bedrooms and the Riverside Room restaurant's modern English cuisine come together to create the perfect setting for a totally relaxing break.

Whether for a special night out or as a touring base of the very best of Derbyshire, the Riverside House Hotel delivers.

LOCATION

1 ½ miles outside Bakewell on the A6 to Buxton.
The entrance to the hotel is at the edge of the
village by the Sheepwash Bridge.

232

Map p.470
ref: D6

THE ROYALIST HOTEL

10th century inn

**Digbeth Street,
Stow-on-the-Wold,
Gloucestershire GL54 1BN**

**Telephone 01451 830670
Fax 01451 870048**

E-mail: *royalist@bestloved.com*

OWNERS
Alan and Georgina Thompson

ROOM RATES
Single occupancy	£50 - £130
6 Doubles/Twins	£90 - £130
1 Four-poster	£110 - £150
1 Suite	£130 - £170

Includes continental breakfast and VAT

CHARGE/CREDIT CARDS

 • DC • JCB • MC • VI

RATINGS & AWARDS
E.T.C. ★★★ *Silver Award*
A.A. ★★★ ✿✿✿ 72%

FACILITIES
On site: *Bar*
1 meeting room/max 70 people
Nearby: *Riding, fishing,
quad biking, clay pigeon shooting*

RESTRICTIONS
*No facilities for disabled guests
No children under 6 years in restaurant
Smoking in bar only
Pets by arrangement*

ATTRACTIONS
*Warwick Castle, The Cotswolds, Oxford,
Blenheim Palace, Hidcote Gardens,
Stratford-upon-Avon*

AFFILIATIONS
Independent

NEAREST
*MAJOR CITY:
Oxford - 35 miles/40 mins*

*MAJOR AIRPORT:
Birmingham - 43 miles/1 ¼ hrs*

*RAILWAY STATION:
Kingham - 4 miles/10 mins*

RESERVATIONS
*Direct with hotel
Quote **Best Loved***

ACCESS CODES
Not applicable

MIDSHIRES

A restaurant, an hotel and an inn.
Three into one does go!

The Royalist is the oldest inn in England dating back to 947 AD when it was a hospice and almshouse owned by the Knights of St John. It is truly atmospheric with antique beams and spooky marks to ward off witches, leper holes and a Babylonian frieze dating from the Crusades.

While it would be hard to improve on this hospitable landmark, the owners of The Royalist, Alan and Georgina Thompson, have completed a superb major refurbishment of the hotel. Behind the mellow 17th-century Cotswold stone façade, there are a dozen bedrooms, each different and inspired by top British designers. For something really unusual, check out the jewel-like Porch House Room created out of the 1615 porch and glassed-in on three sides.

A noted chef, Alan presides over the excellent 947 AD Restaurant. As an Australian, he and Georgina are determined to keep the atmosphere relaxed. For those seeking draught ale and great pub food, take a stroll over the flagstones to the 'Eagle and Child'. This is a real find, so book now before word gets out.

LOCATION
*At Stow-on-the-Wold turn off A429 for
Chipping Norton. The hotel is 300 yards
on left, behind The Green.*

Best Loved Hotels of the World

I want to share a wonderful discovery with your readers . . .

Patricia Morris, Readers Write column, Los Angeles Times

233

• Map p.470
ref: E6

14th century abbey — THE SHAVEN CROWN

600 years of history, a medieval hall and a family welcome

The Shaven Crown hotel is beautifully situated in the heart of the Cotswolds. Originally a 14th century hospice to Bruern Abbey, it is built of local honey-coloured stone around a central medieval courtyard garden. It has the mellowed charm of 600 years of hospitality. The hotel is owned by the Burpitt family who are actively engaged in its daily running.

The pride of the Shaven Crown Hotel, in addition to its original 14th century gateway, is the medieval hall - now the residents' lounge. All the bedrooms have tea and coffee-making facilities, TV and private bathrooms. The hotel is centrally heated throughout.

An intimate candlelit restaurant serves food fresh every day. The bar offers an imaginative array of bar meals, beside the log fire, at lunch and dinner seven days a week. You may eat al fresco in the courtyard when you choose to.

The area is justly renowned for antiques-hunting. Cheltenham and the other towns and villages of the Cotswolds are within easy reach, as are Oxford, Stratford-upon-Avon and Cirencester. Blenheim Palace, birthplace of Sir Winston Churchill, is one of the many great stately homes in the district.

LOCATION

On the A361, 4 miles north of Burford and 6 miles south of Chipping Norton.

**High Street,
Shipton-under-Wychwood,
Oxfordshire OX7 6BA**

**Telephone 01993 830330
Fax 01993 832136**

E-mail: *shaven@bestloved.com*

OWNERS
Robert and Jane Burpitt

ROOM RATES
Single occupancy £55
8 Doubles/Twins £95 - £120
1 Four-poster £120
Includes full breakfast and VAT

CHARGE/CREDIT CARDS

 • MC • VI

RATINGS & AWARDS
E.T.C. ★★

FACILITIES
On site: *Garden, bowling green*
1 meeting room/max 60 people
Nearby: *Golf, fishing, riding*

RESTRICTIONS
Limited facilities for disabled guests

ATTRACTIONS
*The Cotswolds, Burford,
Blenheim Palace,
Bourton-on-the-Water,
Stow-on-the-Wold*

AFFILIATIONS
Independent

NEAREST
MAJOR CITY:
Oxford - 26 miles/30 mins

MAJOR AIRPORT:
London Heathrow - 70 miles/1 ½ hrs
Birmingham - 55 miles/1 ¼ hrs

RAILWAY STATION:
Charlbury - 6 miles/10 mins

RESERVATIONS
Direct with hotel
Quote **Best Loved**

ACCESS CODES
Not applicable

MIDSHIRES

" *A wonderful retreat from the hustle and bustle of London life, being only a short distance away* "

Claire & Mark Grabiner, London

THE SPRINGS HOTEL & GOLF CLUB   *Country house*

**Wallingford Road,
North Stoke,
Oxfordshire OX10 6BE**

**Telephone 01491 836687
Fax 01491 836877**

E-mail: *springs@bestloved.com*

GENERAL MANAGER
George Briffa

ROOM RATES
Single occupancy   £90 - £155
29 Doubles/Twins   £115 - £155
2 Suites   £140 - £165
Includes full breakfast and VAT

CHARGE/CREDIT CARDS

 • DC • JCB • MC • VI

RATINGS & AWARDS
R.A.C. ★★★ *Dining Award 2*
A.A. ★★★ ❦ *71%*

FACILITIES
On site: *Garden, fishing, croquet,
18-hole golf course,
outdoor pool, sauna, jacuzzi
Licensed for weddings
4 meeting rooms/max 100 people*
Nearby: *Riding*

RESTRICTIONS
*Limited facilities for disabled guests
Pets by arrangement, £10 surcharge*

ATTRACTIONS
*Blenheim Palace, Oxford,
Windsor, Henley-on-Thames,
The Chilterns, The Cotswolds,
Newbury Race Course*

AFFILIATIONS
Thames Valley Hotels

NEAREST
MAJOR CITY:
*Oxford - 12 miles/20 mins
Reading - 12 miles/20 mins*

MAJOR AIRPORT:
London Heathrow - 30 miles/1 hr

RAILWAY STATION:
Reading - 12 miles/20 mins

RESERVATIONS
Direct with hotel
*Quote **Best Loved***

ACCESS CODES
Not applicable

A secret hideaway by The Thames for peace and relaxation

The Springs lies in a small Thames-side village midway between the M40 and M4. Its proximity to Oxford, Windsor and Henley makes it an ideal base to explore the wonderful countryside and villages of the Chilterns and Cotswolds or for a relaxing and peaceful break.

The Springs, one of the first mock-tudor houses to be built in England, lies in six acres of wooded grounds and formalised gardens, overlooking a spring-fed lake from which it takes its name. In the panelled lounge, traditional furnishings and glowing log fires in winter reinforce a warm and friendly atmosphere. The bedrooms are attractively decorated and complete with every luxury. Some rooms have balconies overlooking the lake and a few have jacuzzi baths.

The magical setting of the balcony restaurant overlooking the floodlit lake with swans and ducks makes up a very English scene. The imaginative executive chef bases his cooking on English culinary heritage.

For the sporty, there is use of a guitar shaped outdoor swimming pool (open May to September), croquet, putting and 18 hole, par 72 golf course.

LOCATION
Just outside the market town of Wallingford on B4009, 20 minutes drive from Oxford.

❝ *I greatly enjoyed the time I spent there and I trust you will experience the same pleasures at one of the most wonderful stately homes in Britain* ❞

The Earl of Lichfield

Stately home

STAPLEFORD PARK

An historic stately home with a sumptuously unique lifestyle

Stapleford is one of England's finest stately homes with a pedigree stretching back to the 14th century. Set in 500 acres of woods, parkland and beautiful gardens, the house is a miraculously balanced and harmonious blend of architectural periods. The interior has been magnificently restored and furnished in spectacular style. During its long and distinguished history, embellishments have included outstanding works of art such as the glorious 17th-century carvings by Grinling Gibbons in the dining room inspired by the Spanish Riding School in Vienna.

From the elegant drawing room or the comfort of the saloon with its leather sofas to the heavenly bedrooms, guests can relax in the lap of luxury. The cosseting continues in the Clarins Spa, with its 22m pool, new state of the art gym, jacuzzi, solarium and beauty therapy rooms. Outside, the challenging 18-hole Championship golf course designed by Donald Steel will enthral all comers, and the new golf club pavilion has stunning views over the 18th Green. Guests can also enjoy six multi-surface tennis courts (including the first artificial clay court in the UK). The Victorian stables in the grounds are soon to become an

Holistic Spa with 16 treatment rooms - a fabulous addition to this quintessentially country house, opening in Spring 2003.

LOCATION

4 miles east of Melton Mowbray on B676 towards Colsterworth and the A1.

**Stapleford Park,
Near Melton Mowbray,
Leicestershire LE14 2EF**

**Telephone 01572 787522
Fax 01572 787651**

E-mail: *stapleford@bestloved.com*

OWNER
William Boulton-Smith

GENERAL MANAGER
Alan Thomas

ROOM RATES

1 Single	£205
48 Doubles/Twins	£205 - £425
2 Suites	£595

Includes breakfast, newspaper and VAT

CHARGE/CREDIT CARDS

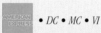 ● *DC* ● *MC* ● *VI*

RATINGS & AWARDS
R.A.C. Gold Ribbon ★★★★ *Dining Award 4*
A.A. ★★★★ ❀❀

FACILITIES
On site: *Garden, croquet, tennis, archery, sauna, jacuzzi, indoor pool, Clarins Spa, gym, snooker, fishing, falconry, 18-hole golf course, pétanque, boules, mountain bikes, clay shooting, off-road driving, heli-pad 8 meeting rooms/max 300 people*
Nearby: *Shooting, riding*

RESTRICTIONS
None

ATTRACTIONS
Burghley House, Belvoir Castle, Rutland Water, Chatsworth House, Belton House, Stamford

AFFILIATIONS
The Celebrated Hotels Collection

NEAREST
MAJOR CITY:
Leicester - 18 miles/35 mins

MAJOR AIRPORT:
East Midlands - 20 miles/45 mins

RAILWAY STATION:
Grantham - 15 miles/25 mins

RESERVATIONS
Toll free in US: 800-322-2403
*Quote **Best Loved***

ACCESS CODES
Not applicable

MIDSHIRES

STRATTONS

Queen Anne villa

Ash Close, Swaffham, Norfolk PE37 7NH

Telephone 01760 723845
Fax 01760 720458

E-mail: strattons@bestloved.com

OWNERS
Les and Vanessa Scott

ROOM RATES
Single occupancy   £75 - £110
6 Doubles/Twins/Suites   £100 - £180
Includes breakfast and VAT

CHARGE/CREDIT CARDS

AMERICAN EXPRESS • MC • VI

RATINGS & AWARDS
E.T.C. ★★ Gold Award &
Gold Environment Award
Green Globe, Global
Achievement Award 2000
Queens Award for Industry Outstanding
Environmental Achievement

FACILITIES
On site: Garden
Nearby: Golf, tennis, riding, fishing, health & beauty

RESTRICTIONS
No facilities for disabled guests
No smoking throughout
Closed 25 - 26 Dec

ATTRACTIONS
North Norfolk Coast, Blakeney Point, Holkham Hall, Blickling Hall, Norwich, Castle Acre Priory, Weeting Heath

AFFILIATIONS
Independent

NEAREST
MAJOR CITY:
Norwich - 28 miles/45 mins

MAJOR AIRPORT:
Stansted - 68 miles/1 ½ hrs

RAILWAY STATION:
King's Lynn - 16 miles/25 mins

RESERVATIONS
Direct with hotel
Quote **Best Loved**

ACCESS CODES
Not applicable

MIDSHIRES

Outstanding care for the environment in the lap of luxury

Strattons is an award-winning family-owned hotel in the Breckland market town of Swaffham in East Anglia. It is in easy reach of the royal Sandringham estate, the Norfolk Broads and Holkham Hall. It is a lovingly restored Queen Anne villa with individually themed rooms that include specially commissioned murals in the bathrooms, antique white linen, and in the lush Red Room Suite, that can sleep a family of five, a secret panel door into a Morroccan-style bathroom. It is internationally recognised as one of the most environmentally-friendly businesses in the UK and beyond.

It has a restaurant that sources local, and wherever possible, organic food on a daily basis. You won't find strawberries at Christmas here; rather, think fresh eggs from hens that roam the gardens and are fed on tasty scraps from the kitchen.

The list of accolades is long: The Green Globe Distinction Award for Outstanding Environmental Performance; UK winners of the BA Tourism for Tomorrow Award; and The Good Food Guide's 'County Restaurant' 2000 Award. But above all, Strattons is also a home.

A home that reflects the taste and personal commitment of proprietors Les and Vanessa Scott, where you can experience a better, greener way of life.

LOCATION
From the centre of Swaffham the entrance to Ash Close is opposite the attractive town sign.

66 We stay in many different hotels, but without exception your standards of friendliness far exceeded any either of us have been to 99

Dave & Rachel Archer, Theale, Berkshire

● Map p.470
ref: D6

237

Historic Cotswold hotel

SWAN HOTEL AT BIBURY

A pride of Cotswold villages with English cooking to be proud of

William Morris, great Victorian aesthete and founder of the Society for the Preservation of Ancient Buildings, listed Bibury as one of the prettiest of Cotswold villages. The Swan was the showpiece of the village when Morris came there. Restored to private ownership and run by a handpicked team of staff, the Swan offers a most splendid base for the Cotswolds.

Guests relax and are cosseted in the parlour with its cosy sofas, or the writing room with a delightful watercolour of the Swan as it was in 1630. Each bedroom is stylishly and comfortably furnished with fluffy white towels and robes, and modern facilities. Some rooms offer king-sized beds and jacuzzi baths.

The richly decorated dining room with its glittering chandelier is the home of great English cooking. Dinner menus change daily and are complemented by a fine wine selection. Alternatively, you can try the more informal Jankowski's Brasserie offering crisp, healthy, traditionally styled cuisine.

Roman and Georgian Bath, Stratford-upon-Avon, the Black Mountains of Brecon, Westonbirt Arboretum and Barnsley House

gardens are within easy reach. Bibury and other soft yellow limestone Cotswold villages are on the doorstep.

LOCATION

On B4425, 7 miles north of Cirencester, 9 miles south of Burford. ½ hour from M4 Swindon and M5 Cheltenham. Easily accessible from M40 via A40 Oxford.

Bibury, Near Cirencester, Gloucestershire GL7 5NW
Telephone 01285 740695
Fax 01285 740473

E-mail: *swanbibury@bestloved.com*

OWNERS
Elizabeth A Rose and Michael O Willcox

GENERAL MANAGER
John P Stevens

ROOM RATES
Single occupancy	£99
16 Doubles/Twins	£125 - £260
3 Four-posters	£154 - £260
1 Family room	£139 - £275

Includes full breakfast, early morning tea, newspaper and VAT

CHARGE/CREDIT CARDS
 ● DC ● JCB ● MC ● VI

RATINGS & AWARDS
E.T.C. ★★★ *Gold Award*
A.A. ★★★ ❀❀ 77%

FACILITIES
On site: *Garden, fishing*
3 meeting rooms/max 50 people
Nearby: *Golf, riding, hot-air ballooning, leisure centre, jet skiing*

RESTRICTIONS
No pets

ATTRACTIONS
Roman Baths, Stratford-upon-Avon, Black Mountains, Barnsley House Gardens, Westonbirt Arboretum, Cotswold villages, Cheltenham Racecourse, Cotswold Water Park

AFFILIATIONS
The Celebrated Hotels Collection
Cotswolds Finest Hotels

NEAREST
MAJOR CITY:
Cheltenham - 12 miles/20 mins

MAJOR AIRPORT:
Birmingham - 55 miles/1 ½ hrs
Bristol - 48 miles/1 hr

RAILWAY STATION:
Cheltenham - 12 miles/20 mins
Kemble - 12 miles/15 mins

RESERVATIONS
Toll free in US: 800-322-2403
*Quote **Best Loved***

ACCESS CODES
Not applicable

MIDSHIRES

> *" We would sincerely like to thank yourself, Claire and the rest of your wonderful staff for everything you did to make the wedding day such a memorable one "*
>
> *Liz & John Puddick, Suffolk*

SWYNFORD PADDOCKS | *Country mansion*

MIDSHIRES

Six Mile Bottom, Newmarket, Suffolk CB8 0UE

**Telephone 01638 570234
Fax 01638 570283**

E-mail: *swynford@bestloved.com*

GENERAL MANAGER
Robert Smith

ROOM RATES
Single occupancy   £110 - £140
13 Doubles/Twins   £135 - £165
2 Four-posters   £155 - £195
Includes full breakfast and VAT

CHARGE/CREDIT CARDS

● *DC* ● *MC* ● *VI*

RATINGS & AWARDS
E.T.C. ★★★
R.A.C. ★★★ *Dining Award 1*
A.A. ★★★ ✿ 73%

FACILITIES
On site: *Garden, croquet, tennis, putting green, heli-pad
Licensed for weddings
1 meeting room/max 120 people*
Nearby: *Golf, riding*

RESTRICTIONS
*No facilities for disabled guests
No pets in public rooms*

ATTRACTIONS
Newmarket Racecourse, Museum & National Stud, Ely Cathedral, Cambridge, Lavenham & Long Melford, Duxford Imperial War Museum, Ickworth House

AFFILIATIONS
Independent

NEAREST
MAJOR CITY:
Cambridge - 12 miles/20 mins

MAJOR AIRPORT:
Stansted - 20 miles/30 mins

RAILWAY STATION:
Cambridge - 12 miles/20 mins

RESERVATIONS
Direct with hotel
Quote **Best Loved**

ACCESS CODES
Not applicable

www.swynford.bestloved.com

A classy thoroughbred handily placed for Cambridge and Newmarket

Swynford Paddocks' racing connection is not just confined to its name. There is a working stud farm within the 62-acre grounds, and the hotel's address at Six Mile Bottom refers to its excellent location six miles as the crow flies from the historic university city of Cambridge and Newmarket, the headquarters of British horseracing for over 300 years.

An elegant country house surrounded by its namesake paddocks, Swynford also has a notorious past. In 1813, the Romantic poet Lord Byron conducted a passionate affair with his married half-sister Augusta Leigh, who lived at Swynford. Later the house was owned by Lord and Lady Halifax before it was sympathetically converted into a comfortable country hotel.

Swynford Paddocks makes a great base for exploring East Anglia's diverse attractions. Take a day trip to Cambridge for its medieval churches and ancient colleges, punting on the River Isis or a gentle stroll along the 'Backs' as the riverbanks are known. For fans of the turf, the flat racing at Newmarket is a major draw and there are visits to the National Stud and National Horseracing Museum. The hotel can also arrange behind-the-scenes tours. Other popular side trips include magnificent Ely Cathedral, the picturesque old

wool towns of Lavenham and Long Melford with their half-timbered buildings, pubs and antique shops, and the aircraft collections of the Imperial War Museum at Duxford.

LOCATION

From M11 Exit 9, take A11 towards Newmarket. After 10 miles take A1304 signposted Newmarket. The hotel is ¾ mile on the left.

" The stay at your property was the highlight of my 18 years as a travel agent! "

Kathleen Gustafson, New England Travel

● Map p.470
ref: E6

Tudor castle

THORNBURY CASTLE

Thornbury,
South Gloucestershire BS35 1HH
Telephone 01454 281182
Fax 01454 416188
E-mail: *thornbury@bestloved.com*

OWNER
Countess von Essen

GENERAL MANAGER
Brian A Jarvis

ROOM RATES
2 Singles	£85 - £110
11 Doubles/Twins	£110 - £280
13 Four-posters	£170 - £280
3 Suites	£195 - £350
1 2-Bedroomed Gatehouse	£350

Includes full breakfast, early morning tea, newspaper and VAT

CHARGE/CREDIT CARDS
 ● *DC* ● *MC* ● *VI*

RATINGS & AWARDS
R.A.C. Gold Ribbon ★★★ *Dining Award 3*
A.A. ★★★ 🌸🌸 *Top 200 - 02/03*
'Super Star Hotel' Reed Travel Group, USA

FACILITIES
On site: *Garden, heli-pad, croquet*
Licensed for weddings
4 meeting rooms/max 100 people
Nearby: *Golf, tennis, shooting, riding, ballooning*

RESTRICTIONS
Limited facilities for disabled guests

ATTRACTIONS
Berkeley Castle, Chepstow Castle, The Cotswolds, Tintern Abbey, Bath, Bristol, Wye Valley

AFFILIATIONS
von Essen hotels - A Private Collection
The Celebrated Hotels Collection
Pride of Britain

NEAREST
MAJOR CITY:
Bristol - 15 miles/20 mins
Bath - 23 miles/45 mins
MAJOR AIRPORT:
Bristol - 21 miles/35 mins
RAILWAY STATION:
Bristol Parkway - 12 miles/15 mins

RESERVATIONS
Toll free in US: 800-322-2403 or 800-98-PRIDE
Quote **Best Loved**

ACCESS CODES
APOLLO/GALILEO HT 41651
SABRE/ABACUS HK 36355
WORLDSPAN HK THORN

MIDSHIRES

'The top hotel in Europe' says Conde Nast Traveler Magazine

The building of Thornbury Castle, started in 1511 by Edward Stafford, 3rd Duke of Buckingham, ended in 1521 when he was beheaded by Henry VIII. Buckingham's vast estates, including Thornbury, were confiscated by the King who stayed here with Anne Boleyn in 1535. Henry's daughter, Mary Tudor, lived here as a princess and when she became Queen she returned the Castle to the descendants of the late Duke.

Today, this Tudor castle-palace stands serenely in 15 acres, with distant views of the Severn Estuary and the hills of South Gloucestershire and Wales. Fine old panelling, tapestries and paintings enrich the interiors. There are 30 carefully restored bedchambers, most overlooking the oldest Tudor garden in England or the vineyard. Many have sumptuous four-poster beds and huge Tudor fireplaces.

The three intimate dining rooms have a gracious ambience to suit the superb cuisine.

Thornbury is an ideal base from which to discover the many historic sites, villages and towns located within an hour's drive of the castle, or cross the Severn Bridge into Wales and explore that beautiful country. Pilots should note the following heli-pad grid reference: OS 172 ST 632 907 N51 36.8 W002 32.5.

LOCATION
Exit 20 M4/16 M5 and A38 north for 5 miles, turn left to Thornbury following brown signs.

Map p.470
ref: D6

" *A really lovely stay once more, thanks to all the staff* "

Mr & Mrs Clayton, Pirton

THREE CHOIRS VINEYARDS

Restaurant with rooms

MIDSHIRES

**Newent,
Gloucestershire GL18 1LS**

**Telephone 01531 890223
Fax 01531 890877**

E-mail: *threechoirs@bestloved.com*

MANAGING DIRECTOR
Thomas Shaw

ROOM RATES
Single occupancy   £65 - £85
8 Doubles/Twins   £85 - £105
Includes full breakfast and VAT

CHARGE/CREDIT CARDS

MC • VI

RATINGS & AWARDS
R.A.C. ◆◆◆◆◆ Dining Award 2
A.A. ❀ Restaurant with rooms
R.A.C. Sparkling Diamond, Warm Welcome
& Little Gem Awards

FACILITIES
On site: Garden
1 meeting room/max 30 people
Nearby: Golf, tennis, fishing, riding

RESTRICTIONS
No smoking throughout
No pets, guide dogs only
Closed 24 - 26 Dec

ATTRACTIONS
The Cotswolds, Cheltenham,
Hereford Cathedral & Mappa Mundi,
Royal Worcester Porcelain,
Malvern & The Elgar Trail,
Hay-on-Wye antique book capital

AFFILIATIONS
Independent

NEAREST
MAJOR CITY:
Gloucester - 9 miles/20 mins

MAJOR AIRPORT:
Birmingham - 67 miles/1 ¼ hrs

RAILWAY STATION:
Cheltenham - 18 miles/30 mins
Ledbury - 8 miles/15 mins

RESERVATIONS
Direct with hotel
Quote **Best Loved**

ACCESS CODES
Not applicable

Everything a wine-lover could want in a hotel

Wine lovers and food aficionados have always enjoyed visiting England's leading producer of single estate wines - so much so they often haven't wanted to go home! With popular demand so high, Three Choirs opened its doors to overnight guests in May 2000. Now, there are eight rooms in total, each with a sunny private terrace and dramatic yet peaceful views across the 100-acre estate's immaculately maintained rows of cultivated vines.

Situated amid the rural splendour of the Cotswolds, Three Choirs is ideal for a weekend break - whether in summer when you can eat outside on the vine-covered restaurant patio, or later in the season when the valley is cloaked in romantic swirls of mist and frost. You don't need to be an oenophile to enjoy the many fruity and flavourful wines available, although the hotel does offer numerous courses and special events for those wishing to expand their expertise. There are several winetasting opportunities throughout the year, with English Wine Week a highlight in early June. Summer barbecues with jazz are complemented by a range of affordably priced one-day courses, including cookery and even

vineyard painting. It is certainly worthwhile telephoning or checking the hotel website for details of events in advance.

LOCATION

15 minutes from Junction 11a on the M5 and 10 minutes from Junction 3 of the M50, on the B4215, 2 miles from Newent.

" Truly a haven of peace and tranquillity - with superb service "

Howard Cragg, Sussex

• Map p.470
  ref: E5

Country mansion THE WELCOMBE HOTEL AND GOLF COURSE

Shakespeare once owned the grounds. Theodore Roosevelt stayed here

This magnificent Jacobean-style mansion is set in 157-acres of beautiful parkland and immaculate gardens. Its intricate gables, tall chimneys and projecting bay windows create a distinctive style, which is mirrored throughout the impressive interior. At the heart of the house is a luxurious oak panelled drawing room leading to the award-winning Trevalyn restaurant. The hotel's 7 meeting rooms can accommodate up to 120 people. Leisure facilities include an excellent 18-hole golf club with two resident PGA professionals, gym, and all-weather floodlit tennis courts, making the Welcombe Hotel an ideal corporate destination.

The 63 luxurious and spacious bedrooms, some with four-posters, are all decorated with traditional country house furnishings. Large windows offer sweeping views over the hotel's magnificent grounds. Stunning antique pieces through the hotel reflect its fascinating past as a private home.

The hotel is ideal for exploring Stratford-upon-Avon, Warwickshire and the Cotswolds. Information is available on site, and the concierge is happy to arrange tickets for local attractions.

LOCATION
1 mile from centre of Stratford-upon-Avon on A439. 5 miles from Exit 15 on the M40.

**Warwick Road,
Stratford-upon-Avon,
Warwickshire CV37 0NR**

**Telephone 01789 295252
Fax 01789 414666**

E-mail: *welcombe@bestloved.com*

GENERAL MANAGER
Craig Hughes

ROOM RATES
1 Single	*£120 - £150*
48 Doubles/Twins	*£155 - £205*
5 Suites	*£275*
8 Gallery/Four-posters	*£315*
1 Lady Caroline Suite	*£750*
Includes full breakfast and VAT	

CHARGE/CREDIT CARDS

 • *DC* • *JCB* • *MC* • *VI*

RATINGS & AWARDS
E.T.C. ★★★★ *Silver Award*

FACILITIES
On site: *Garden, gym,
heli-pad, golf, tennis,
18-hole golf course, fitness room
Licensed for weddings
7 meeting rooms/max 120 people*
Nearby: *Boating, riding, swimming*

RESTRICTIONS
*Limited facilities for disabled guests
No children under 12 in restaurant
after 7 pm*

ATTRACTIONS
*Shakespeare's birthplace, Warwick Castle,
Anne Hathaway's Cottage, Blenheim Palace,
Royal Shakespeare Theatre*

AFFILIATIONS
Grand Heritage Hotels

NEAREST
MAJOR CITY:
Birmingham - 28 miles/35 mins

MAJOR AIRPORT:
Birmingham - 25 miles/30 mins

RAILWAY STATION:
Stratford-upon-Avon - 3 miles/5 mins

RESERVATIONS
Toll free in US: 888-93-GRAND
Quote **Best Loved**

ACCESS CODES
Not applicable

MIDSHIRES

● *Map p.470*
ref: E6

❝ You have a great team who provided us with magnificent service for the evening ❞

Michael White, Carlsberg-Tetley

WESTWOOD COUNTRY HOTEL

Country hotel

MIDSHIRES

Hinksey Hill, Near Boars Hill,
Oxford OX1 5BG

Telephone 01865 735408
Fax 01865 736536

E-mail: *westwood@bestloved.com*

OWNER
Anthony Healy

MANAGER
Ben Hechter

ROOM RATES
2 Singles	*£70*
12 Doubles/Twins	*£95*
2 Four-posters	*£120*
3 Family rooms	*£115*
Includes full breakfast and VAT	

CHARGE/CREDIT CARDS

 • *DC* • *MC* • *VI*

RATINGS & AWARDS
E.T.C. ★★★
A.A. ★★★ 64%

FACILITIES
On site: *Garden, woodlands, car park*
Licensed for weddings
4 meeting rooms/max 70 people
Nearby: *Golf, archery, riding, clay pigeon*
shooting, fishing, swimming

RESTRICTIONS
Pets by arrangement
Closed between Christmas and New Year

ATTRACTIONS
Oxford Botanical Gardens,
Oxford University Colleges,
Stratford, The Cotswolds,
Blenheim Palace,
Waddesden Manor

AFFILIATIONS
Minotel International

NEAREST
MAJOR CITY:
Oxford - 2 ½ miles/10 mins

MAJOR AIRPORT:
London Heathrow - 50 miles/1 hr

RAILWAY STATION:
Oxford - 2 ½ miles/10 mins

RESERVATIONS
Direct with hotel
Quote **Best Loved**

ACCESS CODES
Not applicable

An ancient woodland setting close to Oxford's dreaming spires

Just a couple of miles from the heart of Oxford, there is a 400-acre ancient woodland preserve offering sanctuary to numerous species of birds and wildlife. Here, the Westwood basks in the quiet of the countryside surrounded by its own lovely woodland gardens.

The house was built as an Edwardian private residence and has been thoughtfully extended and refurbished as an hotel. The comfortable bedrooms have been decorated with fabrics and papers by the Zoffany design house. Two have four posters, while others have a private terrace or balcony overlooking the grounds. There is a warm welcome in the Oaks Bar and fine cuisine in the Oaks Restaurant. Corporate clients can make use of four well-equipped conference rooms, or enjoy a challenging round of golf at nearby Frilford Heath Golf Course - Anthony Healy is a member and can wholly recommend it! The hotel is a popular venue for weddings and parties both inside and out in the gardens.

Westwood's gardens are a delight. Opened by renowned naturalist David Bellamy in 1995, they are a work in progress and a small lake is currently being 'resurrected' which will have a romantic summer house where guests can barbecue in summer.

LOCATION

From the A34 Hinksey Hill interchange,
take the exit signed Boars Hill. Road curves
to the left, hotel is on the right.

" Tina and Dino are two of the most welcoming and hospitable hosts in the Cotswolds "

Drew Smith, Editor of Taste magazine, Wiltshire

Elizabethan inn

THE WILD DUCK

An attractive 15th century inn of great character

The Wild Duck is a mellow Cotswold stone Elizabethan Inn. A typical local English inn, warm and welcoming, rich in colours and hung with old oil portraits of English ancestors. Large open log fires burn in the bar and the oak panelled residents' lounge in wintertime.

The garden is secluded, delightful and perfect for al fresco dining in the summer. The bar offers six real ales and the wine list is extensive and innovative.

The country-style dining room offers fresh seasonal food; game in winter and fresh fish delivered overnight from Brixham in Devon, which can include such exotic fare as parrot fish and tilapia.

There are eleven bedrooms, two of which have four-poster beds and overlook the garden. All rooms have direct-dial telephone, colour TV and tea/coffee-making facilities.

Within a mile, The Wild Duck is surrounded by the Cotswold Water Park, with 80 lakes providing fishing, swimming, sailing, water and jet-skiing. Polo at Cirencester Park is a regular event. Every March, Cheltenham holds the Gold Cup Race Meeting. Horse trials at Gatcombe Park and Badminton are held annually.

LOCATION

From M4 take Exit 17 and follow Cirencester signs. Before Cirencester, turn right at Kemble and follow signs to Ewen.

Drakes Island, Ewen, Cirencester, Gloucestershire GL7 6BY

Telephone 01285 770310 Fax 01285 770924

E-mail: wilduck@bestloved.com

OWNER
Tina Mussell

ROOM RATES
Single occupancy	£60
8 Doubles	£80
2 Four-posters	£100
1 Directors double	£100

Includes continental breakfast and VAT

CHARGE/CREDIT CARDS

 • MC • VI

RATINGS & AWARDS
R.A.C. ★★ Dining Award 2
A.A. ★★ ❀ 66%

FACILITIES
Nearby: Sailing, jet skiing, golf, riding, fishing

RESTRICTIONS
Limited facilities for disabled guests
Pets by arrangement

ATTRACTIONS
Slimbridge Wild Fowl Sanctuary, Badminton and Gatcombe Horse Trials, Bath, The Cotswolds, Stratford-upon-Avon, Cirencester Park Polo Club

AFFILIATIONS
Independent

NEAREST
MAJOR CITY:
Bath - 25 miles/35 mins

MAJOR AIRPORT:
London Heathrow - 70 miles/1 ¾ hrs
Bristol - 40 miles/45 mins

RAILWAY STATION:
Kemble - 3 miles/3 mins

RESERVATIONS
Direct with hotel
Quote **Best Loved**

ACCESS CODES
Not applicable

MIDSHIRES

WEST

Wide, surf swept beaches, hidden coves and purposeful stone built harbours, backed by a patchwork of moor and farmland, a place rich in history, folklore and literature – this is the West

Glastonbury Tor, in Somerset is said to be home to The King of the Fairies - Gwynn ap Nudd . It is at the centre of a veritable power grid of ley lines and did Joseph of Arimathea bring the cup from The Last Supper here? Is this where the Holy Grail lies buried ?

Tennyson searched for the romantic world of Camelot in the West Country. He came to Tintagel, scaling its rocky path to where perhaps, King Arthur was born; and ventured into Merlin's cave that echoes with the past. If Tennyson's Arthur lived, then on his death he was taken to the Isle of Avalon – that Land of Apples that is Glastonbury today. There he lies buried beside Guinivere, his queen and waits to live again.

Exmoor is Lorna Doone country – written by RD Blackmore and published in 1869, the tale of murder and revenge in an epic setting is interwoven with a desperate love. Based on fact, but reality's end and fiction's beginning is hard to find. Its great success sparked a revival in Romanticism.

Samuel Taylor Coleridge was born, 1772, son of a vicar, in the peaceful market town of Ottery St Mary. As a child he wandered the quiet beech woods overlooking the town, listening to the church bells and later writing about them. His early friendship with Wordsworth resulted in the Lyrical Ballads. They began with Coleridge's Rime of the Ancient Mariner and ended with Wordsworth's Tintern Abbey - one of the most fruitful literary associations of all time.

On a sunny day the clouds sail high over Dartmoor, dappled crags and giant boulders lie littered on sheep cropped hills and there are glorious far-reaching views of a sparkling sea. But when the mist seeps up from the valley floor and the sky darkens the inspiration for Sir Arthur Conan Doyle's famous fiction, The Hound of the Baskervilles, is palpable.

Thomas Hardy came to Boscastle in pursuit of his work as an architect - he was to restore the ruined St Juiliot Church. Whilst he did so it was here that he fell in love with Emma, sister of the rector's wife. He immortalised their meeting with the winding, wooded valleys threading through the hills in his novel 'A Pair of Blue Eyes'.

Treasure – and the pursuit of it, fascinated the Victorians, Robert Louis Stevenson's Treasure Island captured their imagination. Long John Silver haunted dreams, the sound of his wooden leg ringing on the Bristol cobbles. The prospect of hopeless doom engulfing the young hero so skilfully taking the reader to the edge of horror, and then retreating – the book was a worldwide success.

PLACES TO VISIT

The Georgian splendour of Bath provided a perfect world for Jane Austin to populate with fictional heroes and villains. The Assembly Rooms, where she and her contempories enjoyed the social whirl, are her world – drink the waters at The Pump Room and you can taste it. In the city the stone paved streets still echo intimately, evening lights frame elegant windows. The author lived here from 1801 to 1806.

Daphne du Maurier spent her honeymoon on a yacht on the River Helford. The heroine of Du Maurier's book, Frenchman's Creek meets her lover, a French sea captain, on his boat moored in a hidden tributary of the river. It is still a secluded spot, herons stand silently above their reflections, the waters move quietly, deceptively rapidly with the tide and rich, thick woodland clothes the riverbank.

True writer's retreat, Clouds Hill is the isolated cottage TE Lawrence bought to get away from life in the RAF. Today it belongs to the National Trust and is maintained much as it was when the writer stayed there revising The Seven Pillars of Wisdom. Lawrence died in a motorbike accident a few days after he left the Air Force; the cottage feels as if it's waiting for him to come home.

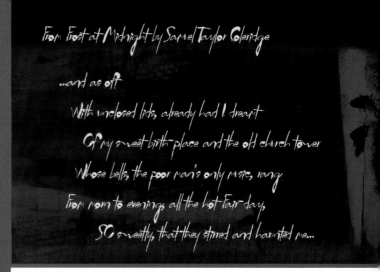

From Frost at Midnight by Samuel Taylor Coleridge

...and as oft

With unclosed lids, already had I dreamt

Of my sweet birth-place and the old church tower

Whose bells, the poor man's only music, rang

From morn to evening, all the hot Fair-day,

So sweetly, that they stirred and haunted me...

BOOKS TO READ

▸ The Life of Samuel Taylor Coleridge by Professor R Ashton: a multitude of excellent reviews testify to this valuable insight into a complex man.

▸ Lorna Doone by RD Blackmore: the essential companion to a stay near Exmoor.

▸ The Body in the Library by Agatha Christie: The Majestic Hotel in the plot was based on the Imperial Hotel in Torquay the town where the author was born and brought up.

A special place to buy books

The knowledgeable owners of Ex Libris Bookseller at 1, The Shambles, Bradford on Avon, in Wiltshire are well versed in local literature. As well as a substantial stock of current titles there's a hoard of older treasures in the Old Book Barn at the back of the shop.

LITERARY ATTRACTIONS & FESTIVALS

▸ Ways with Words, the Dartington Literature Festival: writers, politicians, historians and more, in a superb setting (www.wayswithwords.co.uk).

▸ Jane Austen Festival: a chance to become immersed in Miss Austin's Regency world, readings, performances and dressing up. (www.janeaustenfestival.com).

▸ Daphne du Maurier Festival of Arts and Literature, Fowey, Cornwall. Attended by novelists, biographers, actors and poets of national and international fame, more information on Tel: 01726 223300.

Percy's Restaurant

THE CULINARY West Country

Famous Elizabethan Sir Francis Drake was born in Devon, circumnavigated the world and delighted a queen. Archibald Leach, born in Bristol in 1904, changed his name to Cary Grant, became a Hollywood heartthrob and was loved by millions. Today's legends, in this land of heroes, are creating fabulous flavours from the natural bounty of gorse dotted moorlands, verdant fields and fruitful waters. Rick Stein brought the harbour town of Padstow and its stunningly fresh, locally caught, fish to world prominence. The 'Wild Beef' produced by Lizzy and Richard Vines from their Dartmoor farm is so full of flavour that chefs proclaim its origins on their menus. The Roskilly family farm on the Lizard makes prize-winning ice cream, clotted cream and fabulous fudge with the milk of their Jersey cows that graze lovingly tended acres combining agriculture with conservation. Mr and Mrs Gray immortalised their surname by spelling it backwards to name the delicious nettle wrapped Cornish Yarg cheese that comes from Lyner Dairies, and now graces fine cheese boards all over Britain.

THE RECIPE:

Seared Scallops on broccoli puree with orange pomme fondant and smoked dressing

From Patrick Robert at the superbly restored eighteenth century Binden Country House Hotel.

Bindon Country House

INGREDIENTS - Serves 4.

16 large scallops
4 large potatoes
1 orange
Olive oil
Juice 1 lemon
1 bay leaf
1 clove garlic
300g butter
2 large heads broccoli

For the dressing:-

2 chopped shallots
1 large tomato
4 chives
50ml raspberry vinegar
150ml smoke oil
10 black olives

METHOD

Cook the broccoli in salted, boiling water until soft. Drain and place in a food processor with 80g of the butter and some black pepper. Blend to a very thin puree and keep warm. Heat 200g butter, add orange zest, thyme, garlic and bay leaf. Using 5cm cutter cut the potatoes, place in the pan and cook until soft. Season the scallops and cook them briefly in a very hot pan in a little olive oil turning when well caramelised. Stir in remaining 20g butter, add the lemon juice.

To serve:

Put 4 spoonfuls broccoli puree on each serving plate and place a scallop on the top of each one. Place a potato in the middle and the dressing on the top of it and between the scallops.

THE SIGNATURE: The River Dart flows through Prince Hall's land - and in season provides delicious wild salmon for the restaurant. There are fresh herbs from the garden, all the cheeses are produced in Devon, and the clotted cream is decadently divine. The kitchen, overseen by owner/proprietor Adam Southwell, uses only the very best fresh local produce - and this is an area where 'local' encompasses a cornucopia of delights. Signature dishes include roasted loin and chop of Chagford lamb with minted apricots and a pear and rosemary jus; Dartmoor venison with a Port and Wildberry Compote.

THE BOOK: Not all chefs are prepared to share the innovative recipes that brought them to fame but Proprietor/Head Chef Peter Gorton has a passion for teaching people to cook and he indulges it in his beautiful Horn of Plenty Cookery Book. It's a testament to the superb food served in his hotel and to the highly sought after cookery courses he runs there. A Masterchef of Great Britain, with his own TV series and writer of numerous articles, Peter's ability to pass on his culinary expertise is only one of his many talents.

The Horn of Plenty

THE SPORT: The Arundel Arms, with 20 miles of fishing on the River Tamar and its tributaries, has a faithful following of generations of fishermen and women for its unique sporting facilities - and its gourmet food. A highly renowned fly fishing school offers instruction for all levels of ability, the rod and fishing tackle room is in a 250 year old cockpit - one of the few remaining in England and the menu abounds with succulent local fare. This is West Country food with an international reputation - even the least sport minded guest gets hooked!

Tina Bricknell-Webb

THE PRODUCE: An idyllic, organically managed 150 acre estate surrounds Percy's hotel and provides much of the produce for the contemporary country cuisine cooked so impeccably by Tina Bricknell-Webb. Jacob sheep crop verdant pasture rich with wild flowers and heady with the sound of bees; one and a half acres of glorious kitchen garden provide vegetables that burst with flavour, aromatic herbs and crisp salads; 60 acres of woodland has been planted to provide 'Food from the Forest'. Guests can walk the fields to stimulate their appetite - an unforgettable feast of flavours is their reward.

THE STYLE: The beautifully restored Sugar House, close to the World Heritage docks at Bristol, is now home to an Hotel du Vin & Bistro - great news for lovers of stylish food with a penchant for fine wine. Imaginative design abounds on the plate and in the setting. Dine in a room that could have been painted by Klimpt, or visit the walk in Havana Cigar Humidor. And the food? Perfectly cooked, intriguing menus show a love of good food and stylish creativity, such as Boudin Blanc with Caramelised Lambs Tongues. Modern inspiration with the classic touch and immaculate service.

THE CHEF: Jason Hornbuckle, Head Chef at Lewtrenchard Manor is a man with a mission - to encourage locals and visitors to appreciate the delights of superb lunches in unrivalled surroundings - at remarkably tempting prices. Joining the hotel in 2000, after developing his skills at a succession of Michelin starred and AA Rosetted establishments such as the Four Season Hotel in Park Lane, Tyddyn Llan Country House Hotel in Mid Wales and the Stoke Park Club in Berkshire, Jason has been involved in numerous awards - he won Inspirational Young Chef of the Year, helped Stoke Park enter 'Leading Hotels of the Year', and was at Bistro Bruno in Soho when it won Restaurant of the Year award.

Lewtrenchard Manor

Editor's Extras

Cheese made within the sound of the rolling breakers at sandy Widemouth Bay in Cornwall has to be special - Trelawny - a Modern British Hard Cheese from Whalesborough Dairies was a winner at The British Cheese Awards, and is well worth looking our for.

Cullumpton Farmers' Market is one of the 'best in the West'. Look for local meats, cheese, honey - and

sometimes snails! Held on the second Saturday in every month in this friendly market town.

The fish market at picturesque *Looe harbour* (home to Cornwall's largest fishing fleet after Newquay) provides the perfect 'raw material' for the region's great chefs. It starts at 6.30 in the morning - you have to get up early to see the full catch of the day.

Heather Hay Ffrench
Best Loved Food Editor

" *A really excellent hotel. The meals and service equal the Waldorf Astoria, New York* "

Frank & Margaret Blatchford, Victoria, Australia

● *Map p.472*
ref: B5

Cornish country manor

ALVERTON MANOR

Tregolls Road, Truro, Cornwall TR1 1ZQ

Telephone 01872 276633
Fax 01872 222989

E-mail: *alverton@bestloved.com*

OWNER
Michael Sagin

ROOM RATES

6 Singles	£75
16 Doubles/Twins	£115
8 Deluxe Doubles/Twins	£130
4 Suites	£165

Includes full breakfast and VAT

CHARGE/CREDIT CARDS

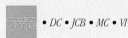 ● DC ● JCB ● MC ● VI

RATINGS & AWARDS
E.T.C. ★★★ *Silver Award*
R.A.C. ★★★ *Dining Award 1*
A.A. ★★★ ❀ 68%

The charm and character of another age

Alverton Manor is a truly impressive sight. Built during the early 19th century, the manor was for many years occupied by the Sisters of the Epiphany. Located on a hillside, the hotel boasts fine period sandstone walls, attractive mullioned windows and an original Cornish Delabole slate roof. The building is Grade II listed, and considered of special historical interest.

Outstandingly comfortable in a discreetly elegant way, it has been lovingly restored and is well appointed, retaining the character and charm of another age. All 34 bedrooms are furnished with all the amenities one expects from a modern luxury hotel. The hotel is renowned in the West Country for its contemporary English and French cuisine and the restaurant has an A.A. rosette. For the golf enthusiast, the hotel offers concessions on its own golf course within the historic Killiow estate situated in over 400 acres of rolling parkland, only five minutes away by car.

Truro has some of the best-preserved Georgian houses in Britain and its own three-spired cathedral. The many reminders from Cornwall's stirring history include Henry VIII's castles at Pendennis and St Mawes.

FACILITIES
On site: *Garden, fishing*
Licensed for weddings
5 meeting rooms/max 200 people
Nearby: *Fishing, sailing, riding, 18-hole golf course*

RESTRICTIONS
Limited facilities for disabled guests
Pets by arrangement

ATTRACTIONS
Truro and Truro Cathedral, Isles of Scilly, Pendennis Castle, St Mawes Castle, Gardens of Cornwall, The Eden Project, Tresco Gardens, Trevano Gardens

AFFILIATIONS
Independent

NEAREST
MAJOR CITY:
Truro - ½ mile/3 mins
Newquay - 12 miles/20 mins

MAJOR AIRPORT:
Exeter - 90 miles/1½ hrs

RAILWAY STATION:
Truro - 1 mile/5 mins

RESERVATIONS
Direct with hotel
Quote **Best Loved**

ACCESS CODES
Not applicable

LOCATION

Situated on the A390 approach road to Truro from St Austell, the hotel is located on your right hand side as you approach the first major roundabout on entering Truro.

WEST COUNTRY

❝ Our meal last night was absolutely superb; I think the best I have ever tasted. Pure genius ❞

George Edwards

THE ARUNDELL ARMS

Country hotel

**Lifton,
Devon PL16 0AA**

**Telephone 01566 784666
Fax 01566 784494**

E-mail: *arundell@bestloved.com*

OWNER
Anne Voss-Bark

ROOM RATES
5 Singles	£79 - £85
17 Doubles/Twins	£120 - £130

Includes full breakfast and VAT

CHARGE/CREDIT CARDS

• DC • MC • VI

RATINGS & AWARDS
E.T.C. ★★★
R.A.C. ★★★ Dining Award 3
A.A. ★★★ ❀❀❀ 74%

FACILITIES
On site: *Garden, fishing, fly-fishing school*
2 meeting rooms/max 100 people
Nearby: *Shooting, golf, walking*

RESTRICTIONS
*Limited facilities for disabled guests
Pets by arrangement
Closed Christmas*

ATTRACTIONS
*Eden Project, Dartmoor National Park,
Buckland Abbey, RHS Rosemoor Gardens,
National Trust Houses and Gardens,
Devonshire coastline*

AFFILIATIONS
Grand Heritage Hotels

NEAREST
*MAJOR CITY:
Plymouth - 30 miles/45 mins*

*MAJOR AIRPORT:
Plymouth - 30 miles/40 mins
London Heathrow - 225 miles/4 hrs*

*RAILWAY STATION:
Exeter - 40 miles/50 mins*

RESERVATIONS
*Toll free in US: 888-93-GRAND
or 800-323-5463*
*Quote **Best Loved***

ACCESS CODES
*AMADEUS UI EXTAAH
APOLLO/GALILEO UI 36794
SABRE/ABACUS UI 58942
WORLDSPAN UI 42412*

WEST COUNTRY

English country pursuits and a little taste of heaven in Devon

The Arundell Arms has long been recognised as one of Britain's top sporting hotels. An old coaching inn, it nestles in a peaceful valley fed by the River Tamar and its tributaries. Devotees of English country sports come here to fish, shoot, ride, play golf and birdwatch, others come to walk or simply relax and enjoy some of the loveliest unspoilt countryside in the southwest.

The hotel has been owned by Anne Voss-Bark since 1961. A highly respected former Woman Hotelier of the Year, she has created just the kind of comfortably elegant surroundings and convivial atmosphere that instantly puts guests at their ease. There is peace and quiet in the sitting room, a buzz of chat in the bar, delightful bedrooms and an award-winning restaurant where Philip Burgess and Nick Shopland, both Master Chefs of Great Britain, share credit for the modern British cuisine.

This is a quiet paradise for experienced and novice fishermen. The hotel owns 20 miles of water frequented by wild brown trout, salmon and sea trout. Advice, lessons and tackle are here for the asking. If fishing is not your bag, there are famous houses, rugged moors and mysterious menhirs to be explored.

LOCATION
*Take Junction 31 from the M5 onto the A30,
signposted Bodmin/Okehampton. After approx
40 miles, take junction signposted Liftondown.
At T-junction, turn right. The hotel is ¾ mile
along on the left.*

“ Some places on earth can't be beaten, you've created one of those places ”

John & Ann Wright, Cambridge

Georgian estate lodge

BATH LODGE HOTEL

Norton St Philip, Bath, Somerset BA2 7NH

Telephone 01225 723040 Fax 01225 723737

E-mail: *bathlodge@bestloved.com*

OWNERS
Richard and Susan Warren

ROOM RATES
1 Single	£45 - £85
3 Doubles/Twins	£75 - £115
3 Four Posters	£95 - £115

Includes full breakfast and VAT

CHARGE/CREDIT CARDS
 • MC • VI

RATINGS & AWARDS
A.A. ◆◆◆◆◆ *Premier Collection*

FACILITIES
On site: *Garden*
Nearby: *Golf, riding, shooting, clay pigeon shooting, fishing*

RESTRICTIONS
No facilities for disabled guests
No children under 10 years
No smoking throughout
No pets

ATTRACTIONS
Bath Spa, Roman Baths, American Museum, Stonehenge, Longleat, Stourhead, Wells, Glastonbury

AFFILIATIONS
Independent

NEAREST
MAJOR CITY:
Bath - 7 miles/15 mins

MAJOR AIRPORT:
London Heathrow - 100 miles/2 hrs
Bristol - 29 miles/45 mins

RAILWAY STATION:
Bath - 7 miles/15 mins

RESERVATIONS
Direct with hotel
Quote **Best Loved**

ACCESS CODES
Not applicable

WEST COUNTRY

Castle comforts amidst the romance of an ancient deer forest

Originally called Castle Lodge, the Bath Lodge Hotel has all the appearance of a pocket-sized medieval castle from its impressive stone structure, portcullis and heraldic shields right up to the battlements and towers above. In fact, the Lodge was built between 1806 and 1813 as the principal of six gate lodges to the Farleigh estate.

The building boasts the original oak beams, natural masonry, a log-burning fireplace and mullioned windows. All the rooms are beautifully decorated and furnished to a high standard with elegant antique furniture happily co-existing with contemporary comforts and facilities. The original lodge rooms benefit from four-poster or brass bedsteads, showers in the turrets and balconies overlooking the grounds.

There's a stream that cascades through the natural garden that clandestinely merges into the ancient deer forest where kings and barons once hunted. All very romantic.

Situated only seven miles outside Bath, the hotel is also ideally located for visiting the heritage sites of Stonehenge, Longleat, Stourhead and Wells with its magnificent cathedral as well as many other attractions of the area. That's why Bath Lodge likes to set its guests up for the day

with an excellent breakfast which has no doubt contributed to the hotel's five diamond A.A. rating. In the evening, the romantic and relaxed atmosphere provides the perfect end to the day.

LOCATION
From Bath take A36 Warminster Road. The hotel is approximately 7 miles along this road on left.

" I rate The Priory the best hotel in town "

David Wickers, The Sunday Times

THE BATH PRIORY HOTEL & RESTAURANT   *Victorian houses*

**Weston Road, Bath,
Somerset BA1 2XT**
Telephone 01225 331922
Fax 01225 448276

E-mail: *priorybath@bestloved.com*

OWNER
Andrew Brownsword

ROOM RATES
1 Single	£145
8 Doubles/Twins	£230 - £260
15 Deluxe doubles	£290
2 Four-posters	£320
2 Junior suites	£320

Includes breakfast, service and VAT

CHARGE/CREDIT CARDS

 • *DC • MC • VI*

RATINGS & AWARDS
R.A.C. Gold Ribbon ★★★★ Dining Award 4
A.A. ★★★★ ❀❀❀
A.A. Top 200 - 02/03

FACILITIES
On site: *Garden, gym, croquet,
indoor pool, health & beauty, outdoor pool,
fitness centre, beauty treatment rooms
3 meeting rooms/max 64 people*
Nearby: *Golf, ballooning, boating, riding*

RESTRICTIONS
*No children under 8 years in the restaurant
No pets, guide dogs only*

ATTRACTIONS
*Roman Baths, Royal Crescent,
Pump Rooms, Bath Abbey,
Costume Museum, Royal Victoria Park,
Lacock, Castle Combe, Longleat*

AFFILIATIONS
*The Celebrated Hotels Collection
Small Luxury Hotels*

NEAREST
MAJOR CITY:
Bath - 1 mile/5 mins

MAJOR AIRPORT:
London Heathrow - 90 miles/1 ½ hrs
Bristol - 15 miles/25 mins

RAILWAY STATION:
Bath Spa - 1 mile/5 mins

RESERVATIONS
Toll free in US: 800-322-2403
Toll free in US: 800-525-4800
*Quote **Best Loved***

ACCESS CODES
AMADEUS LX BRSTPM
APOLLO/GALILEO LX 87851
SABRE/ABACUS LX 41891
WORLDSPAN LX BRSTPM

Utter Sumptuousness in the Roman City of Bath

Set in four acres of award-winning landscaped gardens on the edge of the city, The Bath Priory Hotel was built in 1835 as a private residence and remains one of the finest examples of Gothic architecture of its time. Now beautifully converted, it offers visitors comfort, peace and privacy as well as luxurious health spa facilities.

In the restaurant that overlooks the stunning gardens, guests can enjoy modern French and Mediterranean cuisine from Michelin-starred Chef, Robert Clayton, under the direction of Restaurant Manager Vito Scaduto.

International Designer, Penny Morrison, has created The Priory's 28 sumptuous bedrooms all of which are equipped with ISDN line, voice mail, US/UK modem points, remote control TV with satellite channels, marble bathrooms, fine antique furniture, traditional British fabrics and objets d'art.

Guests are free to use the health club which features a fully equipped gymnasium, heated indoor and outdoor swimming pools, spa, steamroom and solarium.

Theatres, museums, antique shops, and the Roman Baths are within a pleasant walk.

LOCATION
**From London: exit 18 off M4, A46 to Bath.
Follow signs to Bristol (A4) until Victoria Park.
Turn right at Park Lane and left at Weston Road.
The Priory is 300 yards on left.**

" Your home is the epitome of warmth and elegance "

Bungey Travel Inc, California, USA

Gothic mansion   BINDON COUNTRY HOUSE HOTEL

An inspired blend of French and English cuisine and seven acres of tranquillity

'Je trouve bien', 'I find well' - the motto carved on Bindon House could not be more appropriate. The house with its wonderfully Baroque façade all curves and curlicues looks fun and reflects the atmosphere created by owners Mark and Lynn Jaffa. This delightful country house hotel with twelve sumptuous bedrooms has gone from strength to strength over the last six years, and now holds a well-deserved place among Britain's top hotels.

The Jaffas hold frequent themed weekends and offer a really professional and thoughtful service for weddings, private parties or conferences. Indeed thoughtful is the name of the game at Bindon House where service is impeccable and cheerful, whether providing tea in front of the lounge fire, organising a conference or serving meals in the gourmet restaurant. Chef Patrick Robert, whose reputation has grown with the hotel's provides a wide range of top-quality cuisine for every occasion.

The Orangery is now one of two fully equipped conference rooms and with a swimming pool, tennis courts and a croquet lawn within the grounds and Exmoor, Exeter, Wells and the coast in easy reach, there is plenty to do.

LOCATION

Exit 26 /M5; A38 & then B3187 to Wellington. Turn right at second traffic lights. Drive for approx 2 miles, then turn left at sharp S bend to Langford Budville and, after village, right to Wiveliscombe and right again. Hotel is 1 mile on right.

Langford Budville,
Wellington,
Somerset TA21 0RU

Telephone 01823 400070
Fax 01823 400071

E-mail: *bindon@bestloved.com*

OWNERS
Mark and Lynn Jaffa

ROOM RATES
Single occupancy   £95
9 Doubles/Twins   £105 - £205
2 Suites   £135 - £155
1 Four-poster   £205
Includes full breakfast, newspaper and VAT

CHARGE/CREDIT CARDS

 • DC • MC • VI

RATINGS & AWARDS
R.A.C. *Blue Ribbon* ★★★ *Dining Award 3*
A.A. ★★★ ❀❀
A.A. Top 200 - 02/03

FACILITIES
On site: *Garden, heli-pad, heated pool,*
croquet, tennis, health & beauty
Licensed for weddings
3 meeting rooms/max 80 people
Nearby: *Golf, riding, shooting, fishing*

RESTRICTIONS
Limited facilities for disabled guests
Pets by arrangement

ATTRACTIONS
Exeter & Wells Cathedrals,
Hestercombe & National Trust Gardens,
Exmoor & Dartmoor,
Dunster Castle, Bath, Glastonbury

AFFILIATIONS
Preston's Global Hotels
Pride of Britain

NEAREST
MAJOR CITY:
Taunton - 8 miles/15 mins

MAJOR AIRPORT:
Bristol - 50 miles/45 mins
Exeter - 25 miles/25 mins

RAILWAY STATION:
Taunton - 8 miles/15 mins

RESERVATIONS
Toll free in US: 800-544-9993
or 800-98-PRIDE
*Quote **Best Loved***

ACCESS CODES
Not applicable

WEST COUNTRY

> *❝ I must say that speaking as someone who has travelled extensively throughout the world, your hotel is certainly amongst the best ❞*
>
> *Ian Churchill*

THE BRIGSTOW HOTEL

Contemporary hotel

**Welsh Back,
Bristol BS1 4SP**

**Telephone 0117 929 1030
Fax 0117 929 2030**

E-mail: *brigstow@bestloved.com*

GENERAL MANAGER
Peter Lister

ROOM RATES
Single occupancy	£85 - £166
52 Doubles/Twins	£85 - £176
63 Superior Doubles/Twins	£95 - £176
1 Suite	£175 - £270

Includes full breakfast and VAT

CHARGE/CREDIT CARDS

 • *DC* • *MC* • *VI*

RATINGS & AWARDS
A.A. ★★★★ 66%

FACILITIES
On site: *4 meeting rooms/max 120 people*
Nearby: *Gym, squash, watersports*

RESTRICTIONS
No pets, guide dogs only

ATTRACTIONS
*City of Bath, @Bristol, Bristol Historic Docks,
S.S. Great Britain, Bristol Zoo Gardens,
Clifton Suspension Bridge*

AFFILIATIONS
Fullers Hotels

NEAREST
MAJOR CITY:
Bristol

MAJOR AIRPORT:
Bristol - 12 miles/30 mins
London Heathrow - 110 miles/2 hrs

RAILWAY STATION:
Bristol Temple Meads - ½ mile/5 mins

RESERVATIONS
Direct with hotel
*Quote **Best Loved***

ACCESS CODES
Not applicable

WEST COUNTRY

A contemporary and elegant hotel to rival Bristol's maritime history

Surrounded by many outstanding historic and natural landmarks, from the Cheddar Gorge to Wells Cathedral, Bristol has always combined the ancient and the modern with aplomb. Isambard Kingdom Brunel's famous feat of engineering, the Clifton Suspension Bridge, still majestically announces a city that was once the second most important port in Europe and is now known equally for its thriving nightlife and multicultural heritage. Situated directly on the waterfront, and close to the Bristol Millennium development, with its electronic zoo, planetarium and i-max cinema, The Brigstow is a brand new hotel, characterised by sure, clean design - both inside and out.

Business travellers will find it an ideal stop-off: each room has a laptop connection point and dedicated desk area; the secretarial service includes 24-hour business centre. However, state-of-the-art technology is not just for the working guest - weekenders wanting to chill out back at the hotel will also delight in the luxury that includes a walk-in shower and plasma TV screen in every bathroom. Top tip for the guest who wants it all: rooms with '05' numbers are those with a balcony and river views.

LOCATION

*In the centre of Bristol by the historic docks.
Advisable to call first for driving directions.*

Best Loved Hotels of the World

❝ *At last, affordable chic in the West* ❞

Mr & Mrs Woodward, Oxfordshire

● *Map p.472*
ref: D4

Town house

BROWNS HOTEL

Where chic youth meets tradition all in a 4-star Town House

The historic West Country town of Tavistock was the birthplace of one of England's most intrepid explorers, Sir Francis Drake, while back in Victorian times it was renowned as the world's major copper-producing area. Now it is a bustling market town and home to Browns Hotel, a converted 17th century coaching inn, situated right in the town centre and close to the Dartmoor National Park. Inside you will find an interesting blend of trendy and traditional. The brand new gym is pure 21st century and highly acclaimed. The hotel has its own well that is believed to date back as far as Roman times. Positioned under a glass panel in the conservatory, still and sparkling water is drawn from it, bottled on the premises and is provided free to guests in their rooms. The brasserie menu includes regional produce, organic and GM-free foods as available and is a highly regarded local destination for the ubiquitous English Sunday roast.

Tourist attractions in the vicinity include the hugely popular Eden Project, the National Marine Aquarium and various National Trust Properties. Just 20 minutes from Plymouth Airport, and 16 miles from the city itself, the hotel is the ideal base from which to explore the beaches, coves and dramatic landscapes of Cornwall and Devon.

LOCATION
From the town square follow the road up the hill and the hotel is on the right.

---

80 West Street, Tavistock,
Devon PL19 8AQ

Telephone 01822 618686
Fax 01822 618646

E-mail: *brownswb@bestloved.com*

OWNER
Peter Brown

GENERAL MANAGER
Martin Ball

ROOM RATES

6 Singles	£65
12 Doubles/Twins	£90 - £140
1 Four-poster	£150
1 Family room	£140

Includes full breakfast and VAT

CHARGE/CREDIT CARDS

 ● *MC* ● *VI*

RATINGS & AWARDS
E.T.C. ★★★ *Silver Award*
R.A.C. ★★★★ *Town House Dining Award 2*
A.A. ★★★★ ❀❀ *Town House*

FACILITIES
On site: *Gym, courtyard*
Nearby: *Golf, riding, fishing,*
swimming pool, bowls

RESTRICTIONS
Limited facilities for disabled guests
No pets, guide dogs only

ATTRACTIONS
Eden Project,
Dartmoor National Park,
Rosemoor RHS Garden,
National Marine Aquarium,
Padstow, St Mawes

AFFILIATIONS
Independent

NEAREST
MAJOR CITY:
Plymouth - 16 miles/25 mins

MAJOR AIRPORT:
Plymouth - 12 miles/20 mins
Exeter - 47 miles/ 1 hr

RAILWAY STATION:
Plymouth - 16 miles/25 mins

RESERVATIONS
Direct with hotel
Quote **Best Loved**

ACCESS CODES
Not applicable

WEST COUNTRY

Best Loved Hotels of the World

" *Truly spectacular with superb cuisine* "

Lord and Lady Beaumont, Nesbitt, UK

BUCKLAND-TOUT-SAINTS

300-year old mansion

Goveton, Kingsbridge, Devon TQ7 2DS

Telephone 01548 853055
Fax 01548 856261

E-mail: *buckland@bestloved.com*

OWNERS
Mark and Julia Trumble

MANAGER
Julie Hudson

ROOM RATES
Single occupancy	£65 - £120
1 Single	£75 - £95
5 Doubles/Twins	£150 - £240
4 Superior doubles	£170 - £240
2 Suites	£200 - £260

Includes full breakfast and VAT

CHARGE/CREDIT CARDS
MC • JCB • VI

RATINGS & AWARDS
A.A. ★★★ ❀❀
A.A. Top 200 - 02/03

FACILITIES
On site: *Garden, heli-pad, croquet
Licensed for weddings
2 meeting rooms/max 200 people*
Nearby: *Golf, health centre, tennis, sea
fishing, yachting, riding*

RESTRICTIONS
*No facilities for disabled guests
Smoking in bar only
Pets by arrangement, £3.50 surcharge
Closed 6 - 27 Jan*

ATTRACTIONS
*Dartmouth, Salcombe Estuary
Berry Pomeroy Castle, Dartmoor
Dartington Hall Gardens, Plymouth
Mayflower sailing, Eden Project*

AFFILIATIONS
The Celebrated Hotels Collection

NEAREST
MAJOR CITY:
Plymouth - 20 miles/45 mins

MAJOR AIRPORT:
*Exeter - 40 miles/45 mins
London Heathrow - 220 miles/3 ½ hrs*

RAILWAY STATION:
Totnes - 12 miles/25 mins

RESERVATIONS
*Toll free in US: 800-435-8281
or 800-322-2403*
Quote **Best Loved**

ACCESS CODES
Not applicable

www.buckland.bestloved.com

Heavenly hotel and restaurant - one of the West Country's finest

Once upon a time you might have been lucky enough to own a dolls' house modelled on the elegant William and Mary symmetry of Buckland-Tout-Saints. Steeply pitched slate roof pierced by dormers and matching chimneys, neat rows of freshly painted sash windows arranged in a mellow stone façade, yet this gorgeous Grade II listed building is for real and it welcomes visitors.

The house was built in 1690, and set in an idyllic fold of green and wooded hills. Mark and Julia Trumble bought the property in 1998, and set about a 'simple spring clean' which extended over nine months and cost something in the region of £1 million (Mark still doesn't like to think about it). The result is a triumph of luxury tempered by good taste, fine antiques, romantic bedrooms and a brace of splendid original fireplaces discovered during renovations, one of which measures some 16ft across.

Buckland's restaurant serves the best of English and French cuisine devised by head chef Jean-Philippe Bidart. There are set lunch and dinner menus as well as a la carte options and a superb wine list with an impressive selection of half-bottles and house wines by the glass.

LOCATION

**Take the A381 to Kingsbridge. The hotel
is situated 2 miles north of Kingsbridge.
After Halwell and The Mounts,
turn left at the hotel sign.**

❝ Perfection is a very hard commodity to find, and should be cherished. Thank you at Budock for coming so close ❞

The St John Family, Stratford-upon-Avon

Resort hotel BUDOCK VEAN - THE HOTEL ON THE RIVER

Indulgent living and superb sports facilities in a beautiful location

Budock Vean is an elegant, unspoilt retreat on the banks of the Helford River, a designated area of Outstanding Natural Beauty. Beside Britain's most dramatic coastline, it is ideal for a range of country pursuits, including fishing, shooting, golf, tennis, walking, riding and sailing. The climate is so mild that the golf course plays well for the whole year. A spectacular indoor heated pool opens out on to the terrace in summer or, in winter, has its own log fire.

There is a feeling of privacy and exclusivity within the 65 acres of gardens and parkland. Many bedrooms have private sitting rooms with open views across the hotel's golf course and gardens towards the river. Old world cottages in the grounds can be rented. Seafood is a speciality of the award-winning restaurant, with local Helford oysters and mussels. Less formal meals are served in the Country Club Room whose large picture windows overlook the estate.

Cornwall has a unique identity rich in ancient heritage, rites and customs. With breathtaking coastal scenery, picturesque fishing villages and country footpaths, the area has stunning woodland walks beside the estuary. The superb gardens of Glendurgan and Trebah are a short stroll away.

LOCATION

From the A39 Truro to Falmouth Road, follow brown signs to Trebah Gardens, then continue for ½ mile to Budock Vean.

Near Helford Passage, Mawnan Smith, Falmouth, Cornwall TR11 5LG
Telephone 01326 252100
Fax 01326 250892
E-mail: *budock@bestloved.com*

OWNERS
The Barlow Family

RATES PER PERSON
4 Singles	*£66 - £95*
50 Doubles/Twins	*£66 - £95*
1 Four-poster	*£76 - £105*
1 Suite	*£109 - £138*

Includes full breakfast, dinner, and VAT

CHARGE/CREDIT CARDS
DC • MC • VI

RATINGS & AWARDS
E.T.C. ★★★★
R.A.C. ★★★★ *Dining Award 2*
A.A. ★★★★ ❀ *72% Country House*

FACILITIES
On site: *Garden, snooker, heli-pad, fishing, golf, tennis, indoor pool, health & beauty, motor boat, private foreshore*
Licensed for weddings
2 meeting rooms/max 120 people
Nearby: *Water skiing, yachting, riding*

RESTRICTIONS
No facilities for disabled guests
No children under 7 years in restaurant
No pets in public rooms
Closed 2 - 25 Jan

ATTRACTIONS
Lost Gardens of Heligan, Tate Gallery, Trebah Gardens, St Michael's Mount, Seal Sanctuary, Minack Open Air Theatre, National Maritime Museum, Eden Project,

AFFILIATIONS
Grand Heritage Hotels

NEAREST
MAJOR CITY:
Truro - 15 miles/20 mins

MAJOR AIRPORT:
Newquay - 30 miles/45 mins

RAILWAY STATION:
Falmouth - 6 miles/10 mins

FERRY PORT:
Falmouth - 6 miles/10 mins

RESERVATIONS
Toll free in US: 888-93-GRAND
Toll free in UK: 0800 833 927
*Quote **Best Loved***

ACCESS CODES
AMADEUS UI PZEBVC
APOLLO/GALILEO UI 24799
SABRE/ABACUS UI 49775
WORLDSPAN UI 41000

Map p.472
ref: E3

THE CASTLE HOTEL

12th century castle

Castle Green, Taunton, Somerset TA1 1NF

Telephone 01823 272671
Fax 01823 336066

E-mail: castle@bestloved.com

OWNERS
The Chapman Family

GENERAL MANAGER
Kevin McCarthy

ROOM RATES
12 Singles	£108
27 Doubles/Twins	£165
5 Suites	£245
Includes full breakfast and VAT	

CHARGE/CREDIT CARDS

AMERICAN EXPRESS • DC • MC • VI

RATINGS & AWARDS
R.A.C. Gold Ribbon ★★★ Dining Award 4
A.A. ★★★ ✿✿✿
Tatler's 'Best Restaurant Out of London Award 2002'

FACILITIES
On site: *Garden*
4 meeting rooms/max 120 people
Nearby: *Golf, leisure centre, health & beauty, pony trekking*

RESTRICTIONS
Limited facilities for disabled guests
Pets by arrangement

ATTRACTIONS
Bath, Exmoor & The Quantocks, Longleat Safari Park, Blackdown Hills, Forde Abbey, Wells Cathedral, National Trust Properties & Gardens

AFFILIATIONS
Independent

NEAREST
MAJOR CITY:
Bristol - 50 miles/1 hr

MAJOR AIRPORT:
Bristol - 40 miles/45 mins
Exeter - 35 miles/40 mins

RAILWAY STATION:
Taunton - 1 mile/5 mins

RESERVATIONS
Direct with hotel
Quote **Best Loved**

ACCESS CODES
AMADEUS NT BRSCAS
APOLLO/GALILEO NT 29738
SABRE/ABACUS NT 54280
WORLDSPAN NT TAUN

WEST COUNTRY

Twelve centuries of fascinating history and West Country hospitality

The Castle at Taunton is steeped in the drama and romance of English history. As exemplified by the Duke of Monmouth's officers, who in 1685 were heard 'roistering at the Castle Inn' before they were defeated by the forces of King James II. Today the Castle lives at peace with its turbulent past but preserves the atmosphere of its ancient tradition, and having withstood this test of time visitors today can enjoy those very same pleasures.

The Chapman family have been running the hotel for 50 years and in that time it has acquired a worldwide reputation for the warmth of its hospitality. Diners have the choice of gracious and award winning, refined dining or the more relaxed yet innovative Brazz restaurant.

Located in the heart of England's beautiful West Country, the Castle is the ideal base for exploring a region rich in history. This is the land of King Arthur, King Alfred, Lorna Doone's Exmoor and the monastic foundations of Glastonbury and Wells. Roman and Regency Bath, Longleat House and the majestic gardens of Stourhead and Hestercombe. All this and much more can be discovered within easy driving distance of Taunton.

LOCATION

Exit Junction 25 of M5 and follow signs for Taunton town centre. Once in town centre follow signs for the Castle Hotel.

"" *The most delightful situation in the vicinity of Bath* ""

John Wesley, 1781

Country house COMBE GROVE MANOR HOTEL & COUNTRY CLUB

**Brassknocker Hill,
Monkton Combe, Bath,
Somerset BA2 7HS**

**Telephone 01225 834644
Fax 01225 834961**

E-mail: *combegrove@bestloved.com*

GENERAL MANAGER
Julian Ebbutt

ROOM RATES
Single occupancy	£110 - £325
36 Doubles	£110 - £185
2 Four-posters	£155 - £320
2 Suites	£225 - £290

*Includes full breakfast,
all leisure facilities and VAT*

CHARGE/CREDIT CARDS

 ● DC ● MC ● VI

RATINGS & AWARDS
E.T.C. ★★★★ *Silver Award*
R.A.C. ★★★★ *Dining Award 2*
A.A. ★★★★ ❀ *61%*

FACILITIES
On site: *Garden, gym, heli-pad, heated
pool, croquet, golf, tennis, indoor pool,
health & beauty, solaria, sauna, steam
room, jogging trail, creche, jacuzzi,
practice golf/driving range
Licensed for weddings
4 meeting rooms/max 120 people*
Nearby: *Golf, riding, fishing, shooting*

RESTRICTIONS
*No facilities for disabled guests
No pets*

ATTRACTIONS
*Bath, Wells, Longleat,
The Cotswolds, Stonehenge*

AFFILIATIONS
Furlong Hotels

NEAREST
*MAJOR CITY:
Bath - 2 miles/5 mins*

*MAJOR AIRPORT:
London Heathrow - 100 miles/2 hrs
Bristol Airport - 26 miles/45 mins*

*RAILWAY STATION:
Bath Spa - 2 miles/5 mins*

RESERVATIONS
Direct with hotel
Quote **Best Loved**

ACCESS CODES
Not applicable

WEST COUNTRY

Something for everyone on the very edge of Bath

Named after the large fir groves surrounding the house and gardens, Combe Grove Manor was entertaining visitors long before it became an hotel and country club. Built on a hillside site of a Roman settlement, this historic encounter of 18th century elegance with unrivalled 21st century sports and leisure facilities is encompassed by 69 acres of private gardens and woodland which command a spectacular view over the Limpley Stoke Valley.

Situated just two miles from the Georgian splendours of Bath, Combe Grove Manor offers a choice of 40 individually designed bedrooms, nine in the main house, and 31 in the Garden Lodge, from deluxe to four-poster suites. The Manor House boasts two restaurants, the main Restaurant on the first floor offers superb cuisine from both a Table d'Hôte and A La Carte Menu whilst the Eden Bistro on the ground floor offers modern cuisine in a relaxed atmosphere.

Guests have unlimited access to the leisure facilities including four tennis courts, Life Fitness gymnasium, indoor and outdoor heated swimming pools, sauna, steam room, solaria and beauty rooms featuring a range of therapeutic treatments using exclusive Clarins skincare products.

LOCATION
*Two miles south of the city of Bath.
For detailed directions guests are
advise to contact hotel reception.*

● *Map p.472*
ref: F2

THE COUNTY HOTEL

Georgian town house

18/19 Pulteney Road, Bath, Somerset BA2 4EZ

Telephone 01225 425003
Fax 01225 466493

E-mail: *county@bestloved.com*

OWNERS
Maureen and Charles Kent
and Sandra Masson

MANAGER
James Kent

ROOM RATES
2 Singles	£75 - £85
17 Doubles/Twins	£100 - £140
2 Superior Doubles/Twins	£160 - £185
1 Four-poster	£165 - £190

Includes full breakfast and VAT

CHARGE/CREDIT CARDS

AMERICAN EXPRESS ● *DC* ● *JCB* ● *MC* ● *VI*

RATINGS & AWARDS
E.T.C. ◆◆◆◆◆ *Gold Award*
R.A.C. ◆◆◆◆◆
A.A. ◆◆◆◆ *Premier Collection*
R.A.C. Sparkling Diamond and
Little Gem Award
A.A. Guest Accommodation of the Year 2001

FACILITIES
***On site:** Car park, bar*
1 meeting room/max 20 people
***Nearby:** Golf, tennis*

RESTRICTIONS
No facilities for the disabled
No children, No pets
Smoking allowed in bar only
Closed 22 Dec - 8 Jan

ATTRACTIONS
Roman Baths, The Pump Rooms,
Bath Abbey, Museum of Costume,
Castle Combe, Longleat Safari Park

AFFILIATIONS
Independent

NEAREST
MAJOR CITY:
Bath - 1 mile/5 mins

MAJOR AIRPORT:
London Heathrow - 90 miles/1 ½ hrs

RAILWAY STATION:
Bath Spa - 1 mile/5 mins

RESERVATIONS
Direct with hotel
*Quote **Best Loved***

ACCESS CODES
Not applicable

WEST COUNTRY

Put your feet up in comfort with one of the best skylines in Britain

'Perfect', 'Fabulous hotel, fabulous time', 'Nothing too much trouble. Excellent'. With hundreds of similar comments in the visitors' book it's not surprising that the County Hotel has been showered with the highest awards.

The City of Bath is a 'must see' for everyone but, with so many attractions, it is easy to get 'museumed out' and desperate for somewhere friendly and relaxing to recover. Luckily the County Hotel - in easy walking distance of the town centre - offers just that.

A recent refurbishment resulting in a sumptuous ambience, with classical furnishings and generous drapes around the large sash windows and beds, whisked the hotel into a well-deserved, five diamond class. Each luxurious bedroom - equipped with every facility - reflects a different mood, while the gracious public rooms include the Jane Austen reading room and a popular bar, the only place smoking is permitted. The hotel's celebrated Bath breakfast is served in the elegant breakfast room and conservatory. Both revelling in the uninterrupted view over the county cricket ground and Bath's rugby pitch towards the Abbey and River Avon - a real bonus for a hotel in the heart of a city, as is the ample parking.

LOCATION

On entering the City follow signs for the Holbourne Museum. With the Museum on your left, go straight over at roundabout following signs to Bristol/Exeter. The hotel is on your immediate right.

" What a lovely peaceful place! "

Lulu, London

Victorian country house

COURT BARN

Crackling log fires, good food and wine in a romantic Devon hideaway

Built as the 'Sanctuary' around the 16th century, the present house was partly rebuilt in 1853, and had its own chapel. It is a small, but delightful country house, set in park-like grounds with an aura of peace amidst glorious Devon countryside.

The hotel has great charm. Attractive and individually furnished en suite bedrooms, most with bath and shower, offer a wide range of facilities. Cracking log fires and the cosy, well stocked bar, create a warm relaxed atmosphere in which to unwind. For the duller days there is a well stocked library, board games, bridge and perhaps indulgence in an award-winning cream tea.

Robert and Susan are justifiably proud of their reputation for hospitality and good food. A selection of 350 wines accompany the mouth-watering four-course dinner created from fresh, quality produce. While the breakfast room looks over the croquet lawns, the restaurant, candlelit in the evenings and decorated with antiques, fresh flowers and crisp linen, has views of the garden.

You will find good, old-fashioned values of service and hospitality at Court Barn, the perfect

base from which to discover this delightful part of unexplored Devon and Cornwall.

LOCATION

2 ½ miles south of Holsworthy off A388, turn towards North Tamerton for ½ mile. Hotel is next to 12th century Clawton Church.

Clawton, Holsworthy, Devon EX22 6PS

**Telephone 01409 271219
Fax 01409 271309**

E-mail: *courtbarn@bestloved.com*

OWNERS
Robert and Susan Wood

ROOM RATES
Single occupancy	£40 - £55
6 Doubles/Twins	£70 - £86
1 Four-poster	£70 - £90
1 Small suite	£110
Includes full breakfast and VAT	

CHARGE/CREDIT CARDS

 ● *DC* ● *JCB* ● *MC* ● *VI*

RATINGS & AWARDS
E.T.C. ★★ *Silver Award*
A.A. ★★ *72%*
Taste of the West
Tea Council 'Best Teas' in Britain

FACILITIES
On site: *Garden, croquet, tennis, badminton, 9-hole pitch & putt 2 meeting rooms/max 25 people*
Nearby: *Golf, riding, fishing, sailing, archery, clay shooting, indoor pool, leisure centre, water sports, cycle trails*

RESTRICTIONS
*No facilities for disabled guests
Smoking in bar and TV room only
£2 surcharge for pets*

ATTRACTIONS
Boscastle, Clovelly, Tintagel, Docton Mill, Hartland Abbey, Route 3 Cycle Trail, Exmoor, Eden Project, Tate Gallery

AFFILIATIONS
Independent

NEAREST
MAJOR CITY:
Exeter - 35 miles/50 mins

MAJOR AIRPORT:
London Heathrow - 240 miles/4 hrs

RAILWAY STATION:
Exeter - 35 miles/50 mins

RESERVATIONS
Direct with hotel
Quote Best Loved

ACCESS CODES
Not applicable

WEST COUNTRY

• *Map p.472*
ref: E3

" My favourite small hotel on Exmoor. Scrumptious food, oozing with atmosphere and where you are always treated like one of the family "

Christopher Ondaatje C.B.E., O.C., Author and Explorer

THE CROWN HOTEL

Coaching inn

Exmoor National Park, Exford, Somerset TA24 7PP

Telephone 01643 831554
Fax 01643 831665

E-mail: *crowndevon@bestloved.com*

OWNERS
Hugo and Pam Jeune

ROOM RATES
3 Singles   from £55
14 Doubles/Twins   £95 - £110
Includes full breakfast and VAT

CHARGE/CREDIT CARDS

 • *MC • VI*

RATINGS & AWARDS
A.A. ★★★ ✿✿ *71%*

FACILITIES
On site: *Garden, stables*
1 meeting room/max 20 people
Nearby: *Riding, clay pigeon shooting, trout fishing, game shooting, walking*

RESTRICTIONS
No facilities for disabled guests
No children under 8 years
in the dining room for dinner

ATTRACTIONS
Tarr Steps ancient clapper bridge, Lorna Doone Valley, Dunster Castle, Valley of the Rocks, North Devon coast, Lynmouth Cliff Railway

AFFILIATIONS
Great Inns of Britain

NEAREST
MAJOR CITY:
Taunton - 25 miles/45 mins

MAJOR AIRPORT:
Bristol - 63 miles/1 ½ hrs

RAILWAY STATION:
Taunton - 25 miles/45 mins

RESERVATIONS
Direct with hotel
Quote **Best Loved**

ACCESS CODES
Not applicable

WEST COUNTRY

A feast to remember at this out-of-the-way hotel

'It is extremely rare to have the pleasure of eating and relishing such superb food', read the quote at the top of The Crown Hotel's page in the 2000 edition of Best Loved. A closer look reveals that the quote was made by a certain Hugo Jeune, a distinguished West Country hotelier, who was evidently so impressed that earlier this year he bought the hotel.

Surrounded by rolling moorland but nestling in a wooded coombe, The Crown at Exford has long had a reputation for good food but now, under the ownership of Hugo and Pam Jeune, it is excelling itself.

Overseen by Head Chef Scott Dickson and his brigade, the choice of eating in the bar with its log fire or the more formal dining room is entirely up to you. Mouth watering dishes are in both. In the bar, choose, for example, Roast Exmoor venison with braised red cabbage and cider pomme fondant, followed by a choice of exquisite home-made puddings. In the dining room, the special gourmet dinner includes pan seared seabass with braised fennel, open lobster ravioli or slow roast beef with truffle mash.

The ambience of the hotel is first-class for comfort after a day exploring the nearby moors on foot or on horseback - and at The Crown dogs and horses are welcome to bring their well behaved owners with them!

LOCATION
Take Exit 25 off M5 and follow signs for Taunton. Take the A358 out of Taunton, then the B3224 via Wheddon Cross into Exford.

" Quite simply the best hotel I have ever stayed in "

Jan Waldron, Devon

Georgian town house

DUKES HOTEL

Traditional English comfort and elegance in the historic city of Bath

Duke's Hotel is an architecturally important Grade I listed building on one of Europe's most elegant Georgian boulevards. In recent times the hotel has undergone a complete refurbishment and the owners, Philippa and Sebastian Hughes, have gone to great lengths to cleverly recreate the relaxed, country atmosphere of its Dartmoor based sister hotel, Holne Chase (page 273).

Original mouldings, cornices and the magnificent staircase have been retained. The bedrooms, some with four-posters, have been re-decorated to the very highest of standards with elaborate rich fabrics and wall coverings to give a very special feeling of Georgian elegance. All bathrooms have the latest power showers and much attention has been given to the finer details such as the expensive bathroom toiletries.

Fitzroy's restaurant is another great plus point. It has a stylish and relaxed feel and fits the bill whether you're looking for a lively fun evening with friends or just a simple supper on your own, there is also a lovely courtyard for al fresco dining in the summer months.

Exploring the world of Jane Austen's novels is easy from Dukes - the hotel is surrounded by many of Bath's prominent attractions, such as the Pump Room, Roman Baths, and the famous Theatre Royal.

LOCATION

Situated just 5 minutes walk from the centre of Bath and 5 minutes by taxi from the station.

**Great Pulteney Street,
Bath,
Somerset BA2 4DN**

**Telephone 01225 787960
Fax 01225 787961**

E-mail: *dukesbath@bestloved.com*

OWNERS
Sebastian and Philippa Hughes

MANAGER
Christophe Bonneau

ROOM RATES
1 Single £115
10 Doubles/Twins £145 - £185
2 Four-posters £235
5 Suites £215 - £225
Includes continental breakfast and VAT

CHARGE/CREDIT CARDS

 ● *DC* ● *MC* ● *VI*

RATINGS & AWARDS
E.T.C. ★★★
A.A. ★★★ ❀❀ 77%

FACILITIES
On site: 2 meeting rooms/max 30 people
Nearby: Golf, swimming pool,
leisure centre

RESTRICTIONS
No pets in public rooms

ATTRACTIONS
*Roman Baths, American Museum,
Museum of Costume, The Crescent,
Holborne Museum of Art, Prior Park,
Stonehenge*

AFFILIATIONS
Preston's Global Hotels

NEAREST
MAJOR CITY:
Bath

MAJOR AIRPORT:
London Heathrow - 90 miles/1 ½ hrs
Bristol - 15 miles/30 mins

RAILWAY STATION:
Bath Spa - ½ mile/10 mins

RESERVATIONS
Toll free in the US: 800-544-9993
Quote Best Loved

ACCESS CODES
Not applicable

WEST COUNTRY

• *Map p.472*
ref: E3

" Thank you again for the countless ways in which you made our visit so enjoyable and memorable. I'd forgotten that hotels could be like this "

Beryl and Alan Tucker, Oswestry

FARTHINGS HOTEL AND RESTAURANT

Country hotel

Hatch Beauchamp, Taunton, Somerset TA3 6SG

Telephone 01823 480664
Fax 01823 481118

E-mail: *farthings@bestloved.com*

OWNERS
Stephen and Hilary Murphy

ROOM RATES
Single occupancy	£75 - £85
9 Doubles/Twins	£105 - £115
1 Cottage	£90 - £130

Includes full breakfast and VAT

CHARGE/CREDIT CARDS

 • *MC* • *VI*

RATINGS & AWARDS
E.T.C. ★★ *Silver Award*
R.A.C. ★★ *Dining Award 3*
A.A. ★★ ❀ *78%*

FACILITIES
On site: *Garden*
Licensed for weddings
2 meeting rooms/max 50 people
Nearby: *Fitness centre, riding, golf, go-karting, hot-air ballooning*

RESTRICTIONS
No facilities for disabled guests
Children by arrangement
Pets by arrangement
No smoking

ATTRACTIONS
Wells Cathedral, Barrington Court, Montacute House & Gardens, Cheddar Gorge, Hestercombe Gardens, Glastonbury Abbey and Tor

AFFILIATIONS
Independent

NEAREST
MAJOR CITY:
Bristol - 50 miles/1 hr

MAJOR AIRPORT:
Exeter - 35 miles/40 mins

RAILWAY STATION:
Taunton - 7 miles/10 mins

RESERVATIONS
Direct with hotel
Quote **Best Loved**

ACCESS CODES
Not applicable

WEST COUNTRY

West country hospitality in elegant Georgian surroundings

On a warm summer's evening just before dinner, guests at Farthings Hotel in Hatch Beauchamp can enjoy a glass of wine on the two acres of lawn that surround this elegant Georgian country house hotel. Dinner is prepared by owner Stephen Murphy, who has been a chef for 25 years, and the emphasis is on good quality, English food and local produce, including fish, meat and dairy. Beef and lamb are sourced from a butcher who has lived in Somerset all his life, and whose mother still personally inspects the livestock. Eggs are courtesy of a retired Sergeant Major who keeps hens on his farm nearby.

Your host, and co-owner Hilary Murphy will be happy to tell you that a short drive will get you to the cathedral cities of Wells (The Bishop's Garden here is a must), Bath, Exeter and the county town of Taunton which is just five miles away. The Somerset and Dorset coast, Exmoor, Cheddar Gorge and the undulating Mendip hills are also convenient.

While a stay at Farthings is designed to be a pleasure it is also suitable for business, with well-equipped meeting facilities, good communications and friendly and efficient staff who will be happy to tailor a package to suit your needs.

LOCATION

Exit M5 on Junction 25 and take the A358 signed for Ilminster. After the traffic lights in Thornfalcon take a left to Hatch Beauchamp. Bear right at Hatch Inn, hotel is on right.

" Everything was absolutely wonderful - the venue, the food and in particular the excellent staff "

Phil and Sara Knight, Hove, East Sussex

Victorian riverside hotel

THE FOWEY

A Victorian 'grand hotel' restored to its former glory on the banks of the River Fowey

Those Victorian hoteliers certainly appreciated a fine location when they saw one. It would be hard to beat the Fowey's spectacular position, dominating the hillside above the busy river estuary with views across the water to the fishing village of Polruan. Fowey itself is charming, its narrow lanes winding down to the water and the jetty where passenger ferries depart for the short crossing to Polruan. The hotel makes a perfect base for visiting Cornwall's most exciting new attraction, the giant greenhouses of the Eden Project, a 15-minute drive away. Another day trip treat for gardeners is the Lost Gardens of Heligan, near Mevagissey.

The Fowey Hotel was built on a grand scale in 1882, and owners Ann and Keith Richardson have done a terrific job in recreating the handsome Victorian interior using period colour schemes and furnishings. To reach the upper floors, where many of the rooms boast river views, guests can summon the Old Lady, a splendid original Victorian lift. The hotel restaurant enjoys a fine reputation and there are comfortable lounges for relaxing. On a summer's

afternoon, the Victorian Tea Garden is just the place for a Cornish tea on the water's edge.

LOCATION

From the M5 take the A30. At Bodmin take the B3269 Lostwithiel (A390) to Fowey. The hotel is on the right on the Esplanade.

The Esplanade, Fowey,
Cornwall PL23 1HX

Telephone 01726 832551
Fax 01726 832125

E-mail: *fowey@bestloved.com*

OWNERS
Ann and Keith Richardson

GENERAL MANAGER
Andrea Callis

RATES PER PERSON
Single occupancy	£90 - £160
32 Doubles/Twins	£67 - £109
4 Four-posters	£119
1 Suite	£129

Includes full breakfast, dinner and VAT

CHARGE/CREDIT CARDS

 ● *DC ● MC ● VI*

RATINGS & AWARDS
E.T.C. ★★★ *Silver Award*
A.A. ★★★ ❀❀ *73%*
Investors in People

FACILITIES
On site: *Garden, fishing*
1 meeting room/max 70 people
Nearby: *Golf, sailing*

RESTRICTIONS
Limited facilities for disabled guests
Pets by arrangment

ATTRACTIONS
Lanhydrock House & Gardens,
Lost Gardens of Heligan, Carlyon Bay,
Truro, Pencarrow House & Gardens,
The Eden Project, Art Galleries

AFFILIATIONS
Best Western

NEAREST
MAJOR CITY:
Truro - 25 miles/40 mins

MAJOR AIRPORT:
Exeter - 85 miles/1 ¼ hrs
London Heathrow - 270 miles/4 hrs

RAILWAY STATION:
Par - 4 miles/10 mins

RESERVATIONS
Toll free in US: 800-528-1234
Toll free in UK: 0800-243-708
Quote **Best Loved**

ACCESS CODES
Not applicable

WEST COUNTRY

Map p.472
ref: D5

66 At last, enchanting England. We've found heaven 99

Max Malden, Calgary

GABRIEL COURT HOTEL

Manor house

**Stoke Gabriel, Near Totnes,
Devon TQ9 6SF**

**Telephone 01803 782206
Fax 01803 782333**

E-mail: *gabriel@bestloved.com*

OWNER
Mr O M Beacom

ROOM RATES
2 Singles £62
17 Doubles/Twins £86
Includes full breakfast and VAT

CHARGE/CREDIT CARDS

 • *DC* • *MC* • *VI*

RATINGS & AWARDS
R.A.C. ★★★ *Dining Award 1*
A.A. ★★★ *73%*

FACILITIES
On site: *Garden, tennis, outdoor pool
1 meeting room/max 20 people*
Nearby: *Golf, riding, walking, fishing*

RESTRICTIONS
No facilities for disabled guests

ATTRACTIONS
*Dartmoor National Park, Totnes,
River Dart, Dartmouth Castle,
South Devon coastline,
Coleton Fishacre*

AFFILIATIONS
Independent

NEAREST
MAJOR CITY:
Plymouth - 28 miles/40 mins

MAJOR AIRPORT:
Exeter - 28 miles/40 mins
London Heathrow - 190 miles/3 ¼ hrs

RAILWAY STATION:
Totnes - 4 miles/15 mins

RESERVATIONS
Direct with hotel
Quote Best Loved

ACCESS CODES
Not applicable

500 years of heritage and a sunny disposition

For nearly 500 years this was the home of the Churchward family, the Squires of Stoke Gabriel. In 1928 the house was converted into an hotel and since then has earned an excellent reputation for hospitality and comfort. Appealing essentially to those who like peace and quiet it is, nevertheless, a wonderful base for exploring the tourist attractions which abound in a 30 mile radius. Dartmoor, the Heritage Coast, National Trust properties, Totnes and Dartmouth, to name but a few. For guests wishing to visit the Eden Project, trains run from Totnes to St Austell. And to help you enjoy a relaxed day out, packages are available to include train fair, coach transfer and the entrance fee.

The hotel overlooks the very pretty village of Stoke Gabriel which stands by the River Dart. From ancient records it appears that there has been a church in the village since the tenth century.

Set in its own grounds and surrounded by a high stone wall, the hotel faces south and enjoys all available sunshine.

The food is English cooking at its best with salmon from the Dart, sea fish landed at Brixham and game from nearby estates. Vegetables are often from the hotel's own garden. The table

d'hôte menu is changed daily and offers an excellent choice. The Beacom family will warmly welcome you to Gabriel Court.

LOCATION

Leave A38 at Buckfastleigh. Take A384 to Totnes, then A385 towards Paignton. Turn right towards village at Parker's Arms.

"*As usual everything, especially the cuisine, was superb, outshone only by Kilby hospitality*"

Joyce & Bob Hinze, USA

Cornish coastal hotel

GARRACK HOTEL

Burthallan Lane, St Ives,
Cornwall TR26 3AA

Telephone 01736 796199
Fax 01736 798955

E-mail: garrack@bestloved.com

OWNERS
*The Kilby Family
(Frances, Michael, Stephen)*

ROOM RATES
1 Single	£66 - £68
16 Doubles/Twins	£110 - £160
1 Four-poster	£156 - £160

Includes full breakfast and VAT

CHARGE/CREDIT CARDS

 • DC • MC • VI

RATINGS & AWARDS
E.T.C. ★★★ *Silver Award*
A.A. ★★★ ❀❀ 65%

FACILITIES
On site: *Garden, gym ,indoor pool spa, solarium, gym, licensed coffee shop, special facilities for the disabled 1 meeting room/max 30 people*
Nearby: *Golf, riding, fishing*

RESTRICTIONS
Pets by arrangement

ATTRACTIONS
St Ives Tate Gallery, Newlyn, Land's End, Orion Gallery, St Michael's Mount, Cornish coastal path

AFFILIATIONS
Relais du Silence

NEAREST
MAJOR CITY:
Truro - 25 miles/45 mins

MAJOR AIRPORT:
Exeter - 110 miles/ 2 ¼ hrs
London Heathrow - 300 miles/6 hrs

RAILWAY STATION:
St Ives - 1 mile/3 mins

RESERVATIONS
Toll free in UK: 08000 197393
Quote Best Loved

ACCESS CODES
Not applicable

WEST COUNTRY

The connoisseur's choice for seeing Cornwall and south-west England

Cornwall is unique, both for its history and its scenery. It is a land of contrasts from its rugged coastline, precipitous cliffs and often angry seas, to lazy wooded creeks, small fishing harbours and sandy coves.

Originally a private house known in the Cornish language as Chy-an-Garrack, which translates into English as The House on the Rock, it was the home of Lady Ebury prior to becoming a hotel in 1947. Since then the Kilby family has made many changes: new bedrooms have been added and a small leisure centre with swimming pool, sauna and solarium.

It is now a secluded, vine covered granite building standing in two acres of gardens high above Porthmeor Beach with fabulous views of St Ives Bay and the coastal landscape beyond. Of the 18 bedrooms, some have four-poster beds and some have personal spa baths. The hotel is proud of its reputation for good culinary standards, recognised by an award of two rosettes by the A.A., and for an extensive wine list.

The hotel is dedicated to providing comfort in tranquil and beautiful surroundings, accompanied by good food, good service and good company where the customers' interests are paramount. As a base for visiting the many attractions including the renowned Tate Gallery, St Ives and the Garrack have no equal.

LOCATION
From the A30, take 2nd exit to St Ives. Take B3311 then join B3306 towards St Ives. Take third left after petrol station,after 400 yards the hotel is signposted.

*** Words don't often fail me, but I run out of superlatives when talking about Gidleigh! ***

Ruth & Steve, Nottingham

GIDLEIGH PARK

Country house

*Chagford,
Devon TQ13 8HH*

**Telephone 01647 432367
Fax 01647 432574**

E-mail: *gidleigh@bestloved.com*

OWNERS
Kay and Paul Henderson

MANAGER
Catherine Endacott

RATES PER PERSON

Single occupancy	*£275 - £460*
12 Doubles/Twins	*£210 - £275*
2 Suites	*£225 - £275*
1 Cottage	*£550*

*Includes full breakfast, dinner,
morning tea and VAT*

CHARGE/CREDIT CARDS

MC • VI

RATINGS & AWARDS
A.A. ★★★ ❀❀❀❀❀
*The Hideaway Report Grand Award 2000
Wine Spectator Grand Award 2002*

FACILITIES
On site: *Garden, croquet, tennis,
bowls, putting green, heli-pad
1 meeting room/max 22 people*
Nearby: *Fishing, shooting, riding*

RESTRICTIONS
*No facilities for disabled guests
No pets in public rooms*

ATTRACTIONS
*The Eden Project, The Garden House,
Dartmoor National Park, Castle Drogo,
Buckland Abbey, Rosemoor RHS Garden*

AFFILIATIONS
Relais & Châteaux

NEAREST
*MAJOR CITY:
Exeter - 25 miles/30 mins*

*MAJOR AIRPORT:
Exeter - 25 miles/30 mins
London Heathrow - 210 miles/3½ hrs*

*RAILWAY STATION:
Exeter - 25 miles/30 mins*

RESERVATIONS
Toll free in US: 800-735-2478
*Quote **Best Loved***

ACCESS CODES
*AMADEUS WB EXTGID
APOLLO/GALILEO WB 14910
SABRE/ABACUS WB 11551
WORLDSPAN WB GB10*

WEST COUNTRY

The epitome of gracious country living in one of Britain's finest hotels

If one ever needed to prove the dictum that small is perfect, look no further than Gidleigh Park. Americans Kay and Paul Henderson started the hotel in 1977, and together they have created a masterpiece that is widely recognised as one of this country's premier small hotels. It is one of 21 British members of the Relais et Châteaux luxury hotel association and its highly rated restaurant boasts two Michelin stars amongst a galaxy of other prestigious awards.

Gidleigh Park was built as a luxurious country residence for an Australian shipping magnate in the 1920s, surrounded by 45 acres of gardens and secluded beech and oak forest in the Dartmoor National Park. The house has just 15 lovely bedrooms, each individually furnished with antiques and fine English fabrics by Kay Henderson, who has also overseen the decoration of the warmly elegant public rooms. Log fires and cut flowers add a cosy touch and the Gidleigh Siamese cats tend to gravitate to the most comfortable spot in the house.

Guests can enjoy a variety of recreational activities from croquet, tennis and gentle strolls in the grounds to horse riding, fishing and hiking in the National Park.

LOCATION

*From M5, take Junction 31 onto A30.
After 15 miles, turn left onto A382.
Follow signs to Chagford. In Chagford, turn
right at Lloyd's Bank. After 150 yards, take first
fork to right. Hotel is 2 miles along this road.*

*" **Your kindness and consideration was exceptional. Thank you for making our time with you so enjoyable** "*

John Major, former Prime Minister

• *Map p.472*
ref: D4

Country house hotel

GLAZEBROOK HOUSE HOTEL

Tradition, comfort and conviviality in the heart of Dartmoor Park

Glazebrook House is a family-owned hotel in the best tradition of comfort and affability. It is set on an elevated site in Dartmoor Park itself amidst landscaped grounds containing a profusion of colour throughout the year. The original building dates back to around 1600 and was extended in 1879 into a mid-Victorian country house.

The interior of the hotel exhibits a splendidly carved fireplace depicting the events which led to the execution of the Duke of Hamilton. Modern convenience has been added to the grace and elegance of the building's old fabric. There are three honeymoon suites, each with a four-poster bed and all bedrooms have en suite facilities, remote control TV, direct dial telephone and tea/coffee making equipment.

Dinner is prepared by chef David Merriman using fresh local ingredients and the cellar comes to the aid of the party with a wide range of fine wines. Afterwards, in the bar, you will meet your host, Fred Heard, whose easy way encourages everyone in pleasant conversation.

Buckfast Abbey and the River Dart Country Park are nearby. The beauty of Dartmoor is all around. For golfers, Wrangaton Golf Course deserves a special mention: the front nine holes are on Dartmoor, and the back nine cross stunning parkland.

LOCATION

From Exeter take A38. Take South Brent/Avonwick turnoff. Take left lane, follow hotel signs through village, turn right at bottom of village.

Glazebrook, South Brent,
South Devon TQ10 9JE

Telephone 01364 73322
Fax 01364 72350

E-mail: *glazebrook@bestloved.com*

OWNER
Fred Heard

ROOM RATES
3 Singles £50
5 Doubles/Twins £72
3 Four-posters £90 - £125
Includes full breakfast and VAT

CHARGE/CREDIT CARDS

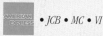 • *JCB* • *MC* • *VI*

RATINGS & AWARDS
A.A. ★★ ❀ 74%

FACILITIES
On site: *Garden*
2 meeting rooms/max 130 people
Nearby: *Golf, fishing, tennis, fitness, riding, shooting, walking*

RESTRICTIONS
No smoking in bedrooms or restaurant
Pets by arrangement

ATTRACTIONS
Saltram House, Eden Project,
River Dart Country Park,
Buckfast Abbey, Dartmouth Castle,
Dartmoor National Park, walking

AFFILIATIONS
Independent

NEAREST
MAJOR CITY:
Plymouth - 12 miles/15 mins

MAJOR AIRPORT:
London Heathrow - 190 miles/3 ½ hrs
Plymouth - 12 miles/15 mins

RAILWAY STATION:
Plymouth - 12 miles/15 mins

RESERVATIONS
Direct with hotel
*Quote **Best Loved***

ACCESS CODES
Not applicable

WEST COUNTRY

" Bursting with hospitality "

Judith Chalmers, 100 Irresistible Weekends

HAYDON HOUSE

Edwardian town house

**9 Bloomfield Park, Bath,
Somerset BA2 2BY**

**Telephone 01225 444919
Fax 01225 427351**

E-mail: *baydon@bestloved.com*

OWNERS
Gordon and Magdalene Ashman-Marr

ROOM RATES
Single occupancy	£50 - £70
3 Doubles/Twins	£75 - £105
1 Four-poster	£90 - £108
1 Suite	£90 - £108
Includes full breakfast and VAT	

CHARGE/CREDIT CARDS

 • *JCB* • *MC* • *VI*

RATINGS & AWARDS
E.T.C. ◆◆◆◆◆ *Silver Award*
A.A. ◆◆◆◆◆ *Premier Collection*
Which? Hotel of the Year 1999

FACILITIES
On site: *Garden, sun terrace*
Nearby: *Golf, riding, health club*

RESTRICTIONS
*No facilities for disabled guests
Children by arrangement
No smoking throughout*

ATTRACTIONS
*Bath, Wells Cathedral,
Glastonbury, Cotswolds,
Avebury, Salisbury,
Stonehenge*

AFFILIATIONS
Independent

NEAREST
MAJOR CITY:
Bath

MAJOR AIRPORT:
*London Heathrow - 90 miles/1 ½ hrs
Bristol - 15 miles/30 mins*

RAILWAY STATION:
Bath Spa - 1 mile/5 mins

RESERVATIONS
*Direct with hotel
Quote **Best Loved***

ACCESS CODES
Not applicable

WEST COUNTRY

Jane Austen wrote about the secrets of Bath ... here's another

Bath needs little introduction as one of the loveliest cities in the world with so much more to enjoy than simply taking the waters, as in Roman times, or the wider range of secret pleasures available in Jane Austen's day. Nowadays, it holds one more secret... a secret you should know - Haydon House.

It looks like any other Edwardian house, so typical of the residential streets of Bath. Inside, however, an oasis of tranquillity and elegance awaits you, where high standards of hospitality prevail.

The reception rooms are tastefully furnished with antiques, whilst the five guest bedrooms are decorated to a very high standard. All rooms have private facilities, colour television and direct-dial telephone and a generous hospitality tray offering complimentary home-made shortbread and a decanter of sherry. Innovative breakfasts are stylishly served and there is a lovely garden in which to relax.

The hosts' aim at Haydon is to make your stay, however short or long, truly happy and memorable by providing a secluded retreat from which you can readily enjoy all the pleasures of Georgian Bath, yet escape the throng.

LOCATION

**Half a mile south of the city centre on the A367,
fork right off Wellsway then turn second right.**

Best Loved Hotels of the World

" A glimpse of paradise at Heddon's Gate "

Paddy Burt, The Daily Telegraph

271

● Map p.472
ref: D3

Country house

HEDDON'S GATE HOTEL

An Exmoor hideaway!

Romantic Exmoor, home of the legendary Lorna Doone, is the stunning location of Heddon's Gate Hotel. Set high above the beautiful wooded Heddon Valley, the hotel enjoys unrivalled views across the western hills of Exmoor. An unspoilt landscape of high rolling moorland and deep valleys, this North Western area of the Exmoor National Park has the most dramatic coastal scenery. The famous South Western Peninsula Footpath can be accessed directly from the hotel.

This Edwardian house, which has a quintessentially English atmosphere, has been run as an hotel for over 30 years by proprietor and cook, Bob Deville. He uses the very best of Exmoor's produce - locally-reared beef and lamb, Devon and Somerset cheeses as well as Devonshire clotted cream.

Heddon's Gate is a very comfortable place, with en suite bedrooms, peaceful lounges with log fires, and outside, terraced lawns and gardens. Every day a complimentary traditional English afternoon tea is offered to all guests. Heddon's Gate is for those seeking to experience Exmoor hospitality at its best.

Please note: the approach is via steep and winding lanes and may not be suitable for just a one night stay!

LOCATION

From A39, 3 miles west of Lynton, take unclassified road signposted 'Martinhoe and Woody Bay'. Left at next crossroads, go downhill for 2 miles - private drive on right.

Heddon's Mouth, Parracombe, Barnstaple, Devon EX31 4PZ

Telephone 01598 763313
Fax 01598 763363

E-mail: *heddons@bestloved.com*

OWNER
Bob Deville

MANAGER
Heather Deville

ROOM RATES
1 Single   £39 - £48
9 Doubles/Twins   £75 - £103
1 Four-poster   £81 - £95
3 Suites   £87 - £117
*Includes full breakfast,
afternoon tea and VAT*

CHARGE/CREDIT CARDS

 ● MC ● VI

RATINGS & AWARDS
E.T.C. ★★ *Silver Award*
A.A. ★★ ❀ 76%

FACILITIES
On site: Garden
Nearby: Riding, coastal walks

RESTRICTIONS
*Limited facilities for disabled guests
Children by arrangement
Closed Nov - Easter*

ATTRACTIONS
*Lynton & Lynmouth Cliff Railway,
Lorna Doone Country, Arlington Court,
South Western Peninsula Footpath,
Exmoor National Park, Marwood Gardens
Rosemoor RHS Garden*

AFFILIATIONS
Independent

NEAREST
MAJOR CITY:
Exeter - 45 miles/1 ½ hrs

MAJOR AIRPORT:
*London Heathrow - 200 miles/4 ½ hrs
Bristol - 95 miles/2 ½ hrs*

RAILWAY STATION:
Barnstaple - 16 miles/40 mins

RESERVATIONS
Direct with hotel
Quote **Best Loved**

ACCESS CODES
Not applicable

WEST COUNTRY

Map p.472
ref: F2

" A haven of tranquillity and comfort, the highlight of our British visit "

Dan Elinghausen, Chicago

HOLLY LODGE

Victorian town house

**8 Upper Oldfield Park,
Bath, Somerset BA2 3JZ**

**Telephone 01225 424042
Fax 01225 481138**

E-mail: *hollylodge@bestloved.com*

OWNER
George Hall

ROOM RATES
1 Single £55 - £65
6 Doubles/Twins £79 - £97
Includes full breakfast and VAT

CHARGE/CREDIT CARDS

 • DC • JCB • MC • VI

RATINGS & AWARDS
E.T.C. ◆◆◆◆◆ *Gold Award*
A.A. ◆◆◆◆◆ *Premier Collection*

FACILITIES
On site: *Garden, car park*
Nearby: *Golf, riding, health spa*

RESTRICTIONS
Limited facilities for disabled guests
No smoking throughout
No pets

ATTRACTIONS
*Castle Combe, Bath, The Cotswolds,
Wells Cathedral Stonehenge,
Glastonbury, Avebury,
Stourhead Gardens*

AFFILIATIONS
Independent

NEAREST
MAJOR CITY:
Bath - ½ mile/5 mins

MAJOR AIRPORT:
London Heathrow - 90 miles/2 ¼ hrs
Bristol - 13 miles/40 mins

RAILWAY STATION:
Bath Spa - ½ mile/5 mins

RESERVATIONS
Direct with hotel
Quote Best Loved

ACCESS CODES
Not applicable

WEST COUNTRY

So much of England's heritage on your award-winning doorstep!

Holly Lodge is a large Victorian town house set in its own grounds and enjoys magnificent views over the world heritage city of Bath. It was rescued from semi-dereliction in 1986 by Carrolle Sellick and George Hall and now boasts seven individually designed rooms, some with queen size beds and others with specially built four-posters. All the rooms have luxury bathrooms, TV and satellite movies, direct-dial telephones, hot drink facilities and a host of extras.

You can enjoy imaginative breakfasts in the conservatory and relax in the beautiful lounge or the floodlit gazebo in the evenings. Holly Lodge is strictly no smoking.

Past winners of an 'England for Excellence' Award, Holly Lodge is graded five diamonds by the English Tourism Council.

Holly Lodge is conveniently placed for touring a wide variety of attractions - Stonehenge, the Cotswolds, Southern Wales, Wells and the Mendip Hills, all within a 40 mile radius of Bath. The magnificent architecture, Roman remains and fine shops of central Bath are on the doorstep.

LOCATION
*½ mile south west of Bath city centre
off A367 Wells Road.*

" **We came for peace and tranquillity and found it in abundance** *"*

David & Sarah Boulay, Ipswich

Victorian country house

HOLNE CHASE HOTEL

A peculiarly secluded and romantic situation

Remarkably, the above description from White's Directory of Devon of 1850, still rings true today. Holne Chase nestles in a woodland clearing overlooking a pocket of sloping lawns within the Dartmoor National Park. Its origins lie back in the 11th century, when the abbots of Buckfast Abbey kept a hunting lodge here, and the present Victorian era country house is very much a sporting retreat as well as a restorative escape from everyday stresses and strains.

Sebastian and Philippa Hughes run the hotel like a private home with the loyal assistance of Batty, the bassett hound, who maintains her own web site and is particularly keen to welcome animal lovers and canine visitors to her patch. The five handsomely converted Stable Suites are ideally suited to sporting visitors keen to fish, ride, shoot, or hike on the moors, and all the rooms in the main hotel have been recently refurbished with pretty English fabrics mirroring fresh flowers from the garden.

Holne Chase's walled garden also provides fruit and vegetables for the kitchen, and the chef's enthusiasm for good food made with top quality local ingredients embraces seafood from Brixham and Looe, and seasonal game dishes.

LOCATION

From M5, join A38 towards Plymouth. Take 2nd turning for Ashburton at Pear Tree Cross, following signs for Dartmeet. The hotel entrance is on the right, 300 metres after Holne Bridge.

Ashburton, Devon TQ13 7NS

**Telephone 01364 631471
Fax 01364 631453**

E-mail: *holnechase@bestloved.com*

OWNERS
Sebastian and Philippa Hughes

ROOM RATES
Single occupancy	£95 - £105
9 Doubles/Twins	£130 - £150
1 Four-poster	£170
7 Suites	£170
Includes full breakfast and VAT	

CHARGE/CREDIT CARDS

 ● *DC* ● *MC* ● *VI*

RATINGS & AWARDS
E.T.C. ★★★
R.A.C. ★★★
A.A. ★★★ ❀❀❀ 74%

FACILITIES
On site: *Garden, heli-pad, fishing, croquet, putting green*
1 meeting room/max 20 people
Nearby: *Riding, golf, shooting*

RESTRICTIONS
Limited facilities for disabled guests
No children under 12 years in restaurant
No pets in public rooms

ATTRACTIONS
Dartmoor National Park, Buckfast Abbey, Darlington Hall, Totnes, Plymouth, Dartmouth Castle

AFFILIATIONS
Preston's Global Hotels
The European Connection

NEAREST
MAJOR CITY:
Exeter/Plymouth - 22 miles/30 mins

MAJOR AIRPORT:
Exeter - 22 miles/30 mins
Bristol - 90 miles/1 ¾ hrs

RAILWAY STATION:
Newton Abbot - 10 miles/20 mins

RESERVATIONS
Toll free in US: 800-544-9993
Quote **Best Loved**

ACCESS CODES
Not applicable

WEST COUNTRY

*** The Horn of Plenty is one of those very rare, special places that one seeks yet rarely finds ***

D Barton, Woodford

THE HORN OF PLENTY

Country house

Gulworthy, Tavistock,
Devon PL19 8JD

Telephone 01822 832528
Fax 01822 832528

E-mail: *hornofplenty@bestloved.com*

OWNERS
Peter Gorton and Paul Roston

ROOM RATES
Single occupancy	£105 - £190
5 Doubles/Twins	£115 - £150
3 Deluxe doubles	£130 - £175
2 Superior doubles	£200

Includes full breakfast and VAT

CHARGE/CREDIT CARDS

 • *MC* • *VI*

RATINGS & AWARDS
A.A. ★★★ ❀❀❀ 77%

FACILITIES
On site: *Garden*
1 meeting room/max 35 people
Nearby: *Golf, riding, fishing,*
sailing, canoeing

RESTRICTIONS
Limited facilities for disabled guests
Closed Christmas
No smoking in bedrooms

ATTRACTIONS
Dartmoor National Park,
Walking, Devon coastline,
Buckland Abbey,
RHS Rosemoor Gardens,
Sailing

AFFILIATIONS
Independent

NEAREST
MAJOR CITY:
Plymouth - 22 miles/35 mins

MAJOR AIRPORT:
Plymouth - 17 miles/30 mins

RAILWAY STATION:
Plymouth - 22 miles/35 mins

RESERVATIONS
Direct with hotel
*Quote **Best Loved***

ACCESS CODES
Not applicable

WEST COUNTRY

A cornucopia overflowing with good food and charm in an English country garden

If you were designing a doll's house, the Horn of Plenty could be your model - with its perfect proportions, wisteria covered porch, sweeping lawns and manicured flowerbeds. Sitting neatly between the rugged areas of Bodmin Moor and Dartmoor, this quintessentially English country house is in lush countryside between the rivers Tamar and Tay, both famous for trout and salmon fishing. Within easy reach of sailing in Plymouth and the famous surfing beaches of the north coast, it is a gem of a hotel.

The Horn of Plenty has five acres of spectacular gardens and untamed orchards in which to wander, with secret arbours and constant changes of vista. The bedrooms in the Coach House have balconies overlooking the fragrant, sunny, walled garden. Indeed the scent of fresh picked flowers fills the house, whether the elegant drawing room, with its welcoming log fire, or the luxuriously furnished bedrooms.

Originally started as a 'restaurant with rooms', the focus here has always been on the food. The cuisine in the elegant restaurant is among the best in Devon with international recognition for its outstanding quality - so eating will be high on your list of things to do!

LOCATION

Exit M5 Junction 31 onto A30 signed Okehampton. After 27 miles turn left on to A386 signed for Tavistock, then onto the A390. After 3 miles turn right at Gulworthy Cross and follow signs to the hotel.

" *The Hotel du Vin is the very best sort of mid-range hotel* "

Walter F Stowry, The Sunday Times

● *Map p.472*
ref: F2

18th century warehouse   HOTEL DU VIN & BISTRO

An impeccable reputation and a coup for the city of Bristol

A neat place, indeed, to open a restaurant let alone a hotel. Showing a familiar skill, the owners of Hotel du Vin & Bistro converted an old warehouse near the Bristol heritage docks and a short walk from its Millennium centrepiece, @Bristol, a state-of-the-art electronic odyssey into the worlds of science and nature.

The Sugar House dates from the 1700's and has been used in a number of ways including the manufacture of clay pipes and tobacco and, more recently, sugar refining. It is fitting, therefore, that the decor of Hotel du Vin draws for inspiration on the city's industrial past and the space age, clean cut design of today. Simple white washed rubble walls contrast with steel columns; a fountain plays in the centre of the flagged courtyard reminiscent of French hostelries often designed in similar manner. The rooms are bright and comfortable with the functionality of a first class hotel designed for the international traveller.

From the opulence of the Lanson Room to the cigar-festooned walls of the Jeanneau Room with its full-size antique billiard table, Hotel du Vin Bristol is already catching the eye of the cognoscente. With its sister hotels having already established their reputations for the excellence

and good value of their cuisine, this one comes with impeccable credentials.

LOCATION

From the end of the M32 into Bristol, aim city centre. 200 yards past the Broadmead Centre, turn right at lights by War Memorial and follow carriageway. The hotel is on the immediate left, on corner of Lewins Mead and Narrow Lewins Mead.

The Sugar House,
Narrow Lewins Mead,
Bristol BS1 2NU

Telephone 0117 925 5577
Fax 0117 925 1199

E-mail: *duvinbris@bestloved.com*

GENERAL MANAGER
Lesley Skelt

ROOM RATES
30 Doubles/Twins	*£120 - £145*
5 Studios	*£170 - £175*
5 Loft Suites	*£190 - £295*

Includes VAT

CHARGE/CREDIT CARDS

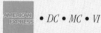 ● *DC* ● *MC* ● *VI*

RATINGS & AWARDS
A.A. ★★★★ ❀ *Town House*

FACILITIES
On site: *Billiard room*
3 meeting rooms/max 80 people
Nearby: *Golf, fitness*

RESTRICTIONS
Limited facilities for disabled guests
No pets

ATTRACTIONS
S.S. Great Britain, @Bristol,
Bristol Cathedral,
Clifton Suspension Bridge,
Bath, Somerset, South Wales

AFFILIATIONS
Hotel du Vin Ltd
Preston's Global Hotels
The European Connection

NEAREST
MAJOR CITY:
Bristol

MAJOR AIRPORT:
London Heathrow - 107 miles/2 hrs
Bristol - 9 miles/30 mins

RAILWAY STATION:
Bristol Temple Meads - 1 mile/10 mins

RESERVATIONS
Toll free in US: 800-544-9993
Quote Best Loved

ACCESS CODES
Not applicable

WEST COUNTRY

" One of the most completely satisfying evenings we have enjoyed for some time. An impeccable example of the marriage of kitchen, cellar, service and setting "

N H Bagot, Bristol

HUNSTRETE HOUSE

18th century country estate

**Hunstrete,
Chelwood, Near Bath,
Somerset BS39 4NS**

**Telephone 01761 490490
Fax 01761 490732**

E-mail: *hunstrete@bestloved.com*

MANAGING DIRECTOR
R H Gillis

ROOM RATES
Single occupancy	£135 - £145
16 Doubles/Twins	£170 - £205
5 Four-posters	£170 - £275
4 Suites	£265 - £275

Includes full breakfast and VAT

CHARGE/CREDIT CARDS

 • *DC* • *MC* • *VI*

RATINGS & AWARDS
A.A. ★★★ 🌺🌺 77%
*The Good Food Guide -
Restaurant of the Year 2000*

FACILITIES
On site: *Garden, heli-pad, croquet,
tennis, heated outdoor pool
Licensed for weddings
3 meeting rooms/max 80 people*
Nearby: *Golf, fishing, riding,
paint balling, orienteering*

RESTRICTIONS
*Limited facilities for disabled guests
Smoking in bar only
Pets by arrangement*

ATTRACTIONS
*Bath, Wells Cathedral, Longleat,
Glastonbury, Stonehenge, Avebury*

AFFILIATIONS
The Celebrated Hotels Collection

NEAREST
*MAJOR CITY:
Bath - 7 miles/15 mins*

*MAJOR AIRPORT:
London Heathrow - 90 miles/2 hrs
Bristol - 11 miles/30 mins*

*RAILWAY STATION:
Bath - 8 miles/15 mins*

RESERVATIONS
*Toll free in US: 800-322-2403
or 800-93-GRAND*
Quote **Best Loved**

ACCESS CODES
*AMADEUS UI BRSHUN
APOLLO/GALILEO UI 22206
SABRE/ABACUS UI 49148
WORLDSPAN UI 40925*

A top restaurant, a stately house and garden near Roman Bath

The 'Houndstreet' estate has a colourful history dating back to 963AD. The diarist, John Evelyn, referred to 'Old Sir Francis (Popham), he lived like a hog at Hownstret in Somerset, with a moderate pittance'. Rest assured guests will find some welcome changes.

Hunstrete House was a private home from the mid-18th century and only became an hotel in 1978. In that time, it has established itself as a first rate restaurant and a splendid country house hotel. Although they play the hotel bit down: one is encouraged to treat the place as your own.

Some invitation! The drawing room and library are splendidly furnished with antiques, original paintings and collections of fine porcelain. They look out onto two acres of formal gardens and beyond to the 90-acre park complete with fallow deer and horse paddocks. The dining room opens into the flower-filled courtyard where al fresco dining makes the best of summer.

The 25 princely bedrooms are an exhibition of romantic design; fairytale settings for very special occasions. And part of the joy is the friendly, efficient way the staff care for you.

The grounds will delight and surprise you with the sweeping lawns, intimate bowers, walled garden with its astonishing botanic variety and woodland walks. Once you have experienced the Hunstrete magic, it will be calling you back. Count on it!

LOCATION

From M4/Exit 18 take A46 to Bath. LeaveBath on A4 to Bristol then take A39 to Wells and Weston. Hunstrete is 5 miles on right.

❝ As always the food was superb. The staff are always so friendly and courteous, and the rooms are so attractive and spotlessly clean ❞

Sarah Flood, Bath

George IV mansion | THE IDLE ROCKS HOTEL

Harbourside, St Mawes, Cornwall TR2 5AN

Telephone 01326 270771 Fax 01326 270062

E-mail: *idlerocks@bestloved.com*

OWNERS
Keith and Ann Richardson

GENERAL MANAGER
Yvonne Scott

ROOM RATES
2 Singles	£63 - £89
26 Doubles/Twins	£89 - £125
4 Four-posters	£73 - £94
1 Suite	£89 - £125

Includes full breakfast, dinner and VAT

CHARGE/CREDIT CARDS

 • *MC* • *VI*

RATINGS & AWARDS
R.A.C. Blue Ribbon ★★★ *Dining Award 2*
A.A. ★★★ ✿✿ 77%
A.A. Romantic Hotel

FACILITIES
On site: *Garden, sea-view terrace*
Nearby: *Tennis, fishing, riding, yachting*

RESTRICTIONS
Limited facilities for disabled guests
No children under 10 yrs allowed in dining room after 7 pm
Pets by arrangement

ATTRACTIONS
The Eden Project, Trelissick Gardens, Heligan Gardens, St Mawes Castle, Lanhydrock House, Trebah Gardens, St Michaels Mount, National Maritime Museum

AFFILIATIONS
The Richardson Group

NEAREST
MAJOR CITY:
Truro - 20 miles/40 mins

MAJOR AIRPORT:
Bristol - 190 miles/3 ½ hrs

RAILWAY STATION:
Truro - 22 miles/45 mins

RESERVATIONS
Toll free in UK: 0800 243020
Quote Best Loved

ACCESS CODES
Not applicable

The Cornish dream, brought to life!

A small idyllic harbour, narrow lanes of fishermen's cottages and green fields sloping to the sea - this is the view from the Idle Rocks, where genuine, personal service and elegantly appointed rooms provide a level of comfort that encourages guests to relax as soon as they arrive. Far from old fashioned, the hotel is being taken into a new era. By Easter, the bar will house a new seafood brasserie style restaurant; the restaurant is soon to have 3 tiers to make the most of the fantastic views, and the terrace extended to have windbreaks and an awning, to prolong the al fresco season. Their six new premier rooms encapsulate this new style, as they are spacious and luxurious with large bathrooms, walk in showers, balconettes and great views!

The food is superb. Breakfast can be traditional with a touch of imagination, or light continental. Dinner is prepared with attention and flair from locally grown Cornish produce, including early season fruit and vegetables, fresh sea-bass and best quality meats and poultry.

The Idle Rocks is on the Roseland Peninsula which is famously picturesque with lovely beaches, breathtaking cliffs, coastal walks, historic castles, pretty villages and a huge range of outdoor activities to enjoy.

LOCATION
M5 to A30 Truro, B3275 to Probus, A3078 to St Mawes. Idle Rocks is first hotel on the left.

WEST COUNTRY

" Wonderful, many thanks "

Elaine Page, Singer

LANGLEY HOUSE HOTEL

16th century country house

Langley, Wiveliscombe, Near Taunton, Somerset TA4 2UF

Telephone 01984 623318 Fax 01984 624573

E-mail: *langley@bestloved.com*

OWNERS
Stuart and Sue Warnock

ROOM RATES
Single occupancy	£95 - £120
4 Doubles/Twins	£120
3 Deluxe Doubles/Twins	£130
1 Four-poster	£140
Includes full breakfast and VAT	

CHARGE/CREDIT CARDS
MC • VI

RATINGS & AWARDS
A.A. ★★ ✿✿
A.A. Top 200 - 02/03
R.A.C. ★★ Dining Award 1

FACILITIES
On site: *Garden, croquet, putting*
1 meeting room/max 30 people
Nearby: *Golf, riding, fishing, shooting*

RESTRICTIONS
No facilities for disabled guests
No children under 10 years
Pets by arrangement

ATTRACTIONS
Exmoor National Park,
Glastonbury Abbey and Tor,
Wells Cathedral,
Knightshayes Gardens,
Dunster Castle,
Hestercombe House & Gardens,
The Quantocks

AFFILIATIONS
Independent

NEAREST
MAJOR CITY:
Exeter - 25 miles/40 mins
Bristol - 63 miles/1 ¼ hrs

MAJOR AIRPORT:
Exeter - 25 miles/40 mins
Bristol - 47 miles/1 hr

RAILWAY STATION:
Taunton - 10 miles/20 mins

RESERVATIONS
Direct with hotel
*Quote **Best Loved***

ACCESS CODES
Not applicable

www.langley.bestloved.com

16th century charm on the edge of the Exmoor National Park

In early spring a 'host of dancing daffodils' surround Langley House Hotel - a 16th century retreat set in four acres of award-winning gardens. Tucked away in the heart of the Brendon Hills, the hotel is both a tranquil hideaway, and the perfect base from which to explore the poetic drama of the adjacent countryside. Exmoor National Park is a vast expanse of protected moorland that is home to deer, ponies and a plethora of habitat-specific wildlife and fauna. Bubbling brooks and secluded pools eventually run out to sea, and the moor continues right to the edge of the cliffs as it meets the Bristol Channel. Somerset also boasts some of England's most ancient and mysterious landmarks, including Glastonbury Tor, and in nearby Taunton local attractions include Hestercombe Gardens and Orchard Wyndham.

At Langley House, inside is as good as out: the eight bedrooms are elegant and individual, with garden views and fresh flowers all adding to the ambience - one reason, perhaps, why the hotel has won the Wedgwood Interior Design Award. Official recognition doesn't stop there: the beamed restaurant has two AA rosettes for its modern English cuisine as cooked by owner Sue Warnock. The hotel is also now recognised by the A.A. as one of the country's top 200.

LOCATION

Exit M5 at Junction 25 and take B3227 to Wiveliscombe. From the town centre follow the signs for Langley Marsh and the hotel is ½ mile along this road.

" In a lifetime of travel, I do not remember more beautiful surroundings or more gracious treatment "

Cordelia May, Pennsylvania

● Map p.472
ref: D4

17th century manor house

LEWTRENCHARD MANOR

**Lewdown,
Near Okehampton,
Devon EX20 4PN**

**Telephone 01566 783256
Fax 01566 783332**

E-mail: *lewtrenchard@bestloved.com*

OWNERS
James and Sue Murray

ROOM RATES
2 Doubles	£130
3 Superior twins	£180
2 Four-posters	£180
2 Suites	£195

Includes full breakfast and VAT

CHARGE/CREDIT CARDS

 ● *DC* ● *MC* ● *VI*

RATINGS & AWARDS
A.A. ★★★ ❀❀
A.A. Top 200 - 02/03

FACILITIES
On site: *Garden, heli-pad, fishing, croquet
Licensed for weddings
2 meeting rooms/max 100 people*
Nearby: *Riding*

RESTRICTIONS
*Limited facilities for disabled guests
Children under 8 years by arrangement
No pets in public rooms*

ATTRACTIONS
*Dartmoor National Park, Eden Project,
Cotehele House, Devon & Cornwall coast,
Buckland Abbey, RHS Rosemoor Gardens,
Lydford Gorge*

AFFILIATIONS
Pride of Britain

NEAREST
*MAJOR CITY:
Exeter/Plymouth - 30 miles/45 mins*

*MAJOR AIRPORT:
Exeter/Plymouth - 30 miles/45 mins
London Heathrow - 195 miles/3 ½ hrs*

*RAILWAY STATION:
Exeter/Plymouth - 30 miles/45 mins*

RESERVATIONS
Toll free in US: 800-98-PRIDE
Quote **Best Loved**

ACCESS CODES
Not applicable

Grandeur and good living in a Jacobean manor

Built by the Monk family, on the site of an earlier house, this Jacobean manor was embellished by the Victorian hymn writer Sabine Baring Gould. There are granite mullion windows with 19th century stained glass and high ceilings with decorative plasterwork set off by rich oak panelling. Bedrooms, some with four-posters, are tastefully decorated and the views are of formal and informal gardens.

The grand oak staircase descends from the long gallery to the imposing entrance hall that gleams with brass. In the panelled lounge, you may welll find the proprietors, James and Sue Murray who love to chat to guests. There are log fires and fresh flowers everywhere. In the dining room, with its crisp white linen, you can enjoy classic English cooking with modern interpretations.

The Murrays offer clay pigeon shooting, fishing and croquet in the grounds and there are riding, golf and tennis facilities nearby. Guests can be met at both Exeter and Plymouth stations and airports.

Lewtrenchard Manor is well placed for National Trust properties, Dartmoor and the Devon or Cornish coasts.

LOCATION

*A30 (Okehampton - Bodmin) from Exeter.
After 25 miles, road to Tavistock/Plymouth.
Follow signs to Lewdown and then Lewtrenchard.
Hotel is signposted.*

WEST COUNTRY

● *Map p.472*
ref: C5

THE LUGGER HOTEL

17th century seaside inn

Portloe, Near Truro, Cornwall TR2 5RD

Telephone 01872 501322
Fax 01872 501691

E-mail: *lugger@bestloved.com*

OWNERS
Sheryl and Richard Young

RATES PER PERSON
20 Doubles/Twins	£125
1 Junior suite	£140

Includes full breakfast, dinner and VAT

CHARGE/CREDIT CARDS

 • *DC* • *JCB* • *MC* • *VI*

RATINGS & AWARDS
R.A.C. Blue Ribbon ★★★ *Dining Award 2*

FACILITIES
On site: *Terrace*
Nearby: *Riding, tennis, bowls, cliff walks*

RESTRICTIONS
No facilities for disabled guests
No children under 12 years
No pets
Closed Dec - Feb

ATTRACTIONS
St Just in Roseland,
St Mawes Castle,
Lands' End, Penzance,
Pendennis Castle,
Trelissick Gardens,
Eden Project

AFFILIATIONS
Preston's Global Hotels

NEAREST
MAJOR CITY:
Truro - 12 miles/25 mins

MAJOR AIRPORT:
Newquay - 20 miles/35 mins
London Heathrow - 220 miles/5 hrs

RAILWAY STATION:
Truro - 12 miles/25 mins

RESERVATIONS
Toll free in US: 800-544-9993
*Quote **Best Loved***

ACCESS CODES
Not applicable

Simplistic perfection and all the romance imaginable

The Lugger is an original 17th century smugglers inn protected from the often wild Atlantic by its setting in a perfectly protected Cornish harbour. Evocative of scenes from Du Maurier's Jamaica Inn and Stevenson's Treasure Island there's no doubt that it's one of most romantic hotels ever.

Richard and Sheryl Young bought The Lugger just over a year ago and have since completed a total refurbishment. It now firmly belongs to the new 'era' of hotel where the essence of the historical property is maintained, but then enhanced by an interior that is luxurious, spacious and stylish, and offers all the up-to-the-minute facilities expected by today's sophisticated guest. In keeping with the current Cornish 'revolution' its classical cuisine makes the very best of the regional produce, particularly the seafood.

For those interested in local traditions, lobster and crab potting are still a part of Portloe life. It is also close to St Mawes and the stunning beaches at Pendower and Carne. There are endless other attractions on the Roseland peninsula as well, of course, as The Eden Project and Lost Gardens of Heligan being nearby.

A place that's hard to do justice to in just 200 words, but one that could be everyone's favourite!

LOCATION
Turn off A390 St Austell to Truro road on to B3287 to Tregony. Then take A3078 (St Mawes road) and after two miles, fork left for Veryan and Portloe, turning left at T-junction for Portloe.

" Great food, great service, great find! "

Nicholas Granger, London

18th century mill

MILL END HOTEL

Mill End is quintessentially English - and proud of it

Think cream teas and cricket, chintz and homemade jam, log fires in winter and the lazy buzz of bumblebees in summer and you will have conjured up an image of an almost forgotten Britain, which we are happy to report is alive and well at Mill End. The term 'country house hotel' does not do justice to this delectable time capsule housed in an 18th-century former flour mill on the River Teign. The experience is far more cosy and personal, rather like staying with a favourite, rather old-fashioned and slightly eccentric branch of the family.

Mill End has been an hotel since 1929, but has preserved all manner of nooks and crannies where guests can hole up with a good book and relax. Upstairs bedrooms have lovely views, while downstairs rooms enjoy private stone-flagged patios. The fine award winning cuisine in the restaurant is augmented by an impressive cheese board laden with local specialities and regular guests rave about the dangerously tempting desserts.

There are plenty of ways to work off the calories around and about. Hiking in the Dartmoor National Park, local walks, pony trekking and golf are easily arranged. Mill End also offers private salmon and trout fishing. Local attractions include the pretty village of Chagford, and Castle Drogo, a Sir Edwin Lutyens-designed National Trust property. The north and south Devon coasts are also within striking distance.

LOCATION

Located on the A382 which is just off the A30, Exeter to Okehampton road, at Whiddon Down. The hotel is not in Chagford village so do not turn into Chagford from A382.

Sandy Park, Chagford,
Newton Abbot,
Devon TQ13 8JN

**Telephone 01647 432282
Fax 01647 433106**

E-mail: *millend@bestloved.com*

OWNER
Keith Green

ROOM RATES
13 Doubles/Twins	£80 - £120
1 Family room	£100 - £150
1 Suite	£140 - £160

Includes full breakfast and VAT

CHARGE/CREDIT CARDS

 ● *JCB* ● *MC* ● *VI*

RATINGS & AWARDS
A.A. ★★★ ❀❀ 74%

FACILITIES
On site: *Garden, fishing, croquet
3 meeting rooms/max 40 people*
Nearby: *Golf, riding, fishing*

RESTRICTIONS
*No facilities for disabled guests
Closed 3 weeks in Jan*

ATTRACTIONS
*Dartmoor National Park,
Rosemoor RHS Gardens,
Drogo Castle, Teign Gorge,
Exeter Cathedral*

AFFILIATIONS
Independent

NEAREST
*MAJOR CITY:
Exeter - 20 miles/35 mins*

*MAJOR AIRPORT:
Exeter - 25 miles/50 mins*

*RAILWAY STATION:
Exeter - 20 miles/35 mins*

RESERVATIONS
Direct with hotel
Quote **Best Loved**

ACCESS CODES
Not applicable

WEST COUNTRY

" There is no greater luxury than to feel at home "

Chris Markiewicz, Barnet

THE MOUNT SOMERSET

Regency country house

**Henlade, Taunton,
Somerset TA3 5NB**

**Telephone 01823 442500
Fax 01823 442900**

E-mail: *somerset@bestloved.com*

OWNER
Countess von Essen

GENERAL MANAGER
Barbara Loadwick

ROOM RATES
Single occupancy	£95
16 Doubles/Twins	£135
5 Suites	£185
2 Four-poster suites	£200

*Includes morning tea/coffee,
newspaper and VAT*

CHARGE/CREDIT CARDS

 • DC • JCB • MC • VI

RATINGS & AWARDS
R.A.C. ★★★ *Dining Award 3*
A.A. ★★★ ❀❀ *72%*

FACILITIES
On site: *Garden, heli-pad, croquet
3 meeting rooms/max 60 people*
Nearby: *Riding, fishing, tennis,
health & fitness club*

RESTRICTIONS
Limited facilities for disabled guests

ATTRACTIONS
*Somerset County Cricket Ground,
Cheddar Gorge, Bath, Wells Cathedral,
Exmoor and Dartmoor, Stonehenge,
Taunton Racecourse*

AFFILIATIONS
*Preston's Global Hotels
von Essen hotels - A Private Collection*

NEAREST
*MAJOR CITY:
Taunton - 2 miles/10 mins
Exeter - 30 miles/30 mins*

*MAJOR AIRPORT:
Bristol - 40 miles/45 mins
London Heathrow - 120 miles/2 hrs*

*RAILWAY STATION:
Taunton - 2 miles/10 mins*

RESERVATIONS
Toll free in US: 800-544-9993
Quote **Best Loved**

ACCESS CODES
Not applicable

WEST COUNTRY

Arrive as a guest -
leave as a friend

High on the slopes of the Blackdown Hills, stands The Mount Somerset. It was built in 1805 by an Italian architect and much of its original plasterwork has been preserved to blend with the decor, antiques and lavish furnishings giving a feeling of maturity, elegance and great character. It is very much more a home than an hotel and every encouragement is given to make you feel at ease.

Both the dining room and garden room, with its French doors opening onto a sunny terrace, create the perfect setting for some grand repast. Inspired dishes make the most of local produce as well as delicacies from home and abroad. A well-chosen wine list completes a truly delightful experience.

There are 23 sumptuously furnished bedrooms and suites rich in colour co-ordinated fabrics and carpeting, including the Barrington Suite which, with its elaborately carved and decorated Queen-sized bed, is palatial both in size and decor. The luxurious bathrooms, most with double whirlpool spa baths and twin hand basins set in marble are a perfect complement to the bedrooms.

The local area is rich in places to visit and

things to do: sport, wildlife, natural phenomena, museums, churches, stately homes and lots more.

LOCATION
**Exit 25 off M5, A358 towards Chard.
After passing through Henlade, turn right
towards Stoke St Mary. Turn left at T-junction
and hotel's drive is 100 yards on the right.**

" The food there really does rival anything you can get in London and was one of the best meals I ever had "

Anna Pursglave, Journalist, Elle Magazine

• *Map p.472*
ref: E4

Georgian country house

ORESTONE MANOR

A delightful clifftop eyrie - head and shoulders above the English Riviera

Strategically perched on the South Devon cliffs, Orestone Manor commands fabulous views down to the glittering expanse of Tor Bay in one direction, and across the tranquil village of Maidencombe and along the coast to Exmouth in the other. The house dates from 1809, and during 2000 was fully restored and stylishly renovated by owners Peter Morgan and Freiderike Etessami.

Orestone is very much a country house rather than a typical Riviera hotel. With its high ceilings, spacious rooms, Lloyd loom furniture in the palm-fringed conservatory and cosy drawing room warmed in winter by open fires, it has a touch of the Old Colonial but all the creature comforts are up-to-the-minute. Generously-sized bedrooms are each decorated with a special theme and most enjoy wonderful sea views. The dining room serves a contemporary English menu, which makes full use of local seafood, and is widely regarded as one of South Devon's finest.

Orestone is just 300 yards from the South Devon Heritage Coast footpath, which takes in spectacular scenery as well as access to glorious beaches and coves. Dartmoor, Dartmouth and a plethora of National Trust properties, gardens and historic sites all lie within an hour's drive.

LOCATION

Located 4 miles from Torquay on the A379 (formerly B3199) coastal road. The hotel is opposite Brunel Manor on the coastal side.

Rockhouse Lane,
Maidencombe, Torquay,
Devon TQ1 4SX

Telephone 01803 328098
Fax 01803 328336

E-mail: *orestone@bestloved.com*

GENERAL MANAGER
Rosemary Dallas

ASSISTANT MANAGER
Rachael Thompson

ROOM RATES
1 Single £55
11 Doubles/Twins £110 - £180
Includes full breakfast and VAT

CHARGE/CREDIT CARDS

 • MC • VI

RATINGS & AWARDS
R.A.C. Blue Ribbon ★★★ *Dining Award 3*
A.A. ★★★ ❀❀ *77%*

FACILITIES
On site: *Garden, snooker, outdoor pool*
1 meeting room/max 80 people
Nearby: *Golf, fishing, water skiing,*
yachting, tennis, shooting, riding

RESTRICTIONS
Limited facilities for disabled guests
Closed 2 - 23 Jan

ATTRACTIONS
Dartmoor, Powderham Castle,
Berry Pomeroy and Dartmouth Castles,
Cockington Village, coastal walks

AFFILIATIONS
Independent

NEAREST
MAJOR CITY:
Exeter - 20 miles/30 mins

MAJOR AIRPORT:
Exeter - 25 miles/45 mins
London Heathrow - 190 miles/3 ½ hrs

RAILWAY STATION:
Newton Abbot - 6 miles/15 mins

RESERVATIONS
Direct with hotel
Quote **Best Loved**

ACCESS CODES
Not applicable

WEST COUNTRY

● *Map p.472*
ref: E4

❝ From the magnificent views to the friendly and professional service, everything is first class ❞

Mrs Jill Wood, Caversham, Reading

THE OSBORNE HOTEL & LANGTRY RESTAURANT *Seaside hotel*

Hesketh Crescent, Meadfoot, Torquay, Devon TQ1 2LL

Telephone 01803 213311
Fax 01803 296788

E-mail: *osborne@bestloved.com*

OWNER
Ian Davies

ROOM RATES
1 Single	£52 - £102
20 Doubles/Twins	£124 - £168
8 Suites	£154 - £198

Includes full breakfast and VAT

CHARGE/CREDIT CARDS

 • MC • VI

RATINGS & AWARDS
E.T.C. ★★★★ *Silver Award*
R.A.C. ★★★★ *Dining Award 3*
A.A. ★★★★ ❀ *65%*

FACILITIES
On site: *Garden, gym, snooker, tennis, health & beauty, sauna, indoor/outdoor pool, putting lawn 1 meeting room/max 60 people*
Nearby: *Fishing, water skiing, yachting, golf*

RESTRICTIONS
No facilities for disabled guests
No pets

ATTRACTIONS
Dartmoor National Park, Plymouth, Dartmouth, Dartmouth & Totnes Castles, Exeter Cathedral

AFFILIATIONS
Independent

NEAREST
MAJOR CITY:
Exeter - 22 miles/35 mins

MAJOR AIRPORT:
London Heathrow - 190 miles/3 ½ hrs
Exeter - 25 miles/45 mins

RAILWAY STATION:
Torquay - 2 miles/10 mins

FERRY PORT:
Plymouth - 32 miles/45 mins

RESERVATIONS
Direct with hotel
Quote Best Loved

ACCESS CODES
Not applicable

www.osborne.bestloved.com

Elegant Regency grandeur and a panoramic view over Tor Bay

The Osborne Hotel is situated in its own five acres of beautiful gardens at the centre of an elegant Regency terrace, looking straight out across the vivid, wide, blue panorama of Tor Bay. The Osborne has often been described as 'Bath by the Sea'. For grace, grandeur, peace and quiet, it matches that Regency showplace, but nowhere in Bath will you find the golden sands, tropical palm trees and luxuriant vegetation that delight the Osborne's guests.

The public rooms and some of the bedrooms benefit from magnificent views that rank high among Britain's most spectacular land and seascapes. In Langtry's Restaurant Head Chef Peter Roberts consistently produces interesting and imaginative dishes, and the less formal brasserie provides appetising meals and refreshments throughout the day.

Torquay is renowned for its leisure facilities, and the Osborne has a good range of its own. A heated swimming pool, putting green and hard tennis courts are in the grounds. The indoor choices include heated swimming pool, satellite TV, full size snooker table, pool table, gymnasium, plunge

pool and solarium - outdoors too there is generally a good supply of sunshine.

LOCATION

A38 to centre of Torquay. Follow Torbay Road along harbour. Turn left at clock tower and right at traffic lights. Follow road over hill and down to Meadfoot Beach. Hotel is on right.

Best Loved Hotels of the World

" Percy's is a very rare place indeed "

Giles Coren, Saturday Times

285

● *Map p.472*
ref: D4

16th century estate PERCY'S COUNTRY HOTEL & RESTAURANT

Take the organic route to sublime food and tranquillity

Deep in the Devon countryside, one of England's three designated areas of tranquillity, Percy's offers an opportunity to surrender utterly to the peace and beauty of this gentle landscape. Secluded in a 130-acre estate with vistas of Bodmin Moor and rugged Dartmoor this is a place that will appeal hugely to lovers of both the countryside and fine food. Its noise-free, smoke-free and child-free environment is an unrivalled setting for a restorative get-away.

The lovingly restored 16th-century Devon grannary provides exceptional accommodation with bedrooms that are luxurious, spacious, uncluttered and bright. The restaurant provides a chic setting for Tina Bricknell-Webb's 'contemporary country cuisine'. Celebrated as Devon's top female chef, she recently received an unprecedented 9/10 from Giles Coren in the Saturday Times who described Percy's 'as a very rare place indeed'. As you would expect Tina takes great care in choosing her ingredients. Fish is sourced straight from the quayside and much of the organic produce used comes from their own estate, which is of course, maintained by good land practices.

When not being 'gastronomically' spoilt this is a place to don a pair of wellies and explore the estate with its lakes, woodlands, wildflowers and undisturbed wildlife.

LOCATION

Leave A30 at Launceston and take A388 towards Holsworthy. At St Giles-on-the-Heath, turn right to Virginstowe. Follow brown signs and hotel is 2 ½ miles on right. From Okehampton take A3079 for 8.3 miles to Metherell Cross. Turn left and follow road for 6 ½ miles. Percy's is on left.

**Coombeshead Estate,
Virginstow,
Near Okehampton,
Devon EX21 5EA**

**Telephone 01409 211236
Fax 01409 211275**

E-mail: *percy@bestloved.com*

OWNERS
Tony and Tina Bricknell-Webb

ROOM RATES
Single occupancy £90 - £135
8 Doubles/Twins £145 - £195
Includes full breakfast and VAT

CHARGE/CREDIT CARDS

 ● *DC* ● *MC* ● *VI*

RATINGS & AWARDS
E.T.C. ★★ *Gold Award*
R.A.C. Gold Ribbon ★★ *Dining Award 4*
E.T.C. Excellence in England Award 2002
E.T.C. Best Small Hotel of the Year
WHICH? Hotel of the Year 2003

FACILITIES
On site: *Garden, heli-pad, Equestrian Hunter - Trial Circuit*
1 meeting room/max 10 people
Nearby: *Golf, water skiing, yachting, fishing, riding*

RESTRICTIONS
No children
No smoking throughout
Pets by arrangement

ATTRACTIONS
Rosemoor RHS Garden, Eden Project, Dartmoor, Bodmin Moor, Roadford Lake, National Trust Properties

AFFILIATIONS
Independent

NEAREST
MAJOR CITY:
Plymouth - 25 miles/30 mins

MAJOR AIRPORT:
London Heathrow - 250 miles/4 hrs
Exeter - 40 miles/50 mins

RAILWAY STATION:
Plymouth - 25 miles/30 mins
Exeter - 40 miles/50 mins

RESERVATIONS
Direct with hotel
*Quote **Best Loved***

ACCESS CODES
Not applicable

WEST COUNTRY

> *Everyone should experience Prince Hall once in a lifetime, we'll be back soon* "
>
> *Ann, John and Sophie, Wiltshire*

PRINCE HALL HOTEL

Georgian country house

Near Two Bridges, Dartmoor, Devon PL20 6SA

Telephone 01822 890403
Fax 01822 890676

E-mail: *princehall@bestloved.com*

OWNERS
Adam and Carrie Southwell

RATES PER PERSON
Single occupancy	£85
6 Doubles/Twins	£83 - £105
2 Four-posters	£92

Includes full breakfast, dinner, service and VAT

CHARGE/CREDIT CARDS

 • DC • MC • VI

RATINGS & AWARDS
E.T.C. ★★ *Silver Award*
A.A. ★★ ❀❀
A.A. Top 200 - 02/03
West Country Cooking Awards
'Best Hotel Restaurant' 2000

FACILITIES
On site: *Garden, fishing, croquet, clay pigeon shooting, fly fishing*
1 meeting room/max 20 people
Nearby: *Golf, fishing, shooting, riding, walking trails*

RESTRICTIONS
No facilities for disabled guests
No children
Closed mid Dec - mid Feb

ATTRACTIONS
Dartmoor, Buckland Abbey, Merrivale Prehistoric Settlement, Cotehele House, Castle Drogo, Lanhydrock Gardens, Eden Project

AFFILIATIONS
Independent

NEAREST
MAJOR CITY:
Plymouth - 12 miles/30 mins

MAJOR AIRPORT:
London Heathrow - 150 miles/3 hrs

RAILWAY STATION:
Plymouth - 12 miles/30 mins

RESERVATIONS
Direct with hotel
*Quote **Best Loved***

ACCESS CODES
Not applicable

The joy of the great outdoors combined with conviviality and good food

What was a former stable and hunting lodge of the Duke of Cornwall (aka The Prince of Wales) Prince Hall, hence the name, is today an elegantly and attractively furnished country house hotel. A perennial favourite of those seeking a few days rest and relaxation in magnificent Dartmoor, Prince Hall combines peace and quiet with fresh air, stunning scenery, comfort, good food and unfussy hospitality.

You will find no nicer nor more easy-going hosts than Adam and Carrie Southwell who bought Prince Hall in 1995. Their insistence on everyone having a good time is evident in the relaxed and friendly atmosphere where their commitment and caring approach play an important part.

If you enjoy outdoor activities look no further. Once you deposit your car you need not think about it until you leave. From walking and shooting, to fishing, riding and mountain biking Dartmoor is the perfect setting for working up a hearty appetite. Fortunately, Adam obliges with creative menus reflecting his passion for Dartmoor and West Country produce. An ample wine list rounds out what is, no doubt, a truly memorable off-the-beaten-track experience.

LOCATION
From the M5, take the A38 towards Plymouth, then the B3357 towards Princetown. The hotel is 10 miles further on, on the left, a mile before Two Bridges Junction.

❝ *Our stay at the Queensberry ranks as our most memorable hotel stay in England* ❞

Heather Cameron, New York

● *Map p.472*
ref: F2

Regency house — QUEENSBERRY HOTEL

An architecturally acclaimed house in the Roman city of Bath

The Queensberry - luxurious, decorative and intimate - a few minutes' walk from the Roman Baths but itself in the heart of Georgian Bath. Built by John Wood of Royal Crescent fame, for the Marquis of Queensberry in 1772, the house retains its splendid period plasterwork and fireplaces, all now complemented by Penny Ross's interiors. There is a delightful courtyard garden, drawing room and cocktail bar.

The focal point of the hotel is The Olive Tree Restaurant which Patron Stephen Ross describes as a contemporary restaurant - informal, modestly priced, with English cooking that combines excellent local produce with the robust flavours of the Mediterranean.

The Queensberry could not be better placed for visiting the highlights of Bath; the Roman Baths, Theatre Royal, Assembly Rooms and Royal Crescent are all close by. A meander downhill takes you past the antiques markets, the best shops outside London and on to Bath Abbey. The famous spa waters are there to be tested.

LOCATION

Exit 18/M4, A46 to Bath. Turn right at T-junction, right at mini-roundabout to next lights, sharp right at Lansdown Road, 2nd left into Bennet Street and Russell Street is 1st right.

Russel Street, Bath,
Somerset BA1 2QF

Telephone 01225 447928
Fax 01225 446065

E-mail: *queensberry@bestloved.com*

OWNERS
Stephen and Penny Ross

ROOM RATES
Single occupancy	*£100 - £145*
29 Doubles	*£120 - £225*
Includes continental breakfast and VAT

CHARGE/CREDIT CARDS

 ● *MC* ● *VI*

RATINGS & AWARDS
E.T.C. ★★★ *Gold Award*
R.A.C. Gold Ribbon ★★★ *Dining Award 3*
A.A. ★★★ 🌸🌸
A.A. Top 200 - 02/03

FACILITIES
On site: *Courtyard garden*
1 meeting room/max 40 people
Nearby: *Golf, riding, leisure centre*

RESTRICTIONS
Limited facilities for disabled guests
No pets
Closed 22 - 27 Dec

ATTRACTIONS
Bath Abbey , Roman Baths,
Stonehenge, Wells, Longleat,
Stourhead Gardens,
Museum of Costume

AFFILIATIONS
Preston's Global Hotels

NEAREST
MAJOR CITY:
Bath

MAJOR AIRPORT:
London Heathrow - 90 miles/1 ¾ hrs
Bristol - 15 miles/30 mins

RAILWAY STATION:
Bath Spa - 1 mile/5 mins

RESERVATIONS
Toll free in US: 800-544-9993
*Quote **Best Loved***

ACCESS CODES
Not applicable

HOTEL RIVIERA

Georgian seaside hotel

The Esplanade, Sidmouth, Devon EX10 8AY

Telephone 01395 515201
Fax 01395 577775

E-mail: *riviera@bestloved.com*

OWNER
Peter S Wharton

RATES PER PERSON
7 Singles	£95 - £125
18 Doubles/Twins	£85 - £115
2 Suites	£115 - £125

*Includes full breakfast,
7-course dinner and VAT*

CHARGE/CREDIT CARDS

 • *DC* • *MC* • *VI*

RATINGS & AWARDS
E.T.C. ★★★★ *Gold Award*
R.A.C. *Blue Ribbon* ★★★★ *Dining Award 3*
A.A. ★★★★ ❀ *72%*
A.A. Courtesy and Care Award
WHICH? Hotel Guide 'Hotel of the Year 1999'

FACILITIES
On site: *Patio*
1 meeting room/max 120 people
Nearby: *Golf, riding, fishing, tennis,
croquet, game shooting*

RESTRICTIONS
Pets at management's discretion

ATTRACTIONS
*Killerton House,
Exeter Cathedral,
Bicton Park and Gardens,
Dartmoor and Exmoor*

AFFILIATIONS
Independent

NEAREST
MAJOR CITY:
Exeter - 13 miles/30 mins
London - 165 miles/3 ½ hrs

MAJOR AIRPORT:
London Heathrow - 153 miles/3 ½ hrs
Exeter - 10 miles/30 mins

RAILWAY STATION:
Exeter - 13 miles/30 mins

RESERVATIONS
Direct with hotel
*Quote **Best Loved***

ACCESS CODES
Not applicable

WEST COUNTRY

The charm of a unique hotel set in an 18th century seaside resort

Is there any finer place in Devon to sit and watch the world go by than the terrace at the Hotel Riviera, on Sidmouth's famous Georgian esplanade? With the beach a stone's throw across the broad promenade, here is the perfect place to drink coffee, take tea or sip a sundowner. Welcome to the Which? Hotel Guide Hotel of the Year, 1999 - and one of the few hotels in Britain with the coveted Courtesy and Care award from the Automobile Association. Little wonder then that Peter Wharton's Hotel Riviera, with its fine, Regency façade and bow fronted windows, handsome public rooms and beautifully appointed en suite bedrooms - many with sea views - is arguably one of the most comfortable and certainly the most welcoming in this ancient and beautiful South West corner of England. Perfectly located in the town which England's Poet Laureate and lover of architecture, Sir John Betjeman, called his favourite holiday place, the Riviera enjoys four-star categories of both the AA and the RAC. Here is superb cuisine, prepared by Swiss and French trained chefs, a fine cellar and elegant dining in a handsome salon overlooking Lyme Bay. Close by are gardens, coastal walks, golf, bowling, croquet,

putting, tennis, fishing, sailing and riding, whilst the cathedral city of Exeter is nearby and everywhere around, lush countryside and stunning coastline to explore.

LOCATION

Sidmouth is 13 miles from M5, Exit 30 (then follow A3052).

" In 1492 Columbus discovered America, in 1992 my husband and I discovered the Isles of Scilly "

Denise & Frank Lucibello Paramus, New Jersey

Island hotel   ST MARTIN'S ON THE ISLE

Everything on St Martin's is unspoilt - except the guests!

St Martin's is one of the Isles of Scilly, just two miles long and half a mile wide, pitched into the Atlantic 28 miles off Lands End. Ocean rollers and the warming Gulf Stream have created one of the loveliest settings you will find in this book. To get to St Martin's on the Isle, you arrive at the hotel's private quay by launch from the main island, St Mary's. It is like stepping back in time; no noise but the sea and the gulls, no pollution and none of the leftovers of tourism. Marvellous.

You may feel moved to come for the rare beauty of the place. But there is another siren song: the hotel has one of the best restaurants in the islands and possibly one of the finest views you could wish for. The speciality is seafood (of course) but the crustacia are divine. The Tean Restaurant and the Round Island Bar are the focus of the island's social life. The rooms, named after local legends, are more than worthy of their three stars, very comfortable and prettily furnished.

On this secluded idyll you will find some of the most wonderful wildlife including Atlantic seals and an abundance of bird-life. The hotel is also a perfect base for fishing, snorkelling - or simply swimming. Alternatively, you can visit the Botanical Gardens of Tresco or . . ., the list just goes on and on.

LOCATION

On the island of St Martin, one of the Isles of Scilly.

The Island of St Martin, Isles of Scilly, Cornwall TR25 0QW

Telephone 01720 422092
Fax 01720 422298

E-mail: *stmartin@bestloved.com*

OWNERS
Peter and Penny Sykes

GENERAL MANAGER
Keith Bradford

RATES PER PERSON
Single occupancy	*£115 - £165*
28 Doubles/Twins	*£105 - £180*
2 Suites	*£160 - £205*
Includes full breakfast, dinner and VAT	

CHARGE/CREDIT CARDS

 • DC • MC • VI

RATINGS & AWARDS
R.A.C. Gold Ribbon ★★★ Dining Award 4
A.A. ★★★ ❀❀❀
A.A. Top 200 - 02/03

FACILITIES
On site: *Garden, tennis, indoor pool, private beach, snooker, sailing, clay pigeon shooting*
3 meeting rooms/max 60 people
Nearby: *Golf, riding*

RESTRICTIONS
No pets
Closed Nov - Mar

ATTRACTIONS
Naturalist's Paradise, Botanical gardens, uninhabited islands and beaches, bird watching, Tresco Abbey Gardens

AFFILIATIONS
Pride of Britain

NEAREST
MAJOR CITY:
Penzance - 40 miles/2 ½ hrs (ferry)
(20 mins by helicopter)

MAJOR AIRPORT:
London Heathrow - 320 miles/2 hrs
(by air via Newquay or Plymouth)

RAILWAY STATION:
Penzance - 40 miles/2 ½ hrs (ferry)
(20 mins by helicopter)

RESERVATIONS
Toll free in US: 800-98-PRIDE
*Quote **Best Loved***

ACCESS CODES
Not applicable

WEST COUNTRY

• Map p.472
ref: E4

" *An oasis of calm in the heart of the city* "

Mr Mitchell, London

ST OLAVES HOTEL

Georgian town house

Mary Arches Street, Exeter, Devon EX4 3AZ

Telephone 01392 217736
Fax 01392 413054

E-mail: *stolaves@bestloved.com*

OWNERS
Sebastian and Philippa Hughes

ROOM RATES
1 Single	£95 - £115
12 Doubles/Twins	£95 - £115
2 Suites	£125 - £145

Includes continental breakfast and VAT

CHARGE/CREDIT CARDS

 • *MC* • *VI*

RATINGS & AWARDS
E.T.C. ★★★ *Silver Award*
A.A. ★★★ ❀❀ *73%*

FACILITIES
On site: *Secluded walled gardens, private car park*
Licensed for weddings
3 meeting rooms/max 80 people
Nearby: *Golf, leisure centre*

RESTRICTIONS
No facilities for disabled guests
No pets in public rooms

ATTRACTIONS
Exeter Cathedral, Roman Walls, Royal Albert Museum, Theatre, Exe Estuary, Exeter Racecourse, Exeter Quay

AFFILIATIONS
Preston's Global Hotels

NEAREST
MAJOR CITY:
Exeter

MAJOR AIRPORT:
Exeter - 7 miles/12 mins
London Heathrow - 180 miles/3 hrs

RAILWAY STATION:
Exeter - 1 mile/5 mins

RESERVATIONS
Toll free in US: 800-544-9993
Quote **Best Loved**

ACCESS CODES
Not applicable

WEST COUNTRY

A stylish town house hotel within the sound of cathedral bells

Just 400 yards from Exeter Cathedral, this lovely Georgian property boasts a private walled garden right in the heart of the city as well as a long-standing reputation for its welcoming home-from-home atmosphere and fine dining. New owners, Sebastian and Philippa Hughes, who also run the delectable Holne Chase Country House Hotel in the wilds of Dartmoor (see page 273), have carried out a complete refurbishment, creating a new dining room, drawing room and bar whilst carefully preserving the elegant period style of the building. The Hughes' love of the English countryside and traditional pursuits can be seen in the sporting prints decorating the drawing room, and upstairs they have introduced a real breath of country air in the fresh and prettily decorated bedrooms which now include two spacious suites.

St Olaves is a handy touring base for the South Devon coastline, which leads down from the mouth of the River Exe to the seaside towns and beaches of the English Riviera. If you like your scenery rugged, head inland for the windswept beauty of Dartmoor National Park; if you prefer nature tamed, plan a trip to the Killerton or Coleton Fishacre National Trust gardens.

LOCATION
From Exeter city centre follow signs to 'Mary Arches P'. Hotel entrance is directly opposite.

« A statley home with elegance yet a most comfortable country house »

J Taylor, Cricket St. Thomas

Palladian mansion

STON EASTON PARK

Grand in style
and effervescent in spirit

One of Britain's most glorious Palladian mansions, Ston Easton Park epitomises the very essence of the aristocratic English country house set in grounds created by the 18th century landscape supremo, Humphry Repton.

Ston Easton is at once ineffably elegant and stately, yet surprisingly human in scale. A private home until recently, many of its furnishings, paintings and objets d'art have been amassed over the years and are intrinsic to the overall effect. Opulent stucco decorations and trompe-l'oeil murals are highlights of the magnificent Saloon, and Regency mahogany furnishings can be found in the Library and Yellow Dining Room. The bedrooms are delicate and pretty with fine antique beds and garden views. For guests wanting utter privacy, the 17th century Gardener's Cottage is an idyllic retreat on the wooded banks of the River Norr.

Ston Easton's atmosphere mirrors the grand yet human feel of the house. On the one hand, impeccably trained staff squeeze the lemon and stir the sugar into your tea in the manner of an old school butler. On the other, the General Manager and Sorrel the friendly spaniel, materialise, as if by magic, to greet guests as they pull into the drive, adding that elusive personal touch which gives Ston Easton such a special sense of ease. Pilots should note the following heli-pad grid reference: OS 183 ST 624 540 N51 16.9 W002 32.5.

LOCATION

Exit M4 onto M32 signed Bristol.
Then follow signs for A37 Wells/Shepton.
Continue on A37 and the hotel is on this road
on the left hand side, and is well signed.

Ston Easton, Near Bath,
Somerset BA3 4DF
Telephone 01761 241631
Fax 01761 241377
E-mail: *stoneaston@bestloved.com*

OWNER
Countess von Essen

GENERAL MANAGER
Andrew Chantrell

ROOM RATES
12 Doubles/Twins	£185
3 Superior Doubles/Twins	£245
6 Four-posters	£245
3 Suites	£345

Includes early morning tea,
newspaper and VAT

CHARGE/CREDIT CARDS

 • DC • MC • VI

RATINGS & AWARDS
R.A.C. Gold Ribbon ★★★★ Dining Award 3
A.A. ★★★★ ❀❀ Top 200 - 02/03

FACILITIES
On site: *Garden, heli-pad, fishing,*
croquet, golf, tennis, ballooning, laser
shooting, hunting, off-road driving,
falconry displays, billiards
Licensed for weddings
8 meeting rooms/max 150 people
Nearby: *Clay pigeon shooting, riding*

RESTRICTIONS
No facilities for disabled guests
Pets by arrangement

ATTRACTIONS
Bath, Longleat House, Glastonbury,
Wells Cathedral, American Museum,
Stourhead Gardens, Cheddar Gorge,
Wookey Hole Caves, Lacock Abbey

AFFILIATIONS
von Essen hotels - A Private Collection
The Celebrated Hotels Collection
Pride of Britain

NEAREST
MAJOR CITY:
Bath - 15 miles/25 mins

MAJOR AIRPORT:
Bristol - 12 miles/20 mins

RAILWAY STATION:
Bath Spa - 15 miles/25 mins
Castle Cary - 4 miles/10 mins

RESERVATIONS
Toll free in US: 800-322-2403 or
800-98-PRIDE
Quote Best Loved

ACCESS CODES
Not applicable

WEST COUNTRY

● *Map p.472*
ref: C5

TALLAND BAY HOTEL   *Cornish manor house*

**Talland-by-Looe,
Cornwall PL13 2JB**

**Telephone 01503 272667
Fax 01503 272940**

E-mail: *tallandbay@bestloved.com*

OWNERS
George and Mary Granville

GENERAL MANAGER
Maureen Le Page

ROOM RATES
2 Singles	*£50 - £84*
17 Doubles/Twins	*£100 - £168*
2 Four-posters	*£100 - £168*

*Includes full breakfast,
afternoon tea and VAT*

CHARGE/CREDIT CARDS

MC • VI

RATINGS & AWARDS
A.A. ★★★ ❀❀ *77%*

FACILITIES
On site: *Garden, croquet, putting
green, outdoor pool*
Nearby: *Golf, riding, sailing, boating,
sea fishing, tennis*

RESTRICTIONS
*No facilities for disabled guests
Pets by arrangement*

ATTRACTIONS
*The Eden Project, Lanhydrock Gardens,
St Catherine's Castle, Bodmin Moor,
Fowey, St Michael's Mount,
Lost Gardens of Heligan*

AFFILIATIONS
Independent

NEAREST
*MAJOR CITY:
Plymouth - 25 miles/30 mins*

*MAJOR AIRPORT:
Plymouth - 25 miles/30 mins*

*RAILWAY STATION:
Liskeard - 10 miles/15 mins*

RESERVATIONS
*Direct with hotel
Quote* **Best Loved**

ACCESS CODES
Not applicable

WEST COUNTRY

A rare example of a fine country house hotel by the sea

Hidden down a sunken lane that leads to the sea, the Talland Bay Hotel is a real charmer. The stylishly converted old manor, parts of which date back to the 16th century, is nestled in two acres of glorious gardens and enjoys splendid views of the twin headlands flanking its namesake bay.

Comfort and quiet are two key components in Talland Bay's unpretentious and relaxing atmosphere. The Library and sitting room open onto a pool terrace, where palm trees add a distinctly Mediterranean air in summer. The bright and airy bedrooms are decorated with pretty chintzes, and nine have sea views. Two cottages in the walled garden offer an appealing alternative.

Cornwall's bracing sea air is bound to build up an appetite and menus display a healthy bias in favour of traditional local ingredients. Fresh crab and lobster from the fish markets of Looe, and Cornish lamb and West Country cheeses are staples.

Local explorations range from coastal walks to visits to the famous Lost Gardens of Heligan and the spectacular biomes of the Eden Project. Sporting types can try their hand at golf, riding, sailing, and sea fishing.

LOCATION

***From Plymouth take the A38 south.
Then the B3251 to Looe. Head towards
Polperro for 2 miles. Left at crossroads.***

" Completely relaxed, wholly pampered and now totally addicted "

George Turner III, Washington

Map p.472
ref: D5

Beachside resort

TIDES REACH HOTEL

An ideal holiday location for total relaxation

Elegant and luxuriously appointed the Tides Reach Hotel has been under the personal supervision of the owners, Mr and Mrs Roy Edwards, for more than 30 years. They have built up an enviable reputation for cuisine and standards of service complementing the hotel's situation which must be one of the most naturally beautiful in the British Isles.

Set in a commanding position, facing south in the tree-fringed sandy cove of South Sands, it is the ideal location for a short break or relaxing holiday. The hotel stands just inside the mouth of the outstandingly scenic Salcombe Estuary.

At Tides Reach, one of the most important ingredients is the service. Highly trained staff, carefully chosen for their caring and courteous service, are dedicated to making your stay a pleasant and memorable one. In the Garden Room Restaurant the connoisseur of fine food and wine will find great satisfaction. Fresh

fish and carefully selected local produce are expertly prepared to uphold the hotel's international reputation.

LOCATION

Leave A38 at Totnes, then follow A381 to Kingsbridge and thereafter to Salcombe as signposted.

South Sands, Salcombe, Devon TQ8 8LJ

**Telephone 01548 843466
Fax 01548 843954**

E-mail: *tidesreach@bestloved.com*

OWNER
Roy Edwards

MANAGER
John Edwards

RATES PER PERSON
2 Singles	£71 - £120
28 Doubles/Twins	£60 - £140
2 Suites	£75 - £125
3 Family suites	£65 - £150

Includes full breakfast, dinner and VAT

CHARGE/CREDIT CARDS

 • *DC* • *MC* • *VI*

RATINGS & AWARDS
E.T.C. ★★★ *Silver Award*
R.A.C. ★★★ *Dining Award 2*
A.A. ★★★ ✿ *75%*

FACILITIES
On site: *Garden, indoor pool, health & beauty, squash, snooker, fitness centre, sauna, windsurfing, sailing, water skiing*
Nearby: *Golf, riding, beaches*

RESTRICTIONS
*No facilities for disabled guests
No children under 8 years
Closed 1 Dec - 14 Feb*

ATTRACTIONS
National Maritime Aquarium, Dartmoor, Dartmouth & Totnes Castles, Plymouth, Overbeck Museum, South Devon coast

AFFILIATIONS
Independent

NEAREST
MAJOR CITY:
Plymouth - 24 miles/40 mins

MAJOR AIRPORT:
London Heathrow - 220 miles/4 ½ hrs
Plymouth - 24 miles/40 mins

RAILWAY STATION:
Totnes - 20 miles/30 mins

RESERVATIONS
Direct with hotel
Quote **Best Loved**

ACCESS CODES
Not applicable

WEST COUNTRY

❝ *After leaving you, we went on to stay at another hotel. We paid twice as much and didn't enjoy it half as much. You are the best innkeeper in the UK* **❞**

Name withheld, USA

THE WELL HOUSE | *Victorian country manor*

***St Keyne, Liskeard,
Cornwall PL14 4RN***

Telephone 01579 342001
Fax 01579 343891

E-mail: *wellhouse@bestloved.com*

OWNERS
Nick Wainford and Ione Nurdin

MANAGER
Denise Manning

ROOM RATES
Single occupancy   £75 - £95
9 Doubles/Twins   £100 - £175
Includes full breakfast and VAT

CHARGE/CREDIT CARDS
MC • JCB • VI

RATINGS & AWARDS
A.A. ★★ ❀❀❀
A.A. Top 200 - 02/03
West Country Cookings
'Best Hotel in Cornwall'
Courvoisier's Book of the Best
WHICH? 'Secluded Charm Award 2000'

FACILITIES
On site: *Garden, croquet,
tennis, outdoor pool*
1 meeting room/max 60 people
Nearby: *Golf, riding, fishing*

RESTRICTIONS
No facilities for disabled guests
No children under 8 years at dinner

ATTRACTIONS
*The Eden Project,
Heligan and 70 other gardens,
Restormel Castle, St Michael's Mount,
Cothele, Polperro and Fowey,
Land's End, fishing villages of Looe*

AFFILIATIONS
Independent

NEAREST
MAJOR CITY:
Plymouth - 16 miles/25 mins

MAJOR AIRPORT:
London Heathrow - 220 miles/3 ½ hrs
Plymouth - 16 miles/25 mins

RAILWAY STATION:
Liskeard - 3 miles/5 mins

FERRY PORT:
Plymouth - 18 miles/35 mins

RESERVATIONS
Direct with hotel
*Quote **Best Loved***

ACCESS CODES
Not applicable

Discover Cornwall from this delightful secluded manor

An intimate nine-bedroomed Victorian country manor, The Well House is tucked away down a country lane deep in Cornwall's Looe Valley, just beyond the River Tamar. Its facade, wrapped in rambling wisteria and jasmine trailers, is just one of the hotel's continuous series of delights that include top quality service, modern luxury and impeccable standards of comfort.

The dining room, with its magnificent bay windows and sun terrace overlooking the lawns, has a contemporary style which is echoed in the cooking though the traditions of the area are clearly in evidence. Cornish fish soup and freshly caught sea bass, turbot or lobster, along with wild boar, partridge and local English cheeses are all a feature of the daily changing menu at this internationally acclaimed restaurant.

The hotel is set in four acres of gardens, with an all-weather tennis court, swimming pool and croquet lawn - in a spectacular setting. Excellent fishing, riding and golf can be found nearby and the coastline offers matchless scenery and walking territory.

LOCATION

*From Liskeard, take the B3254 to St Keyne,
3 miles south of Liskeard. Take the left fork by
the church and the hotel is ½ mile from there.*

" A friendly service and relaxing atmosphere. The gardens are peaceful and the warm indoor swimming pool is seductive "

A.A. Inspector

Georgian country house — WIDBROOK GRANGE

**Trowbridge Road,
Bradford-on-Avon, Near Bath,
Wiltshire BA15 1UH**

**Telephone 01225 864750
Fax 01225 862890**

E-mail: *widbrook@bestloved.com*

OWNERS
Peter and Jane Wragg

ROOM RATES
1 Single   £95 - £105
11 Doubles/Twins   £110 - £120
6 Four-posters   £125 - £140
2 Family rooms   £140 - £170
Includes full breakfast and VAT

CHARGE/CREDIT CARDS

 • DC • MC • VI

RATINGS & AWARDS
E.T.C. ◆◆◆◆◆
R.A.C. ◆◆◆◆◆ *Dining Award 1*
A.A. ◆◆◆◆◆ *Premier Collection*
*R.A.C. Sparkling Diamond, Warm Welcome
& Little Gem Awards*

FACILITIES
On site: *Garden, gym, indoor pool
3 meeting rooms/max 50 people*
Nearby: *Golf, horse riding, cycle hire*

RESTRICTIONS
*No pets, guide dogs only
Closed 24 - 30 Dec*

ATTRACTIONS
*Narrow boat hire on the Kennet & Avon,
Bath, Bradford Saxon Church,
Longleat House & Safari Park,
Stonehenge, Wells, Salisbury*

AFFILIATIONS
Independent

NEAREST
MAJOR CITY:
Bath - 8 miles/17 mins

MAJOR AIRPORT:
*London Heathrow - 90 miles/2 hrs
Bristol Airport - 27 miles/50 mins*

RAILWAY STATION:
*Bath Spa - 8 miles/17 mins
Bradford-on-Avon - 1 mile/5mins*

RESERVATIONS
Direct with hotel
Quote **Best Loved**

ACCESS CODES
Not applicable

A homely base from which to explore historic Bath

This elegant 250-year-old Georgian country house hotel and restaurant is also home to resident owners, Jane and Peter Wragg. Its position is a peaceful one surrounded as it is by rolling Wiltshire countryside. The name Widbrook dates back as far as 1279 and relates to the stream that runs through the hotel's 11 acres of lovely gardens.

The Grange itself is impressive and stands in a courtyard surrounded by converted stables and barns which house some of the 20 bedrooms, the heated indoor pool and gymnasium, and the purpose built conference suite - which is quite superb. The award-winning Medlar Tree Restaurant, housed within the main building, serves authentic and imaginative British regional cuisine. One interesting dish that has appeared on the menu in season is the Elizabethan dish of peacock and pomegranate. The overall feeling is one of a warm, homely and comfortable house, enhanced with open log fires burning in the cooler months.

Widbrook Grange is only 17 minutes from the historic city of Bath and just outside the medieval town of Bradford-upon-Avon, near the Kennet and Avon canal. This is a great base to sightsee and explore the countryside, not to mention the local waterways by hired narrow boat.

LOCATION

On A363 Bradford-upon-Avon to Trowbridge Road, one mile from Bradford-upon-Avon centre and 2 miles from Trowbridge.

WEST COUNTRY

THE WINDSOR

Georgian town house

69 Great Pulteney Street, Bath, Somerset BA2 4DL

Telephone 01225 422100
Fax 01225 422550

E-mail: *windsor@bestloved.com*

OWNERS
Cary and Sachiko Bush

ROOM RATES

2 Executive singles	£85 - £115
7 Doubles/Twins	£135 - £175
2 Four-posters	£195
2 Junior suites	£195
1 Suite	£275

Includes full breakfast, tea or coffee on arrival, newspaper, morning tea and VAT

CHARGE/CREDIT CARDS

 • *DC* • *JCB* • *MC* • *VI*

RATINGS & AWARDS
R.A.C. ★★★★ *Dining Award 1*
A.A. ★★★★ ❀ *69% Town House*

FACILITIES
On site: *Restaurant, internet access*
1 meeting room/max 24 people
Nearby: *Golf, swimming pool, leisure centre*

RESTRICTIONS
No facilities for disabled guests
No children under 12 years
No smoking throughout
No pets

ATTRACTIONS
Roman Baths, American Museum, Museum of Costume, Wells, Wells Cathedral, Royal Crescent, Stonehenge, The Assembly Rooms, Bath Abbey

AFFILIATIONS
Independent

NEAREST
MAJOR CITY:
Bath

MAJOR AIRPORT:
Bristol - 15 miles/30 mins
London Heathrow - 90 miles/1 ½ hrs

RAILWAY STATION:
Bath Spa - ½ mile/10 mins

RESERVATIONS
Direct with hotel
Quote Best Loved

ACCESS CODES
Not applicable

Gracious Georgian Bath infused with a touch of the Orient

This grand town house in the historical city of Bath is located on the famous Great Pulteney Street. The street was built by Sir Thomas Baldwin in 1789 who was also involved in the creation of The Pump Room and The Guildhall and who himself lived on the street. Reminiscent of the wide French Boulevards, it remains one of Bath's major attractions, and The Windsor - a wonderful attraction within it.

Spacious, elegant bedrooms are individually named, and antique furnishings and fine English fabrics pervade throughout. The Bathwick Suite is modern in design with stylish lighting and large comfy sofas. All double rooms, such as the Abbey, Laura and Victoria are large, but cosy and traditional with modern bathrooms. The Windsor is certainly ideal for both corporate and leisure guests.

There is, however, something of a surprise - owners Cary and Sachiko Bush have created Bath's first Japanese restaurant, Sakura. Here you can choose from three styles of authentic Japanese food - Shabu Shabu, Sukiyaki or Seafood Nabe. The décor is also traditionally Japanese, and has views out onto a small Japanese garden decorated in bamboo and stone.

An exceptional base from which to explore the many sights and delights of this perfect Georgian city.

LOCATION

From the South and West approach the City on the A36 and follow signs for London and the M4. The hotel is just off Walcot Street on Great Pulteney Street.

WEST COUNTRY

Nearest place to heaven (outside Scotland)

Jim & Christine Riddle, Galashiels, Scotland

Victorian country house WOODLANDS COUNTRY HOUSE HOTEL

Relax and unwind in the shadow of history

This mellow country house hotel nestles at the foot of Brent Knoll, in an extraordinarily peaceful corner of West Somerset. This is the land of Arthurian legend; Glastonbury, mythical burial site of King Arthur and final resting place of the Holy Grail, is nearby, as is the cathedral city of Wells.

Owners Colin and Angie Lapage are the epitome of the perfect hosts - nothing, it seems, is ever too much trouble and you do get the feeling that you are more of a family friend than a guest.

The very comfy bedrooms are mostly furnished in traditional pine and decorated in pretty fabrics. There are many thoughtful touches and the views through the sash windows unfold way into the distance. The restaurant has built up an enthusiastic local following, always a good sign, and thoughtfully created and well prepared dishes are served in the charming Victorian dining room.

With the M5 just 5 minutes away, the hotel is also very popular with business travellers. A challenging team-building course has been set up

within the grounds, as has a secluded 'picnic' corner in a small meadow.

Woodlands really is a place for that rare escape!

LOCATION

Exit the M5 at Junction 22 and then take the A38 north for ½ mile. Turn left following the signs to Brent Knoll.

Hill Lane, Brent Knoll, Somerset TA9 4DF

Telephone 01278 760232
Fax 01278 769090

E-mail: *woodlands@bestloved.com*

OWNERS
Colin and Angie Lapage

ROOM RATES
8 Doubles/Twins	£79 - £90
1 Four-poster	£115
1 Deluxe Bridal Suite	£115

Includes full breakfast and VAT

CHARGE/CREDIT CARDS

 • MC • VI

RATINGS & AWARDS
A.A. ★★ ❀ 72%

FACILITIES
On site: *Garden, outdoor pool, team building activities*
2 meeting rooms/max 90 people
Nearby: *Golf, fishing, water skiing, tennis, shooting, yachting, fitness, riding, para-gliding*

RESTRICTIONS
No facilities for disabled guests

ATTRACTIONS
Cheddar Gorge, Wookey Hole, Wells Cathedral, Glastonbury, Bath, Quantock Hills

AFFILIATIONS
Independent

NEAREST
MAJOR CITY:
Bristol - 33 miles/40 mins

MAJOR AIRPORT:
Bristol - 16 miles/25 mins

RAILWAY STATION:
Highbridge - 3 miles/10 mins

RESERVATIONS
Direct with hotel
Quote **Best Loved**

ACCESS CODES
Not applicable

WEST COUNTRY

Map p.472
ref: D3

YEOLDON HOUSE HOTEL

Country hotel

**Durrant Lane,
Northam, Bideford,
Devon EX39 2RL**

**Telephone 01237 474400
Fax 01237 476618**

E-mail: *yeoldon@bestloved.com*

OWNERS
Brian and Jennifer Steele

ROOM RATES
Single occupancy   £60 - £65
10 Doubles/Twins   £95 - £105
Includes full breakfast and VAT

CHARGE/CREDIT CARDS

 • MC • VI

RATINGS & AWARDS
E.T.C. ★★
A.A. ★★ ✿ 74%

FACILITIES
On site: *Garden*
Nearby: *Golfing, fishing, shooting*

RESTRICTIONS
*No facilities for disabled guests
Smoking in lounge only
Closed 24 - 27 Dec*

ATTRACTIONS
*Tapeley Park Gardens, Lundy Island,
Exmoor, Westward Ho,
Arlington Court,
Combe Martin Wildlife Park*

AFFILIATIONS
Independent

NEAREST
*MAJOR CITY:
Exeter - 45 miles/1 ¼ hrs*

*MAJOR AIRPORT:
Bristol - 110 miles/2 ¼ hrs*

*RAILWAY STATION:
Barnstaple - 10 miles/15 mins*

RESERVATIONS
*Direct with hotel
Quote* **Best Loved**

ACCESS CODES
Not applicable

WEST COUNTRY

A family-run home from home in glorious Devon

A rambling stone family house perched above the River Torridge with lawns leading down towards the water's edge, Yeoldon House has an easy charm that is apparent from the moment you arrive. Brian and Jennifer Steele, with a helping hand from sons Colin and Christopher, welcome visitors with genuine warmth and guests find Yeolodon's casual yet comfortable ambience supremely relaxing. So much so, reports Jennifer, that it is not unusual to find particularly 'at home' guests snoozing on the sofa with their feet up after a delicious three-course dinner!

Brian is in charge of the menu in Soyer's Restaurant. He is an advocate of simple but imaginative cooking using the finest fish, meat and seasonal vegetables available from local producers. Typical dishes might include grilled goat's cheese atop mediterranean vegetables, West Country lamb cutlets with parsnip mash, and homemade marmalade bread and butter pudding. When it is time to retire to bed, there are cosy country style rooms, a romantic four-poster, or a suite with private veranda and seating area.

Northam is ideally placed for day trips to the North Devon beaches and Exmoor. Another entertaining option is a steamer trip to the Lundy Island seabird sanctuary.

LOCATION
*Exit M5 at Junction 27 onto A361 to Barnstaple,
then A39 to Bideford. At Torridge Bridge
roundabout turn onto A386 signed Northam.
Take 3rd turning right and follow left fork.
Hotel is at end of lane.*

SOUTH

Beautiful, impressive houses, with remarkable gardens, set in magnificent country – and not too far from London. Many successful authors have come from, or aspired to, such properties in the South. For some, such as Kipling, his country house, Bateman's in Sussex, was as well as being a quiet place to work, somewhere to entertain people of influence and advance a career. For others such as Gilbert White at Selborne in Hampshire, the comfortable lifestyle and rural surroundings provided a place to study, to research and to write ones findings in peace before spreading them to a wider audience.

Vita Sackville West and her husband bought Sissinghurst in Kent when it was in a ruined state. They established a printing press there, and meanwhile drew up a plan for turning their country home and specifically the garden into a place of great beauty. Intriguingly, while they discussed and planted roses and vines Vita lead a life linked with scandal and notoriety.

Benjamin Disraeli, major political figure of the 19th century was also a literary great. His home at Hugenden, in Buckinghamshire, provided him with a quiet haven, a place to admire the trees and plan to reposition himself via his early novels. All of these works were based to a major part on Disraeli's own life, when he republished them after 1850 he had removed passages that referred to his mental breakdown and others that were defamatory to leading personages of the day.

The combination of the romantic, flowery garden design skills of Vita Sackville West and her husband Harold Nicolson's strict, geometric plans have created the glorious gardens at Sissinghurst .Vita Sackville West wrote and published over 50 books including The Edwardians, believed by many to be her best work. Poet, novelist and journalist, her novel The Edwardians brings that era to life with its meticulous observation.

Eighteenth century writer and naturalist Gilbert White lived almost all his life at The Wakes in Selborne. Fascinated by the dependence of one type of creature on another he wrote a multitude of scholarly letters over his life describing his observations. Gathered together and published some 200 years ago, his 'The Natural History and Antiquities of Selborne' has been continually in print, and is the 4th most published book in the English language.

The annual Victorian Christmas Festival at Rochester in Kent is an event Charles Dickens would have loved. Pretty ladies in bonnets and velvet capes are escorted by gentlemen with beaver hats and 'mutton chop' whiskers. The streets are scented with roasting chestnuts and organ grinders make music for the throng. Eastgate House is the Dickens Centre, with memorabilia to see and readings to hear, in the garden is Dickens's Summer House from Gads' Hill – where he wrote up until his death.

PLACES TO VISIT

The atmosphere inside Rudyard Kipling's beautiful stone house, Bateman's is one of intense calm, of beeswaxed floors, of cool, charming rooms, a place to think – a house of restrained opulence. The gardens are similarly tranquil, wide lawns, places to sit and contemplate, a formal pond. In the garage is a splendid car; Rudyard Kipling enjoyed the wealth he created with his remarkable talent as generations have enjoyed the fruits of his effort.

Christopher Robin's world was inhabited by Tiggers, by bears that loved honey and other delightful, furry creatures that had wills of their own. The setting that AA Milne populated with these memorable characters is Ashdown Forest in Sussex, with small stands of Scots Pines, where Christopher and his friends played hide and seek. The little river where Pooh Sticks is played – an amusement for children of all ages – is very popular – go early or late and your own game can be just as secret as Christopher's.

Hitchcock's film interpretation of John Buchan's classic, The Thirty Nine Steps, doesn't identify the real location of the immortalised steps, but Buchan spent the summer of 1914 recuperating from an illness in a friend's house Broadstairs and based the climax to his book on narrow, steep stairs down to the beach nearby. There are actually 108 steps, but the fictionalised version is shorter. The sandy charms of this pretty town attracted another literary great, and the Dickens Museum here is in 'Bleak House', where the writer finished David Copperfield.

From The Naturalist's Summer Evening Walk by Gilbert White

Each rural sight, each sound, each smell, combine;
The tinkling sheep bell, or the breath of kine;
The new mown hay that scents the swelling breeze,
Or cottage chimney smoking through the trees.

The chilling night dews fall away, retire;
For see, the glowworm lights her amorous fire!

Thus e'er night's veil had half obscur'd the sky,
Th' impatient damsel hung her lamp on high:

True to the signal, by love's meteor led,
Leander hasten'd to his hero's bed.

BOOKS TO READ

▶ Gilbert White by Richard Mabey; an award winning biography about the man whose work has formed a cornerstone of modern ecology.

▶ Portrait of a Marriage by Nigel Nicholson: this is Vita Sackville West's son's account of the unusual, and turbulent relationship between his parents.

▶ PG Wodehouse's books about Jeeves and his house, Blandings – any of them for a comic glimpse at how life was lived in the English Country House.

A special place to buy books:

P & J Wells, College Street, and Winchester. Stockists of Jane Austen Society Publications, and close to her house there. Plus the chance to explore the cathedral and surroundings that inspired Trollope.

LITERARY ATTRACTIONS & FESTIVALS

▶ Henry James, major American Novelist, lived at Lamb House in Rye, where he entertained Rudyard Kipling among other literary contempories. James' connection with Rye is celebrated with an annual lecture at the Rye Festival (www.ryefestival.co.uk).

▶ The Brighton Festival is a feast of present day literary talent in the unique setting of Regency/cosmopolitan Brighton: readings, performances and workshops (www.brighton-festival.org).

▶ Edward Bulwer-Lytten was one of the nineteenth century's most popular novelists. The bicentenary of his birth is celebrated this year at his ancestral home, Knebworth House in Hertfordshire (www.knebworthhouse.com).

THE CULINARY
South

Seasonal larders in the South of England overflow with fruit and preserves. From the geometric perfection of apple and pear orchards in Kent to the meandering, ancient orchards of Dorset, this is an area to revel in ciders and perrys, jams and chutneys and crisp, ripe fruit. Flemish weavers brought hops to Kent in the 15th century, adding the unique 'bite' to ale that has inspired generations of brewers. Hop growing still influences the countryside, 'gardens' of tall poles, linked with a cats' cradles of wires are festooned, in late summer, with the flowing tassels of aromatic hop vines. The New Forest, once the hunting ground of Kings, is still rich with game as are the parks of historic houses such as Penshurst Place in Kent, ancestral home of the Sidney family and Petworth Place in West Sussex where the kitchens contain a copper batterie de cuisine of over 1000 pieces - proof of centuries of good living. Vineyards cover south facing slopes - many offering tastings of red, white or sparkling wines. Artisan smokers fuel their kilns with locally hewn wood and sell at farmers markets and small, speciality shops that, like Aladdin's cave, are full of treasure and well worth finding.

Hartwell House

THE MENU:
Summer Lodge

The Drawing Room at Summer Lodge was designed by Thomas Hardy - a seriously literary claim to fame. The menus are also designed and fulfilled with remarkable talent, locally sourced ingredients are much in evidence, taste and presentation are given equal importance and everything is served perfectly. The following are just some of the dishes offered on the Country Cooking Dinner Menu:-

Starter
Pressed Terrine of Ham Hock served with a Pear Chutney

Home cured Gravadlax with Wild Parsley and Caperberries, Cream Cheese and Chive Dressing

Main Course
Breast of Gressingham Duck served on Braised Fennel with a Saffron Fondant and a Star Anise infused Sauce

Pork Fillet in a Herb and Mustard Crust set on a Ratatouille Tatin with Parisian Potatoes and a Wild Mushroom Cream

Dessert
Chocolate Parfait studded with Griottines of Cherries accompanied by a crisp Mille Feuille

THE SIGNATURE: Head Chef Alan Ford came to Hintlesham Hall via some very famous kitchens including Maxim's in Paris, the Inter-Continental in Sydney and The Dorchester. Hintlesham's renowned herb garden - a summer riot of scent and colour - is as much a product of Alan's enthusiasm as the head gardener's.

A special example amongst his signature dishes is:

Seared supreme of wild seabass, couscous, chickpeas and tomatoes, citrus dressing.

The combination of flavours and textures works beautifully. The charred skin of the seabass contrasts with the bittersweet flavour of the sauce. Served with crisp french beans, baked red onions and roasted tomatoes, the flavour and texture loop is complete.

THE CHEF: Stephen Toward, Head Chef at Langshott Manor, is a true European; his route to this well respected hotel has covered much of the gastronomic Continent. Time spent as Head Chef at a German Michelin starred establishment, owned by a hunting, shooting and fishing Baron, honed wide ranging game skills. On to Italy, furthering a passion for the finest vegetables and fruit, pasta and pulses. Spells at several Relais Chateau establishments in Portugal and France have further influenced his menus at Langshott that offer a contemporary European concept of the finest cuisine. Indulging an enthusiasm for local sourcing has lead Stephen to discover ingredients from the rivers, ponds, fields and woods of the surrounding counties of Surrey, Sussex and Kent - easy access to Covent Garden and Billingsgate completes the story.

Hintlesham Hall

Langshott Manor

THE SURPRISE: The village of Teffont Evias is a 17th century architectural gem In the ownership of the same, conservatively minded, family from 1692, little has outwardly changed since the time of King William and Queen Mary - it may well be the most untouched village in England. In this remarkable setting, surrounded by ancient yew hedges, nestling in the most perfect country garden is Howards House Hotel - with a restaurant that has won innumerable awards for food and service. With the surrounding county of Wiltshire abundantly represented on the menu along with homegrown vegetables and herbs, this is a place to come for superb food, beautifully presented, in an idyllic setting.

THE HISTORY: This is a truly ancient site, a Priory has existed here, on the banks of the River Frome, for some 13 hundred years; King Alfred the Great created great fortifications to protect this precious part of his kingdom. The Abbots Cellar Restaurant at the Priory of Lady St Mary is in a vaulted stone undercroft, the perfect setting to savour 'kiln roasted salmon' or 'sauteed pigeon breast', cooked with expertise, beautifully presented and providing inspiration for a choice of fine wine from a well stocked cellar. Time, and the seasons, pass slowly here in sight of the Purbeck Hills: alfresco lunch on the lawn in summer - lobster, crab and strawberries, or an after dinner moonlight walk over frosted lawns to the silvery river. Peace and plenty.

Editor's Extras

Dane John Gardens in historic Canterbury is the setting for a new British Food and Drink Festival held in September. In the shadow of the old city walls is a bustling market, lots of stalls, live entertainment, a real ale pub and a feast of specialities from all over Britain.

At The Clergy House in Alfriston you'll be told a strange use for sour milk - sealing a chalk floor! This picture postcard village, close to the remarkable Cuckmere Valley, has 'olde worlde' teashops, an intriguing history of smuggling, and the Village Stores - once a Victorian Drapers - is one of those special finds, full of character and edible, local 'goodies'.

The Hamble Valley offers all sorts of visitor attractions from a strawberry fair, to the largest purpose built contemporary arts and craft gallery in Britian. The locals call it the strawberry coast - that has to be worth exploring!

P.S. Strawberries have an amazing affinity for spices - try them sprinkled with black or Sichuan pepper, they're also great soaked in balsamic vinegar and poured over vanilla ice cream.

Heather Hay Ffrench
Best Loved Food Editor

Map p.474
ref: E4

ALEXANDER HOUSE HOTEL

17th century country house

Turners Hill,
West Sussex RH10 4QD

Telephone 01342 714914
Fax 01342 717328

E-mail: *alexander@bestloved.com*

GENERAL MANAGER
Mark Fagan

ROOM RATES
1 Single	£145
11 Doubles	£185
3 Feature doubles	£265
2 Four-posters	£310
1 Master suite	£310

Includes full breakfast and VAT

CHARGE/CREDIT CARDS

 • DC • MC • VI

RATINGS & AWARDS
R.A.C. Gold Ribbon ★★★ Dining Award 4
A.A. ★★★ ✿✿✿
A.A. Top 200 - 02/03

FACILITIES
On site: *Garden, heli-pad,*
croquet, tennis,
Licensed for weddings
4 meeting rooms/max 60 people
Nearby: *Golf, fishing, rifle shooting,*
archery, team building activities, riding

RESTRICTIONS
No facilities for disabled guests
No children under 7 years
No pets, No smoking in bedrooms

ATTRACTIONS
Hever Castle, Chartwell House,
Glyndebourne, Wakehurst Place, Brighton

AFFILIATIONS
The Celebrated Hotels Collection
Small Luxury Hotels

NEAREST
MAJOR CITY:
Brighton - 24 miles/35 mins

MAJOR AIRPORT:
London Gatwick - 9 miles/15 mins

RAILWAY STATION:
East Grinstead - 4 miles/10 mins
Gatwick - 9 miles/15 mins

RESERVATIONS
Toll free in US: 800-322-2403
or 800-525-4800
*Quote **Best Loved***

ACCESS CODES
AMADEUS LX LGWALE
APOLLO/GALILEO LX 64741
SABRE/ABACUS LX 20136
WORLDSPAN LX ALEXT

SOUTH

Comfort and dedicated service in Shelley's historic home

The Alexander House estate has a recorded history dating back to 1332. Some of England's most important families have made it their home, including Percy Bysshe Shelley, the famous romantic poet, and William Campbell, Governor of the Bank of England.

Today Alexander House is an exclusive country house hotel set in 175 acres of private parkland. With 18 bedrooms and a wealth of public rooms and meeting rooms, it successfully combines tradition with all the modern comforts and amenities. From the moment guests arrive, the dedicated staff attend to their every wish.

A superb daily choice of menus are served in the dining room. The chef has established a fine reputation for particularly delicious classic English and French cuisine. Menus emphasise fresh natural foods carefully prepared and artistically presented.

The hotel has a range of amenities for those of an active disposition: croquet and tennis. The area is rich in places of interest, from the opera at Glyndebourne, racing at Lingfield to National Trust properties at Wakehurst Place and Chartwell, home of Sir Winston Churchill.

LOCATION

Exit 10 off M23 for East Grinstead. At 2nd roundabout follow signs for Turners Hill (B2028). At Turners Hill turn left (B2110) for East Grinstead. Hotel is 1 ½ miles along on left.

" Amberley Castle - the friendliest castle in the world "

Mrs R Simpson

● *Map p.474*
  ref: E4

12th century castle

AMBERLEY CASTLE

Peace and serenity within the 60 foot walls of a 900-year-old castle

Amberley Castle, which celebrates its 900th anniversary in 2003, stands in a serene landscape of undulating downland and hauntingly beautiful water meadows. Built originally by Bishop Luffa of Chichester as a country retreat, the magnificent building has extended hospitality to Henry VIII, Elizabeth I and Charles II.

Lovingly restored by its resident owners, Joy and Martin Cummings, Amberley Castle was transformed into England's only medieval castle hotel in 1988. With its 19 bedrooms, each with jacuzzi bathroom, Amberley Castle offers superb luxury and every convenience, while retaining all its authentic grandeur.

The 12th century Queen's Room, with its barrel vaulted ceiling and 17th century mural, and the Great Room offer a splendid setting for award-winning castle cuisine based on English culinary heritage with a modern-day interpretation.

Just 60 miles from London and convenient for air and channel ferry ports, Amberley Castle lies beside one of the prettiest Sussex downland villages, amidst a host of historic landmarks such as Arundel Castle and Petworth House. There is

shopping and theatre in Brighton and Chichester, Glorious Goodwood for horse racing, Cowdray Park for polo and much more besides.

LOCATION
Amberley Castle is on the B2139, off the A29 between Fontwell and Bury.

Amberley, Arundel, West Sussex BN18 9ND
Telephone 01798 831992
Fax 01798 831998
E-mail: *amberley@bestloved.com*

OWNERS
Joy and Martin Cummings
GENERAL MANAGER
Clive Cummings
ROOM RATES
6 Doubles/Twins	£145 - £210
7 Four-posters	£195 - £340
6 Suites	£275 - £325

Includes VAT

CHARGE/CREDIT CARDS
 ● *DC* ● *MC* ● *VI*

RATINGS & AWARDS
A.A. ★★★ ❀❀
A.A. Top 200 - 02/03

FACILITIES
On site: *Garden, heli-pad, croquet, tennis, en suite jacuzzis, professional class putting course Licensed for weddings 2 meeting rooms/max 48 people*
Nearby: *Golf, riding, shooting, fishing*

RESTRICTIONS
No facilities for disabled guests
No children under 12 years
No smoking in bedrooms, No pets

ATTRACTIONS
Arundel Castle, Petworth, Brighton Royal Pavillion, Amberley Chalk Pits Museum, Goodwood House, Chichester, Parham House

AFFILIATIONS
Pride of Britain
Small Luxury Hotels
The Celebrated Hotels Collection

NEAREST
MAJOR CITY:
London - 55 miles/1 ¼ hrs
MAJOR AIRPORT:
London Gatwick - 30 miles/45 mins
RAILWAY STATION:
Amberley - 1 mile/5 mins

RESERVATIONS
Toll free in US: 800-322-2403
or 800-98-PRIDE
*Quote **Best Loved***

ACCESS CODES
AMADEUS LX LONAMB
APOLLO/GALILEO LX 4517
SABRE/ABACUS LX 26404
WORLDSPAN LX ESHAC

SOUTH

● *Map p.474*
ref: E4

" *The Angel is our private little haven* "

Philip & Barbara Gosden, Eastbourne

THE ANGEL HOTEL

16th century coaching inn

**North Street, Midhurst,
West Sussex GU29 9DN**

**Telephone 01730 812421
Fax 01730 815928**

E-mail: *angelmidhurst@bestloved.com*

GENERAL MANAGER
Tony Gilmore

ROOM RATES
4 Singles £80 - £115
24 Doubles/Twins £110 - £150
Includes full breakfast and VAT

CHARGE/CREDIT CARDS

 ● *DC* ● *MC* ● *VI*

RATINGS & AWARDS
E.T.C. ★★★

FACILITIES
On site: *Garden*
Licensed for weddings
2 meeting rooms/max 80 people
Nearby: *Golf, riding, shooting, fishing*

RESTRICTIONS
Pets by arrangement

ATTRACTIONS
*Winchester & Chichester Cathedrals,
Arundel Castle, Petworth House,
Chawton House,
Cowdray Polo Park,
Goodwood, South Downs*

AFFILIATIONS
Preston's Global Hotels

NEAREST
MAJOR CITY:
Chichester - 15 miles/20 mins

MAJOR AIRPORT:
London Gatwick - 40 miles/50 mins

RAILWAY STATION:
Haslemere - 8 miles/10 mins

RESERVATIONS
Toll free in US: 800-544-9993
Quote **Best Loved**

ACCESS CODES
Not applicable

A stay at The Angel will delight all the senses

Sheltered by the rounded chalk hills of the South Downs, Midhurst has been an important staging post on the London to Chichester road since the Middle Ages. Here, The Angel Hotel first opened its doors to travellers in the 16th century and five centuries on its reputation has never been more illustrious.

The hotel lies a couple of minute's walk from the Market Square, yet its views stretch across the fields to the picturesque ruins of Cowdray, a stone manor house damaged by fire in 1793. The interior is a delight from the scent of fresh flowers and sound of crackling log fires in the sitting room to the charming and luxurious bedrooms and the culinary delights whipped up in the kitchens. The Angel Brasserie serves some of the best food in the area in a relaxed and informal atmosphere. Its Sussex Menu has received considerable praise and might feature such treats as herb-crusted fillet of lamb with a rosemary jus and rhubarb crumble.

The Angel is perfect weekend get-away and a great base from which to explore the cathedral city of Chichester, visit the races at Goodwood, or watch polo at Cowdray Park.

LOCATION

*From Junction 10 of the M25, take the A3 south.
At the junction with the A287, head south.
Midhurst is about 6 miles south on the A286.*

« *Hard to believe it's 1998 when here! Absolutely charming* »

Alan & Sandy Werft, Sarasota, Florida

• *Map p.474*
ref: C3

15th century inn

AT THE SIGN OF THE ANGEL

**6 Church Street, Lacock,
Chippenham,
Wiltshire SN15 2LB**

**Telephone 01249 730230
Fax 01249 730527**

E-mail: *atthesign@bestloved.com*

OWNERS
George and Lorna Hardy

ROOM RATES
Single occupancy	£72 - £89
7 Doubles/Twins	£99 - £125
3 Superior rooms	£126 - £150

Includes full breakfast and VAT

CHARGE/CREDIT CARDS

 • *DC* • *JCB* • *MC* • *VI*

RATINGS & AWARDS
A.A. ◆◆◆◆◆ *Premier Collection*

FACILITIES
On site: *Garden*
2 meeting rooms/max 18 people
Nearby: *Golf, riding*

RESTRICTIONS
*Limited facilities for disabled guests
No smoking in bedrooms
Pets by arrangement
Closed 20 - 30 Dec*

ATTRACTIONS
*Lacock Abbey and village,
Bath, Stonehenge,
Avebury, Corsham Hall,
Fox-Talbot Museum of Photography,
Bradford-on-Avon*

AFFILIATIONS
Independent

NEAREST
*MAJOR CITY:
Bath - 15 miles/30 mins*

*MAJOR AIRPORT:
London Heathrow - 90 miles/2 hrs*

*RAILWAY STATION:
Chippenham - 4 miles/15 mins*

RESERVATIONS
Direct with hotel
Quote **Best Loved**

ACCESS CODES
Not applicable

The quintessential English inn in a National Trust village

In the 15th century, a wool merchant built a house for his family in the Wiltshire village of Lacock. The oak panelled lounge reflects the warmth of his family home. The beautiful old staircase looks down on courtyard and gardens. Crackling, log fires, squeaky floor boards, oak panels and beams add up to the quintessential English inn. Since 1953 the Levis family has run it with enthusiasm and friendship.

The restaurant is renowned for traditional English cooking. Breakfasts feature the inn's own eggs, locally cured bacon, home-made bread and Mrs Levis's marmalade. Lunch and dinner concentrate on traditional roasts, fish fresh from Cornwall and herbs, vegetables and asparagus from the kitchen garden. All the puddings are made on the premises.

Lacock is the archetypal English village, with winding streets, Gothic-arched grey-stone houses and half-timbered cottages. William Fox-Talbot, maker of the world's first photographic prints in 1833, lived here and his house is now a world-famous Museum of Photography. The Roman city of Bath, Stonehenge and Avebury are within

40 minutes' drive, as are historic houses in Wiltshire, Somerset and Gloucestershire and the cathedral cities of Salisbury and Wells.

LOCATION
From M4 Exit 17 take A350 towards Chippenham. Then follow signs into Lacock. The hotel is in Church Street.

SOUTH

Map p.474
ref: E4

" *This is our favourite place on earth* "

Mark Elliott, London

BAILIFFSCOURT HOTEL

Medieval manor house

Climping, Near Arundel,
West Sussex BN17 5RW

Telephone 01903 723511
Fax 01903 723107

E-mail: *bailiffscourt@bestloved.com*

DIRECTORS
Sandy and Anne Goodman

GENERAL MANAGER
Mr Kerry Turner

ROOM RATES
26 Doubles/Twins   £210 - £260
5 Suites   £300 - £375
Includes full breakfast and VAT

CHARGE/CREDIT CARDS

 • DC • MC • VI

RATINGS & AWARDS
Independent

FACILITIES
On site: *Garden, heli-pad,*
heated pool, croquet, tennis
Licensed for weddings
2 meeting rooms/max 100 people
Nearby: *Golf, riding, fishing*

RESTRICTIONS
No facilities for disabled guests

ATTRACTIONS
Arundel Castle, Petworth,
Chichester, Brighton,
Goodwood House

AFFILIATIONS
The Celebrated Hotels Collection
Historic Sussex Hotels

NEAREST
MAJOR CITY:
Chichester - 8 miles/15 mins

MAJOR AIRPORT:
London Gatwick - 35 miles/45 mins

RAILWAY STATION:
Littlehampton - 3 miles/5 mins

RESERVATIONS
Toll free in US: 800-322-2403
Quote Best Loved

ACCESS CODES
Not applicable

SOUTH

A *luxurious and magnificent caprice with the pleasures of the seaside nearby*

Gothic mullioned windows wink through the trees along the approach to Bailiffscourt. As you walk under the gnarled 15th century beams you can sense the dignity of the Middle Ages. Yet Bailiffscourt is an extraordinary architectural fantasy a medieval manor built in the 1930s at immense cost to satisfy a caprice of the late Lord Moyne, from materials dating as far back as the 13th century.

Bailiffscourt has a unique atmosphere and specially captivating charm. The 31 bedrooms are luxuriously furnished, many with four-poster beds, oak beams and log fires for winter nights. There is a truly magnificent master suite with cathedral ceiling, four-poster bed, open log fire and two baths side-by-side.

A special feature is the walled-courtyard filled with climbing roses, occasionally visited by the peacocks who have made Bailiffscourt their home for many years. Thatched cottages and mellow stone buildings are grouped around the courtyard and surrounded by 32 acres of idyllic parkland bordering the beach.

The innovative young head chef is receiving the highest accolades for his imaginative cuisine and the restaurant is renowned for its superb food accompanied by the finest wines.

LOCATION
Off the A259 at Climping, near Arundel,
'next to the sea'.

309

"" *...superb comfort and decor accompanied by the excellent food served in your delightful conservatory more than justify the awards and acclaim of your hotel* ""

Mr & Mrs G Jay, Isle of Wight

● *Map p.474*
ref: C4

Georgian town house   # BEECHLEAS HOTEL & RESTAURANT

Georgian elegance with Anglo-Mediterranean cuisine in Hardy country

Beechleas is a delightful Grade II listed Georgian house, five minutes' walk from the centre of Wimborne Minster. It offers the traditional welcome of a good family hotel. The Lodge and Coach House feature cosy beamed rooms with the atmosphere of yesteryear and the comforts of today while the Georgian rooms offer a spacious and elegant ambience.

The charming restaurant, overlooking a pretty walled garden, features modern English cooking, with a Mediterranean influence. It has three Dining Awards from the R.A.C. and a rosette from the A.A. Welcoming log fires during the chillier months enhance a warm, friendly atmosphere, as does the conservatory in spring and summer.

Beechleas is perfectly situated for visiting the beautiful Thomas Hardy countryside. Within easy reach are The Dorset World Heritage Coast, Brownsea Island, Sandbanks, Kingston Lacy House, Corfe Castle and the Iron Age defensive earthworks of Badbury Rings. Walking, riding, fishing and golf are close by. Sailing can be arranged from Poole Harbour on the hotel's own yacht to coves such as Lulworth, Old Harry Rocks or The Needles. Sandy beaches, shopping at Poole and Bournemouth, the New Forest and Purbeck Hills are all within 20 minutes' drive.

LOCATION

From London: A31 to Wimborne. From large roundabout take B3073 which becomes Leigh Road after 2 miles. At next roundabout bear left (A349). Beechleas is on right hand side.

**17 Poole Road,
Wimborne Minster,
Dorset BH21 1QA**

**Telephone 01202 841684
Fax 01202 849344**

E-mail: *beechleas@bestloved.com*

OWNER
Josephine McQuillan

ROOM RATES
Single occupancy   £69 - £99
9 Doubles/Twins   £79 - £119
Includes newspaper, early morning tea, breakfast and VAT

CHARGE/CREDIT CARDS

 ● DC ● JCB ● MC ● VI

RATINGS & AWARDS
E.T.C. ★★ *Silver Award*
R.A.C. *Blue Ribbon* ★★*Dining Award 3*
A.A. ★★ ❀ 78%

FACILITIES
On site: *Garden, parking*
1 meeting room/max 20 people
Nearby: *Fishing, golf, sailing, riding, tennis, swimming*

RESTRICTIONS
*Limited facilities for disabled guests
Smoking in drawing room only
Pets by arrangement
Closed 24 Dec - mid Jan*

ATTRACTIONS
*Kingston Lacy House,
Purbecks, New Forest,
Poole Harbour, Brownsea Island,
Wimborne Minster,
Dorset Coast World Heritage Site*

AFFILIATIONS
Independent

NEAREST
MAJOR CITY:
Bournemouth/Poole - 6 miles/15 mins

MAJOR AIRPORT:
London Heathrow - 85 miles/1 ½ hrs
Bournemouth Airport - 8 miles/20 mins

RAILWAY STATION:
Poole - 6 miles/15 mins
Bournemouth - 6 miles/15 mins

RESERVATIONS
Direct with hotel
*Quote **Best Loved***

ACCESS CODES
Not applicable

SOUTH

www.beechleas.bestloved.com

❝ *Warm, friendly, totally relaxing. What more can I say* ❞

Phillip Ness

BISHOPSTROW HOUSE

Hotel and spa

**Warminster,
Wiltshire BA12 9HH**
Telephone 01985 212312
Fax 01985 216769

E-mail: *bishopstrow@bestloved.com*

OWNER
Countess von Essen

GENERAL MANAGER
Mark Dicks

ROOM RATES
19 Doubles/Twins	£160
9 Deluxe doubles	£245
4 Suites	£330

Includes full breakfast and VAT

CHARGE/CREDIT CARDS

 • DC • JCB • MC • VI

RATINGS & AWARDS
A.A. ★★★★ ✿✿ 74%
WHICH? Hotel of the Year 2000

FACILITIES
On site: *Garden, gym, heli-pad,
heated pool, fishing, croquet, tennis,
health & beauty, indoor & outdoor pool,
full spa, hair & beauty salon
Licensed for weddings
3 meeting rooms/max 120 people*
Nearby: *Golf, riding*

RESTRICTIONS
None

ATTRACTIONS
*Salisbury Cathedral, Bath,
Stonehenge & Old Sarum, Avebury,
Longleat, Stourhead, Sherbourne Castle*

AFFILIATIONS
*von Essen hotels - A Private Collection
Preston's Global Hotels
Small Luxury Hotels*

NEAREST
*MAJOR CITY:
Salisbury - 20 miles/ ½ hr*

*MAJOR AIRPORT:
Bristol - 34 miles/1 hr
London Heathrow - 88 miles/1 ¾ hrs*

*RAILWAY STATION:
Westbury - 4 miles/10 mins*

RESERVATIONS
*Toll free in US: 800-525-4800
or 800-544-9993*
Quote **Best Loved**

ACCESS CODES
*AMADEUS LX BRSBID
APOLLO/GALILEO LX 4509
SABRE/ABACUS LX 22223
WORLDSPAN LX BRSBH*

SOUTH

An inviting house in the country with luxury spa

There's a great deal to say about Bishopstrow House, as it's a place, which manages to be 'all things to all people', and does them all exceptionally well.

This is the kind of place where you'll find welly boots and walking sticks by the front door. The public rooms including the Drawing Room, Bar and Library are comfortable and welcoming with antique furnishings and open log fires. The bedrooms are the epitome of English country house elegance and some of the suites have extravagant bathrooms, a must for any one taking a romantic getaway.

For leisure visitors it couldn't be more perfect. The grounds are a paradise with a Rotunda Temple, pretty summerhouse and riverbank. The Mulberry Restaurant offers superb West Country Cooking and to cap it all The Ragdale Spa offers everything from a wonderful pool to all manner of pampering treatments including a world-class hair salon. From a corporate perspective, the hotel has two well-appointed rooms that are ideal for private functions or meetings.

All this doesn't leave much room to say that being situated between Bath and Salisbury opens up all sorts of sightseeing opportunities. To make the most of your visit plan to stay an extra day.

L O C A T I O N
**Situated on the B3414 1 mile south of
Warminster, off the A36.**

"*Every single member of staff is an absolute credit to you ... The excellent service even extended to the Bistro, and every meal we had in the restaurant was of the highest quality*"

Mrs Susan Chisham, Fareham, Hampshire

- Map p.474
  ref: D4

311

Country hotel

CAREYS MANOR HOTEL

Everything you'd ever need for your New Forest stay

Brockenhurst means 'the home of the badger', which is an entirely appropriate soubriquet for this mellow village in the heart of the New Forest. Just inside the village, but secluded in its own quiet landscaped grounds, the redbrick Victorian façade of Careys Manor offers an unpretentious welcome to this wonderfully comfortable spa hotel.

Careys appeals equally to the business and leisure traveller combining all the ingredients for a relaxing break with a friendly and professional staff and excellent facilities for meetings and corporate retreats. Many of the thoughtfully-appointed bedrooms are in the Garden Wing and offer private terraces or balconies overlooking the grounds. Guests are welcome at The Carat Club, the hotel's superbly equipped health club and spa which centres on the magnificent ozone pool and also offers a sauna, steam room, solarium, gym and beauty treatments.

If you can tear yourself away from Careys' numerous attractions, the New Forest is on the doorstep and activities range from mountain biking to sailing and pony trekking. In addition, the hotel can arrange a variety of tailor-made, high quality corporate team building activities too! A whole host of easy sidetrips include the National Motor Museum at Beaulieu, the picturesque waterfront village of Bucklers Hard, Romsey Abbey and Winchester.

LOCATION

Exit M27 at Junction 1, signed for the New Forest. Take A337 to Brockenhurst. Hotel is first on the left after 30 mph speed limit sign.

Brockenhurst,
Hampshire SO42 7RH

Telephone 01590 623551
Fax 01590 622799

E-mail: *careys@bestloved.com*

GENERAL MANAGER
Christopher Biggin

ROOM RATES

2 Singles		£89
71 Doubles/Twins	£129	£149
5 Four-posters		£179
1 Suite		£199

Includes full breakfast, newspaper and VAT

CHARGE/CREDIT CARDS

 • DC • MC • VI

RATINGS & AWARDS
A.A. ★★★ ❀ 74%

FACILITIES
On site: *Garden, croquet, indoor pool, health & beauty, jacuzzi, sauna, steam room, fitness room*
Licensed for weddings
9 meeting rooms/max 200 people
Nearby: *Riding, shooting, golf, sailing*

RESTRICTIONS
No facilities for disabled guests
No children under 7 years
No pets

ATTRACTIONS
New Forest, Isle of Wight, Beaulieu Motor Museum, Salisbury & Winchester Cathedrals, Exbury Gardens, Wilton House, Winchester, Salisbury

AFFILIATIONS
Independent

NEAREST
MAJOR CITY:
Southampton - 13 miles/25 mins

MAJOR AIRPORT:
Southampton - 15 miles/30 mins
London Heathrow - 80 miles/1 ½ hrs

RAILWAY STATION:
Brockenhurst - ¼ mile/5 mins

RESERVATIONS
Direct with hotel
*Quote **Best Loved***

ACCESS CODES
Not applicable

SOUTH

● *Map p.474*
ref: E3

" This delightful country house hotel is hidden from the hustle and bustle of modern life...truly an oasis and our special place "

Ian Thomson, Los Gatos, California, USA

CHALK LANE HOTEL

Country hotel

Chalk Lane, Epsom, Surrey KT18 7BB

Telephone 01372 721179
Fax 01372 727878

E-mail: *chalklane@bestloved.com*

MANAGING DIRECTOR
Steven McGregor

ROOM RATES
4 Singles	£85
17 Doubles/Twins	£100 - £150
1 Four-poster	£150
Includes full breakfast and VAT

CHARGE/CREDIT CARDS

● DC ● MC ● VI

RATINGS & AWARDS
A.A. ★★★ ✿ 72%

FACILITIES
On site: *Garden*
3 meeting rooms/max 150 people
Nearby: *Golf, riding, complimentary use of local leisure centre/health club*

RESTRICTIONS
No facilities for disabled guests
No smoking in bedrooms
Pets by arrangement

ATTRACTIONS
Hampton Court, Epsom Racecourse, Windsor Castle, Runnymede, Richmond Park, Hever Castle, Chessington World of Adventure

AFFILIATIONS
Independent

NEAREST
MAJOR CITY:
London - 16 miles/35 mins

MAJOR AIRPORT:
London Gatwick - 20 miles/25 mins

RAILWAY STATION:
Epsom - 1 mile/5 mins

RESERVATIONS
Direct with hotel
Quote **Best Loved**

ACCESS CODES
Not applicable

SOUTH

A thoroughbred winner at the foot of the Epsom Downs

A 20-minute train ride from Central London, Epsom lies in the sheltering lee of its chalk Downs. This leafy, English town just south of the capital offers easy access to Heathrow and Gatwick airports, and makes a great alternative base for visiting the city as well as numerous well-known sightseeing attractions.

The Chalk Lane Hotel combines old world charm with the services of a splendidly efficient and courteous staff under the direction of Steven McGregor, whose years of experience in five-star hotels in Scotland is very much in evidence. The hotel is a convenient 10-minute stroll from the famous Derby racecourse and half-a-mile from the town centre and station. Spacious and extremely comfortable bedrooms offer a quiet retreat at the end of the day, but not before dinner in the highly-rated restaurant. The eclectic contemporary menu contains such temptations as a starter of yellow courgette and chickpea soup and roasted Welsh lamb.

On the sightseeing front, top of the list might be the royal palaces of Hampton Court and Windsor Castle, a boat trip on the Thames from Kingston, or Chessington World of Adventures theme park. Other diversions include weekly markets, shopping and walking on the Downs.

LOCATION

From the M25, take Junction 9 onto the A24 towards Epsom. In Epsom, turn right at the BP Garage. Turn left into Avenue Road, then sharp right onto Worple Road. At T-junction, turn left. The hotel is on the right.

" Having had tea at the Mandarin in Hong Kong, Singapore Slings at Raffles in Singapore and tea at the Ritz, none of them come close to Donnington Valley Hotel "

H S, Newbury

Hotel and golf course — DONNINGTON VALLEY HOTEL

Old Oxford Road, Donnington, Newbury, Berkshire RG14 3AG

Telephone 01635 551199
Fax 01635 551123

E-mail: *donnington@bestloved.com*

MANAGING DIRECTOR
Andrew McKenzie

GENERAL MANAGER
Gordon Riddell

ROOM RATES
Single occupancy £150
53 Doubles/Twins £185
5 Suites £220
Includes VAT

CHARGE/CREDIT CARDS

 ● DC ● MC ● VI

RATINGS & AWARDS
E.T.C. ★★★★ *Silver Award*
R.A.C. *Blue Ribbon* ★★★★ *Dining Award 2*
A.A. ★★★★ ❀ 76%

FACILITIES
On site: *Garden, heli-pad,
18-hole golf course
Licensed for weddings
9 meeting rooms/max 140 people*
Nearby: *Fishing, tennis, shooting, riding*

RESTRICTIONS
No pets

ATTRACTIONS
*Oxford, Bath,
London, Highclere Castle,
Newbury Racecourse*

AFFILIATIONS
Independent

NEAREST
*MAJOR CITY:
Oxford - 25 miles/30 mins*

*MAJOR AIRPORT:
London Heathrow - 50 miles/50 mins*

*RAILWAY STATION:
Newbury - 2 miles/5 mins*

RESERVATIONS
Toll free in US: 800-856-5813
Quote Best Loved

ACCESS CODES
*AMADEUS UI EWYDON
APOLLO/GALILEO UI 25903
SABRE/ABACUS UI 30972
WORLDSPAN UI 42936*

Set in Royal Berkshire
with historic cities in every direction

In the beautiful countryside of Royal Berkshire, Donnington Valley Hotel blends charm and elegance with the luxury and personal service expected from a privately owned hotel. As well as having its own 18-hole par 71 golf course, the hotel is a 40 minute drive from England's top championship courses of Sunningdale and Wentworth. Inside, uncompromising quality extends to each of the 58 guest rooms and suites which all enjoy peaceful views and ensure total comfort.

The Wine Press Restaurant offers an intimate, yet informal atmosphere where guests can enjoy superb cuisine complemented by wines from an excellent cellar, whilst the uniquely designed 'Greens' is the perfect setting for exclusive private parties and gourmet dinners.

A host of activities are available on the estate offering any combination of golfing, clay pigeon shooting or a day at Newbury Races. Being at the crossroads of England, you have the perfect touring base for visits to the historic cities of Oxford, Windsor and Bath, and still are only an hour's drive from central London. Personal service, and attention to detail will ensure a warm welcome and a memorable stay.

LOCATION

*Exit 13/M4, A34 southbound to Newbury.
Leave A34 at first exit signed Donnington Castle.
Turn right then left towards Donnington.
Donnington Valley Hotel is 1 mile on right.*

SOUTH

Map p.474
ref: F3

❝ *Your charm was only exceeded by the hospitality* ❞

Kathryn & Francis Williams

EASTWELL MANOR

19th century manor

Eastwell Park, Boughton Lees, Ashford, Kent TN25 4HR

**Telephone 01233 213000
Fax 01233 635530**

E-mail: *eastwell@bestloved.com*

GENERAL MANAGER
Graham Rothwell

ROOM RATES
Single occupancy	£170 - £325
18 Doubles/Twins	£200 - £245
44 Suites	£265 - £400

Includes newspaper, full breakfast and VAT

CHARGE/CREDIT CARDS

 • DC • JCB • MC • VI

RATINGS & AWARDS
E.T.C. ★★★★ *Gold Award*
R.A.C. *Blue Ribbon* ★★★ *Dining Award 4*
A.A. ★★★★ ❀❀ 76%

FACILITIES
On site: *Garden, gym, heli-pad, croquet, tennis, indoor pool, outdoor pool, beauty salon, Pavilion Club & Spa, Brasserie*
Licensed for weddings
7 meeting rooms/max 180 people
Nearby: *Golf, fishing, riding*

RESTRICTIONS
Pets by arrangement

ATTRACTIONS
Leeds Castle, Canterbury Cathedral, Sissinghurst Gardens, Hever Castle, Dover Castle

AFFILIATIONS
Marston Hotels

NEAREST
MAJOR CITY:
Canterbury - 10 miles/30 mins

MAJOR AIRPORT:
London Gatwick - 70 miles/1 ¼ hrs

RAILWAY STATION:
Ashford - 4 miles/10 mins

FERRY PORT:
Folkestone/Dover - 20 miles/30 mins

RESERVATIONS
Direct with hotel
Quote **Best Loved**

ACCESS CODES
Not applicable

SOUTH

The Garden of England with Paris and Brussels a day trip away

Gloriously positioned in the tranquil Kent countryside, Eastwell Manor lies in 62 acres of picturesque gardens and grounds set in the midst of a 3,000-acre estate. Queen Victoria and King Edward VII were frequent visitors to the manor a century ago. Today it is an independent, family owned hotel offering an appealing combination of exceptional service, fine cuisine and luxurious surroundings.

There are 23 sumptuous guest rooms in the main house and a further 39 in one, two or three bedroom mews cottages converted from the original Victorian stables. The hotel's superb facilities include The Pavillion Leisure Spa, which is one of the finest in England, complete with a 20-metre pool, large hydro therapy pool, steam room, sauna and jacuzzi. The state-of-the-art gymnasium contains the very latest equipment, while Dreams is dedicated to an extensive range of beauty and therapy treatments for men and women.

Eastwell is ideally situated for visiting historic Canterbury, Leeds Castle and other attractions in the aptly named Garden of England. Fast trains from Ashford Station can also whisk you to Paris or Brussels for the day and home in time for dinner in the traditional Manor Restaurant, or the informal Brasserie.

LOCATION
Take the M20 to Exit 9 at Ashford, then follow the A251 Faversham Road.

" You have managed to make your hotel welcoming and friendly....this is a winning combination, please don't ever change! "

Mr & Mrs Pack, Hampshire

• Map p.474 ref: D3

Country house hotel

ESSEBORNE MANOR

Close by Stonehenge in the heart of southern England

Esseborne Manor, set in rich farmland high on the north Wessex Downs, is an ideal location for exploring the South with Highclere Castle, mystical Stonehenge, Avebury and the Iron Age Danebury Rings, famous gardens and the great cathedral cities of Salisbury and Winchester close by. London and the historic towns of Bath and Oxford are within an hour and a half's drive. Altogether one of the finest places to discover an aspect of Britain's heritage that goes back over almost 4,000 years!

Privately owned, the hotel, once described as 'invitingly snug', has 15 individually designed bedrooms with comfortable sitting rooms that complement the elegant dining room, which itself reflects the importance placed by the owners on their cuisine and celebrated cellar.

The gardens are for enjoying and lazing and traffic free walks abound. The more energetic may in summer play croquet on the finely manicured lawns, tennis year round on the all weather court or golf on a nearby course.

Esseborne Manor is essentially a centre for staying and touring where every comfort is provided by hospitable hosts and caring staff.

LOCATION

Leave the M4 at Exit 13 to Newbury. Take A343 towards Andover. The hotel is 1 ½ miles north of Hurstbourne Tarrant on A343, (or M3/A303 to Andover).

Hurstbourne Tarrant,
Andover,
Hampshire SP11 0ER

Telephone 01264 736444
Fax 01264 736725

E-mail: esseborne@bestloved.com

OWNERS
Ian and Lucilla Hamilton

GENERAL MANAGER
Richard Beasley

ROOM RATES
Single occupancy   £95 - £105
15 Doubles/Twins   £100 - £180
Includes full breakfast and VAT

CHARGE/CREDIT CARDS

 • DC • MC • VI

RATINGS & AWARDS
A.A. ★★★ ❀❀ 72%

FACILITIES
On site: *Garden, heli-pad, croquet, tennis*
Licensed for weddings
2 meeting rooms/max 50 people
Nearby: *Golf, riding, fitness centre*

RESTRICTIONS
No pets in public rooms
Closed 24 Dec - 2 Jan

ATTRACTIONS
Stonehenge, Highclere Castle,
Broadlands, Windsor,
Salisbury Cathedral,
Winchester Cathedral

AFFILIATIONS
Independent

NEAREST
MAJOR CITY:
Andover - 6 miles/15 mins

MAJOR AIRPORT:
London Heathrow - 55 miles/1 hr

RAILWAY STATION:
Andover - 6 miles/15 mins

RESERVATIONS
Direct with hotel
Quote Best Loved

ACCESS CODES
Not applicable

SOUTH

" *Wonderful hotel . . . unpretentious, warm and friendly* "

Barry D Jones, Singapore

● Map p.474
ref: F4

FLACKLEY ASH HOTEL

Georgian country house

**Peasmarsh, Rye,
East Sussex TN31 6YH**

**Telephone 01797 230651
Fax 01797 230510**

E-mail: *flackley@bestloved.com*

OWNERS
Clive and Jeanie Bennett

GENERAL MANAGER
Bernice McDonald

ROOM RATES
Single occupancy	£79 - £90
38 Doubles/Twins	£124 - £159
3 Four-posters	£139
4 Suites	£159 - £169

Includes full breakfast and VAT

CHARGE/CREDIT CARDS

 • DC • MC • VI

RATINGS & AWARDS
E.T.C. ★★★
R.A.C. ★★★
A.A. ★★★ 71%

FACILITIES
On site: *Garden, gym, heli-pad, croquet,
indoor pool, health & beauty, putting green,
sauna, spa, steam-room, mini-gym
Licensed for weddings
2 meeting rooms/max 100 people*
Nearby: *Riding, cycle hire*

RESTRICTIONS
Limited facilities for disabled guests

ATTRACTIONS
*Cinque Port of Rye,
Bodian & Sissinghurst Castles,
Kent & East Sussex Steam Railway,
Canterbury Cathedral,
Tenterden Steamtrain*

AFFILIATIONS
Best Western

NEAREST
*MAJOR CITY:
London - 60 miles/2 hrs*

*MAJOR AIRPORT:
London Heathrow - 86 miles/1 ¾ hrs
London Gatwick - 40 miles/1 ¼ hrs*

*RAILWAY STATION:
Rye - 4 miles/10 mins*

RESERVATIONS
Toll free in US: 800-528-1234
Quote **Best Loved**

ACCESS CODES
*AMADEUS BW VLW138
APOLLO/GALILEO BW 13106
SABRE/ABACUS BW 11492*

SOUTH

A Georgian country house near Rye, the perfect place to relax

Deep in the Sussex countryside nestles the pretty village of Peasmarsh near Rye and the delightful Flackley Ash Hotel. A far cry from the hustle and bustle of modern city life, this attractive Georgian country house is the ideal place to enjoy a relaxing holiday.

The fine traditions of comfort and service are retained by Clive and Jeanie Bennett, the owners, who for over twenty years have provided a warm and friendly welcome for their guests. The bedrooms are furnished in the style of a traditional country home and have all the modern facilities. In the friendly lounge you can read the morning paper, meet other guests or relax with coffee after a dinner in the candlelit restaurant.

In such a place it is easy to drift back in time. Wander the cobbled streets of medieval Rye with its potteries, antique shops, taverns and tea shops. Discover the enchantingly beautiful Bodiam Castle and Bateman's, the house where Kipling lived. Follow in the footsteps of William the Conqueror, visit the fields where the first 'Battle of Britain' was fought and see the abbey built to mark his victory.

You can relax with croquet or putting in the pretty gardens, and in the indoor swimming pool and leisure centre with its mini-gym, sauna, whirlpool spa, steam room and beauty parlour.

LOCATION

From M25 Exit 5 (signposted A21 Hastings). Turn left on to A268 at Flimwell traffic lights. Proceed through Hawkhurst and Northiam to Peasmarsh.

*" **The best spit-roasted duck I have ever tasted** "*

Kevin Brant, Berkshire

● *Map p.474*
ref: D3

Riverside hotel

FRENCH HORN HOTEL

**Sonning on Thames,
Berkshire RG4 6TN**

**Telephone 0118 9692204
Fax 0118 9442210**

E-mail: *frenchhorn@bestloved.com*

OWNERS
The Emmanuel Family

ROOM RATES
*16 Doubles/Twins   £105 - £165
5 Luxury suites   £160 - £195
Includes full breakfast and VAT*

CHARGE/CREDIT CARDS

 ● *DC* ● *MC* ● *VI*

RATINGS & AWARDS
A.A. ★★★ ✿✿ 77%

FACILITIES
On site: *Garden, heli-pad, fishing*
1 meeting room/max 24 people
Nearby: *Golf, riding, health centre*

RESTRICTIONS
*Limited facilities for disabled guests
No pets
Closed 25 - 31 Dec*

ATTRACTIONS
*Blenheim Palace,
Windsor Castle,
Mapledurham House,
Stratfield Saye House,
Ascot Racecourse,
Windsor, Newbury*

AFFILIATIONS
Pride of Britain

NEAREST
*MAJOR CITY:
London - 36 miles/1 hr
Reading - 3 miles/5 mins*

*MAJOR AIRPORT:
London Heathrow - 20 miles/45 mins*

*RAILWAY STATION:
Reading - 4 miles/15 mins*

RESERVATIONS
Toll free in US: 800-98-PRIDE
Quote **Best Loved**

ACCESS CODES
Not applicable

Peace and plenty on the banks of the River Thames

At the foot of the Chilterns, beside the tranquil River Thames, is a very special English country house - The French Horn at Sonning. For over 150 years the hotel has provided a riverside retreat from the cares of the world. Today it offers comfortable rooms and outstanding cooking in the most beautiful of settings.

By day the sunny restaurant is the perfect rendezvous for an enjoyable lunch. At night the graceful weeping willows fringing the Thames are romantically floodlit. The cuisine is a traditional mixture of French and English cooking using the freshest ingredients, many local. The French Horn's wine list is amongst the finest in Europe and includes many rare and unusual bottles. In the old panelled bar, ducks roast on a spit before an open fire. Upstairs, the beautifully decorated suites and rooms look out over landscaped grounds.

The French Horn has five luxury suites and 16 well-appointed suites and double rooms. Each has a TV, alarm radio and direct dial telephone.

The Emmanuels continue the tradition of family ownership at the French Horn, ensuring that the standard of excellence is maintained throughout.

LOCATION

Sonning is just off the A4, 5 miles east of Reading. The hotel is signed from the village.

SOUTH

● Map p.474
ref: E3

To find an hotel with such a balance of comfort and historical integrity is rare, but to stumble across one within such a short distance of London and its airport must be unique

A Salisbury-Jones, Boston, USA

GREAT FOSTERS

Elizabethan manor house

Stroude Road, Egham, Surrey TW20 9UR

Telephone 01784 433822
Fax 01784 472455

E-mail: *greatfosters@bestloved.com*

GENERAL MANAGER
Richard Young

ROOM RATES
17 Singles	£110 - £120
22 Doubles/Twins	£140 - £195
1 Four-poster	£295
2 Suites	£195 - £295
2 Historic rooms	£295 - £325

Includes early morning tea, newspaper and VAT

CHARGE/CREDIT CARDS
 ● DC ● MC ● VI

RATINGS & AWARDS
E.T.C. ★★★

FACILITIES
On site: *Garden, heli-pad, heated pool, croquet, tennis*
Licensed for weddings
5 meeting rooms/max 200 people
Nearby: *Golf, riding, boating, windsurfing*

RESTRICTIONS
No pets

ATTRACTIONS
Windsor Castle, Eton Colleges, Hampton Court, Ascot Racecourse, Thames Valley villages, London

AFFILIATIONS
The Celebrated Hotels Collection
Small Luxury Hotels

NEAREST
MAJOR CITY:
London - 25 miles/40 mins
Windsor - 5 miles/10 mins

MAJOR AIRPORT:
London Heathrow - 7 miles/20 mins

RAILWAY STATION:
Egham - 1 mile/5 mins

RESERVATIONS
Toll free in US: 800-322-2403
or 800-525-4800
*Quote **Best Loved***

ACCESS CODES
AMADEUS LX LHRGRE
APOLLO/GALILEO LX 33646
SABRE/ABACUS LX 44661
WORLDSPAN LX LHRGF

SOUTH

An illustrious historical pedigree spanning four centuries

Great Fosters can genuinely claim to offer the best of both worlds. An atmospheric former manor house, where Elizabethan courtiers once strolled the corridors and warmed themselves beside roaring log fires, it has one foot in an enviably rich and fascinating past. Meanwhile, the other foot is firmly planted in the present, conveniently close to the M25, and within half an hour of Central London and Heathrow airport.

This unusual combination offers an alluring opportunity to travel-weary visitors keen to experience a side of England only usually found deep in the distant shires. Great Fosters is a scheduled historic monument which still displays a plethora of original features in the grand public rooms, the dining room and lavishly decorated bedrooms.

The hotel's magnificent gardens cover some 50 landscaped acres liberally adorned with topiary and statuary. A highlight is the intricate Knot Garden, which is surrounded by a Saxon moat and despite its Tudor overtones actually dates from the early 20th-century Arts and Crafts Movement era. There are rose gardens and a lily pond as well, and guests can take a little gentle exercise on the croquet lawn, in the swimming pool, or on the tennis court.

LOCATION

7 miles from Heathrow Airport. Exit 13 on M25 and take A30 for gham. From Egham head towards Virginia Water and hotel is in Stroude Road on left.

Best Loved Hotels of the World

“ Altogether delightful. Very comfortable accommodation, an excellent dinner and a superb spa. We shall return yet again ”

The Wakefields, Hampshire

319

• Map p.474 ref: D2

Stately home

HARTWELL HOUSE

'Why wouldst thou leave calm Hartwell's green abode?' pondered Lord Byron

Why indeed, though the subject of Byron's musings, Louis XVIII of France, had more reason than most: he was returning home to claim the throne of France after a five-year sojourn at Hartwell. Set in 90 acres of landscaped parkland in the Vale of Aylesbury, Hartwell's long and distinguished history stretches back to the Domesday Book, though the present house dates from the early 17th century when it was built for ancestors of General Robert E. Lee.

This is a stately home hotel in the classical mould with large and historic public rooms filled with fine antiques and oil paintings and an ornate rococo style Morning Room which boasts a superb carved plaster ceiling.

There are 30 rooms and suites in the main house (several named after the members of the Bourbon family who once occupied them), while the converted stable block, Hartwell Court, houses a further 16 rooms. Guests are free to explore the grounds and seek out the various 18th-century pavilions and monuments. The Hartwell Spa has a large swimming pool, steam room, saunas and a gym, as well as beauty salons offering a range of treatments.

LOCATION

M40 Junction 7, follow signs to Aylesbury In Aylesbury take A418 towards Oxford. Hartwell House is 2 miles along this road on the right hand side.

Oxford Road, Near Aylesbury, Buckinghamshire HP17 8NL

Telephone 01296 747444 Fax 01296 747450

E-mail: *hartwell@bestloved.com*

DIRECTOR AND GENERAL MANAGER
Jonathan Thompson

ROOM RATES
7 Singles	£145 - £175
16 Doubles/Twins	£235
5 Four-posters	£345 - £395
18 Suites	£335 - £335

Includes early morning tea, service and VAT

CHARGE/CREDIT CARDS

 • MC • VI

RATINGS & AWARDS
R.A.C. Gold Ribbon ★★★★ Dining Award 4
A.A. ★★★★ 🏵🏵🏵
A.A. Top 200 - 02/03

FACILITIES
On site: *Garden, heli-pad, fishing, croquet, tennis, indoor pool, health & beauty 4 meeting rooms/max 100 people*
Nearby: *Golf, riding*

RESTRICTIONS
No children under 8 years Pets by arrangement

ATTRACTIONS
Waddesdon Manor, Blenheim Palace, Woburn Abbey, Stowe Landscape Gardens, Chiltern Hills, Oxford

AFFILIATIONS
The Celebrated Hotels Collection Historic House Hotels Relais & Châteaux

NEAREST
MAJOR CITY:
Oxford - 21 miles/30 mins

MAJOR AIRPORT:
London Heathrow - 35 miles/45 mins

RAILWAY STATION:
Aylesbury - 2 miles/5 mins

RESERVATIONS
Toll free in US: 800-322-2403 or800-735-2478
*Quote **Best Loved***

ACCESS CODES
AMADEUS WB LHRBO5
APOLLO/GALILEO WB 15217
SABRE/ABACUS WB 32002
WORLDSPAN WB G05

SOUTH

www.hartwell.bestloved.com

• Map p.474
ref: G2

" **Surely one of the finest in England in all respects** *"*

Diana Noronha

HINTLESHAM HALL

Elizabethan manor house

Hintlesham, Ipswich,
Suffolk IP8 3NS
Telephone 01473 652334
Fax 01473 652463

E-mail: *hintlesham@bestloved.com*

GENERAL MANAGER
Timothy Sunderland

ROOM RATES
Single occupancy	£98 - £125
27 Doubles/Twins	£110 - £235
2 Four-posters	£165 - £325
4 Suites	£225 - £375

Includes continental breakfast and VAT

CHARGE/CREDIT CARDS

 • *DC* • *MC* • *VI*

RATINGS & AWARDS
E.T.C. ★★★★ *Gold Award*
R.A.C. Gold Ribbon ★★★★ *Dining Award 4*
A.A. ★★★★ ✿✿✿
A.A. Top 200 - 02/03

FACILITIES
On site: *Garden, outdoor heated pool,*
heli-pad, croquet, golf, tennis,
health & beauty, gym, sauna, snooker,
18-hole golf course
Licensed for weddings
4 meeting rooms/max 120 people
Nearby: *Riding, fishing*

RESTRICTIONS
Pets by arrangement
No children under 12 years in
restaurant for dinner

ATTRACTIONS
Suffolk Heritage Coast, Cambridge,
Sutton Hoo, Norwich, Constable Country,

AFFILIATIONS
Small Luxury Hotels

NEAREST
MAJOR CITY:
Ipswich - 5 miles/10 mins

MAJOR AIRPORT:
London Heathrow - 111 miles/2 hrs
London Gatwick - 103 miles/2 hrs
Stansted - 50 miles/1 hr

RAILWAY STATION:
Ipswich - 5 miles/10 mins

RESERVATIONS
Toll free in US: 800-525-4800
Quote **Best Loved**

ACCESS CODES
AMADEUS LX IPWHHH
APOLLO/GALILEO LX 21652
SABRE/ABACUS LX 31110
WORLDSPAN LX IPWHH

SOUTH

A great house with an international reputation for excellence

More than fifteen monarchs have been on the throne of England since Hintlesham Hall was built in the mid 1400s, and for much of that time the Lord of the manor has been in residence. David Allan, owner since 1990, acquired the title in 1995, thus reviving this long-held tradition. A Grade I listed Elizabethan manor, the Hall is set within a generous 175 acres of inspiring Suffolk countryside.

Leisure facilities are impressive and include an array of treatments at the Health and Fitness Club and a par-72 championship golf course, whose clubhouse won an architectural award. There are 80 plus staff and the hotel can be booked exclusively for house parties. Weddings ceremonies and receptions are welcomed and a full planning service is available.

Dining is as required: there are three private rooms, climaxing in the elegant grandeur of the Salon which can seat up to 81; the restaurant has extensive a la carte and set menus with vegetarian options. Fish is well represented, as you would expect in this neck of the woods, and seasonal delicacies include pheasant, grouse, crayfish, crab

and truffles. The wine-list is award-winning and fresh herbs are cut from the garden. All of the 33 rooms are sumptuously furnished.

LOCATION
Take A12 towards Ipswich. At the A12/A14
interchange, turn left on to A1071 signed for
Hadleigh. Follow road for 2 miles into
Hintlesham village. Entrance to Hall is
past church on the right.

" We felt so at home, we forgot we would have to pay "

Peter Goulandris

Sporting estate & hotel

HORSTED PLACE

A grand place to indulge your most trivial pursuit or gourmet desire

Horsted Place and its surrounding 1,100-acre estate represents a way of life which has now largely disappeared. It is a magnificent Victorian manor house designed by Augustus Pugin and overlooks the tenth tee of the West Course of East Sussex National Golf Club - arguably one of the most challenging and picturesque holes in England. In the recent past, when the estate was privately owned, the Royal Family were regular guests but they could not have been better cared for than today's guests, all of whom are treated royally.

The gracious living of Victorian times is nicely balanced with modern amenities like the all weather tennis court and full conference facilities for up to 100 people. Both the Pugin Dining Room and the private dining room have the warmth and intimacy which is impossible to capture in a larger establishment, whilst the cuisine is of a standard worth travelling some distance to experience.

With its rich woods, beautiful furnishings, individually decorated bedrooms and suites, Horsted Place is a country house hotel of distinction. Stay for a night or two and you'll carry the memory with you for a long time.

LOCATION

*45 miles from Central London,
2 miles south of Uckfield on A26 to Lewes.*

**Little Horsted, Uckfield,
East Sussex TN22 5TS**

**Telephone 01825 750581
Fax 01825 750459**

E-mail: *horsted@bestloved.com*

HOTEL MANAGER
Elizabeth Brown

ROOM RATES
Single occupancy	£130 - £285
6 Doubles/Twins	£130 - £155
14 Suites	£185 - £330

Includes full breakfast and VAT

CHARGE/CREDIT CARDS

 ● DC ● MC ● VI

RATINGS & AWARDS
R.A.C. Blue Ribbon ★★★ Dining Award 3
A.A. ★★★ ❀❀
A.A. Top 200 - 02/03

FACILITIES
On site: *Garden, heli-pad, fishing,
croquet, golf, tennis
Licensed for weddings
5 meeting rooms/max 100 people*
Nearby: *Riding*

RESTRICTIONS
*No facilities for disabled guests
No children under 7 years
No pets*

ATTRACTIONS
*Glyndebourne, Sheffield Park,
The Bluebell Railway, Wakehurst Place,
Lewes Castle*

AFFILIATIONS
Independent

NEAREST
*MAJOR CITY:
London - 45 miles/1 ¼ hrs*

*MAJOR AIRPORT:
London Gatwick - 25 miles/35 mins*

*RAILWAY STATION:
Lewes - 7 miles/10 mins*

RESERVATIONS
*Direct with hotel
Quote **Best Loved***

ACCESS CODES
Not applicable

SOUTH

HOTEL DU VIN & BISTRO

Town house

**Ship Street, Brighton,
East Sussex BN1 2AD**

**Telephone 01273 718588
Fax 01273 718599**

E-mail: *duvinbright@bestloved.com*

GENERAL MANAGER
Nigel Buchanan

ROOM RATES
34 Doubles/Twins   £115 - £125
3 Suites   £185 - £350
Includes VAT

CHARGE/CREDIT CARDS

 • DC • MC • VI

RATINGS & AWARDS
Awards Pending

FACILITIES
On site: *Courtyard*
2 meeting rooms/max 48 people
Nearby: *Golf, leisure centre, tennis, beach*

RESTRICTIONS
No pets, guide dogs only

ATTRACTIONS
*Bodium Castle,
Herstmonceux Castle,
The Bluebell Railway,
Wilderness Wood,
Eastbourne, Hastings*

AFFILIATIONS
*Hotel du Vin Ltd
Preston's Global Hotels
The European Connection*

NEAREST
MAJOR CITY:
Brighton

MAJOR AIRPORT:
London Gatwick - 29 miles/35 mins
London Heathrow - 70 miles/1 ¼ hrs

RAILWAY STATION:
Brighton - 1 ½ miles/3 mins

RESERVATIONS
Toll free in US: 800-544-9993
*Quote **Best Loved***

ACCESS CODES
Not applicable

SOUTH

A touch of decadence in Britain's trendiest city

Strictly speaking Hotel du Vin Brighton is part of a chain - but what a chain! Each of the five hotels in the Hotel du Vin group has been carefully chosen with an eye for the beautiful, the eccentric and the stunning. Among the group are a tobacco warehouse and a Victorian eye hospital, but this quirky building can happily compete with these. Once inside the massive Gothic-revival hall with its soaring cathedral-like ceiling, heavily carved staircase and bizarre gargoyles, you would never guess you were only 50 yards from Brighton's trendy seafront. Brighton bustles with a Bohemian and flamboyantly sexy air - its trademark for many years - and the Brighton Pavilion and the narrow streets of The Lanes with their maze of antique, bric-a-brac and jewellery shops are popular with artists and celebrities.

Into this mêlée has come a haven of luxury with good food, good wine and that something extra - entering fully into the spirit of Brighton, the Lofts Suite offers a 'party' shower room and an eight foot bed, while three other suites have a pair of side by side baths with sea views - perfect for that 'dirty weekend'!

LOCATION

In the heart of Brighton just off the Kings Road.

*" **Every town in England should have an Hotel du Vin** "*

Janis Miller, San Rafael, USA

Georgian town house

HOTEL DU VIN & BISTRO

A 'must visit' hotel in the centre of historic and scenic Kent

This sandstone Grade-II listed building in the heart of the historic spa town of Royal Tunbridge Wells was built as a private residence for the Earl of Egremont in 1762, and converted into an hotel in the mid-19th century. Princess Victoria was a frequent visitor. The conversion came in 1997 following the acclaimed success of its sister hotel in Winchester (see next page).

Hotel du Vin continues a theme of an easygoing life style within an ambience of sophisticated luxury; where the attention to detail is fastidiously attended to by the friendly staff. The bistro presents reasonably priced, high-quality food and wine, now becoming the signature of all Hotel du Vin establishments. The Burgundy Bar features a selection of exceptional but affordable vintages chosen personally by Henri Chapon, and the Havana Room has an antique billiard table and a range of fine Cuban cigars.

The Tunbridge Wells Hotel du Vin has caught the eye of food critics, all of whom have awarded it full marks. The concept is a good one and deserves its growing reputation.

LOCATION

In town centre, on Crescent Road across from Town Council and Assembly Hall.

Crescent Road,
**Tunbridge Wells,
Kent TN1 2LY**

**Telephone 01892 526455
Fax 01892 512044**

E-mail: *duvinton@bestloved.com*

GENERAL MANAGER
Matthew Callard

ROOM RATES
24 Doubles/Twins   £85 - £130
12 Principal rooms   £140 - £165
Includes VAT

CHARGE/CREDIT CARDS

 • DC • MC • VI

RATINGS & AWARDS
A.A. ★★★★ ❀❀ *Town House*

FACILITIES
On site: *Garden, petanque, snooker
2 meeting rooms/max 100 people*
Nearby: *Golf, tennis*

RESTRICTIONS
*Limited facilities for disabled guests
No pets, guide dogs only*

ATTRACTIONS
*The Pantiles, Hever Castle,
Chartwell, Groombridge,
Scotney Castle,
Sissinghurst Gardens*

AFFILIATIONS
*Hotel du Vin Ltd
Preston's Global Hotels
The European Connection*

NEAREST
*MAJOR CITY:
Tunbridge Wells*

*MAJOR AIRPORT:
London Gatwick - 27 miles/40 mins*

*RAILWAY STATION:
Tunbridge Wells - ¼ mile/2 mins*

RESERVATIONS
Toll free in US: 800-544-9993
Quote **Best Loved**

ACCESS CODES
Not applicable

SOUTH

" *The best bed I've ever slept in* "

Emma Thompson, actress

HOTEL DU VIN & BISTRO

Georgian town house

Southgate Street, Winchester, Hampshire SO23 9EF

Telephone 01962 841414
Fax 01962 842458

E-mail: *duvinwin@bestloved.com*

GENERAL MANAGER
Mark Huntley

ROOM RATES
22 Doubles/Twins   £105 - £115
1 Suite   £185 - £205
Includes VAT

CHARGE/CREDIT CARDS

 • *DC* • *MC* • *VI*

RATINGS & AWARDS
A.A. ★★★★ ❀❀ *Town House*
A.A. Best Dessert Wine List in the UK 2000

FACILITIES
On site: *Garden, petanque*
2 meeting rooms/max 48 people
Nearby: *Golf, riding, fishing*

RESTRICTIONS
Limited facilities for disabled guests
No pets, guide dogs only

ATTRACTIONS
Winchester Cathedral,
Portsmouth Naval Base,
New Forest, Stonehenge,
King Alfred's Round Table

AFFILIATIONS
Hotel du Vin Ltd
Preston's Global Hotels
The European Connection

NEAREST
MAJOR CITY:
Winchester

MAJOR AIRPORT:
London Heathrow - 50 miles/45 mins
Southampton - 10 miles/15 mins

RAILWAY STATION:
Winchester - ½ mile/2 mins

RESERVATIONS
Toll free in US: 800-544-9993
Quote **Best Loved**

ACCESS CODES
Not applicable

A 'total experience' just minutes away from Winchester Cathedral

In the heart of Winchester, near the Cathedral, is Hotel du Vin & Bistro. The red brick Georgian Grade II listed building was built as a private house in 1715; and was first converted to an hotel about 70 years ago.

After distinguished careers in the world's top hotels, Robin Hutson and Gerard Basset made Hotel du Vin & Bistro a remarkable town house hotel. Emphasis is on casual comfort at sensible prices. This is a relaxed establishment with a true warmth of welcome in an unpretentious way. Great attention has been paid to detail and the wine theme is evident throughout. Each bedroom has been sponsored by a leading wine house. They all feature top quality essentials such as excellent beds, deep baths and power showers.

Basset has been Britain's leading sommelier for many years, and has won countless national and international competitions. The food and wine, which are carefully prepared and chosen, offer really great value for money. The chef has a passion for fresh local produce, which shows in the simple yet innovative style of food.

LOCATION
Take M3 to Winchester. Southgate Street is between city centre and St Cross.

Best Loved Hotels of the World

" Perfect "

Richard E. Grant

325

• *Map p.474*
ref: C4

Country house

HOWARD'S HOUSE

A truly tasteful experience in every sense!

Teffont Evias is stunningly pretty and has hardly changed in 300 years - a real trip back in time, the quintessential pastoral setting.

Howard's House, itself, sits in two acres of meandering Wiltshire country garden and croquet lawn. Ancient box hedges and secret corners add to the romance. The House was built in 1623 and extended and renovated in 1837 following a previous owner's trip to Switzerland, which inspired the steeply pitched Swiss style roof.

Having taken over this lovely property in February 2002, Bill and Noële Thompson have redecorated and added their own tasteful touches. The result is a relaxed, yet confident air of style and comfort that carries right through to the kitchen.

Chef, Boyd McIntosh, whose credentials include a coveted Bib Gourmand from Michelin, produces a menu that yields a treasure trove of delights. This place is all about good food, utter charm and comfort. If you can't relax here, you can't relax anywhere.

This is, of course, also a lovely peaceful base from which to explore the many fascinating sights in the vicinity including the Cathedral at Salisbury, Old Sarum and Stonehenge.

LOCATION

From Salisbury follow signs for A36 Warminster. At Wilton fork left onto the A30. At Barford St. Martin fork right onto the B3089. The turning for Teffont Evias is on the left just before Teffont Magna.

Teffont Evias, Near Salisbury, Wiltshire SP3 5RJ

Telephone 01722 716392
Fax 01722 716820

E-mail: *howardshse@bestloved.com*

OWNERS
Bill and Noële Thompson

ROOM RATES
Single occupancy	£95
7 Doubles/Twins	£145
1 Four-poster	£165
1 Family room	£175

Includes full breakfast and VAT

CHARGE/CREDIT CARDS
 • *MC* • *VI*

RATINGS & AWARDS
Independent

FACILITIES
On site: *Garden, croquet*
1 meeting room/max 36 people
Nearby: *Golf, swimming, riding*

RESTRICTIONS
No facilities for disabled guests
Closed 23 - 26 Dec

ATTRACTIONS
Salisbury town and Cathedral,
Stonehenge, Old Sarum, Bath,
Stourhead Gardens,
Longleat House and Safari Park

AFFILIATIONS
Independent

NEAREST
MAJOR CITY:
Salisbury - 10 miles/20 mins

MAJOR AIRPORT:
London Heathrow - 84 miles/1 ¾ hrs

RAILWAY STATION:
Salisbury - 10 miles/20 mins

RESERVATIONS
Direct with hotel
Quote **Best Loved**

ACCESS CODES
Not applicable

SOUTH

● *Map p.474*
ref: C3

" The restaurant must rate one of the best in the country and the staff are pleasant and accommodating. The overall package is excellent! "

Ken Wattam, Information Systems Practitioners

THE IVY HOUSE

Georgian residence

High Street, Marlborough, Wiltshire SN8 1HJ

Telephone 01672 515333
Fax 01672 515338

E-mail: *ivyhouse@bestloved.com*

GENERAL MANAGER
Julian Roff

ROOM RATES
Single occupancy	£75 - £85
31 Doubles/Twins	£75 - £98
4 Family rooms	£110
1 Suite	£95 - £115

Includes full breakfast and VAT

CHARGE/CREDIT CARDS

 ● *MC* ● *VI*

RATINGS & AWARDS
R.A.C. ★★★ *Dining Award 2*
A.A. ★★★ ❀❀ *74%*

FACILITIES
On site: *Terrace*
3 meeting rooms/max 100 people
Nearby: *Golf, health & beauty, leisure centre, clay shooting, quad biking*

RESTRICTIONS
Limited facilities for disabled guests
No pets

ATTRACTIONS
Stonehenge, Avebury, White Horses Trail, Crop Circles, Bath, Glastonbury Abbey and Tor, Newbury Racecourse, Salisbury Cathedral

AFFILIATIONS
Independent

NEAREST
MAJOR CITY:
Swindon - 13 miles/20 mins

MAJOR AIRPORT:
London Heathrow - 63 miles/1 ¼ hrs

RAILWAY STATION:
Great Bedwyn - 7 miles/10 mins

RESERVATIONS
Direct with hotel
*Quote **Best Loved***

ACCESS CODES
Not applicable

A Georgian residence in a mythical landscape

This Grade II listed Georgian residence was built for the Earl of Aylesbury in 1707 and is now a family-run hotel that prides itself on its ability to provide an intimate, personal service for both business and leisure clientele. Overlooking Marlborough High Street, which enjoys a rather particular claim to fame as the widest high street in England, the hotel has 36 bedrooms, including the Vines Annex with seven rooms across the road. The restaurant faces south over the Courtyard Bar terrace, and offers an extensive modern English menu.

There are too many noteworthy architectural and ancient local sites to list here, but suffice to say history is as prolific in this region as the lush, green ivy cladding which gives the hotel its name. Many dramatic crop circles have appeared locally and to the south of the town is Avebury, the largest stone circle and henge in the world, with the equally famous Merlin's Mound, Glastonbury Tor and Stonehenge also nearby.

Heritage aside, commercial visitors will find the facilities onsite, or at the adjacent Beeches Conference Centre, reassuringly modern; and the

many partnership leisure arrangements - from golf, shooting and fishing to massage and manicures - absolutely magic!

LOCATION
10 minutes from Junction 15 on the M4. Follow the A345 into town and the hotel is located on High Street, just past the Town Hall.

" Fantastic evening, beautiful room, lovely food and all round wonderful service - thank you "

Peter & Jo Jackman, Reading

16th century manor house

LANGSHOTT MANOR

Horley, Near Gatwick, Surrey RH6 9LN
Telephone 01293 786680
Fax 01293 783905
E-mail: *langshott@bestloved.com*

OWNERS
Peter and Deborah Hinchcliffe

GENERAL MANAGER
Robert Tether

ROOM RATES
Single occupancy   £165 - £270
16 Doubles/Twins   £185 - £260
5 Four-posters   £250 - £260
1 Suite   £275 - £290
Includes full breakfast, newspaper, service, transfer to the airport and VAT

CHARGE/CREDIT CARDS

 ● DC ● MC ● VI

RATINGS & AWARDS
R.A.C. Gold Ribbon ★★★ Dining Award 3
A.A. ★★★ ❀❀ Top 200 - 02/03

FACILITIES
On site: *Garden, croquet, Licensed for weddings*
3 meeting rooms/max 80 people
Nearby: *Golf, fishing, fitness centre, shooting, riding*

RESTRICTIONS
Limited facilities for disabled guests
No children under 12 years in the restaurant for dinner
No pets

ATTRACTIONS
Windsor, Brighton, Chartwell House, Glyndebourne, R.H.S. Wisley, London

AFFILIATIONS
The Celebrated Hotels Collection
Small Luxury Hotels
Selected British Hotels

NEAREST
MAJOR CITY:
London - 28 miles/30 mins

MAJOR AIRPORT:
London Gatwick - 3 miles/8 mins

RAILWAY STATION:
Horley - ½ mile/5 mins

RESERVATIONS
Toll free in US: 800-322-2403
or 800-525-4800
Quote Best Loved

ACCESS CODES
AMADEUS LX LGW249
APOLLO/GALILEO LX 92710
SABRE/ABACUS LX 42115
WORLDSPAN LX 11674

SOUTH

Such antiquity, style and seclusion next door to Gatwick ... astonishing!

Cocooned by the centuries and a three-acre award-winning garden, complete with moat, is Langshott Manor. As if by some historical sleight of hand it stands just eight minutes drive from Gatwick airport but once within its embrace, the strident sounds of today ebb in diminuendo; only far, far away might you catch the occasional reminder of our age.

The illusion of time in reverse continues inside the house. Two cottages dating from the 1500's, were joined by the Victorians, adding a bell tower and a mews. The eccentricities of the building give great character to the rooms which a recent refurbishment has exploited to great effect. The picturesque bedrooms, despite their great age, have a fresh individuality given greater charm by posies of flowers in every nook and cranny. Concessions are made, however, to the modern world, so the facilities are luxuriously right up to the minute!

The dining room will tempt you to an array of classic delights and a tempting wine list that is a wonderful compliment to the chef's gastronomic inspirations.

An enchanted place, so near and yet so far from London, Brighton and the South East.

LOCATION

From the A23 in Horley, take Ladbroke Road to Langshott. The hotel is ¾ mile further on.

• *Map p.474*
ref: F2

" The Ritz of the East "

Beverley Byrne, The Lady Magazine

MAISON TALBOOTH

Riverside hotel & restaurant

**Dedham, Colchester,
Essex CO7 6HN**

**Telephone 01206 322367
Fax 01206 322752**

E-mail: *talbooth@bestloved.com*

OWNERS
Gerald and Paul Milsom

ROOM RATES
*Single occupancy   £120 - £150
5 Doubles/Twins   £155 - £170
5 Suites   £190 - £210
Includes continental breakfast and VAT*

CHARGE/CREDIT CARDS

 • *DC • MC • VI*

RATINGS & AWARDS
*R.A.C. Blue Ribbon ★★★ Dining Award 3
A.A. ★★★ ❀❀
A.A. Top 200 - 02/03*

FACILITIES
On site: *Garden, heli-pad,
croquet, garden chess
Licensed for weddings
1 meeting room/max 120 people*
Nearby: *Golf, river fishing, shooting, riding*

RESTRICTIONS
*Limited facilities for disabled guests
No pets*

ATTRACTIONS
*Constable country,
Flatford and Willy Lott's cottages,
Cambridge, Lavenham,
Colchester Castle Museum,
Beth Chatto's Gardens*

AFFILIATIONS
*The Celebrated Hotels Collection
Pride of Britain*

NEAREST
*MAJOR CITY:
Colchester - 6 miles/10 mins*

*MAJOR AIRPORT:
London Heathrow - 90 miles/1 ½ hrs
Stansted - 45 miles/50 mins*

*RAILWAY STATION:
Colchester - 10 miles/15 mins*

RESERVATIONS
*Toll free in US: 800-322-2403
or 800-98-PRIDE
Quote **Best Loved***

ACCESS CODES
Not applicable

SOUTH

Fine art and great cooking in beautiful Constable country

A Victorian country house blessed with a superb position overlooking the Stour river valley and the medieval church of Stratford St. Mary, Maison Talbooth is the hotel arm of the renowned Le Talbooth restaurant which lies just a short distance along the riverbank. The hotel is a charmer, with ten spacious and appealing bedrooms decorated with a real eye for colour and thoughtful touches which emphasise the Milsom family's dedication to guests comfort. A courtesy car is on hand to whisk guests between the hotel and restaurant at lunch and dinner (breakfast and light meals are available at the hotel).

Le Talbooth itself occupies a delightful 16th-century timber framed house with a riverside terrace that is transformed into a glorious outdoor dining room in summer. A gourmet pilgrimage of note, Le Talbooth's other claim to fame is that the building featured in John Constable's famous painting of Dedham Vale. Do make time to explore around Dedham and Flatford admiring the scenery which inspired England's greatest landscape painter. There is another artistic connection at Sudbury, where the great portraitist Gainsborough's family home can be visited, conveniently close to the old wool towns and antiques centres of Lavenham and Long Melford.

LOCATION

**Follow A12 to Ipswich bypassing Colchester.
Take exit for Stratford St Mary. Turn right at
bottom of hill to Dedham. The hotel is
situated after the bridge 300 yards on.**

❝ *This is a wonderful, wonderful hotel. I can't fault it* **❞**

Jilly Cooper, author

● *Map p.474*
ref: C4

18th century town house

MANSION HOUSE HOTEL

Georgian elegance and a highly-rated dining experience

Set down a quiet cul-de-sac a few minutes stroll from the quayside, the Mansion House was Poole's original 'Mayoral House' dating back to the 1780s. This charming corner of Old Poole is redolent with the town's distinguished maritime history, and the house itself was built for a leading merchant family whose fortunes were founded on the Newfoundland cod-fish trade. An unusual memento of their New World connections is the 'cod fillet' fireplace in the Benjamin Lester suite.

The privately owned hotel has been sympathetically restored and furnished with period antiques while providing every modern luxury for today's discerning guest. Its pretty bedrooms are named after famous Georgian and Victorian characters and contain many thoughtful extras. Guests can dine in the informal surroundings of JJ's bistro, or enjoy the ambience of the cherry panelled restaurant, where chef Gerry Godden's outstanding modern British menu might feature signature dishes such as Dorset mussels with Thai spices, roast wood pigeon, and a catch of the day.

Poole is a noted yachting centre and excellent base for exploring Thomas Hardy country and the New Forest. Golf, sailing and watersports are easily arranged.

LOCATION

In Poole follow signs to Channel Ferry. Take inside lane on approaching Poole Bridge & turn left into Poole Quay. Turn left after 200 yards into Thames Street - hotel is on left.

Thames Street, Poole, Dorset BH15 1JN

Telephone 01202 685666
Fax 01202 665709

E-mail: *mansionpoole@bestloved.com*

OWNERS
Jackie and Gerry Godden

ROOM RATES
9 Singles	£70 - £90
21 Doubles/Twins	£110 - £130
2 Four-posters	£135

Includes full breakfast, early morning tea, newspaper and VAT

CHARGE/CREDIT CARDS

 ● *DC* ● *JCB* ● *MC* ● *VI*

RATINGS & AWARDS
R.A.C. ★★★ *Dining Award 3*
A.A. ★★★ ❀❀

FACILITIES
On site: *Restaurant, Bistro*
Licensed for weddings
3 meeting rooms/max 50 people
Nearby: *Golf, fishing, sailing, yachting, fitness centre, shooting, riding*

RESTRICTIONS
No facilities for disabled guests
No pets

ATTRACTIONS
Poole Old Town, Corfe Castle, Hurst Castle, Hardy Country, The New Forest, Abbotsbury Abbey, Dorset villages, Blue flag beaches

AFFILIATIONS
Best Western

NEAREST
MAJOR CITY:
Poole

MAJOR AIRPORT:
London Heathrow - 100 miles/2 ¼ hrs

RAILWAY STATION:
Poole - 1 mile/5 mins

FERRY PORT:
Poole - ½ mile/3 mins

RESERVATIONS
Toll free in US: 800-528-1234
Quote **Best Loved**

ACCESS CODES
AMADEUS BW BOH382
APOLLO/GALILEO BW 58155
SABRE/ABACUS BW 14103
WORLDSPAN BW 83382

SOUTH

Map p.474
ref: D4

❝ I have stayed at many hotels in the area in recent years and this is the first one that I have enjoyed so much that I will return. Excellent service, beautiful location and charming staff ❞

Ms Portingell, North Wales

THE MONTAGU ARMS HOTEL

Country hotel

Palace Lane, Beaulieu, Hampshire SO42 7ZL

Telephone 01590 612324
Fax 01590 612188

E-mail: *montaguarms@bestloved.com*

GENERAL MANAGER
James Hiley-Jones

ROOM RATES
4 Singles	£90
12 Doubles/Twins	£140 - £150
5 Junior suites	£165
3 Suites	£185 - £210

Includes breakfast and VAT

CHARGE/CREDIT CARDS

 • *DC* • *MC* • *VI*

RATINGS & AWARDS
A.A. ★★★ ❀❀ 75%

FACILITIES
On site: *Garden, croquet*
Licensed for weddings
3 meeting rooms/max 50 people
Nearby: *Complimentary leisure club, shooting, fishing, riding*

RESTRICTIONS
No facilities for disabled guests
No children under 7 years in the Terrace Restaurant

ATTRACTIONS
National Motor Museum, Stonehenge, Bucklers Hard, Isle of Wight, Exbury Gardens

AFFILIATIONS
Independent

NEAREST
MAJOR CITY:
Southampton - 10 miles/15 mins

MAJOR AIRPORT:
London Heathrow - 80 miles/2 hrs

RAILWAY STATION:
Brockenhurst - 5 miles/10 mins

RESERVATIONS
Direct with hotel
Quote **Best Loved**

ACCESS CODES
Not applicable

SOUTH

Atmosphere, character and a great location in the New Forest

The picturesque village of Beaulieu nestles quietly in the depths of the New Forest, yet it would be hard to find a more convenient touring base for exploring central southern England. Adventurous visitors can strike out for Dorchester and Thomas Hardy country to the west, head north to ancient Stonehenge and the cathedral cities of Salisbury and Winchester, or east to Portsmouth's Royal Naval Dockyard, home to Lord Nelson's flagship, the Victory, and the salvaged Tudor battleship, Mary Rose. Closer to home are the glorious Exbury Gardens, Lymington's steep cobbled streets, Saturday market and ferries to the Isle of Wight. The National Motor Museum at the Montagu family estate is right on the doorstep.

The Montagu Arms can trace its origins back to the 17th century and has retained many atmospheric period features such as panelled walls and beamed ceilings. The luxurious bedrooms are a delight, charmingly decorated in traditional English fabrics and several of the spacious suites have four poster beds. Guests can dine in the cosy pub atmosphere of Monty's bar brasserie, enjoy the elegant restaurant with views over lovely terraced gardens, or a private dining room is available for business and special occasions.

LOCATION

From M3 take M27 signed Bournemouth. Exit at Junction 2 and take A326 signed Beaulieu. Take B3054 to Beaulieu. Hotel is on the left as you enter village.

331

" We celebrated our wedding here and the whole experience was something of a lovely dream, a lovely place to return to "

Mr & Mrs Michael Bower

• *Map p.474*
ref: D4

16th century hunting lodge

NEW PARK MANOR

Once King Charles II's favourite hunting lodge

New Park Manor has the most magical setting deep within the New Forest, an area that was once the royal hunting ground of William the Conqueror. The Forest fringes the hotel grounds on all sides bringing with it not only the squirrels and fallow deer but a certain hush, an insulation from the outside world - yet this is of course little over an hour's drive from London.

In the main house the bedrooms are traditional in style with classic fabrics and furnishings, some rooms have period features and four-posters. The exciting news however is the recent total refurbishment of the rooms in the Forest Wing. These are highly stylised and indulgent with some of the most fabulous beds you've ever slept in. The bathrooms are complete with LCD TVs and their good humoured brochure invites you to 'lie back in the bubbles and enjoy a good old weepy movie'. The transformation also extends to the restaurant, Stags, which now serves modern rustic English cuisine with an emphasis on local specialities.

The Forest can be explored on a hired bike or on horseback, arranged through the hotel's own equestrian centre. If the Forest lets you out of its grip, the area offers endless ideas for local outings!

LOCATION

From M27, follow A337 for 6 miles south past Lyndhurst. Turn right at sign for New Park Manor. The hotel is ¼ mile into the forest.

Lyndhurst Road, Brockenhurst,
Hampshire SO42 7QH

**Telephone 01590 623467
Fax 01590 622268**

E-mail: *newparkmanor@bestloved.com*

OWNER
Countess von Essen

GENERAL MANAGER
Nick Romano

ROOM RATES
7 Classic doubles   £110
6 Manor rooms   £150
8 Forest rooms   £170
3 Four-posters   £190
Includes full breakfast and VAT

CHARGE/CREDIT CARDS

 • *DC* • *MC* • *VI*

RATINGS & AWARDS
R.A.C. ★★★ *Dining Award 3*
A.A. ★★★ ❀❀ *73%*

FACILITIES
On site: Garden, heli-pad, croquet, riding,
tennis, swimming pool, equestrian centre
Licensed for weddings
5 meeting rooms/max 150 people
Nearby: Golf, fishing

RESTRICTIONS
Limited facilities for disabled guests

ATTRACTIONS
*New Forest, Exbury Gardens,
Beaulieu Motor Museum, Highcliffe Castle,
Stonehenge, Broadlands at Romsey,
Isle of Wight*

AFFILIATIONS
von Essen hotels - A Private Collection

NEAREST
MAJOR CITY:
Southampton - 10 miles/20 mins

MAJOR AIRPORT:
London Heathrow - 80 miles/1 ½ hrs
London Gatwick - 93 miles/2 hrs

RAILWAY STATION:
Brockenhurst - 1 ½ miles/5 mins

RESERVATIONS
Direct with hotel
Quote **Best Loved**

ACCESS CODES
Not applicable

SOUTH

● Map p.474
ref: E4

One night is much too brief a stay in this delightful place. Delicious food, friendly and welcoming staff - a real haven. Thank you

The Longs, Shropshire

OCKENDEN MANOR

16th century manor house

Ockenden Lane, Cuckfield, West Sussex RH17 5LD

Telephone 01444 416111
Fax 01444 415549

E-mail: ockenden@bestloved.com

OWNERS
Mr and Mrs Sandy Goodman

GENERAL MANAGER
Adam Smith

ROOM RATES
1 Single	£105
15 Doubles/Twins	£160 - £300
6 Four-posters	£265 - £300
Includes full breakfast and VAT	

CHARGE/CREDIT CARDS

 • DC • MC • VI

RATINGS & AWARDS
E.T.C. ★★★ *Gold Award*
A.A. ❀❀❀

FACILITIES
On site: *Garden, croquet*
Licensed for weddings
1 meeting room/max 100 people
Nearby: *Golf, riding, fishing*

RESTRICTIONS
Limited facilities for disabled guests
No pets

ATTRACTIONS
Brighton, Bluebell Railway, Leonardslee Gardens, Chartwell, Wakehurst Place, Hever Castle, Charleston, Penshurst Place, Sheffield Park Gardens

AFFILIATIONS
The Celebrated Hotels Collection
Pride of Britain
Historic Sussex Hotels

NEAREST
MAJOR CITY:
London - 40 miles/1 hr

MAJOR AIRPORT:
London Gatwick - 13 miles/20 mins

RAILWAY STATION:
Haywards Heath - 2 miles/10 mins

RESERVATIONS
Toll free in US: 800-322-2403
or 800-98-PRIDE
Quote **Best Loved**

ACCESS CODES
AMADEUS HK LGWOCK
APOLLO/GALILEO HK OCKEN
SABRE/ABACUS HK 36354
WORLDSPAN HT 41648

SOUTH

Gastronomic excellence in a 400 year-old family manor

Ockenden Manor is a 16th century manor house set in the tranquil Tudor village of Cuckfield, just 20 minutes away from Gatwick Airport. The setting offers peace and quiet but is in easy reach of major cities such as London and Brighton.

The 22 bedrooms, of which six have four-poster beds, either overlook the splendid nine-acre gardens surrounding the manor, or over to the rolling South Downs. The public rooms offer log fires in the winter and superb views all year round.

Ockenden Manor is well known for its Elizabethan oak panelled dining room with its unique gold leaf painted ceiling. Chef Steve Crane uses only the finest local produce and ingredients such as fresh crab from Chichester. His cuisine has a delicate but excellent touch and this is borne out by the many return visits from satisfied guests! The wine cellar is extensive with over 200 bins of both New World and the more traditional French varieties available.

Ockenden Manor is well situated for visits to the opera at Glyndebourne and antique hunting in many of the nearby villages. National Trust properties abound within easy reach, as do golf courses. The seaside is close by, as well as the countryside for walking and outdoor pursuits.

LOCATION

Take A23 south of Crawley towards Brighton. Proceed east at exit B2115 marked Cuckfield. Drive 3 ½ miles to village.

" Forest is great: it is true old wild English Nature, and then the fresh heath-sweetened air is so delicious. The Forest is grand "

Alfred Lord Tennyson

Country house hotel

PASSFORD HOUSE HOTEL

A rather special country house on the edge of the New Forest

Passford House Hotel, the former home of Lord Arthur Cecil, is situated on the edge of the New Forest in nine acres of grounds and beautifully maintained gardens. The hotel boasts a compact leisure centre featuring indoor and outdoor pools, a sauna, gym, a hard tennis court and a croquet lawn.

The informal charm of the panelled oak lounge and bar is matched by the deluxe bedrooms all with private bathroom, some of which are on the ground floor. The elegant restaurant offers an imaginative and tempting menu complemented by fine wines.

Two miles away, the old Georgian town of Lymington has a superb shopping centre, thriving Saturday market, two impressive marinas and superior yachting facilities. A short drive away are Beaulieu, the cathedral cities of Winchester and Salisbury, and ferry ports to the Isle of Wight and France.

There are numerous golf courses within easy driving distance, horse riding stables, the glorious New Forest on the very doorstep, cycling paths, beautiful walks and, of course, sailing on the Solent.

LOCATION

Exit 1/M27 (West), A337 to Brockenhurst. After railway bridge & mini roundabout, right at Tollhouse Pub & bear right into Mount Pleasant Lane. Hotel is 1 mile past garden centre.

Mount Pleasant Lane, Lymington, Hampshire SO41 8LS

Telephone 01590 682398
Fax 01590 683494

E-mail: *passford@bestloved.com*

OWNER
Ian Hudleston

ROOM RATES
4 Singles   £65 - £105
46 Doubles/Twins   £120 - £300
Includes full breakfast and VAT

CHARGE/CREDIT CARDS

 ● DC ● MC ● VI

RATINGS & AWARDS
E.T.C. ★★★ *Silver Award*
A.A. ★★★ *73%*

FACILITIES
On site: *Garden, gym, heli-pad, heated pool, croquet, tennis, indoor pool heated indoor/outdoor pool, petanque, gym, sauna, table tennis*
4 meeting rooms/max 100 people
Nearby: *Golf, riding, fishing, sailing*

RESTRICTIONS
No facilities for disabled guests
Smoking in designated areas only
No children under 7 years
Pets by arrangement

ATTRACTIONS
Salisbury and Winchester Cathedrals, New Forest, Beaulieu Motor Museum, Exbury Gardens, Isle of Wight, Broadlands, Wilton House

AFFILIATIONS
Independent

NEAREST
MAJOR CITY:
Southampton - 17 miles/30 mins
Bournemouth -15 miles/25 mins

MAJOR AIRPORT:
London Heathrow - 80 miles/1 ¼ hrs
Southampton - 17 miles/30 mins

RAILWAY STATION:
Brockenhurst - 4 miles/10 mins

RESERVATIONS
Direct with hotel
Quote **Best Loved**

ACCESS CODES
Not applicable

SOUTH

" Pretty, Polished, Professional, Perfect "

Paddy Burt, The Daily Telegraph

PEAR TREE AT PURTON

Former vicarage

**Church End, Purton,
Wiltshire SN5 4ED**

**Telephone 01793 772100
Fax 01793 772369**

E-mail: *peartree@bestloved.com*

OWNERS
Francis and Anne Young

ROOM RATES
Single occupancy	£115 - £155
10 Doubles/Twins	£115 - £135
7 Executive Doubles/Twins	£135
2 Suites	£145 - £155
Includes full breakfast and VAT	

CHARGE/CREDIT CARDS

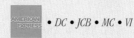 • *DC • JCB • MC • VI*

RATINGS & AWARDS
R.A.C. Blue Ribbon ★★★ *Dining Award 3*
A.A. ★★★ ❀❀ *76%*

FACILITIES
On site: *Garden, heli-pad, croquet
Licensed for weddings
4 meeting rooms/max 60 people*
Nearby: *Leisure centre, riding,
shooting, jet-skiing*

RESTRICTIONS
Closed 26 - 31 Dec

ATTRACTIONS
*Steam GWR Rail Exhibition,
Designer outlet village,
Bowood House, Cirencester,
Cotswold Water Park, The Cotswolds*

AFFILIATIONS
Pride of Britain

NEAREST
*MAJOR CITY:
Swindon - 5 miles/10 mins*

*MAJOR AIRPORT:
Bristol - 30 miles/30 mins*

*RAILWAY STATION:
Swindon - 5 miles/10 mins*

RESERVATIONS
Toll free in the US: 800-98-PRIDE
*Quote **Best Loved***

ACCESS CODES
*AMADEUS HK SWIPEA
APOLLO/GALILEO HT 14848
SABRE/ABACUS HK 30135
WORLDSPAN HK PEART*

Peaceful retreat in the lovely Vale of the White Horse

Not far from the source of the River Thames in the gently rolling landscape of north Wiltshire, The Pear Tree's rural surroundings belie its convenient location minutes from the M4 with easy access to Heathrow and four-star sightseeing attractions such as Oxford and Bath. For those of a more mystical persuasion, the ancient Avebury Stone Circle and even Stonehenge are within striking distance, as are the white horses carved into the chalk hills of the Vale of the White Horse and Vale of Pewsey.

The Pear Tree occupies a handsome 16th-century former vicarage moved brick by brick from its original position next to the unusual twin-towered church of St. Mary's 400 yards away in 1921. Each of the pretty and extremely comfortable rooms are named after famous local characters from Anne Hyde, mother of Queen Mary and Queen Anne, to cricketer E.H. Budd. The conservatory restaurant is a key feature with lovely views of the traditional English gardens scented with roses and fragrant stocks in summer. The hotel has a charmingly relaxed family-run air lent by hosts Francis and Anne Young, and the service is memorable for its genuine consideration and care towards guests.

LOCATION
*From M4 Exit 16 follow signs to Purton.
At Spar Grocers turn right. The hotel is
¼ mile along on the left hand side.*

SOUTH

> " *You have managed to find the perfect mix of great service, marvellous accommodation and magnificent dining* "

Sarah Lomas, Colchester

Restaurant with rooms

THE PIER AT HARWICH

Quayside seafood restaurants with rooms and bustling harbour views

The Harbourside Restaurant and its more casual little sister, The Ha-Penny Bistro, sit right on Old Harwich Quay. Over the years, they have established an enviable reputation for the quality and variety of their seafood menus, which will come as no surprise to foodies when they realise that the owners are the Milsom family of Le Talbooth fame (a watchword for fine dining in East Anglia).

Adjacent to the restaurants, one of The Pier's chief charms is its harbour views constantly enlivened by the coming and going of yachtsmen and traditional fishing boats. The 14 bedrooms breathe a distinctly nautical chic of their own after a fresh and modern seaside themed redecoration programme completed under the talented guidance of Geraldine Milsom. The imaginative use of seashells and rope, weatherboarding and natural fibre floor coverings augmented by marine paintings and photographs lends a wonderfully briny air and there are numerous creative touches to amuse and entertain throughout the hotel. The Pier makes a welcome overnight stop en route to the continent, or take advantage of the hotel's

great value sailing weekends. There are also short break offers in conjunction with Maison Talbooth (see page 328).

LOCATION

Take the A120 to Harwich and continue straight on this road until it comes to an end on the quayside of Old Harwich. The Pier is on the right, opposite the Life Boat Station.

The Quay, Harwich,
Essex, CO12 3HH

Telephone 01255 241212
Fax 01255 551922

E-mail: *pier@bestloved.com*

OWNERS
Gerald and Paul Milsom

CHEF DIRECTOR
Chris Oakley

ROOM RATES
Single occupancy	*£62 - £100*
13 Doubles/Twins	*£80 - £100*
1 Suite	*£150*
Includes continental breakfast and VAT

CHARGE/CREDIT CARDS

 • *DC* • *MC* • *VI*

RATINGS & AWARDS
R.A.C. ★★★ *Dining Award 2*
A.A. ★★★ ❀❀ 74%

FACILITIES
On site: *Licensed for weddings*
1 meeting room/100 people
Nearby: *Pool, golf, tennis,*
boating, fishing, sailing

RESTRICTIONS
Limited facilities for disabled guests
No pets

ATTRACTIONS
Harwich Maritime & Lifeboat Museums,
Kentwell Hall & Lavenham,
Beth Chatto's Gardens, Colchester Castle,
Flatford Mill & Constable Country

AFFILIATIONS
Great Inns of Britain
Preston's Global Hotels

NEAREST
MAJOR CITY:
Harwich

MAJOR AIRPORT:
Stansted - 60 miles/50 mins

RAILWAY STATION:
Harwich - ½ mile/2 mins

FERRY PORT:
Harwich International Port - 1 mile/3 mins

RESERVATIONS
Toll free in US: 800-544-9993
Quote **Best Loved**

ACCESS CODES
Not applicable

SOUTH

> *The most comfortable, friendly and relaxing 'restaurant with rooms' in which we have had the good fortune to stay - and you have a magician in the kitchen* "

Mrs D E Raymond, Haywards Heath

PLUMBER MANOR

17th century manor

Sturminster Newton, Dorset DT10 2AF

Telephone 01258 472507
Fax 01258 473370

E-mail: *plumber@bestloved.com*

OWNER
Richard Prideaux-Brune

ROOM RATES
Single occupancy   £90
16 Doubles/Twins   £105 - £165
Includes full breakfast, newspaper, service and VAT

CHARGE/CREDIT CARDS

 • DC • MC • VI

RATINGS & AWARDS
A.A. ★★★ ❀ 70%

FACILITIES
On site: *Garden, heli-pad, croquet, tennis 1 meeting room/max 25 people*
Nearby: *Golf, fishing, shooting, riding, clay pigeon shooting*

RESTRICTIONS
Smoking in bar only
No pets in public rooms
Closed 1 - 28 Feb

ATTRACTIONS
Dorset villages, Kingston Lacy, Corfe Castle, Cerne Abbas, Lulworth Cove, Poole Harbour, Brownsea Island, Starhead Longleys, Salisbury Cathedral

AFFILIATIONS
Pride of Britain

NEAREST
MAJOR CITY:
Salisbury - 30 miles/1 hr

MAJOR AIRPORT:
London Heathrow - 100 miles/2 ½ hrs

RAILWAY STATION:
Gillingham - 10 miles/20 mins

RESERVATIONS
Toll free in US: 800-98-PRIDE
*Quote **Best Loved***

ACCESS CODES
Not applicable

SOUTH

A Devilish place to satisfy the senses

Plumber Manor is a wonderful Jacobean manor house lost in the lush green countryside of Thomas Hardy's Dorset. The five-acre lawns are edged by the Devilish Stream, an idyllic picture of sublime peace in pastoral bliss.

Inside the house there are homely touches like family heirlooms and jars of homemade shortbread that refute any notion that this is an hotel! One look at the plumped-up, oversized furniture tells you comfort is the keynote here. There are six rooms in the original manor and another ten in the stable courtyard across the lawn. The original drawing room is now a part of a trio of richly decorated dining rooms. The bar is what used to be the dining room.

The Prideaux-Brunes still live here and that's what gives the place such an authentic feeling of home. Richard attends to front of house duties while his younger brother, Brian, is the chef whose unfussy style of cuisine fits the Plumber philosophy like a rind to its fruit. His imaginative menu based on the goodness of Dorset has won a loyal following and well-earned recognition from the major guides.

The world seems oblivious of little Dorset's huge inheritance; making Plumber Manor your base, your senses, all of them, will be in for a treat.

LOCATION

Located 1 ½ miles south west of Sturminster Newton on the Hazelbury Bryan road. Turn off the A357 towards Hazelbury Bryan and the hotel is situated 2 miles further on.

" A style uniquely its own, tremendous hospitality. It's the hosts that make the inn "

General K Israel, US Air Force

• Map p.474
ref: F4

337

Country house

POWDER MILLS HOTEL

Powdermill Lane, Battle, East Sussex TN33 0SP

Telephone 01424 775511
Fax 01424 774540

E-mail: *powdermills@bestloved.com*

OWNERS
Douglas and Julie Cowpland

MANAGER
Nick Walker

ROOM RATES

2 Singles	£80 - £95
17 Doubles/Twins	£110 - £140
10 Four-posters	£110 - £180
6 Junior suites	£180
Includes full breakfast and VAT	

CHARGE/CREDIT CARDS

 • DC • MC • VI

RATINGS & AWARDS
R.A.C. ★★★ Dining Award 2
A.A. ★★★ ❀ 71%

FACILITIES
On site: *Garden, heated outdoor pool*
Licensed for weddings
3 meeting rooms/max 300 people
Nearby: *Golf, riding*

RESTRICTIONS
None

ATTRACTIONS
Battle Abbey, Rye, Hastings, Sissinghurst Gardens, Herstmonceaux Castle, Bodiam Castle, local antique shops

AFFILIATIONS
Grand Heritage Hotels

NEAREST
MAJOR CITY:
Hastings - 6 miles/10 mins

MAJOR AIRPORT:
London Gatwick - 48 miles/1 hr

RAILWAY STATION:
Battle - 1 mile/2 mins

RESERVATIONS
Toll free in US: 888-93-GRAND
*Quote **Best Loved***

ACCESS CODES
AMADEUS UI LGWPMP
APOLLO/GALILEO UI 94007
SABRE/ABACUS UI 43023
WORLDSPAN UI 40664

SOUTH

Many would argue British history started here back in 1066 AD

Powder Mills is a stunning 18th century country house hotel set in 150 acres of parks and woodland just outside the historic town of Battle. This is '1066 country' - where William the Conqueror fought and killed King Harold. The hotel, with its historic atmosphere and legendary surroundings, is ideally located for exploring the most beautiful and ancient parts of Sussex and Kent.

A seven-acre specimen fishing lake and three smaller lakes are available to guests. There are plenty of opportunities to relax and wander around the grounds. Proprietors Douglas and Julie Cowpland and their staff are on hand to make you feel at home in warm and friendly surroundings.

This corner of the country is like a treasure trove to the antiques enthusiast and the hotel itself has been furnished with antiques from many of the local antique shops.

The Orangery Restaurant has received glowing ratings and awards for its fine classical cooking prepared under the direction of Chef James Penn. It is open to residents and non-residents for lunch, afternoon tea and dinner.

LOCATION

Through town of Battle on A2100, direction Hastings. First turning right into Powdermill Lane. After 1 mile Hotel is on right-hand side of lane after sharp bend.

PRIORY HOTEL

16th century priory

Church Green, Wareham, Dorset BH20 4ND

Telephone 01929 551666
Fax 01929 554519

E-mail: *prioryware@bestloved.com*

GENERAL MANAGER
Jeremy Turner

ROOM RATES
2 Singles	£80 - £140
12 Doubles/Twins	£110 - £185
2 Four-posters	£230
2 Suites	£265

Includes full breakfast, early morning tea or coffee, newspaper and VAT

CHARGE/CREDIT CARDS
DC • MC • JCB • VI

RATINGS & AWARDS
E.T.C. ★★★ Gold Award
R.A.C. Gold Ribbon ★★★ Dining Award 3

FACILITIES
On site: *Garden, croquet*
1 meeting room/max 20 people
Nearby: *Fishing, sailing, riding, cycling, golf*

RESTRICTIONS
No facilities for disabled guests
No children under 8 years
No smoking in bedrooms
No pets

ATTRACTIONS
Corfe Castle, Purbeck, Lulworth Cove, Kingston Lacey, Poole Harbour, Hardy Country, Blue Flag Beaches

AFFILIATIONS
Independent

NEAREST
MAJOR CITY:
Salisbury - 35 miles/45 mins
Southampton - 94 miles/2 hrs

MAJOR AIRPORT:
London Heathrow - 100 miles/1 ½ hrs

RAILWAY STATION:
Wareham - 1 mile/5 mins

RESERVATIONS
Direct with hotel
Quote **Best Loved**

ACCESS CODES
Not applicable

SOUTH

Steeped in history, an idyllic sanctuary for the world-weary

Dating from the early 16th century, the one-time Lady St Mary Priory has offered sanctuary for years. Far from the hustle and bustle of city life, The Priory stands in four acres of immaculate gardens on the banks of the River Frome, surrounded by idyllic Dorset countryside.

Steeped in history, The Priory has undergone a sympathetic conversion to a charming yet unpretentious hotel. Each bedroom is distinctively styled with family antiques lending character. Many rooms have commanding views of the Purbeck Hills. A 16th century clay barn has been transformed into the Boathouse, consisting of four spacious luxury suites at the river's edge.

Tastefully furnished, the drawing room, residents' lounge and intimate bar, together create a convivial atmosphere. The 'Garden Room' is open for breakfast and lunch, while dinner is served in the 'Abbots Cellar Restaurant'. There are moorings for guests arriving by boat.

Dating back to the 9th century, the market town of Wareham has more than 200 listed buildings. Corfe Castle, Lulworth Cove, Poole and Swanage are all close by.

LOCATION
Wareham is on the A351 to the west of Bournemouth and Poole. The hotel is beside the River Frome to the east of Wareham.

Ancient hostelry — THE RED LION HOTEL

One of the country's oldest hotels now voted Best Historic Inn in Britain

Salisbury is a city rich with history and architectural antiquity. Centre stage is the awe-inspiring cathedral, which was built some 750 years ago. Astonishingly, The Red Lion Hotel is not only surrounded by history, with Stonehenge, the New Forest, Broadlands and the Museum of Army Flying all nearby, it is also an integral part of it.

Believed to be the oldest purpose-built hotel in Britain it was constructed in the 13th century to house the draughtsmen working on the Cathedral. Further testament to these artisanial origins is the discovery of an intricately carved medieval fireplace (circa 1220) which was uncovered during a recent refurbishment.

The hotel occupies a very central location and is accessed via a charming, vine bedecked, courtyard. The owners, Jill and Michael Maidment were recently delighted, for themselves and their dedicated staff, to be voted the Best Historic Inn in Britain by British Heritage magazine - a most prestigious accolade. However, whilst maintaining the heritage of the property is paramount all 54 bedrooms are amply equipped with modern facilities and cater well for

both leisure and business guests. Additionally, the hotel has five conference rooms making it an ideal site for corporate events.

LOCATION

In the town centre, just off the Market Square.

4 Milford Street, Salisbury, Wiltshire SP1 2AN

Telephone 01722 323334
Fax 01722 325756

E-mail: *redlion@bestloved.com*

OWNERS
Michael and Jill Maidment

ROOM RATES
10 Singles	£88
38 Doubles/Twins	£109 - £125
2 Four-posters	£127
2 Suites	£127
2 Family rooms	£130
	Includes VAT

CHARGE/CREDIT CARDS

 • *DC* • *MC* • *VI*

RATINGS & AWARDS
R.A.C. ★★★ *Dining Award 1*
A.A. ★★★ *70%*
R.A.C. Hospitality Award

FACILITIES
On site: *5 meeting rooms/max 120 people*
Nearby: *Swimming, leisure centre, tennis, golf*

RESTRICTIONS
Limited facilities for disabled guests
No pets, guide dogs only

ATTRACTIONS
Salisbury Cathedral, Old Sarum, New Forest, Stonehenge, Broadlands, Wilton House

AFFILIATIONS
Best Western

NEAREST
MAJOR CITY:
Salisbury

MAJOR AIRPORT:
London Heathrow - 73 miles/1 ½ hrs

RAILWAY STATION:
Salisbury - ¼ mile/5 mins

RESERVATIONS
Toll free in US: 800-528-1234
Quote Best Loved

ACCESS CODES
AMADEUS BW SOU062
APOLLO/GALILEO BW 13333
SABRE/ABACUS BW 28009
WORLDSPAN BW 83062

SOUTH

● Map p.474
ref: F3

" *The hotel & Spa exceeded our expectations in every way. The food and service was outstanding and our room stunning ...* "

Mr & Mrs P Diamond, Potters Bar

ROWHILL GRANGE HOTEL & SPA   *Country house*

Wilmington, Dartford, Kent DA2 7QH

Telephone 01322 615136
Fax 01322 615137

E-mail: *rowhill@bestloved.com*

GENERAL MANAGER
Martial Chaussy

ROOM RATES
Single occupancy	£150 - £265
29 Doubles/Twins	£175 - £325
5 Four-posters	£165 - £325
4 Junior suites	£185 - £215
Includes VAT	

CHARGE/CREDIT CARDS
● DC ● MC ● VI

RATINGS & AWARDS
R.A.C. Blue Ribbon ★★★★ *Dining Award 3*
A.A. ★★★★ ❀❀ 78%

FACILITIES
On site: *Garden, gym, croquet, indoor pool, health & beauty, spa, hair salon, gym, aerobics studio*
Licensed for weddings
7 meeting rooms/max 200 people
Nearby: *Golf*

RESTRICTIONS
Limited facilities for disabled guests
No smoking in bedrooms
No pets, guide dogs only

ATTRACTIONS
Brands Hatch Race Circuit, Eltham Place, London, Leeds Castle, Rochester, Canterbury

AFFILIATIONS
Independent

NEAREST
MAJOR CITY:
London - 20 miles/40 mins

MAJOR AIRPORT:
London Gatwick - 35 miles/40 mins
London Heathrow - 60 miles/1 hr
Stansted - 40 miles/45 mins

RAILWAY STATION:
Swanley - 1 ½ miles/5 mins

RESERVATIONS
Direct with hotel
Quote **Best Loved**

ACCESS CODES
Not applicable

www.rowhill.bestloved.com

The ultimate relaxing location for business or pleasure

The Mail on Sunday rated Rowhill Grange's Utopia Spa as one of the top 50 in the world. With 15 treatment rooms, Japanese showers, underwater massage beds and Jacuzzi, guests are invited to completely indulge themselves. Reflexology, Indian head massages, and therapy pool are just a few of the treats on offer. A wonderful range of customised spa breaks and gift vouchers are available – an excellent way to treat someone.

This sense of relaxation extends to the accommodation. All rooms are tastefully and lavishly furnished, with solid wood furniture and designer fabrics. Many have four-posters or sleigh beds and all have luxury Egyptian linen. Dining options include an a la carte restaurant with conservatory dining, a more casual brasserie or private dining rooms.

Set within nine acres of mature woodland, including a walled Victorian garden, Rowhill is an ideal venue for a wedding. The Clockhouse Suite, with its own courtyard area accommodates up to 150 guests. The hotel's corporate facilities are popular with many large companies, partly due to its surprisingly convenient location for the M25, M20, London and Brands Hatch.

In short - an attractive Kentish country house with a spectacular 21st century spa and unparalleled conference facilities all only 20 miles from London.

LOCATION
From the M25, turn off at Junction 3 and follow signs for Swanley on the B2173. At Swanley, follow signs for B258 Hextable through 3 small roundabouts. 1 ½ miles from the last roundabout you will see the entrance to the hotel on the left.

SOUTH

341

❝ *We could not have been better looked after from our breakfast in bed through to our most excellent dinner. I will have no hesitation in recommending Rye Lodge to friends* ❞

Brigadier H G W Hamilton C.B.E. D.L. Banbury, Oxon

Town house

RYE LODGE

Rare attention to detail, elegance and restful charm in historic Rye

The English Channel once lapped at the very toes of Rye, an ancient hilltop town and Cinque Port that now lies on the sheltered Rother Estuary surrounded by the wetlands of Romney Marsh. Before the sea receded the only access to the citadel was through the medieval Landgate, still standing a stone's throw from Rye Lodge.

The hotel occupies a wonderful position on East Cliff with panoramic views down to the harbour where the Rye fishing fleet gathers. A few steps away is the bustling High Street, Rye Castle and picturesque cobbled streets of quaint Tudor and Elizabethan buildings festooned with flower-filled window boxes and hanging baskets.

Rye Lodge is a labour of love for the de Courcy family and their small, dedicated staff. Relaxation and attention to detail are two key elements in the hotel's ethos - the guests relax and the service is second to none. There are 19 attractive bedrooms, a friendly bar and a scenic terrace for sunny days. In the elegant Terrace Restaurant, with a real marble floor, guest can enjoy local specialities such as Rye Bay plaice and Romney

Marsh lamb, and the extensive wine list features wines from around the world, the 'R' de Ruinart setting the standard as the house Champagne!

LOCATION

Exit M20 at Junction 10. Take A2070 signposted Lydd. At Brooklands roundabout take A259 to Rye. In Rye, follow signs to town centre. After passing through Landgate arch hotel is 100yds on right.

Hilders Cliff, Rye,
East Sussex TN31 7LD

Telephone 01797 223838
Fax 01797 223585

E-mail: *rye@bestloved.com*

OWNERS
The de Courcy Family

ROOM RATES
1 Single £55
18 Doubles/Twins £90 - £170
Includes full breakfast and VAT

CHARGE/CREDIT CARDS

 • *DC* • *MC* • *VI*

RATINGS & AWARDS
E.T.C. ★★★ *Silver Award*
R.A.C. ★★★ *Dining Award 1*
A.A. ★★★ *70%*

FACILITIES
On site: *Indoor pool, health & beauty treatments, sauna, spa bath, steam cabinet, private car park*
Nearby: *Golf, fishing, sailing*

RESTRICTIONS
Limited facilities for disabled guests

ATTRACTIONS
Leeds Castle, Rye Town, Canterbury Cathedral, Battle Abbey & Battlefield, Sissinghurst Gardens, Hever Castle, Bodiam Castle

AFFILIATIONS
Grand Heritage Hotels

NEAREST
MAJOR CITY:
Ashford - 10 miles/20 mins
Canterbury - 35 miles/50 mins

MAJOR AIRPORT:
London Gatwick - 50 miles/1 ¼ hrs

RAILWAY STATION:
Rye - ½ mile/5 mins

RESERVATIONS
Toll free in US: 888-93-GRAND
Quote **Best Loved**

ACCESS CODES
Not applicable

SOUTH

● Map p.474
ref: C4

SALTERNS HOTEL

Waterside hotel

**Salterns Way, Poole,
Dorset BH14 8JR**

**Telephone 01202 707321
Fax 01202 707488**

E-mail: *salterns@bestloved.com*

GENERAL MANAGER
Jim Beedham

ROOM RATES
10 Singles £96
10 Doubles/Twins £126
Includes VAT

CHARGE/CREDIT CARDS

 ● DC ● MC ● VI

RATINGS & AWARDS
R.A.C. ★★★ *Dining Award 2*
A.A. ★★★ ❀❀
A.A. Top 200 - 02/03

FACILITIES
On site: *Garden, heli-pad*
Licensed for weddings
3 meeting rooms/max 120 people
Nearby: *Golf, fishing*

RESTRICTIONS
No facilities for disabled guests
Pets by arrangement

ATTRACTIONS
*Corfe Castle, Stonehenge,
Thomas Hardy country,
Poole pottery*

AFFILIATIONS
Independent

NEAREST
MAJOR CITY:
Poole

MAJOR AIRPORT:
London Heathrow - 100 miles/2 ½ hrs
Hurn - 8 miles/30 mins

RAILWAY STATION:
Poole - 2 miles/10 mins

FERRY PORT:
Southampton - 23 miles/40 mins

RESERVATIONS
Direct with hotel
*Quote **Best Loved***

ACCESS CODES
Not applicable

SOUTH

Romantic dining and bedrooms with glorious views of Poole Harbour

Salterns Hotel has certainly picked a glorious location: right on the edge of Poole Harbour. As if this isn't enough to tempt you, it also ranks as one of the top three star hotels in the country.

You are made welcome from the moment you enter the hotel and you soon begin to appreciate what makes it such an attractive place to visit. It has its own waterside patio, lawn and pretty borders of carefully kept shrubs.

At its heart is the waterside bar in which to enjoy not just the drink or the company but the compelling view of the harbour. There are 20 themed bedrooms offering high standards of comfort with all the extras to enhance your stay and, of course, they all enjoy that stunning view.

Dinner in the candlelit restaurant is a romantic affair; peachy table cloths, fluted peach starched napkins and food that has earned two AA Rosettes for the past seven years.

But, at the end of the day, as you gaze at the sunset across the harbour, you have to reflect on your good fortune at having found such a place.

LOCATION

**Leave Poole in the direction of Sandbanks,
B3369. After approximately 1 ½ miles turn
right into Salterns Way at Lilliput.**

❝ *The Spread Eagle of Midhurst, that oldest and most revered of all the prime inns of this world* ❞

Hilaire Belloc

● Map p.474
ref: E4

Hotel and Health Spa   THE SPREAD EAGLE HOTEL & SPA

This famous and historic hotel has been welcoming guests since 1430

The Spread Eagle is one of England's oldest hotels, dating back to 1430. Successive influences have been reflected both in the architecture and the decorative features; superb, heavy polished timbers, Flemish stained glass windows and Tudor bread ovens are amongst them. Whilst the past makes this hotel the venerable character it is, recent changes have dramatically increased its appeal: a conservatory lounge has been added along with two new bedroom suites. There is now an outdoor terrace and a conference centre but the pride of the Spread Eagle is the Aquila Club which, eschewing tradition, offers the very latest in health, beauty and fitness facilities.

For all that, history lives here; you get British cooking at its traditional best served in the restaurant with its coppered inglenook fireplace and dark oak beams. The bedrooms match the mood with co-ordinated fabrics and antique furnishings but with modern facilities added.

The 17th century Jacobean Hall is available for meetings or maybe a medieval banquet with minstrels and all! There is a secluded courtyard flanked by climbing roses and clematis.

There are many stately homes in the area, Chawton, Jane Austen's home, and the attractions of Chichester are within easy reach.

LOCATION

Situated in the historic town of Midhurst, Spread Eagle can be found just off the A272 near the old market square.

South Street, Midhurst,
West Sussex GU29 9NH

Telephone 01730 816911
Fax 01730 815668

E-mail: *spread@bestloved.com*

OWNERS
*Sandy and Anne Goodman,
Pontus and Miranda Carminger*

GENERAL MANAGER
Tim Hall

ROOM RATES
Single occupancy	from £85
31 Doubles/Twins	from £135
6 Four-posters	from £225
2 Suites	from £225

Includes full breakfast and VAT

CHARGE/CREDIT CARDS

 ● DC ● MC ● VI

RATINGS & AWARDS
Awards Pending

FACILITIES
On site: *Garden, indoor pool,
health & beauty, health spa
Licensed for weddings
5 meeting rooms/max 120 people*
Nearby: *Golf, riding*

RESTRICTIONS
No facilities for disabled guests

ATTRACTIONS
*Chawton, Goodwood House, Petworth,
Cowdray polo, Arundel town and castle,
Uppark Country House*

AFFILIATIONS
*Historic Sussex Hotels
The Celebrated Hotels Collection*

NEAREST
*MAJOR CITY:
London - 52 miles/1 ½ hrs
Chichester - 12 miles/ 20 min*

*MAJOR AIRPORT:
London Gatwick - 40 miles/50 mins
London Heathrow - 46 miles/1 hr*

*RAILWAY STATION:
Haslemere - 8 miles/10 mins*

RESERVATIONS
Toll free in US: 800-322-2403
Quote **Best Loved**

ACCESS CODES
Not applicable

SOUTH

---

www.spread.bestloved.com

● *Map p.474*
ref: E2

> *" A wonderful place - wonderful people - wonderful time, not far from home in miles but a different peaceful world. Thank you "*
>
> *R D Higgis, Bank of England, London*

St Michael's Manor

16th century lakeside hotel

St Michael's Village, Fishpool Street, St Albans, Hertfordshire AL3 4RY
Telephone 01727 864444
Fax 01727 848909

E-mail: *stmichaels@bestloved.com*

OWNERS
The Newling Ward Family

GENERAL MANAGER
Richard Newling Ward

ROOM RATES
3 Singles	£135
17 Doubles/Twins	£170
1 Four-poster	£270
1 Junior suite	£270

Includes full breakfast, newspaper and VAT

CHARGE/CREDIT CARDS

 • *DC* • *MC* • *VI*

RATINGS & AWARDS
E.T.C. ★★★ *Silver Award*
R.A.C. Blue Ribbon ★★★ *Dining Award 3*
A.A. ★★★ ❀❀ *77%*

FACILITIES
On site: *Garden, fishing, croquet*
Licensed for weddings
3 meeting rooms/max 90 people
Nearby: *Golf, fitness, tennis, riding, fishing, water skiing, yachting*

RESTRICTIONS
No facilities for disabled guests
No pets

ATTRACTIONS
St Albans Abbey, Knebworth House, Roman Museum, Hatfield House, RAF Museum, Whipsnade Zoo

AFFILIATIONS
Independent

NEAREST
MAJOR CITY:
St Albans - ¼ mile/10 mins

MAJOR AIRPORT:
London Heathrow - 25 miles/45 mins
Luton - 10 miles/15 mins

RAILWAY STATION:
St Albans City - 2 miles/10 mins

RESERVATIONS
Toll free in US: 800-544-9993
*Quote **Best Loved***

ACCESS CODES
AMADEUS HK LTMSTH
APOLLO/GALILEO HT 69464
SABRE/ABACUS HK 25783
WORLDSPAN HK STMIS

SOUTH

Village charm and hidden lakeside gardens in historic St Albans

In the shadow of Verulamium, ancient Roman heart of St Albans, and the imposing abbey and cathedral named for the Roman soldier who became Britain's first Christian martyr in 209 AD, the gentle curve of Fishpool Street winds through the picturesque heritage district of St Michael's Village. Here, St Michael's Manor fronts five acres of beautiful gardens arranged around a peaceful lake and shaded by mature trees.

The original manor was built on medieval foundations for the Gape family in around 1512, and the site of the family's tannery business was discovered at the bottom of the lake during the drought of 1976. The manor has been harmoniously altered and extended over the centuries but remains rich in character and architectural detail while offering an enviable degree of comfort and unparalleled service to leisure and business travellers alike. The charming bedrooms have been thoughtfully supplied with games, books and magazines, many feature fine antiques and some have views over the garden. The notable Terrace Room restaurant with its ornate Victorian conservatory specialises in seasonally-influenced British regional cooking, and guests will find one of the finest selections of malt whiskys outside Scotland in the Garden Bar.

LOCATION

By road, M1/M25 or M4/M40 motorways.
By train 20 minutes from London's Kings Cross - short taxi ride from St Albans station.

❝ Oh to be in England now that Summer Lodge is here! ❞

Peter Stephens, Ottawa

• *Map p.474*
ref: B4

Georgian dower house

SUMMER LODGE

The house that Thomas Hardy built in the county he wrote about

A weekend break at Summer Lodge will take you far away from the 'madding crowd' and deep into the heart of Hardy country. Dorset's famous son brought the area to life with such classics as Tess of the d'Urbevilles, and in his capacity as architect, he gave new life to this country house hotel by adding the sitting room and master bedroom. This Georgian dower house was constructed for the Earls of Ilchester, who along with much of the English aristocracy favoured this tranquil corner of the world. Set in picturesque grounds, with a charming walled garden that is overlooked by many of the bedrooms, as well as the restaurant, it was built in around 1788.

Current owners Nigel and Margaret Corbett have lovingly restored the property to its original glory after they bought the place in 1979. Menu highlights include home-cured Gravadlax with wild parsley and caperberries and breast of Gressingham duck served on braised fennel with a saffron and star anise sauce.

The hotel is licensed for wedding ceremonies and Yeovil, Sherborne Castle and Jane Austen's Lyme Regis are all nearby. The coast lies 12 miles to the south and many National Trust properties are in the locality.

LOCATION
1 mile west of A37, halfway between Dorchester and Yeovil. In village take Summer Lane turning.

**Eversbot,
Dorset DT2 0JR**

**Telephone 01935 83424
Fax 01935 83005**

E-mail: *summerlodge@bestloved.com*

OWNER
Nigel and Margaret Corbett

MANAGER
Vincent Gullon

ROOM RATES
1 Single	£95 - £145
16 Doubles/Twins	£145 - £295
1 Cottage	£225 - £305

*Includes early morning tea, newspaper,
full breakfast and VAT*

CHARGE/CREDIT CARDS

 • *DC* • *MC* • *VI*

RATINGS & AWARDS
R.A.C. Gold Ribbon ★★★ Dining Award 4
A.A. ★★★ ❀❀❀
A.A. Top 200 - 02/03

FACILITIES
On site: *Garden, croquet,
tennis, outdoor heated pool
Licensed for weddings
1 meeting room/max 20 people*
Nearby: *Golf, riding, fishing, shooting*

RESTRICTIONS
None

ATTRACTIONS
*Kingston Lacey,
Stourhead Gardens,
World Heritage Coast,
Thomas Hardy's Cottage,
Cerne Giant, Corfe Castle,
Abbotsbury Swannery*

AFFILIATIONS
Relais & Châteaux

NEAREST
*MAJOR CITY:
Bath - 50 miles/1 ¼ hrs*

*MAJOR AIRPORT:
London Heathrow - 100 miles/2 hrs*

*RAILWAY STATION:
Dorchester - 10 miles/15 mins*

RESERVATIONS
Toll free in US: 800-735-2478
Quote **Best Loved**

ACCESS CODES
*AMADEUS WB BRSSUM
APOLLO/GALILEO WB 14963
SABRE/ABACUS WB 11553
WORLDSPAN WB GB09*

SOUTH

www.summerlodge.bestloved.com

« The staff could not have been more helpful. Nothing we have asked for has caused any problems. We have been treated with friendly efficiency throughout our stay »

Margaret Hawkes, Bristol

TAPLOW HOUSE

Stately home

Berry Hill, Taplow, Berkshire SL6 0DA

Telephone 01628 670056
Fax 01628 773625

E-mail: *taplow@bestloved.com*

GENERAL MANAGER
Neal Matthews

ROOM RATES
7 Singles	£65
21 Doubles/Twins	£130 - £210
3 Junior suites	£170 - £250
1 Suite	£220 - £320

Includes full breakfast and VAT

CHARGE/CREDIT CARDS

 • DC • MC • VI

RATINGS & AWARDS
A.A. ★★★ 72%

FACILITIES
On site: *Garden, croquet*
Licensed for weddings
7 meeting rooms/max 150 people
Nearby: *Golf, river cruises, cycling, walking, riding*

RESTRICTIONS
No facilities for disabled guests
No smoking in bedrooms
No pets

ATTRACTIONS
Windsor Castle, Legoland, Royal Ascot, Henley-on-Thames, Thorpe Park, Windsor Races, boating on the Thames, Cliveden National Trust Properties

AFFILIATIONS
Grand Heritage Hotels
Preston's Global Hotels
Thames Valley Hotels

NEAREST
MAJOR CITY:
London - 20 miles/35 mins

MAJOR AIRPORT:
London Heathrow - 10 miles/15 mins

RAILWAY STATION:
Maidenhead - 3 miles/2 mins

RESERVATIONS
Toll free in US: 800-544-9993
or 888-93-GRAND
*Quote **Best Loved***

ACCESS CODES
AMADEUS UI LHR100
APOLLO/GALILEO UI 94922
SABRE/ABACUS UI 19742
WORLDSPAN UI 40754

SOUTH

A stately welcome and princely comfort not an hour from London

American readers might be amused to know that 22 years before the Pilgrim Fathers landed on Plymouth Rock (1620), the Taplow House estate was given by King James I to the first Governor of Virginia. Its splendid six acres include a tree said to have been planted by Queen Elizabeth I and Europe's tallest tulip tree. The park is virtually unchanged since it was originally landscaped.

The mansion stands out of earshot, but within 15 minutes, of Heathrow Airport so providing a fitting welcome and a convenient home-from-home for our newly-arrived New World cousins. It is a fine example of Georgian classicism with Doric columns, high decorative ceilings, chandeliers and chiselled brass balusters. A recent refurbishment programme has rejuvenated the old fabric and installed the latest technology so that the period design is subtly combined with contemporary amenities and creature comforts.

This is no ordinary hotel. All the 32 luxury bedrooms could happily feature in a mega-budget period drama. And to be seated in the dining room, enjoying award-winning cuisine, is quite the stately occasion. Memories are made of this!

As you stroll like a lord through your very own estate, it is hard to believe you are so close to the capital - within an hour of London's West End. And so near Windsor, Oxford, Henley and other Royal beauty spots along the Thames Valley.

LOCATION

Exit 7/M4 on to A4 (signposted Maidenhead). Follow A4 for 2 ½ miles. Go under large railway arch. Turn right at traffic lights into Berryhill. The hotel is 200 yards up on the right hand side.

"An oasis in the heart of Canterbury, a truly five diamond experience"

Jim Laurel, Seattle, USA

Georgian town house

THANINGTON HOTEL

An attractive Georgian residence minutes from the centre of Canterbury

Situated just ten minutes from Canterbury city centre, in the historic Wincheap Conservation area, the Thanington Hotel offers outstanding hospitality and accommodation. A Grade II listed Georgian house, it was built in 1800, extended in 1830 when the second floor was added, and opened as a hotel in 1987. Its convenient location makes it the ideal base from which to tour the lush countryside of Kent, the county which is known as the 'garden of England'. The hotel has its own, pretty walled garden, overlooking a heated indoor pool, which by all accounts is something of a sun trap in the summer months. Other leisure facilities on-site include a snooker room and games table. Four of the hotel's 15 bedrooms are on the ground floor, and therefore perfect for those unable to climb stairs. Many are furnished with antique bedsteads and romantic four-posters.

Those who wish to explore further afield will find themselves realistically placed for day trips to France and Belgium. The Channel Tunnel, Eurostar International Station and Dover seaport are all half an hour away.

The seaside towns of Deal, Broadstairs, Folkestone and Whitstable are in the vicinity and the cathedral and various castles are additional local attractions.

LOCATION

Situated on the A28 Canterbury to Ashford road just outside the city walls.

---

140 Wincheap, Canterbury, Kent CT1 3RY

**Telephone 01227 453227
Fax 01227 453225**

E-mail: *thanington@bestloved.com*

OWNER
Jennie and Iain Chapman

ROOM RATES
Single occupancy	£55 - £68
8 Doubles/Twins	£73 - £82
4 Superior doubles	£85 - £110
2 Family rooms	£100 - £125

Includes full breakfast and VAT

CHARGE/CREDIT CARDS

 • DC • MC • VI

RATINGS & AWARDS
E.T.C. ◆◆◆◆◆ *Gold Award*
R.A.C. ◆◆◆◆◆ *Warm Welcome &
Sparkling Diamond Awards*
A.A. ◆◆◆◆ *Premier Collection*

FACILITIES
On site: *Garden, indoor heated pool,
games room, car park*
Nearby: *Golf, riding*

RESTRICTIONS
*No facilities for disabled guests
No smoking in bedrooms
Pets by arrangement*

ATTRACTIONS
*Canterbury Cathedral,
Town's museums,
Canterbury Festival,
Whitstable & Broadstairs,
Mount Ephraim Gardens,
Leeds Castle*

AFFILIATIONS
Independent

NEAREST
*MAJOR CITY:
Canterbury*

*MAJOR AIRPORT:
Gatwick - 70 miles/1 ¼ hrs*

*RAILWAY STATION:
Canterbury East - 1 mile/10 mins*

*FERRY PORT:
Dover - 17 miles/30 mins*

RESERVATIONS
Direct with hotel
*Quote **Best Loved***

ACCESS CODES
Not applicable

SOUTH

" The place is so magical that I was unable to resist proposing to my girlfriend "

M Thompson, Addlestone, Surrey

THATCHED COTTAGE HOTEL

17th century cottage

**16 Brookley Road,
Brockenhurst,
Hampshire SO42 7RR**

**Telephone 01590 623090
Fax 01590 623479**

E-mail: *thatchedcottage@bestloved.com*

OWNERS
The Matysik Family

ROOM RATES
2 Doubles/Twins	£90 - £140
2 Four-posters	£130 - £160
1 Suite	£150 - £170

Includes full breakfast, newspaper and VAT

CHARGE/CREDIT CARDS

 • *JCB* • *MC* • *VI*

RATINGS & AWARDS
A.A. Restaurant with Rooms ❀❀

FACILITIES
On site: *Garden*
1 meeting room/max 40 people
Nearby: *Golf, fishing, yachting, riding,
mountain biking*

RESTRICTIONS
*No facilities for disabled guests
No children under 10 years
Closed 1 Jan - 10 Feb*

ATTRACTIONS
*New Forest, Stonehenge,
Beaulieu Motor Museum,
Winchester, Salisbury,
Exbury Gardens, Isle of Wight,
Athelhampton House*

AFFILIATIONS
Independent

NEAREST
MAJOR CITY:
Southampton - 12 miles/20 mins

MAJOR AIRPORT:
London Heathrow - 76 miles/1 ½ hrs

RAILWAY STATION:
Brockenhurst - ½ mile/5 mins

RESERVATIONS
Direct with hotel
Quote **Best Loved**

ACCESS CODES
Not applicable

A cottage for the happy few

The Thatched Cottage nestles in a pretty village in the heart of the New Forest. Built in 1629 it is today one of Britain's most romantic small hotels. It is run by the Matysik family who bring well over a century's combined experience of managing top hotels to the personal care of their guests. The five bedrooms, decorated with antiques and objets d'art, combine old world charm with the modern essentials.

The quality and individuality of the dinners have won numerous awards, and are much acclaimed by the British and international press. Local specialities include New Forest venison and mushrooms. The newest recruit to the Matysik family is a leading chef from Japan, she adds Japanese flare to the signature dishes. Gastronomic highlights are late breakfast in bed and wicker picnic hampers. The hotel with its tea garden was recently named as one of England's top 50 establishments for afternoon tea.

The New Forest is the oldest of England's great forests, but it was new to William the Conqueror when he decreed it as his hunting ground in 1079. The Forest verderers look after its unique wildlife. The Conqueror's red deer and the protected New Forest ponies stroll freely when you walk through the beautiful 200 square miles of forest and heath land.

LOCATION
Take exit 1 from the M27 and drive south on the A337 to Brockenhurst. Turn right onto Brookley Road just before the level crossing.

SOUTH

“ *Very cosy and comfortable rooms and the cooking was exquisite* ”

Mr & Mrs A Conway

• Map p.474
ref: C4

Restaurant with rooms

THE THREE LIONS

Cooking from the heart on the edge of the New Forest

Built in 1863 as a farmhouse in the hamlet of Stuckton on the edge of the New Forest, the Three Lions is now a destination for enthusiasts of good food. It is personally owned and run by Mike and Jayne who live on the premises. Mike learnt his craft over ten years in two and three-star Michelin restaurants in France and Britain. His personal style of cuisine is based on the best local produce available - most of it organically grown and reared in the vicinity. They succeeded well enough to be named Restaurant of the Year a few years ago by The Times and were the recipient of the WHICH? Hotel Guide's Newcomer of the Year 2002. The 180 bin wine list is compiled from personally tasted and selected wines from all over the world.

The rooms are very comfortable and quiet, and a spacious conservatory connected to the accommodation overlooks manicured gardens. Guests can also relax in the Catalina whirlpool spa and jacuzzi or in the hotel's sauna. The Three Lions is a comfortable environment in which to unwind, a place where you can come and go as you please without the formality of an hotel.

Ideally situated for exploring the New Forest. The inviting sandy beaches of the South Coast or Studland's nature reserve are half an hour away.

A little further afield are Salisbury, Poole, Rockbourne, Winchester and many picturesque Dorset villages which you can visit in a day and still be back for dinner.

LOCATION

Located ½ mile east of Fordingbridge on the A338 or B3078. From the Q8 garage follow the brown tourists signs marked Three Lions.

Stuckton, Fordingbridge, Hampshire SP6 2HF

Telephone 01425 652 489
Fax 01425 656 144

E-mail: *threelions@bestloved.com*

OWNERS
Mike and Jane Womersley

ROOM RATES
Single occupancy	£59 - £75
5 Doubles/Twins	£70 - £85

Includes continental breakfast and VAT

CHARGE/CREDIT CARDS

 • MC • VI

RATINGS & AWARDS
E.T.C. ◆◆◆◆◆ *Gold Award*
A.A. ◆◆◆◆◆ ❀❀❀ *Premier Collection*
WHICH? Hotel National Newcomer of the Year 2002

FACILITIES
On site: *Garden, jacuzzi/hot tub, sauna*
Licensed for weddings
1 meeting room/max 40 people
Nearby: *Golf, river and sea fishing, water skiing, yachting, tennis, fitness centre, hunting/shooting, riding, cycling*

RESTRICTIONS
Limited facilities for disabled guests
Smoking in bar only
Pets by arrangement
Closed mid Jan - mid Feb

ATTRACTIONS
Salisbury Cathedral, Stonehenge & Avebury, Beaulieu Motor Museum, Exbury Gardens, Brockenhurst & Burley, the New Forest, Broadlands, Poltons Park

AFFILIATIONS
Independent

NEAREST
MAJOR CITY:
Salisbury - 14 miles/20 mins

MAJOR AIRPORT:
London Heathrow - 83 miles/1 ½ hrs
Bournmouth Airport - 16 miles/25 mins

RAILWAY STATION:
Salisbury - 16 miles/20 mins

RESERVATIONS
Direct with hotel
Quote **Best Loved**

ACCESS CODES
Not applicable

SOUTH

• *Map p.474*
ref: D2

VILLIERS HOTEL

17th century coaching inn

3 Castle Street, Buckingham,
Buckinghamshire MK18 1BS

Telephone 01280 822444
Fax 01280 822113

E-mail: *villiers@bestloved.com*

GENERAL MANAGER
Henry Scrase

ROOM RATES
3 Singles	£115
31 Doubles/Twins	£135
8 Premium doubles	£155
4 Suites	£180

Includes full breakfast, service and VAT

CHARGE/CREDIT CARDS

AMERICAN EXPRESS • DC • MC • VI

RATINGS & AWARDS
A.A. ★★★★ ✿✿ 69%

FACILITIES
On site: *Licensed for weddings*
6 meeting rooms/max 250 people
Nearby: *Complimentary use of local leisure club*

RESTRICTIONS
None

ATTRACTIONS
Althorpe, Sulgrave Manor, Stowe Landscape Gardens, Woburn Abbey, Claydon House, Silverstone

AFFILIATIONS
Independent

NEAREST
MAJOR CITY:
Milton Keynes - 10 miles/20 mins

MAJOR AIRPORT:
London Heathrow - 50 miles/1 ¼ hrs

RAILWAY STATION:
Milton Keynes - 10 miles/20 mins

RESERVATIONS
Direct with hotel
*Quote **Best Loved***

ACCESS CODES
Not applicable

SOUTH

A 400-year tradition of hospitality continues unabated

The antique walls of the Villiers Hotel literally ooze history - and a few ghostly visitors if the stories are to be believed. In Cromwellian times, this 400-year-old hostelry was Buckingham's most important coaching inn, and Cromwell himself is reputed to have billeted his troops here during a visit in 1643. Perhaps one of these guests stayed behind, as an expert in the supernatural detected the presence of a large bearded man with a sword and red sash after a series of unexplained incidents in an upstairs bedroom! A ghostly grey-suited gentleman has also been spotted in the library bar.

While steeped in history, the Villiers is up to the minute when it comes to guests' comfort. Warm pastel tones, soft fabrics, and fresh flowers create a restful ambience in the main building. Across the courtyard is Henry's Restaurant and the splendid old Swan & Castle bar, where the dark oak panelling, flagstone floor and large inglenook fireplace hark back to the inn's Jacobean origins.

Around Buckingham, sightseeing opportunities range from the grandeur of Blenheim Palace and the dreaming spires of Oxford to Sulgrave Manor, home of George Washington's ancestors. Just four miles from Buckingham, the Stowe Landscape Gardens are renowned for their 32 temples and are open during the school summer holidays. For motor racing enthusiasts, a few miles further on lies Silverstone Race Circuit.

LOCATION

In the town centre. Castle Street is to the right of the Old Town Hall.

Best Loved Hotels of the World

" You really do have a 'gem' in The Vineyard "

Raymond Blanc

• Map p.474
ref: D3

351

Restaurant with suites ## THE VINEYARD AT STOCKCROSS

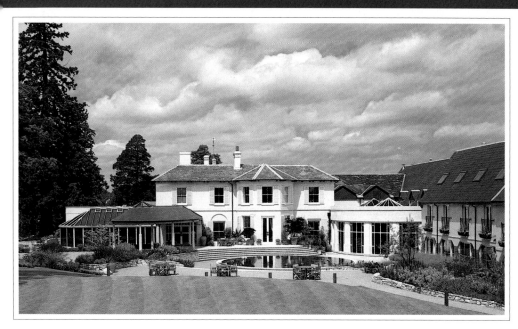

Sublime food and wine in an elegant environment

The Vineyard at Stockcross was opened in 1998 by Sir Peter Michael, founder of Classic FM radio. This restaurant with suites is a showcase for the finest Californian wines, including those from his renowned Peter Michael Winery. Head Sommelier, Edoardo Amadi, has created a Burke's Peerage of wines in a wide, innovative wine list. Awarded five red stars and four rosettes by the AA, the Michelin-starred restaurant, under the direction of chef, John Campbell, offers a combination of modern British and classical French elements.

The Vineyard at Stockcross was built in the 19th century as the country retreat of the Lords of the Manor of Stanford Dingley. The purpose-built restaurant matches the original warm Bath stone, featuring full-length windows set between contemporary pillars. Suites and rooms provide an elegant, spacious and well-appointed environment. They have been designed in French provincial style with both authentic French and contemporary furniture. Another stimulating feature of The Vineyard, is the collection of paintings and sculptures.

The new Vineyard Spa is a paragon of luxury

and tranquillity in which to relax or exercise. Altogether an indulgence for all the senses.

LOCATION

From Exit 13 of the M4, take A34 to Newbury. At first roundabout, take Hungerford exit (A4), at the second head for Stockcross. The hotel is on the right.

Stockcross, Newbury,
Berkshire RG20 8JU

Telephone 01635 528770
Fax 01635 528398

E-mail: *vineyard@bestloved.com*

OWNER
Sir Peter Michael

MANAGING DIRECTOR
Andrew McKenzie

ROOM RATES

6 Singles	£188
9 Doubles/Twins	£269
14 Suites	£335 - £464
2 Four-posters	£705
Includes breakfast and VAT	

CHARGE/CREDIT CARDS

 • DC • MC • VI

RATINGS & AWARDS
E.T.C. ★★★★★ *Gold Award*
R.A.C. *Blue Ribbon* ★★★★★
Dining Award 4
A.A. ★★★★★ ❀❀❀❀
A.A. Top 200 - 02/03
A.A. Wine Award

FACILITIES
On site: *Garden, gym, indoor pool, health & beauty, sauna, spa bath, steam room, gym*
Licensed for weddings
3 meeting rooms/max 140 people
Nearby: *Golf, fishing, tennis, shooting, riding*

RESTRICTIONS
No facilities for disabled guests
No pets

ATTRACTIONS
Oxford, The Cotswolds, Windsor Castle, Newbury Racecourse, Highclere Castle

AFFILIATIONS
The Celebrated Hotels Collection
Small Luxury Hotels
Relais & Châteaux

NEAREST
MAJOR CITY:
Oxford - 29 miles/30 mins

MAJOR AIRPORT:
London Heathrow - 50 miles/1 hr

RAILWAY STATION:
Newbury - 2 miles/15 mins

RESERVATIONS
Toll free in US: 800-322-2403
Toll free in UK: 0800-VINEYARD
Quote Best Loved

ACCESS CODES
AMADEUS LX EWYVST
APOLLO/GALILEO LX 18934
SABRE/ABACUS LX 30971
WORLDSPAN LX EWYVS

SOUTH

WALLETT'S COURT

Country house hotel

**Westcliffe,
St Margaret's-At-Cliffe, Dover,
Kent CT15 6EW**

**Telephone 01304 852424
Fax 01304 853430**

E-mail: *walletts@bestloved.com*

OWNERS
Christopher and Leonora Oakley

GENERAL MANAGER
Gavin Oakley

ROOM RATES
Single occupancy £75 - £115
12 Doubles/Twins £90 - £110
2 Four-posters £150
2 Suites £150
Includes VAT

CHARGE/CREDIT CARDS

 • *DC* • *JCB* • *MC* • *VI*

RATINGS & AWARDS
E.T.C. ★★★ *Silver Award*
R.A.C. ★★★ *Dining Award 2*
A.A. ★★★ ✿✿ *75%*

FACILITIES
On site: *Garden, gym, heli-pad,
croquet, tennis, indoor pool,
health & beauty, sauna, steam room,
jacuzzi, golf practice area
3 meeting rooms/max 80 people*
Nearby: *Golf, fishing, shooting, yachting,
windsurfing, surfing*

RESTRICTIONS
*Limited facilities for disabled guests
No pets*

ATTRACTIONS
*Canterbury Cathedral, Dover Castle,
Leeds Castle, Sissinghurst Gardens,
Eurostar to Paris, Tenterden*

AFFILIATIONS
Independent

NEAREST
MAJOR CITY:
Canterbury - 15 miles/20 mins

MAJOR AIRPORT:
London Gatwick - 60 miles/1 hr

RAILWAY STATION:
Dover Priory - 3 miles/10 mins

FERRY PORT:
Dover - 3 miles/10 mins

RESERVATIONS
Direct with hotel
*Quote **Best Loved***

ACCESS CODES
Not applicable

SOUTH

A glorious retreat close to Canterbury, in the heart of white cliffs country

Wallett's Court is owned and run by the Oakley family. They first discovered it, near derelict, on a summer's day in 1975. It was listed as the Manor of Westcliffe in the Domesday Book and its history embraces such luminaries as Bishop Odo of Bayeux, Queen Eleanor of Castille, historian Edward Gibbon, Admiral Lord Aylmer and Prime Minister William Pitt.

Today it is a family home and country house hotel with 16 large, comfortable bedrooms. The style is homely: you can settle in the old leather sofa by a blazing fire, hear the grandfather clock ticking, or relax in the conservatory.

The indoor pool, sauna, steam and fitness rooms as well as the luxurious health spa housed within a Kentish barn, add an attractive dimension to the hotel. As indeed, does its location: close to Canterbury and on the doorstep of the continent - the ever expanding Cruise Terminal is only four miles away.

The surrounding area is designated as being of Outstanding Natural Beauty. A mile away is St Margaret's Bay and on a clear day you can see France. On others, you can visit Leeds Castle,

Canterbury Cathedral and the secret wartime tunnels of Dover Castle.

LOCATION

*From M2/A2 or M20/A20 follow signs for
A258 Deal. After Swingate Inn take right turn
to Westcliff, St Margaret's. Hotel is 1 mile
down road on the right.*

BESTLOVEDHOTELS.com

Business Travel

Offering a variety of city centre accomodation, from town house to traditional grand hotel, in cities from London to Dublin, from Edinburgh to Exeter.
BESTLOVEDHOTELS.COM is perfect for the traveller who wants to combine the comforts of home with the functions demanded by todays executives.

With a multitude of characterful places to stay, Best Loved is an ideal means to help you find the hotel that suits you… …whatever your needs

For all your travel needs visit BESTLOVEDHOTELS.COM and register your details on-line now to receive special offers, discounts and benefits.

- Fast and efficient search capabilities
- Reliable quality content
- Search for great places to stay close to the motorways
- Excellent route planning maps and location details
- Send a postcard home

For all your business travel needs - register today at bestlovedhotels.com

LONDON

London is still, in many ways, a collection of villages each with its own distinctive atmosphere and many of them with strong literary links. Virginia Woolf, 1882 – 1941, and her literary and artistic friends including Lytton Strachey, Leonard Woolf and Clive Bell became known as the Bloomsbury Group because they originally met and socialised in Virginia's home in Gordon Square. This was, and still is, elegant town living with grassy squares and beautiful Georgian houses. Later, Virginia and her husband founded the Hogarth Press that published TS Elliot and Freud as well as Vanessa's own work.

TS Elliott is still very much in vogue - the long running West End musical 'Cats' was based on his original poem, 'Old Possum's Book of Practical Cats'.

Charles Dickens' first taste of London life was in cheap lodgings in Southwark, his father was deeply in debt and the young Dickens had to work for his keep – his experiences in dingy back streets became part of the precious stock of knowledge he drew on in his novels. In 1853 he began the series of articles 'Sketches of London Life' that became the Pickwick Papers - the public was captivated, Dickens was prolific, backing up his writing with dramatic readings bringing his characters to vivid life.

The misty, streets of Dickensian London find an echo in Conan Doyle's tales of Sherlock Holmes. The famous sleuth and his partner Dr Watson solved puzzling crimes in dark, Victorian alleys then stepped back into their comfortable lives – the gentleman's club, the servants, the polished, elegant interiors.

In 17th century London, the' Great Coffee House' at Covent Garden was the place for men about town to be seen, the poet Dryden had a seat reserved here and Samuel Pepys recorded his first visit. There were then more than 2000 coffee houses in London – even more than today! The government of the time tried to ban them – and failed.

Glittering and fascinating, at the time of Oscar Wilde, London Society savoured the many delights of the Café Royal. A fantastic wine list - some said the best in the world, clever, creative food and the company of writers and artists, the rich and the famous. Scandals and intrigue, assignations and amours were indulged to the accompaniment of cigars and champagne.

William Blake 1757 – 1827 was born and died in London, poet and printmaker; he was fascinated with the Gothic World and a firm believer in the power and importance of imagination in art and literature. Christened at the Wren church, St James's in Westminster, he spent almost his entire life in the city.

PLACES TO VISIT

It was in 48 Doughty St, WC1 that Charles Dickens wrote the Pickwick Papers, Oliver Twist and Nicholas Nickleby. Very much the up and coming popular literary man of the day Dickens was enjoying his new found prosperity and fame during the 2 years he lived here. Dickens Museum 020 7405 2127

Follow the steps of George Orwell and Dylan Thomas to the Fitzroy Tavern on the corner of Windmill Street and Charlotte Street. Ideally situated between Soho and Bloomsbury this Bohemian meeting place was the 'watering hole' for writers and artists, actors and thinkers.

The dedication and passion of American Actor' Director Sam Wannamaker brought the Globe Theatre to life again on the banks of the Thames. Visually stunning, it is the setting for a cornucopia of performances, workshops and routes to further information and enjoyment.
www.shakespeares-globe.org

Why sir you find no man, at all an intellectual, who is willing to leave London.

No Sir, when a man is tired of London, he is tired of life; for there is in London all that life can afford.

Dr Johnson

BOOKS TO READ

▶ Mrs Dalloway by Virginia Woolf: thought provoking novel about the society and times the author lived in and the role and aspirations of women.

▶ London: The Biography by Peter Ackroyd: the author's fascination for this unique city translates into the concept of the capital as a living being.

▶ Dr Johnson's London by Liza Pickard: remarkable insight into life and culture of the 18th century Londoner.

A special place to buy books:

Chelsea Old Town Hall Antiquarian Bookfair in November (www.aba.org.uk).

LITERARY ATTRACTIONS & FESTIVALS

▶ Poetry International at the Royal Festival Hall (biennial). The biggest poetry festival in the UK with a wide range of international poets – workshops, debates and readings. Tel: 020 7921 0971.

▶ Charing Cross Road - made world famous as a book browser's paradise in Helen Hanff's book, 84 Charing Cross Road. Foyles, at nos 119-125 was founded in 1906 and hosts superb literary lunches at the Grosvenor House Hotel.
More details on 020 7437 5660.

▶ The British Library contains more than 150 million items. It uses over 650km of shelves, it has treasures ranging from the Magna Carta to the Beatles manuscripts. The building at St Pancreas is the largest public building constructed in the UK in the 20th Century. (www.bl.uk).

Blakes Restaura[nt]

A CULINARY London

You can enjoy food from all over the world in London - and intriguing tastes of the past. There are hundreds of restaurants featuring contemporary cuisines from far away places, and others, like Rules in Covent Garden, specialising in classic, traditional British food - including game from their own estate in the North. Bramah's Tea and Coffee Museum in Bankside has a fascinating collection of tea and coffee memorabilia, a London tea and coffee trail - and serves pots of delicious tea with timers so that you can enjoy the perfect 'brew'. Eel and pie shops used to be commonplace, now they are a rarity, but visit F.Cooke in Hackney's thriving Broadway Market - in the same family for over 100 years - to find sawdust on the floor as it's always been and a true flavour of Victorian London. For the ultimate in time travel, watch the magnificent kitchens at Hampton Court come alive with the bustle, heat and the hands-on expertise of Tudor Stuart or Georgian times during November and December.

THE MENU:
The Enigma Restaurant

The Enigma Restaurant offers something different - Modern European cuisine with a Californian twist. Strikingly contemporary in design it's a great find in tranquil Little Venice, the following are just some of the dishes on their stylish menu:

Starter
Fried Buffalo Mozzarella in Breadcrumbs
on a Bed of Grilled Vegetables and Basil

Octopus Salad with New Potatoes, Green Beans and Rocket Pesto

Thinly Sliced Scotch Beef Fillet with Lemon Dressing,
Artichoke and Shaved Parmesan

Main Course
Roast Guinea Fowl Stuffed with Ricotta, Sultanas and Leeks,
served on a bed of Saffron Mashed Potatoes and Rosemary Jus

Pan Fried Scottish Salmon with Olive Paste
and Crispy Potato on a bed of Swiss Chard

Dessert
Bramley Apple Mousse with a Granny Smith Sorbet
Rhubarb and Vanilla Cassonade, Confit Pineapple
Warm Bitter Chocolate Fondant with Agen Prune Ice Cream

A Selection of British and French Cheese with Fresh Fruit

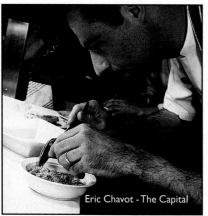
Eric Chavot - The Capital

THE QUOTE: AA Gill, Sunday Times columnist and possibly the most discriminating of all food journalists, wasn't stinting in his praise for the food he had at The Capital restaurant (2 Michelin Stars), under Head Chef Eric Chavot. In his words it was, ' a faultlessly assured, elegant, thoughtful, poignant, intelligent, top-of-the-range, exceedingly rare handmade dinner.' Praise indeed!

THE VIEW: La Terrazza at the Grosvenor Hotel receives rave reviews - for its delicious contemporary Italian food, its faultless service, superb ambiance and a view over Hyde Park that runs out of superlatives. Bought in 1536 by Henry VIII who was eager to posses the excellent hunting afforded by its 360 acres, this is still a Royal Park. There's boating on the Serpentine in the summer, the first daffodils of the year in the spring, riding on Rotten Row all year round. But perhaps the best way to appreciate one of the most famous parks in the world, is to sip a glass of fine wine, taste some of the very best Italian food, look out from the Terrazzo windows and watch its day go by.

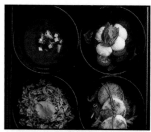

THE STYLE: Dramatic, fashionable, intimate - daring, all adjectives that have been used in abundance to describe Blakes Hotel and its inimical restaurant. Everything here is designed by Anouska Hempel - internationally renowned designer and creator of this unique venue. The originality of the menu, a skilful blend of cuisines from the East and West, is matched by the setting and enhanced by a magnificent wine list. Superlatives abound - where else can you indulge a taste for caviar by enjoying Roasted Five Spiced Lobster with Wasabi Cream, Tobiko Caviar and Coriander Risottini?

THE CLUB: The combination of Harvey Nichols, Harrods and Sloane Street, offer serious shopping opportunities - and the perfect haven to recover from indulgence is The Parrot Club at the Basil Hotel, in the centre of this 'Tiara Triangle'. Exclusively for women, the superb, Art Deco style club is provided with the same impeccable, Edwardian standards of food and service that has ensured this hotel -'an English country house in the heart of Knightsbridge', a dedicated following.

The Capital

THE RECIPE: From Head Chef Stephen Henderson at The Chesterfield.

Harissa Chicken on Cous Cous, Mint, Garlic, Yoghurt and Aubergine Salad.

INGREDIENTS

4 Chicken Supremes (skin left on)

Harissa Paste:

3 Red Chillies
1 tsp Paprika
500g bunch of Coriander
4 Cloves of Garlic
1 pinch of Saffron
Juice of 3 Limes
1 tbsp ground cumin
250ml olive oil
salt and pepper to taste

METHOD

Put the ingredients for Harissa paste in the food processor until smooth. Add to the prepared and trimmed chicken supreme and marinade for 24 hours.

Using a hot pan, or ideally a skillet, seal the chicken to a dark brown colour finish off in the oven for about 15 minutes until cooked.

Stephen prepares an aromatic couscous and a delicious Aubergine salad .to compliment the spiciness of the chicken.

This is Harissa at its pungent best, bursting with flavour and great with meat, fish or stirred into vegetable stews - NB it's very strong, start using a little and taste before adding more.

Editor's Extras

Borough Market, on Fridays and Saturdays, is foodie heaven. Every seasonal delight, from wild mushrooms in autumn to edible flowers in summer is on sale. There are great wines, beers and cider - and enthusiasts like Barry Topp and his New Forest Cider who'll give you hints on cider making techniques while you're choosing your tipple. Add to that meats from all over Britain, and lots, lots more

Neal's Yard in Covent Garden is crammed full of delicious cheese, all in perfect condition, being sold by people who really know and care about their product. They have another, larger shop beside Borough Market - as you've probably gathered, I'm a fan of the area.

Billingsgate fish market has 98 stands, 30 shops, a shellfish boiling room and is the essential market for serious fish buyers from world renowned chefs to fish and chip shop proprietors - they don't run regular tours but can often organise them, contact details on www.billingsgate-market.org.uk.

Heather Hay Ffrench
Best Loved Food Editor

Map p.476
ref: F3

" *Best 'Rapport, Qualite, Prix' in London for me. I will come back soon* "

Philppe Peverelli

10 MANCHESTER STREET

City centre hotel

10 Manchester Street,
London W1U 4DG

Telephone 020 7486 6669
Fax 020 7224 0348

E-mail: *10manchester@bestloved.com*

GENERAL MANAGER
Neville Isaac

ROOM RATES
Single occupancy	£120
37 Doubles/Twins	£150
9 Suites	£195
Includes continental breakfast and VAT

CHARGE/CREDIT CARDS

 • *MC* • *VI*

RATINGS & AWARDS
E.T.C. ◆◆◆◆

FACILITIES
Nearby: *Health club*

RESTRICTIONS
No facilities for disabled guests
No pets

ATTRACTIONS
Wallace Collection,
Madam Tussaud's,
London Planetarium,
Theatreland, Bond Street,
Oxford Street

AFFILIATIONS
The European Connection

NEAREST
MAJOR CITY:
London

MAJOR AIRPORT:
London Heathrow - 15 miles/50 mins
London Gatwick - 30 miles/1 ¼ hrs

RAILWAY STATION:
Paddington - ½ mile/10 mins
Baker Street Underground

RESERVATIONS
Direct with hotel
Quote **Best Loved**

ACCESS CODES
AMADEUS UI LONTEN
APOLLO/GALILEO UI 31791
SABRE/ABACUS UI 21060
WORLDSPAN UI LONTEN

LONDON

Location, location, location!
The best of London on your doorstep

Manchester Street is in the heart of London's West End, with everything the 'big smoke' has to offer right on its doorstep. Tourist attractions such as Madame Tussaud's and the London Planetarium are a short walk away, as is Regent's Park - the emerald jewel in the capital's crown. Lesser known places of interest in the vicinity include The Wallace Collection, one of the world's finest exhibitions of 18th Century French furniture. You won't need to catch a cab home from Oxford Street, unless you're too laden down with the many bargains on offer - although the more upmarket shopper will no doubt prefer the luxury fashion houses of Bond Street and St Christopher's Place.

Number 10 is a 'boutique townhouse' and as such is the ideal alternative to an hotel. Purpose-built as a hostelrie in 1919, this elegant red-brick residence provides stylish, high-quality accommodation, that includes nine suites and 37 bedrooms, all with satellite television and the requisite mini-bar and trouser press. There is also a public internet access terminal and a lift to all floors. Continental breakfast is included in the tariff and there are a good number of special deals that run throughout the year.

LOCATION

5 minutes walk from Baker Street Underground.

> *" The entire staff was gracious and the facilities were impeccable "*
>
> *Kim & Mark Riley, Englewood, NJ, USA*

Georgian town house — THE ACADEMY TOWN HOUSE

Top marks and top value in the bookish quarter of central London

Mention Bloomsbury and the mind conjures up names like Virginia Woolf, Lytton Strachey and J M Keynes; English writers, aesthetes and philosophers whose contribution to 20th-century British culture is widely acknowledged today. The presence of the British Museum lends the area the hush of a library, but the bright lights of Covent Garden and the West End are within a few minutes' walk.

The Academy, The Bloomsbury Town House, occupies five Georgian terraced houses in the heart of this secluded yet accessible corner of London. At the rear, there are private gardens where guests can take tea or drinks in summer, a conservatory for cooler days, and the newly refurbished hotel has a delightful country feel that is both welcoming and elegant. There is a choice of cosy lounges and an informal basement restaurant. Luxurious bedrooms benefit from gleaming new bathrooms, pure linen bedsheets, carefully chosen ornaments and prints, and Internet access. Each one is completely different so regular guests develop particular favourites.

The Academy has one very special trick up its sleeve: it can devote one whole house with eight guest bedrooms and exclusive use of a garden and the library for a private party. It is the only hotel in London to offer this unique feature, perfect for a corporate 'do' or a wedding party.

LOCATION

The hotel is in Bloomsbury on Gower Street equidistant from Tottenham Court Road and Goodge Street underground stations.

**21 Gower Street,
London WC1E 6HG**

**Telephone 020 7631 4115
Fax 020 7636 3442**

E-mail: *academy@bestloved.com*

GENERAL MANAGER
Margaret Kavanagh

ROOM RATES
12 Singles	£160 - £168
26 Doubles/Twins	£187 - £222
11 Studio suites	£252 - £265

Includes full breakfast, service and VAT

CHARGE/CREDIT CARDS

 • DC • JCB • MC • VI

RATINGS & AWARDS
Independent

FACILITIES
On site: *Courtyard gardens*
1 meeting room/max 14 people
Nearby: *Leisure centre*

RESTRICTIONS
No facilities for disabled guests
No pets, guide dogs only

ATTRACTIONS
British Museum, Theatreland,
Covent Garden, National Gallery,
Bloomsbury squares

AFFILIATIONS
The Eton Group
Summit Hotels and Resorts

NEAREST
MAJOR CITY:
London

MAJOR AIRPORT:
London Heathrow - 15 miles/45 mins
London Gatwick - 40 miles/1 hr

RAILWAY STATION:
Euston - ½ mile/5 mins
Goodge Street Underground

RESERVATIONS
Toll free in US: 800-457-4000
*Quote **Best Loved***

ACCESS CODES
AMADEUS XL LONACA
APOLLO/GALILEO XL 62068
SABRE/ABACUS XL 20496
WORLDSPAN XL 41062

LONDON

Map p.476
ref: F5

ASCOTT MAYFAIR

Mayfair apartments

**49 Hill Street, Mayfair,
London W1J 5NB**

**Telephone 020 7499 6868
Fax 020 7499 0705**

E-mail: *ascott@bestloved.com*

GENERAL MANAGER
Christine Malcolm

ROOM RATES
7	Studios	£241
27	1-Bedroom apts	£306 - £347
21	2-Bedroom apts	£511
1	3-Bedroom apts	£699

Includes continental breakfast and VAT

CHARGE/CREDIT CARDS

 • *DC* • *JCB* • *MC* • *VI*

RATINGS & AWARDS
E.T.B. ★★★★

FACILITIES
On site: *Garden, sauna, solarium, gym,
steam room, business services,
use of The Hothouse Health Club
2 meeting rooms/max 50 people*
Nearby: *Riding, boating, tennis,
squash, parking*

RESTRICTIONS
*No facilities for disabled guests
No pets*

ATTRACTIONS
*Hyde Park, Piccadilly Circus, Harrods,
Leicester Square, Selfridges, Oxford Street,
Buckingham Palace, Covent Garden*

AFFILIATIONS
The Celebrated Hotels Collection

NEAREST
*MAJOR CITY:
London*

*MAJOR AIRPORT:
London Heathrow - 15 miles/40 mins
London Gatwick - 30 miles/1 ¼ hrs*

*RAILWAY STATION:
Victoria - 2 miles/10 mins
Green Park Underground*

RESERVATIONS
*Toll free in US: 1 886-246-7054
or 800-322-2403*
Quote **Best Loved**

ACCESS CODES
*AMADEUS UI LONASC
APOLLO/GALILEO UI 75023
SABRE/ABACUS UI 14921
WORLDSPAN UI 25130*

*Your residence
in stylish Mayfair*

With high quality accommodation, a wide range of facilities and excellent service, the Ascott Mayfair is a very desirable address in London. You will enjoy all the facilities and services of a luxury hotel, with the privacy, comfort and relaxed environment of a home.

The studios and the one, two and three-bedroom apartments are all luxuriously furnished. Each has a lounge, dining and study area, kitchen and bathroom, satellite TV and computer games, video, music system, and telephone. Breakfasts, concierge and daily maid service are all included. The building's Art Deco heritage achieves an elegant and refined style that is welcoming and relaxing. Original artworks in the Ascott's exclusive Club will delight you.

Mayfair's attractions stem from the elegance of its Georgian architecture and its central location. It is bound by Hyde Park, the department stores of Oxford Street and Regent Street and Piccadilly. It is a perfect place for shopping; international fashion houses rub shoulders with small specialist shops. Almost every kind of cuisine is available around Shepherd's Market. The Royal Academy, the Museum of Mankind and, of course, the West End theatres are close at hand.

LOCATION
Between Berkeley Square and Park Lane.

" It is so nice to keep seeing familiar faces amongst the staff and to be recognised "

Clare Fellows, Kingston, Ontario

• Map p.476
ref: E6

Traditional English hotel

BASIL STREET HOTEL

The Basil - an excellent hotel steeped in tradition

The Basil is an island of hospitality in an increasingly brusque, modern life, and that is why their guests come back again and again. Many of their returning guests have said that The Basil is just like coming home. Tradition is respected, nothing is contrived and there is warmth and friendliness in the air. The interior is full of English and Oriental antiques, and at every turn there is something to delight the eye. Plants and flowers are in abundance.

Each of the 78 comfortable bedrooms is different in shape and decor and regular visitors are given their favourites whenever possible.

Fully furnished rooms are available for private parties. The Basil is large enough to contain all the amenities expected in a cosmopolitan hotel, yet not too large to become impersonal.

General Manager Charles Lagares and his colleagues carry on the traditions which have become synonymous with The Basil. They will do their utmost to ensure that your visit is an enjoyable one. Few world class hotels in a city centre are so perfectly situated for both business and pleasure.

LOCATION

In Knightsbridge, a few steps away from Harrods, Harvey Nichols and Knightsbridge Underground Station.

Basil Street, Knightsbridge, London SW3 1AH

Telephone 020 7581 3311
Fax 020 7581 3693

E-mail: *basil@bestloved.com*

GENERAL MANAGER
Charles Lagares

ROOM RATES
29 Singles	£170
44 Doubles/Twins	£240
5 Family rooms	£323
Includes VAT	

CHARGE/CREDIT CARDS

 • *JCB* • *MC* • *VI*

RATINGS & AWARDS
R.A.C. ★★★
A.A. ★★★ 73%

FACILITIES
On site: *Restaurant, business centre, The Parrot Club (for women) 3 meeting rooms/max 200 people* **Nearby:** *Pool, gym, riding, tennis*

RESTRICTIONS
Limited facilities for disabled guests No pets in public rooms

ATTRACTIONS
Harrods, Victoria & Albert Museum, Royal Academy of Art, Theatreland, Houses of Parliament, Bond Street, Tower of London, Buckingham Palace

AFFILIATIONS
Preston's Global Hotels

NEAREST
MAJOR CITY:
London

MAJOR AIRPORT:
London Heathrow - 18 miles/45 mins
London Gatwick - 30 miles/1 ¼ hrs

RAILWAY STATION:
Victoria - 1 ¼ miles/15 mins
Knightsbridge Underground

RESERVATIONS
Toll free in US: 800-544-9993
or 800-448-8355
Quote **Best Loved**

ACCESS CODES
AMADEUS UI LONBAS
APOLLO/GALILEO UI 18513
SABRE/ABACUS UI 264
WORLDSPAN UI 3896

LONDON

" If you want to be treated as an individual, stay with the people who know how "

Dyan Cannon

THE BEAUFORT

Private house hotel

**33 Beaufort Gardens,
Knightsbridge,
London SW3 1PP**

**Telephone 020 7584 5252
Fax 020 7589 2834**

E-mail: *beaufort@bestloved.com*

OWNER
Ahmed Jajbhay

GENERAL MANAGER
Sue Gregory

ROOM RATES
3 Singles	£182
10 Doubles	£229
9 Deluxe Doubles/Twins	£306
7 Junior suites	£364

Includes breakfast, afternoon tea, all drinks (including champagne) and VAT

CHARGE/CREDIT CARDS

 ● *DC* ● *JCB* ● *MC* ● *VI*

RATINGS & AWARDS
A.A. ★★★★ *72% Town House
Courvoisier's Book of the Best
Zagat - Highest Rated Hotel in London for
Service (26/30)*

FACILITIES
On site: *1 meeting room/max 6 people*
Nearby: *Health club & pool, riding*

RESTRICTIONS
*No facilities for disabled guests
No pets*

ATTRACTIONS
*Harrods, Theatreland,
Victoria & Albert Museum,
Buckingham Palace,
Royal Academy of Art*

AFFILIATIONS
Independent

NEAREST
*MAJOR CITY:
London*

*MAJOR AIRPORT:
London Heathrow - 14 miles/45 mins
London Gatwick - 30 miles/1 ¼ hrs*

*RAILWAY STATION:
Victoria -1 mile/20 mins
Knightsbridge Underground*

RESERVATIONS
Toll free fax in US: 800-548-7764
Quote **Best Loved**

ACCESS CODES
*AMADEUS UI LONBEA
APOLLO/GALILEO UI 42508
SABRE/ABACUS UI 31342
WORLDSPAN UI 16376*

LONDON

Great value, service and much more awaits you in London's Knightsbridge

High quality, individual attention, the best value for money and of course wonderful staff are what makes The Beaufort so successful. 100 yards from Harrods in a quiet tree-lined Victorian square, The Beaufort offers everything it can to make guests feel comfortable and at home.

Complimentary breakfast in the rooms is served on fine bone Wedgwood china with solid silver cutlery - hot croissants and rolls, fresh orange juice and steaming coffee. The rooms are beautifully decorated in warm pastel colours - and are air-conditioned. Each room is provided with Belgian chocolates, fresh fruit and biscuits.

A complimentary limousine is available to or from the airport for guests booking junior suites. The hotel's direct dial telephone service provides guests with their own private number plus the use of a personal fax. All rates include service, and there is no tipping. There is CNN, a video, cassette and CD library, and portable CD player. There is a closed front door - only guests have front door keys.

The Beaufort is home to the world's largest collection of over 400 original English floral watercolours. All drinks including champagne and cream teas are served free of charge in the drawing room.

LOCATION

Quietly situated in the heart of Knightsbridge.

" Everyone made us feel so at home - thankyou "

Ann Key, USA

Regency town house BEAUFORT HOUSE APARTMENTS

Fully-serviced traditional apartments just around the corner from Harrods

Situated in Beaufort Gardens, a quiet, tree-lined Regency cul-de-sac in the heart of Knightsbridge, 250 yards from Harrods, Beaufort House is an exclusive establishment comprising 21 self-contained, fully serviced luxury apartments. All the comforts of a first-class hotel are combined with privacy, discretion and the relaxed atmosphere of home.

Accommodation ranges in size from an intimate one-bedroomed to a spacious four-bedroomed apartment. Each apartment has been decorated in a traditional style to a standard which is rigorously maintained. All apartments have telephones with voice mail, personal safes, satellite TV, CD players, videos and DVD players. A number of the apartments also feature private balconies or patios - a definite luxury in the centre of London! All the kitchens are fully equipped with everything guests will need for their stay, together with a daily maid service. Full laundry and dry-cleaning services are also available.

For your extra security, a concierge is on duty 24 hours a day from whom taxis, theatre tickets, restaurant reservations and other services are available. Complimentary membership to exclusive health and leisure facilities at Champney's Piccadilly is offered to all guests for the duration of their stay.

LOCATION
Beaufort Gardens is 250 yards from Harrods, off the Brompton Road.

**45 Beaufort Gardens,
Knightsbridge,
London SW3 1PN**

**Telephone 020 7584 2600
Fax 020 7584 6532**

E-mail: *beauforthouse@bestloved.com*

GENERAL MANAGER
Bettina Hoff

ROOM RATES
9	1-Bedroom apts	£276 - £411
2	2-Bedroom apts	£470 - £564
9	3-Bedroom apts	£599 - £787
1	4-Bedroom apt	£776 - £881

*Includes daily maid service,
24-hour concierge and VAT*

CHARGE/CREDIT CARDS

 • *DC* • *MC* • *VI*

RATINGS & AWARDS
E.T.C. ★★★★★

FACILITIES
On site: *Laundry facility*
Nearby: *Health & fitness club*

RESTRICTIONS
*No facilities for disabled guests
No pets*

ATTRACTIONS
*Hyde Park, Harrods, Buckingham Palace,
West End Theatre, Science Museum,
Apsley House*

AFFILIATIONS
The Celebrated Hotels Collection

NEAREST
*MAJOR CITY:
London*

*MAJOR AIRPORT:
London Heathrow - 15 miles/45 mins
London Gatwick - 30 miles/ 1 ¼ hrs*

*RAILWAY STATION:
Victoria - 1 mile/5 mins
Knightsbridge Underground*

RESERVATIONS
Toll free in US: 800-322-2403
Quote Best Loved

ACCESS CODES
Not applicable

LONDON

• *Map p.476*
ref: D7

BLAKES HOTEL

Victorian mansion

" *If ever dreams can become reality, then Blakes is where it will happen* "

Nina Prommer, London

**33 Roland Gardens,
South Kensington,
London SW7 3PF**

**Telephone 020 7370 6701
Fax 020 7373 0442**

E-mail: *blakes@bestloved.com*

OWNER
Anouska Hempel

GENERAL MANAGER
Edward Wauters

ROOM RATES
18 Singles   £194
20 Doubles/Twins   £299 - £393
11 Suites   £640 - £1,443
Includes service and VAT

CHARGE/CREDIT CARDS

 • DC • MC • VI

RATINGS & AWARDS
*Andrew Harper's Hideaway Report
Courvoisier's Book of the Best*

FACILITIES
On site: *Blake's Restaurant
Licensed for weddings
1 meeting room/max 80 people*
Nearby: *Health club*

RESTRICTIONS
*No facilities for disabled guests
No pets*

ATTRACTIONS
*South Kensington Museums, King's Road,
Harrods and Knightsbridge,
Kensington Gardens,
Christies Auction Room,
antique shops*

AFFILIATIONS
Preferred Hotels & Resorts

NEAREST
MAJOR CITY:
London

MAJOR AIRPORT:
*London Heathrow - 15 miles/45 mins
London Gatwick - 30 miles/1 ¼ hrs*

RAILWAY STATION:
*Victoria - 1 mile/20 mins
South Kensington Underground*

RESERVATIONS
Toll free in US: 800-926-3173
Quote **Best Loved**

ACCESS CODES
*APOLLO/GALILEO PH 87401
SABRE/ABACUS PH 21718*

LONDON

Exclusive and stylish -
the haunt of the famous

Blakes was created just over ten years ago out of two Victorian mansions in South Kensington by Anouska Hempel, the London hotelier and internationally renowned designer.

Blakes is a statement about what good design can achieve; daring and dramatic, each of the rooms are individually designed to provide the ideal blend of colour, texture and atmosphere. Respected for protecting the privacy of its clients, it's the London base for film stars, musicians and top designers. Blakes is now established as unique, the model for 'the fashionable small hotel'.

To the international business man or woman, it is convenience and efficiency: private faxes, telephone and all the other high-tech paraphernalia for modern living.

Blakes Restaurant, 'an opium den managed by Coco Chanel' has an unrivalled reputation for the originality and contents of its superb menu devised and designed by Anouska Hempel, classic cooking with oriental twists, stunning presentation and spectacular tastes ensures Blakes continues to attract critical acclaim as one of the top three restaurants in London.

LOCATION
**A few minutes' walk from
South Kensington tube station.**

" *This is as good as you can eat in London. A top-of-the-range, exceedingly rare handmade dinner* "

A.A. Gill, The Sunday Times

Luxury hotel

THE CAPITAL

Matured Excellence

'It takes a long time to bring excellence to maturity', so the maxim goes, but this cannot be true of The Capital. In just 30 years David Levin and family have achieved absolute perfection in this elegantly traditional 'grand' hotel, more closely resembling a fine private residence.

Here at The Capital everything is exceptional. The interiors are the work of two of Britain's most prominent designers, Nina Campbell and David Linley, nephew of the Queen. The antique furnishings have all been chosen by the Levin family themselves and their private art collection adorns the walls. In the bedrooms there are Egyptian cotton sheets, hand-made mattresses and luxurious, spacious marble bathrooms.

The restaurant at The Capital is widely celebrated in its own right. As the possessor of two Michelin stars, no further description of the food is required, however, an interesting inclusion on the wine list is the Le Vin du Levin, from the family's own vineyard in the Loire.

Finally, the hotel's location is superb for accessing the best of London and Head

Concierge, Clive Smith, will ensure that you do. Whether you're planning on residing or dining, book well in advance.

LOCATION

In Knightsbridge, just a few yards from Harrods and Harvey Nichols.

Basil Street, Knightsbridge, London SW3 1AT

Telephone 020 7589 5171
Fax 020 7225 0011

E-mail: *capital@bestloved.com*

OWNER
David Levin

GENERAL MANAGER
Henrik Mueble

ROOM RATES
12 Singles	£223
22 Doubles/Twins	£288
6 Deluxe doubles	£370
8 Junior suites	£441
Includes VAT	

CHARGE/CREDIT CARDS

 • DC • JCB • MC • VI

RATINGS & AWARDS
R.A.C. Gold Ribbon ★★★★ Dining Award 5
A.A. ★★★★ ❀❀❀
A.A. Top 200 - 02/03

FACILITIES
On site: *2 meeting rooms/max 35 people*
Nearby: *Health club*

RESTRICTIONS
Limited facilities for disabled guests
Pets by arrangement

ATTRACTIONS
Buckingham Palace,
Royal Academy of Art,
Victoria & Albert Musuem,
Harrods & Harvey Nichols,
Sloane Street, Theatreland

AFFILIATIONS
Small Luxury Hotels

NEAREST
MAJOR CITY:
London

MAJOR AIRPORT:
London Heathrow - 18 miles/45 mins
London City - 10 miles/35 minutes

RAILWAY STATION:
Victoria - ¼ mile/15 mins
Knightsbridge Underground

RESERVATIONS
Toll Free in US: 800-525-4800
*Quote **Best Loved***

ACCESS CODES
AMADEUS LX LON800
APOLLO/GALILEO LX 01074
SABRE/ABACUS LX 45738
WORLDSPAN LX 00800

LONDON

" *Taking customer comfort to a new level* "

THE CHESTERFIELD MAYFAIR

Deluxe hotel

**35 Charles Street, Mayfair,
London W1J 5EB**

**Telephone 020 7491 2622
Fax 020 7491 4793**

E-mail: *chesterfield@bestloved.com*

GENERAL MANAGER
Alex Bray

ROOM RATES
11 Singles	£170 - £245
56 Doubles/Twins	£194 - £277
30 King bedded	£212 - £305
4 Themed rooms	£294 - £465
5 Junior suites	£294 - £465
4 Executive suites	£410 - £617

Includes service and VAT

CHARGE/CREDIT CARDS

 • *DC* • *JCB* • *MC* • *VI*

RATINGS & AWARDS
A.A. ★★★★ ✿ 74%

FACILITIES
On site: *Valet, 24-hour room service
Licensed for weddings
6 meeting rooms/max 150 people*
Nearby: *Use of leisure facilities*

RESTRICTIONS
*No facilities for disabled guests
Pets by arrangement*

ATTRACTIONS
*Buckingham Palace, Bond Street,
Regent Street, Piccadilly, Harrods,
Royal Academy of Art*

AFFILIATIONS
*Red Carnation Hotels
The European Connection*

NEAREST
*MAJOR CITY:
London*

*MAJOR AIRPORT:
London Heathrow - 15 miles/45 mins
London Gatwick - 30 miles/1 ¼ hrs*

*RAILWAY STATION:
Victoria - ½ mile/10 mins
Green Park Underground*

RESERVATIONS
Toll free in US: 877-955-1515
Quote **Best Loved**

ACCESS CODES
*AMADEUS VE LONCHE
APOLLO/GALILEO VE 5219
SABRE/ABACUS VE 274
WORLDSPAN VE 0327*

Gracious living just off Berkeley Square

Named after the third Earl of Chesterfield, a noted Mayfair resident in the 18th century, this hotel combines the gracious living standards of an elegant past with every modern comfort, service and convenience.

Traditional fabrics and exquisite furnishings are featured in the nine suites, four themed rooms and 97 deluxe guest rooms, all fully air-conditioned. Guests are pampered with thoughtful personal comforts that include nightly turndown service, plush bathrobes, hairdryer, potpourri sachets, bottled mineral water and deluxe toiletries. As for technology, you can relax while watching full cable TV or see one of the many movies on demand. Great care has been taken in providing for the needs of the business traveller including generous desk space, modem/fax facilities and Internet access in most rooms.

The Restaurant's seasonal menus place emphasis on both English specialities, like table carved roasts, as well as the finest international cuisine. A small wine room, adjacent to the restaurant, offers opportunities for exclusive wine tastings. A highly enjoyable feature of the hotel is the resident pianist who plays nightly in the hotel's club-style Terrace Bar. The Chesterfield is close to the famous West End theatres and nightlife, and a short stroll to famous shops, museums and landmarks.

LOCATION
In the heart of exclusive Mayfair.

LONDON

• *Map p.476
ref: G5*

" Beautiful and charming - lovely place, we highly recommend it "

Mr & Mrs C Ramin, San Francisco, USA

Victorian town house — THE COLONNADE TOWN HOUSE

2 Warrington Crescent,
London W9 1ER

Telephone 020 7286 1052
Fax 020 7286 1057

E-mail: colonnade@bestloved.com

GENERAL MANAGER
Oliver Brown

ROOM RATES
6 Singles   £148
10 Doubles   £173
18 Deluxe Doubles/Twins   £210
8 Suites   £270 - £289
Includes service and VAT

CHARGE/CREDIT CARDS

 • DC • JCB • MC • VI

RATINGS & AWARDS
E.T.C. ★★★★ Silver Award
London Tourist Board Hotel of the Year

FACILITIES
On site: Enigma Restaurant with Terrace
Nearby: Golf, tennis, riding, squash

Indulgent luxury in leafy Little Venice - relaxed, convenient and good value

Contrary to expectations, five-star luxury does not have to be contained to the likes of Mayfair - and The Colonnade, The Little Venice Town House, is the exception that proves the rule. It stands amongst the leafy gardens of Little Venice within easy reach of Piccadilly and Heathrow (25 minutes) yet it competes room-for-room on equal terms with the highest standards of service and luxury you will find anywhere in central London.

The Colonnade is the result of the conversion of an elegant Victorian mansion frequented by Sigmund Freud and birthplace of Alan Turing, breaker of the Enigma Code in WW2. The furnishings are lavish, the fabrics sumptuous, the objets d'art genuinely antique. There are only 42 bedrooms, some with a four-poster bed and even a private terrace (not one central London hotel can make such a boast) and all of them have the latest e-facilities.

The Colonnade's new Enigma restaurant is named in honour of Turing. Here, modern and sophisticated décor is matched by contemporary European cuisine. Whilst at lunch you can indulge in some homemade Bruschetta or smoked swordfish; for dinner you may sample fried buffalo mozzarella or octopus salad. And the price of such indulgent luxury? Like its location - a breath of fresh air!

LOCATION
50 yards to Warwick Avenue Underground with direct trains to central London. 5 minutes from Paddington and the Heathrow Express, 12 minutes from Oxford Circus

RESTRICTIONS
Limited facilities for disabled guests
Pets by arrangement

ATTRACTIONS
Little Venice, Regents Park,
Camden Market, Lords Cricket Ground,
Portobello Road, London Zoo,
Madame Tussaud's Museum

AFFILIATIONS
The Eton Group
The Celebrated Hotels Collection
Summit Hotels and Resorts

NEAREST
MAJOR CITY:
London

MAJOR AIRPORT:
London Heathrow - 15 miles/25 mins

RAILWAY STATION:
Paddington - 1 mile/5 mins
Warwick Avenue Underground

RESERVATIONS
Toll free in US: 800-457-4000
or 800-322-2403
Quote **Best Loved**

ACCESS CODES
AMADEUS XL LONMCO
APOLLO/GALILEO XL 82381
SABRE/ABACUS XL 41050
WORLDSPAN XL 40747

LONDON

❝ This second visit confirms my first thought, that after ten years of looking, I've finally found my London hotel ❞

Brent Stevens, Beverly Hills, California

THE CRANLEY ON BINA GARDENS   *Victorian mansion*

10-12 Bina Gardens,
South Kensington,
London SW5 0LA
Telephone 020 7373 0123
Fax 020 7373 9497

E-mail: *cranley@bestloved.com*

DIRECTOR OF OPERATIONS
Robert Wauters

ROOM RATES
3 Singles   £182
24 Doubles/Twins   £212 - £223
3 Four-posters   £259
3 Junior suites   £247
2 Executive suites   £294
Includes afternoon tea, champagne,
service and VAT

CHARGE/CREDIT CARDS

 • *DC* • *JCB* • *MC* • *VI*

RATINGS & AWARDS
A.A. ★★★★ *72% Town House*

FACILITIES
On site: *Air conditioning,*
honesty bar, patio, room service
Nearby: *Use of local health club, pool*

RESTRICTIONS
No facilities for disabled guests
No pets

ATTRACTIONS
Harrods, Museums of South Kensington,
Royal Albert Hall, Buckingham Palace,
Kensington Gardens, Westminster,
King's Road, London Eye,
House of Commons

AFFILIATIONS
Argyll Townhouse Hotels
Selected British Hotels
Grand Heritage Hotels

NEAREST
MAJOR CITY:
London

MAJOR AIRPORT:
London Heathrow - 15 miles/40 mins

RAILWAY STATION:
Victoria - 3 miles/15 mins
Gloucester Road Underground

RESERVATIONS
Toll free in US: 800-98-GRAND
or 888-989-1768
Quote **Best Loved**

ACCESS CODES
AMADEUS UI LONCRA
APOLLO/GALILEO UI 61263
SABRE/ABACUS UI 32652
WORLDSPAN UI 21563

LONDON

Your relaxed and luxurious home in Royal Kensington and Chelsea

Most first-time visitors do a double-take and recheck the address when they arrive outside The Cranley. It looks so quiet, so private, blending seamlessly into one of London's smartest residential neighbourhoods. However, closer inspection reveals the discrete gold plaque confirming that these three elegant mansion houses are indeed a hotel.

The captivating first impression is created by the bold Prussian blue lounge, where the reception arrangements are confined to an unobtrusive desk next to the honour bar. Already, you feel at home, and tempted to sink gratefully into the depths of a comfy sofa after your journey. Relieved of luggage by enthusiastic staff (who, miraculously, appear to know your name already), you'll be offered a complimentary glass of sherry or whisky, or the opportunity to relax in your room first. Most of the bedrooms have been recently refurbished in soft gold, beige and cream tones, and equipped with custom-built desks and ISDN access; some luxurious suites also boast four-posters and seating/breakfasting areas in bay windows.

A short step beyond The Cranley's front door, several excellent restaurants serve lunch and

dinner, and the celebrated Victoria & Albert, Science and Natural History museums vie for your attention with world-class shopping.

LOCATION
4 minutes walk south of Gloucester Road
Underground Station, just north of the Old
Brompton Road.

" Your hotel was a real find for us and we look forward to making The Darlington our regular home away from home "

Phil Lewis, Dallas, Texas

Victorian town house THE DARLINGTON HYDE PARK

20 minutes from Heathrow, in the centre of London, earning top marks for value

The fastest way to and from London Heathrow these days is the high speed, high tech, non-stop Heathrow Express linking the airport with Paddington Station in 15 minutes, every 15 minutes. Paddington to The Darlington is so close, you ll earn a derisory quip from a cabbie if you stop him; it s not five minutes on foot.

The other feature about The Darlington is that it is one of a new breed of places to stay in London: clean and comfortable, simple without being stark, and provisioned with all the facilities you need as a business or leisure traveller. It is centrally located but in a quieter part of town, living up to the highest standards of hotel keeping but without the frills. Result: great value! You are free to enjoy your stay without the need of paramedical support when you check out.

The Conservatory Restaurant serves a freshly cooked traditional breakfast or you can help yourself to a Continental Buffet. For lunch and dinner, there are many excellent places on the doorstep with a cosmopolitan choice of cuisine. If you are more ambitious, the glitter of the West End and the World s highest concentration of

theatres, concert halls and galleries are about 20 minutes away by cab. The Darlington may well appeal beyond the budget-conscious traveller, its convenience and comfort factors get top marks.

LOCATION

5 minutes walk from both Paddington Station (Heathrow Express Terminal) and LancasterGate Underground Station next to Hyde Park.

111-117 Sussex Gardens, London W2 2RU

Telephone 020 7460 8800 Fax 020 7460 8828

E-mail: *darlington@bestloved.com*

GENERAL MANAGER
Jo Douch

ROOM RATES
5 Singles	£90 - £130
27 Doubles/Twins	£120 - £140
6 Suites	£145 - £155
2 Family rooms	£135 - £145

Includes breakfast and VAT

CHARGE/CREDIT CARDS

 ● DC ● MC ● VI

RATINGS & AWARDS
Independent

FACILITIES
On site: *Self-service guest laundry*
Nearby: *Tennis, fitness*

RESTRICTIONS
*No facilities for disabled guests
No pets*

ATTRACTIONS
*Hyde Park, Knightsbridge,
Theatreland, Oxford Street,
Windsor Castle, Hampton Court*

AFFILIATIONS
Preston's Global Hotels

NEAREST
MAJOR CITY:
London

MAJOR AIRPORT:
*London Heathrow - 15 miles/45 mins
London Gatwick - 30 miles/1 ½ hrs*

RAILWAY STATION:
*Paddington - ¼ mile/5 mins
Paddington Undergound*

RESERVATIONS
Toll free in US: 800-544-9993
*Quote **Best Loved***

ACCESS CODES
Not applicable

LONDON

❝ The hotel in the square is London's best kept secret ❞

Lord Peter Graves

DOLPHIN SQUARE HOTEL

Luxury suites

Dolphin Square, Westminster, London SW1V 3LX

Telephone 020 7798 8890
Fax 020 7798 8896

E-mail: *dolphin@bestloved.com*

HOTEL MANAGER
Clare Stewart

ROOM RATES
Single occupancy		£140 - £255
110	1-Bedroom suites	£170 - £400
35	2-Bedroom suites	£225 - £320
3	3-Bedroom suites	£450

Includes newspapers, service and VAT

CHARGE/CREDIT CARDS

 • *DC* • *JCB* • *MC* • *VI*

RATINGS & AWARDS
E.T.C. ★★★★ *Silver Award*
A.A. ★★★★ ❀❀ *68%*

FACILITIES
On site: *Garden, tennis, indoor pool, gym, squash, shops, bureau de change, business centre, Gary Rhodes's restaurrant Rhodes in the Square*
3 meeting rooms/max 200 people
Nearby: *Golf, riding*

RESTRICTIONS
Limited facilities for disabled guests
No pets, guide dogs only

ATTRACTIONS
Houses of Parliament, London Eye, Tate Britain Gallery, West End Theatres, Knightsbridge, Buckingham Palace

AFFILIATIONS
Preston's Global Hotels
Grand Heritage Hotels
Utell International

NEAREST
MAJOR CITY:
London

MAJOR AIRPORT:
London Heathrow - 15 miles/30 mins
London Gatwick - 30 miles/40 mins
London City - 8 miles/30 mins

RAILWAY STATION:
Victoria - ½ mile/10 mins
Pimlico Underground

RESERVATIONS
Toll free in US: 800-544-9993 or
800-207-6900 or 888-93-GRAND
Toll free in UK: 0800 616607

ACCESS CODES
AMADEUS UI LONDSH
APOLLO/GALILEO UI 96713
SABRE/ABACUS UI 32611
WORLDSPAN UI 40411

A unique property by the river with its own shops, bar and restaurants

Despite its size and prominent position on the Embankment, Dolphin Square maintains a remarkably low profile - a fact much appreciated by residents and visitors, many of whom are well-known public figures. The building is, in effect, a self-contained village with its own security system, small shopping area, health spa and 3 ½-acre flowering garden which surprises everyone who discovers it.

Located on the north side of the Square, the hotel offers apartment-style accommodation in studios, one-, two- and three-bedroom suites ideal for short or long lets. The studios and suites are complemented by full kitchens, bathrooms and living areas, suitable for all types of guests from a single person to a whole family. Guests can also enjoy the facilities at the Zest! Health and Fitness Spa, which include an extensively equipped gymnasium, 18-metre swimming pool, aerobics classes, and squash and tennis courts. There are pampering treatments, too: facials, massage, reflexology and aromatherapy to name but a few.

Also within the hotel, you can sample celebrity chef Gary Rhodes' modern British cuisine at the Rhodes in the Square restaurant, or dine in the less formal surroundings of the Brasserie. For drinks and a relaxing meeting place for friends, look no further than the nautically-themed Clipper Bar.

LOCATION
Central London beside the Thames off Grosvenor Road.

" The total ambience of the hotel is delightful, and the staff really caring and sensitive to the needs of the guests "

John C Groome, Hull

• Map p.476
ref: G5

Mayfair hotel & apartments

FLEMINGS MAYFAIR

**7 - 12 Half Moon Street,
London W1J 7BB**

**Telephone 020 7499 2964
Fax 020 7499 1817**

E-mail: *flemings@bestloved.com*

GENERAL MANAGER
Simon Scarborough

ROOM RATES
30 Standard/Executive singles	£222
69 Doubles/Twins	£234
18 Executive rooms	£258
4 Junior suites	£299
10 Apartments	£382 - £499

Including VAT

CHARGE/CREDIT CARDS
 • *DC* • *JCB* • *MC* • *VI*

RATINGS & AWARDS
Independent

FACILITIES
On site: *Restaurant, Bodeca Bar
3 meeting rooms/max 55 people*
Nearby: *Tennis, riding, golf, gym*

RESTRICTIONS
*No facilities for disabled guests
No pets, guide dogs only*

ATTRACTIONS
*Buckingham Palace, Bond Street,
Regents Street, Piccadilly Circus,
Trafalgar Square, Hyde Park*

AFFILIATIONS
Independent

NEAREST
*MAJOR CITY:
London*

*MAJOR AIRPORT:
London Heathrow - 15 miles/45 mins
London Gatwick - 30 miles/1 ¼ hrs*

*RAILWAY STATION:
Victoria - 2 miles/15 mins
Green Park Underground*

RESERVATIONS
*Toll free in US: 800-348-4685
or 800-44-UTELL*
*Quote **Best Loved***

ACCESS CODES
*AMADEUS UI LONFLE
APOLLO/GALILEO UI 5265
SABRE/ABACUS UI 13258
WORLDSPAN UI 0393*

A high quality hotel with London on your doorstep

The elegance of the Georgian age, together with the best of English hospitality, can be found in the heart of London's exclusive Mayfair, where Flemings Hotel has been welcoming guests since the early 1900s. Its location is superb. It is within a couple of minutes walk of Green Park underground station, within easy reach of all the West End's attractions, yet it is in a quiet street tucked away from the bustle of Piccadilly.

The opulent lounge is a pleasant place for afternoon tea, and the magnificent restaurant offers a fine à la carte menu of traditional British and Continental cuisine.

There are ten luxury self-contained apartments, which have been recently refurbished to a five star standard, in addition to the 121 bedrooms. Flemings has full 24 hour room service, and the experience of the concierge team is there to help you make the most of your visit.

London really does belong to you when you stay at Flemings. Buckingham Palace, Regent Street, Bond Street, Piccadilly Circus, West End theatreland, the Royal Academy of Arts and Trafalgar Square are all within easy walking distance.

LOCATION

Turn right out of the Piccadilly north side exit at Green Park station and walk for two minutes down Piccadilly, past Bolton Street towards Hyde Park Corner.

LONDON

● *Map p.476*
ref: G6

❝ *The Goring is that great rarity, a smart, privately owned one-off hotel* ❞

Craig Brown, The Sunday Times

THE GORING

Luxury hotel

**15 Beeston Place,
London SW1W 0JW**

**Telephone 020 7396 9000
Fax 020 7834 4393**

E-mail: *goring@bestloved.com*

OWNER
George Goring

MANAGING DIRECTOR
William Cowpe

ROOM RATES
20 Singles	£194 - £223
31 Doubles/Twins	£229 - £276
16 Deluxe doubles	£288 - £335
7 Suites	£317 - £429

Includes service and VAT

CHARGE/CREDIT CARDS

AMERICAN EXPRESS • *DC* • *MC* • *VI*

RATINGS & AWARDS
E.T.C. ★★★★★ *Gold Award*
R.A.C. ★★★★★ *Dining Award 3*
A.A. ★★★★★ ❀❀
A.A. Top 200 - 02/03

FACILITIES
On site: *Garden*
Licensed for weddings
4 meeting rooms/max 100 people
Nearby: *Golf, riding,
free use of local health club*

RESTRICTIONS
*Limited facilities for disabled guests
No pets, guide dogs only*

ATTRACTIONS
*Buckingham Palace, Royal Parks,
West End, Houses of Parliament*

AFFILIATIONS
*Pride of Britain
Virtuoso*

NEAREST
*MAJOR CITY:
London*

*MAJOR AIRPORT:
London Heathrow - 16 miles/45 mins*

*RAILWAY STATION:
Victoria - 100 yards/2 mins
Victoria Underground*

RESERVATIONS
Toll free in US: 800-98-PRIDE
Quote **Best Loved**

ACCESS CODES
*AMADEUS HK LONGOR
APOLLO/GALILEO HK 14860
SABRE/ABACUS HK 30136
WORLDSPAN HK GORIN*

LONDON

A prestigious and privately owned London residence

Chairman, George Goring is proud to operate one of London's most prestigious hotels, which has been in his family since 1910.

The 67 bedrooms and 7 suites are designed to cater for guests' every need. Beds are made with goose down pillows and fine Egyptian cotton sheets, and the marble bathrooms are wholly indulgent. Each room has air conditioning and is fitted with modern conveniences such as the latest TV's, ISDN and voice-mail. Fresh flowers provide that final thoughtful touch.

The Garden Bar overlooks the 'secret garden' and is a lovely setting for afternoon tea. In the evenings it comes alive with warmth of atmosphere, which makes it one of the most delightful meeting places in London.

The Dining Room is renowned for its excellent English food, with a few continental touches. The wine list is regarded among the best in the capital and the hotel is unusual among its peers as it continues in laying down some of the finest wines for the future enjoyment of guests.

The Goring is located in a quiet haven, adjacent to Buckingham Palace, the Queen's Gallery and the Royal Mews. It is close to the principal shopping areas and West End.

LOCATION

Beeston Place is a small, quiet street between Grosvenor Gardens and Buckingham Palace. It is very close to Victoria British Rail and Underground stations.

" The rooms in the main house and the gardens are delightful and the staff are extremely helpful "

Mr A Hughes, Wiltshire

Victorian country house

GRIM'S DYKE HOTEL

A country setting with a theatrical twist close to Central London

The original Grim's Dyke is an ancient earthwork set in Harrow Weald north of London. The name was adopted by Victorian painter Frederick Goodall for his country home designed by well-known architect Norman Shaw and constructed parallel to the earthwork between 1870 and 1872. Later the house was home to librettist W.S. Gilbert, the wordsmith of Gilbert and Sullivan fame.

Shaw's design was a splendid Tudoresque affair adorned with numerous gables and tall chimney stacks, mullioned windows and decorative half-timbering. The Grade II-listed house sits in 40 acres of lovely grounds with lawns, shrubberies ablaze with rhododendrons and azaleas in spring, and quiet woodlands criss-crossed by paths. The immaculate interior has retained its ornate ceilings and cornices as well as several magnificent fireplaces. One of these, in Cornish alabaster, graces the Music Room, which was used in Gilbert's time to stage operas and is now the scene of monthly evenings of costumed operetta with dinner. The recently refurbished Gilberts restaurant serves modern English food and has a significant local following. At weekends, diners can enjoy the sound of the piano in the background and in the summer, guests can eat out on the terrace overlooking the lawn. The location is convenient, with tube and train connections nearby and the West End is 35 minutes away.

LOCATION

Exit M25 at Junction 23. Take A1 south to London. Follow A411 signed Watford/Elstree, then A411 signed Bushey. Then take A409 signed Harrow/Harrow Weald. Turn right into Old Redding. Hotel is well signed.

Old Redding, Harrow Weald, London HA3 6SH

**Telephone 020 8385 3100
Fax 020 8954 4560**

E-mail: *grimsdyke@bestloved.com*

DIRECTOR
Paul Follows

ROOM RATES
Single occupancy   £125
35 Doubles/Twins   £152
9 Suites   £173 - £300
Includes full breakfast and VAT

CHARGE/CREDIT CARDS

• DC • MC • VI

RATINGS & AWARDS
E.T.C. ★★★ Silver Award
R.A.C. ★★★ Dining Award 2
A.A. ★★★ ❀ 66%

FACILITIES
On site: *Garden, croquet*
Licensed for weddings
6 meeting rooms/max 95 people
Nearby: *Golf, riding*

RESTRICTIONS
No facilities for disabled guests
Pets by arrangement

ATTRACTIONS
*London's West End,
The London Eye, Windsor Castle,
RNRS Gardens of the Rose,
Kew Gardens, Kenwood House*

AFFILIATIONS
Grand Heritage Hotels

NEAREST
MAJOR CITY:
London - 14 miles/35 mins

MAJOR AIRPORT:
London Heathrow - 16 miles/30 mins

RAILWAY STATION:
Watford Junction - 4 miles/10 mins
Stanmore Underground - 2 miles/5 mins

RESERVATIONS
Toll free in US: 888-93-GRAND
*Quote **Best Loved***

ACCESS CODES
AMADEUS UI LONGDH
APOLLO/GALILEO UI 84449
SABRE/ABACUS UI 38999
WORLDSPAN UI 40704

LONDON

• Map p.476
ref: C6

> *We were very happily surprised and thrilled at the reasonable rates, lovely location, the beauty of the hotel and the fabulous service*
>
> Beth Sobel, USA

KENSINGTON HOUSE

Contemporary town house

15-16 Prince of Wales Terrace, Kensington, London W8 5PQ

Telephone 020 7937 2345
Fax 020 7368 6700

E-mail: *kensingtonhse@bestloved.com*

OPERATIONS MANAGER
Samantha Fitzgerald

ROOM RATES
11 Singles	£150
8 Doubles/Twins	£175
20 Executive doubles	£195
2 Junior suites	£215

Includes continental breakfast and VAT

CHARGE/CREDIT CARDS

 • DC • JCB • MC • VI

RATINGS & AWARDS
R.A.C. Blue Ribbon ★★★★
A.A. ★★★★ *67% Town House*

FACILITIES
On site: *Tiger Bar*
Nearby: *Fitness, riding, tennis*

RESTRICTIONS
No facilities for disabled guests
No pets

ATTRACTIONS
Natural History Museum, Hyde Park, Science Museum, Royal Albert Hall, Knightsbridge, Victoria & Albert Museum, Kensington Palace and Gardens

AFFILIATIONS
Utell International
Preston's Global Hotels

NEAREST
MAJOR CITY:
London

MAJOR AIRPORT:
London Heathrow - 15 miles/40 mins

RAILWAY STATION:
Victoria - 3 miles/15 mins
High St Kensington Underground

RESERVATIONS
Toll Free in US: 800-544-9993
Quote **Best Loved**

ACCESS CODES
AMADEUS UI LONKNS
APOLLO/GALILEO UI 26891
SABRE/ABACUS UI 51957
WORLDSPAN UI 42351

Understatement is the key to this modern take on hospitality

A welcome addition to the capital's boutique hotel scene, Kensington House opened its doors in April 2000. This is a thoroughly modern hotel created with an understated but distinctive style within the traditional setting of a quiet 19th-century site off fashionable High Street Kensington.

The aim of any city centre hotel is to provide guests with a respite from the hurly-burly of urban street life - no minor feat in the heart of London. Kensington House achieves this enviable state of calm through what appears to be an effortless blend of simplicity, sophistication and a sense of informality that relaxes guests, yet standards of service never fall short of utter professionalism. Guest bedrooms are light and airy, decorated in restful combinations of oatmeal and white with sleek contemporary fittings and communications facilities including voicemail/modem. The hotel has its own bar open throughout the day and serving anything from a coffee to a three course meal, with the menu reflecting its own individual style.

Kensington House is a terrific base for exploring London. Just a short step from a whole range of fine shops and restaurants, Kensington Palace and the wide green spaces of Hyde Park, it is also well-placed for the West End, museums, galleries, and nightlife.

LOCATION

The turning into Prince of Wales Terrace is off Kensington Gardens, opposite Kensington Palace. The hotel is a short way down on the right.

❝ *For more than ten years, Knightsbridge Green has been my 'home' in London . . . it is a very nice place to come back to* ❞

Mr Peter Yeo

• *Map p.476*
ref: E6

Town house | KNIGHTSBRIDGE GREEN HOTEL

159 Knightsbridge,
London SW1X 7PD

Telephone 020 7584 6274
Fax 020 7225 1635

E-mail: *knightsbridge@bestloved.com*

OWNERS
The Marler Family

MANAGER
Paul Fizia

ROOM RATES
7 Singles	£110
9 Doubles/Twins	£145
12 Suites	£170
Includes service and VAT	

CHARGE/CREDIT CARDS

 • *DC • MC • VI*

RATINGS & AWARDS
E.T.C. ◆◆◆◆
R.A.C. ◆◆◆◆
B&B Award Scheme
Commended Past Winner of BTA London
Certificate of Distinction

FACILITIES
Nearby: *Riding*

RESTRICTIONS
Limited facilities for disabled guests
No smoking throughout
No pets

ATTRACTIONS
Harrods, Harvey Nichols,
Kensington Palace, West End Theatre,
Victoria & Albert Museum,
Natural History Museum

AFFILIATIONS
Preston's Global Hotels

NEAREST
MAJOR CITY:
London

MAJOR AIRPORT:
London Heathrow - 15 miles/45 mins
London Gatwick - 30 miles/1 ¼ hrs

RAILWAY STATION:
Victoria - ½ mile/10 mins
Knightsbridge Underground

RESERVATIONS
Toll free in US: 800-544-9993
*Quote **Best Loved***

ACCESS CODES
Not applicable

LONDON

A family-owned hotel with a personal touch

Knightsbridge Green is a small hotel with a big difference: with Harrods just across the street and Hyde Park virtually on your doorstep, it is hard to believe that, these days, a family-owned establishment could exist in such a wonderfully central position. And yet, here it is combining the comforts and pleasures of the larger consortia hotels with the personality and friendliness you can only find in a privately-owned business.

The hotel has recently been transformed: new furnishings, new lighting, new colours; new marbled bathrooms with top quality fittings and fixtures. Double glazing keeps the peace in one of London's busiest areas and air-conditioning in all the bedrooms and suites allows you to find your own comfort level. The rooms are exceptionally large, a single at the Knightsbridge Green being the size of many a double anywhere else.

The area is blessed with a great range of cafés, restaurants, pubs, wine bars and bistros offering all kinds of cuisine. So a restaurant in the hotel is superfluous although a hearty breakfast will be served in your room as you wish.

When you want help in booking a restaurant, theatre tickets, limousine or hire car, all you have to do is ask.

LOCATION

In Knightsbridge, central London,
adjacent to Hyde Park.

> ❝ *The staff were superb, the accommodation outstanding and the facilities good. Please convey my appreciation to everyone involved in making my visit so memorable* ❞
>
> *Doug Rhymes, Scottsdale, USA*

LE MÉRIDIEN GROSVENOR HOUSE   *City centre hotel*

**86-90 Park Lane,
London W1K 7TN**

**Telephone 020 7499 6363
Fax 020 7493 3341**

E-mail: *grosvenorhse@bestloved.com*

GENERAL MANAGER
James McBride

ROOM RATES
154 Superior Double/Twins	£195 - £225
77 Deluxe Doubles/Twins	£225 - £255
40 Superior Suites	£690 - £720
187 Le Royal Club rooms	£255 - £820
139 Apartments	£310 - £1,665
Includes service and VAT	

CHARGE/CREDIT CARDS

 • *DC* • *JCB* • *MC* • *VI*

RATINGS & AWARDS
E.T.C. ★★★★★
R.A.C. ★★★★★ *Dining Award 5*
A.A. ★★★★★ ❁❁❁ 70%

FACILITIES
On site: *Indoor pool, gym, sauna,
health & beauty, hair salon, business centre
Licensed for weddings
19 meeting rooms/max 2000*
Nearby: *Golf, riding*

RESTRICTIONS
No pets, guide dogs only

ATTRACTIONS
*Royal Parks, Victoria & Albert Museum,
Knightsbridge, Bond Street,
Oxford Street, Theatreland,
National Gallery, Tower of London*

AFFILIATIONS
Le Meridien Hotels

NEAREST
MAJOR CITY:
London

MAJOR AIRPORT:
*London Heathrow - 15 miles/40 mins
London Gatwick - 30 miles/1¼ hrs*

RAILWAY STATION:
*Victoria - 2 miles/10 mins
Hyde Park Corner Underground*

RESERVATIONS
*Toll free in US/Canada: 800-543-4300
Toll free in UK: 0800 40 40 40*
Quote **Best Loved**

ACCESS CODES
*APOLLO/GALLILEO MD 5455
AMADEUS FE LON250
SABRE/ABACUS MD 11250
WORLDSPAN MD 5932*

Luxury, comfort and style in Mayfair, London's best address

In 1927 Le Meridien Grosvenor House opened as the first hotel on prestigious Park Lane. It was built on the site of the 18th century residence of the Duke of Westminster. The facade was designed by Sir Edwin Lutyens, creator of the imperial city of Delhi. He designed the building to capture natural light and provide extensive views of Hyde Park. The hotel won a reputation for high quality and exclusivity. Its huge ice rink became The Great Room, Europe's largest hotel ballroom, hosting grand gala balls from the 1930s on.

The flagship property of Le Meridien Hotels and Resorts, Grosvenor House recently underwent a £35 million refurbishment programme, introducing a new style and concept in luxury. The impressive facilities include Le Royal club, a new Italian restaurant, La Terraza, the stylish Bollinger Bar and a state of the art health club featuring the largest indoor swimming pool in London.

At the heart of Mayfair, Le Meridien Grosvenor House is minutes away from haute couture shopping in Bond Street and the West End theatres. For travellers who value the opportunity to mingle with leaders in business, fashion and society, the hotel offers a winning combination of luxury and comfort, with flawless service.

LOCATION
**Situated on Park Lane between
Hyde Park Corner and Marble Arch.**

" The scale of the lavishly decorated suites alone means The Leonard offers the ultimate urban luxury space "

Christine Temin, Boston Globe

Georgian town house

THE LEONARD

A discreet luxury Town House address

Since its opening in 1996 The Leonard has gained a reputation for being a very discrete luxury residence and has become a regular bolt hole for many high profile guests, especially from the worlds of business and entertainment.

Created out of four 18th Century town houses, The Leonard is exquisitely decorated and furnished throughout, retaining a wonderful air of understated Georgian elegance. There are 21 suites and 23 bedrooms in total, all of which have lavish interiors and marble bathrooms. The Grand Suites on the first floor are very spacious indeed and all the larger suites come with either a fully equipped kitchen or Butlers Pantry. Each room has air-conditioning and all the other modern facilities you would expect such as hi-fi, video, and modem access.

The café bar serves a fine breakfast as well as light meals throughout the day. They really have overlooked nothing and provide; 24-hour room service, full secretarial support services, a compact exercise room and a beautiful roof terrace.

The service, as you would expect of an exclusive residence, is outstanding. And the final

plus point - the shops of Oxford Street and Bond Street are just around the corner!

LOCATION

Situated on the south side of Seymour Street, just west of Portman Square. Car parking is available in Bryanston Street.

**15 Seymour Street,
Marble Arch,
London W1H 7JW**

**Telephone 020 7935 2010
Fax 020 7935 6700**

E-mail: *leonard@bestloved.com*

HOUSE MANAGER
Angela Stoppani

ROOM RATES
Single occupancy   £235
23 Doubles/Twins   £259
21 Suites   £329 - £588
Includes VAT

CHARGE/CREDIT CARDS

 • *DC* • *JCB* • *MC* • *VI*

RATINGS & AWARDS
E.T.C. ★★★★ *Silver Award*
A.A. ★★★★ *Town House*
A.A. Courtesy & Care Award

FACILITIES
On site: *Gym, roof terrace*
1 meeting room/max 50 people
Nearby: *Riding*

RESTRICTIONS
Limited facilities for disabled guests
No pets

ATTRACTIONS
*Buckingham Palace, Hyde Park,
Bond Street, Victoria & Albert Museum,
Wallace Collection*

AFFILIATIONS
*Small Hotel Company
The European Connection
The Celebrated Hotels Collection*

NEAREST
MAJOR CITY:
London

MAJOR AIRPORT:
London Heathrow - 15 miles/45 mins
London Gatwick - 30 miles/1 ¼ hrs

RAILWAY STATION:
Paddington - 1 mile/5 mins
Marble Arch Underground

RESERVATIONS
Toll free in US: 800-322-2403
*Quote **Best Loved***

ACCESS CODES
Not applicable

LONDON

THE MONTAGUE ON THE GARDENS *Luxury Georgian hotel*

**15 Montague Street,
Bloomsbury,
London WC1B 5BJ**

**Telephone 020 7637 1001
Fax 020 7637 2516**

E-mail: *montague@bestloved.com*

GENERAL MANAGER
Andrew Pike

ROOM RATES
26 Singles	£140 - £200
44 Doubles/Twins	£160 - £235
23 Kings	£170 - £260
5 Junior suites	£247 - £376
6 Executive suites	£317 - £494

Includes service and VAT

CHARGE/CREDIT CARDS

 ● *DC* ● *JCB* ● *MC* ● *VI*

RATINGS & AWARDS
R.A.C. ★★★★ *Dining Award 1*
A.A. ★★★★ ❀ 70%

FACILITIES
On site: *Garden, bar-b-que,
health suite, conservatory
Licensed for weddings
5 meeting rooms/max 150 people*

RESTRICTIONS
*No facilities for disabled guests
Pets by arrangement*

ATTRACTIONS
*The British Museum, Theatre District,
Trafalgar Square, Tower of London,
Covent Garden, Westminster Abbey*

AFFILIATIONS
*Red Carnation Hotels
The European Connection*

NEAREST
MAJOR CITY:
London

MAJOR AIRPORT:
*London Heathrow - 18 miles/45 mins
London Gatwick - 30 miles/1 ¼ hrs*

RAILWAY STATION:
*Euston/King's Cross - ½ mile/6 mins
Holborn/Russell Square Underground*

RESERVATIONS
Toll free in US: 877-955-1515
Quote **Best Loved**

ACCESS CODES
*AMADEUS VE LONMON
GALILEO VE 18505
SABRE/ABACUS VE 10896
WORLDSPAN VE 0366*

Comfort and personal service in a unique London setting

In Georgian times, Bloomsbury was the home of rich merchants and aristocrats. Later it was famed for the Bloomsbury group of writers that included Virginia Woolf. From the Montague's garden setting beside the British Museum, the attractions of London's West End theatres are a stroll away and the Tower of London and The City are within easy reach.

The townhouse style Montague on the Gardens has been completely refurbished for modern business and leisure. Its 104 guest rooms are fully air-conditioned and include 11 split-level and deluxe suites. 'Business ready' rooms provide office supplies, speaker phones, fax machines on request, good desk space and lighting. Laptop users will find hooking up to each bedroom's UK/US modem lines a snap. For relaxation, you can take advantage of the hotels in-room movies on demand capability or work out in the recently installed gym and fitness centre.

Montague staff members proudly wear red carnations, symbolising personal service and attention to detail. The Blue Door Bistro offers a gastronomic treat with superb lunchtime selections and à la carte dinner menu. You can relax on the terrace or, during the summer, enjoy live jazz in the private gardens, and be miles away from today's pressures.

LOCATION

*In Bloomsbury, close to Russell
Square Underground and Airbus A1 stop.
Convenient parking facilities nearby.*

" I have been frequenting The Montcalm for over twenty years. It has changed little - it is small, private, discreet and with friendly impeccable service "

Frederick Forsyth, Author

Georgian town house

THE MONTCALM HOTEL

A discreet residence just two minutes from Marble Arch and Oxford Street

Tucked away in a quiet, tree-lined crescent behind Marble Arch and the bustling Oxford Street shopping district, The Montcalm makes an exceptional base for the discerning traveller in one of the greatest cities in the world.

The hotel was named after an 18th-century general, the Marquis de Montcalm, who was renowned for his dignity and style. These two qualities are admirably reflected in the surroundings and atmosphere of this London outpost of the highly-regarded Nikko Hotel group. Behind the discreet Georgian façade, comfortable traditional bedrooms and duplex suites feature modern conveniences from private fax machines and voicemail to satellite and CNN television channels. The spacious lobby is an ideal meeting point for friends and business colleagues, or there is the wood panelled bar where afternoon tea is served, and an open fire provides a cosy focus in winter.

The Montcalm's elegant Crescent Restaurant has a light and airy feel with tall windows and an Arcadian mural of a formal English garden stretching off into distant countryside. The menu features the inspired modern British cuisine of talented chef Stephen Whitney (ex-Mosimann's and the Savoy). Typical offerings include

tournedos of Scottish beef with woodland mushrooms and a delice of salmon on spinach and wild rice with a caviar and vodka butter. Private dining rooms are also available.

LOCATION

Two minutes walk from Marble Arch and Oxford Street.

Great Cumberland Place, London W1H 7TW

**Telephone 020 7402 4288
Fax 020 7724 9180**

E-mail: montcalm@bestloved.com

GENERAL MANAGER
Jonathan Orr-Ewing

ROOM RATES
43 Singles	£180 - £260
63 Doubles/Twins	£180 - £290
14 Suites	£370 - £705

Includes VAT

CHARGE/CREDIT CARDS

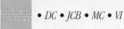 • DC • JCB • MC • VI

RATINGS & AWARDS
R.A.C. ★★★★ Dining Award 3
A.A. ★★★★ ❀❀ 77%

FACILITIES
On site: In-room fax, voicemail, modem, photocopier and printer, chauffeur service, secretarial services, bicycles
3 meeting rooms/max 120 people
Nearby: Jogging, riding

RESTRICTIONS
Limited facilities for disabled guests
Pets by arrangement

ATTRACTIONS
Buckingham Palace, Wellington Museum, The Wallace Collection, Bond Street, Madame Tussauds, Shopping on Oxford Street

AFFILIATIONS
Nikko Hotels International
The Celebrated Hotels Collection
Macdonald Hotels

NEAREST
MAJOR CITY:
London

MAJOR AIRPORT:
London Heathrow - 15 miles/50 mins
London Gatwick - 30 miles/1 ¼ hrs

RAILWAY STATION:
Paddington - ½ mile/10 mins
Marble Arch Underground

RESERVATIONS
Toll free in US: 800-645-5687
or 800-322-2403 or 888-892-0038
Toll free in UK: 0800 282502
Quote **Best Loved**

ACCESS CODES
AMADEUS NK LON001
APOLLO/GALILEO NK 26211
SABRE/ABACUS NK 14527
WORLDSPAN NK 14527

LONDON

● Map p.476
ref: G6

THE RUBENS AT THE PALACE

Victorian luxury

**39 Buckingham Palace Road,
London SW1W 0PS**

**Telephone 020 7834 6600
Fax 020 7233 6037**

E-mail: rubens@bestloved.com

GENERAL MANAGER
Paul Hemmings

ROOM RATES
40 Singles	£155 - £200
75 Doubles/Twins	£185 - £235
46 King-bedded rooms	£205 - £285
7 Junior suites	£275 - £365
6 Executive/Master suites	£295 - £530

Includes VAT

CHARGE/CREDIT CARDS

 • DC • JCB • MC • VI

RATINGS & AWARDS
R.A.C. ★★★★ *Dining Award 3*
A.A. ★★★★ ❀❀ 74%

FACILITIES
On site: *Fully air-conditioned*
6 meeting rooms/max 150 people
Nearby: *Tennis, fitness centre, riding*

RESTRICTIONS
*No facilities for disabled guests
Pets by arrangement*

ATTRACTIONS
*Buckingham Palace, Hyde Park,
Houses of Parliament, Westminster Abbey,
Tower of London, Royal Mews*

AFFILIATIONS
*Red Carnation Hotels
The European Connection*

NEAREST
MAJOR CITY:
London

MAJOR AIRPORT:
London Heathrow - 15 miles/45 mins

RAILWAY STATION:
Victoria - 200 metres/2 mins

RESERVATIONS
Toll free in US: 877-955-1515
Quote **Best Loved**

ACCESS CODES
*AMADEUS VE LONRUB
GALILEO VE 10977
SABRE/ABACUS VE 10687
WORLDSPAN VE LONRB*

LONDON

Luxurious sanctuary in a Royal neighbourhood

An old rule suggests that an hotel's location is essential to its success. The Rubens at the Palace goes a long way to proving this rule. Look out your bedroom window and directly across the street are the grounds of Buckingham Palace. Westminster is a short stroll and Victoria Station provides easy access in and around town.

Red Carnation Hotels has invested heavily in upgrading this landmark to a luxury standard. Lush fabrics and furnishings throughout create a calm mood. In the Cavalry Bar and Palace Lounge, you can enjoy a traditional tea or in the evening listen to a live piano while sipping a night-cap. Dining options include the elegant Library Restaurant serving superb international cuisine or the more relaxed Carvery, where the obvious emphasis is on mouth-watering roasts.

Bedrooms have received serious attention and redecorating has meant sparing no expense in creating comfortable and luxurious environments. Suites and bedrooms include king and queen-sized beds. The new Royal Wing features eight magnificent rooms, each individually styled after historic Kings and Queens of Great Britain. Business travellers will appreciate their needs have been properly addressed with bedrooms that

can be transformed into virtual offices with ample workspace and state-of-the-art communication facilities.

LOCATION

*Opposite the Royal Mews of Buckingham Palace.
Only 200 metres from Victoria Station.*

• Map p.476
ref: C7

Apartments

SOMERSET ROLAND GARDENS

**121 Old Brompton Road,
South Kensington,
London SW7 3RX**

**Telephone 020 7341 6800
Fax 020 7341 6801**

E-mail: *roland@bestloved.com*

GENERAL MANAGER
Eddy Brosse

ROOM RATES

1	1-Bedroom apt	£183
15	2-Bedroom apts	£212
74	Studios	£147

Includes continental breakfast and VAT

CHARGE/CREDIT CARDS

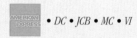 • DC • JCB • MC • VI

RATINGS & AWARDS
Independent

FACILITIES
Nearby: *Tennis, riding, fishing*

RESTRICTIONS
*No facilities for disabled guests
No pets, guide dogs only*

ATTRACTIONS
*Harvey Nichols and Harrods,
Kensington Gardens, Hyde Park,
Natural History Museum,
Victoria & Albert Museum,
Science Museum*

AFFILIATIONS
The Ascott Group

NEAREST
*MAJOR CITY:
London*

*MAJOR AIRPORT:
London Heathrow - 15 miles/40 mins*

*RAILWAY STATION:
Victoria - 3 miles/15 mins
Gloucester Road Underground*

RESERVATIONS
*Toll free in US: 866-246-7054
Quote **Best Loved***

ACCESS CODES
*AMADEUS UI LONROL
APOLLO/GALILEO UI 81175
SABRE/ABACUS UI 34300
WORLDSPAN UI 25729*

A home from home even when you're on holiday

For frequent travellers hotel hopping can take its toll and there are times when you simply want to kick back and relax, just as if you were at home. This is where a serviced residence, such as Somerset Roland Gardens in South Kensington comes in. Unlike other private accommodation, you can book here for just one night, with a two-bedroom apartment in a top London location costing as little as £211.50. It will have its own modern kitchen facilities, including microwave and hob cooker. If you are planning on eating in, there is a grocery service - just tell them your favourite food and they'll make sure the fridge is stocked up with it.

Internet and fax connection, hi-fi, CD, DVD and cable television will ensure that the majority of business and leisure requirements are catered for. And a six day-a-week maid service means you don't have to waste precious moments on household chores. Instead, pop over to Harrods and Harvey Nichols for a spot of retail therapy, or soak in the culture at the many galleries, museums, exhibitions and royal parks and gardens nearby.

LOCATION

**10 minutes walk from the
Gloucester Road Underground.**

LONDON

IRELAND

WB Yeats said, 'The place that has really influenced my life most is Sligo'. As a child he spent his holidays in this beautiful place, later he bought a ruined tower here and turned it into a summer home for himself and his wife. He was an avid collector of local myths and stories. Yeats used his feelings about the places around him in his poetry, invoking a true sense of landscape and locality – as did, and still do, many writers of Irish birth.

The list of great authors and poets born in Dublin is remarkable, add those produced by the rest of Ireland and it is amazing! Even writers who left their homeland carried its inspiration with them. James Joyce left Ireland for ever in 1912, He was living on the Continent when he wrote Ulysses – the tale of one day in Dublin: June 16th 1904, in the book he created his own Dublinesque world that devotees create maps of and scholars argue over. Like Dickens in London, Joyce's father's fell on 'hard times' and as a young man the author roamed city streets, absorbing character and language and turning it into a unique world of fiction.

George Bernard Shaw was another famous son of Dublin, his father a shopkeeper and his mother a singer. He left Ireland at 20, attaining international fame and prestige whilst retaining forever an eccentric Irish 'crustiness'.

Oscar Fingle O'Flahertie Wills Wilde was born in Dublin in 1854, son of a wealthy surgeon who was also an author and a mother who was an innovative poet studying Celtic literature. Oscar's literary heritage was rich - and Irish, his creative genius is increasingly recognised as a product of his origins.

The power of Edna O'Brien's writing is carried in a prose so lyrical you hear the words as you read. Born into a village in County Clare, she spoke Irish at school and English at home, and was stifled by her environment; perhaps that is why her writing is so compelling. A real storyteller in the great Irish tradition, her works combine scenery, character and opinions, forcefully put, linking past and present.

This is a Celtic land, a place for bards, where ancient history and myth live side by side and sometimes mingle. Irish author Morgan Llywelyn writes historical novels that bring past Celtic culture to life – and Irish history to the world. She also writes pure fantasy, creating other worlds conjured from the imagination.

Nobel prizewinner, Seamus Heany was born in 1939, on a farm in County Derry. His father was a cattle dealer with 50 acres; others of his family were in service or worked in industry.

His writing and inspiration, he's said, stems from a combination of his family's cattle herding Gaelic past and Industrial Revolution Ulster. Rural County Derry is his 'country of the mind', and where much of his poetry stems from.

PLACES TO VISIT

The 16th of June is Bloomsday worldwide – when enthusiasts dress up in straw boaters and stripy blazers to breakfast on kidneys and other unusual delights taken from Joyce's Ulysses then embark on a day of inventive eccentricity. And all of this clutching the required copy of Ulysses, the more thumbed, and well read, the better. The Dublin celebrations are tremendous.

The relatively humble origins of George Bernard Shaw are on show at 33 Synge Street in Dublin. This small house, with its small garden was, Shaw said 'loveless'. Today, restored to convey the atmosphere of the home of his first 10 years, visiting is thought provoking, a step towards understanding some of his motivations.

Oscar Wilde went to school in Enniskillen, on holidays he visited Fort Hill and climbed the 108 steps that lead to the monument to Sir Galbraith Lowry Cole, one of Wellington's generals. It's thought that the monument inspired Wilde to write his fairy tale, The Happy Prince'. It begins, 'High above the town, on a tall column, stood the statue of the Happy Prince…' A new literary festival celebrates Wilde's links with the handsome town.

I will a rise and go now, and go to Innisfree,
And a small cabin build there, of clay and wattles made:
Nine bean-rows will I have there, a hive for the honeybee,
And live alone in the bee-loud glade.

And I shall have some peace there, for peace comes dropping slow,
Dropping from the veils of morning to where the cricket sings;
There midnight's all a glimmer, and noon a purple glow,
And evening full of linnet's wings.

From The Lake of Innisfree by William Butler Yeats 1865-1939

BOOKS TO READ

▶ The Thief of Reason: Oscar Wilde and Modern Ireland by Richard Pine: a fascinating insight into how Wilde's Irish origins affected his work.

▶ The New Bloomsday Book: A Guide Through Ulysses: whether you read this before the book itself, or afterwards, the well researched and readable information adds to the Joyce 'experience'.

▶ WB Yeats, The Love Poems edited by AN Jeffries: an evocative collection of poems from youthful idealism to later disillusion.

A special place to buy books:

The Book Nest, Sligo, specialising in Irish Literature – with an emphasis on local authors past and present - just the place to buy Yeats - www.booknest.ie.

LITERARY ATTRACTIONS & FESTIVALS

▶ Yeats Festival - a summer celebration of literature, drama, poetry, music and art at Sligo.
Tel: +353 (0)71 42693.

▶ Oscar Wilde House Museum, Dublin: Tours and events in recently restored childhood home of Oscar Wilde. Tel: +353 (0) 1662 0281.

▶ Ireland's oldest literary festival held at Listowel, County Kerry, an area of rich literary heritage.
Tel: +353 (0) 68 2174.

A CULINARY Ireland

With pastures an emerald green, and a sea as blue as the proverbial Irish eyes it's not surprising that the quality of meat, fish and shellfish is legendary. There's a wonderful tradition of home cooking too, of rich soups and stews, of soft breads and crisp rolls. Buttermilk recipes are still in use today alongside the most contemporary cuisine, and the potato is enjoyed in all its versatility, with local butter or farmhouse cheese, with a slice o dry cured ham cut off the bone, perhaps as part of the famou Irish breakfast - to 'set you up for the day'. Great chefs love cooking in Ireland - for the quality of the local ingredients, fo the appreciative locals and enthusiastic visitors and for the quality of the 'craic' - such an essential part of Irish hospitality.

THE WINE:

The Wineport's remarkably apt name isn't an advertising agency's designer creation but comes from the sixth century when epicurean monks at nearby St Ciaran's Abbey enjoyed importing wines from France. Today's very special wines served at the waterside Wineport Lodge are from all over the world. Enjoy them sitting on the private balcony of your bedroom, or at dinner in the restaurant - gorgeous food, such as steamed lobster with spicy crab samosa, as befits such a stunning setting. And the vinious theme continues - each bedroom is 'sponsored' by a leading wine importer, a night in the Champagne Bollinger room is sure to add fizz to your stay!

Wineport Lodge

THE SETTING: Take a magnificent early eighteenth century limestone mansion - in need of some tender loving care. Spend four years restoring, renovating and pampering the Queen Anne structure and its surrounding 30 acres of gardens and you have Castle Durrow. Add Peter Stokes' final touch, all his experience and ability from twenty-seven successful years in the fast moving Dublin restaurant business. The result is an eclectic mix of modern Irish cooking and new world cuisine beneath original ornate ceilings and twinkling crystal chandeliers.

THE SERVICE: The quality of service at Aghadoe Heights is legendary - past guests reminisce about it in far flung corners of the world - and can't wait to come back. Enjoy afternoon tea in the lounge and it's brought to you by staff wearing white gloves. The view from the restaurant is so spectacular that it could be hard to concentrate on the food - but the food is so delicious, so immaculately French in concept and Irish in quality that the whole experience becomes one of 'Magic place, magic people, magic peace.' in the words of a recent guest.

THE SCHOOL: One of the wonderful things about a session at the Dunbrody Cookery School is that you can experience Masterchef Kevin Dundon's 'state of the art' dinners in the beautiful Dunbrody Hotel at the end of each educating day. Kevin is adept at passing on his exceptional skills and students learn the secrets of producing fine food using only the best of quality Irish ingredients. It is a totally win-win situation because you improve hands on skills at the same time as appreciating the fantastic choice of local produce and specialities. The cookery school itself is in a stylishly designed contemporary kitchen with cherrywood and granite and lots of Neff appliances - you even get a Dunbrody Cookery School chef jacket and apron to take home!

THE LOCATION: As they say in the movies: location! location! location! Brownes Brasserie at their renowned Town House overlooking St Stephen's Green - the oldest and most prestigious square in Dublin, has it all. The interior is a step back in time to an age of opulence and indulgence. But the atmosphere, like the food, has a distinctly contemporary flavour. 'Fois gras terrine with a salad of carrots and sugar snaps, served with an apple and Muscat sauce and toasted brioche' could be followed by, 'Pumpernickel crusted loin of lamb served on a bed of broccoli puree with a mint and apricot jus', and all just a few steps away from the best shopping in the city.

THE AMBIENCE: It may be the mild climate in this corner of Kerry, or the glorious garden, or perhaps the spectacular view, but the atmosphere at Caragh Lodge seems to inspire guests to relax and take time to enjoy the delicious food in this beautifully furnished hotel that retains a sense of intimacy. Mary and Graham Gaunt are wonderful hosts, making sure their bright, young staff perform to perfection. Home made breads and cakes, locally caught wild salmon, a touch of Guinness around a sublime fillet steak - edible memories to take away - and ask for the recipe for Mary's delectable chocolate cake to take away as well, she's so nice that she'll give it to you!

THE SPORT: Lahinch golf course is home to every major amateur Irish competition and the Home internationals. Its mighty sand dunes and hidden

greens make it a 'must play'. It's also beautifully positioned to take advantage of Gregans Castle where delicious organic Burren lamb and beef feature on a menu rich with fish from the nearby Atlantic. In this glorious wilderness fantastic views are everywhere, but one of the best is from the hotel's windows, when the setting sun sends shimmering beams across Galway Bay to strike the limestone mountains.

Editor's Extras

The annual Irish Country Sports Fair features all sorts of country pursuits and has a food tent crammed with home grown delights - there's even a Guinness Traditional Beer Tent.

Paddy O'Reilly suggested to Seamus Clarke and Tommy Brady that they should host an event... sounds very like the beginning of an Irish novel, but it was the start of the Ballyjamesduff Pork Festival - Mardi Gras Irish style - held in June, more on www.ballyjamesduffporkfestival.com.

The ultimate taste of Ireland? Impossible to single out just one, but Irish beef cooked in Irish Stout with a few Irish oysters is hard to beat.

" This is truly all that one expects of a private hotel, the Edwardian features, the personal service and the surroundings "

Brian Sanker, Los Gatos, California

Edwardian town house

ABERDEEN LODGE

A peaceful, private address in Dublin's fashionable Embassy District

Dublin's elegance has many facets: wide streets and Georgian facades, parks and gardens, the vibrant city centre with its bright lights, shops and night life and the quiet, secluded leafy areas just off the city centre. In one of these more exclusive areas, world's embassies are located. So is the Aberdeen Lodge.

Aberdeen Lodge, a converted Edwardian house, is an affordable, well-located option for any visitor, providing high standards of comfort and service within the generous proportions of its rooms. Each bedroom is en suite, and lists multichannel TV, direct dial telephone, trouser press and hairdryer amongst its facilities. The suites additionally include a whirlpool spa and fine period furniture.

The hotel is owned and run by the Halpin family who, as well established hoteliers, know the needs of their guests and how to indulge them. This particularly applies to the dining room where, overlooking the garden, you can dine on good food and wine. Indeed, the hotel has enjoyed excellent reviews from the Irish Tourist Board, the AA and the RAC. In short, the Aberdeen Lodge can match most of the qualities of Dublin's city centre hotels but adds to them greater seclusion and great value.

LOCATION

From city centre take Merrion Road towards Sydney Parade DART station and then first left into Park Avenue.

53 Park Avenue, off Ailesbury Rd, Ballsbridge, Dublin 4, Republic of Ireland
Telephone +353 (0)1 283 8155
Fax +353 (0)1 283 7877
E-mail: *aberdeenlodge@bestloved.com*

OWNER
Pat Halpin

ROOM RATES (EUROS)
3 Singles   €106 - €129
10 Doubles/Twins   €139 - €179
2 Four-posters   €169 - €219
2 Suites   €190 - €290
Includes full breakfast, newspaper and VAT

CHARGE/CREDIT CARDS
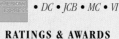 • DC • JCB • MC • VI

RATINGS & AWARDS
I.T.B. ★★★★
R.A.C. ◆◆◆◆◆
A.A. ◆◆◆◆◆
R.A.C. Warm Welcome and Sparkling Diamond Awards
Galtee Breakfast Award

FACILITIES
On site: *Garden, health & beauty, car park*
2 meeting rooms/max 30 people
Nearby: *Golf, riding, fitness centre, tennis, shooting, fishing, water skiing*

RESTRICTIONS
Limited facilities for disabled guests
No pets

ATTRACTIONS
Gardens of Wicklow, National Art Gallery, Christchurch, Trinity College, New Grange, Powerscourt Gardens, Druids Glen Golf Course

AFFILIATIONS
Preston's Global Hotels
Charming Hotels
The Green Book of Ireland

NEAREST
MAJOR CITY:
Dublin

MAJOR AIRPORT:
Dublin - 6 miles/20 mins

RAILWAY STATION:
Sydney Parade - ¼ mile/5 mins

RESERVATIONS
Toll free in US: 800-544-9993
or 1800-617-3178
Toll free in UK: 0800 0964748
Quote **Best Loved**

ACCESS CODES
AMADEUS UI DUBABE
APOLLO/GALILEO UI 1400
SABRE/ABACUS UI 35428
WORLDSPAN UI 19689

IRELAND

AGHADOE HEIGHTS HOTEL — *Luxury hotel*

**Lakes of Killarney,
Killarney, Co Kerry
Republic of Ireland**
Telephone +353 (0)64 31766
Fax +353 (0)64 31345
E-mail: *aghadoe@bestloved.com*

GENERAL MANAGERS
Pat and Marie Chawke

ROOM RATES *(EUROS)*
Single occupancy	€310 - €786
55 Doubles/Twins	€310 - €478
7 Junior suites	€534 - €646
1 Four-poster	€730 - €786
1 Suite	€730 - €786

Includes full breakfast and VAT

CHARGE/CREDIT CARDS

 • DC • MC • VI

RATINGS & AWARDS
I.T.B. ★★★★★
R.A.C. Gold Ribbon ★★★★ Dining Award 3
A.A. ★★★★ ✿✿✿ Top 200 - 02/03
A.A. Hotel of the Year 2001/2002
Irish Hotel of the Year 2001/2002
Regional Winner of Barry's Afternoon
Tea Award 2001

FACILITIES
On site: *Garden, gym, fishing, tennis,
indoor pool, health & beauty, hair salon
3 meeting rooms/max 120 people*
Nearby: *Golf, beach, walking*

RESTRICTIONS
*Limited facilities for disabled guests
Pets by arrangement
Closed 29 Dec - 7 Mar*

ATTRACTIONS
*Ring of Kerry, Muckross House & Gardens,
Killarney National Park, Gap of Dunloe,
Torc Waterfall, Ballybunion,
Waterville & Tralee Golf Courses*

AFFILIATIONS
Preferred Hotels & Resorts

NEAREST
MAJOR CITY:
Cork - 60 miles/1 ½ hrs

MAJOR AIRPORT:
Cork - 60 miles/1 ½ hrs

RAILWAY STATION:
Killarney - 3 miles/5 mins

RESERVATIONS
Toll free in US: 800-323-7500
*Quote **Best Loved***

ACCESS CODES
*AMADEUS PH KIRAGH
APOLLO/GALILEO PH 36489
SABRE/ABACUS PH 21798
WORLDSPAN PH AGHAD*

The luck of the Irish will grant you hospitality in 'this little bit of heaven'

Images of Ireland are often of quaint crofts, rough walled tracks, limpid lakes and mist-swirled mountains - perhaps enhanced by a dancing leprechaun. Well, the lakes and mountains are certainly there when you visit Aghadoe Heights in its enviable location right in the Lakes of Killarney National Park, but the hotel will prevent any bouts of whimsy by bringing you bang into the 21st century. The contemporary design with its large upstairs lounge, picture windows and balconies does justice to the outstanding surroundings. The well-equipped suites and rooms are spacious and comfortably furnished with a mix of contemporary styles and carefully selected antiques. The swimming pool, fitness and spa facilities are top-class while the internationally applauded Fredrick's Restaurant is among the top ten in Ireland.

What is really admirable about Aghadoe is the warmth and professionalism of the service - plenty of genuine Irish hospitality from staff who have dedicated many years to the well-being of the guests bringing delightful touches such as

traditional smoking rules in the Cigar Room and tea served by white-gloved waiters. With superb salmon and trout fishing and several championship golf courses nearby - what more could anyone want?

LOCATION

*From the centre of Killarney head
out towards the N22 Tralee Road.
Where the road forks with the N22 veer
right and follow the hotel signs.*

IRELAND

" They are surrounded by the finest fish in the sea "

The Guardian

• *Map p.478*
  ref: E9

Hotel and restaurant

AHERNES

**163 North Main St,
Youghal, Co Cork,
Republic of Ireland**

***Telephone +353 (0)24 92424
Fax +353 (0)24 93633***

E-mail: *ahernes@bestloved.com*

OWNERS
The Fitzgibbon Family

ROOM RATES *(EUROS)*
Single occupancy   €100 - €110
13 Doubles/Twins   €140 - €205
Includes full breakfast and VAT

CHARGE/CREDIT CARDS

 • *DC* • *MC* • *VI*

RATINGS & AWARDS
I.T.B. ★★★★ *Guest House*
R.A.C. ◆◆◆◆◆ *Dining Award 2*
A.A. ◆◆◆◆◆ *Restaurant with rooms
& Romantic hotel*
*R.A.C. Sparkling Diamond, Warm Welcome
& Little Gem Awards*

FACILITIES
On site: *1 meeting room/max 40 people*
Nearby: *Golf, fishing, riding, hill walking*

RESTRICTIONS
*Limited facilities for disabled guests
No pets, guide dogs only
Closed 23 - 28 Dec*

ATTRACTIONS
*Fota Island Golf Course, Waterford Crystal,
Jameson Heritage Centre, Blarney Castle,
Cobh Heritage Centre, National Hunt Racing*

AFFILIATIONS
*Preston's Global Hotels
Ireland's Blue Book*

NEAREST
MAJOR CITY:
Cork - 30 miles/45 mins

MAJOR AIRPORT:
Cork - 30 miles/45 mins

RAILWAY STATION:
Cork - 30 miles/45 mins

RESERVATIONS
*Toll free in US: 800-544-9993
or 800-323-5463*
Quote **Best Loved**

ACCESS CODES
Not applicable

Luxury rooms with a 'seafood view'

Ahernes is in the heart of the picturesque Youghal (pronounced Yawl), the old historic walled port at the mouth of the River Blackwater. It is a family pub that the Fitzgibbons (3rd generation) have changed into a renowned restaurant that specialises in the freshest local seafood. Lobsters, crab, sole, salmon, monkfish, mussels, clams all feature on menus that change daily.

The twelve luxurious bedrooms, generous in size, have been tastefully decorated and furnished. They combine modern features (six-foot beds, hairdryer, TV, direct-dial telephone and trouser press) with carefully chosen antiques that blend perfectly together.

East Cork is a primary tourist area on the splendid south coast of Ireland. Ancient historic buildings include the still used 12th century Collegiate Church, the unique Clock Tower and Ireland's first post-Norman University, founded in 1464.

Close by are an 18-hole golf course, deep sea and river angling, riding, two Blue Flag beaches and superb walks through beautiful countryside. From the moment you are first greeted by the family, you will find Ahernes is a marvellous place to relax and enjoy yourself.

LOCATION
On the N25, on Youghal's main street.

Map p.478
ref: B9

> ❝ *The days at Ard na Sidhe are the highlight of our visit in Ireland* ❞
>
> *Hans Jürgen Linschind*

ARD NA SIDHE

Victorian country house

**Caragh Lake,
Killorglin, Co Kerry,
Republic of Ireland**

**Telephone +353 (0)66 9769105
Fax +353 (0)66 9769282**

E-mail: *ardnasidhe@bestloved.com*

RESIDENT MANAGER
Kathleen Dowling

ROOM RATES *(EUROS)*
Single occupancy	€215 - €309
12 Doubles/Twins	€215 - €260
7 Superior Doubles/Twins	€260 - €309

Includes full breakfast, service and VAT

CHARGE/CREDIT CARDS

 • *DC* • *MC* • *VI*

RATINGS & AWARDS
I.T.B. ★★★★
National Garden Competition Winner

FACILITIES
On site: *Garden, fishing, boating*
Nearby: *Golf, horse-riding*

RESTRICTIONS
No facilities for disabled guests
No children
No pets
Closed 1 Oct - 30 Apr

ATTRACTIONS
*Ring of Kerry, Caragh Lake, Ballybunion,
Killarney National Park, Dingle Peninsula,
Waterville and Tralee golf courses*

AFFILIATIONS
*Killarney Hotels Ltd
Preston's Global Hotels*

NEAREST
MAJOR CITY:
Cork - 67 miles/2 ¼ hrs

MAJOR AIRPORT:
Shannon - 95 miles/2 ¼ hrs
Cork - 95 miles/2 ½ hrs

RAILWAY STATION:
Killarney - 17 miles/40 mins

RESERVATIONS
*Toll free in US: 800-544-9993
or 800-537-8483*
*Quote **Best Loved***

ACCESS CODES
Not applicable

The house of your dreams
in an award-winning garden

Ard na Sidhe translates as 'the Hill of the Fairies'. This 20-bedroom mansion hotel on the edge of Caragh Lake has modern facilities, high standards of cuisine and service you would expect from Killarney Hotels, one of Ireland's leading leisure groups. It stands in an award-winning garden. Yet it also has a mystic history that reaches deep into the country's distant and magical past.

Lady Gordon, a lady of titled Irish lineage, built the house in 1913. It is long and low and gabled, with casement windows set in stone mullions, 'and never', said Lady Gordon, 'looked new'. The ghost of her ancestor, Bess Stokes, is said to haunt the grounds, but it was 'The Hill of the Fairies' long before Bess.

The house fits harmoniously into superbly romantic scenery, beside Ireland's highest mountain, McGillicuddy's Reeks. All around is magnificently beautiful countryside for fishing, cycling and boating on the lakes. Several of the country's finest golf courses are within an easy and delightful drive away.

At the Ard na Sidhe you will enjoy the full range of holiday leisure and historical touring attractions that have made Killarney one of the best-loved places in the world. And there is an extra special something in the unique and mystical history of The Hill of the Fairies.

LOCATION
*Right at the edge of the beautiful
Caragh Lake at Killarney.*

"*I just wish that I had the eloquence of diction or the brilliance of metaphor to adequately describe this fine castle*"

Mr J O'Neil, Texas, USA

13th century castle

ASHFORD CASTLE

**Cong, Co Mayo,
Republic of Ireland**

**Telephone +353 (0)92 46003
Fax +353 (0)92 46260**

E-mail: *ashford@bestloved.com*

GENERAL MANAGER
Niall Rochford

ROOM RATES (EUROS)
Single occupancy   €189 - €932
40 Standard Doubles/Twins €204 - €414
32 Deluxe Doubles/Twins €317 - €489
5 State rooms   €543 - €687
6 Suites   €653 - €947
Includes service and VAT

CHARGE/CREDIT CARDS

 • DC • MC • VI

RATINGS & AWARDS
I.T.B. ★★★★★

FACILITIES
On site: *Garden, gym, heli-pad, fishing,
riding, golf, tennis, health & beauty
archery, snooker, clay pigeon shooting,
gym, falconry
1 meeting room/max 110 people*

RESTRICTIONS
*No facilities for disabled guests
No pets*

ATTRACTIONS
*Westport, Clifden,
Connemara National Park,
Kylemore Abbey, Galway,
Ceidhe Fields*

AFFILIATIONS
Independent

NEAREST
MAJOR CITY:
Galway - 35 miles/45 mins

MAJOR AIRPORT:
Shannon - 90 miles/1 ½ hrs

RAILWAY STATION:
Galway - 35 miles/45 mins

RESERVATIONS
*Toll free in US: 800-346-7007
Quote Best Loved*

ACCESS CODES
Not applicable

A stately home, sporting complex and the best of the West of Ireland

Until 1939, Ashford Castle was part of an estate owned by the Guinness family and the residence of Lord Ardilaun. It was transformed into a luxury hotel and many of its lavish furnishings, the rich panelling of the Great Hall, the objets d'art and masterpiece paintings came into the domain of those guests fortunate enough to stay there.

The estate provides an almost inexhaustable array of sporting pleasures: a nine-hole golf course, indoor equestrian centre, clay pigeon shooting, archery, fishing, a fully equipped gymnasium, a health centre and some of the most magnificent walks in Ireland.

Everything about Ashford Castle reflects its aristocratic antecedents: the comfort, the service and, not least, the food. This area of Ireland is famous for the quality of its produce especially the seafood which comes from the cleanest waters in Europe. You have a choice between traditional and French cuisine dining in either the George V or The Connaught restaurants. An evening drink in the Dungeon Bar is accompanied by a resident pianist and harpist.

The lordly bedrooms are sumptuously furnished to the highest standards and most overlook the lough or the river.

LOCATION

*From Galway take the N84 north to Headford
then the R334 forking left onto the R346 to Cong.
At the village of Cross, turn left at the church
and drive through the castle gates.*

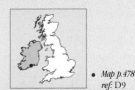

ASHLEE LODGE

Luxury guesthouse

❝ *We found it as it was described to us, Absolutely Beautiful* ❞

The Breeze Family, New Zealand

**Tower, Blarney,
Co Cork,
Republic of Ireland**

**Telephone +353 (0)21 4385346
Fax +353 (0)21 4385726**

E-mail: *ashlee@bestloved.com*

OWNERS
John and Anne O'Leary

ROOM RATES (EUROS)
Single occupancy   €100 - €160
6 Executive Doubles/Twins   €120
2 Mini-suites   €140
2 Master-suites   €160
Includes full breakfast and VAT

CHARGE/CREDIT CARDS

 • DC • MC • VI

RATINGS & AWARDS
I.T.B. ★★★★ *Guest House*
A.A. ◆◆◆◆◆

FACILITIES
On site: *Garden, sauna, jacuzzi*
Nearby: *Golf, fishing, riding, leisure centre*

RESTRICTIONS
*No children under 12 years
No smoking throughout
Closed 20 Dec - 5 Jan*

ATTRACTIONS
*Blarney Castle, Blarney Woollen Mills,
Cork City Gaol, English Market,
Cobh - Queenstown Story,
Jameson Heritage Centre*

AFFILIATIONS
Independent

NEAREST
MAJOR CITY:
Cork - 9 miles/15 mins

MAJOR AIRPORT:
Cork - 11 miles/20 mins

RAILWAY STATION:
Cork - 9 miles/15 mins

RESERVATIONS
Direct with hotel
Quote **Best Loved**

ACCESS CODES
Not applicable

IRELAND

Offering sheer luxury and the very best of Irish Hospitality

John and Anne O'Leary are justifiably proud of Ashlee Lodge, which they built entirely with the discerning guest in mind. Every detail was carefully considered so visitors from all over the world would instantly feel cocooned by the best of Irish hospitality.

Only ten minutes from Cork, it is near many of Ireland's greatest sights and in a golfer's paradise. To reflect this, the ten spacious bedrooms are named after famous local golf courses. Each light, airy room is exceptionally well equipped with a king-size bed, independent heating, a wide-screen TV, modem access and a luxurious bathroom. The two Master Suites and the two Garden Suites also have whirlpool baths, but for all guests a Canadian hot-tub and sauna are discreetly placed in an attractive roof-top garden.

Within a few minutes walk of pubs and restaurants, only breakfast is served here. But what a breakfast! Taken in the greenery-filled Conservatory, there is a superb cold buffet plus a choice of ten hot dishes cooked with the best of local produce.

Although all visitors may end up kissing the Blarney Stone at the nearby castle, no one is exaggerating when Ashlee Lodge is described as a place 'that puts you first'.

LOCATION
***On the R617 Blarney to Killarney Road,
just 2 km outside of Blarney.***

" I have travelled the globe for 30 years. This house equals most and tops the rest. It's a credit to you "

Mr Shanks, Dublin, Ireland

• Map p.478
ref: B9

Country house

BALLYGARRY HOUSE

A wonderful welcome and the drama of Ireland's breathtaking Atlantic coast

For fifty years the family-run Ballygarry House has invited all who stay there to make themselves at home. This traditional, warm welcome is authentic to this South Western corner of Ireland that is also home to some of the country's premier championship and links golf courses, including Tralee, Ballybunion and Mahoney's Point. This hospitality is echoed in the décor: well chosen antiques, blazing open fires and freshly cut flowers all contribute to the cordial environment, and the surrounding grounds are equally enticing.

Ballygarry is really all about style and imagination. The staff are quite simply the backbone of the hotel and nothing, but nothing is too much trouble. The bedrooms are spacious and individually designed; fluffy towels and bathrobes adorn elegant bathrooms.

In the split-level dining room, culinary delights may include char grilled black Angus Beef on a bed of Chive Mash, or Seared Pepper Crusted Yellow Fin Tuna on a Warm Spinach Salad.

Set in six acres of mature gardens at the foot of the Kerry Mountains, the local countryside also offers a variety of lake, woodland and sea with a plethora of fascinating walks and trails in the vicinity. A host of outdoor activities can also be arranged.

LOCATION

2 km from Tralee on the Killarney road.

**Killarney Road,
Tralee, Co Kerry,
Republic of Ireland**

**Telephone +353 (0)66 7123322
Fax +353 (0)66 7127630**

E-mail: *ballygarry@bestloved.com*

OWNER
Eoin McGillicuddy

ROOM RATES *(EUROS)*
Single occupancy   €120
7 Doubles/Twins   €150
32 Superior Doubles/Twins €190
7 Junior suites   €250
Includes full breakfast and VAT

CHARGE/CREDIT CARDS

 • MC • VI

RATINGS & AWARDS
I.T.B. ★★★★

FACILITIES
On site: *Garden, heli-pad*
1 meeting room/max 400
Nearby: *Golf, fishing, riding,*
clay pigeon shooting

RESTRICTIONS
No pets
Closed 16 - 28 Dec & 6 - 20 Jan

ATTRACTIONS
*Dingle Peninsula,
Ring of Kerry,
Killarney National Park,
Muckross House,
Jeanie Johnston Emigrant Ship,
Blennerville Windmill*

AFFILIATIONS
Independent

NEAREST
MAJOR CITY:
Tralee

MAJOR AIRPORT:
Shannon - 82 miles/2 hrs
Kerry - 5 miles/10 mins

RAILWAY STATION:
Tralee - 1 mile/5 mins

RESERVATIONS
Direct with hotel
*Quote **Best Loved***

ACCESS CODES
*AMADEUS LM KIR030
APOLLO/GALILEO LM 52861
SABRE/ABACUS LM 8228
WORLDSPAN LM 09030*

IRELAND

BAYVIEW HOTEL

Seaside hotel

Ballycotton, Co Cork, Republic of Ireland

Telephone +353 (0)21 4646746
Fax +353 (0)21 4646075

E-mail: *bayview@bestloved.com*

OWNER
John O'Brien

GENERAL MANAGER
Stephen Belton

ROOM RATES *(EUROS)*
Single occupancy	€121 - €139
33 Doubles/Twins	€178 - €214
2 Suites	€242 - €278

Includes full breakfast and VAT

CHARGE/CREDIT CARDS

 • *DC • MC • VI*

RATINGS & AWARDS
I.T.B. ★★★★ *Hotel*
R.A.C. ★★★ *Dining Award 2*

FACILITIES
On site: *Garden, fishing, sea fishing*
2 meeting rooms/max 40 people
Nearby: *Golf, fishing, tennis, riding*

RESTRICTIONS
Limited facilities for disabled guests
No pets
Closed 1 Nov - 1 April

ATTRACTIONS
Cobb Heritage Centre, Youghal Cathedral, Titanic Trail, Fota Wildlife Park, Jameson Heritage Centre, Fota House

AFFILIATIONS
Manor House Hotels of Ireland

NEAREST
MAJOR CITY:
Midleton - 12 miles/30 mins

MAJOR AIRPORT:
Cork - 23 miles/45 mins

RAILWAY STATION:
Cork - 23 miles/45 mins

RESERVATIONS
Toll free in US/Canada: 800-44-UTELL
Quote **Best Loved**

ACCESS CODES
AMADEUS UI ORKBAY
APOLLO/GALILEO UI 91672
SABRE/ABACUS UI 27287
WORLDSPAN UI 40022

Superb food and marvellous views of a spectacular coastline

Bayview Hotel at Ballycotton overlooks a small, unspoilt, fishing harbour. Every bedroom is a room with a view over miles of spectacular coastline. The hotel was caringly restored in 1991, and now combines modern luxury with the charm and warmth of bygone days. The style is informal and friendly. The dinners are superb, based on the best use of fresh local produce to provide dishes with the right balance of flavour, texture and presentation to make them truly delightful. The hotel's original garden offers invigorating air and an insight into the work of a traditional fishing harbour.

The hotel is excellently placed for sea angling, especially for warm water fish such as shark and conger, and for bird watching, coastal walking and swimming. Six golf courses, links and woodland, are within 30 minutes' drive.

Ballycotton is a traditional fishing village dating back to 1250. It is ideally located for exploring the many treasures of East Cork and the wider environs of counties Cork and Waterford. Close at hand are Fota Wildlife Park, Jameson Whiskey Heritage Centre, Queenstown

Harbour with its Titanic connections, and the Queenstown Story at Cobh, where many Irish emigrants set sail for America from the mid 19th century to the 1950s.

LOCATION
At Castlemartyr on the N25 turn onto the R632 towards Garryvoe. From Garryvoe follow signs for Shanagarry and Ballycotton.

IRELAND

395

" In great appreciation to you both for providing hours of pleasure in your wonderful cooking and very beautiful restaurant "

A devoted fan (name witheld)

● Map p.478
ref: B10

Georgian country house

BLAIRS COVE HOUSE

Self-catering, B&B, and an acclaimed restaurant in 4½ tropical acres by the sea

Blairs Cove House is a beautiful Georgian country house set on the shores of Dunmanus Bay in four and a half acres of lawns and sub-tropical gardens. The old stone buildings that are arranged around the cobbled courtyard have been converted into two houses, a duplex apartment and a studio, all of which can be rented year round on either a self-catering or a bed-and-breakfast basis (This is not an hotel). There are also two cottages, one in its own grounds with direct access to the sea, the other on Dunmanus Pier, both self-catering. All are delightful.

Local craftsmen have been employed to blend old and new in the conversion of the very different living spaces, making the best of spectacular views over the cove or the hills and valleys. The owners have furnished each one in an individual style, with a good eye for colour, using carefully chosen fabrics and floor coverings, antiques and locally made modern furniture, works of art and choice pieces of bric-à-brac. Facilities include washing machine/driers or use of a laundry, and some of the suites have a video and stereo system. In the old stable block, with high stone walls and lofty, beamed roof, is the

much-acclaimed restaurant (open March to late October for dinner only). Plan to stay for as long as you can.

LOCATION

1 ½ miles from Durrus along the Coleen/Barleycove Road. The hotel's entrance (blue gates) is on the right hand side.

**Near Bantry,
Durrus, Co Cork,
Republic of Ireland**

**Telephone +353 (0)27 61127
Fax +353 (0)27 61487**

E-mail: *blairs@bestloved.com*

OWNERS
Philippe and Sabine De Mey

ROOM RATES *(EUROS)*
Single occupancy   €105 - €135
3 Suites   €140 - €200
*Includes continental breakfast,
service and VAT*

CHARGE/CREDIT CARDS

 ● DC ● MC ● VI

RATINGS & AWARDS
*Bridgestone Top 100 Best Places
to Stay in Ireland*

FACILITIES
On site: *Garden*
Nearby: *Golf, tennis, fitness,
yachting, fishing, riding*

RESTRICTIONS
*No facilities for disabled guests
Closed 30 Nov - 15 Mar
No pets*

ATTRACTIONS
*Bantry House, Ring of Beara,
Garnish Island Italian Gardens,
Mizenhead Lighthouse, Ring of Kerry,
Schull Planetarium*

AFFILIATIONS
Ireland's Blue Book

NEAREST
*MAJOR CITY:
Cork - 80 miles/1 ¼ hrs*

*MAJOR AIRPORT:
Cork - 80 miles/1 ¼ hrs*

*RAILWAY STATION:
Cork - 80 miles/1 ¼ hrs*

RESERVATIONS
Toll free in US: 800-323-5463
*Quote **Best Loved***

ACCESS CODES
Not applicable

IRELAND

● *Map p.478*
ref: G7

"A wonderful town house, can't wait to come back"

Margaret Clarke, New Jersey, USA

BLAKES TOWNHOUSE

Town house

**50 Merrion Road,
Ballsbridge, Dublin 4,
Republic of Ireland**

**Telephone +353 (0)1 6688324
Fax +353 (0)1 6684280**

E-mail: *blakestown@bestloved.com*

OWNER
Pat Halpin

ROOM RATES (EUROS)
Single occupancy	€99 - €129
5 Doubles/Twins	€126 - €169
5 Superior Doubles/Twins	€159 - €189
2 Suites	€190 - €290

Includes full breakfast, service and VAT

CHARGE/CREDIT CARDS

 ● *DC* ● *JCB* ● *MC* ● *VI*

RATINGS & AWARDS
A.A. ◆◆◆◆◆ *Premier Collection*

FACILITIES
On site: *Garden, car park
1 meeting room/ max 30 people*
Nearby: *Complimentary use of nearby
leisure centre, golf, riding, fishing*

RESTRICTIONS
*Limited facilities for disabled guests
No pets, guide dogs only*

ATTRACTIONS
*Trinity College, National Art Gallery,
Christchurch, St Stephen's Green,
Grafton Street, Powerscourt Gardens*

AFFILIATIONS
*The Green Book of Ireland
Preston's Global Hotels
Luxe Boutique Hotels*

NEAREST
*MAJOR CITY:
Dublin*

*MAJOR AIRPORT:
Dublin - 6 miles/20 mins*

*RAILWAY STATION:
Sandymount - ¼ mile/5 mins*

RESERVATIONS
*Toll free in US: 800-888-1199
or 1800-671-73178
or 800-544-9993
Toll free in UK: 0800 0964748
Quote **Best Loved***

ACCESS CODES
*AMADEUS LE DUB987
APOLLO/GALILEO LE 27207
SABRE/ABACUS LE 52264
WORLDSPAN LE 52264*

IRELAND

*Small is beautiful (and affordable)
in the fair city of Dublin*

If you are looking for a home-from-home that won't break the bank in Eire's increasingly fashionable capital city, Blakes' Townhouse is a very useful address to know. One of a row of three-storey Edwardian homes in the quiet residential quarter of Ballsbridge (also known as the Embassy District for the proliferation of foreign embassies that have established themselves here), Blakes' combines century-old style and an intimate ambience with modern facilities. Easy access to the city centre is a major attraction - it is close enough to walk - yet without the inflated prices.

The very comfortable bedrooms are equipped with the latest in-room technology to suit the most discerning professional and leisure traveller, while the executive rooms and four-poster suites also feature whirlpool spas. There is a direct luxury coach link to and from Dublin Airport, and private car parking is available to guests. And if you are keen to escape the city for the day, the hotel can arrange golfing packages and scenic country tours. A private hotel chauffeur service is also available.

LOCATION

From Dublin centre follow signs to East Link toll bridge. Cross bridge and follow South City sign to 1st set of lights & turn left along seafront. Continue for ½ km turning right at Sidney Parade junction. Cross Dart Line and turn right into Merrion Road.

" Sumptuous food in splendid surroundings "

Lucinda O Sullivan, Irish Independent

● *Map p.478*
ref: G7

Georgian town house

BROWNES TOWNHOUSE

The talk of Dublin stylishly set in its cultural centre

Sophisticated but relaxed - this is the atmosphere that pervades this Georgian town house whose tall windows overlook St Stephen s Green, the spacious and prestigious park right in the heart of Dublin. Close by are the buildings of Trinity College and the National Museum, Grafton Street s fashionable shopping district, many of the city s most popular pubs and all the gathering places of trendy Temple Bar.

Brownes is a city-centre hotel, yet it has the intimacy and warmth of a country house. The twelve bedrooms and suites are equipped with all the facilities a business guest requires (including ISDN and a direct fax line), but each is individually designed and traditionally decorated and furnished with comfort and luxury in mind.

Brownes Brasserie is a gracious, split-level dining room whose plush deep-red seating is set off by the crisp white table linen. Known by locals for its sumptuous cuisine, the Brasserie is, like the townhouse, stylish in a traditional manner with a contemporary, relaxed ambience. It prides itself on being the perfect setting for a casual meal with friends, a lunch with business colleagues, or a romantic dinner deux. There is a

suite for small, private meetings, and a private dining room with view of St Stephen's Green.

Full of life. A place to see and be seen.

LOCATION

From the airport follow the signs to City Centre and then St Stephen's Green. Brownes is on the North side of St Stephen's Green.

---

22 St Stephen's Green, Dublin 2, Republic of Ireland

Telephone +353 (0)1 638 3939
Fax +353 (0)1 638 3900

E-mail: *brownes@bestloved.com*

OWNER
Barry Canny

ROOM RATES *(EUROS)*
2 Singles	€180
7 Doubles/Twins	€210 - €255
1 Four-poster	€255
2 Suites	€445 - €510

Includes full breakfast and VAT

CHARGE/CREDIT CARDS

 ● *MC* ● *VI*

RATINGS & AWARDS
I.T.B. ★★★★ *Guest House*
R.A.C. ★★★★ *Town House Dining Award 3*
A.A. ◆◆◆◆◆
Gilbey's Gold Medal Award for Excellence in Catering 2000
Bridgestone Best in Ireland 2001

FACILITIES
On site: *1 meeting room/max 40 people*
Nearby: *Golf, tennis, fitness, water skiing, fishing, riding, shooting*

RESTRICTIONS
Limited facilities for disabled guests
No pets
Closed 24 Dec - 3 Jan

ATTRACTIONS
St Stephen's Green, Trinity College, National Museum, Grafton Street, Temple Bar

AFFILIATIONS
The Celebrated Hotels Collection

NEAREST
MAJOR CITY:
Dublin

MAJOR AIRPORT:
Dublin - 15 miles/30 mins

RAILWAY STATION:
Heuston - 6 miles/15 mins

RESERVATIONS
Toll free in US: 800-322-2403
or 800-44-UTELL
Quote **Best Loved**

ACCESS CODES
Not applicable

IRELAND

" It's one of those places where you hope it rains all day so you have an excuse to snuggle indoors "

Ian Cruikshank, Journalist, Canada

THE BUSHMILLS INN

Coaching inn and restaurant

9 Dunluce Road, Bushmills, Co Antrim BT57 8QG Northern Ireland

Telephone +44 (0)28 207 3 2339 Fax +44 (0)28 207 3 2048

E-mail: *bushmills@bestloved.com*

MANAGERS
Alan Dunlop and Stella Minogue

ROOM RATES
4 Singles   £68 - £78
28 Doubles/Twins   £88 - £188
Includes full breakfast and VAT

CHARGE/CREDIT CARDS
MC • VI

RATINGS & AWARDS
N.I.T.B. ★★★
R.A.C. ★★★ *Dining Award 2*
Taste of Ulster
BA Tourism Awards - Best Hotel 2000
Gilbeys Gold Medal for Catering Excellence 2001

FACILITIES
On site: *Garden, heli-pad, fishing 3 meeting rooms/max 40 people*
Nearby: *Golf, riding, fishing*

RESTRICTIONS
No pets
No smoking in bedrooms or restaurant

ATTRACTIONS
Giant's Causeway, Dunluce Castle, Old Bushmills Distillery, Carrick-a-Rede rope bridge, Royal Portrush Golf Club, Bushmills Steam Railway

AFFILIATIONS
Ireland's Blue Book
Northern Ireland's Best Kept Secrets

NEAREST
MAJOR CITY:
Belfast - 60 miles/1 hr

MAJOR AIRPORT:
Belfast - 48 miles/1 hr
City of Derry - 35 miles/55 mins

RAILWAY STATION:
Coleraine - 9 miles/15 mins

RESERVATIONS
Toll free in US: 800-323-5463
Quote **Best Loved**

ACCESS CODES
Not applicable

An intriguing inn by the world's oldest distillery near The Giant's Causeway

The Giant's Causeway Coast is reckoned the most spectacular in Europe - wide sandy beaches washed by Atlantic rollers, neat fishing harbours nestling between craggy cliffs and grassy dunes supporting a wealth of wildlife. The area is a golfer's paradise with no less than eight courses, including Royal Portrush, within easy driving range while, for anglers, the River Bush is within casting distance of the hotel gardens.

The welcoming glow of, not one but four, turf fires is just one of many features that give this historic inn its unique and intriguing character. There is a secret room, if you can find it and, in the bar, still lit by gaslight, you can treat yourself to a glass of 25 year old Bushmills malt whiskey from the hotel's private cask before anticipating the pleasures of the Taste of Ulster Restaurant. Within its white washed walls and intimate snugs you can enjoy excellent, freshly prepared dishes and a glass (or two) of expertly chosen wines.

Bedrooms in the Coaching Inn are individually furnished in comfortable cottage style. The oak-beamed Loft is the gateway to the Mill House on the banks of the River Bush and here the spacious bedrooms have their own sitting room area.

The inn has come to epitomise the true spirit of Ulster hospitality and is regularly featured by television presenters and travel writers from all over the world.

LOCATION
On the A2 Antrim coast road. From Ballymoney take the B62 turning right on to the B17 from Coleraine. Follow the Giant's Causeway signs.

IRELAND

« Even before I leave I cherish the thought of returning to your magical house »

Bruce & Noreen Finnamore, Bath

Dublin town house

BUTLERS TOWN HOUSE

A haven of calm in the heart of cosmopolitan Dublin

On a quiet, leafy avenue in the Victorian quarter of Ballsbridge, the red brick façade of Butlers Town House is pierced by one of the city's characteristic painted doors. Behind this particular one you will find peaceful and stylish surroundings, and service that regular visitors to Butlers value so highly.

This elegant town house has retained many of its original features imaginatively interwoven with 21st-century conveniences from air-conditioning and modem points in the bedrooms to a computer for guests' use in the reception area. The ambience is intimate, even clubby, with a degree of personalised service that belongs to another more leisured age and the skilled staff appear positively telepathic in their ability to anticipate your needs.

The gourmet Irish breakfast is designed to set up the most demanding appetite for the day. Menu choices include traditional favourites such as black and white puddings and scrambled eggs with Irish cheddar and tomatoes, as well as more exotic fare from poached eggs with salmon and hollandaise sauce to French toast with maple syrup. There is also a light room service menu and a plethora of excellent restaurants nearby.

LOCATION

Travel along the M1 to the City, follow signs for East Link Toll Bridge. Drive to the top of Bath Avenue and take a left - Butlers is 100 yards on the right.

---

44 Lansdowne Road, Ballsbridge, Dublin 4, Republic of Ireland

Telephone +353 (0)1 667 4022
Fax +353 (0)1 667 3960

E-mail: *butlers@bestloved.com*

GENERAL MANAGER
Adrian Harkins

ROOM RATES *(EUROS)*
Single occupancy	€140
16 Doubles/Twins	€190
4 Deluxe doubles	€215

Includes buffet breakfast, 24 hour complimentary tea and coffee, service and VAT

CHARGE/CREDIT CARDS

 • DC • MC • VI

RATINGS & AWARDS
I.T.B. ★★★★ *Guest House*
R.A.C. ◆◆◆◆◆ *Sparkling Diamond & Warm Welcome Award*
A.A. ◆◆◆◆◆ *Town House*

FACILITIES
On site: *Garden*
1 meeting room/max 22 people
Nearby: *Golf, tennis, fitness, riding, sea fishing*

RESTRICTIONS
Limited facilities for disabled guests
Closed 23 Dec - 3 Jan
No pets

ATTRACTIONS
Trinity College, National Museum, St Stephen's Green, National Gallery, Christchurch, Grafton Street,

AFFILIATIONS
The Charming Hotels
Manor House Hotels of Ireland

NEAREST
MAJOR CITY:
Dublin

MAJOR AIRPORT:
Dublin - 8 miles/25 mins

RAILWAY STATION:
Heuston - 3 miles/15 mins

FERRY PORT:
Dun Laoghaire - 2 miles/10 mins

RESERVATIONS
Toll free in US: 800-44-UTELL
Quote Best Loved

ACCESS CODES
AMADEUS UI DUBBUT
APOLLO/GALILEO UI 82012
SABRE/ABACUS UI 3779
WORLDSPAN UI 26133

IRELAND

Map p.478
ref: B9

" This is why Irish Americans sing and cry over Ireland "

Mike & Mary O'Malley, Kansas City, USA

CARAGH LODGE

**Caragh Lake, Co Kerry,
Republic of Ireland**

**Telephone +353 (0)66 9769115
Fax +353 (0)66 9769316**

E-mail: *caragh@bestloved.com*

OWNER
Mary Gaunt

ROOM RATES *(EUROS)*
1 Single   €130
13 Doubles/Twins   €180 - €230
1 Suite   €325
Includes full breakfast, service and VAT

CHARGE/CREDIT CARDS

 • DC • MC • VI

RATINGS & AWARDS
I.T.B. ★★★★ *Guest House*
R.A.C. Gold Ribbon ★★ *Dining Award 3*
Karen Brown Recommended
Gilbeys Hotel and Catering Award

FACILITIES
On site: *Garden, fishing, tennis, sauna*
1 meeting room/max 15 people
Nearby: *Golf, riding, beaches*

RESTRICTIONS
Limited facilities for disabled guests
No children under 8 years
No pets
Closed 12 Oct - 25 Apr

ATTRACTIONS
*Ring of Kerry, Dingle Peninsula,
Killarney, Skelligs Rock*

AFFILIATIONS
Preston's Global Hotels
Ireland's Blue Book

NEAREST
MAJOR CITY:
Cork - 70 miles/2 hrs

MAJOR AIRPORT:
Shannon/Cork - 70 miles/2 hrs
Kerry Airport - 16 miles/30 mins

RAILWAY STATION:
Killarney - 16 miles/30 mins

RESERVATIONS
*Toll free in US: 800-544-9993
or 800-323-5463*
Quote **Best Loved**

ACCESS CODES
Not applicable

A gracious house a stone's throw from the spectacular Ring of Kerry

Less than one mile from the spectacular Ring of Kerry and four miles from the golden beaches of Dingle Bay, Caragh Lodge sits on the shore of Caragh Lake, looking towards the breathtaking slopes of the McGillycuddy Reeks, Ireland's highest mountains.

The rooms are sumptuously decorated with period furnishings and antiques. The converted garden rooms offer spectacular views. Each looks out onto stunning displays of magnolias, rhododendrons, azaleas, camelias and many rare shrubs. Exquisite furnishings and welcoming log fires in the main house's lounges provide the perfect place to end the day.

Overlooking the lake, the dining room features only the finest Irish cuisine, freshly caught wild salmon, succulent Kerry lamb, garden grown vegetables and home baked breads, all personally prepared by Mary Gaunt.

Golfers will find Caragh Lodge the perfect base. With eight courses nearby, tee-off times can be easily arranged prior to your stay. Salmon and brown trout fishing are on the doorstep and two boats are available for guests. Ghillies or any necessary permits for fishing in the two local rivers can easily be arranged.

LOCATION
**Caragh Lodge is situated just off N70.
Travelling from Killorglin to Glenbeigh,
take road signposted 'Caragh Lodge 1 mile'.
Turn left at lake, lodge is on right.**

> *" We left feeling more relaxed than we have felt in years "*
>
> J Buchanon, The Netherlands

• *Map p.478*
ref: E8

18th century manor house

CASTLE DURROW

Feel like Lord and Lady of the manor and get a taste of the high-life

Sweeping up the Castle Durrow's drive, guests are transported to the elegant world of the Irish country house. Looking out over its own 30 acres of rolling countryside, manicured gardens and the River Erkina, the four-year restoration of the 18th-century mansion has worked miracles. True to its origins, the high-ceilinged, colonnaded reception rooms are furnished with the best quality antiques cleverly complemented by outstanding modern classics.

Glitteringly lavish, polished oak floors gleam with the light from tall, elegantly draped windows or the light from sparkling chandeliers. Each of the 26 bedrooms is individual from the huge 'mistress' rooms with four-poster beds, antiques and sumptuous drapes to the contemporary deluxe rooms, with their king-size sleigh beds and classic Colonial furnishings. The top floor rooms are idiosyncratic with beamed, sloping ceilings and antique Oriental furnishings in the fashion of the 18th century. Everywhere the incredible attention to detail is apparent.

The restaurant, with its classical Georgian décor, serves inspired international and regional favourites using the fresh produce for which

Ireland is famed. Only 90 minutes from Dublin and with up to date facilities for meetings and unlimited attractions and activities nearby, Castle Durrow is also ideal for conferences or weddings.

LOCATION

From Dublin take the N7 to Portlaoise and then the N8 signed for Cork. Once in the village of Durrow the hotel is on the right.

**Durrow, Co Laois,
Republic of Ireland**

**Telephone +353 (0)502 36555
Fax +353 (0)502 36559**

E-mail: *durrow@bestloved.com*

OWNERS
Peter and Shelly Stokes

RATES PER PERSON *(EUROS)*
Single occupancy	*€130 - €190*
6 Standard Doubles	*€90*
6 Deluxe Doubles/Twins	*€110*
10 Master rooms	*€130*
1 Suite	*€150*
4 Deluxe Family rooms	*POA*
Includes full breakfast and VAT	

CHARGE/CREDIT CARDS

 • *MC* • *VI*

RATINGS & AWARDS
Awards Pending

FACILITIES
On site: Garden, heli-pad, snooker room, fishing, riding, Equestrian Centre
3 meeting rooms/max 180 people
Nearby: Golf, fishing, walking

RESTRICTIONS
*No pets in bedrooms
Closed Christmas & New Year*

ATTRACTIONS
Mount Juliet Golf Course, Rock of Cashel, Kilkenny Town & Castle, Holycross Abbey, Irish National Stud and Japanese Gardens, Curragh Racecourse, Dunmore Caves

AFFILIATIONS
Independent

NEAREST
*MAJOR CITY:
Kilkenny - 16 miles/25 mins*

*MAJOR AIRPORT:
Dublin - 70 miles/1 ½ hrs*

*RAILWAY STATION:
Portlaoise - 15 miles/20 mins*

RESERVATIONS
Direct with hotel
Quote **Best Loved**

ACCESS CODES
Not applicable

IRELAND

● *Map p.478*
ref: D9

CASTLEHYDE HOTEL

17th century country house

**Castlehyde, Fermoy,
Co Cork,
Republic of Ireland**

**Telephone +353 (0)25 31865
Fax +353 (0)25 31485**

E-mail: *castlehyde@bestloved.com*

OWNERS
Erik and Helen Speekenbrink

ROOM RATES *(EUROS)*
Single occupancy   €105 - €140
14 Doubles/Twins   €145 - €195
5 Self-catering cottages   €415 - €990
*Includes full breakfast, service and VAT
(Cottages quoted per week)*

CHARGE/CREDIT CARDS

 ● *MC* ● *VI*

RATINGS & AWARDS
A.A. ★★★ ❀❀ 71%

FACILITIES
On site: *Garden, outdoor pool
1 meeting room/max 40 people*
Nearby: *Golf, river and sea fishing, pony
trekking*

RESTRICTIONS
*Limited facilities for disabled guests
No smoking in bedrooms or restaurant
No pets*

ATTRACTIONS
*Mitchelstown Caves, Rock of Cashel,
Jameson Heritage Centre, Cahir Castle,
Lismore Castle and gardens,
Cobh Heritage Centre,
Lusitania - Titanic trail*

AFFILIATIONS
Preston's Global Hotels

NEAREST
*MAJOR CITY:
Cork - 25 miles/40 mins*

*MAJOR AIRPORT:
Cork - 30 miles/30 mins*

*RAILWAY STATION:
Mallow - 18 miles/30 mins*

*FERRY PORT:
Cork - 35 miles/45 mins*

RESERVATIONS
Toll free in US: 800-544-9993
Quote **Best Loved**

ACCESS CODES
Not applicable

IRELAND

From pre-Raphaelite ruins to a sanctuary of luxury. The stuff of legend.

The transformation of CastleHyde is a tribute to the vision, energy and enterprise of Erik and Helen Speekenbrink. In two years, its decaying pre-Raphaelite ruins have been converted into a grand house with every contemporary comfort and indulgence hidden discretely within its stone walls. It is an amazing feat made all the more remarkable by the fact that the haunting romance remains strong as ever. Full marks go to Helen. Her inate ability to spot a treasure in a builder s tip has provided the 200-year old Pitchpine columns supporting the walkways, the Chinese slate floor in the reception area and the wood floors in the dining room. She also has an eagle eye for colour and contrasting materials. Tensions simply melt just to look at the harmony of it all.

Erik is a professional hotelier making his debut as an owner/manager. He is well aware of what satisfies guests and has ensured the amenities live up to their expectations: a choice between well-appointed bedrooms and luxurious self-catering cottage suites, a heated outdoor swimming pool set in the sanctuary of beautiful gardens and a dining room which will inevitably find honour in the good food guides. Erik is supported by a cheerful, attentive staff who enjoy meeting and looking after his guests.

The Blackwater Valley is an angler's paradise and a horse breeding centre; a magical place where legends are made - like CastleHyde!

LOCATION

On the Dublin side of Fermoy take the N72 to Mallow. The hotel is by the N72, between Ballyhooly and 3 kms from Fermoy.

" Dinner by candlelight and beech wood fire. Bushmills Malt, Bordeaux and Burgundy; roast lamb, roast duck and Sheila's chocolate mousse. Thank you for the last two weeks "

Lucy Tan and Christof Geyer, Zurich, Switzerland

- Map p.478
ref: D5

Georgian mansion

COOPERSHILL

A fine Georgian mansion, a family welcome and sumptuous cooking

The fine Georgian mansion Coopershill has been home to seven generations of the O'Hara family since it was built in 1774. Six of its bedrooms have four-poster or canopy beds, and all have their own private bathrooms. The furniture dates from the 18th century.

Brian and Lindy O'Hara welcome guests to their home. Candle-lit dinners with family silver and crystal glass, a wide choice of wines and Lindy's sumptuous cooking make a Coopershill holiday memorable.

There are delightful walks and abundant wildlife on the 500 acres of farm and woodland. Facilities include an all-weather tennis court, trout and coarse fishing on the River Arrow which flows through the estate, and a croquet lawn. A boat for fishing or exploring is available on nearby Lough Arrow. Uncrowded beaches, the top-ten rated County Sligo championship golf course and the spectacular mountains and lakes of WB Yeats country are in the vicinity. Lissadell House, the Famine Museum at Strokestown, the Abbey and historic King House at Boyle, and Ireland's largest collection of megalithic tombs are part of the district's fascinating history.

LOCATION

Coopershill is 2 miles from Riverstown and 12 miles from Sligo town, clearly signposted on the N4 Sligo-Dublin road.

Riverstown, Co Sligo, Republic of Ireland

Telephone +353 (0)71 65108
Fax +353 (0)71 65466

E-mail: coopershill@bestloved.com

OWNERS
Brian and Lindy O'Hara

ROOM RATES *(EUROS)*
Single occupancy   €97 - €118
5 Doubles/Twins   €156 - €184
3 Superior doubles   €170 - €198
Includes full breakfast, service and VAT

CHARGE/CREDIT CARDS

  • DC • JCB • MC • VI

RATINGS & AWARDS
Independent

FACILITIES
On site: *Garden, fishing, croquet, tennis*
Nearby: *Fishing, riding*

RESTRICTIONS
No facilities for disabled guests
No smoking in bedrooms and dining room
No pets
Closed 1 Nov - 31 Mar

ATTRACTIONS
Lissadell House, King House,
Slieve League Donegal, Keide Fields - Mayo,
Strokes Townhouse & Famine Museum,
Megalithic Monuments

AFFILIATIONS
Ireland's Blue Book
Preston's Global Hotels

NEAREST
MAJOR CITY:
Sligo - 13 miles/25 mins

MAJOR AIRPORT:
Knock - 24 miles/45 mins
Dublin - 125 miles/2 ½ hrs

RAILWAY STATION:
Ballymote - 7 miles/15 mins

FERRY PORT:
Dun Laoghaire - 135 miles/3 hrs

RESERVATIONS
Toll free in US: 800-323-5463
or 800-544-9993
Quote **Best Loved**

ACCESS CODES
Not applicable

IRELAND

Map p.478
ref: C8

« Everyone is so eager to please - this alone makes you world class »

Dr James Van Ness, Laguna Beach, California

DROMOLAND CASTLE   *16th century castle*

Newmarket-on-Fergus,
Co Clare,
Republic of Ireland

Telephone +353 (0)61 368144
Fax +353 (0)61 363355

E-mail: *dromoland@bestloved.com*

GENERAL MANAGER
Mark Nolan

ROOM RATES *(EUROS)*

Single occupancy	*€204 - €370*
29 Doubles/Twins	*€204 - €370*
26 Deluxe rooms	*€317 - €459*
24 Club rooms	*€360 - €492*
15 Staterooms	*€390 - €762*
6 Suites	*€547 - €547*

Includes VAT

CHARGE/CREDIT CARDS

 • *DC* • *MC* • *VI*

RATINGS & AWARDS
I.T.B. ★★★★★ *Silver Award*
A.A. ★★★★★ ❀❀
A.A. Top 200 - 02/03
Travel & Leisure Magazine
'19th Best Hotel in the World'

FACILITIES
On site: *Garden, gym, snooker, heli-pad,*
fishing, riding, golf, indoor pool,
health & beauty, sauna
6 meeting rooms/max 250 people

RESTRICTIONS
Limited facilities for disabled guests
No pets

ATTRACTIONS
Cliffs of Moher, The Burren, Bunratty Castle,
King John's Castle, Craggaunowen Project,
Aran Islands, Hunt Museum, Ballybunion,
Doonbeg & Lahinch golf courses

AFFILIATIONS
Preferred Hotels & Resorts

NEAREST
MAJOR CITY:
Canterbury - 35 miles/50 mins

MAJOR AIRPORT:
London Gatwick - 50 miles/1 ¼ hrs

RAILWAY STATION:
Rye - ½ mile/5 mins

RESERVATIONS
Toll free in US: 800-346-7007
Quote Best Loved

ACCESS CODES
Not applicable

IRELAND

www.dromoland.bestloved.com

Supreme comfort in a castle on an historic estate

In the 16th century, the Dromoland Estate became the seat of the O'Brien clan, descendants of 'Brian Boru', High King of Ireland. Today the castle is one of Europe's top luxury hotels. Its rooms and suites blend period pieces with modern comfort. Its gallery has one of Ireland's largest collections of portraits, most notably Lucius O'Brien painted by the Swedish artist Michael Dahl. The 17th Baron Inchiquin gave musical recitals in the drawing room where guests now take tea or coffee. His study has become the Library Bar.

The 375 acre estate is supremely beautiful. There are many private facilities for guests. Fine trout have been caught on the lake and the Castle has its own 18-hole championship golf course and club house with a brassiere restaurant and health and beauty spa. Fishing, shooting, horse riding, jogging trails and tennis are all on the estate.

The splendid dining room gives panoramic views of the lake and golf course. David McCann, Head Chef of international repute, presents house specialities such as lamb with foie gras, and steamed fillets of turbot in fennel. There is an outstanding list of wines from the cellar, which guests are welcome to visit. Dromoland

sets out to provide the highest standard of personal service. Your home will be your castle when you make Dromoland Castle your home.

LOCATION

8 miles north of Shannon airport.

" Thank you for the 'Fáilte' "

Mary McAleese, President of Ireland

● Map p.478
ref: F9

Georgian country house

DUNBRODY COUNTRY HOUSE

**Arthurstown, Near Waterford,
Co Wexford
Republic of Ireland**
Telephone +353 (0)51 389 600
Fax +353 (0)51 389 601

E-mail: *dunbrody@bestloved.com*

OWNERS
Kevin and Catherine Dundon

ROOM RATES *(EUROS)*
Single occupancy	*€120 - €385*
15 Doubles/Twins	*€225 - €295*
7 Suites	*€300 - €385*

Includes full breakfast and VAT

CHARGE/CREDIT CARDS

 ● DC ● MC ● VI

RATINGS & AWARDS
I.T.B. ★★★★ *Hotel*
R.A.C. Blue Ribbon ★★★ *Dining Award 3*
A.A. ★★★ ✿✿ *Top 200 - 02/03*
Andrew Harper's Grand Award 2002

FACILITIES
On site: *Garden, croquet,
clay pigeon shooting, cookery school
3 meeting rooms/max 200 people*
Nearby: *Golf, fishing, polo cross*

RESTRICTIONS
*No children in restaurant after 8 pm
Pets accommodated in stables
Closed 24 - 28 Dec*

ATTRACTIONS
*Waterford Crystal, Tintern Abbey,
Hook Peninsula and Lighthouse,
JFK Arboretum, beaches, shark fishing*

AFFILIATIONS
*The Celebrated Hotels Collection
Ireland's Blue Book
Small Luxury Hotels*

NEAREST
*MAJOR CITY:
Waterford - 10 miles/15 mins*
*MAJOR AIRPORT:
Dublin - 100 miles/2 hrs*
*RAILWAY STATION:
Waterford - 10 miles/15 mins*
*FERRY PORT:
Rosslare - 40 miles/45 mins*

RESERVATIONS
*Toll free in US: 800-323-5463
or 800-525-4800
or 800-322-2403*
*Quote **Best Loved***

ACCESS CODES
*AMADEUS LX DUBDCH
APOLLO/GALILEO LX 30267
SABRE/ABACUS LX 55137
WORLDSPAN LX DUBDH*

All the attributes of a fine country house with a restaurant to grace any great city

Epicures amongst you who reckon they can tell the difference between a restaurant in a country hotel and its modish city counterpart, may have to adjust their mind sets. Dunbrody House is your archetypal country house alright with big, spacious bedrooms all beautifully appointed, a 20-acre woodland and manicured garden setting etc, etc but there the cliché ends. Its restaurant has the gastronomic authority you will find in any European capital and a discerning, well-travelled, appreciative clientele to prove it. Gone is that ghastly hush; this place buzzes with enthusiasm - as true of the diners as of the cheerful young staff who attend them.

Now offering a delightful new cookery school with two and four day residential courses, Dunbrody will become more and more of a destination for food lovers. Kevin Dundon acquired star-status as a Master Chef in Canada before returning as the Executive Chef at the Shelbourne in Dublin.

The Front of House is managed by Catherine Dundon whose marketing background blends perfectly with Kevin's creative talents. They must be very happy with their achievement; their welcome says it all.

The garnish on this unexpected pleasure is the hotel's gorgeous location: on Ireland's Sunshine Coast on a long promontory in historic and luscious Co Wexford.

LOCATION

*From Wexford take the R733 to Duncannon
and Arthurstown. Dunbrody is located on
the left coming into Arthurstown village.*

IRELAND

Map p.478
ref: B9

❝ Your property is outstanding; its pastoral setting, magnificent ❞

Lynn Dixson, North Carolina

DUNLOE CASTLE

Luxury hotel

Killarney, Co Kerry, Republic of Ireland

Telephone +353 (0)64 44111
Fax +353 (0)64 44583

E-mail: *dunloe@bestloved.com*

RESIDENT MANAGER
Michael Brennan

ROOM RATES *(EUROS)*
74 Doubles/Twins   €192
28 Superior Doubles/Twins €224 - €251
1 Suite   €575
Includes service and VAT

CHARGE/CREDIT CARDS

• DC • MC • VI

RATINGS & AWARDS
I.T.B. ★★★★★
R.A.C. ★★★★ *Dining Award 2*

FACILITIES
On site: *Garden, riding, tennis, indoor pool, steam room, sauna 6 meeting rooms/max 250 people*
Nearby: *Golf*

RESTRICTIONS
No facilities for disabled guests
No pets
Closed 30 Nov - 1 Mar

ATTRACTIONS
Gap of Dunloe, Dunloe Castle, Ring of Kerry, Dingle Peninsula, Killarney National Park, numerous golf courses

AFFILIATIONS
Killarney Hotels Ltd

NEAREST
MAJOR CITY:
Cork - 57 miles/1 ¼ hrs

MAJOR AIRPORT:
Cork - 60 miles/1 ¼ hrs
Shannon - 90 miles/2 hrs

RAILWAY STATION:
Killarney - 7 miles/20 mins

RESERVATIONS
Toll free in US: 800-537-8483
*Quote **Best Loved***

ACCESS CODES
Not applicable

Peace and birdsong in a historic Killarney setting

The five-star Hotel Dunloe Castle is in the midst of a fascinating park landscape. The Green Isle's magic is reflected in the hotel park, an award-winning botanic collection of international renown. An unbelievable assortment of flowers and plants flourish here, and there are Haflinger horses grazing nearby. The park looks out to the famous Gap of Dunloe, and the beauties of unspoilt nature. The hotel is a member of the Historic Houses and Gardens Association.

The hotel's furnishings are elegant and comfortable. Its decor is stylish with exquisite details. The 103 rooms and mini-suites, have each been designed to include world class deluxe appointments.

In the most beautiful natural settings, you can enjoy the best of international and Irish cuisine in the gourmet restaurant. A magnificent list of wines is there to complement your meal, and you can have a Guinness, an Irish whiskey or anything else you fancy in the cocktail bar. The countless opportunities for leisure activities within easy reach include no fewer than ten golf courses.

LOCATION
From Killarney take N72 Killorglin road. After 4 ¼ miles take a left turn towards Gap of Dunloe. Hotel is then signposted.

> ❝ *A joy to behold. The courtesy, friendship and attention to detail of the management and staff. An enriching experience* ❞
>
> *David and Sheila Power, Douglas, Co Cork*

• *Map p.478*
ref: B9

Neo-Georgian country house

EMLAGH HOUSE

**Dingle, Co Kerry,
Republic of Ireland**

**Telephone +353 (0)66 91 52345
Fax +353 (0)66 91 52369**

E-mail: *emlagh@bestloved.com*

OWNERS
Michael and Marion Kavanagh

ROOM RATES *(EUROS)*
Single occupancy €140 - €160
10 Doubles/Twins €200 - €240
Includes full breakfast and VAT

CHARGE/CREDIT CARDS

MC • VI

RATINGS & AWARDS
I.T.B. ★★★★ *Guest House*
R.A.C. ◆◆◆◆◆ *Sparkling Diamond,
Warm Welcome & Little Gem Awards*
A.A. ◆◆◆◆◆ *Premier Collection
Bridgestone Top 100 Hotels*

FACILITIES
Nearby: *Riding, fishing, watersports*

RESTRICTIONS
*No children under 8 years
No smoking in bedrooms
No pets
Closed Christmas and 7 Jan - 7 Mar*

ATTRACTIONS
*Ring of Kerry, Marine Eco Tours,
Inch Strand, Blasket Islands,
Slea Head Drive, Archeological Sites,
Walking*

AFFILIATIONS
Preston's Global Hotels

NEAREST
*MAJOR CITY:
Cork - 105 miles/2 ½ hrs*

*MAJOR AIRPORT:
Cork - 105 miles/2 ½ hrs*

*RAILWAY STATION:
Tralee - 32 miles/50 mins*

RESERVATIONS
Toll free in US: 800-544-9993
*Quote **Best Loved***

ACCESS CODES
Not applicable

Tailor-made comfort and style on the outskirts of Dingle

It could be said that celebrated film maker David Lean shot the first travelogue for this stunningly beautiful corner of Ireland when he chose the Kerry coast as the setting for the 1970 movie Ryan's Daughter. It alerted a worldwide audience to the scenic splendours of the Dingle Peninsula, the sandy beaches set against a backdrop of hills, countryside that invites exploration on foot or on horseback, and picturesque fishing communities and harbourside towns such as Dingle itself.

Emlagh House enjoys a superb position on the seashore overlooking Dingle Harbour. Combining the graciousness of neo-Georgian architecture with all the comforts and conveniences expected by a discerning 21st-century traveller, the Kavanagh family's purpose-built country house hotel is a terrific find. A clever dovetailing of the old and the new marries the period setting of the foyer with its imposing antique Georgian fireplace and a chic, light-filled conservatory dining room, where breakfast and light meals are served during the day (Dingle offers a number of dining choices for the evening). Emlagh's stylish bedrooms, named after local wildflowers, with soothing colour schemes and artworks to match, are all air-conditioned and feature deluxe bathrooms, satellite television, video and CD players.

LOCATION

**N86 from Tralee to Dingle. On entering
Dingle, take first left after Shell station.**

• *Map p.478*
ref: H5

GLASSDRUMMAN LODGE

Country house

**85 Mill Road, Annalong,
Co Down BT34 4RH
Northern Ireland**

**Telephone +44 (0)28 437 68451
Fax +44 (0)28 437 67041**

E-mail: *glassdrumman@bestloved.com*

OWNER
Joan Hall

ROOM RATES
Single occupancy	£80 - £115
8 Doubles/Twins	£100 - £135
2 Suites	£135 - £145

Includes full breakfast and VAT

CHARGE/CREDIT CARDS

 • *DC* • *MC* • *VI*

RATINGS & AWARDS
N.I.T.B. ★★★

FACILITIES
On site: *Garden*
1 meeting room/max 70 people
Nearby: *Golf, fishing, riding, health club*

RESTRICTIONS
No facilities for disabled guests
No pets, kennel available

ATTRACTIONS
*Silent Valley, Navanfort,
Armagh, Mountains of Mourne,
Royal County Down golf course,
National Trust Properties*

AFFILIATIONS
Ireland's Blue Book

NEAREST
MAJOR CITY:
Belfast - 40 miles/1 hr

MAJOR AIRPORT:
Belfast - 55 miles/1 ½ hrs

RAILWAY STATION:
Newry - 25 miles/30 mins

RESERVATIONS
Toll free in US: 800-323-5463
*Quote **Best Loved***

ACCESS CODES
Not applicable

IRELAND

A seductive taste of the 'good life' in a five-star farmhouse

'Simple excellence' is the watchword at Glassdrumman Lodge, home to the Hall family for over 20 years. Graeme and Joan Hall came to Annalong to escape the stresses of modern life and bring up their family in quiet rural foothills of the Mountains of Mourne overlooking the Irish Sea. From modest beginnings growing organic vegetables, business boomed and soon they were retailing homemade breads, pies and cheeses, rearing meat and poultry and serving meals in the front parlour. Today, the Halls' farming days are over, allowing them to devote all their formidable energies to hospitality and welcoming guests to the family home with a warmth and attention to detail that is truly amazing.

The Lodge is a happy marriage of home from home informality and comfort and dedicated round-the-clock service that gets shoes cleaned and cars washed overnight. There are beamed ceilings, comfy chairs, crackling log fires and gorgeous views. Delicious food is a given and most of the ingredients are local, from garden herbs to Dundrum Bay oysters. No wonder this is such a popular spot with golfers who come to play the famous Royal County Down golf course just down the road.

LOCATION

From Dublin: to Newry, then A2 coast road to Warrenpoint, Kilkeel, Annalong. Turn left at Halfway House. From Belfast: to Newcastle, then A2 coast road to Annalong. Turn right at Halfway House.

408

*" **Wonderful hotel, warm people, beautiful setting** "*

Jean Kennedy Smith, US Ambassador to Ireland, Dublin

18th century manor   GLENLO ABBEY HOTEL

The Orient Express awaits you at Galway's most luxurious hotel

Built in 1740, Glenlo Abbey was the ancestral home of the Ffrench family, one of the fourteen tribes that ruled Galway for five centuries. Set on 138 acres on the shores of Lough Corrib, the estate has a nine-hole golf course, driving range, fishing rights and opportunities for boating.

Owners Peggy and John Bourke spent many years painstakingly restoring the property into a luxury hotel, but one with a difference. Three centuries of antiques furnish the house, recent works by local artists hang up on its walls and the skilled plasterwork and hand woven carpets are by local craftsmen. The overall effect is very stylish without being overbearing, and comfortably grand.

But what gives the hotel its novelty is the Pullman Restaurant housed in two of the original carriages from The Orient Express. Indeed one of the carriages 'starred' in Murder on the Orient Express and long before that carried many a celebrity such as Sir Winston Churchill. The restaurant's menu is themed on some of the famous train's destinations: Paris, St Petersburg, Istanbul ... A more local destination, just three miles away, is the medieval city of Galway which offers infinite pleasures - not least the pubs, boutiques, and heritage shops as well as the excellent theatre and concerts.

LOCATION

The hotel is located on the N59, just 2 ½ miles from Galway.

Bushypark, Galway, Co Galway, Republic of Ireland
Telephone +353 (0)91 526666
Fax +353 (0)91 527800
E-mail *glenlo@bestloved.com*

OWNER
John Bourke

ROOM RATES *(EUROS)*
Single occupancy   €145 - €250
43 Doubles/Twins   €185 - €310
3 Suites   €400 - €770
Includes VAT

CHARGE/CREDIT CARDS

 ● *DC* ● *MC* ● *VI*

RATINGS & AWARDS
I.T.B. ★★★★★ *Hotel*
R.A.C. Gold Ribbon ★★★★ *Dining Award 2*
A.A. ★★★★ ❀ *74%*
A.A. Romantic Hotel

FACILITIES
On site: *Garden, heli-pad, fishing, golf, Driving range, putting green, boating, clay pigeon shooting, business centre 9 meeting rooms/max 220 people*
Nearby: *Yachting, tennis, fitness centre, shooting, riding, watersports*

RESTRICTIONS
No pets, guide dogs only

ATTRACTIONS
Lough Corrib, Aran Islands, The Burren, Cliffs of Moher, Connemara, Galway City

AFFILIATIONS
Small Luxury Hotels

NEAREST
MAJOR CITY:
Galway - 2 ½ miles/10 mins

MAJOR AIRPORT:
Shannon - 56 miles/1 ½ hrs

RAILWAY STATION:
Galway - 2 miles/10 mins

RESERVATIONS
Toll free in US: 800-525-4800
UK: 00800-4536-5666
*Quote **Best Loved***

ACCESS CODES
AMADEUS LX GWYGAH
APOLLO/GALILEO LX 58443
SABRE/ABACUS LX 13705
WORLDSPAN LX GWYGA

IRELAND

Map p.478
ref: C8

" Glin is surely the beau ideal of an Irish country house, grand yet intimate "

Hugh Montgomery Massingberd, Great Houses of Ireland

GLIN CASTLE

Historic house

Glin, Co Limerick, Republic of Ireland
Telephone +353 (0)68 34173
Fax +353 (0)68 34364
E-mail: glin@bestloved.com

OWNERS
Desmond FitzGerald, Knight of Glin and Madam FitzGerald

GENERAL MANAGER
Bob Duff

ROOM RATES (EUROS)
Single occupancy   €280 - €440
3 Standard Doubles/Twins €280 - €360
11 Superior Doubles/Twins   €350
3 Deluxe rooms   €440
Includes full breakfast and VAT

CHARGE/CREDIT CARDS

 • DC • MC • VI

RATINGS & AWARDS
R.A.C. Blue Ribbon ★★★ *Dining Award 1*

FACILITIES
On site: *Garden, croquet, tennis*
1 meeting room/max 20 people
Nearby: *Golf, riding, yachting*

RESTRICTIONS
No facilities for disabled guests
No children under 10 years
No smoking in bedrooms
No pets
Closed 7 Nov - 15 Mar

ATTRACTIONS
Cliffs of Moher, The Burren, Ring of Kerry, Dingle Peninsula, Birr Castle and Demesne, Adare and Limerick, Bunratty

AFFILIATIONS
The Celebrated Hotels Collection
Ireland's Blue Book

NEAREST
MAJOR CITY:
Limerick - 32 miles/45 mins
MAJOR AIRPORT:
Shannon - 45 miles/1 hr
RAILWAY STATION:
Limerick - 32 miles/45 mins
FERRY PORT:
Cork - 70 miles/2 hrs

RESERVATIONS
Toll Free in US: 800-322-2403
or 800-323-5463
*Quote **Best Loved***

ACCESS CODES
AMADEUS SNN 599
APOLLO/GALILEO SNN 22779
SABRE/ABACUS SNN 49606
WORLDSPAN SNN 05599

IRELAND

Art and architecture in a unique, historic home

Glin Castle took pride of place in a recent exhibition of Irish Country Houses. The 29th Knight of Glin and Madam FitzGerald welcome visitors in style. The present Glin Castle succeeds the medieval ruin in the village of Glin and was built in the late 18th century with entertaining in mind. It is steeped in Ireland's history and its architectural pleasures. The entrance hall has a screen of Corinthian pillars, a superb neo-classical plaster ceiling and a unique collection of Irish mahogany furniture. Family portraits and Irish pictures line the walls. The library bookcase has a secret door. The hall has a rare flying staircase.

The drawing room is a superb setting for coffee and conversation. It has an Adam period ceiling, a beautiful Bossi chimney piece and six long windows looking out to the croquet lawn. Upstairs are sets of bedrooms, bathrooms and dressing rooms with wall-to-wall carpets, chaises longues and comfortable chintz-covered beds.

The cooking is good Irish country house, using vegetables from the walled garden, fresh local fish, poultry and meats. The castle garden grows its own flowers and fruit, bees for honey and hens

for free-range eggs. The staff take great care to welcome visitors, and make sure they enjoy their visit to a unique, historic home.

LOCATION
Off N69, 32 miles to the west of Limerick.

Best Loved Hotels of the World

" *A perfect find!* "

Lisa Duff, Automobile Association, Ireland

411

● *Map p.478*
ref: H9

Coastal hotel GORMANS CLIFFTOP HOUSE & RESTAURANT

**Glaise Bheag, Ballydavid,
Dingle Peninsula, Co Kerry,
Republic of Ireland**

Telephone +353 (0)66 91 55162
Fax +353 (0)66 91 55003
E-mail: *gormans@bestloved.com*

OWNERS
Sile and Vincent Gorman

ROOM RATES *(EUROS)*
Single occupancy	*€75 - €100*
5 Doubles/Twins	*€100 - €125*
2 Family rooms	*€115 - €135*
2 Mini suites	*€125 - €150*
Includes full breakfast and VAT	

CHARGE/CREDIT CARDS
MC • VI

RATINGS & AWARDS
I.T.B. ★★★★ *Guest House*
A.A. ◆◆◆◆◆ *Premier Collection*
Les Routiers 'Hidden Gem Ireland 2000'
Les Routiers 'Hotel of the Year 2001'
*Georgina Campbell 'Guest House
of the Year 2002'*

FACILITIES
On site: *Garden, cycle hire*
Nearby: *Golf, fishing, riding, walking*

RESTRICTIONS
*Limited facilities for disabled guests
Smoking in Lounge only
No pets, guide dogs only
Closed Nov - Mar*

ATTRACTIONS
*Inch Strand, Gallerus Oratory,
Slea Head, Blasket Islands,
Killarney National Park,
Ring of Kerry, Hill walking*

AFFILIATIONS
Independent

NEAREST
MAJOR CITY:
Cork - 105 miles/2 ½ hrs

MAJOR AIRPORT:
Shannon - 150 miles/3 hrs
Kerry Airport - 36 miles/1 hr

RAILWAY STATION:
Tralee - 40 miles/1 hr

FERRY PORT:
Cork - 105 miles/2 ½ hrs

RESERVATIONS
Direct with hotel
Quote **Best Loved**

ACCESS CODES
Not applicable

A welcoming clifftop refuge at the tip of the glorious Dingle Peninsula

Gorman's Clifftop is surely one of the most westerly establishments in Europe. The house looks out over Smerwick Harbour to the Three Sisters and the vastness of the Atlantic beyond. Vincent Gorman's family settled this land in the 1700s, and his wife, Sile (pronounced Sheila), proudly proclaims that she came here on holiday over 20 years ago and if anything loves it more than ever.

Dingle is all about long sandy beaches and tall cliffs peppered with little coves and harbours. There are mountains in the background, and hedgerows burgeoning with wild fuschias. Irish is the first language of the local people, and traditional culture is very much part of everyday life from the fishermen hauling in lobster pots to spontaneous outbreaks of music and dance. Around and about there are walks, golf, and archaeological sites to visit.

Every room at Gorman's Clifftop pays homage to the landscape offering breathtaking views of mountains or the ocean. The spacious bedrooms are furnished in pine offset by hand-thrown pottery lamps and tapestry wall hangings. Downstairs guests can gather around the fire to read or chat, dine handsomely, and sit out in the garden to watch the sun set behind Ballydavid Head on a summer's evening.

LOCATION
*Go through Dingle with the harbour on your left
to roundabout west of town. Go straight across,
taking the road signposted for 'An Fheothanach'.
Road forks approx 5 miles out, keep left.
Hotel is approx 8 miles from roundabout.*

IRELAND

• *Map p.478*
ref: C7

> *" Like The Burren itself, Gregans Castle is one of the quiet treasures of Ireland. First among its charms are the owners, whose superb management is matched only by the warmth of their welcome "*
>
> *Gibbons & Kay Ruark, Pennsylvania*

GREGANS CASTLE

18th century country house

Ballyvaughan, Co Clare, Republic of Ireland

Telephone +353 (0)65 707 7005
Fax +353 (0)65 707 7111

E-mail: *gregans@bestloved.com*

OWNERS
The Haden Family

ROOM RATES *(EUROS)*
Single occupancy   €125 - €260
14 Doubles/Twins   €150 - €280
4 Suites   €270 - €440
Includes full breakfast and VAT

CHARGE/CREDIT CARDS

 • *MC* • *VI*

RATINGS & AWARDS
I.T.B. ★★★★ *Hotel*
R.A.C. Blue Ribbon ★★★ *Dining Award 2*
A.A. ★★★ ❀❀
A.A. Top 200 - 02/03

FACILITIES
On site: *Garden, croquet*
1 meeting room/max 65 people
Nearby: *Golf, riding, fishing*

RESTRICTIONS
Limited facilities for disabled guests
No pets
Closed 1 Dec - 13 Feb

ATTRACTIONS
The Burren, Cliffs of Moher,
Galway Bay, Aran Islands,
Lahinch Golf Club,
Guided walking tours

AFFILIATIONS
Ireland's Blue Book
Preston's Global Hotels

NEAREST
MAJOR CITY:
Galway - 33 miles/45 mins

MAJOR AIRPORT:
Shannon - 36 miles/1 hr

RAILWAY STATION:
Gort - 22 miles/25 mins

RESERVATIONS
Toll free in US: 800-544-9993
or 800-323-5463
Quote Best Loved

ACCESS CODES
Not applicable

IRELAND

Sheer excellence after nearly 30 years of private family ownership

Gregans Castle Hotel is a welcome surprise in a remote part of the West of Ireland. Nestling at the foot of Corkscrew Hill with majestic views of bare limestone mountains and Galway Bay, this country house offers warmth, welcome and every possible comfort.

Only one hour's scenic drive from Shannon airport, this area is called The Burren and is known worldwide for its wild flowers and distinctive scenery. A rich legacy of ancient monuments tells the story of inhabitants as far back as 5,000 years. The seascapes are dramatic: Atlantic Ocean, Galway Bay, the famous Cliffs of Moher, two golden beaches and several small local fishing harbours of character.

Gregans Castle Hotel was built as a private house more than 150 years ago for the Martyn family to replace their home in the old castle nearby. Recently converted into an hotel, it is now one of the most comfortable hostelries on the west coast of Ireland.

Dinner is an essential part of the day and a special emphasis is placed on local produce. The expert cooking has earned the hotel many ratings & awards in all the better travel guide books.

Gregans Castle Hotel is owner-managed by the Haden family, and is an elected member of the prestigious Ireland's Blue Book.

LOCATION
On the west coast of Ireland, 3 ½ miles south of the village of Ballyvaughan in Co Clare.

> **❝ What an experience again, the rugged coastline, the resort of Kilkee and then the warmth of Halpin ❞**
>
> *Professor Trevor Elliott, University of Liverpool*

Town house hotel

HALPIN'S HOTEL

Welcoming, friendly, the place to find the true taste of Ireland

Western Ireland has many attractions but two in particular are fundamental to the others: the rugged beauty of its coast and the warm, unpolluted waters of the gulf stream that wash over it. The picturesque Victorian resort of Kilkee, recently awarded a Blue Flag from the EU for its beach, stands in a horseshoe bay midway between the Cliffs of Moher and the Ring of Kerry. There is plenty of scenic variety and all sorts of attractions - one of them being the well-known, privately owned and managed Halpin's Town House Hotel.

This small townhouse has been owned and run by the Halpin family for 15 years, and has earned a reputation for its excellent standards and welcoming atmosphere. Modestly priced and as unpretentious as the town it stands in, its looks belie its true character. The bedrooms are comfortable and offer every modern facility. The hotel bar, with its open hearth fire and flag-stoned floor, is the perfect place to relax at the end of the day and chat with the locals.

Local attractions include scenic drives, heritage sites, cliffs, beaches and caves and all kinds of sports including golf at nearby Doonbeg Golf

Course. Halpin's is surely a place to discover the true taste of Ireland.

LOCATION

50 minutes from Shannon Airport on the N67. The hotel is in the centre of Kilkee.

**Erin Street, Kilkee, Co Clare
Republic of Ireland**
**Telephone +353 (0)65 9056032
Fax +353 (0)65 9056317**
E-mail: *balpins@bestloved.com*

OWNER
Pat Halpin

MANAGER
Ann Keane

ROOM RATES *(EUROS)*
2 Singles	€69 - €99
8 Doubles/Twins	€89 - €129
2 Executive rooms	€99 - €159

Includes full breakfast, newspaper and VAT

CHARGE/CREDIT CARDS
 • DC • JCB • MC • VI

RATINGS & AWARDS
I.T.B. ★★★
R.A.C. ◆◆◆◆ *Dining Award 1*
R.A.C. Sparkling Diamond

FACILITIES
On site: *Garden*
1 meeting room/max 40 people
Nearby: *Golf, riding, leisure centre,
tennis, fishing, water skiing*

RESTRICTIONS
*Limited facilities for disabled guests
No pets
Closed 15 Nov - 15 Mar*

ATTRACTIONS
*Cliffs of Moher, The Burren,
Bunratty Castle, Aran Islands,
Lakes of Killarney, Doonbeg Golf Course
Lahinch and Ballybunion golf courses*

AFFILIATIONS
*Preston's Global Hotels
The Green Book of Ireland
Elegant Small Hotels*

NEAREST
*MAJOR CITY:
Limerick - 50 miles/1 hr*

*MAJOR AIRPORT:
Shannon - 40 miles/50 mins*

*RAILWAY STATION:
Kilkee - ¼ mile/5 mins*

RESERVATIONS
*Toll free in US: 800-544-9993
or 1800-6173178
Toll free in UK: 0800 0964 748
Quote **Best Loved***

ACCESS CODES
*AMADEUS UI SNNHAL
APOLLO/GALILEO UI 1437
SABRE/ABACUS UI 35170
WORLDSPAN UI 19690*

IRELAND

" *A superb union of country house charm and elegance, only minutes from the city centre* "

Ann Cahill, writer, Ireland

HAYFIELD MANOR

Country house in the city

**Perrott Avenue, College Road,
Cork, Co Cork,
Republic of Ireland**

Telephone **+353 (0)21 4845900**
Fax **+353 (0)21 4816839**

E-mail: *bayfield@bestloved.com*

OWNERS
Margaret and Joseph Scally

GENERAL MANAGER
Margaret Naughton

ROOM RATES *(EUROS)*
Single occupancy €215 - €280
73 Doubles/Twins €300 - €365
15 Suites €420 - €900
Includes full breakfast, service and VAT

CHARGE/CREDIT CARDS

 ● *DC* ● *MC* ● *VI*

RATINGS & AWARDS
I.T.B. ★★★★★ *Hotel*
R.A.C. Gold Ribbon ★★★★ *Dining Award 3*
A.A. ★★★★ ❀❀
A.A. Top 200 - 02/03

FACILITIES
On site: *Garden, gym, indoor pool,
health & beauty, steam room, jacuzzi
4 meeting rooms/max 80 people*
Nearby: *Riding, golf, tennis, fishing,
water skiing*

RESTRICTIONS
No pets

ATTRACTIONS
*Midleton Distillery, Cobh Heritage Centre,
Waterford Crystal, Blarney Castle,
Ring of Kerry/Killarney, Kinsale*

AFFILIATIONS
*The Celebrated Hotels Collection
Small Luxury Hotels*

NEAREST
MAJOR CITY:
Cork - 1 mile/5 mins

MAJOR AIRPORT:
Cork - 6 miles/20 mins

RAILWAY STATION:
Cork (Kent Station) - 2 miles/15 mins

RESERVATIONS
*Toll free in US:800-322-2403
or 800-525-4800*
Quote **Best Loved**

ACCESS CODES
*AMADEUS LX ORKHMR
APOLLO/GALILEO LX 78411
SABRE/ABACUS LX 31327
WORLDSPAN LX ORKHM*

IRELAND

The best of town and country, of traditional and modern

Hayfield Manor offers the best of both worlds in several respects. It is an elegant 19th century mansion, yet it is Cork's only five-star hotel with every modern comfort. It is a country house standing among the old parkland trees of its own quiet, two-acre mature gardens with its private well-concealed car park, yet it is within a mile of the city centre.

The spacious guest rooms are matched by luxurious marble bathrooms. The grandeur and style of the Manor Room restaurant combine with a superb cuisine to create a magnificent gourmet experience.

From your room, you have direct access to an executive health club where even the pool has views across the formal garden. Whether you wish to work out in the fitness suite, enjoy the steam room or simply relax in the outdoor jacuzzi, Hayfield is the complete health facility.

Cork has much to commend it as a touring centre. Hayfield Manor is well placed for the Cobh Heritage Centre and Midleton Distillery and within easy reach of Killarney, the Ring of Kerry, Kinsale, Blarney Castle and Waterford, famous for its crystal.

LOCATION
Travelling west from City Centre, take N70 for Killarney. Turn left at University Gates off Western Rd, at top of road turn right and immediate left - hotel is at top of avenue.

> **The rooms were spacious and spotless, the staff exceptionally friendly; the service outstanding and the food first class**
>
> *John Walker, Walker Travel Group, Virginia*

● *Map p.478*
ref: G7

Contemporary hotel   HERBERT PARK HOTEL

**Ballsbridge, Dublin 4,
Republic of Ireland**

**Telephone +353 (0)1 667 2200
Fax +353 (0)1 667 2595**

E-mail: *herbertpark@bestloved.com*

GENERAL MANAGER
Ewan Plenderleith

ROOM RATES (EUROS)
9 Singles	€230
103 Doubles/Twins	€275
11 Superior doubles	€300
27 Executive Doubles/Twins	€340
3 Suites	€430

Includes service and VAT

CHARGE/CREDIT CARDS

 • *DC* • *MC* • *VI*

RATINGS & AWARDS
I.T.B. ★★★★
R.A.C. *Blue Ribbon* ★★★★ *Dining Award 1*
A.A. ★★★★ ❁❁ 77%
A.A. Courtesy & Care Award 2002/03

FACILITIES
On site: *Gym, car park*
5 meeting rooms/max 150 people
Nearby: *Golf, tennis, fitness, fishing, yachting, water skiing*

RESTRICTIONS
No pets, guide dogs only

ATTRACTIONS
Tours of Dublin City, National Art Gallery, National Library, Guinness Hopstore, Horseracing, Wicklow Mountains

AFFILIATIONS
Utell International

NEAREST
MAJOR CITY:
Dublin

MAJOR AIRPORT:
Dublin - 8 miles/30 mins

RAILWAY STATION:
Lansdowne Road - ½ mile/5 mins

FERRY PORT:
Dun Laoghaire - 3 miles/20 mins

RESERVATIONS
Toll free in US: 800-44-UTELL
Quote Best Loved

ACCESS CODES
AMADEUS UI DUBHER
APOLLO/GALILEO UI 76888
SABRE/ABACUS UI 23542
WORLDSPAN UI 25224

Contemporary Irish design finds a spectacular showcase in vibrant Dublin

Cocooned in the leafy parklands of the Embassy District, the Herbert Park is a very special modern Irish hotel. Its warm honey-coloured stone and glass façade has been purposely designed as a continuation of the park and bathes the striking two-storey public areas in natural light. Vistas range over trees and city to the countryside and mountains beyond, and the view west from the Mezzanine is spectacular at sunset.

A sense of calm and space is intrinsic to the airy inside-out design of the hotel. The style is clean and contemporary, but softened by clever use of colour and collections of Irish abstract art and portraiture. Facilities are excellent from the king size double beds and outstanding dining options to the fully-equipped meeting rooms. And let's not forget the all-important human touch evident in the superb service.

As well as offering a grand base for exploring Dublin, Herbert Park is a favourite with golfers, ideally placed for all the major links and parkland courses to the south and west of the city. Druids Glen, home to the Irish Open, is also easily accessible, and the hotel is delighted to arrange tee times for guests.

LOCATION

From the City Centre follow signs to Ballsbridge. Take the first right after the Ball's Bridge down Anglesey Road and next right again into the hotel.

IRELAND

" *One of the five most stylish hotels in the Irish Capital* "

Conde Nast Traveller Magazine

HIBERNIAN HOTEL

Victorian town house

Eastmoreland Place,
Ballsbridge, Dublin 4,
Republic of Ireland

Telephone +353 (0)1 668 7666
Fax +353 (0)1 660 2655

E-mail: *hibernian@bestloved.com*

DIRECTOR
David Butt

RESIDENT MANAGER
Briege Dobbin

ROOM RATES *(EUROS)*
Single occupancy	€220
30 Doubles/Twins	€220
10 Junior suites	€275
Includes breakfast service and VAT	

CHARGE/CREDIT CARDS

 ● *DC* ● *MC* ● *VI*

RATINGS & AWARDS
R.A.C. ★★★ *Dining Award 3*
A.A. ★★★ ❀❀ 74%

FACILITIES
On site: *Restaurant, car park*
1 meeting room/max 45 people
Nearby: *Golf, health centre, riding*

RESTRICTIONS
No pets, guide dogs only
Closed 24 - 27 Dec

ATTRACTIONS
National Art Gallery, Grafton Street,
Trinity College, Temple Bar

AFFILIATIONS
The Celebrated Hotels Collection
Manor House Hotels of Ireland
Small Luxury Hotels

NEAREST
MAJOR CITY:
Dublin

MAJOR AIRPORT:
Dublin - 8 miles/30 mins

RAILWAY STATION:
Connolly - 2 miles/10 mins

RESERVATIONS
Toll free in US/Canada: 800-322-2403
or 800-525-4800
Toll free in UK: 00800 525 48000
Quote **Best Loved**

ACCESS CODES
AMADEUS LX DUBTHH
APOLLO/GALILEO LX 58480
SABRE/ABACUS LX 35282
WORLDSPAN LX DUBHH

IRELAND

A taste of gracious city living,
an experience to be savoured

A previous recipient of the Hotel of the Year award from Small Luxury Hotels, the Hibernian Hotel is a tranquil haven of true hospitality in bustling downtown Dublin. This splendid Victorian building, built at the end of the 19th century, offers a very warm welcome with friendly smiles and an impeccable service.

Each of the hotel's 40 elegant and luxurious bedrooms is individually decorated in true historic style. Professionalism and care prevail throughout, creating, for the guest, a 'home-away-from-home' feeling. The drawing room, library and sun lounge are graced by antiques, original oil paintings, fresh flowers and rich furniture, recreating an inviting atmosphere of relaxation and times past. For business meetings and private gatherings the wood-panelled boardroom is the ideal setting.

The hotel really is a wonderful place to relax and discover the charms of Dublin. There are museums to visit, shopping on Grafton Street, the Theatre or a fun night of Irish music and dance in one of the many quaint local pubs.

The Hibernian is classical and enchanting and offers the ultimate in relaxation, intimacy and professional care. The Hibernian, sister hotel to The McCausland, Belfast, (page 428) and the Woodstock, Ennis, Co. Clare, (page 447), is a taste of gracious city living, an experience to be savoured.

LOCATION

Turn right from Mespil Road into Baggot Street
Upper; then left into Eastmoreland Place.
The Hibernian is at the end on the left.

" *I have been to many places in the south of Ireland but I find this lovely spot the most peaceful and charming of them all* "

W D Doherty FRCS, London

• Map p.478
ref: G7

18th century coaching inn

HUNTER'S HOTEL

Good food and old-world charm - a family tradition of five generations

Hunter's Hotel, one of Ireland's oldest coaching inns, has been established for over 270 years, since the days of post horses and carriages. Run by the same family for five generations, the hotel has built up a strong tradition based on good food, comfortable surroundings and unique, old world charm.

Set in one of Ireland's most beautiful counties, the hotel stands in gardens bordering the River Vartry. All the rooms retain the character of bygone days, with antique furniture, open fires, fresh flowers and polished brass. Most of the 16 attractive bedrooms overlook the gardens.

Sea angling, riding, hunting, tennis, swimming and hiking are all in the immediate locality. There are 18 golf courses within 30 minutes' drive including Druids Glen and The European Club. The beautiful Wicklow countryside, known as 'Garden of Ireland', lies at your doorstep. Lovely sandy beaches, breathtaking mountain scenery, quiet glens and well known beauty spots such as Mount Usher Gardens, Powerscourt, Russborough House, Avondale House, Glendalough, the Devil's Glen and Roundwood are all within easy reach.

Whether you want a country base from which to visit Dublin, a peaceful rural holiday or a pleasant overnight stop after the ferry, Hunter's Hotel is the ideal location.

LOCATION

Take N11 to Rathnew village. Turn left just before the village on Dublin side.

Newrath Bridge, Rathnew, Co Wicklow, Republic of Ireland

Telephone +353 (0)404 40106
Fax +353 (0)404 40338

E-mail: *hunters@bestloved.com*

OWNERS
The Gelletlie Family

ROOM RATES *(EUROS)*
2 Singles   €95 - €115
14 Doubles/Twins   €178 - €216
Includes full breakfast and VAT

CHARGE/CREDIT CARDS

 • *MC* • *VI*

RATINGS & AWARDS
I.T.B. ★★★ *Hotel*
A.A. ★★★ ❀ *67%*

FACILITIES
On site: *Garden*
1 meeting room/max 40 people
Nearby: *Golf, riding, fishing, walking*

RESTRICTIONS
No pets
Closed Christmas

ATTRACTIONS
Mount Usher Gardens,
Powerscourt Gardens and Waterfall,
Russborough House,
Glendalough

AFFILIATIONS
Ireland's Blue Book

NEAREST
MAJOR CITY:
Dublin - 28 miles/45 mins

MAJOR AIRPORT:
Dublin - 40 miles/1 ¼ hrs

RAILWAY STATION:
Wicklow - 3 miles/5 mins

RESERVATIONS
Toll free in US: 800-323-5463
Quote **Best Loved**

ACCESS CODES
Not applicable

IRELAND

www.hunters.bestloved.com

THE KILKENNY HIBERNIAN HOTEL

City centre hotel

**1 Ormonde Street,
Kilkenny, Co Kilkenny,
Republic of Ireland**

**Telephone +353 (0)56 7771888
Fax +353 (0)56 7771877**

E-mail: *ckhibernian@bestloved.com*

OWNERS
Gerry Byrne and David Lawlor

ROOM RATES *(EUROS)*
40 Doubles/Twins   €150 - €200
3 Junior suites   €220 - €250
3 Penthouse suites   €250 - €300
Includes full breakfast, service and VAT

CHARGE/CREDIT CARDS

 • DC • MC • VI

RATINGS & AWARDS
R.A.C. ★★★

FACILITIES
On site: *1 meeting room/max 25 people*
Nearby: *Golf, riding, tennis,
fishing, leisure centre*

RESTRICTIONS
*No pets
Closed 24 & 25 Dec*

ATTRACTIONS
*Kilkenny Castle, Waterford Crystal,
Rock of Cashel, Smithicks Brewery,
Craft Trail, Walking Tours,
Saint Canices Cathedral*

AFFILIATIONS
Preston's Global Hotels

NEAREST
*MAJOR CITY:
Waterford - 30 miles/40 mins
Dublin - 80 miles/1 ¾ hrs*

*MAJOR AIRPORT:
Dublin - 85 miles/2 hrs*

*RAILWAY STATION:
Kilkenny - 1 mile/5 mins*

RESERVATIONS
Toll free in US: 800-544-9993
Quote **Best Loved**

ACCESS CODES
Not applicable

IRELAND

Bank on a comfortable stay in the 'Marble City'

Large tracts of County Kilkenny in the southeast of Ireland are formed of a limestone rock which turns black when polished. Much of the historic city of Kilkenny is built with this characteristic local stone hence the 'Marble City'. Marble is no stranger to the handsome purlieus of the Kilkenny Hibernian Hotel. This gracious old Victorian bank, in the shadow of Kilkenny Castle, has been sympathetically transformed and substantially extended into a welcoming boutique hotel with a grand lobby area and many original features, such as the marble fireplaces in the bedrooms, which survive from an even earlier incarnation as a private residence.

The Hibernian's 46 comfortable bedrooms, including Junior suites and Penthouses, feature generous king-size beds, sleek bathrooms and Irish fabrics in soft, warm tones with floral touches. Guests can relax over a drink, morning savouries or afternoon tea and the daily newspapers in the traditional Hibernian Bar, or sample the more lively ambience of Morrissons Bar. Jacobs Cottage restaurant, one of the region's leading restaurants, offers an eclectic menu of Irish and International cuisine including the ubiquitous but utterly delicious sticky toffee pudding. If you need to work off a surfeit of pudding, guests enjoy complimentary membership of a health and leisure centre with pool, gym, sauna and steam room close to the hotel.

LOCATION

*Situated on main cross-roads in
Kilkenny town centre, secure parking
available at multi-storey opposite.*

" The hotel is beautiful and impeccably maintained, but it is the consistent willingness and helpfulness of every member of staff which makes my guests stay in Ireland such a memorable experience "

Jerry Quinlan, Jerry Quinlan's Celtic Golf

Luxury hotel

KILLARNEY PARK

Old-world courtesy and charm honed to perfection by three generations of expertise

Marrying together the many and varied vital ingredients that make a successful hotel is a complex art form. To start from scratch with a new building and create a gracious Victorian-style country house hotel takes a minor miracle. Fortunately Janet and Padraig Treacy can call on three generations of expertise in the hotel industry, and they have indeed performed miracles at the Killarney Park.

The Treacys' attention to detail is phenomenal from traditional fabrics and furnishings to the oh-so-Victorian potted plants. Soft, relaxing colour schemes lend a restful air to the bedrooms, and there are splendid antique beds and open fires in the generously proportioned suites. The quiet, half-panelled Library actually contains books you want to read, and the clubby Billiards Room almost demands a fat cigar and snifter of brandy for accompaniment. The ladies' preserve is the elegant Drawing Room, though gentlemen are certainly welcome. Meanwhile, everybody appreciates the warm welcome in the Garden Bar with its choice of newspapers, sheltered outdoor terrace, and a barman who can concoct the most delicious Irish coffee imaginable.

However, Killarney Park is far from locked in

the amber of the Victorian era. Queen Victoria herself might have been impressed by the lavishly-equipped Health Spa. She would also have heartily endorsed the horse-riding, golf, fishing, and other country sports available, perhaps interspersed with a spot of sightseeing.

LOCATION

Situated in the centre of Killarney town. Kenmare Place is a continuation of Main Street and the hotel is on the right hand side.

Kenmare Place, Killarney, Co Kerry, Republic of Ireland
Telephone +353 (0)64 35555
Fax +353 (0)64 35266
E-mail: *killarneypark@bestloved.com*

OWNERS
Padraig and Janet Treacy

GENERAL MANAGER
Donagh Davern

ROOM RATES *(EUROS)*
50 Deluxe Doubles/Twins €240 - €360
18 Junior suites €340 - €515
3 Superior suites €560 - €700
Includes full breakfast and VAT

CHARGE/CREDIT CARDS

 ● MC ● VI

RATINGS & AWARDS
I.T.B. ★★★★★ *Hotel*
R.A.C. *Blue Ribbon* ★★★★ *Dining Award 3*
A.A. ★★★★ ❀❀ *Top 200 - 02/03*
CIE Tours National Award of Excellence 1999

FACILITIES
On site: *indoor pool, health & beauty 3 meeting rooms/max 150 people*
Nearby: *Fishing, golf, cycling, shooting, riding*

RESTRICTIONS
No pets
Closed 17 Nov - 1 Feb

ATTRACTIONS
Killarney National Park, Muckross House, Ring of Kerry, Gap of Dunloe, Ross Castle, Torc Waterfalls, Hill and mountain walking

AFFILIATIONS
The Celebrated Hotels Collection

NEAREST
MAJOR CITY:
Cork - 54 miles/1 ½ hrs

MAJOR AIRPORT:
Cork - 54 miles/1 ½ hrs
Kerry - 15 miles/20 mins

RAILWAY STATION:
Killarney - ¼ mile/1 min

RESERVATIONS
Toll free in US: 800-322-2403
Lexington 800-537-8483
Quote Best Loved

ACCESS CODES
AMADEUS LM KIR744
APOLLO/GALILEO LM 25271
SABRE/ABACUS LM 50359
WORLDSPAN LM 05744

IRELAND

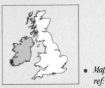

Map p.478
ref: B9

" The wonderful service, the great accommodation, your fantastic dining room and staff make the Royal a truly first class establishment "

Mrs Desmond, London

KILLARNEY ROYAL HOTEL

Victorian town house

**College Street,
Killarney, Co Kerry,
Republic of Ireland**

**Telephone +353 (0)64 31853
Fax +353 (0)64 34001**

E-mail: *killarney@bestloved.com*

OWNERS
Joe and Margaret Scally

ROOM RATES *(EUROS)*
Single occupancy	€140 - €200
24 Doubles/Twins	€225 - €320
5 Junior suites	€320 - €380

Includes full breakfast and VAT

CHARGE/CREDIT CARDS

 • DC • MC • VI

RATINGS & AWARDS
R.A.C. ★★★★ *Dining Award 2*

FACILITIES
On site: *1 meeting room/max 50 people*
Nearby: *Golf, tennis, leisure centre,
fishing, riding, leisure centre*

RESTRICTIONS
No pets
Closed 23 - 26 Dec

ATTRACTIONS
*Ring of Kerry, Dingle Peninsula,
Gap of Dunloe, Lakes of Killarney,
Muckross House & Gardens,
Torc Waterfall*

AFFILIATIONS
Independent

NEAREST
MAJOR CITY:
Cork - 55 miles/1 ¼ hrs

MAJOR AIRPORT:
Kerry Airport - 9 miles/15 mins

RAILWAY STATION:
Killarney

RESERVATIONS
Toll free in UK: 00800 4748 4748
*Quote **Best Loved***

ACCESS CODES
AMADEUS LM KIR170
APOLLO/GALILEO LM 38135
SABRE/ABACUS LM 60601
WORLDSPAN LM 08170

IRELAND

Right royal hospitality and good food in Ireland's romantic south west

Killarney is a popular touring base for the southwest of Ireland: visitors come to explore the legendary Ring of Kerry, the scenic Dingle Peninsula or the 21-mile long Bantry Bay; to walk in the 25,000 acres of Killarney National Park, to play golf on the town's two championship courses or to taste the excellent local brown trout; to visit Victorian Muckross House and Gardens and Kate Kearney's Cottage. Yet many visitors have said the highlight of their trip was their stay at the Killarney Royal, in the centre of town.

The Scally family pride themselves on the excellent, personal service they offer their guests. All bedrooms are well designed, airy and decorated with antiques (all personal treasures) all are air-conditioned. Comfort is the key to their brand of hospitality and is as evident here as it is in the sister hotel, Hayfield Manor (pg 414) in Cork.

The dining room attracts a big local following - its traditional, fine-dining menu offers good Irish beef, lamb and salmon. The bar has a homely, local feel to it, and in the lounge you can take tea and scones by an open fire. A touch of pure luxury in Ireland's wild west

LOCATION

Killarney Royal is situated in the centre of Killarney on College Street off the N22.

> **❝ I have to thank you all here for looking after me so well. I had a terrific time and hope to return here soon for more of the same. Thanks for everything ❞**
>
> *Derbhla Kirwan, actress*

● *Map p.478*
ref: F7

Victorian manor house — KILLASHEE HOUSE HOTEL

Twenty-first century sophistication in the timeless grace of a fine country manor

Set in 80 acres of landscaped gardens and woodland 20 minutes from Dublin, Killashee House is reached by an elegant curving driveway. Guests are treated to tantalizing views of its Jacobean-style façade and eye-catching bell tower as they arrive, though the house actually dates from Victorian times when it was built for the influential Moore family in the early 1860s.

From estate house to convent and school run by an order of French nuns, Killashee's latest transformation into a luxury hotel and country club was completed in March 2001. Its finest Victorian features have been painstakingly restored and the décor carefully chosen to complement the period surroundings. A perfect example is Turner's Restaurant where, amidst exquisite plasterwork and imposing faux marble columns, traditional Irish and Mediterranean cuisine is served with views of the lovely Fountain Garden. Meanwhile, sumptuous guest rooms successfully combine traditional furnishings and the latest technology including voice mail and highspeed data ports. The conference and banqueting facilities are equally impressive.

Sporting guests will enjoy the superbly equipped Country Club offering a 25m pool and fully equipped gymnasium. Close by, Kildare boasts famous racecourses, topflight golf, glorious gardens and stately homes.

LOCATION

From Dublin take N7 to Naas.
Through Naas town and onto the old
Kilcullen Road. Hotel is 1 mile on the left.

Killashee, Naas,
Co Kildare,
Republic of Ireland

Telephone +353 (0)45 879277
Fax +353 (0)45 879266

E-mail: *killashee@bestloved.com*

OWNERS
Jack and Jenny Tierney

GENERAL MANAGER
Odhran Lawlor

ROOM RATES (EUROS)
Single occupancy   €144 - €174
66 Doubles/Twins   €198 - €220
2 Four-posters   €230 - €258
16 Suites   €215 - €419
Includes full breakfast and VAT

CHARGE/CREDIT CARDS

 ● MC ● VI

RATINGS & AWARDS
R.A.C. ★★★★ Dining Award 2
A.A. ★★★★ ❀❀

FACILITIES
On site: *Garden, indoor pool, archery, cycling, sauna, jacuzzi, gym, clay pigeon shooting*
20 meeting rooms/max 1600 people
Nearby: *Golf, riding*

RESTRICTIONS
Closed 25 - 27 Dec

ATTRACTIONS
St Fiachra's Gardens, Japanese Gardens, National Stud Farm, Mondello Race Track, Punchestown and Naas Racecourses, Glendalough, Russborough House, Dublin, Curragh

AFFILIATIONS
Independent

NEAREST
MAJOR CITY:
Dublin - 22 miles/35 mins

MAJOR AIRPORT:
Dublin - 26 miles/35 mins

RAILWAY STATION:
Sallins - 5 miles/15 mins

RESERVATIONS
Direct with hotel
*Quote **Best Loved***

ACCESS CODES
Not applicable

IRELAND

• Map p.478
ref: G7

" As usual, the food was outstanding, but we also appreciated the warm welcome that you gave to everyone in our group. We all felt as if it was home from home "

Tamsin Varley, Hampshire

KING SITRIC

Restaurant with rooms

**East Pier,
Howth, Co Dublin,
Republic of Ireland**

**Telephone +353 (0)1 832 5235
Fax +353 (0)1 839 2442**

E-mail: *sitric@bestloved.com*

OWNERS/CHEF
Joan and Aidan MacManus

ROOM RATES *(EUROS)*
Single occupancy   €89 - €121
8 Doubles/Twins   €126 - €190
Includes breakfast and VAT

CHARGE/CREDIT CARDS

 • *MC* • *VI*

RATINGS & AWARDS
I.T.B. ★★★★ *Guest House
Karen Brown Recommended
Gilbeys Gold Medal for Catering Excellence*

FACILITIES
On site: *Private dining room*
Nearby: *Golf, boating, beaches, watersports*

RESTRICTIONS
*No facilities for disabled guests
No smoking in bedrooms
No pets
Closed 20 Jan - 3 Feb*

ATTRACTIONS
*Port of Howth and Yacht Marina,
National Transport Museum,
Howth Head, Malahide Castle, Dublin City,
Newbridge House Donabate*

AFFILIATIONS
Ireland's Blue Book

NEAREST
*MAJOR CITY:
Dublin - 9 miles/25 mins*

*MAJOR AIRPORT:
Dublin - 6 miles/20 mins*

*RAILWAY STATION:
Howth - ⅓ mile/2 mins*

RESERVATIONS
Toll free in US: 800-323-5463
Quote **Best Loved**

ACCESS CODES
Not applicable

www.sitric.bestloved.com

Rooms with a view add extra appeal to Co Dublin's best-known fish restaurant

A deft flick of the wrist could launch a fish from Dublin Bay into a waiting pan in Aidan MacManus' kitchen. As it is, the ocean's finest tends to travel the 400 yards from Howth Pier in a rather more sedate fashion since only the pick of the morning's catch passes muster in this renowned fish restaurant. Aidan and Joan MacManus first opened their restaurant business over 30 years ago and have nurtured a network of trusty suppliers who can rustle up everything from locally caught lobster and crab to organically grown vegetables. To complement the menu there is a well-stocked cellar where guests can enjoy a pre-dinner drink while choosing from the award-winning wine list.

In 2000, the MacManus' completed a major refurbishment of the old Harbour Master's house. The new look is light and bright with a subtle nautical theme, a first floor restaurant offering splendid bay views, and eight comfortable sea-facing guest rooms.

Howth is just 25 minutes from central Dublin by Dart rail link and a great base for golfers and sailors. Horse riding can be arranged, and walkers can hike the unspoiled cliff path and trails around Howth Head.

LOCATION

At end of M50 (North) take link road towards Malahide. Look for signs to Howth. All the way across the harbour front, end of the road on the right.

&#6 *Our first visit to Westport has been brilliant, largely due to our choice of accommodation which has been splendid in every respect* &#8

Annette, Martin & Claire Murphy, Belfast

• *Map p.478*
ref: C5

Victorian style house   KNOCKRANNY HOUSE HOTEL

Irish hospitality and an island for every day of the year in Clew Bay

Locals claim there is an island for every day of the year anchored in the broad and peaceful embrace of Clew Bay. On the shore, the seaside town of Westport, often described as the cultural capital of Mayo, is a marvellous touring base for Co. Mayo and neighbouring Co. Galway. One of the great charms of Knockranny House is its enviable position with views over the Bay and of Croagh Patrick, Ireland's famous pilgrimage mountain.

Knockranny is a classic Victorian-built hotel successfully combining period style with modern comforts and very friendly and efficient staff headed by welcoming hosts Adrian and Geraldine. From the moment you walk in, a sense of spaciousness and brightness extends throughout. The dining room enjoys yet more wonderful views and dinner is accompanied by a classical pianist. Head Chef Philip Brazil concentrates on presenting the very best of Irish cuisine with an international flavour. His menu has a multitude of dishes, many using local fish, and fresh herbs from their own garden.

With three meeting rooms, Knockranny offers excellent conference facilities for up to 500

delegates. And for both leisure and business travellers, a new spa is opening in Autumn 2003, set to be one of the best in Ireland, so watch this space!

LOCATION
Take N5/N60 from Castlebar. Hotel is on left before entering Westport.

Westport, Co Mayo,
Republic of Ireland

Telephone +353 (0)98 28600
Fax +353 (0)98 28611

E-mail: *knockranny@bestloved.com*

OWNERS
Adrian and Geraldine Noonan

ROOM RATES *(EUROS)*
Single occupancy	€175
42 Doubles/Twins	€230
9 Deluxe Doubles/Twins	€268
3 Four-posters	€294
Includes full breakfast and VAT	

CHARGE/CREDIT CARDS

 • *MC* • *VI*

RATINGS & AWARDS
I.T.B. ★★★★

FACILITIES
On site: *Garden, heli-pad, full spa & leisure facilities opening Autumn 2003*
3 meeting rooms/max 500 people
Nearby: *Golf, riding, fishing, tennis, complimentary leisure facilities*

RESTRICTIONS
No pets
Closed 22 - 27 Dec

ATTRACTIONS
Croagh Patrick Mountain,
Westport House, Clew Bay,
Clare Island, Ceide Fields,
Kylemore Abbey,
Connemara National Park,
Blue Flag beaches

AFFILIATIONS
Independent

NEAREST
MAJOR CITY:
Galway - 55 miles/1 hr

MAJOR AIRPORT:
Shannon - 125 miles/1 ¾ hrs
Knock - 45 miles/50 mins

RAILWAY STATION:
Westport - ½ miles/5 mins

RESERVATIONS
Direct with hotel
*Quote **Best Loved***

ACCESS CODES
AMADEUS LW GWYKNO
APOLLO/GALILEO LM 91477
SABRE/ABACUS LM 17342
WORLDSPAN LM KNOC1

IRELAND

● *Map p.478*
ref: C10

> **" The location is wonderful - a must for anyone who is passionate about the sea - and the Thalassotherapy Centre is an experience not to be missed "**
>
> *Top Sante UK*

LODGE & SPA AT INCHYDONEY ISLAND — *Resort hotel*

Clonakilty, Co Cork, Republic of Ireland

Telephone +353 (0)23 33143
Fax +353 (0)23 35229

E-mail: *inchydoney@bestloved.com*

MANAGING DIRECTOR
Michael Knox-Johnston

ROOM RATES *(EUROS)*
Single occupancy	€154 - €182
63 Doubles/Twins	€265 - €310
4 Suites	€350 - €650

Includes full breakfast and VAT

CHARGE/CREDIT CARDS

 ● *DC* ● *MC* ● *VI*

RATINGS & AWARDS
I.T.B. ★★★★
R.A.C. Blue Ribbon ★★★★ *Dining Award 3*
A.A. ★★★★ ❀❀ *74%*

FACILITIES
On site: *heli-pad, indoor pool, health & beauty, beach, spa 4 meeting rooms/max 750 people*
Nearby: *Fishing, cycling, golf, deep sea diving, sailing*

RESTRICTIONS
No pets, guide dogs only
Closed 25 - 26 Dec

ATTRACTIONS
Castle Freke, Drombeg Stone Circle, Fota Wildlife Park, Blarney Castle, West Cork Scenic Drive, Cobh Heritage Centre

AFFILIATIONS
Knox Hotels and Resorts

NEAREST
MAJOR CITY:
Cork - 35 miles/55 mins

MAJOR AIRPORT:
Cork - 30 miles/45 mins

RAILWAY STATION:
Cork - 35 miles/55 mins

RESERVATIONS
Direct with hotel
Quote **Best Loved**

ACCESS CODES
Not applicable

Refreshed and revitalised - a tonic for body and soul in West Cork

The mesmerizing vista of sea and sky stretching off to the distant horizon from Inchydoney cannot fail to soothe and relax visitors to this magical spot. The sea is an intrinsic element of any stay at the Lodge & Spa, which sits on a promontory flanked by glorious beaches. Every guestroom is ocean facing, and there are more sea views from the indoor marine pool, centrepiece of the Thalasso Spa. Derived from the Greek words for seawater (thalassa) and medical treatment, thalassotherapy promotes the curative, calming and regenerative powers of seawater. The Spa at Inchydoney is the only accredited thalassotherapy facility outside mainland Europe, and offers a full range of treatments from soothing seaweed wraps to hydro massage as well as a sauna and Hammam steam room. Additional treats for the mind and body include reflexology, an aquatonic pool, and beauty treatments using Elemis and Guinot products.

There is plenty to see and do in this corner of West Cork. Sea fishing, riding and golf are easily arranged, and if you visit at New Year, a bracing charity swim takes place off the beach.

Special break packages are available, and include dinner and a variety of treatments - making them exceptional value for money.

LOCATION

Follow N71 from Cork to Clonakilty. Take 2nd left at roundabout and proceed for 3 miles.

> **" Longfield's has proved to be a tranquil haven in an active city. Wonderful to have been cared for by an excellent team of staff "**
>
> *Mrs Sandra Hamilton, London*

● *Map p.478*
ref: G7

18th century Georgian house

LONGFIELD'S

A home in the centre of Dublin you could almost call your own

'During this morning walk in Dublin, I continued to believe that no matter where I looked I would find traces of the faces, the laughter and the voices which gave birth to this city and whose buildings and streets had a way of making you feel they belonged to you'. This is how J P Donleavy, the Irish-American novelist described one of Europe's smallest cities and, arguably, its most endearing and entertaining.

Within walking distance of the principal attractions of the city is Longfield's gracing one of the many elegant Georgian terraces for which this part of Dublin is famous. If you were not staying there, you might be tempted by Number Ten, the below stairs restaurant, whose intimate ambience, excellent cuisine and splendid cellar entice and satisfy its business and residential neighbours.

If you find the acquaintance of the restaurant to your liking, you will surely fall for the other pleasures of this erstwhile home of Lord Longfield. The high-ceilinged rooms have all the refinements of which his lordship would have thoroughly approved and many he could never have dreamed of, introduced as some were, in an ongoing major refurbishment of the property.

Indeed, as the charming staff put you at your ease, you may reflect, like Donleavy, that this haven in some way belongs to you.

LOCATION

Only 10 minutes (¼ mile) from Grafton Street and the City Centre.

9-10 Fitzwilliam Street Lower, Dublin 2, Republic of Ireland

Telephone +353 (0)1 676 1367 Fax +353 (0)1 676 1542

E-mail: *longfield@bestloved.com*

GENERAL MANAGER
Chris Vos

ROOM RATES *(EUROS)*
2 Singles	€145 - €185
22 Doubles/Twins	€215
2 Four-posters	€255

Includes full breakfast and VAT

CHARGE/CREDIT CARDS

 ● *DC* ● *JCB* ● *MC* ● *VI*

RATINGS & AWARDS
I.T.B. ★★★ *Hotel*
R.A.C. ★★★ *Dining Award 2*
A.A. ★★★ ✿✿ *67%*

FACILITIES
On site: 'No 10' Restaurant
1 meeting room/max 22 people
Nearby: *Tennis, fishing, fitness, riding, golf*

RESTRICTIONS
No facilities for disabled guests
No pets
Smoking in Drawing Room only

ATTRACTIONS
Trinity College, National Library,
St Stephen's Green, National Art Gallery,
Grafton Street, Christchurch Cathedral

AFFILIATIONS
Manor House Hotels of Ireland

NEAREST
MAJOR CITY:
Dublin

MAJOR AIRPORT:
Dublin - 7 miles/30 mins

RAILWAY STATION:
Dublin - ½ mile/5 mins

FERRY PORT:
Dun Laoghaire - 4 miles/20 mins

RESERVATIONS
Toll free in US: 800-44-UTELL
*Quote **Best Loved***

ACCESS CODES
AMADEUS UI DUBLON
APOLLO/GALILEO UI 91673
SABRE/ABACUS UI 33792
WORLDSPAN UI 40025

IRELAND

❝ *Addiction is the word that springs to mind. Had a fabulous weekend.*
Thanks a million again. See you next time ❞

Colman Finlay & Claire Bolan, Ireland

LOUGH INAGH LODGE HOTEL   *Victorian lodge*

Recess,
Connemara, Co Galway,
Republic of Ireland

Telephone +353 (0)95 34706
Fax +353 (0)95 34708

E-mail: *loughinagh@bestloved.com*

OWNER
Maire O'Connor

ROOM RATES *(EUROS)*
Single occupancy   €111 - €129
12 Doubles/Twins   €178 - €213
Includes full breakfast and VAT

CHARGE/CREDIT CARDS

 • DC • MC • VI

RATINGS & AWARDS
I.T.B. ★★★★ Hotel
A.A. ★★★ ❀❀ 77%
A.A. Romantic Hotel

FACILITIES
On site: *Garden, heli-pad, fishing,*
shooting, walking, cycle hire
1 meeting room/max 24 people
Nearby: *Golf, sea fishing, riding,*
scuba diving

RESTRICTIONS
No facilities for disabled guests
Closed 8 Dec - 14 March

ATTRACTIONS
Connemara National Park,
Twelve Bens Mountain Range,
Letterfrack Furniture College,
The Victoria Walled Garden,
Kylemore Abbey, local craft shops

AFFILIATIONS
Manor House Hotels of Ireland

NEAREST
MAJOR CITY:
Galway - 42 miles/1 hr

MAJOR AIRPORT:
Shannon - 99 miles/2 ½ hrs
Knock - 75 miles/2 ½ hrs

RAILWAY STATION:
Knock - 75 miles/2 ½ hrs

RESERVATIONS
Direct with hotel
Quote **Best Loved**

ACCESS CODES
Not applicable

The most beautiful place to go hill walking and see Connemara

The lodge is set on the shores of Lough Inagh, one of Connemara's most beautiful lakes. Amidst the most spectacular scenery in Ireland, visitors can fish, shoot, pony trek, cycle, play golf or simply relax. Sturdily built in the 1880s, Lough Inagh Lodge combines the comforts and pleasures of a modern hotel with its own old-world charm. The original lodge record books make fascinating reading for fishermen, and everyone else can take in Ireland's finest panoramic views that accompany morning coffee or afternoon tea in the sitting room. Each bedroom has a separate dressing room, and fabulous vistas over the lake and The Twelve Bens mountains. Open log fires in the library and the oak-panelled bar symbolise the warmth of Inagh hospitality. Seafood and wild game dishes are specialities of the house, and are complemented by an excellent wine list.

Outdoor action is unlimited. There is game fishing on Lough Inagh, sea fishing within ten miles, driven woodcock shooting, riding and golf. All Irish craftware is available in the many shops at Recess, Kylemore and Clifden.

The lodge is the ideal base for a tour of

Connemara. It is surrounded by noted beauty spots, including the Connemara National Park. Kylemore Abbey is nearby.

LOCATION

Take the N59 towards Clifden as far as Recess.
Turn right onto the R344 just after Recess and
head towards Letterfrack. The hotel is situated
approximately 7 kms from this junction.

IRELAND

" *Ireland's finest castle of its period* "

Lord Clark, 'Civilisation' television programme

• *Map p.478*
ref: D5

17th century castle

MARKREE CASTLE

The Coopers have lived here for 350 years - the welcome is as warm as ever

Home of the Cooper family for over 350 years, Markree Castle is now run as a small family hotel by Charles and Mary Cooper, the 10th generation of the Coopers to live at Markree.

Set in a large estate with lovely gardens, the original house has been altered many times over the years, the main addition being in 1802 by the architect Francis Johnston. The enormous oak staircase is overlooked by a stained glass window depicting the Cooper family tree going back 20 generations, and the Louis Philippe style plasterwork in the dining-room makes it one of Ireland's most spectacular rooms.

Charles Cooper worked in hotels in many other countries before returning to Markree in 1989. Since then much has been restored creating a family hotel of character. The bedrooms all have private bathrooms, telephones, and efficient heating, yet great care has been taken to retain the character of the old building and the family atmosphere, rather than the formal, impersonal atmosphere of more luxurious hotels.

The restaurant has also become well known for carefully prepared meals of a high standard.

LOCATION

8 miles south of Sligo town, just off N4 and N17 junction.

Collooney, Co Sligo, Republic of Ireland

Telephone +353 (0)71 67800
Fax +353 (0)71 67840

E-mail: *markree@bestloved.com*

OWNERS
Charles and Mary Cooper

ROOM RATES *(EUROS)*
Single occupancy   €99 - €108
30 Doubles/Twins   €170 - €190
Includes full breakfast and VAT

CHARGE/CREDIT CARDS

 • DC • MC • VI

RATINGS & AWARDS
I.T.B. ★★★ Hotel
A.A. ★★★ ❀ 56%
Bewley's Best Coffee Award
Bridgestone Top 100 Best Hotels

FACILITIES
On site: *Garden, fishing, riding*
Nearby: *Golf, fishing*

RESTRICTIONS
Limited facilities for disabled guests
No smoking throughout
No pets, guide dogs only
Closed 24 - 26 Dec

ATTRACTIONS
Yeats country, Lough Gill,
Carrowmore megalithic remains,
Parke's Castle

AFFILIATIONS
Independent

NEAREST
MAJOR CITY:
Galway - 80 miles/2 hrs

MAJOR AIRPORT:
Dublin/Shannon - 125 miles/3 hrs
Knock - 40 miles/30 mins

RAILWAY STATION:
Collooney - 1 ½ miles/5 mins

RESERVATIONS
Direct with hotel
Quote **Best Loved**

ACCESS CODES
Not applicable

IRELAND

● Map p.478
ref: G4

" A stylish hotel, an oasis of comfortable calm "

Karen Brown's Charming Inns & Itineraries

THE MCCAUSLAND HOTEL

19th century warehouse

**34 - 38 Victoria Street,
Belfast BT1 3GH
Northern Ireland**
**Telephone +44 (0)28 9022 0200
Fax +44 (0)28 9022 0220**
E-mail: *mccausland@bestloved.com*

DIRECTOR
David Butt

GENERAL MANAGER
Niall Coffey

ROOM RATES
Single occupancy	from £140
51 Doubles/Twins	from £140
9 Junior suites	from £180

Includes breakfast service and VAT

CHARGE/CREDIT CARDS
 ● *DC* ● *JCB* ● *MC* ● *VI*

RATINGS & AWARDS
N.I.T.B. ★★★★
R.A.C. ★★★★ *Dining Award 1*
A.A. ★★★★ 68%

FACILITIES
On site: *restaurant and café bar
3 meeting rooms/max 80 people*
Nearby: *Golf, fishing, water skiing,
yachting, tennis, fitness centre, riding*

RESTRICTIONS
*No pets, guide dogs only
Closed 24 - 27 Dec*

ATTRACTIONS
*Waterfront Hall, The Grand Opera House,
Castle Court shopping centre, The Odyssey,
Ulster Museum, Botanical Gardens*

AFFILIATIONS
*The Celebrated Hotels Collection
Small Luxury Hotels
Manor House Hotels of Ireland*

NEAREST
*MAJOR CITY:
Belfast*

*MAJOR AIRPORT:
Belfast International - 11 miles/15 mins
Belfast City - 3 miles/10 mins*

*RAILWAY STATION:
Belfast Central - ⅔ mile/5 mins*

RESERVATIONS
*Toll free in US: 800-322-2403
or 800-525-4800*
Toll free in UK: 00800 525 48000
Quote **Best Loved**

ACCESS CODES
*AMADEUS LX BFSTMH
APOLLO/GALILEO LX 96467
SABRE/ABACUS LX 44462
WORLDSPAN LX BFSMH*

Belfast's hotel of the future with traditional standards of luxury

The area of Belfast known as Laganside was once a busy port whose great warehouses were built by eminent Victorian architects. Its recent and dramatic rejuvenation has been spearheaded by the Waterfront Hall entertainment centre. Laganside heralds a resurgence of the good times with bistros, restaurants, bars, boutiques, galleries and penthouse apartments. The McCausland Hotel, built as two warehouses in the 1850s, is an integral part of this exciting renaissance.

The hotel is Italianate in concept. Behind the splendid four-storey Victorian façade, is an elegant blend of technology, imagination and contemporary design. When its doors opened in late 1998, a luxury hotel was revealed providing 60 rooms with every possible facility launching it into world class exclusivity.

Conceptually, it is a hotel of tomorrow: there are I.T. options to satisfy the technophile, bedrooms specifically designed for the lady traveller and rooms that cater for wheelchairs. Guests can enjoy the contemporary Irish dishes served in the hotel's restaurant and relax with a coffee or cocktail in the café bar. Business meetings are also catered for in the well-equipped conference rooms. This is a sister property to The Hibernian Hotel, Dublin (page 416) and the Woodstock Hotel, Ennis, Co. Clare (page 447), and shares with them a provenance of excellence.

This is a place to come, see and be conquered!

LOCATION
*Located on Victoria Street between Anne
Street and the Albert Clock Tower.*

Deluxe hotel

MERRION HOTEL

Dublin's most gracious Georgian hotel with 5-star modern facilities

Four Georgian houses were sensitively restored and two magnificent 18th century formal landscaped gardens combined to create The Merrion, Dublin's most gracious hotel. It opened in autumn 1997, an oasis of tranquillity close to exclusive Grafton Street and even closer to the leafy walks and shady lawns of Merrion Square.

The 145 rooms and suites are designed to recall the elegance of the Georgian era and achieve five-star standards of luxury. Each has individually controllable air conditioning, in-room safe and 24-hour valet and room service. The splendid salons are in authentic period style. Contemporary Irish art from the country's finest collection is on display.

Restaurant Patrick Guilbaud presents a renowned gastronomic menu in classical style. Mornington's Brasserie offers superb contemporary Irish cuisine in a more relaxed environment. The Cellar Bar is graced by the vaulted ceilings of the original Georgian wine cellars.

In the heart of Dublin, the Merrion is directly opposite Government Buildings. Trinity College, the National Museum and National Gallery are among its nearest neighbours. Yet, such is the peace in the gardens that the only sounds are the songs of the birds.

LOCATION

In the heart of Dublin.

Upper Merrion St, Dublin 2, Republic of Ireland
Telephone +353 (0)1 603 0600
Fax +353 (0)1 603 0700
E-mail: *merrion@bestloved.com*

GENERAL MANAGER
Peter MacCann

ROOM RATES *(EUROS)*
45 Singles €300 - €380
80 Doubles/Twins €325 - €415
20 Suites €610 - €995
Includes newspaper and VAT

CHARGE/CREDIT CARDS

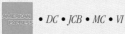

• *DC* • *JCB* • *MC* • *VI*

RATINGS & AWARDS
I.T.B. ★★★★★ *Hotel*
R.A.C. Gold Ribbon ★★★★ *Dining Award 5*
A.A. ★★★★★ 🌸🌸🌸🌸
A.A. Top 200 - 02/03
The American Academy of Hospitality
Science Five Star Diamond Award 2002
Top Irish Hotel, Zagat Survey 2001

FACILITIES
On site: *Garden, gym, indoor pool,*
health & beauty, steam room
6 meeting rooms/max 100 people
Nearby: *Golf, riding, fishing, tennis*

RESTRICTIONS
No smoking in bedrooms
No pets, guide dogs only

ATTRACTIONS
Trinity College, National Art Gallery,
Grafton Street, Newgrange,
Christchurch Cathedral,
Powerscourt House and Gardens

AFFILIATIONS
Leading Hotels of the World
The Celebrated Hotels Collection

NEAREST
MAJOR CITY:
Dublin

MAJOR AIRPORT:
Dublin - 4 miles/25 mins

RAILWAY STATION:
Heuston - 2 miles/15 mins

RESERVATIONS
Toll free in US: 800-223-6800
or 800-322-2403
Toll free in UK: 0800 181123
Quote **Best Loved**

ACCESS CODES
AMADEUS LW DUB430
APOLLO/GALILEO LW 93859
SABRE/ABACUS LW 8715
WORLDSPAN LW 8430

IRELAND

MORRISON HOTEL

City centre hotel

**Ormond Quay, Dublin 1
Republic of Ireland**

**Telephone +353 (0)1 887 2400
Fax +353 (0)1 878 3185**

E-mail: *morrison@bestloved.com*

MANAGING DIRECTOR
Anthony Kenna

ROOM RATES *(EUROS)*
Single occupancy   €222 - €292
87 Doubles/Twins   €222
3 Georgian rooms   €317
2 Suites   €444
1 Penthouse   €1,587
Includes VAT

CHARGE/CREDIT CARDS

 • DC • MC • VI

RATINGS & AWARDS
I.T.B. ★★★★ *Hotel*

FACILITIES
On site: *2 meeting rooms/max 50 people*
Nearby: *Golf, tennis, fitness, sauna, gym, sailing, fishing*

RESTRICTIONS
*No pets
Closed 24 - 28 Dec*

ATTRACTIONS
National Art Gallery, Trinity College, Temple Bar, Dublin Castle, Grafton Street shopping, Guiness Hopstore

AFFILIATIONS
Sterling Hotels

NEAREST
*MAJOR CITY:
Dublin*

*MAJOR AIRPORT:
Dublin - 8 miles/15 mins*

*RAILWAY STATION:
Connolly - 1 mile/5 mins*

RESERVATIONS
*Direct with hotel
Quote* **Best Loved**

ACCESS CODES
*AMADEUS WR DUB461
APOLLO/GALILEO WR 98026
SABRE/ABACUS WR 13172
WORLDSPAN WR 8461*

IRELAND

'*This is the place to come for a slice of cool Ireland*'

One of dozens of rave reviews received from the travel press and publications as disparate as The Irish Times and the New York Post, the above quote from the Evening Standard sums up the latest ultra hip arrival on Dublin's hotel scene. "The hotel of the moment" declares Interiors Magazine, "Everything about the hotel screams style" enthuses Ulster Tatler, and the plaudits keep on coming.

The Morrison is blessed with everything from a superb central location at the foot of the new Millennium bridge overlooking the River Liffey to award-winning architecture. Behind the unassuming façade of a Georgian townhouse, architect Douglas Wallace and interior designer John Rocha have created a sleek contemporary masterpiece where Irish modernism dovetails seamlessly with Oriental minimalism to produce an innate sense of tranquillity. The luxurious and soothingly monochromatic guest rooms are a seductive blend of crisp linen and soft velvet, limestone bathrooms and state-of-the-art sound systems. Modern international cuisine is served to Dublin's most fashionable crowd in the Halo restaurant, where the atrium setting is as stunning as it is romantic. There's the Morrison bar, or enjoy cocktails and sushi in the basement club, Lobö, beneath the gaze of a giant African head.

LOCATION

Located on Ormaond Quay, just three minutes walk from O'Connell Bridge and close to Temple Bar

❝ I came here and thought it would be just another guesthouse. Few times in my life have I been this wrong! ❞

Robert Bjark, USA

• Map p.478
ref: C7

Country house

MOY HOUSE

Lahinch, Co Clare, Republic of Ireland

Telephone +353 (0)65 708 2800
Fax +353 (0)65 708 2500

E-mail: *moyhouse@bestloved.com*

GENERAL MANAGER
Bernadette Merry

ROOM RATES *(EUROS)*
2 Singles   €127
7 Doubles/Twins   €190
Includes full breakfast and VAT

CHARGE/CREDIT CARDS

 • *JCB* • *MC* • *VI*

RATINGS & AWARDS
I.T.B. ★★★★ *Guest House*
A.A. ◆◆◆◆◆ *Premier Collection*

FACILITIES
On site: *Garden*
Nearby: *Golf, beach, cycling, swimming pool, sauna & jacuzzi*

RESTRICTIONS
No facilities for disabled guests
No children under 6 years
No pets

ATTRACTIONS
Cliffs of Moher, Bunratty Castle, King John's Castle, Aran Islands, Doonbeg and Lahinch golf courses, Hunt Museum

AFFILIATIONS
Ireland's Blue Book

NEAREST
MAJOR CITY:
Limerick - 42 miles/1 hr

MAJOR AIRPORT:
Shannon - 35 miles/50 mins

RAILWAY STATION:
Ennis - 20 miles/30 mins

RESERVATIONS
Toll free in US: 800-323-5463
Quote **Best Loved**

ACCESS CODES
Not applicable

Romantic Atlantic - an idyllic Irish retreat on Lahinch Bay

Moy House was originally built for Sir Augustine Fitzgerald in the mid-18th century and occupies a superb position overlooking Lahinch Bay on the Co. Clare coast. This country house is set in 15 acres of gardens and grounds with mature woodlands and a picturesque river, beyond which there is a sweeping sandy beach renowned for surfing and sunbathing, while the Atlantic Ocean itself contributes breathtaking seascapes year-round.

Major restoration has transformed Moy House into a wonderfully stylish and appealing country retreat deftly blending traditional character and antiques with the best of contemporary design and comfort. The spacious and delightful bedrooms benefit from wonderful views, and the kitchen, where breakfast and dinner are prepared, is open for guests to use at their leisure.

Fortified by a hearty breakfast, there are any number of sightseeing and sporting activities to choose from. Lahinch is synonymous with golf, offering both the famous Castle Golf Course and the Greg Norman-designed links course at Doonberg. Golfers, walkers, cyclists (there are two house bikes) and sea bathers can depart from the front door. Further afield, things to see include the Cliffs of Moher, the Burren and the Ailwee Caves.

LOCATION

Situated on the coast road
1 mile south of Lahinch.

IRELAND

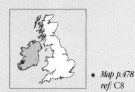

" Fabulous decor, we felt like we were at home. The food was fantastic and service impeccable "

G Lamson, Travel & Leisure, San Diego

MUSTARD SEED AT ECHO LODGE   *Country house restaurant*

**Ballingarry, Co Limerick,
Republic of Ireland**

Telephone +353 (0)69 68508
Fax +353 (0)69 68511

E-mail: *mustard@bestloved.com*

OWNER
Daniel Mullane

ROOM RATES *(EUROS)*
Single occupancy   €106 - €180
13 Doubles/Twins   €172 - €280
1 Four-poster   €280
2 Suites   €280
Includes full breakfast and VAT

CHARGE/CREDIT CARDS

 ● *DC* ● *JCB* ● *MC* ● *VI*

RATINGS & AWARDS
I.T.B. ★★★★ *Hotel*
Bridgestone 100 Best Ireland
*Gilbeys Gold Medal Award for Catering
Excellence in Ireland*
*Bushmills 'Best Restaurant Outside of
Dublin Award 2002/2003'*

FACILITIES
On site: *Garden, health & beauty,
sauna, massage room, exercise room
1 meeting room/max 20 people*
Nearby: *Golf, riding, fishing*

RESTRICTIONS
*Pets by arrangement
Closed 23 - 26 Dec*

ATTRACTIONS
*Glin Castle & Gardens, Islandmore Gardens,
Ring of Kerry, Adare's antique shops,
Clonshire Equestrian Centre,
Cliffs of Moher, The Burren*

AFFILIATIONS
*Preston's Global Hotels
Ireland's Blue Book*

NEAREST
MAJOR CITY:
Limerick - 20 miles/35 mins

MAJOR AIRPORT:
Shannon - 33 miles/1 hr

RAILWAY STATION:
Limerick - 20 miles/45 mins

RESERVATIONS
*Toll free in US/Canada: 800-544-9993
or 800-323-5463*
Quote **Best Loved**

ACCESS CODES
Not applicable

IRELAND

*Share your Irish country home
with a top Irish restaurant*

Daniel Mullane's Mustard Seed Restaurant in Adare village is one of Ireland's most respected. In 1995 he bought Echo Lodge, a fine Victorian country house built in 1884 in the tranquil village of Ballingarry near Adare. Into it he has put his restaurant, his love for the space and elegance of a bygone age, plus today's comforts and amenities. Guests are welcomed for dinner with an overnight stay. The 16 bedrooms are beautifully decorated and furnished. There are seven acres of lawns, pleasure grounds and peace. The library has an unusual and excellent book collection.

The restaurant is memorable. Great care is taken to source ingredients from the best of Ireland's organic farms and cheese makers. The herbs are grown in the garden. The menu is made up of the delightful flavour of the very best of Irish cuisine, both traditional and modern. It is complemented by a serious wine list.

Peaceful countryside with delightful walks is all around. The air is enchanting. Cycling, five golf courses, angling and horse riding are within the locality.

LOCATION

*From the top of Adare Village, take the N21
Killarney Road for ¼ mile. Turn left at the first
junction and follow signs to Ballingarry where
the hotel is signed as Mustard Seed.*

Best Loved Hotels of the World

" Set fair to become the outstanding hotel in Ireland "

Travel & Leisure

● Map p.478
ref: B9

433

Victorian country hotel

PARK HOTEL KENMARE

Relaxation and luxury in the heart of Ireland's Lake District

The building was constructed in 1897 by the Great Southern and Western Railway Company to provide overnight accommodation for passengers travelling to Parknasilla 17 miles away. Ownership continued in the hands of the GS&W Company until 1977 when the hotel was sold. In 1980, refurbishment began and the hotel was re-opened in late 1980 under its new name 'the Park Hotel Kenmare'. Since then, it has become renowned for its splendid collection of antiques and interior furnishings.

In 1985, Mr Francis Brennan, the then manager, took complete control becoming the proprietor and managing director. In the quest for superior comfort, a refurbishment programme was undertaken to double the size of the bedrooms and to add balconies to some rooms to allow wonderful views of the river. This latest development has firmly established the hotel as one of Ireland's most luxurious. The hotel lays special emphasis on personalised service and has won many accolades to date.

Numerous outdoor activities are available, including an 18-hole golf course, fishing (sea and lake), horse riding, and many scenic walks.

The pressures of modern living can easily be forgotten at the Park Hotel Kenmare where the staff are waiting to make your stay - whether for a holiday or on business - most memorable.

LOCATION
Southwest Ireland, off the N70 from Killarney on the 'Ring of Kerry'.

***Kenmare, Co Kerry,
Republic of Ireland***
**Telephone +353 (0)64 41200
Fax +353 (0)64 41402**
E-mail: *kenmare@bestloved.com*

OWNER
Francis Brennan

GENERAL MANAGER
John Brennan

ROOM RATES *(EUROS)*
4 Singles	*€158 - €181*
19 Standards	*€138 - £172*
17 Superiors	*€172 - €204*
9 Suites	*€248 - €294*
Includes VAT, excludes service charge of 15%

CHARGE/CREDIT CARDS
 ● DC ● MC ● VI

RATINGS & AWARDS
I.T.B. ★★★★★ *Hotel*
R.A.C. Gold Ribbon ★★★★ *Dining Award 4*
A.A. ★★★★ ❀❀❀ *Top 200 - 02/03*
*Courvoisier's Book of the Best
Hideaway Report 'Hotel of the Year'*

FACILITIES
On site: *Garden, heli-pad, croquet,
tennis, fitness, golf adjacent
2 meeting rooms/max 30 people*
Nearby: *Fishing, cycling, riding*

RESTRICTIONS
*No children in restaurant after 6 pm
No pets in hotel, kennels available
Closed 29 Oct - 19 Apr open Xmas & New Year*

ATTRACTIONS
*Ring of Kerry, Lakes of Killarney,
World renowned gardens*

AFFILIATIONS
*Small Luxury Hotels
The Celebrated Hotels Collection
Ireland's Blue Book*

NEAREST
*MAJOR CITY:
Cork - 60 miles/1 ½ hrs*

*MAJOR AIRPORT:
Cork - 60 miles/1 ½ hrs*

*RAILWAY STATION:
Killarney - 20 miles/45 mins*

RESERVATIONS
*Toll free in US: 800-322-2403 or
800-323-5463*
*Quote **Best Loved***

ACCESS CODES
*AMADEUS LX KIRPHK
APOLLO/GALILEO LX 32328
SABRE/ABACUS LX 30947
WORLDSPAN LX KIRPH*

IRELAND

Map p.478
ref: D10

66 Your establishment is beautiful and comfortable and run with the perfect blend of professionalism and unobtrusiveness. I'll keep a fond memory of Perryville house and Kinsale 99

Andrew Colman, Editor-in-Chief, Saveur

PERRYVILLE

Georgian residence

Kinsale, Co Cork
Republic of Ireland
Telephone +353 (0)21 477 2731
Fax +353 (0)21 4772298
E-mail: *perryville@bestloved.com*

OWNERS
Andrew and Laura Corcoran

GENERAL MANAGER
Barry McDermott

ROOM RATES *(EUROS)*
Single occupancy	€200
13 Doubles/Twins	€200
4 Superior doubles	€255
3 Deluxe doubles	€300
6 Superior Deluxe	€380

Includes continental breakfast and VAT

CHARGE/CREDIT CARDS
MC • VI

RATINGS & AWARDS
I.T.B. ★★★★ *Guest House*

FACILITIES
On site: *Garden*
Nearby: *Golf, sailing, fishing, riding, cycling*

RESTRICTIONS
No facilities for disabled guests
No children under 13 years
No smoking throughout
No pets
Closed 1 Nov - 6 Apr

ATTRACTIONS
Charles Fort, Desmond Castle, West Cork Scenic Drive, Cobh Heritage Centre, Fota Wildlife Park, The Titanic Trail, Old Head of Kinsale Golf links, Fota Island Golf Course

AFFILIATIONS
The Celebrated Hotels Collection
Manor House Hotels of Ireland

NEAREST
MAJOR CITY:
Cork - 18 miles/30 mins

MAJOR AIRPORT:
Cork - 15 miles/25 mins

RAILWAY STATION:
Cork - 18 miles/30 mins

RESERVATIONS
Toll free in US: 800-322-2403
*Quote **Best Loved***

ACCESS CODES
AMADEUS UI ORKPVH
APOLLO/GALILEO UI 97839
SABRE/ABACUS UI 45457
WORLDSPAN UI 40551

Pretty town, pretty hotel and pretty good breakfast too!

The legacy of Kinsale's past as a flourishing port shows in the elegant façade of Perryville House. The Georgian building with its ornate front door and fine wrought-iron balcony was evidently created for a wealthy merchant or sea-captain. In prime position overlooking the busy marina, it is one of the prettiest houses in a pretty town with twisting streets festooned with hanging baskets. Nestled above its rocky harbour since medieval times, Kinsale has witnessed invasions by the Spanish, the French and the English, resulting in two strong forts nearby. Now, the invaders are tourists, tempted to visit Ireland's Gourmet Capital with its annual food festival and top-class restaurants.

Laura Corcoran has taken Perryville House to heart and recreated a classic interior with Irish antiques, four-poster beds and blazing turf fires. The generously proportioned bedrooms boast equally sumptuous bathrooms, crisp cotton bed linen and fresh flowers grown in Laura's own garden. With so many restaurants nearby, only breakfast is offered but one irresistible to any food lover!

In easy reach of Cork, there are excellent coastal walks, sailing, riding, fishing and golfing - plenty of opportunity to work up an appetite for those gourmet meals!

LOCATION
In the centre of Kinsale overlooking marina.

66 The friendly Irish welcome, the traditional love of golf and the beauty of the place leave you with just one regret - that the visit was not for longer. 99

John Prince, Manchester Evening News

• Map p.478
ref: G7

Golf resort PORTMARNOCK HOTEL AND GOLF LINKS

Sea views with Dublin on the doorstep for golfers and non-golfers alike

The Jameson family of Irish whiskey fame built Portmarnock, though it was known as St. Marnock's House back in 1864. In the 1880s, expert yachtsman Willy Jameson entertained the Prince of Wales (later Edward VII) here. He gave the prince a yacht named Britannia, but turned down a knighthood on the grounds that "the name Jameson was known world-wide by those who drank anyway". A golf course was laid out on the seashore in 1894, and the old Portmarnock Golf Club hosted several classic events before Bernard Langer's magnificent championship course was opened in 1996. It makes optimum use of the challenging links terrain and is the only PGA European Tour course in Ireland.

Each of the hotel's 100 bedrooms has a view of the golf course or the sea, and guests can choose between comfortable modern executive suites, deluxe rooms and bedrooms in the original house furnished with historic four-poster beds. There is a choice of restaurants too, with the more formal Osborne Restaurant, named for the artist who painted several well known views from the house, and the casual Links Restaurant. Portmarnock is

just 15 miles from Dublin and convenient for the airport.

LOCATION

From Dublin airport, take N1 (Drogheda). At junction for Swords, take 2nd exit. Take R106 (Malahide) Junction with R107, turn left. Hotel is approx 4 miles on the left.

Strand Road, Portmarnock, Co Dublin, Republic of Ireland

**Telephone +353 (0)1 846 0611
Fax +353 (0)1 846 2442**

E-mail: *portmarnock@bestloved.com*

GENERAL MANAGER
Shane Cookman

ROOM RATES *(EUROS)*
Single occupancy   €220 - €320
98 Doubles/Twins   €295 - €367
2 Four-poster suites   €500
Includes full breakfast and VAT

CHARGE/CREDIT CARDS

 • DC • JCB • MC • VI

RATINGS & AWARDS
I.T.B. ★★★★ Hotel
A.A. ★★★★ ❀❀❀❀
A.A. Top 200 - 02/03

FACILITIES
On site: *Garden, gym, golf, health & beauty, sauna*
3 meeting rooms/max 350 people
Nearby: *riding, sailing, fishing*

RESTRICTIONS
*Limited facilities for disabled guests
No pets, guide dogs only*

ATTRACTIONS
*Dublin, Malahide Castle,
Talbot Botanical Gardens,
Fry Model Railway,
Newbridge House & Farm,
Lusk Heritage Centre, New Grange*

AFFILIATIONS
Summit Hotels & Resorts

NEAREST
MAJOR CITY:
Dublin - 15 miles/25 mins

MAJOR AIRPORT:
Dublin - 9 miles/15 mins

RAILWAY STATION:
Portmarnock - 1 mile/5 mins

RESERVATIONS
Toll free in US: 800-457-4000
*Quote **Best Loved***

ACCESS CODES
*AMADEUS UI DUBPOR
APOLLO/GALILEO UI 72712
SABRE/ABACUS UI 29752
WORLDSPAN UI 22052*

IRELAND

" My bedroom overlooked rolling lawns and ancient oaks. The bed was the size of a croquet lawn "

Alan Bestic - The Sunday Telegraph

RATHSALLAGH HOUSE

Queen Anne stables

Dunlavin, Co Wicklow, Republic of Ireland
Telephone +353 (0)45 403112
Fax +353 (0)45 403343
E-mail: *rathsallagh@bestloved.com*

OWNERS
The O'Flynn Family

ROOM RATES *(EUROS)*
Single occupancy	€175 - €250
26 Doubles/Twins	€250 - €290
1 Four-poster	€290
2 Suites	€290

Includes full breakfast and VAT

CHARGE/CREDIT CARDS
• DC • JCB • MC • VI

RATINGS & AWARDS
I.T.B. ★★★★
4 National Breakfast Awards
Irish Country House Restaurant
of the Year 2002

FACILITIES
On site: *Garden, snooker, heli-pad, croquet, golf, tennis, indoor pool, clay pigeon shooting, archery, sauna, steam room, jacuzzi*
3 meeting rooms/max 150 people
Nearby: *Fishing, riding*

RESTRICTIONS
No children under 12 years
Smoking in Bar and Drawing room only
Pets by arrangement
Closed 6 - 31 Jan

ATTRACTIONS
Russborough House, National Stud, Curragh Racecourse, Glendalough, Punchestown Racecourse

AFFILIATIONS
Ireland's Blue Book
Small Luxury Hotels

NEAREST
MAJOR CITY:
Dublin - 35 miles/1 hr

MAJOR AIRPORT:
Dublin - 45 miles/1 ½ hrs

RAILWAY STATION:
Kildare - 15 miles/30 mins

RESERVATIONS
Toll free in US: 800-323-5463
or 800-525-4800
*Quote **Best Loved***

ACCESS CODES
AMADEUS LX DUBRHG
APOLLO/GALILEO LX 52732
SABRE/ABACUS LX45779
WORLDSPAN LX DUBRH

The most stylish and entertaining nineteenth hole you'll ever find!

Take 530 acres of gorgeous Irish parkland at the foot of the Wicklow Mountains, convert some ivy-covered Queen Anne stables into a country house and surround it with an 18-hole championship golf course and you have the prospect of a superb holiday - whether or not you play golf!

This is the home of Joe and Kay O'Flynn and their welcome is as big as the countryside around them. The house has a happy and relaxed atmosphere and is fully centrally heated. But nothing can match the genial warmth of the log and turf fires that blaze away in the well-proportioned reception rooms. Upstairs, the bedrooms are luxuriously appointed with views of the park.

The food is country house cooking at its best with a light modern influence from Head Chef John Luke; game in season, fresh fish from the Wexford coast and breakfasts to drool over! Rathsallagh has won the National Breakfast Awards four times! All this is a tribute to Kay's imagination and mastery of the culinary arts.

The championship golf course was designed by former world amateur champion, Peter McEvoy and leading Irish professional Christie O'Connor. Rathsallagh is set on lush parkland amidst mature trees and natural water hazards. Other facilities include a heated indoor pool, tennis court, billiard room and spa room.

LOCATION
From Dublin Airport take the M50 to Naas N7.
Take the Naas bypass (M7) south and exit for the
M9 south towards Carlow. After 6 miles pass Priory
Inn on left. After 2 miles turn left for Rathsallagh.

" The way your reception welcomed us, your restaurant and bar-team hosted us, and the perfection your chef and his team cooked for us was a daily pleasure for me, my family and our friends from Hamburg "

Dr Beckord, Germany

● Map p.478
ref: B6

Country hotel

RENVYLE HOUSE HOTEL

Fresh air and first class relaxation on the Connemara coast

Set on a peninsula jutting out into the Atlantic, Renvyle was once home to one of the oldest and most powerful Gaelic clans in ancient Connacht. Perhaps it is the superb location that explains the house's phoenix-like quality for over the centuries it has been built, rebuilt, reduced to ashes and risen yet again until it took its present form of country house hotel.

The Gogarty family opened the first hotel here in 1883, and illustrious visitors have included Augustus John, who came to paint the great Irish poet W.B. Yeats, and Sir Winston Churchill. There are spacious and comfortable bedrooms, a relaxing lounge leading on to the sunny conservatory, a cosy bar and a dining room where local delicacies such as Connemara lamb, game and fresh fish are served. The hotel organises theme weekends and activities include tennis courts, a heated swimming pool, trout fishing and a challenging nine-hole golf course in the grounds. Golfers can also play the championship Westport and Connemara courses nearby.

If a sightseeing appeals, Renvyle Castle was the home of Elizabethan 'pirate queen' Grace O'Malley, there is peaceful Kylemore Abbey, and the Renvyle peninsula is a noted archaeological site.

LOCATION

From the N59 at Letterfrack take the road to Tully Cross and Tully End. Entrance to the hotel is at the end of the village.

Renvyle, Connemara, Co Galway, Republic of Ireland

Telephone +353 (0)95 43511
Fax +353 (0)95 43515

E-mail: *renvyle@bestloved.com*

CHIEF EXECUTIVE
Ronnie Counihan

RATES PER PERSON (EUROS)
Single occupancy €70 - €195
65 Doubles/Twins €70 - €145
5 Suites €120 - €195
Includes breakfast, 5-course Gourmet dinner and VAT

CHARGE/CREDIT CARDS

 ● DC ● MC ● VI

RATINGS & AWARDS
I.T.B. ★★★ Hotel
R.A.C. ★★★ Dining Award 2
A.A. ★★★ ❀ 68%
Irelands Best Service Award

FACILITIES
On site: Garden, snooker, heli-pad, fishing, croquet, golf, tennis, outdoor pool, bowls, boating
3 meeting rooms/max 200 people
Nearby: Riding, cycling, salmon fishing, shooting, sailing, windsurfing, scuba diving, mountain climbing

RESTRICTIONS
Pets by arrangement
Closed 6 Jan - 12 Feb

ATTRACTIONS
Connemara National Park, Kylemore Abbey, Clare Island, Cliffs of Moher, Church of the Seven Sisters

AFFILIATIONS
Independent

NEAREST
MAJOR CITY:
Limerick - 120 miles/3 hrs

MAJOR AIRPORT:
Shannon - 110 miles/2 ¾ hrs

RAILWAY STATION:
Galway - 60 miles/1 ½ hrs

RESERVATIONS
Direct with hotel
Quote **Best Loved**

ACCESS CODES
Not applicable

IRELAND

❝ *Thank you once more and most heartily for the unforgettable experience of your hospitality at Rosleague Manor* ❞

Richard Weiszècker, President of former German Federal Republic

ROSLEAGUE MANOR

18th century country house

Letterfrack, Co Galway, Republic of Ireland

Telephone +353 (0)95 41101
Fax +353 (0)95 41168

E-mail: *rosleague@bestloved.com*

OWNER
Edmund Foyle

MANAGER
Mark Foyle

ROOM RATES *(EUROS)*
Single occupancy   €115 - €140
16 Doubles/Twins   €130 - €200
4 Junior suites   €180 - €220
Includes full breakfast and VAT

CHARGE/CREDIT CARDS

 • *JCB • MC • VI*

RATINGS & AWARDS
I.T.B. ★★★★ *Hotel*

FACILITIES
On site: *Garden, heli-pad, tennis*
Nearby: *Golf, fishing, riding, swimming, gym*

RESTRICTIONS
No facilities for disabled guests
Closed 1 Nov - 14 Mar

ATTRACTIONS
Connemara National Park, Kylemore Abbey, Cliffs of Moher, the Sky Road, scuba diving, hill walking

AFFILIATIONS
Preston's Global Hotels
Ireland's Blue Book

NEAREST
MAJOR CITY:
Galway - 50 miles/1 ¼ hrs

MAJOR AIRPORT:
Shannon - 110 miles/2 ½ hrs
Galway - 50 miles/1 ¼ hrs

RAILWAY STATION:
Galway - 50 miles/1 ¼ hrs

RESERVATIONS
Toll free in US: 800-544-9993
or 800-323-5463
Quote **Best Loved**

ACCESS CODES
Not applicable

IRELAND

Character, charm and good food on the rugged Connemara coast

On the wild western shores of Co. Galway, romantic and evocative Connemara combines scenic grandeur with a strong folkloric tradition and genuine Irish hospitality. It is a land of extraordinary and constantly changing natural beauty, of sea and sky, blue mountains and peat-stained streams, doughty homesteads and sturdy little ponies. Here, sandwiched between sheltered Ballinakill Bay and the glories of the Connemara National Park, father and son, Edmund and Mark Foyle preside over a delightful small hotel with a well-deserved reputation for wonderful food.

A Georgian country house with sympathetic later additions, Rosleague Manor is surrounded by 30 acres of landscaped gardens with a path leading down to the bay. There is an all-weather tennis court, the Connemara Golf Course nearby, and a host of beautiful and almost deserted beaches, plus numerous opportunities for hiking, horse riding and superb salmon and trout fishing. Another good way to work up an appetite is a spot of sea fishing or boat trip to the island of Inishbofin from the fishing village of Cleggan. Fresh seafood is speciality of the hotel restaurant, which prides itself on featuring the finest seasonal local produce from Connemara lamb to homegrown vegetables.

LOCATION

Letterfrack is 7 miles north of Clifden, the capital of Connemara off the N59.

" It is indeed a rare luxury today to experience such a warm, friendly and family atmosphere that you both so naturally provide at Ross Lake House "

Paddy & Clodagh Donovan, Dublin

• Map p.478
ref: C6

Country house

ROSS LAKE HOUSE HOTEL

A wonderful old house at the gateway to Connemara

Ross Lake is a wonderful old country house whose former glory has been revived by owners Henry and Elaine Reid. This 19th century mansion was formerly an estate house of the landed gentry, who prized it for its serenity. It has three suites and ten comfortable, well appointed double bedrooms.

From the moment you arrive, Henry and Elaine will make you feel at home. The intimate bar is ideal for a drink before dinner. A high quality Irish menu is delightfully prepared and presented featuring a tempting variety of fresh produce from the nearby Connemara hills, streams and lakes, as well as fish straight from the Atlantic.

Ross Lake House has its own magnificent gardens, with hardcourt tennis. Oughterard golf course is two miles away. Lough Corrib and local lakes are famous for game and coarse fishing. The surrounding countryside is rich in superb mountain walks and climbs. Nearby attractions include Aughnanure Castle, Kylemore Abbey, Connemara National Park, the Aran Islands, the Cliffs of Moher and The Burren.

LOCATION
The hotel is situated 14 miles from Galway City on the N59, the main Galway to Clifden road. Turn left after village of Rosscahill.

Rosscahill, Oughterard, Co Galway, Republic of Ireland

Telephone +353 (0)91 550109
Fax +353 (0)91 550184

E-mail: *rosslake@bestloved.com*

OWNERS
Henry and Elaine Reid

ROOM RATES *(EUROS)*
Single occupancy   €100 - €125
7 Doubles/Twins   €150 - €170
3 Suites   €260 - €300
3 Superior rooms   €170 - €200
Includes full breakfast and VAT

CHARGE/CREDIT CARDS

   • DC • MC • VI

RATINGS & AWARDS
I.T.B. ★★★ Hotel

FACILITIES
On site: *Garden, tennis*
1 meeting room/max 150 people
Nearby: *Golf, fishing, riding*

RESTRICTIONS
Limited facilities for disabled guests
No pets in public rooms
Closed 1 Nov - 15 Mar

ATTRACTIONS
Aughnanure Castle,
Connemara National Park,
Cliffs of Moher, Kylemore Abbey,
Aran Islands, The Burren

AFFILIATIONS
Preston's Global Hotels
The Green Book of Ireland

NEAREST
MAJOR CITY:
Galway - 14 miles/30 mins

MAJOR AIRPORT:
Shannon - 65 miles/2 hrs

RAILWAY STATION:
Galway - 14 miles/30 mins

RESERVATIONS
Toll free in US: 800-544-9993
or 800-888-1199
Toll free in UK: 0800 371425
Quote Best Loved

ACCESS CODES
AMADEUS LE GWY279
APOLLO/GALILEO LE 26193
SABRE/ABACUS LE 42799
WORLDSPAN LE 42799

IRELAND

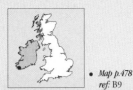
" We are back, but wish we were back there! Thank you again for such wonderful hospitality, service and friendship "

Morris and Sandy Gregory, Texas, USA

SALLYPORT HOUSE

Country house

**Kenmare, Co Kerry,
Republic of Ireland**

**Telephone +353 (0)64 42066
Fax +353 (0)64 42067**

E-mail: *sallyport@bestloved.com*

OWNERS
The Arthur Family

ROOM RATES *(EUROS)*
Single occupancy	€100
4 Doubles/Twins	€140
1 Four Poster	€140
Includes breakfast and VAT	

CHARGE/CREDIT CARDS
None

RATINGS & AWARDS
A.A. ◆◆◆◆◆ *Premier Collection*

FACILITIES
On site: *Garden*
Nearby: *Golf, fishing, walking, pony trekking, watersports*

RESTRICTIONS
*No facilities for disabled guests
No children under 13 years
No smoking throughout
No pets
Closed 1 Nov - 1 April*

ATTRACTIONS
*BearaPeninsula, Ring of Kerry,
Lakes of Killarney, Mizen Head,
Killarney National Park, Gouyan Barra*

AFFILIATIONS
Independent

NEAREST
MAJOR CITY:
Cork - 60 miles/1 ¼ hrs

MAJOR AIRPORT:
*Cork - 60 miles/1 ¼ hrs
Kerry - 30 miles/1 hr*

RAILWAY STATION:
Killarney - 20 miles/50 mins

RESERVATIONS
Direct with hotel
Quote **Best Loved**

ACCESS CODES
Not applicable

IRELAND

A luxurious and welcoming country house that is truly a family affair

An elegant country house on the outskirts of Kenmare, Sallyport House was built by the Arthur family in 1932. Three generations on, the family home has been transformed into a gem of a bed and breakfast by Janie Arthur, together with her brother and sister, all of whom were born in the house. Sallyport has many charms, but chief of these is the warm and unpretentious welcome extended by the Arthurs and the sense that one is a valued guest in a private home. The quiet and secluded setting in lawned gardens with views across Kenmare Bay to the surrounding mountains is undoubtedly another significant plus, as are the comfortable bedrooms furnished with antiques and king or queen size beds, and the magnificent full Irish breakfast menu and buffet.

Kenmare itself combines old-world charm with award-winning restaurants and interesting craft shopping. Nestled in the green hills of Kerry, the town is also known as 'An Neidín' ('little nest'), and makes a fantastic touring base for visits to the Ring of Kerry, Killarney National Park and Bantry Bay, and for hiking the Kerry Way or tackling the majestic heights of McGillycuddy Reeks.

LOCATION

In Kenmare, go in direction of Bantry on N71 for 500 yards. Sallyport House is on the left before bridge.

> **Thank you for such a lovely stay. Sea View House was utterly charming. It's just my kind of place - elegant but not pretentious**
>
> *Bill Sertl, Travel Editor, Saveur Garden Design, New York*

19th century country house — SEA VIEW HOUSE HOTEL

Resplendent and secluded amongst the delights of Ireland

This exceptional hotel offers perfect location and food which is worth going out of your way for. This is possibly one of the most romantic areas in the world; all mountains, lakes and a coast line praised in song that has passed down the generations across the world. Culturally, it is a rich seam of gold that spans prehistory, the Celts, the dawn of Christendom and modern history. Relics and remains are preserved for all to see.

Seashore and landscapes provide never-ending pleasure: golfing to walking, pony trekking, fishing. Whatever your interest, there is nowhere more beautiful in which to enjoy it.

Sea View House nestles comfortably into this idyllic picture. An elegant house that stands aloof from worldly pressures, basking in a reputation for good food that has spread far and wide. "It's really a country house with country house cooking" says Kathleen O'Sullivan, who owns and runs the hotel. She has a 'nose' for good wine so it stands to reason the cellar is a veritable treasure trove!

She also has an eye for beauty; her splendid collection of antiques is displayed throughout the house and in the charming well-appointed bedrooms. It is, after all, her home. What makes it so special is that so many of her guests have been encouraged to call it theirs, too!

LOCATION

70 yards off the N71 Bantry to Glengarriff road close by Ballylickey Bridge.

**Ballylickey,
Bantry, Co Cork,
Republic of Ireland**

**Telephone +353 (0)27 50462
Fax +353 (0)27 51555**

E-mail: *seaview@bestloved.com*

OWNER
Kathleen O'Sullivan

ROOM RATES (EUROS)
Single occupancy   €70 - €100
21 Doubles/Twins   €140 - €175
2 Suites   €175 - €190
Includes newspaper, full breakfast and VAT

CHARGE/CREDIT CARDS
 • DC • MC • VI

RATINGS & AWARDS
I.T.B. ★★★★ Hotel
R.A.C. ★★★
A.A. ★★★ ✿✿ 77%
I.T.B. Award for Excellence
Gilbeys Gold Medal Award for Catering
Excellence in Ireland

FACILITIES
On site: *Garden*
1 meeting room/max 20 people
Nearby: *Golf, fishing, tennis, riding*

RESTRICTIONS
*No pets in public rooms
Closed 15 Nov - 15 Mar*

ATTRACTIONS
*Gougane Barra, Killarney,
Bantry House, Armada Centre,
Garnish Island, Peninsula Barra*

AFFILIATIONS
Manor House Hotels of Ireland

NEAREST
MAJOR CITY:
Cork - 56 miles/1 ½ hrs

MAJOR AIRPORT:
Cork - 56 miles/1 ½ hrs
Shannon - 120 miles/3 hrs

RAILWAY STATION:
Cork - 56 miles/1 ½ hrs

RESERVATIONS
Direct with hotel
Quote **Best Loved**

ACCESS CODES
Not applicable

IRELAND

SHEEN FALLS LODGE

Luxury resort hotel

Kenmare, Co Kerry, Republic of Ireland
Telephone +353 (0)64 41600
Fax +353 (0)64 41386
E-mail: *sheenfalls@bestloved.com*

OWNER
Mr B Hoyer

GENERAL MANAGER
Adriaan Bartels

ROOM RATES *(EUROS)*
44 Deluxe rooms	*€229 - €362*
8 Superior deluxe rooms	*€355 - €550*
9 Suites	*€455 - €595*
1 Presidential Suite	*€1,200 - €1,500*
Little Hay Cottage	*€950 - €1,675*

Includes VAT

CHARGE/CREDIT CARDS
 • DC • MC • VI

RATINGS & AWARDS
I.T.B. ★★★★★ De Luxe
R.A.C. Gold Ribbon ★★★★ Dining Award 3
A.A. ★★★★ ✿✿ Top 200 - 02/03
A.A. Hotel of the Year 2002/2003
American Academy of Hospitality Sciences
Five Star Diamond Award

FACILITIES
On site: *Garden, gym, heli-pad, croquet, riding, tennis, indoor pool, health & beauty, clay shooting, billiards 3 meeting rooms/max 120 people*
Nearby: *Two 18-hole golf courses*

RESTRICTIONS
No pets
Closed 2 Jan - 7 Feb

ATTRACTIONS
Beara Peninsula and the Healy Pass, Ring of Kerry, Killarney National Park

AFFILIATIONS
The Celebrated Hotels Collection
Relais & Chateaux

NEAREST
MAJOR CITY:
Cork - 60 miles/1 ½ hrs

MAJOR AIRPORT:
Kerry - 30 miles/50 mins
Cork - 60 miles/1 ½ hrs

RAILWAY STATION:
Killarney - 23 miles/30 mins

RESERVATIONS
Toll free in US: 800-735-2478
or 800-322-2403
*Quote **Best Loved***

ACCESS CODES
AMADEUS LM KEH275
APOLLO/GALILEO LM 96346
SABRE/ABACUS LM 30264
WORLDSPAN LM 04275

IRELAND

Dedicated to your indulgence in Ireland's most lyrical landscape

If ever there was an hotel that existed to exploit the beauty of its surroundings, none does it better or with greater panache than Sheen Falls Lodge. Set amongst the lyrical beauty of south west Ireland is the resort's 300-acre estate complete with a 15 mile stretch of river that tumbles and sparkles in a picturesque cascade in front of the sub-tropical garden of this 17th century retreat.

The scene is set for all kinds of country pursuits: walking and horse riding through the woodlands, clay pigeon shooting and fishing for salmon in the Sheen River (rods supplied). The fully equipped Health Spa attends one's corporal needs with a heated swimming pool, extensive range of facial and body treatments, jacuzzi, steam room and gym. And there's a tennis court. In short, working up an appetite is not difficult.

La Cascade Restaurant is your reward. It's not enough to say it is award-winning, so many others make a similar claim. The food really is exceptional, an assembly of gorgeous Irish produce and terrific culinary flair. You can also dine at Oscar's Bistro where you will find a lighter bite in a less formal atmosphere. Now you begin to see why Sheen Falls is so highly rated.

The rooms breathe quality from the rich, polished woods to the authentic Irish linen. This is a luxury hotel with irresistible Irish charm; famous in Ireland but for the rest of us, what a find!

LOCATION
The hotel is 1 mile outside Kenmare. Follow the Glengarriff road, take first turn on left and hotel is ½ mile on the left.

> *In a world of hotels where the anodyne and the anonymous are the norm, Tinakilly House is a beacon to restore hope to the traveller's heart*
>
> *1996 Bon Appetit Special Collector's Edition*

• *Map p.478*
ref: G7

Victorian country house

TINAKILLY HOUSE

Splendid fresh food in rich and elegant Victorian surroundings

Truly a romantic secret hideaway, Tinakilly is just south of Dublin. This gracious Victorian Italianate manor stands on seven acres of gardens that sweep down to the Irish Sea. Built for Captain Halpin, who laid the world's telegraph cables, the ornate interiors are rich in period furnishings, oil paintings and seafaring memorabilia. Tinakilly is now the home of the Power family, who together with their friendly staff bid you a warm welcome.

Each of the 51 bedrooms is a perfect blend of Victorian splendour and modern comfort. The Captain Suites and four-poster Junior Suites enjoy breathtaking sea and garden views.

Chef Jason Wall uses fresh local produce such as fish and Wicklow lamb flavoured with herbs from Tinakilly's own gardens. Jason's creations are complemented by an award-winning wine cellar. Brown bread is baked daily, which is especially delicious with the locally smoked Irish salmon.

Excellent local golf courses include the links European Club and parkland Druid's Glen, home of the 1996-1999 Irish Open. A host of nearby visitor attractions include the Wicklow Mountains and the 6th century monastic city Glendalough.

LOCATION

From Dublin follow the N11/M11 to Rathnew and then R570 towards Wicklow. Entrance is on the left, 500 metres outside of Rathnew.

Wicklow, (Rathnew), Co Wicklow, Republic of Ireland
Telephone +353 (0)404 69274
Fax +353 (0)404 67806
E-mail: *tinakilly@bestloved.com*

OWNERS
Raymond and Josephine Power

ROOM RATES *(EUROS)*

Single occupancy	€163 - €376
12 Doubles/Twins	€204 - €250
10 Four-posters	€252 - €320
23 Junior suites	€252 - €320
5 Captain suites	€340 - €428
1 Admirals State Room	€630

Includes full breakfast and VAT

CHARGE/CREDIT CARDS

 • *DC • MC • VI*

RATINGS & AWARDS
I.T.B. ★★★★ *Hotel*
R.A.C. Gold Ribbon ★★★ *Dining Award 3*
A.A. ★★★★ ❀ *68%*
Georgina Campbell Hotel of the Year 2001

FACILITIES
On site: *Garden, heli-pad, croquet, tennis, health & beauty*
3 meeting rooms/max 80 people
Nearby: *Golf, riding, biking*

RESTRICTIONS
No pets

ATTRACTIONS
Glendalough, Mount Usher, Powerscourt Gardens & Waterfall, Dublin City, Trinity College

AFFILIATIONS
The Celebrated Hotels Collection
Ireland's Blue Book
Small Luxury Hotels

NEAREST
MAJOR CITY:
Dublin - 29 miles/45 mins

MAJOR AIRPORT:
Dublin - 35 miles/1 ½ hrs

RAILWAY STATION:
Wicklow - 2 miles/5 mins

FERRY PORT:
Dun Laoghaire - 20 miles/40 mins

RESERVATIONS
Toll free in US: 800-322-2403
or 800-323-5463
Quote Best Loved

ACCESS CODES
AMADEUS LX DUBTCH
APOLLO/GALILEO LX 67443
SABRE/ABACUS LX 30077
WORLDSPAN LX DUBTC

IRELAND

● *Map p.478*
ref: F9

WATERFORD CASTLE HOTEL

15th century castle

**The Island, Ballinakill,
Waterford,
Republic of Ireland**
Telephone +353 (0)51 878203
Fax +353 (0)51 879316
E-mail: *waterford@bestloved.com*

GENERAL MANAGER
Gillian Butler

ROOM RATES *(EUROS)*
Single occupancy   €155 -
€230
14 Doubles/Twins   €180 -
€420
4 Deluxe four-poster suites
€355 - €525
1 Presidential Suite   €435 -
€600
Includes VAT

CHARGE/CREDIT CARDS

 • DC • MC • VI

RATINGS & AWARDS
A.A. ★★★★ ❀❀
A.A. Top 200 - 02/03

FACILITIES
On site: *Garden, heli-pad, golf, tennis,
18 hole golf course,
clay pigeon shooting, archery and team
building events, driving range, scenic walks
2 meeting rooms/max 82 people*
Nearby: *Fishing, riding, free use of local
fitness centre*

RESTRICTIONS
*Limited facilities for disabled guests
No pets, guide dogs only
Closed Christmas*

ATTRACTIONS
*Waterford Crystal showrooms,
Waterford Walking tours,
Christchurch Cathedral,
Reginalds Tower Museum,
The Waterford Show,
Waterford Treasures Museum*

AFFILIATIONS
The Celebrated Hotels Collection

NEAREST
MAJOR CITY:
Waterford - 3 miles/10 mins

MAJOR AIRPORT:
Dublin - 109 miles/3 hrs

RAILWAY STATION:
Waterford - 3 miles/10 mins

FERRY PORT:
Rosslare 50 miles/1 hr

RESERVATIONS

Take the ferry to a secluded island with luxury hotel and golf course

Waterford Castle, former home of the Fitzgerald family, dates back to the 15th century. To stay here is to pass into another world of legend and folklore. It starts as you take the car ferry across from reality onto this enchanted island. From there, the drive leads to the greystone castle, as proud and romantic as your imagination will allow. The carved granite archway leads into the grand entrance hall, dominated by the cavernous fireplace. This gracious hotel, filled with antiques, is redolent of an elegant past. In contrast, the bedrooms are bright and airy with stunning views of the surrounding island estate.

The fairy tale illusion is continued at dinner: With the menu as your guide book, crested plates bear culinary delights and confections dreamed up by the castle's gifted chefs. The food is divine, as bewitching as the castle itself.

Completing the picture is the spectacular 18 hole championship golf course, laid out over 200 acres of beautiful and mature parkland. First class leisure facilities are just two minutes drive from the car ferry, and activities such as riding and fishing are also available.

LOCATION

*Take N9 to Waterford. Cross bridge and stay by
River Suir. At the Tower Hotel turn left into
Dunmore Road for 3 miles passing Hospital, take
4th turn on left. Follow signs for ferry.*

Don't change anything in this house, you can't make it better

Grislind & Helmut Glaser, Munich, Bavaria

• Map p.478
ref: D8

Country house

WATERMAN'S LODGE

Become a part of village life - this is country living at its best

Perched on a hill overlooking the River Shannon, the Clare Hills and the lovely, unspoilt village of Killaloe, Waterman's Lodge oozes charm, peace and tranquillity. Old stone steps, high ceilings, timber floors, brass and cast iron beds, together with open fires and books add up to the perfect rural retreat. The ten bedrooms are all beautifully furnished with rugs, antiques and books.

The kitchen is the heart of this country house. Using organic produce and excellent cooking skills, it provides wonderful food for dinner guests in the converted courtyard restaurant with its high timbered ceiling.

The Lough Derg Bar completes the relaxed atmosphere while the village of Killaloe has some great pubs and people - no cars required, just stroll home. Fishing, boat hire, ghillies, rods etc. are all available in the village. There are excellent golf courses within a short drive, and Cork, Galway and Kerry are all within easy reach.

The philosophy is simple - provide a beautiful rural retreat, good food, and a warm welcome. The ideal home-from-home, it is a real escape from the hurly burly and offers guests the chance to experience country village life at its best.

LOCATION

On the N7 Limerick to Dublin road, turn left in Birdhill on to a road signposted Killaloe/Ballina. Drive through Ballina and the house is just outside the village on the left.

**Ballina/Killaloe,
Co Clare,
Republic of Ireland**

**Telephone +353 (0)61 376333
Fax +353 (0)61 375445**

E-mail: *watermans@bestloved.com*

OWNER
Marcus McMahon

GENERAL MANAGER
John Downes

ROOM RATES *(EUROS)*
Single occupancy	€77 - €110
3 Standard Doubles/Twins	€126 - €165
7 Superior Doubles/Twins	€154 - €198

Includes full breakfast and VAT

CHARGE/CREDIT CARDS

 • MC • VI

RATINGS & AWARDS
I.T.B. ★★★
*Bridgestone 100 Best Places
to Stay in Ireland*

FACILITIES
On site: *Garden*
1 meeting room/max 60 people
Nearby: *Lake and river fishing - ghillie
provided, walking, riding, golf,
sailing, boat hire, clay shooting*

RESTRICTIONS
*Limited facilities for disabled guests
No smoking in bedrooms
No pets
Closed 24 - 25 Dec*

ATTRACTIONS
*The Burren, Cliffs of Moher,
Bunratty Castle, Killaloe Cathedral,
Birr Castle & Demesne,
Galway, Shannon*

AFFILIATIONS
Manor House Hotels of Ireland

NEAREST
*MAJOR CITY:
Limerick - 12 miles/30 mins*

*MAJOR AIRPORT:
Shannon - 20 miles/40 mins*

*RAILWAY STATION:
Bird Hill - 3 miles/5 mins*

RESERVATIONS
*Direct with hotel
Quote **Best Loved***

ACCESS CODES
Not applicable

IRELAND

WINEPORT LODGE

Luxury accommodation

**Glasson, Athlone,
Co Westmeath,
Republic of Ireland**

**Telephone +353 (0)902 85466
Fax +353 (0)902 85471**

E-mail: *wineport@bestloved.com*

OWNERS
Ray Byrne and Jane English

MANAGER
Norma Wilson

ROOM RATES *(EUROS)*
Single occupancy   €175 - €275
10 Doubles/Twins   €200 - €275
Includes full breakfast and VAT

CHARGE/CREDIT CARDS

  • DC • MC • VI

RATINGS & AWARDS
A.A. ❀
*Evian/Food & Wine Magazine -
Best Leinster restaurant 2002*

FACILITIES
On site: *2 meeting rooms/max 125 people*
Nearby: *Golf, riding, leisure centre*

RESTRICTIONS
*No smoking in bedrooms
No pets
Closed 24 - 26 Dec*

ATTRACTIONS
*Belvedere House & Gardens,
Athlone Castle, Killbeggan Racecourse,
Lockes Distillery, Fore Abbey,
Dun na Si Heritage Centre*

AFFILIATIONS
Ireland's Blue Book

NEAREST
*MAJOR CITY:
Galway - 57 miles/1 ¼ hrs*

*MAJOR AIRPORT:
Dublin - 79 miles/1 ¾ hrs*

*RAILWAY STATION:
Athloe - 4 miles/10 mins*

RESERVATIONS
*Toll free in US: 800-323-5463
Quote **Best Loved***

ACCESS CODES
Not applicable

An epicurean oasis with stunning lakeside views

As the name suggests Wineport has a long and distinguished connection with imported fine wines. In the sixth Century cases were dispatched from France, transported by boat up the River Shannon, and then distributed to the local monastery. This tradition continues today and the restaurant offers a prolific selection of artfully chosen vintages from around the world. Attention to sourcing quality, local produce is evidenced by a menu that includes Dublin prawns, Irish Angus beef and braised saddle of rabbit. Private dining can cater for 50 and is perfect high-level executive entertaining.

Sponsorship has afforded the luxurious Tattinger Bubble Lounge, which is reserved for residents. The love of the grape doesn't stop there: each room is named after a specific vintner or drinks company and the relevant complimentary bottle awaits within. Magnificently appointed on the water's edge, the hotel can be accessed via road or river: all the rooms have private balconies overlooking the lakes and the bathrooms have heated floors and power showers.

Nothing is too much trouble for the hospitable staff, and the dress code, like the hotel itself, is 'casually elegant'. One quiet word of warning: do not stay for one night - it won't be long enough!

LOCATION

*From Athlone take the N55 Longford Road.
After 3 miles take the left-hand fork at the
Dog & Duck. The hotel is 1 mile further on,
on the left-hand side.*

IRELAND

" *I for a short time had the privilege of residing in its magic* "

Margaret Johnson, Travel Writer, USA

● Map p.478
ref: C7

Luxury hotel — WOODSTOCK HOTEL

**Shanaway Road, Ennis,
Co Clare,
Republic of Ireland**
**Telephone +353 (0)65 684 6600
Fax +353 (0)65 684 6611**
E-mail: *woodstock@bestloved.com*

DIRECTOR
David Butt

RESIDENT MANAGER
Edward Farrell

ROOM RATES (EUROS)
Single occupancy   from € 200
38 Doubles/Twins   from € 200
29 Junior suites   from € 260
Includes service, full breakfast and VAT

CHARGE/CREDIT CARDS

 ● DC ● JCB ● MC ● VI

RATINGS & AWARDS
I.T.B. ★★★★ Hotel
R.A.C. ★★★★ Dining Award 1
A.A. ★★★★ 68%

FACILITIES
On site: *Garden, gym, heli-pad, golf,
indoor pool, health & beauty
4 meeting rooms/max 200 people*
Nearby: *Riding, hunting, fishing,
tennis, cycling, watersports*

RESTRICTIONS
*No pets, guide dogs only
Closed 24 - 26 Dec*

ATTRACTIONS
*Cliffs of Moher, Bunratty Castle, The Burren,
Ailwee Caves, Traditional music and dance*

AFFILIATIONS
*The Celebrated Hotels Collection
Small Luxury Hotels
Manor House Hotels of Ireland*

NEAREST
MAJOR CITY:
Limerick - 22miles/40 mins

MAJOR AIRPORT:
Shannon - 18 miles/30 mins

RAILWAY STATION:
Ennis - 2 miles/5 mins

FERRY PORT:
Cork - 85 miles/2 hrs

RESERVATIONS
*Toll free in US:800-322-2403 or 800-525-4800
Toll free in UK: 00800 525 48000*
*Quote **Best Loved***

ACCESS CODES
*AMADEUS LX SNNWOO
APOLLO/GALILEO LX 28974
SABRE/ABACUS LX 54323
WORLDSPAN LX SNNWO*

Unadulterated luxury and superb golfing in Clare

The Woodstock is one of the most exciting Irish hotel developments of recent years. Opened in the spring of 2000, it is a luxurious country cousin of the highly acclaimed Hibernian Hotel in Dublin (page 416), and the McCausland Hotel in Belfast (page 428), two of Ireland's top addresses for discerning visitors.

For a start, the Woodstock's setting is glorious. Just off the West Coast tourist trail between Limerick and Galway, it revels in 155 acres of rolling green countryside and a championship standard golf course generously supplied with handsome vistas. The hotel's architecture is dynamic to say the least - an harmonious blend of modern and classical that is both striking and stylish. From the first view of the soaring reception area with its marble floors, stained glass windows and fabulous outsize chandelier, the Woodstock continues to impress. Charming bedrooms, delicious contemporary Irish cuisine, a well-equipped leisure club featuring swimming pool, sauna, and gym, and superb service are all an integral part of the Woodstock experience.

Difficult though it may be to tear yourself away from Woodstock's sybaritic charms, golfers will find another eight courses within a 45-minute drive, including Doonbeg Golf Course, the notable links course at Lahinch. There is also fishing and riding close by as well as good walking in the Burren. The many sightseeing attractions include the Cliffs of Moher and Bunratty Castle.

LOCATION

*From Ennis, take the Lahinch Road (N85),
turning left at the One Mile Inn. The hotel
is ½ mile on the left.*

IRELAND

AMBERLEY CASTLE

COTSWOLD HOUSE HOTEL

ELEVEN DIDSBURY PARK

HOLNE CHASE HOTEL

INVERLOCHY CASTLE

THE MALT HOUSE

● = Children Welcome. Please telephone hotels directly for any applicable restrictions

PIER AT HARWICH

ROWHILL GRANGE

WIDBROOK GRANGE

County/ Hotel	Price range	Grid ref	Page
SCOTLAND			
ARGYLL			
Ardanaiseig	●	D9	18
Bridge of Orchy	●	E8	24
Cairnbaan Hotel	●	D9	26
Enmore Hotel	●	D10	41
Isle of Eriska	●	D8	58
Kirkton House	●	E10	63
Loch Melfort	●	D9	70
Royal Hotel	●	D10	83
Stonefield Castle	●	D10	85
Taychreggan	●	D9	87
AYRSHIRE			
Culzean Castle	●	E11	35
Enterkine House	●	E11	42
Glenapp Castle	●	D12	46
Ladyburn	●	E11	68
Piersland House Hotel	●	E10	77
BANFFSHIRE			
Craigellachie Hotel	●	G6	31
DUMFRIES & GALLOWAY			
Cavens Country House	●	F12	27
Dryfesdale Country House	●	F11	37
Knockinaam Lodge	●	D12	66
DUNBARTONSHIRE			
Inverbeg Inn	●	E10	56
EAST LOTHIAN			
Green Craigs	●	G9	48
Greywalls	●	G9	49
EDINBURGH			
Bonham	●	G10	23
Channings	●	G10	28
Dalhousie Castle & Spa	●	G10	36
Howard	●	G10	50
Knight Residence	●	G10	65
Melvin House Hotel	●	G10	71
Prestonfield House	●	G10	80
FIFE			
Balbirnie House Hotel	●	G9	19
Fernie Castle	●	G9	43
Inn At Lathones	●	G9	53
Old Manor Hotel	●	G9	73
Peat Inn	●	G9	76
Woodside Hotel	●	G9	90
GLASGOW			
Inn on the Green	●	E10	54
One Devonshire Gardens	●	E10	74
HIGHLAND			
Boat Hotel	●	F7	22
Kinloch Lodge	●	D7	61
INVERNESS-SHIRE			
Bunchrew House Hotel	●	E6	25
Corriegour Lodge	●	E7	29
Culloden House	●	F6	34
Dunain Park Hotel	●	E6	38
Glenmoriston Arms Hotel	●	E7	47
Inn at Ardgour	●	D8	52
Inverlochy Castle	●	D7	57
ISLE OF SKYE			
Flodigarry	●	C5	44
Hotel Eilean Iarmain	●	C7	40
KINCARDINESHIRE			
Banchory Lodge	●	H7	21
MORAY			
Archiestown Hotel	●	G6	17
Culdearn House	●	F6	33
Knockomie Hotel	●	F6	67
PERTHSHIRE			
Ballathie House Hotel	●	F8	20
Cromlix House	●	F9	32
Dunalastair Hotel	●	E8	39
Four Seasons Hotel	●	E9	45
Huntingtower Hotel	●	F8	51
Kinfauns Castle	●	F9	59
Kinloch House Hotel	●	F8	60
Kinnaird	●	F8	62
Lake of Menteith Hotel	●	E9	69
Roman Camp Country House	●	E9	81
ROSS-SHIRE			
Coul House Hotel	●	E6	30
Summer Isles	●	D5	86
Tigh an Eilean	●	D6	88
ROXBURGHSHIRE			
Roxburghe Hotel	●	H11	82
STIRLINGSHIRE			
Monachyle Mhor	●	E9	72
Park Lodge Hotel	●	F9	75
SUTHERLAND			
Inver Lodge Hotel	●	D4	55
Royal Marine Hotel	●	F5	84
Tongue Hotel	●	E4	89
WESTER ROSS			
Plockton Hotel	●	D6	78
Pool House Hotel	●	D5	79
WIGTOWNSHIRE			
Kirroughtree House	●	E12	64

● *Double room: up to £95 per night* ● *Double room: £96 - £145 per night* ● *Double room: £146 - £195 per night* ● *Double room: £196+ per night*

Regional Index

● *Double room: up to £95 per night* ● *Double room: £96 - £145 per night* ● *Double room: £146 - £195 per night* ● *Double room: £196+ per night*

MIDSHIRES

WEST COUNTRY

County/ Hotel	Price range	Grid ref	Page
DEVON			
Arundell Arms	●	D4	250
Browns Hotel	●	D4	255
Buckland-Tout-Saints	●	D5	256
Court Barn	●	C4	261
Gabriel Court Hotel	●	D5	266
Gidleigh Park	●	D4	268
Glazebrook House Hotel	●	D4	269
Heddon's Gate Hotel	●	D3	271
Holne Chase Hotel	●	D4	273
Horn of Plenty	●	D4	274
Hotel Riviera	●	E4	288
Lewtrenchard Manor	●	D4	279
Mill End Hotel	●	D4	281
Orestone Manor	●	E4	283
Osborne Hotel	●	E4	284
Percy's	●	D4	285
Prince Hall Hotel	●	D4	286
St Olaves Hotel	●	E4	290
Tides Reach Hotel	●	D5	293
Yeoldon House Hotel	●	D3	298
SOMERSET			
Bath Lodge Hotel	●	F3	251
Bath Priory Hotel	●	F2	252
Bindon Country House Hotel	●	E3	253
Castle at Taunton	●	E3	258
Combe Grove Manor Hotel	●	F2	259
County Hotel	●	F2	260
Crown Hotel	●	E3	262
Dukes Hotel	●	F2	263
Farthings Hotel	●	E3	264
Haydon House	●	F2	270
Holly Lodge	●	F2	272
Hunstrete House	●	F2	276
Langley House Hotel	●	E3	278
Mount Somerset	●	E3	282
Queensberry Hotel	●	F2	287
Ston Easton Park	●	F3	291
Windsor	●	F2	296
Woodlands Country House Hotel	●	E3	297
WILTSHIRE			
Widbrook Grange	●	G2	295

SOUTH

County/ Hotel	Price range	Grid ref	Page
BERKSHIRE			
Donnington Valley Hotel	●	D3	313
French Horn Hotel	●	D3	317
Taplow House	●	E3	346
Vineyard At Stockcross	●	D3	351

County/ Hotel	Price range	Grid ref	Page
BUCKINGHAMSHIRE			
Hartwell House	●	D2	319
Villiers Hotel	●	D2	350
DORSET			
Beechleas Hotel	●	C4	309
Mansion House Hotel	●	C4	329
Plumber Manor	●	C4	336
Priory Hotel	●	C4	338
Salterns Hotel	●	C4	342
Summer Lodge	●	B4	345
EAST SUSSEX			
Flackley Ash Hotel	●	F4	316
Horsted Place	●	F4	321
Hotel du Vin & Bistro	●	E4	322
Powder Mills Hotel	●	F4	337
Rye Lodge	●	F4	341
ESSEX			
Maison Talbooth	●	F2	328
Pier at Harwich	●	G2	335
HAMPSHIRE			
Careys Manor Hotel	●	D4	311
Esseborne Manor	●	D3	315
Hotel du Vin & Bistro	●	D4	324
Montagu Arms Hotel	●	D4	330
New Park Manor	●	D4	331
Passford House Hotel	●	D4	333
Thatched Cottage Hotel	●	D4	348
Three Lions	●	C4	349
HERTFORDSHIRE			
St Michael's Manor	●	E2	344
KENT			
Eastwell Manor	●	F3	314
Hotel Du Vin & Bistro	●	F4	323
Rowhill Grange Hotel	●	F3	340
Thanington Hotel	●	G3	347
Wallett's Court	●	G3	352
SUFFOLK			
Hintlesham Hall	●	G2	320
SURREY			
Chalk Lane Hotel	●	E3	312
Great Fosters	●	E3	318
Langshott Manor	●	E3	327
WEST SUSSEX			
Alexander House Hotel	●	E4	304
Amberley Castle	●	E4	305
Angel Hotel	●	E4	306
Bailiffscourt Hotel	●	E4	308
Ockenden Manor	●	E4	332
Spread Eagle Hotel	●	E4	343
WILTSHIRE			
At The Sign Of The Angel	●	C3	307
Bishopstrow House	●	C3	310
Howard's House	●	C4	325
Ivy House	●	C3	326
Pear Tree at Purton	●	C3	334
Red Lion Hotel	●	C4	339

● *Double room: up to £95 per night*   ● *Double room: £96 - £145 per night*   ● *Double room: £146 - £195 per night*   ● *Double room: £196+ per night*

County/Hotel	Price range	Grid ref	Page

LONDON

County/Hotel	Price range	Grid ref	Page
10 Manchester Street	●	F3	358
Academy Town House	●	H3	359
Ascott Mayfair	●	F5	360
Basil Street Hotel	●	E6	361
Beaufort	●	E6	362
Beaufort House Apartments	●	E6	363
Blakes Hotel	●	D7	364
Capital	●	E6	365
Chesterfield Mayfair	●	G5	366
Colonnade Town House	●	A2	367
Cranley on Bina Gardens	●	C7	368
Darlington Hyde Park	●	D4	369
Dolphin Square Hotel	●	H8	370
Flemings Mayfair	●	G5	371
Goring	●	G6	372
Grim's Dyke Hotel	●	I6	373
Kensington House	●	C6	374
Knightsbridge Green Hotel	●	E6	375
Le Meridien Grosvenor House	●	F5	376
Leonard	●	F4	377
Montague On The Gardens	●	I3	378
Montcalm Hotel	●	E4	379
Rubens At The Palace	●	G6	380
Somerset Roland Gardens	●	C7	381

IRELAND

County/Hotel	Price range	Grid ref	Page
CO ANTRIM			
Bushmills Inn	●	G3	398
BELFAST			
McCausland Hotel	●	G4	428
CO CLARE			
Dromoland Castle	●	C8	404
Gregans Castle	●	C7	412
Halpin's Hotel	●	B8	413
Moy House	●	C7	431
Waterman's Lodge	●	D8	445
Woodstock Hotel	●	C7	447
CO CORK			
Ahernes	●	E9	389
Ashlee Lodge	●	D9	392
Bayview Hotel	●	D10	394
Blairs Cove House	●	B10	395
CastleHyde Hotel	●	D9	402
Hayfield Manor	●	D10	414
Lodge & Spa	●	C10	424
Perryville House	●	D10	434

County/Hotel	Price range	Grid ref	Page
Sea View House Hotel	●	C10	441
CO DOWN			
Glassdrumman Lodge	●	H5	408
DUBLIN			
Aberdeen Lodge	●	G7	387
Blakes Townhouse	●	G7	396
Brownes Townhouse	●	G7	397
Butlers Town House	●	G7	399
Herbert Park Hotel	●	G7	415
Hibernian Hotel	●	G7	416
Longfield's	●	G7	425
Merrion Hotel	●	G7	429
CO DUBLIN			
King Sitric	●	G7	422
Morrison Hotel	●	G7	430
Portmarnock Hotel and Golf Links	●	G7	435
CO GALWAY			
Glenlo Abbey Hotel	●	C6	409
Lough Inagh Lodge Hotel	●	C6	426
Renvyle House Hotel	●	B6	437
Rosleague Manor	●	B6	438
Ross Lake House Hotel	●	C6	439
CO KERRY			
Aghadoe Heights Hotel	●	B9	388
Ard na Sidhe	●	B9	390
Ballygarry House	●	B9	393
Caragh Lodge	●	B9	400
Dunloe Castle	●	B9	406
Emlagh House	●	B9	407
Gormans Clifftop	●	A9	411
Killarney Park	●	C9	419
Killarney Royal Hotel	●	B9	420
Park Hotel Kenmare	●	B9	433
Sallyport House	●	B9	440
Sheen Falls Lodge	●	B10	442
CO KILDARE			
Killashee House Hotel	●	F7	421
CO KILKENNY			
Kilkenny Hibernian Hotel	●	F8	418
CO LAOIS			
Castle Durrow	●	E8	401
CO LIMERICK			
Glin Castle	●	C8	410
Mustard Seed At Echo Lodge	●	C8	432
CO MAYO			
Ashford Castle	●	C6	391
Knockranny House Hotel	●	C5	423
CO SLIGO			
Coopershill	●	D5	403
Markree Castle	●	D5	427
CO WATERFORD			
Waterford Castle Hotel	●	F9	444
CO WESTMEATH			
Wineport Lodge	●	E6	446
CO WEXFORD			
Dunbrody Country House	●	F9	405
CO WICKLOW			
Hunter's Hotel	●	G7	417
Rathsallagh House	●	F7	436
Tinakilly House	●	G7	443

● *Double room: up to £95 per night*   ● *Double room: £96 - £145 per night*   ● *Double room: £146 - £195 per night*   ● *Double room: £196+ per night*

Hotel Facilities

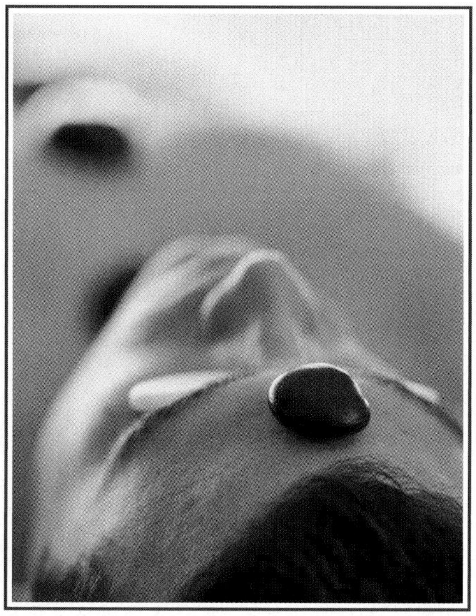

Budock Vean - The Hotel on the River 257
Combe Grove Manor 259
Osborne Hotel & Langtry Restaurant 284
Tides Reach Hotel 293

SOUTH

Bishopstrow House 310
Careys Manor Hotel 311
Eastwell Manor 314
Flackley Ash Hotel 316
Hartwell House 319
Hintlesham Hall 320
Rowhill Grange Hotel & Spa 340
Rye Lodge 341
Spread Eagle Hotel & Spa 343
Vineyard At Stockcross 351
Wallett's Court 352

LONDON

Dolphin Square Hotel 370
Le Meridien Grosvenor House 376
Montague On The Gardens 378

IRELAND

Aberdeen Lodge 387
Aghadoe Heights Hotel 388
Ashford Castle 391
Dromoland Castle 404
Mayfield Manor 414
Killarney Park 419
Killashee House Hotel 421
Lodge & Spa at Inchydoney Island 424
Merrion Hotel 429
Mustard Seed At Echo Lodge 432
Park Hotel Kenmare 433
Portmarnock Hotel and Golf Links 435
Sheen Falls Lodge 442
Tinakilly House 443
Woodstock Hotel 447

TENNIS

Definition: *Hotels reporting that they have either indoor/outdoor or all weather tennis courts on their premises.*

HOTEL **PAGE**

SCOTLAND

Ardanaiseig 18
Craigellachie 31
Cromlix House 32
Culloden House 34
Glenapp Castle 46
Greywalls 49
Inverlochy Castle 57
Isle of Eriska 58
Kinnaird 62
Kirroughtree House 64
Roxburghe Hotel 82

NORTH

Armathwaite Hall Hotel 96
Chevin Country Park Hotel 101
Crewe Hall 102
Devonshire 105
Feversham Arms 108
Graythwaite Manor Hotel 113
Holbeck Ghyll Hotel & Spa 115

WALES

Bodysgallen Hall 152
Lake Country House 161
Lake Vyrnwy Hotel 162
Lamphey Court Hotel 163
Llangoed Hall 164
Warpool Court Hotel 174

MIDSHIRES

Brockencote Hall 183
Calcot Manor 187
Charingworth Manor 189
Congham Hall 193
Corse Lawn House Hotel 194
Fawsley Hall 204
Heythrop Park 208
Norfolk Mead Hotel 221
Stapleford Park 235
Swynford Paddocks 238
Welcombe Hotel 241

WEST COUNTRY

Bindon Country House Hotel 253
Budock Vean 257
Combe Grove Manor 259
Court Barn 261
Gabriel Court Hotel 266
Gidleigh Park 268
Hunstrete House 276
Osborne Hotel 284
St Martin's On The Isle 289
Ston Easton Park 291
Well House 294
Widbrook Grange 295

SOUTH

Alexander House Hotel 304
Amberley Castle 305
Bailiffscourt Hotel 308
Bishopstrow House 310
Eastwell Manor 314
Esseborne Manor 315
Great Fosters 318
Hartwell House 319
Hintlesham Hall 320
Horsted Place 321
New Park Manor 331
Passford House Hotel 333
Plumber Manor 336
Summer Lodge 345
Wallett's Court 352

LONDON

Dolphin Square Hotel 370

IRELAND

Aghadoe Heights Hotel 388
Ashford Castle 391
Caragh Lodge 400
Coopershill 403
Dunloe Castle 406
Glin Castle 410
Park Hotel Kenmare 433
Rathsallagh House 436
Renvyle House Hotel 437
Rosleague Manor 438
Ross Lake House Hotel 439
Sheen Falls Lodge 442
Tinakilly House 443
Waterford Castle Hotel 444

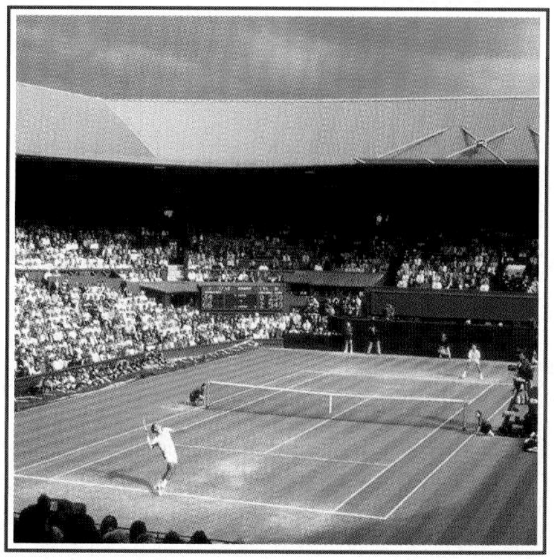

Hotel Facilities

FISHING

Definition: *Hotels reporting fishing on, or adjacent to, their premises.*

RIDING

Definition: *Hotels who report that they have horseback riding available on site.*

Meeting Facilities

MOST BEST LOVED HOTELS *have facilities for meetings, conferences, receptions and weddings, some small and comfortable, some large and sophisticated. Take your choice from this list, get full details from the page on which your choice appears and telephone to find out more.*

Definition: *Hotels reporting the maximum number of individuals they could accommodate for a cocktail reception and the number of meeting and reception rooms they maintain.*

CAPACITY: UP TO 25 PEOPLE

HOTEL	MEETING ROOMS	PAGE
SCOTLAND		
Archiestown Hotel	1	17
Enterkine House	1	42
Glenmoriston Arms Hotel	1	47
Howard	2	50
Kinloch Lodge	1	61
Kinnaird	3	62
Knight Residence	0	65
Ladyburn	1	68
Monachyle Mhor	1	72
Peat Inn	1	76
Pool House Hotel	1	79
NORTH		
Broadoaks Country House	1	99
Crosby Lodge	2	103
Lakeshore House	3	117
Quebecs Town House	3	129
Samling	1	131
Swinside Lodge Hotel	1	135
Waren House Hotel	1	138
Woolton Redbourne Hotel	1	143
WALES		
Crown at Whitebrook	2	154
Groes Inn	1	160
Hotel Maes-y-Neuadd	1	165
Penally Abbey	1	169
MIDSHIRES		
Broadway Hotel	2	182
Brookhouse	1	184
Cottage in the Wood	1	197
Dannah Farm	1	199
Dial House Hotel	1	200
Hotel des Clos	1	210
Hotel on the Park	1	213
Lords of the Manor	1	217
Malt House	1	218
New Inn At Coln	1	220
Raven Hotel & Restaurant	1	229
WEST COUNTRY		
County Hotel	1	260
Court Barn	2	261
Crown Hotel	1	262
Gabriel Court Hotel	1	266
Gidleigh Park	1	268
Holne Chase Hotel	1	273
Percy's	1	285
Prince Hall Hotel	1	286
Windsor	1	296
SOUTH		
At The Sign Of The Angel	2	307
French Horn Hotel	1	317
Plumber Manor	1	336
Priory Hotel	1	338
Summer Lodge	1	345
LONDON		
Beaufort	1	362
IRELAND		
Butlers Town House	1	399
Caragh Lodge	1	400
Glin Castle	1	410
Kilkenny Hibernian Hotel	2	418
Longfield's	1	425
Lough Inagh Lodge Hotel	1	426
Sea View House Hotel	1	441

CAPACITY: 26 TO 50 PEOPLE

HOTEL	MEETING ROOMS	PAGE
SCOTLAND		
Ardanaiseig	1	18
Cavens Country House Hotel	1	27
Channings	2	28
Craigellachie	3	31
Enmore Hotel	2	41
Flodigarry	1	44
Glenapp Castle	3	46
Greywalls	1	49
Hotel Eilean Iarmain	1	40
Inver Lodge Hotel	1	55
Inverlochy Castle	1	57
Isle of Eriska	3	58
Kinloch House Hotel	1	60
Kirroughtree House	1	64
Knockinaam Lodge	1	66
Lake of Menteith Hotel	2	69
Loch Melfort	1	70
One Devonshire Gardens	3	74
Royal Hotel	1	83
Taychreggan	2	87
Tongue Hotel	1	89
NORTH		
Blue Lion	2	97
Broxton Hall	1	100
Eleven Didsbury Park	1	107
Feversham Arms	1	108
General Tarleton Inn	1	109
Graythwaite Manor Hotel	2	113
Hipping Hall	1	114
Lovelady Shield	2	119
Manor House	1	120
Miller Howe Hotel	2	124
Rothay Manor	1	130
Studley Hotel	1	133
White House Manor	4	140
White Swan	1	141
Yorke Arms	2	145
WALES		
Egerton Grey Hotel	1	155
Empire	1	156
Fairyhill	1	157
George III Hotel	1	159
Pale Hall Country House	2	168
Penmaenuchaf Hall	2	170
Tyddyn Llan Country House	2	173
MIDSHIRES		
Brockencote Hall	2	183
Crown at Blockley	1	198
Feathers	2	205
Greenway	2	207
Hoste Arms	3	209
Langar Hall	2	215
Le Manoir Aux Quat' Saisons	1	216
Manor House	2	219
Old Vicarage	3	225
Owlpen Manor	2	226
Plough At Clanfield	2	228
Riverside House Hotel	1	231
Swan Hotel At Bibury	3	237
Three Choirs Vineyards	1	240
WEST COUNTRY		
Dukes Hotel	2	263
Farthings	2	264

HOTEL	MEETING ROOMS	PAGE
Garrack Hotel	1	267
Horn of Plenty	1	274
Langley House Hotel	1	278
Mill End Hotel	3	281
Queensberry Hotel	1	287
Widbrook Grange	3	295
SOUTH		
Amberley Castle	2	305
Beechleas	1	309
Esseborne Manor	2	315
Hotel du Vin & Bistro	2	322
Hotel du Vin & Bistro	2	324
Howard's House	1	325
Mansion House Hotel	3	329
Montagu Arms Hotel	3	330
Thatched Cottage Hotel	1	348
Three Lions	1	349
LONDON		
Ascott Mayfair	2	360
Capital	2	365
Leonard	1	377
Academy Town House	1	359
IRELAND		
Aberdeen Lodge	2	387
Ahernes	1	389
Bayview Hotel	2	394
Blakes Townhouse	1	396
Brownes Townhouse	1	397
Bushmills Inn	3	398
CastleHyde Hotel	1	402
Halpin's Hotel	1	413
Hibernian Hotel	1	416
Hunter's Hotel	1	417
Killarney Royal Hotel	1	420
Morrison Hotel	2	430
Mustard Seed At Echo Lodge	1	432
Park Hotel Kenmare	2	435

CAPACITY: 51 TO 75 PEOPLE

HOTEL	MEETING ROOMS	PAGE
SCOTLAND		
Ardanaiseig	1	18
Cavens Country House Hotel	1	27
Channings	2	28
Craigellachie	3	31
Enmore Hotel	2	41
Flodigarry	1	44
Glenapp Castle	3	46
Greywalls	1	49
Hotel Eilean Iarmain	1	40
Inver Lodge Hotel	1	55
Inverlochy Castle	1	57
Isle of Eriska	3	58
Kinloch House Hotel	1	60
Kirroughtree House	1	64
Knockinaam Lodge	1	66
Lake of Menteith Hotel	2	69
Loch Melfort	1	70
One Devonshire Gardens	3	74
Royal Hotel	1	83
Taychreggan	2	87
Tongue Hotel	1	89
NORTH		
Blue Lion	2	97
Broxton Hall	1	100
Eleven Didsbury Park	1	107
Feversham Arms	1	108

Hotel	Meeting Rooms	Page
General Tarleton Inn	1	109
Graythwaite Manor Hotel	2	113
Hipping Hall	1	114
Lovelady Shield	2	119
Manor House	1	120
Miller Howe Hotel	2	124
Rothay Manor	1	130
Studley Hotel	1	133
White House Manor	4	140
White Swan	1	141
Yorke Arms	2	145
WALES		
Egerton Grey Hotel	1	155
Empire	1	156
Fairyhill	1	157
George III Hotel	1	159
Pale Hall Country House	2	168
Penmaenuchaf Hall	2	170
Tyddyn Llan Country House	2	173
MIDSHIRES		
Brockencote Hall	2	183
Crown at Blockley	1	198
Feathers	2	205
Greenway	2	207
Hoste Arms	3	209
Langar Hall	2	215
Le Manoir Aux Quat' Saisons	1	216
Manor House	2	219
Old Vicarage	3	225
Owlpen Manor	2	226
Plough At Clanfield	2	228
Riverside House Hotel	1	231
Swan Hotel At Bibury	3	237
Three Choirs Vineyards	1	240
WEST COUNTRY		
Dukes Hotel	2	263
Farthings	2	264
Garrack Hotel	1	267
Horn of Plenty	1	274
Langley House Hotel	1	278
Mill End Hotel	3	281
Queensberry Hotel	1	287
Widbrook Grange	3	295
SOUTH		
Amberley Castle	2	305
Beechleas	1	309
Esseborne Manor	2	315
Hotel du Vin & Bistro	2	322
Hotel du Vin & Bistro	2	324
Howard's House	1	325
Mansion House Hotel	3	329
Montagu Arms Hotel	3	330
Thatched Cottage Hotel	1	348
Three Lions	1	349
LONDON		
Ascott Mayfair	2	360
Capital	2	365
Leonard	1	377
Academy Town House	1	359
IRELAND		
Aberdeen Lodge	2	387
Cahernes	1	389
Bayview Hotel	2	394
Lakes Townhouse	1	396
Crownes Townhouse	1	397
Bushmills Inn	3	398
CastleHyde Hotel	1	402
Halpin's Hotel	1	413
Hibernian Hotel	1	416
Hunter's Hotel	1	417
Killarney Royal Hotel	1	420
Morrison Hotel	2	430
Mustard Seed At Echo Lodge	1	432
Park Hotel Kenmare	2	433

CAPACITY: 76 TO 100 PEOPLE

Hotel	Meeting Rooms	Page
SCOTLAND		
Ballathie House Hotel	5	20
...nham	1	23
Bridge of Orchy	2	24
Cromlix House	3	32

Hotel	Meeting Rooms	Page
Dunalastair Hotel	3	39
Inn At Lathones	1	53
Inverbeg Inn	2	56
Kinfauns Castle	3	59
Knockomie Hotel	2	67
Melvin House Hotel	4	71
Plockton Hotel	0	78
Roxburghe Hotel	3	82
NORTH		
Holbeck Ghyll Hotel & Spa	2	115
Linthwaite House	3	118
Middlethorpe Hall	2	123
WALES		
Bodysgallen Hall	2	152
Llangoed Hall	3	164
MIDSHIRES		
Arrow Mill Hotel	2	180
Bignell Park Hotel	2	181
Broom Hall Country Hotel	1	185
Charingworth Manor	3	189
Cockliffe Country House	1	191
Corse Lawn House Hotel	2	194
Cottage Country House Hotel	4	196
Dinham Hall	1	201
Lace Market Hotel	3	214
Royalist Hotel	1	232
Shaven Crown	1	233
Westwood Country Hotel	4	242
WEST COUNTRY		
Bath Priory Hotel	3	252
Mount Somerset	3	282
Osborne Hotel	1	284
St Martin's On The Isle	3	289
Well House	1	294
Woodlands Country	2	297
SOUTH		
Alexander House Hotel	4	304
Pear Tree at Purton	4	334
LONDON		
Flemings Mayfair	3	371
IRELAND		
Glassdrumman Lodge	1	408
Gregans Castle	1	412
Waterman's Lodge	1	445

CAPACITY: 101 TO 150 PEOPLE

Hotel	Meeting Rooms	Page
SCOTLAND		
Banchory Lodge	2	21
Cairnbaan Hotel	2	26
Dalhousie Castle & Spa	5	36
Dryfesdale Country House Hotel	3	37
Four Seasons Hotel	3	45
Woodside Hotel	2	90
NORTH		
Devonshire	4	105
Mere Court Hotel	10	122
Seaham Hall Hotel	4	132
Swan Hotel	3	134
Swinton Park	7	136
Westmorland Hotel	6	139
Wordsworth Hotel	3	144
WALES		
Bae Abermaw	1	151
Bontddu Hall Hotel	2	153
Lake Country House	1	161
Lake Vyrnwy Hotel	3	162
Peterstone Court	3	171
MIDSHIRES		
Colwall Park Hotel	4	192
Fawsley Hall	7	204
Risley Hall	4	230
Swynford Paddocks	1	238
Welcombe Hotel	7	241
WEST COUNTRY		
Brigstow Hotel	4	254
Budock Vean	2	257
Castle at Taunton	4	258
Combe Grove Manor Hotel	4	259
Glazebrook House Hotel	2	269
Hotel Riviera	1	288

Hotel	Meeting Rooms	Page
Ston Easton Park	8	291
SOUTH		
Bishopstrow House	3	310
Chalk Lane Hotel	3	312
Donnington Valley Hotel	9	313
Hintlesham Hall	4	320
Maison Talbooth	1	328
New Park Manor	5	331
Red Lion Hotel	5	339
Salterns Hotel	3	342
Spread Eagle Hotel & Spa	5	343
Taplow House	7	346
Vineyard At Stockcross	3	351
LONDON		
Chesterfield Mayfair	6	366
Montague On The Gardens	5	378
Montcalm Hotel	3	379
Rubens At The Palace	6	380
IRELAND		
Aghadoe Heights Hotel	3	388
Ashford Castle	1	391
Herbert Park Hotel	5	415
Rathsallagh House	3	436
Ross Lake House Hotel	1	439
Sheen Falls Lodge	3	442
Wineport Lodge	2	446

CAPACITY: OVER 150 PEOPLE

Hotel	Meeting Rooms	Page
SCOTLAND		
Balbirnie House Hotel	8	19
Fernie Castle	3	43
Green Craigs	1	48
Huntingtower Hotel	6	51
Old Manor Hotel	3	73
Park Lodge Hotel	3	75
Piersland House Hotel	3	77
Prestonfield House	6	80
Stonefield Castle Hotel	4	85
NORTH		
Chevin Country Park Hotel	5	101
Crewe Hall	17	102
Judges Country House Hotel	7	116
Matfen Hall	7	121
Willington Hall	4	142
WALES		
Warpool Court Hotel	2	174
MIDSHIRES		
Dormy House	5	203
Grafton Manor	2	206
Heythrop Park	60	208
Nuthurst Grange	3	222
Stapleford Park	8	235
WEST COUNTRY		
Alverton Manor	5	249
Buckland-Tout-Saints	2	256
SOUTH		
Careys Manor Hotel	9	311
Eastwell Manor	3	314
Great Fosters	5	318
Powder Mills Hotel	3	337
Rowhill Grange Hotel & Spa	7	340
Villiers Hotel	6	350
LONDON		
Basil Street Hotel	3	361
Dolphin Square Hotel	3	370
Le Meridien Grosvenor House	19	376
IRELAND		
Ballygarry House	1	393
Castle Durrow Country House	3	401
Dromoland Castle	6	404
Dunbrody Country House	3	405
Dunloe Castle	6	406
Glenlo Abbey Hotel	9	409
Killarney Park	3	419
Killashee House Hotel	20	421
Knockranny House Hotel	3	423
Lodge & Spa - Inchydoney Island	4	424
Portmarnock Hotel	3	435
Renvyle House Hotel	3	437
Woodstock Hotel	4	447

On Site Golf Courses

Best Loved Hotels with a golf course on site

Ashford Castle	*391*
Balbirnie House Hotel	*19*
Budock Vean	*257*
Combe Grove Manor	*259*
Coul House Hotel	*30*
Donnington Valley Hotel	*313*
Dromoland Castle	*404*
Glenlo Abbey Hotel	*409*
Heythrop Park	*208*
Hintlesham Hall	*320*
Horsted Place	*321*
Isle of Eriska	*58*
Lake Country House	*161*
Matfen Hall	*121*
Park Hotel Kenmare	*433*
Portmarnock Hotel	*435*
Prestonfield House	*80*
Rathsallagh House	*436*
Renvyle House Hotel	*437*
Roxburghe Hotel	*82*
Springs Hotel	*234*
Stapleford Park	*235*
Ston Easton Park	*291*
Swinton Park	*136*
Waterford Castle Hotel	*444*
Welcombe Hotel	*241*
Woodstock Hotel	*447*

HOTEL	COURSE	MILES AWAY	PAGE

SCOTLAND

HOTEL	COURSE	MILES AWAY	PAGE
Archiestown Hotel	Rothes	5	17
Ardanaiseig	Taynuilt	10	18
Ballathie House Hotel	Blairgowrie	5	20
Banchory Lodge	Banchory	1	21
Boat Hotel	Boat of Garten	Adjacent	22
Bonham	Murrayfield	3	23
Bridge of Orchy	Loch Lomond	35	24
Bunchrew House Hotel	Inverness	4	25
Cairnbaan Hotel	Lochgilphead	4	26
Cavens Hotel	Southerness	1	27
Channings	Braid Hills	3	28
Corriegour Lodge	Fort Augustus	17	29
Coul House Hotel	Strathpeffer Spa	2	30
Craigellachie	Elgin	12	31
Cromlix House	Gleneagles	15	32
Culdearn House	Grantown-on-Spey	1	33
Culloden House	Nairn	18	34
Culzean Castle	Turnberry	4	35
Dalhousie Castle & Spa	Broomieknowe	1	36
Dryfesdale Country House	Lockmaben	2	37
Dunain Park Hotel	Inverness	2	38
Dunalastair Hotel	Taymouth Castle	18	39
Enmore Hotel	Cowal	1/4	41
Enterkine House	Royal Troon	4	42
Fernie Castle	Ladybank	2	43
Flodigarry Country House	Skeabost	20	44
Four Seasons Hotel	St Fillans	1/2	45
Glenapp Castle	Stranraer	18	46
Glenmoriston Arms Hotel	Fort Augustus	5	47

HOTEL	COURSE	MILES AWAY	PAGE
Green Craigs	Kilspindie	1	48
Greywalls	Muirfield	Adjacent	49
Hotel Eilean Iarmain	Sconcer	10	40
Howard	Murrayfield	5	50
Huntingtower Hotel	Craigie Hill	3	51
Inn at Ardgour	Fort William	13	52
Inn At Lathones	Crail	7	53
Inn on the Green	Dougalston	7	54
Inver Lodge Hotel	Ullapool	35	55
Inverbeg Inn	Helensburgh	10	56
Inverlochy Castle	Fort William	1/2	57
Isle of Eriska	Oban	10	58
Kinfauns Castle	King James VI	2	59
Kinloch House Hotel	Blairgowrie	4	60
Kinloch Lodge	Sconser	15	61
Kinnaird	Blairgowrie	5	62
Kirkton House	Cardross	1	63
Kirroughtree House	Newton Stewart	1	64
Knight Residence	Braid Hills	2	65
Knockinaam Lodge	Dunskey Portpatrick	3	66
Knockomie Hotel	Forres	2	67
Ladyburn	Brunston Castle	3	68
Lake of Menteith Hotel	Aberfoyle	2	69
Loch Melfort	Oban	20	70
Melvin House Hotel	Murrayfield	2	71
Monachyle Mhor	Callander	17	72
Old Manor Hotel	Lundin Links	1/4	73
One Devonshire Gardens	Dougalston	7	74
Park Lodge Hotel	Kings Park	Adjacent	75
Peat Inn	St Andrews	6	76
Piersland House Hotel	Royal Troon	Adjacent	77
Plockton Hotel	Loch Carron	20	78
Pool House Hotel	Gairloch	6	79
Roman Camp	Callander	1/3	81
Royal Hotel	Kyles of Bute	1	83
Royal Marine Hotel	Brora	Adjacent	84
Stonefield Castle Hotel	Tarbert	1 1/2	85
Summer Isles	Ullapool	25	86
Taychreggan	Taynuilt	7	87
Tigh an Eilean	Lochcarron	17	88
Tongue Hotel	Durness	30	89
Woodside Hotel	Aberdour	1/4	90

NORTH

HOTEL	COURSE	MILES AWAY	PAGE
Armathwaite Hall Hotel	Keswick	8	96
Blue Lion	Masham	5	97
Borrowdale Gates	Keswick	7	98
Broadoaks Country House	Windermere	2	99
Broxton Hall	Aldersley	2	100
Chevin Country Park Hotel	Otley	3	101
Crewe Hall	Western	2	102
Crosby Lodge	Eden	1/2	103
Dale Head Hall	Keswick	5	104
Devonshire	Ilkley	6	105
Devonshire Fell	Skipton	6	106
Eleven Didsbury Park	Didsbury	1/4	107
Feversham Arms	Kirbymoorside	6	108
General Tarleton Inn	Knaresborough	3	109
Gilpin Lodge Hotel	Windermere	1/2	110
Grange Hotel	Fulford	4	111
Grants Hotel	Oakdale	1/2	112
Graythwaite Manor Hotel	Grange	1	113
Hipping Hall	Kirkby Lonsdale	3	114
Holbeck Ghyll Hotel & Spa	Windermere	4	115
Judges at Kirklevington	Eaglescliffe	1	116
Lakeshore House	Windermere	3	117
Linthwaite House	Windermere	1	118
Lovelady Shield	Alston Moor	2	119
Manor House	Beverley	2	120
Mere Court Hotel	Mere	1/4	122
Middlethorpe Hall	Forest Park	5	123
Miller Howe Hotel	Windermere	2	124
Monk Fryston Hall	Scarthingwell	4	125

HOTEL	COURSE	MILES AWAY	PAGE
Northcote Manor	Wilpshire	10	126
Nunsmere Hall	Sandiway	2	127
Pheasant Hotel	Kirkbymoorside	4	128
Quebecs Town House	Leeds	2	129
Rothay Manor	Windermere	5	130
Samling	Windermere	1	131
Seaham Hall Hotel	Durham City	10	132
Studley Hotel	Oakdale	1	133
Swan Hotel	Windermere	3	134
Swinside Lodge Hotel	Keswick	5	135
Underscar Manor	Keswick	4	137
Waren House Hotel	Bamburgh Castle	2	138
Westmorland Hotel	Penrith	17	139
White House Manor	Prestbury	1	140
White Swan	Kirbymoorside	7	141
Willington Hall	Priors Hays	2	142
Woolton Redbourne Hotel	Woolton	1	143
Wordsworth Hotel	Windermere	12	144
Yorke Arms	Masham	10	145

WALES

HOTEL	COURSE	MILES AWAY	PAGE
Bae Abermaw	Royal St David's	15	151
Bodysgallen Hall	Conwy	3	152
Bontddu Hall Hotel	Royal St David's	15	153
Crown at Whitebrook	Rolls of Monmouth	6	154
Egerton Grey Hotel	Bryshill	2	155
Empire	North Wales	1	156
Fairyhill	Pennard	8	157
Felin Fach Griffin	Brecon	5	158
George III Hotel	Dolgellau	3	159
Groes Inn	Conwy	3	160
Hotel Maes-y-Neuadd	Royal St David's	3	165
Lake Country House	Builth Wells	6	161
Lake Vyrnwy Hotel	Llanymynech	20	162
Lamphey Court Hotel	Tenby	6	163
Llangoed Hall	Cradoc	11	164
Old Rectory	Conwy	3	166
Osborne House	North Wales	1	167
Pale Hall Country House	Bala Lake	4	168
Penally Abbey	Tenby	2	169
Penmaenuchaf Hall	Royal St David's	20	170
Peterstone Court	Cradoc	5	171
Tan-y-Foel Country House	Betws-y-Coed	2	172
Tyddyn Llan	Bala	8	173
Warpool Court Hotel	St David's City	3	174

MIDSHIRES

HOTEL	COURSE	MILES AWAY	PAGE
Arrow Mill Hotel	Stratford-upon-Avon	8	18
Bignell Park Hotel	Bicester	1	18
Broadway Hotel	Broadway	3	18
Brockencote Hall	Ombersley	12	18
Brookhouse	Craythorne	1/2	18
Broom Hall	Richmond Park	1/2	18
Burford House	Burford	1	18
Calcot Manor	Cotswold Edge	3	18
Castle House	Belmont	4	18
Charingworth Manor	Broadway	6	18
Close Hotel	Minchinhampton	4	19
Cockliffe Country House	Ramsdale	2	19
Colwall Park Hotel	Worcestershire	3 1/2	19
Congham Hall	Middleton	5	19
Corse Lawn House Hotel	Puckrup Hall	6	19
Cotswold House Hotel	Broadway	4	19
Cottage Country House	Ruddington Grange	1	19
Cottage in the Wood	Worcestershire	1	19
Crown at Blockley	Broadway	3	19
Dannah Farm	Chevin	3	19
Dial House Hotel	Naunton Downs	3	20
Dinham Hall	Ludlow	2	20
Dog and Partridge	Branston	10	20
Dormy House	Broadway	Adjacent	20
Fawsley Hall	Farthingstone	5	20

HOTEL	COURSE	MILES AWAY	PAGE
Feathers	Kirtlington	5	205
Grafton Manor	Bromsgrove	3	206
Greenway	Lilley Brook	3	207
Hoste Arms	Royal West Norfolk	5	209
Hotel des Clos	Cotgrave	10	210
Hotel du Vin & Bistro	Edgbaston	2	211
Hotel Felix	Cambridge	5	212
Hotel on the Park	Lilley Brook	3	213
Lace Market Hotel	Cotgrave	7	214
Langar Hall	Cotgrave Place	3	215
Le Manoir	Oxfordshire	6	216
Lords of the Manor	Naunton Downs	4	217
Malt House	Broadway	4	218
Manor House	Royal West Norfolk	17	219
New Inn At Coln	Cirencester	7	220
Norfolk Mead Hotel	Sprowston	7	221
Nuthurst Grange	Henley in Arden	2	222
Old Mill	Brailes	5	223
Old Parsonage	Studley Wood	8	224
Old Vicarage	Worfield	1 1/2	225
Owlpen Manor	Stinchcombe	3	226
Painswick Hotel	Painswick	1	227
Plough At Clanfield	Carswell	7	228
Raven Hotel	Shrewsbury	10	229
Risley Hall	Maywood	1	230
Riverside House Hotel	Bakewell	2	231
Royalist Hotel	Naunton Downs	6	232
Shaven Crown	Burford	5	233
Strattons	Swaffham	1/4	236
Swan Hotel At Bibury	Cirencester	7	237
Swynford Paddocks	Gog Magog	12	238
Thornbury Castle	Thornbury	1	239
Three Choirs Vineyards	Newent	1	240
Westwood Country Hotel	Frilford Heath	5	242
Wild Duck	Oaksey Park	3	243

WEST COUNTRY

HOTEL	COURSE	MILES AWAY	PAGE
Alverton Manor	Killiow	2	249
Arundell Arms	Okehampton	15	250
Bath Lodge Hotel	Orchardsleigh	5	251
Bath Priory Hotel	Cumberwell Park	5	252
Bindon Hotel	Oak Manor	3	253
Brigstow Hotel	Bath	12	254
Browns Hotel	Tavistock	1	255
Buckland-Tout-Saints	Dartmouth	8	256
Castle at Taunton	Taunton Vale		258
Combe Grove Manor	Bath	1	259
County Hotel	Sham Castle	1/2	260
Court Barn	Holsworthy	2 1/2	261
Crown Hotel	Minehead	14	262
Dukes Hotel	Sham Castle	2	263
Farthings Hotel	Taunton Vale	6	264
Fowey Hotel	Looe	10	265
Gabriel Court Hotel	Dainton Park	4	266
Garrack Hotel	West Cornwall	5	267
Gidleigh Park	Manor House	15	268
Glazebrook House Hotel	Wrangaton	1	269
Haydon House	Bath	2	270
Heddon 's Gate Hotel	Saunton	15	271
Holly Lodge	Bath	3	272
Holne Chase Hotel	Hele Park	8	273
Horn of Plenty	Tavistock	4	274
Hotel du Vin & Bistro	Bath	12	275
Hotel Riviera	Woodbury Park	6	288
Hunstrete House	Farrington	7	276
Idle Rocks Hotel	Truro	15	277
Langley House Hotel	Oak Manor	3	278
Lewtrenchard Manor	Hurdwick	6	279
Lugger Hotel	Truro	12	280
Mill End Hotel	The Manor House	8	281
Mount Somerset	Vivary Park	5	282
Orestone Manor	Torquay	1/2	283

HOTEL	COURSE	MILES AWAY	PAGE
Osborne Hotel	Dainton Park	6	284
Percy's	Holsworthy	3	285
Prince Hall Hotel	St Mellion	12	286
Queensberry Hotel	Bath	2	287
St Martin's On The Isle	Isle of Scilly	3 (by boat)	289
St Olaves Hotel	Exeter	4	290
Ston Easton Park	Farrington	Adjacent	291
Talland Bay Hotel	Looe Bindown	10	292
Tides Reach Hotel	Thurlestone	6	293
Well House	Looe	3	294
Widbrook Grange	Cumberwell	2	295
Windsor	Sham Castle	2	296
Woodlands Hotel	Burnham & Berrow	2	297
Yeoldon House Hotel	Royal North Devon	2	298

SOUTH

HOTEL	COURSE	MILES AWAY	PAGE
Alexander House Hotel	Chartham	4	304
Amberley Castle	West Sussex	5	305
Angel Hotel	Cowdray Park	1/2	306
At The Sign Of The Angel	Bowood	3	307
Bailiffscourt Hotel	Littlehampton	2	308
Beechleas	Canford Magna	2	309
Bishopstrow House	West Wiltshire	1	310
Careys Manor Hotel	Brockenhurst Manor	1	311
Chalk Lane Hotel	Epsom	2	312
Eastwell Manor	Ashford	2	314
Esseborne Manor	Hampshire	10	315
Flackley Ash Hotel	Lydd	14	316
French Horn Hotel	Sonning	1	317
Great Fosters	Wentworth	4	318
Hartwell House	Aylesbury Park	1	319
Horsted Place	East Sussex	1	321
Hotel du Vin & Bistro	Brighton & Hove	1/2	322
Hotel Du Vin & Bistro	Dale Hill	10	323
Hotel du Vin & Bistro	South Winchester	3	324
Howard's House	Rushmore	18	325
Ivy House	Marlborough	3/4	326
Langshott Manor	Lingfield	7	327
Maison Talbooth	Stoke by Nayland	10	328
Mansion House Hotel	Parkstone	4	329
Montagu Arms Hotel	Brockenhurst	5	330
New Park Manor	Brockenhurst Manor	3	331
Ockenden Manor	Paxhill Park	3	332
Passford House Hotel	Brockenhurst Manor	4	333
Pear Tree at Purton	Wiltshire	3	334
Pier at Harwich	Harwich Dovercourt	2	335
Plumber Manor	Sherborne	10	336
Powder Mills Hotel	Battle	3	337
Priory Hotel	Wareham	1/2	338
Red Lion Hotel	Salisbury	3	339
Rowhill Grange	Birchwood Park	5	340
Rye Lodge	Lydd Golf Club	6	341
Salterns Hotel	Parkstone	1/2	342
Spread Eagle Hotel & Spa	Cowdray Park	1	343
St Michael's Manor	Batchwood	1	344
Summer Lodge	Dorchester	12	345
Taplow House	Stoke Poges	2	346
Thanington Hotel	Canterbury	3	347
Thatched Cottage Hotel	Brockenhurst	1	348
Three Lions	Brook	10	349
Villiers Hotel	Buckingham	2	350
Vineyard At Stockcross	Donnington Valley	2 1/2	351
Wallett's Court	Royal St Georges	10	352

LONDON

HOTEL	COURSE	MILES AWAY	PAGE
10 Manchester Street	Hendon	10	358
Academy Town House	Old Thorns	46	359
Ascott Mayfair	Richmond	9	360
Basil Street Hotel	Richmond	6	361
Beaufort	Stoke Poges	20	362
Beaufort House Apts	Richmond	10	363
Blakes Hotel	Richmond	7	364

HOTEL	COURSE	MILES AWAY	PAGE
Capital	Liphook	45	365
Chesterfield Mayfair	Richmond	10	366
Colonnade Town House	Stoke Poges	20	367
Cranley on Bina Gardens	Richmond	10	368
Darlington Hyde Park	Stoke Park	25	369
Dolphin Square Hotel	Richmond	10	370
Flemings Mayfair	Bushey Hall	25	371
Goring	Royal Mid Surrey	5	372
Grim's Dyke Hotel	Grim's Dyke	Adjacent	373
Kensington House	Richmond	10	374
Knightsbridge Green Hotel	Richmond	8	375
Le Meridien Grosvenor	Stockley Park	15	376
Leonard	Wentworth	10	377
Montague On The Gdns	Richmond	10	378
Montcalm Hotel	Hendon	10	379
Rubens At The Palace	Richmond	6	380
Somerset Roland Gardens	Richmond	10	381

IRELAND

HOTEL	COURSE	MILES AWAY	PAGE
Aberdeen Lodge	Portmarnock	8	387
Aghadoe Heights Hotel	Killarney	2	388
Ahernes	Youghal	1	389
Ard na Sidhe	Beaufort	6	390
Ashlee Lodge	Moskerry	1/4	392
Ballygarry House	Tralee	7	393
Bayview Hotel	East Cork	12	394
Blairs Cove House	Bantry	7	395
Blakes Townhouse	Portmarnock	8	396
Brownes Townhouse	Elm Park	2	397
Bushmills Inn	Royal Portrush	4	398
Butlers Town House	Elm Park	1	399
Caragh Lodge	Dooks	4	400
Castle Durrow	Abbeyleix	6	401
CastleHyde Hotel	Fermoy	5	402
Coopershill	County Sligo	20	403
Dunbrody Country House	Waterford Castle	10	405
Dunloe Castle	Dunloe	1/4	406
Emlagh House	Dingle	10	407
Glassdrumman Lodge	Royal County Down	9	408
Glin Castle	Newcastle West	10	410
Gormans Clifftop	Dingle	6	411
Gregans Castle	Lahinch	16	412
Halpin's Hotel	Kilkee	1/4	413
Hayfield Manor	Fota Island	12	414
Herbert Park Hotel	Elm Park	1 1/2	415
Hibernian Hotel	Portmarnock	8	416
Hunter's Hotel	Wicklow	3	417
Kilkenny Hibernian Hotel	Kilkenny	1	418
Killarney Park	Killarney	2 1/2	419
Killarney Royal Hotel	Killarney	2	420
Killashee House Hotel	Craddockstown	3	421
King Sitric	Howth	2	422
Knockranny House Hotel	Westport	2	423
Lodge & Spa	Old Head of Kinsale	17	424
Longfield's	Elm Park	2	425
Lough Inagh Lodge Hotel	Connemara	20	426
Markree Castle	Strandhill	5	427
McCausland Hotel	Royal Belfast	5	428
Merrion Hotel	Portmarnock	8	429
Morrison Hotel	Royal Dublin	7	430
Moy House	Lahinch	1	431
Mustard Seed	Adare Manor	8	432
Perryville House	Old Head of Kinsale	5	434
Rosleague Manor	Connemara	14	438
Ross Lake House Hotel	Oughterard	2	439
Sallyport House	Kenmare	1/2	440
Sea View House Hotel	Bantry Park	1	441
Sheen Falls Lodge	Kenmare	1	442
Tinakilly House	Wicklow	2	443
Waterman's Lodge	East Clare	12	445
Wineport Lodge	Glasson	2	446

SCOTLAND

KEY TO HOTELS

The rosettes indicate the page number of the hotel. The colour of the rosette is a rough guide to the price of a twin or double room (see colour key below).

- Double room: up to £95 per night
- Double room: £96 - £145 per night
- Double room: £146 - £195 per night
- Double room: £196+ per night

Base map © MAPS IN MINUTES™ 2000
©Crown Copyright, Ordnance Survey 2000
Design and modification
© 2003 Best Loved Hotels of the World

ORKNEY ISLANDS

KIRKWALL
Balfour
Stromness
Hoy

John O'Groats
Castletown
Scrabster
Thurso
Melvich
Bettyhill
Tongue
Durness
Altnaharra
Ullapool
Lochinver
Achiltibuie
Ullapool
Gairloch
Poolewe
Port of Ness
Stornoway
Tarbert
Lochmaddy
Lochboisdale
Castlebay
BENBECULA

Wick
WICK
Latheron
Kinbrace
Helmsdale
Brora
Dornoch
Lairg
Bonar Bridge
Tain
Alness
Dingwall
Garve
Contin
Achnasheen
Cannich
Kinlochewe
Shieldaig
Lochcarron
Plockton
Kyle of
Domie
Kinloch
Ardvasar
Mallaig
Arisaig
Staffin
Portree
Dunvegan
Isle of Skye

Peterhead
Fraserburgh
ABERDEEN
Portlethen
Stonehaven
Inverurie
Banchory
Alford
Rhynie
Huntly
Keith
Dufftown
Elgin
Forres
Nairn
Craigellachie
Archiestown
Grantown-on-Spey
Boat of Garten
Aviemore
Braemar
Dalwhinnie
Newtonmore
Laggan
Invergarry
Spean
Culloden
INVERNESS
Beauly
Drumnadrochit
Invermoriston
Whitebridge
Fort Augustus

Moray Firth
Pentland Firth
Cromarty Firth

HIGHLAND
ABERDEENSHIRE
MORAY
WESTERN ISLES
OUTER HEBRIDES

The Minch
The Little Minch
Cuillin Sound

Hotel numbers: 21, 31, 17, 33, 22, 67, 34, 38, 25, 30, 47, 29, 84, 89, 55, 86, 79, 88, 78, 61, 40, 44

NORTH SEA

MAP KEY

- Region border
- National border
- Motorways
- Major throughroutes
- Other roads
- Ferry routes
- River
- Urban area
- Airport
- Lake/Loch
- Capital
- Major town
- Minor town
- Other town
- Other settlement

PLYMOUTH
LONDON
KING'S LYNN
Braintree
Pwllheli
Mumbles

NORTH
see pages
466 ~ 467

IRELAND
see pages
478 ~ 479

North Channel

Firth of Clyde

Solway Firth

Firth of Forth

Inner Hebrides

Montrose
Collieston
Arbroath
Carnoustie
Monifieth
Newport-on-Tay
St Andrews
Largoward
Leven
Buckhaven
Kirkcaldy
Aberdour
Dunbar
Gullane
Aberlady
EDINBURGH
Bonnyrigg
Penicuik
Peebles
Eyemouth
Kelso
Jedburgh
Selkirk
Hawick
Langholm
Canonbie
Gretna
Lockerbie
Dryfesdale
Lochmaben
Dumfries
Kirkbean
Newton Stewart
New Galloway
Whithorn
Drummore
Cairnryan
Stranraer
Portpatrick
Ballantrae
Girvan
Maybole
Ayr
Prestwick
Troon
Irvine
Ardrossan
Largs
Dalmellington
Dalry
Annbank
Strathaven
Darvel
Kilmarnock
Barrhead
Paisley
Dumbarton
GLASGOW
East Kilbride
Lanark
Carluke
Biggar
Abington
Shotts
Airdrie
Falkirk
Bo'ness
Roxburgh
Dunfermline
Port of Menteith
Stirling
Callander
Comrie
St Fillans
Lochearnhead
Balquhidder
Killin
Crianlarich
Bridge of Orchy
Tarbet
Helensburgh
Greenock
Dunoon
Tighnabruaich
Kennacraig
Tarbert
Stonefield
Lochgilphead
Arduaine
Kilmore
Oban
Kilchrenan by Taynuilt
Kilchenan
Strachur
Brodick
Campbeltown
Tayinloan
Port Askaig
Port Ellen
Colonsay
Islay
Jura
Isle of Mull
Tobermory
Killiechronan
Fionnphort
Arinagour
Scarinish
Coll
Tiree
Kentallen by Appin
Onich
Ardgour
Lochaline
Fort William
Glencoe
Pitlochry
Aberfeldy
Dunkeld
Blairgowrie
Kirriemur
Spittal of Glenshee
Forfar
Brechin
Auchterhouse
Dundee
Perth
Bridge of Earn
Auchterarder
Crieff
Cupar
Markinch
Kinross
Blairgowrie
Kinloch Rannoch
Kinlochard
Glasgow

SCOTLAND

NORTH

KEY TO HOTELS

The rosettes indicate the page number of the hotel. The colour of the rosette is a rough guide to the price of a twin or double room (see colour key below).

Double room: up to £95 per night

Double room: £96 - £145 per night

Double room: £146 - £195 per night

Double room: £196+ per night

Base map © MAPS IN MINUTES™ 2000
©Crown Copyright, Ordnance Survey 2000
Design and modification
© 2003 Best Loved Hotels of the World

30 Miles

NORTH SEA

SCOTLAND
see pages
464 - 465

NORTHUMBERLAND

DURHAM

Berwick-upon-Tweed
Cornhill-on-Tweed
Holy Island
Bamburgh
Waren Mill
Belford
Alnwick
Amble
Ashington
Newbiggin-by-the-Sea
Morpeth
Ridsdale
Whitley Bay
Blyth
South Shields
NEWCASTLE UPON TYNE
Gosforth
Ponteland
Matfen
Corbridge
Hexham
Prudhoe
Consett
Castleside
Wear Head
Alston
SUNDERLAND
Seaham
Houghton le Spring
Gateshead
Washington
Stanley
Peterlee
Wingate
Durham
Brandon
Crook
Stanhope
Willington
Spennymoor
Bishop Auckland
Gainford
Newton
Aycliffe
Hartlepool
Billingham
Redcar
Brotton
Stockton-on-Tees
Middlesbrough
Longtown
High Crosby
CARLISLE
Carlisle
Brampton
Penrith
Temple Sowerby
Appleby-in-Westmorland
Wigton
Bassenthwaite
Applethwaite
Keswick
Newlands
Maryport
Cockermouth
Workington

Firth of Forth
Solway Firth

DUMFRIES AND GALLOWAY

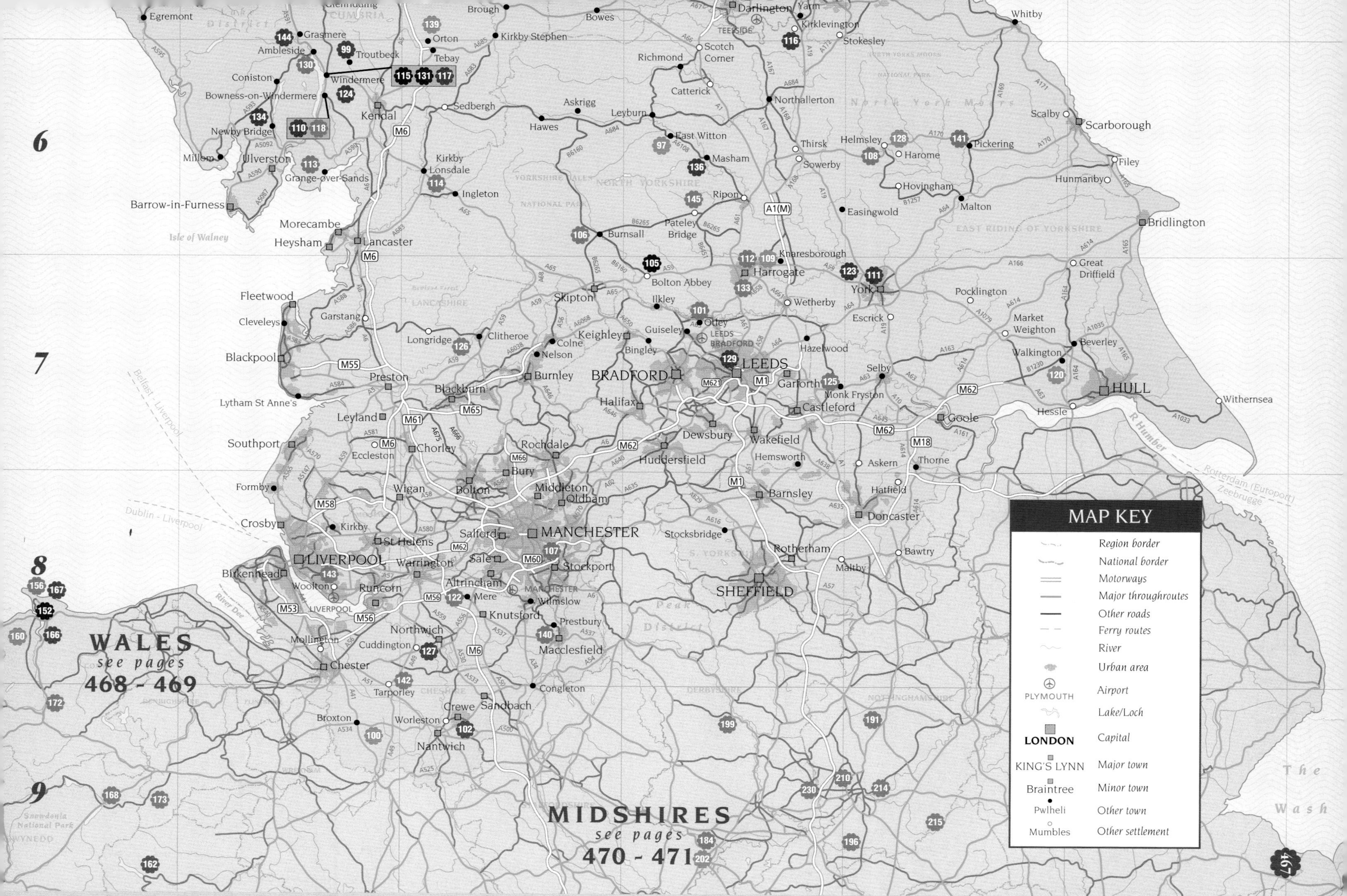

MAP KEY
Region border
National border
Motorways
Major throughroutes
Other roads
Ferry routes
River
Urban area
Airport
PLYMOUTH
Lake/Loch
LONDON
Capital
KING'S LYNN
Major town
Braintree
Minor town
Pwlheli
Other town
Mumbles
Other settlement
WALES
see pages
468 - 469
MIDSHIRES
see pages
470 - 471
6
7
8
9
467
Egremont
Brough
Bowes
Darlington
Yarm
Kirklevington
Stokesley
Whitby
Grasmere
Ambleside
Troutbeck
Orton
Tebay
Kirkby Stephen
Richmond
Scotch Corner
Catterick
Northallerton
Coniston
Windermere
Bowness-on-Windermere
Kendal
Sedbergh
Hawes
Askrigg
Leyburn
East Witton
Masham
Thirsk
Sowerby
Helmsley
Harome
Pickering
Scalby
Scarborough
Filey
Hunmanby
Newby Bridge
Millom
Ulverston
Grange-over-Sands
Kirkby Lonsdale
Ingleton
Hovingham
Malton
Easingwold
Ripon
Barrow-in-Furness
Isle of Walney
Morecambe
Heysham
Lancaster
Burnsall
Pateley Bridge
Knaresborough
Harrogate
York
Bridlington
Great Driffield
Bolton Abbey
Fleetwood
Cleveleys
Garstang
Longridge
Clitheroe
Skipton
Ilkley
Otley
Wetherby
Escrick
Pocklington
Market Weighton
Beverley
Walkington
Blackpool
Lytham St Anne's
Preston
Blackburn
Burnley
Nelson
Colne
Keighley
Bingley
Guiseley
BRADFORD
LEEDS
Garforth
Hazelwood
Selby
Monk Fryston
Castleford
HULL
Hessle
Withernsea
Leyland
Chorley
Eccleston
Southport
Halifax
Dewsbury
Wakefield
Huddersfield
Hemsworth
Askern
Thorne
Goole
R Humber
Formby
Wigan
Bolton
Rochdale
Bury
Middleton
Oldham
Barnsley
Hatfield
Doncaster
Crosby
Kirkby
St Helens
Salford
MANCHESTER
Stocksbridge
Rotherham
Bawtry
Maltby
LIVERPOOL
Warrington
Sale
Stockport
Birkenhead
Wootton
Runcorn
Altrincham
Mere
Wilmslow
SHEFFIELD
Knutsford
Prestbury
Macclesfield
Northwich
Mollington
Cuddington
Chester
Tarporley
Congleton
Crewe
Sandbach
Broxton
Worleston
Nantwich
River Dee
Peak District
North York Moors
EAST RIDING OF YORKSHIRE
NORTH YORKSHIRE
LANCASHIRE
CUMBRIA
Belfast - Liverpool
Dublin - Liverpool
Rotterdam (Europort) Zeebrugge
The Wash
Snowdonia National Park
GWYNEDD
M6
M55
M61
M65
M66
M62
M58
M60
M56
M53
M621
M1
M18
A1(M)

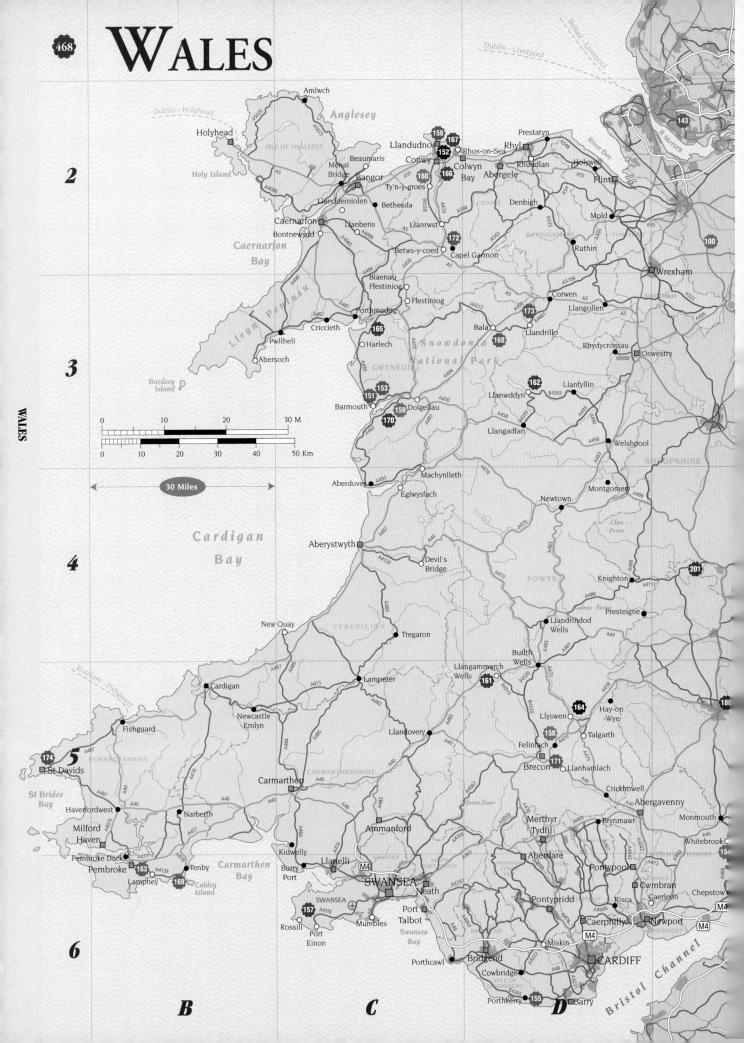

WALES

Anglesey

Amlwch

Holyhead

ISLE OF ANGLESEY

Holy Island

Beaumaris

Menai Bridge

Bangor

Llanddeiniolen

Bethesda

Caernarfon

Bontnewydd

Llanberis

Caernarfon Bay

Llandudno
156
167
152
Conwy
Colwyn Bay
160
166
Ty'n-y-groes

Prestatyn

Rhyl

Rhos-on-Sea

Rhuddlan

Abergele

Holywell

Flint

Denbigh

Mold

100

Lleyn Peninsula

Criccieth

Pwllheli

Abersoch

Llanrwst

172
Betws-y-coed
Capel Garmon

Ruthin

Wrexham

Bardsey Island

Blaenau Ffestiniog

Ffestiniog

Porthmadog

165

Harlech

GWYNEDD

Snowdonia National Park

Bala
168

173
Corwen
Llandrillo

Llangollen

Rhydycroesau

Oswestry

151
153
Barmouth
159
Dolgellau
170

Llanwddyn

162
Llanfyllin

Llangadfan

Welshpool

Montgomery

SHROPSHIRE

Cardigan Bay

Aberdovey

Machynlleth

Eglwysfach

Newtown

Aberystwyth

Devil's Bridge

POWYS

Knighton

201

Clun Forest

Radnor Forest

Presteigne

New Quay

CEREDIGION

Tregaron

Llandrindod Wells

Builth Wells

Llangammarch Wells
161

164
Hay-on-Wye

Llyswen

158
Talgarth

Rosslare - Fishguard

Cardigan

Lampeter

Newcastle Emlyn

Llandovery

Fishguard

174
St Davids

PEMBROKESHIRE

Carmarthen

CARMARTHENSHIRE

Felinfach
171
Brecon
Llanhamlach

188

Crickhowell

Abergavenny

Monmouth

Whitebrook

Haverfordwest

Narberth

Milford Haven

Pembroke Dock
163
Pembroke
Lamphey
169
Caldey Island

Tenby

Carmarthen Bay

Kidwelly

Burry Port

Llanelli

Ammanford

Forest Fawr

Merthyr Tydfil

Brynmawr

Aberdare

Pontypool

Cwmbran

Caerleon

Chepstow

SWANSEA
M4

157

Mumbles

Rossili

Port Einon

Neath

Port Talbot

Pontypridd

Risca

Newport

M4

Swansea Bay

Porthcawl

Bridgend

Miskin

Caerphilly

M4

CARDIFF

Cowbridge

155
Porthkerry
Barry

Bristol Channel

Dublin - Holyhead
Dublin - Liverpool
Belfast - Liverpool
River Dee
R Mersey
143

0   10   20   30 M

0   10   20   30   40   50 Km

30 Miles

St Brides Bay

St David's

NORTH
see pages
466 - 467

MIDSHIRES
see pages
470 - 471

WALES

MAP KEY

	Region border
	National border
	Motorways
	Major throughroutes
	Other roads
	Ferry routes
	River
	Urban area
⊕ PLYMOUTH	Airport
	Lake/Loch
LONDON	Capital
■ KING'S LYNN	Major town
■ Braintree	Minor town
• Pwlheli	Other town
○ Mumbles	Other settlement

KEY TO HOTELS

The rosettes indicate the page number of the hotel. The colour of the rosette is a rough guide to the price of a twin or double room (see colour key below).

- Double room: up to £95 per night
- Double room: £96 - £145 per night
- Double room: £146 - £195 per night
- Double room: £196+ per night

Base map © MAPS IN MINUTES™ 2000
©Crown Copyright, Ordnance Survey 2000
Design and modification
© 2003 Best Loved Hotels of the World

SOUTH
see pages
474 - 475

LONDON
see pages
476 - 477

WEST
see pages
472 - 473

E   F   G   H

MIDSHIRES

NORTH
see pages
466 - 467

MIDSHIRES

126
129
M180
107
A1(M)
Bawtry
Woodhead
Glossop
Worksop
Retford
143
New Mills
122
Whaley Bridge
Ashford in
the Water
Chesterfield
140
Buxton
231
166
Bakewell
Clay
Cross
M1
Mansfield
127
Matlock
Sutton in
Ashfield
191
Burnt Hill Stump
142
Biddulph
Leek
199
Shottle
Ripley
100
Kidsgrove
Dovedale
Belper
230
NOTTINGHAM
102
STOKE-ON-TRENT
Ashbourne
Duffield
210
214
Bingham
172
Newcastle-
under-Lyme
Uttoxeter
DERBY
Risley
215
Langar
Tutbury
184
Long
Eaton
196
Ruddington
168
173
Whitchurch
202
Burton upon
Trent
EAST
MIDLANDS
Melton
Mowbray
Ellesmere
Market
Drayton
Stone
M1
Ashby-de-
la-Zouch
Loughborough
162
Oswestry
Eccleshall
Stafford
Rugeley
Coalville
LEICESTER
Newport
M6
Cannock
Lichfield
M42
Shrewsbury
Telford
Tamworth
M69
229
M54
Sutton
Coldfield
Much
Wenlock
WOLVERHAMPTON
Worfield
Nuneaton
Hinckley
Bridgnorth
225
West Bromwich
M6
BIRMINGHAM
211
Market
Harborough
Dudley
Stourbridge
Halesowen
Solihull
COVENTRY
M6
M1
201
Ludlow
Kidderminster
183
Kings
Norton
222
Binley
Rugby
Presteigne
Stourport-
on-Severn
206
Redditch
Hockley
Heath
COVENTRY
M45
Kington
Leominster
Bromyard
Bromsgrove
Droitwich
Studley
Warwick
Leamington
Spa
Daventry
161
Alcester
241
Northampton
Worcester
180
Stratford
upon Avon
204
Fawsley
164
192
Great Malvern
Pershore
Alderminster
Banbury
M40
M1
158
188
197
Colwall
Evesham
182 203
189 195
223
Chipping Campden
Shipston
350
Hereford
Ledbury
218
Broadway Broad
Campden
198
Moreton-in-Marsh
171
194
Tewkesbury
Stow-on-the-Wold
Chipping Norton
M50
232 217
Upper Slaughter
Kingham
208
Ross-
on-Wye
240
Corse Lawn
213
Cheltenham
200
Bledington
233
Enstone
205
Chesterton
181
Bicester
Newent
207
Withington
Bourton-
on-water
Shipton-under
-Wychwood
Witney
Woodstock
Gloucester
Shurdington
Burford
186
Kidlington
M40
Coleford
227
Bibury
237
OXFORD
Thame
154
Stroud
Cirencester
220
242
224
Lydney
Rodborough
Coln St-Aldwyns
228
Clanfield
216
Ewen
Abingdon
Great
Milton
155
226
Didcot
187 190
243
Wallingford
239
Thornbury
Tetbury
234
North Stoke
Chipping
Sodbury
M49
317
M4 Hinton
313
254 275
351
276
287
315
259 263 270
272 252 296
260
297

WALES
see pages
468 - 469

WEST
see pages
472 - 473

SOUTH
see pages
474 - 475

B   C   D   E

KEY TO HOTELS

The rosettes indicate the page number of the hotel. The colour of the rosette is a rough guide to the price of a twin or double room (see colour key below).

- Double room: up to £95 per night
- Double room: £96 - £145 per night
- Double room: £146 - £195 per night
- Double room: £196+ per night

Base map © MAPS IN MINUTES™ 2000
©Crown Copyright, Ordnance Survey 2000
Design and modification
© 2003 Best Loved Hotels of the World

MAP KEY

- Region border
- National border
- Motorways
- Major throughroutes
- Other roads
- Ferry routes
- River
- Urban area
- ⊕ PLYMOUTH   Airport
- Lake/Loch
- ■ **LONDON**   Capital
- ■ KING'S LYNN   Major town
- ■ Braintree   Minor town
- • Pwlheli   Other town
- ○ Mumbles   Other settlement

MIDSHIRES

120

Barton-upon-Humber
Scunthorpe
M181   M180   Immingham   Grimsby
Brigg   Cleethorpes
Caistor
Rotterdam (Europort) Zeebrugge

Gainsborough   Market Rasen   Louth   Mablethorpe

Lincoln   Washingborough   Horncastle   Ingoldmells   Skegness

LINCOLNSHIRE

Newark-on-Trent   Coningsby

Sleaford   Boston

Grantham   **The Wash**

235   Stapleford   Pinchbeck   Spalding   Long Sutton   Holbeach   King's Lynn

RUTLAND   Bourne

Oakham   Stamford   The Fens   Wisbech   193   Congham   236   Swaffham

Thornham   Hunstanton   209   Burnham Market   Great Snoring   219   Sheringham   Cromer

Dersingham   Fakenham   Aylsham   North Walsham   221   Coltishall

Dereham   NORWICH   Norwich   Caister-on-Sea   Great Yarmouth

NORFOLK   185   Saham Toney   Wymondham   The Broads   Lowestoft

Peterborough   Downham Market   Attleborough   Bungay   Beccles

Corby   Oundle   March   Brandon   Thetford   Diss

Kettering   Chatteris   CAMBRIDGESHIRE   Ely   Eye

Rushden   Huntingdon   Mildenhall   Saxmundham

St Ives   Newmarket   Bury St Edmunds   Aldeburgh

St Neots   CAMBRIDGE   212   Six Mile Bottom   238   SUFFOLK   Stowmarket   Orford Ness

BEDFORDSHIRE   M11   Haverhill   Long Melford   Woodbridge   Ipswich   320

Sudbury   Felixstowe   335

Esbjerg, Hamburg, Hoek Van Holland

328

HERTFORDSHIRE   ESSEX

SOUTH see pages **474 - 475**

344

LONDON see pages **476 - 477**

346   318   340   347

30 Miles

0   10   20   30 M
0   10   20   30   40   50 Km

F   G   H   I

2   3   4   5   6   7

WALES
see pages
468 - 469

MAP KEY

~~	Region border
~~	National border
≡	Motorways
—	Major throughroutes
—	Other roads
- - -	Ferry routes
~~	River
	Urban area
✈ PLYMOUTH	Airport
~	Lake/Loch
■ LONDON	Capital
■ KING'S LYNN	Major town
■ Braintree	Minor town
• Pwlheli	Other town
○ Mumbles	Other settlement

KEY TO HOTELS

The rosettes indicate the page number of the hotel. The colour of the rosette is a rough guide to the price of a twin or double room (see colour key below).

Double room: up to £95 per night

Double room: £96 - £145 per night

Double room: £146 - £195 per night

Double room: £196+ per night

Base map © MAPS IN MINUTES™ 2000
©Crown Copyright, Ordnance Survey 2000
Design and modification
© 2003 Best Loved Hotels of the World

St Brides Bay

Skomer Island

Skokholm Island

163

169

CARMARTHENSHIRE

Carmarthen Bay

SWANSEA

157

Swansea Bay

VALE OF GLAMORGAN

155

Bristol

174

C E L T I C

S E A

Lynton
271
Lynmouth
Parracombe
Porlock
Ilfracombe
Mortehoe
Williton
Minehead
262
Exford
Exmoor Forest
Barnstaple
298
Northam
Bideford
South Molton
Dulverton
278
Wivelscombe
Great Torrington
Burrington
Tiverton
Cullompton
Bude
Holsworthy
Hatherleigh
Crediton
M5
261
Okehampton
290 Exeter
285
Virginstow
DEVON
EXETER
Tintagel
Launceston
Lewdown
Chagford
Doddiscombsleigh
Exmouth
Lifton
279
268 281
Dawlish
250
Dartmoor
Bovey Tracey
Kingsteignton
Two Bridges
Rock
286
Teignmouth
Padstow
Bodmin Moor
Tavistock
274
Newton Abbot
273 Ashburton
Kingskerswell
283
Wadebridge
CORNWALL
255
Princetown
Buckfastleigh
284
Torquay
NEWQUAY
Bodmin
Gulworthy
269 Totnes
Paignton
Newquay
PLYMOUTH
South Brent
266
Brixham
St Keyne
294
Galmpton
Truro
249
Widegates Saltash
PLYMOUTH
Ivybridge
267
Tregrehan
Looe
Goveton
St Ives
St Austell
265
292
256 Dartmouth
Redruth
Camborne
280
Fowey
293 Kingsbridge
St Just
Hayle
Portloe
Salcombe
Penzance
Helston
257
277
Start Point
Sennen
Falmouth
Mawnan Smith
Mount's Bay
A3063

Santander (summer only)
St Malo (winter only)
Roscoff

30 Miles

289
Isles of Scilly

Lizard

B

C

D

158
171
154
194
218
198
232
252
217
207
213
227
200
208
205
181
350
473
233
237
186
228
242
224
216
187 190
226
243
334
317

Forest of Dean

MONMOUTHSHIRE

GLOUCESTERSHIRE

River Severn

239

Avonmouth
Portishead
Long Ashton
254 275
M32
BRISTOL
Clevedon
Nailsea
Yatton
BRISTOL
Congresbury
Winscombe
Weston-super-Mare
M5
Cheddar
Brent Knoll
Burnham-on-Sea
Highbridge
Watchet

260
296 252 263
270 272 287
295
Bradford-on-Avon
276
Hunstrete
Bath
259
Radstock
Norton St Philip
291
Ston Easton
251
Frome
310
307
326
313
351
315

WILTSHIRE
BERKSHIRE
Lambourn Downs
Cotswolds
Chilterns

SOUTH
see pages
474 - 475

Salisbury Plain

HAMPSHIRE

Wells
Shepton Mallet
Glastonbury
Street
Bridgwater
Langford Budville
Taunton
Langport
Wincanton
325
339
324
349

253
258
Henlade
282
264
Hatch Beauchamp
Wellington
M5
Ilminster
Yeovil
336
Chard
Crewkerne
345
SOMERSET
DORSET

Honiton
Gittisham
Axminster
288
Sidmouth
Budleigh Salterton
Seaton
Lyme Bay

311 331
348
333
309
329
342
338
330
New Forest
The Solent
ISLE OF WIGHT
Isle of Wight

Channel

2
3
4
5

WEST COUNTRY

Guernsey and Jersey
Cherbourg
St Malo (summer only)
Channel Islands

E N G L I S H
C H A N N E L

0   10   20   30 M
0   10   20   30   40   50 Km

E   F   G   H

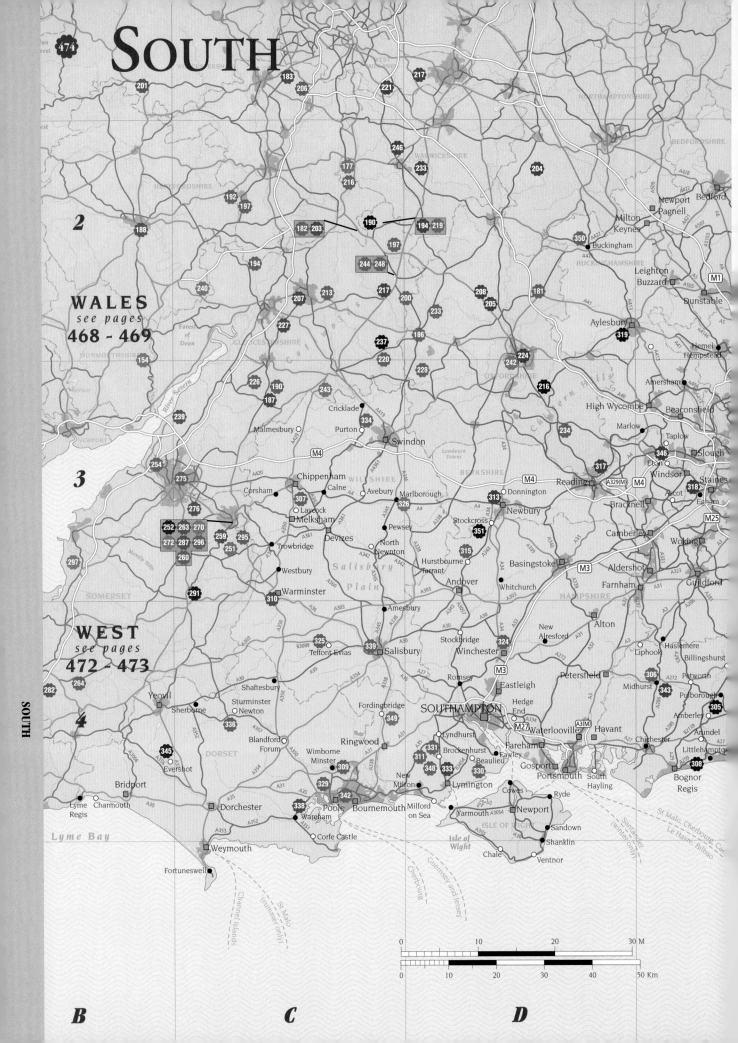

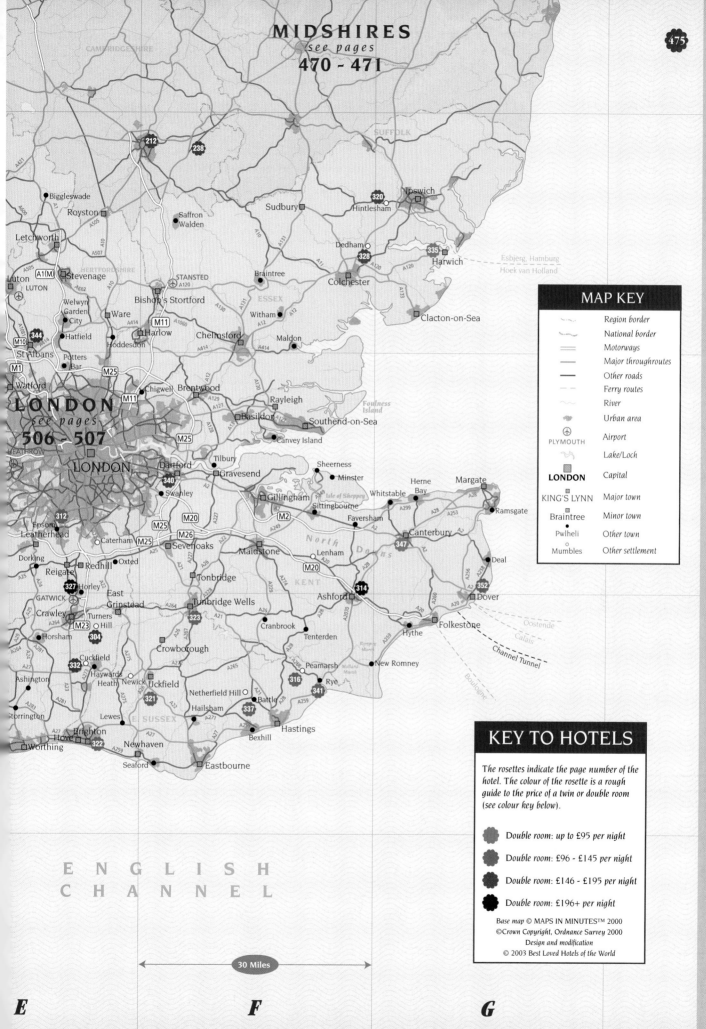

MIDSHIRES
see pages
470 – 471

SOUTH

MAP KEY

	Region border
	National border
	Motorways
	Major throughroutes
	Other roads
	Ferry routes
	River
	Urban area
PLYMOUTH	Airport
	Lake/Loch
LONDON	Capital
KING'S LYNN	Major town
Braintree	Minor town
Pwlheli	Other town
Mumbles	Other settlement

KEY TO HOTELS

The rosettes indicate the page number of the hotel. The colour of the rosette is a rough guide to the price of a twin or double room (see colour key below).

Double room: up to £95 per night

Double room: £96 - £145 per night

Double room: £146 - £195 per night

Double room: £196+ per night

Base map © MAPS IN MINUTES™ 2000
©Crown Copyright, Ordnance Survey 2000
Design and modification
© 2003 Best Loved Hotels of the World

ENGLISH CHANNEL

30 Miles

LONDON
see pages
506 – 507

E   F   G

LONDON

KEY TO HOTELS

The rosettes indicate the page number of the hotel. The colour of the rosette is a rough guide to the price of a twin or double room (see colour key below).

Double room: up to £95 per night

Double room: £96 - £145 per night

Double room: £146 - £195 per night

Double room: £196+ per night

KEY

Parks & Gardens

Lakes & Rivers

Motorways

Through routes

Other Important Roads

Canal

Mainline Railway Station

Underground Station

Tourist Information Centre

Pier

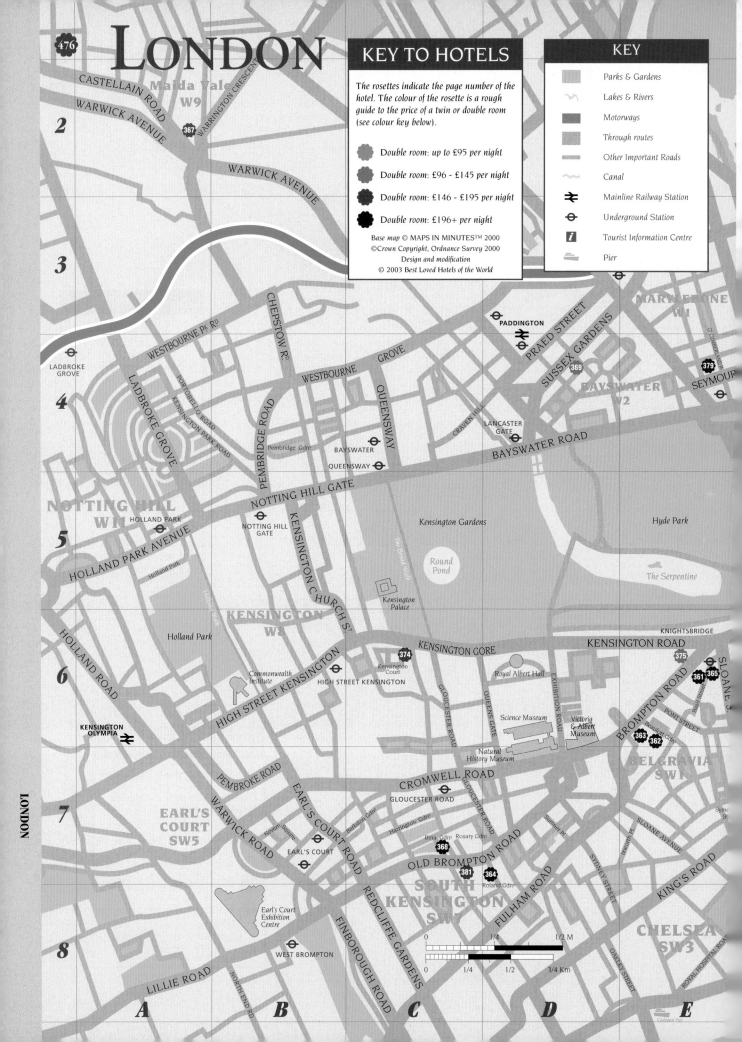

Map labels

CASTELLAIN ROAD

WARWICK AVENUE

Maida Vale W9

WARRINGTON CRESCENT

367

WARWICK AVENUE

2

3

CHEPSTOW RD

WESTBOURNE PK RD

PADDINGTON

PRAED STREET

SUSSEX GARDENS

MARYLEBONE W1

369

LADBROKE GROVE

LADBROKE GROVE

PORTOBELLO ROAD

KENSINGTON PARK ROAD

PEMBRIDGE ROAD

WESTBOURNE GROVE

QUEENSWAY

CRAVEN HILL

LANCASTER GATE

BAYSWATER W2

379

SEYMOUR

4

Pembridge Gdns.

BAYSWATER

QUEENSWAY

BAYSWATER ROAD

NOTTING HILL GATE

NOTTING HILL W11

HOLLAND PARK

NOTTING HILL GATE

KENSINGTON CHURCH ST.

Kensington Gardens

The Broad Walk

Round Pond

Hyde Park

The Serpentine

5

HOLLAND PARK AVENUE

Holland Park

Holland Park

Holland Walk

KENSINGTON W8

Kensington Palace

6

HOLLAND ROAD

Holland Park

Commonwealth Institute

HIGH STREET KENSINGTON

HIGH STREET KENSINGTON

374

Kensington Court

KENSINGTON GORE

Royal Albert Hall

GLOUCESTER ROAD

QUEENS GATE

EXHIBITION ROAD

Science Museum

Victoria & Albert Museum

KNIGHTSBRIDGE

KENSINGTON ROAD

375

361 365

Sloane St

BROMPTON ROAD

PONT STREET

Beauchamp Gdns.

363 362

BELGRAVIA SW1

KENSINGTON OLYMPIA

Natural History Museum

7

EARL'S COURT SW5

WARWICK ROAD

PEMBROKE ROAD

EARL'S COURT ROAD

Nevern Square

EARL'S COURT

EARL'S COURT

Barkston Gdns.

CROMWELL ROAD

GLOUCESTER ROAD

GLOUCESTER ROAD

Harrington Gdns.

Bina Gdns. Rosary Gdns.

368

OLD BROMPTON ROAD

381 364

Roland Gdns.

FULHAM ROAD

Sumner Pl.

SYDNEY STREET

SLOANE AVENUE

KING'S ROAD

Sydney St.

8

West Brompton

FINBOROUGH ROAD

REDCLIFFE GARDENS

Earl's Court Exhibition Centre

SOUTH KENSINGTON SW7

CHELSEA SW3

OAKLEY STREET

ROYAL HOSPITAL ROAD

LILLIE ROAD

NORTH END RD

A   B   C   D   E

Scale

0   1/4   1/2 M

0   1/4   1/2   3/4 Km

KING'S CROSS
PENTONVILLE ROAD
PANCRAS RD
YORK WAY
ST PANCRAS
EUSTON
EUSTON ROAD
SWINTON ST
JUDD STREET
EVERSHOLT STREET
HAMPSTEAD RD
ALBANY STREET
Regent's Park
ST JOHN
CLERKEN
FARRINGDON ROAD
GRAY'S INN ROAD
CHARTERHO
Regent's Park
WARREN STREET
GT PORTLAND ST
GOWER STREET
RUSSELL SQUARE
BERNARD STREET
GUILFORD STREET
BLOOMSBURY WC1
THEOBALDS ROAD
HATTON GARDEN
MARYLEBONE ROAD
GREAT PORTLAND STREET
TOTTENHAM COURT ROAD
GOODGE STREET
359
378
The British Museum
SOUTHAMPTON ROW
HOLBORN
CHANCERY LANE
FETTER LANE
HOLBORN VIADUCT
SHOE LANE
PADDINGTON ST
358
BEDFORD
MONTAGUE
KINGSWAY
NEW BRIDGE ST
WIGMORE ST
CANENDISH
OS CANENDISH
NEW OXFORD STREET
377
BAKER ST
MANCHESTER STREET
STREET
OXFORD STREET
TOTTENHAM COURT ROAD
WARDOUR STREET
CHARING CROSS RD
ENDELL ST
ALDWYCH
TEMPLE
BLACKFRIARS
Blackfriars Bridge
OXFORD STREET
BOND STREET
SOHO W1
SHAFTESBURY AVENUE
MONMOUTH AV
ST MARTIN'S LA
LONG ACRE
BOW ST
Theatre Museum
THE STRAND
BOND STREET
NEW BOND STREET
REGENT STREET
BREWER STREET
COVENT GARDEN
British Transport Museum
CONDUIT ST
OLD BOND STREET
LEICESTER SQUARE
British Travel Centre
Museum of Mankind
Royal Academy of Arts
National Gallery & National Portrait Gallery
VICTORIA EMBANKMENT
Waterloo Bridge
OS GROSVENOR
Upper Grosvenor
Mount Street
Hill Street
Albemarle St
Arlington St
PICCADILLY CIRCUS
PICCADILLY
TRAFALGAR
376
PARK LANE
360
MOUNT STREET
PALL MALL
SQUARE
CHARING CROSS
EMBANKMENT
Charing Cross Pier
366
MAYFAIR W1
371
PICCADILLY
Scotland
NORTHUMBERLAND AV
VICTORIA EMBANKMENT
South Bank Festival Pier
PARK LANE
Northern Ireland
GREEN PARK
HYDE PARK CORNER
Green Park
CONSTITUTION HILL
Buckingham Palace
Royal Mews
380
BUCKINGHAM PALACE ROAD
WILTON
BELGRAVE
GROSVENOR PLACE
GROSVENOR CR
Beeston Pl
372
Westminster Cathedral
BELGRAVE PL
PONT STREET
SLOANE
BELGRAVE
VICTORIA
WILTON RD
EATON SQUARE
ECCLESTON ST
EBURY STREET
BUCKINGHAM PALACE ROAD
BELGRAVE ROAD
SLOANE SQUARE
WARWICK WAY
PIMLICO ROAD
EBURY BRIDGE RD
PIMLICO SW1
CHELSEA BRIDGE ROAD
GROSVENOR ROAD
Dolphin Sq
370
Vauxhall Bridge
1/2 Mile
NINE ELMS LANE
Chelsea Bridge
Battersea Power Station
Battersea Park
F G H I J

GREATER LONDON

A1M
M1
M11
M25
South see pages 474 - 475
A417
A1
A10
A406
A12
A118
A13
Harrow
373
A409
Hampstead
A4020
M40
A5
M4
A4
A316
A207
HEATHROW
A30
A4
A205
A20
A2
340
318
South see pages 474 - 475
312
A21
M20
M3
A3
A243
A24
M25
M26
A217
M23
A22
M25
The Oval Cricket Ground

IRELAND

SCOTLAND
see pages
464 – 465

*North
Channel*

KEY TO HOTELS

The rosettes indicate the page number of the hotel. The colour of the rosette is a rough guide to the price of a twin or double room(see colour key below), note prices are listed in Euros.

🌸 Double room: up to €156 per night

🌸 Double room: €157 - €238 per night

🌸 Double room: €239 - €320 per night

🌸 Double room: €321+ per night

Base map © MAPS IN MINUTES™ 2001

©Crown Copyright, Ordnance Survey Northern Ireland 2001
Permit No. N1 1675 &©Government of Ireland,
Ordnance Survey Ireland

Design and modification © 2002 Best Loved Hotels of the World

MAP KEY

〰〰	Region border
═══	National border
▌▌▌	Motorways
▬▬▬	Major throughroutes
────	Other roads
〰〰〰	Ferry routes
〰〰	River
	Urban area
✈	Airport
	Lake/Loch
LONDON	Capital
■ PLYMOUTH	Major town
■ KING'S LYNN	
Braintree	Minor town
• Pwlheli	Other town
○ Mumbles	Other settlement

Place names

Tory Island

Aran Island

Inishtrahull

Inishowen Head

Malin Head

Fahan, Buncrana, Milford, Rathmullan, Cresslough, Letterkenny, Ballybofey, Castlederg, Ballyshannon, Donegal, Bundoran, Killybegs

Moville, CITY OF DERRY, LONDONDERRY, Strabane, Newtownstewart, Omagh, Enniskillen, Lisnaskea

Portrush, Portstewart, Coleraine, Bushmills, Ballycastle, Ballymoney, Limavady, Dungiven, Maghera, Magherafelt, Moneymore, Cookstown, Dungannon, Coalisland

Cushendall, Larne, Whitehead, Ballymena, Ballyclare, Ballymena, Bangor, Holywood, Newtownards, Portaferry, Portavogie

BELFAST, BELFAST INTERNATIONAL, Crumlin, Lisburn, Portadown, Dromore, Banbridge, Ballynahinch, Downpatrick, Castlewellan, Newcastle, Annalong, Kilkeel, Warrenpoint, Newry, Armagh, Tandragee, Keady, Crossmaglen, Castleblayney, Carlingford, Dundalk, Ardee, Carrickmacross, Castleblayney, Monaghan, Clones, Cootehill, Newtownbutler, Ballybay, Cavan, Ballyjamesduff, Ballieborough, Kells, Navan, Trim

Balbriggan, Skerries, Rush, Malahide, Drogheda

Sligo, Ballysadare, Riverstown, Collooney, Boyle, Carrick-on-Shannon, Ballaghaderreen, Castlerea, Roscommon, Longford, Granard, Mullingar, Athlone

Swinford, Ballyhaunis, Ballina, Claremorris, Ballinrobe, Tuam, Caherlistrane, Castlebar, Westport, Cong, Oughterard, Recess, Ballinafad, Clifden, Letterfrack, Renvyle, Belmullet

Inishbofin, Inishturk, Inishshark, Clare Island, Achill Island, Inishkea North, Inishkea South, Inishmurray

MAYO, GALWAY, ROSCOMMON, LONGFORD, CAVAN, MONAGHAN, FERMANAGH, TYRONE, LONDONDERRY, ANTRIM, DOWN, ARMAGH, DONEGAL, SLIGO, LEITRIM, WESTMEATH, MEATH

Rosette numbers
478, 46, 66, 26, 85, 390, M5, 428, M2, M22, A26, 108, M1, M11, 446, 403, 427, 391, 439, 423, 426, 437, 438

WALES
see pages
468 - 469

St George's Channel

IRELAND

DUBLIN
Dun Laoghaire
Bray
Greystones
Rathnew
Wicklow
Celbridge
Naas
Dunlavin
Kildare
Monasterevin
Portarlington
Tullamore
Kilcormac
Mountmellick
Portlaoise
Mountrath
Clara
Moate
Banagher
Ballinasloe
Loughrea
Oranmore
Galway
Ballyvaughan
Ennistymon
Lahinch
Liscannor
Aran Islands
Inishmore
Mutton Island
Kilkee
Kilrush
Killaloe
LIMERICK
Newmarket-on-Fergus
SHANNON
Ennis
Gort
Nenagh
Roscrea
Templemore
Thurles
Cashel
Golden
Tipperary
Adare
Ballingarry
Rathkeale
Glin
Ballybunion
Listowel
Abbeyfeale
Castleisland
KERRY COUNTY
Tralee
Killorglin
Caragh Lake
Killarney
Kenmare
Glenbeigh
Cahersiveen
Valentia Island
Dingle
An Daingean
Gt. Blasket Island
Blasket Islands
Mutton Island
Mountrath
Abbeyleix
Castlecomer
Durrow
Kilkenny
Callan
Clonmel
Carrick-on-Suir
Cahir
Mitchelstown
Fermoy
Mallow
Charleville
Kilmallock
Kanturk
Millstreet
Macroom
Blarney
CORK
Midleton
Cobh
Kinsale
Bandon
Dunmanway
Clonakilty
Skibbereen
Durrus
Bantry
Clear Island
Bear Island
Dursey Island
Cahir
Dungarvan
Youghal
Ballycotton
Castle Hyde
WATERFORD
Arthurstown
New Ross
Graiguenamanagh
Borris
Bagenalstown
Carlow
Athy
Enniscorthy
Wexford
Tagoat
Rosslare
Saltee Islands
Rathdrum
Arklow
Enfield
Moate

Cherbourg
Rosslare - Fishguard
Rosslare - Pembroke Dock
Dublin - Liverpool
Dublin - Holyhead

Cork - Swansea
Le Havre (Summer Only)
Cherbourg (Summer Only)
St Malo (Summer Only)
Roscoff

CLARE
TIPPERARY
LIMERICK
KERRY
CORK
WATERFORD
KILKENNY
LAOIS
OFFALY
KILDARE
WICKLOW
WEXFORD

30 M
20
10
0

50 Km
40
30
20
10
0

30 Miles

7
8
9
10
11
12

FREE BROCHURE SERVICE

If you see a hotel in this book and want to know more about it, simply circle its page number below, fill in your name and address details, and post the card to us.

As soon as we receive your request, we shall arrange for the brochures to be delivered to you as soon as the postal services allow. This card can be used to request a maximum of ten brochures only.

There will be no delivery or postage charge for this service.

BEST LOVED HOTELS 2003

Suite 11, The Linen House, 253 Kilburn Lane, London W10 4BQ, United Kingdom
Tel: +44 (0)20 8962 9555 ◆ Fax: +44 (0)20 8962 9550
E-mail: freebrochure@bestlovedhotels.com
Website: www.bestlovedhotels.com

BEST LOVED HOTELS 2003
Free Brochure Service

Please send me full details on the hotel(s) circled opposite.

Name _____

Address _____

_____

_____

City _____

Postcode _____

Tel: _____

Fax: _____

E-mail: _____

BLD03/BR

17	46	75	109	138	172	206	235	269	298	332	366	400	429
18	47	76	110	139	173	207	236	270	304	333	367	401	
19	48	77	111	140	174	208	237	271	305	334	368	402	430
20	49	78	112	141	180	209	238	272	306	335	369	403	431
21	50	79	113	142	181	210	239	273	307	336	370	404	
22	51	80	114	143	182	211	240	274	308	337	371	405	432
23	52	81	115	144	183	212	241	275	309	338	372	406	433
24	53	82	116	145	184	213	242	276	310	339	373	407	
25	54	83	117	151	185	214	243	277	311	340	374	408	434
26	55	84	118	152	186	215	249	278	312	341	375	409	435
27	56	85	119	153	187	216	250	279	313	342	376	410	
28	57	86	120	154	188	217	251	280	314	343	377	411	436
29	58	87	121	155	189	218	252	281	315	344	378	412	437
30	59	88	122	156	190	219	253	282	316	345	379	413	
31	60	89	123	157	191	220	254	283	317	346	380	414	438
32	61	90	124	158	192	221	255	284	318	347	381	415	
33	62	96	125	159	193	222	256	285	319	348	387	416	439
34	63	97	126	160	194	223	257	286	320	349	388	417	440
35	64	98	127	161	195	224	258	287	321	350	389	418	
36	65	99	128	162	196	225	259	288	322	351	390	419	441
37	66	100	129	163	197	226	260	289	323	352	391	420	442
38	67	101	130	164	198	227	261	290	324	358	392	421	
39	68	102	131	165	199	228	262	291	325	359	393	422	443
40	69	103	132	166	200	229	263	292	326	360	394	423	444
41	70	104	133	167	201	230	264	293	327	361	395	424	
42	71	105	134	168	202	231	265	294	328	362	396	425	445
43	72	106	135	169	203	232	266	295	329	363	397	426	446
44	73	107	136	170	204	233	267	296	330	364	398	427	
45	74	108	137	171	205	234	268	297	331	365	399	428	447

GUEST SURVEY

Please tell us about your stay, the more we know the more reliable our future editions will be.

Hotel name _____

Name of guest _____ / _____

Address _____

_____

Postcode _____

Tel: _____ Fax: _____

E-mail: _____

Reason for stay

Business ☐   Conference ☐

Pleasure ☐   Dining ☐

How did you find your visit?

	Excellent	Good	Not Good	Poor
Public Rooms				
Bedrooms				
Restaurant/Food				
Comfort				
Facilities				
Service				
Courtesy/friendliness				
Value for money				

Please tick only one box for each aspect of your stay

Additional comments:

_____

_____

_____

Do you have a best loved hotel?

Name of hotel _____

Location _____

_____

Hire car information:

Did you rent a car to get to the hotel?
☐ Yes   ☐ No

From where:

Hertz   **Avis**   **Europcar**   Other
(please circle)

Airline information:

What airline did you use to arrive in the British Isles?

BLD03/GS

Use this £5 voucher at selected Best Loved hotels

*Y*OUR PURCHASE of this 2003 Directory of Best Loved Hotels of the World entitles you to the four £5 tear-off vouchers opposite.

To redeem them, just make a reservation to stay at any of the participating hotels (see other side of opposite page) or book a table for two for a meal at one of them. When making your reservation, you must tell the hotel of your intention to use the voucher.

£5 off your stay or..

If you use your voucher in association with booking accommodation, you will have £5 deducted from the standard charge (rack rate) for the room.

... two free glasses of wine

If you choose to take a meal, there must be two of you, your voucher will entitle you to a glass of house wine each. It is as simple as that.

It's a gift!

If you wish to give the voucher to someone else, there is no problem, it is entirely transferable. The rules, however, are the same.

Please refer to full terms and conditions on the voucher.

Hotel bedroom copies do not contain any vouchers.
If you would like to purchase your own copy please see order card or go to www.bestlovedhotels.com

---

No stamp
needed
UK only

Best Loved Hotels of The World
FREEPOST LON16342
LONDON
W10 4BR

No stamp
needed
UK only

Best Loved Hotels of The World
FREEPOST LON16342
LONDON
W10 4BR